Indomitable Sarah

Indomitable Sarah

The Life *of*
Judge Sarah T. Hughes

DARWIN PAYNE

Foreword by Barefoot Sanders
Afterword by Sarah Weddington

SOUTHERN METHODIST
UNIVERSITY PRESS
Dallas

Requests for permission to reproduce material from this work should be sent to:
    Rights and Permissions
    Southern Methodist University Press
    PO Box 750415
    Dallas, Texas 75275-0415

Jacket and text design by Tom Dawson
Cover photo courtesy of University of North Texas Archives

LIBRARY OF CONGRESS CATALOGING-IN-PUBLICATION DATA
Payne, Darwin.
    Indomitable Sarah : the life of Judge Sarah T. Hughes / Darwin Payne ; foreword by
    Barefoot Sanders ; afterword by Sarah Weddington.
        p. cm.
    Includes bibliographical references and index.
    ISBN 0-87074-487-9 (alk. paper)
        1. Hughes, Sarah T. (Sarah Tilghman), 1896- 2. Women judges—Texas—Biography. 3.
    Women legislators—Texas—Biography. I. Title.

    KF373.H838P39 2004
    347.73'14'09764—dc22
    [B]   2004041668

Printed in the United States of America on acid-free paper

10   9   8   7   6   5   4   3   2   1

Foreword ~

The world remembers Sarah T. Hughes as the judge who swore in Vice President Lyndon B. Johnson as president on that fateful day in November 1963 when President John Kennedy was assassinated in Dallas. But there is more, much more, to the career of this diminutive woman (five feet tall, plus or minus an inch or so), as Darwin Payne demonstrates in this aptly titled and engrossing biography.

Policewoman, lawyer, legislator, state trial judge, federal district judge, author of *Roe v. Wade*, reformer of the Dallas County jail, lifelong fighter for equal rights for women, and early (and relentless) advocate of civil rights for minorities—these are some of the facets of the inspiring career of this remarkable woman, Judge Sarah T. Hughes. Plainspoken to the point of being blunt, she was without guile, a pragmatist, she looked for solutions that worked, in lawsuits and in public problems. Asked in later years, after having received many awards for public service, to recall the biggest thrill of her career, she said that it was being elected to the Texas Legislature in 1930 from Dallas County. (She said her second biggest thrill was becoming a federal district judge in 1962.) Named by Governor Allred to the state district bench back in 1935 while serving in the legislature, she did not have any serious opposition for reelection during the twenty-six years she served. That she was a dedicated Democrat made no difference whatsoever in her courtroom. Her integrity, impartiality, efficiency, and energy were admired by lawyers who practiced in her court, even though some disagreed with her extrajudicial interests and activities.

Chronicled here is her active support of the Democratic ticket in the 1960 presidential campaign. With the election of Kennedy and Johnson, Judge Hughes decided to seek appointment to the federal district bench and campaigned for the post with her characteristic determination and energy. Opposed by the American Bar Association on account of her age (sixty-five), she was strongly supported by Speaker Sam Rayburn, Vice President Johnson, Senator Ralph Yarborough, and many lawyers (including her opponent in her unsuccessful 1946 congressional race, J. Frank Wilson). She was sworn in as a United States District Judge in 1962. Her role as the judge who administered the presidential oath to Lyndon Johnson November 22, 1963, is described here in gripping detail. Interestingly, as proud as she was of her part in this historic event, she did not consider it to be one of her major accomplishments, because, as she later recounted, it was not something that she had worked to achieve.

Judge Hughes brought to the federal court the same qualities that had characterized her service as a state trial judge. Her well-known determination was demonstrated in the contentious Dallas County jail reform case, in which, confronted with the opposition of the county to remedy unconstitutional conditions in the jail, she threatened to shut down the jail completely. No one doubted that she would do just that, and the county commissioners promptly decided to support funds for a new jail. Amid complaints that she was "coddling criminals," she ordered the county to place television sets in the tanks, the common areas where prisoners whiled away the time during the day. After it was found that TV substantially reduced fighting and property destruction, the criticism subsided.

In a ruling affirmed by the United States Supreme Court, Judge Hughes authored the opinion in *Roe v. Wade*, in which, joined by Judges Goldberg and Taylor, she held the Texas anti-abortion law unconstitutional. All are aware that the case continues to generate sharp, sometimes bitter, controversy.

For many years Judge Hughes handled all the criminal cases in the Dallas federal courthouse. She had the reputation for handing out tough sentences to white-collar offenders. Yet she had a firm belief in the merits of rehabilitation, particularly for nonviolent down-and-outers, thus demonstrating her well-known instinct to help the underdog. She often granted probation when another judge might not have, and many of her unusual probation hearings are legendary in the federal courthouse.

After coming to the federal bench, Judge Hughes took no part in partisan politics. However, she continued to speak out strongly for the United Nations and to support organizations in which she had always been active, for example, the Business and Professional Women's Clubs and Zonta Club.

As all of us who knew her realized, Judge Hughes was always looking ahead. She never bragged about her honors or complained about her losses. Her husband, George, died in 1964, shortly after she went on the federal bench. She and he were devoted to each other, and it was obvious to those who saw her often that she was deeply affected by his death. Nevertheless, she did her grieving alone. She handled with the same stoicism the death of her beloved secretary of forty years, Gwen Graul, in 1980.

Felled by a massive stroke in May 1982 and unable to continue her judicial duties, Judge Hughes died in April 1985 at the age of eighty-nine.

Judge Hughes was unique—in her determination, her courage, and her lifelong dedication to the public good. Surely, she must be considered one of the most important women in our state and national history.

Darwin Payne has brought us a superb biography. Read and enjoy.

Barefoot Sanders
November 2003

～ Contents

Prologue ~

ternally etched in the minds of millions of Americans is the anguished image of a moment that abruptly changed a chapter in their history. It is, of course, the stark photograph depicting the swearing-in of Lyndon B. Johnson as the nation's president, taken just two hours after the shocking assassination of John F. Kennedy in 1963 on the streets of downtown Dallas. In the background loom the shadowy, furrowed faces of White House aides, standing in disarray and horror. In the foreground are Johnson, his wife, Lady Bird, and the slain president's widow, Jacqueline. Lady Bird Johnson is composed, obviously deep in thought about the awful event she has witnessed and what it foretells. Jackie Kennedy, wearing a fashionable pink suit still stained with blood from her slain husband, appears to be in shock, her eyes unfocused and her lips apart. Johnson, his right hand uplifted and his left hand flattened atop a Bible, is grim and purposeful as he looks into the face of the small woman who for these few moments commands his attention and that of the others as well.

This diminutive, bespectacled woman, United States District Judge Sarah T. Hughes, had been summoned to *Air Force One* from her home only minutes before. She is the person to whom Lyndon Baines Johnson is swearing that he will faithfully execute the office of president and preserve, protect, and defend the Constitution of the United States. In front of the judge the hand of Assistant Press Secretary Malcolm Kilduff can be seen holding the microphone of a stenographer's Dictaphone machine, the only instrument available for recording for posterity the few words of this occasion.

In this dramatic episode, occurring at a time when all of America and much of the world focused their attention on events in Dallas, Sarah Augusta Tilghman Hughes was thrust suddenly onto center stage. For the rest of her life millions of people would remember her for the role she played in assuring the legitimacy of constitutional presidential succession. Those who knew her only for this, though, knew very little of her.

Long before that fateful day, Sarah T. Hughes had been a maker of head-lines. Beginning in the early 1930s and into the 1980s she was the foremost Democratic woman in Texas. She was a legislator, judge, political leader, and feminist who had devoted her life to the liberal movement that dominated so much of the twentieth century, the effort to extend the full rights and privi-leges of American citizenship especially to women but also to ethnic minori-ties, juveniles, prisoners, and laborers.

She wrote the opinion and was the presiding member of the three-judge panel that overturned Texas's anti-abortion statutes in *Roe v. Wade*, one of the most momentous legal decisions of the twentieth century. It was a ruling that continues to serve as a lightning rod for politicians and judicial candidates well into the present century.

Her favorable ruling in a class-action suit filed by Dallas County jail inmates forced a massive overhaul in the treatment of prisoners. She threat-ened to shut down the jail unless her orders to institute humanitarian reforms and provide a decent environment were followed. When she visited the jail on an inspection tour, inmates recognized her and cheered. Defying public criticisms and the recalcitrant county commissioners, she ultimately ordered the commissioners to construct a modern and expensive facility incorporat-ing the latest advances in penal reform.

Twenty-five years earlier she single-handedly launched a determined campaign to force the Dallas County commissioners to provide a modern and separate facility for juvenile offenders. Her speeches on the subject infuriated county officials but won others to her side. In 1946 voters approved a million-dollar bond program that led to a modern juvenile home.

Overriding all of Judge Hughes's interests was her desire to push women into the public arena, to extend their activities far beyond the mere act of voting awarded them in 1920, when she was a young woman. She encouraged protégés, prodded them to run for public office, lobbied for and promoted legislation that would permit women to serve on juries (a privilege denied them in Texas until 1954), urged equal pay for women in business and all other endeavors, ridiculed and sought to overturn property laws that made women subservient to their husbands, crusaded for the creation of courts dedicated to domestic and juvenile cases, and favored (at a time when almost all women disagreed with her) drafting women by the armed forces and plac-ing them alongside men as equal partners in combat.

The long struggle and triumphant victory to empower women through the Nineteenth Amendment did not, for Sarah T. Hughes, signal a final victory as it did for so many others. Much remained to be done. The brief flurry of female political activity that followed the granting of women's suffrage in 1920 was short-lived. Some bold women enrolled in law schools; a few ran for public office. Then came a surprising lull. There was no significant follow-up to extend further the rights of women beyond the mere privilege of voting. The immediate goal had been attained. The powerful organizations that had coalesced in the fight for suffrage grew quiet. A period of relaxation, even retreat, commenced. Other pressing matters such as the Great Depression, a worldwide war, postwar adjustments, and the Cold War had to be dealt with. Not until the societal upheavals of the 1960s and 1970s would women energize themselves once more to tackle the next phase of their struggle for equality.

There may have been an interregnum for others during these decades, but not so for Sarah T. Hughes. She, along with a few others, labored consistently in what sometimes seemed to be an unappreciated battle to extend the rights of women. Throughout her career, she gave speeches and wrote articles encouraging women to step into the public arena. Her crusades and her own actions always provided an example. Elected to the Texas Legislature in 1930 as one of a handful of women in a predominantly man's world, she lost no time in plunging into the fierce deal-making that typified Texas politics, and she experienced surprising success as a crusader for liberal reform. Five years after her election she became the first woman in Texas history to serve as a state district judge, winning confirmation after a controversial and headline-making battle in which she was admonished to stay in the kitchen, where she and all women belonged. At the Democratic National Convention in 1952 she was placed in nomination for vice president, the second woman accorded that honor, following Mrs. Leroy Springs of South Carolina in 1924. In 1961, after twenty-six years as a state district judge, she thought it time to call in the chips owed to her as a faithful Democratic crusader, and against great odds she sought and won nomination by President John F. Kennedy to become a federal district judge, gaining Senate confirmation despite the initial reluctance of Attorney General Robert Kennedy and opposition by the American Bar Association on the grounds that at sixty-five she was too old.

For much of her career Judge Hughes enjoyed an association with and was supported by a powerful organization that continued to upgrade the

3

status of women even after suffrage was won. The National Federation of Business and Professional Women's Clubs, founded in 1919, was a coalition of local clubs dedicated to the betterment of women. Judge Hughes served as national president of the organization and held many other of its high offices. On a persistent, regular basis, the National Federation and state and local B&PW Clubs worked to improve the status of women through lobbying, research, special programs, commissions, and annual conventions. Their important efforts would be often overlooked after more flamboyant women and organizations surfaced in the late 1960s and grabbed the feminist flag. The B&PW Clubs provided much of the groundwork to make the success of the modern women's movement possible, and younger feminists called upon Judge Hughes for advice and counsel.

From early adulthood to her last years, Sarah T. Hughes never wavered in her convictions. When she identified a goal—and she always had a goal— she pursued it relentlessly. Never disingenuous, she developed instead a reputation for forthrightness, even tartness. She was comfortable with herself, with deep roots planted in the two communities in which she lived all her life, first Baltimore and then Dallas.

As accomplished as Judge Hughes was in her professional life, she was memorable as well for her striking personality. Concerned all her life with staying physically fit, even in her eighties she was rising at dawn, doing her yoga exercises, and swimming laps in the heated swimming pool in her back- yard in Dallas. Her favorite vacation spot was a small village in Norway, but she also journeyed to more remote places such as islands in the South Pacific.

Upon her death in 1985 U.S. district judge Robert Hill summed her up: "She was the most independent individual—notice I said individual, not woman—that I ever met in my life. She didn't lean on anyone; she was a free thinker who would never compromise her beliefs."[1] One of her most success- ful protégés, long-time and leading Democratic congressman Martin Frost, served as her law clerk early in his career. "Had she been ten years younger," he said, "I am convinced she would have been the first woman on the U.S. Supreme Court."[2]

1 ~

Dynamo from Baltimore

In the last decade of the nineteenth century, Baltimore, the place of Sarah Tilghman Hughes's birth, was an American city very comfortable with itself, happy in its commercial prowess as one of the nation's major ports, proud of its rich heritage, and content with the genteel, easy-going ways that marked so many of its half million residents. The Tilghmans were among a number of Baltimore families whose descendants had played important roles in the creation of the nation. Few if any were more distinguished than the Tilghmans. General George Washington himself said the Tilghmans were among the "pillars of the Revolution." He undoubtedly was thinking primarily of Lt. Col. Tench Tilghman, who served as his aide-de-camp along with Alexander Hamilton and who in a dramatic four-day journey sometimes compared to that of Paul Revere, rode horseback from Yorktown to Philadelphia to carry official news of Cornwallis's surrender to the Continental Congress.* Another distant relative, Matthew Tilghman, was active with the Committees of Correspondence and became a member of Congress between 1774 and 1776, resigning to become Talbot County's senator in Maryland's first legislative assembly.[1]

The Tilghman clan's prominence in affairs of the proprietary province had deep roots, beginning with the arrival in 1660 of an English surgeon named Richard Tilghman, who settled on the Eastern Shore and was given a thousand acres of land for bringing twenty persons to the colony. Succeeding generations involved themselves significantly in the colonial government of Maryland, all the way up to Revolutionary times. Sarah's own great-great-great-grandfather Richard Tilghman held high positions in the provincial government, including a stint as chancellor. Her great-great grandfather

---

*Colonel Tilghman, who fought in every action in which the main American army was involved, was Sarah T. Hughes's first cousin "four times removed" (see endnote 2).

James Tilghman took office as Maryland's first attorney general after independence was declared and later served as chief justice of a four-county judicial district.[2]

When the Civil War commenced, many family members of this border state opted for the Southern cause. Brigadier General Lloyd Tilghman, who had moved from his native Maryland to Kentucky prior to the outbreak of war, was killed at the battle of Champion Hill at Vicksburg. Tench Francis Tilghman slipped across federal lines as a civilian, and he helped Jefferson Davis evade pursuing Union troops after the collapse of the Confederacy in the spring of 1865. Oswald Tilghman fought with Terry's Texas Rangers, was captured in Mississippi in July 1863, and spent the rest of the war in Union prison camps. After the war he studied law and eventually became secretary of state for Maryland.[3]

Those days, though, had faded into the past by the time the Tilghman line produced Sarah's father, James Cooke Tilghman, a man of modest means and attainment who was born in 1858, the son of James and Sarah Augusta Tilghman. He sold coal briefly as a young man before taking a job as a "clerk." Precisely what this entailed is uncertain, but for the rest of his working life the Baltimore City directories listed his occupation as "clerk." Such a job was respectable if lacking in prestige and substantial recompense. He was content to live in ordinary circumstances in Baltimore in the bosom of relatives and friends, very conscious of his family's rich heritage.[4]

Sarah's mother, Elizabeth Haughton, was an interesting contrast. The daughter of Malacai and Elizabeth Bradley Haughton, she was orphaned at an early age. Her father died at the age of thirty-five in 1867 when Elizabeth was seven years old. The date of her mother's death is uncertain. Sarah's mother had been reared by an aunt in North Carolina. As an adult she found a job as a saleslady in a department store. Just how she and J. Cooke Tilghman came to know one another, given the geographical distance between them, is not known, but on June 20, 1892, they were married. James, or "Jay," as he sometimes was called, was thirty-four years of age and Elizabeth thirty-two. Elizabeth, having fended for herself for so long, was from all available evidence a strong-willed, practical woman with ambition. The modest economic circumstances in which the couple found themselves in Baltimore gave Elizabeth little reason to appreciate or dwell on her husband's distinguished family heritage.[5]

After the disappointment of a still-born infant, their first surviving child, a little girl who was destined seven decades later to give the oath of office to the thirty-sixth president of the United States, was born at their home on August 2, 1896. A neighborhood physician, Dr. E. A. Smith, was in attendance. The birth certificate issued by the Baltimore City Health Department identified the infant only as "Tilghman," omitting given names, height, and weight.[6] She was named Sarah Augusta—after her father's mother, Sarah Augusta James—but not until seventy years later would Sarah file a document to amend the birth certificate to include her name "Sarah," omitting and seemingly forgetting the middle name she had never used, "Augusta."[7] Two years after Sarah's birth, a brother, Richard Haughton, arrived on August 24, 1898, completing the Tilghman family.

The family lived in one of the classic, three-story row houses so typical of Baltimore. The Tilghmans' home, 1110 Myrtle Avenue, was on the corner at the end of a long stretch of row houses, just a few blocks west of the downtown area.[8] Although the Tilghmans lived in several different houses during Sarah's childhood, she and her parents remained within a three-mile radius of this same neighborhood, from her birth through her undergraduate years at nearby Goucher College. This would not have seemed remarkable to a fellow Baltimorean H.L. Mencken, who graduated from high school in the same year Sarah was born and who lived almost his entire life less than a mile from Sarah's birthplace in the same house he grew up in.

Just north of the Tilghman neighborhood was the vast Druid Hill Park, a popular recreational area where streetcars and "coach and fours" carried families for their Sunday afternoon outings. As late as the 1880s deer occasionally could still be seen on the grounds. Throughout town were streets and alleys still paved with cobblestones and Belgian blocks. Sidewalks were made of red bricks. A large foreign-born population included numbers of Italian fruit vendors who presided over "johnnie" stands at corners throughout the city, and, given the densely populated neighborhood of the Tilghmans, surely one was located near their place.[9]

Even though the Tilghmans' circumstances were modest, the family enjoyed a social life on a small scale. As members of the Episcopal church, they permitted Sarah to learn card games but forbade her to ride her bicycle on Sundays.[10] On rare occasions the Tilghmans might even see their names in the newspaper, such as the time when "Mr. and Mrs. J. Cooke Tilghman" were among the participants in a series of progressive euchres (a card game) at Mount Brook Cottage on Park Heights Avenue. Sarah carefully maintained notations of such items in a scrapbook she filled with clippings, programs, and miscellaneous things typical of a child's mementos. Her own name probably first appeared in the newspaper in a brief notice when "little Miss Tilghman," age six, was the flower girl at a wedding at Associate Congregational Church. In her scrapbook Sarah later noted her role as a school mascot, saying, "I was dressed just like the older girls only I had on socks. My but I felt big sitting down at the table with all the 'big' girls." At the age of seven she was enrolled in the Baltimore Grammar School, starting in the second grade rather than the first. An early undated report card, issued long before the modern collapse of grading standards, showed Sarah with an "E" or excellent for conduct, "Good" for spelling, "Fair" for reading, "Good" for writing, and "Fair" for arithmetic.[11]

Shortly after the turn of the century the Tilghmans moved to Park Heights Avenue near First Avenue, a few blocks from the old house on Myrtle Avenue. Perhaps this coincided with an event that loomed large in the adult memory of Sarah T. Hughes. To bolster the family income Mrs. Tilghman, evidently without the help of her husband, opened a summer boardinghouse in 1900 on the outskirts of Baltimore. Sarah, then four, and her brother, Haughton, two, spent a good part of their future summers there as their mother worked to improve the family's financial situation.[12] Some sixteen years later Sarah herself took over for a summer the job of running the boarding-house while her mother was ill.[13] In the same year the boardinghouse opened, Mr. Tilghman must have tried his luck at an enterprise with more potential reward than clerking. R. L. Polk & Company's Baltimore City Directory for 1900, and only for this year, lists his occupation as "liquors." Thereafter and in succeeding years, his occupation returned once more to "clerk." Try though he did, Sarah's father was unable to interest his daughter in his family's back-ground. Half a century later, when she did develop such an interest, she would recall his saying, "Sarah doesn't give a damn about her ancestors."[14]

It was the more industrious side of her mother after which Sarah would model herself. Her mother's expectations were high. Sarah would designate her as the strongest influence in her life. "She always told me I could do anything I wanted to."[15] When Sarah graduated from elementary school she was pleased to have been fourth in the class. Instead of gushing over her daughter's accomplishments, though, Bessie Tilghman said quietly but firmly, "You should have been first." It was an admonition Sarah never forgot.[16]

In the eighth grade Sarah and her classmates went to Washington, D.C., on a field trip. On the way back, a journey of some thirty miles, Sarah fell asleep in the arms of "Mister Sparks," presumably a teacher or chaperone. "That shows how 'big' I was."[17] Indeed, Sarah was tiny. At maturity, she would reach a height alternately listed as just five feet or sometimes five feet and one-half inch. "And don't forget the half inch," she would sometimes admonish as an adult.

Political events in the nation's capital and changing concepts during this time about the proper role of the federal government surely did not occur without some impact, however small, on an impressionable student such as Sarah. Theodore Roosevelt, having engineered William Howard Taft into the presidency as his successor, now had become estranged from him as Taft veered into conservatism. By 1910, talk already could be heard about the possible formation of a third party if Taft retained the Republican nomination in 1912. Theories behind the Progressive movement had experienced full flower; the old philosophy of laissez-faire individualism had given way to the idea that society should organize itself for collective actions in the public interest. Such organization must occur at governmental levels—federal, state, and municipal. There was a strong impulse to do good. Sarah would adopt and fully subscribe to Progressive or liberal politics for all her life.

In the fall of 1910 first-year student Sarah Tilghman enrolled in Western Female High School. It was a public school, one of two all-girl schools founded in 1844 in Baltimore when the board of school commissioners had observed in their 1843 report to city officials that "females of superior abilities and suitable attainments in the primary schools are as deserving as males of the opportunity to obtain a more liberal English education." Since females were "more delicate" than males and could not attend schools at remote distances, the recommendation that two schools be built was followed—one on the east side of town and another on the west side.[18] By the time of Sarah's enrollment, Western High was in a building constructed in the 1890s at the corner of Lafayette and McCulloh streets, only a few blocks from her house.

At Western, Sarah exhibited the indomitable spirit that would mark the rest of her life. By November she had been elected president of the freshman class. As a note from a friend related, "Here's to the littlest, but not to the least of class presidents! May she live and prosper!" The fierceness of Sarah's personality, coupled with her diminutive stature, seemed to many a remarkable contrast. Another invitation to a high school party reinforces that image. It addressed her as "small but terrible."[19]

Her competitiveness was evidenced especially in her participation in intramural track and field, gymnastics, and basketball. "We won it! Oh how mad the Seniors were," she exclaimed after a class gymnastics victory during her junior year. When a teacher disapproved of the victors' excessive exuberance, Sarah privately recorded her own disgust at the teacher's reaction: "As if everybody doesn't want to win."[20]

Ample opportunity existed for other extracurricular activities. Public speaking and theatrical presentations were emphasized. Sarah saved in her scrapbook many of the programs describing these events, some of which she participated in. In "A Roman Wedding," presented by Latin Department students, she took the role of a flute player. In "Vaudeville" she gave a reading. Dances were held, but at the all-girls' school male partners were not present or necessary. Sarah's dance program in 1913 listed only girls as her partners, as was the custom.[21]

But academics were most important to her. The strong sense of discipline her mother had instilled in her was helpful. Sarah habitually went to bed at 8 P.M., and after eight hours of sleep arose at 4 A.M. She did not trouble herself in applying makeup—for fear of disapproval, she never used lipstick until after her mother died—and she never faced a day of school with her lessons unprepared.[22]

In the summer of 1912, prior to her senior year, Sarah managed to be a spectator at one of the most memorable political conventions ever held, the Democratic National Convention in Baltimore. Champ Clark, the salty old Speaker of the House, appeared to have the presidential nomination locked up, enjoying a large majority in early ballots. But his principal challenger, Woodrow Wilson, the former Princeton president who had electrified the nation with his reform programs as governor of New Jersey, persisted in his bid for the nomination, and when William Jennings Bryan dramatically shifted his vote midway from Clark to Wilson, a corner was turned. In one of the miracles of American politics, on the forty-sixth ballot Wilson won the nomination. The long struggle between the brilliant reformer and the unimaginative old-time politician, the drama of so many ballots, and the machinations of Bryan as kingmaker captured the attention of the nation, and of Sarah, too. She would remember the convention as her earliest exposure to Progressive rhetoric.[23]

The issue of women's suffrage, to be won with Wilson's support during the last months of his second term, loomed large at this all-girls' school. In one debate, "Resolved that women should vote," Sarah's team won. The importance of gaining the vote for women was also the topic for the speaker at the high school graduation ceremony in 1913. More than fifty years later, when she was giving the commencement address herself at a Dallas community college, Sarah T. Hughes said his message made a lasting impression on her.[24]

Sarah was sixteen years of age at her spring graduation and salutatorian of her class. Her mother's comment was not unfamiliar: "You should have been first."[25]

That she would go to college was a foregone conclusion, and the matter of where to go was already decided. "As far as I was concerned, there was only one college, and that was Goucher College," she later said. "There I intended to go and did go in September 1913."[26] Goucher was an all-women's institution (to become coeducational in 1986), located in central Baltimore in a Romanesque building next door to the Methodist church on St. Paul between Twenty-second and Twenty-third streets. It was about a mile from where Sarah had been born, on Myrtle Avenue, even closer to Western High, and no more than two miles from the Tilghman household at Shirley and Ludwig streets, where the family had relocated a year or so earlier.

Even before graduating from high school Sarah participated in a fundraising drive for Goucher as one of four students who spoke on March 27, 1913, before a large audience of high school girls at Ford's Opera House. With no public address system, students with strong voices were needed, and as Sarah said, "I filled the bill." She read a speech prepared by someone else, entitled "A Plea for Goucher."[27]

The choice of Goucher, even if seemingly dictated by proximity, was not a bad one for Sarah Tilghman or for any other young woman. The college had been founded in Baltimore in 1885 under the auspices of the Baltimore Conference of the Methodist Episcopal Church as an extension of the same realization that had led to Western High—women as well as men might profit from higher education. Its original name, the Woman's College of Baltimore, was changed in 1910 to Goucher College in honor of its benefactor and second president, the Reverend Dr. John Franklin Goucher.[28] Requirements for admission included three units of English, two of algebra, one of plane geometry, and three of a foreign language. Entrance examinations were given twice a year, and scholarships were offered to students with special promise. Sarah took the examination with trepidation, carrying a four-leaf clover for luck. The result was all she had hoped for—she was awarded a scholarship. Her mother was pleased, of course, but Sarah dared not tell her about the four-leaf clover.[29]

As an educational institution Goucher had won much favor in its existence of three decades, attracting students from far beyond the Baltimore area. By 1914 its graduates already had organized alumni chapters in Charleston, Philadelphia, Atlanta, New York, Pittsburgh, and Connecticut. John F. Goucher was now president emeritus, succeeded as president by William Westley Guth.[30] One father who enrolled his daughter expressed disappointment when he saw that the college was so near downtown. President Guth explained that this was an advantage, for "all of Baltimore is our laboratory and our classroom."[31]

Sarah A. Tilghman became one of 125 freshmen, class of 1917, to enroll in the fall of 1913. (Attrition would reduce her class size to 92 by 1917.) The college had a total enrollment of about 550 ambitious young women from upper and upper-middle-class families. About a fourth of Sarah's freshman classmates were from Baltimore, a dozen others from the rest of the state, and the remaining from out of state. First-year class members were welcomed to Goucher at a September reception at the YWCA, new students generally wearing the dresses they had purchased a few months earlier for their high school graduation. "We left that night most conscious of the Pride the college must feel in us," the class historian later wrote.[32]

"Goucher was a city college, its only campus the hockey field, tennis courts, and a bright patch of green marking the approach to Goucher Hall," Sarah recalled in a speech to the school's Cleveland alumni years later. "The students would have appeared a rather strange looking lot—skirts an inch from the ground, high button shoes, long hair and no makeup. Even basketball found us completely covered with voluminous bloomers, long stockings and middy blouses."[33]

Regulations were strict. Dancing was permitted, but not with boys. Boys were not even allowed to attend the girls' basketball games. Goucher girls could go to the theater under restrictions, but not to the movies.[34] Students observed formalities that already had been developed as school tradition. Seniors were accorded an honored place in daily life. Yet the college was small enough that all students, no matter their classifications, came to know one another very well. Boarding students lived in residence halls named for Norse gods such as Mardal and Folkvang.

One of the advantages of a small, all-female college such as Goucher was the opportunity for each student to participate fully in extracurricular activities. In fact, each student was required to play on one of her class athletic teams, either field hockey, basketball, swimming, or tennis. The college shunned intercollegiate competition, offering instead a comprehensive intramural schedule in which class teams played one another for the college championship in contests marked by intense spirit. Sarah immediately plunged fully into the athletic program. Despite her short stature, she became captain of the freshman basketball team, and she would continue to be a star on the class basketball team for all her years at Goucher. She also was on the swimming and field hockey teams.

Immersed in athletics, Sarah "learned to lose without bitterness, to get up and try again, to never feel resentment." It was a lesson in sportsmanship, one that she later realized was essential for her long-time devotion to politics. Additionally, she gave sports credit for inculcating in her a habit of exercise that she continued enthusiastically throughout her adult life.[35]

Sarah's intense interest in athletics reflected a competitiveness not limited to sports. In her sophomore year she was elected class president. In her senior year, after two years as assistant business manager, she became business manager for the *Goucher College Weekly* newspaper. An anecdote in the yearbook related her success at this job and suggested her future promise: "After talking all day to a stern business man, she went off with an 'ad' and he called to her as she ran, 'Come back any day—there's a job for you here—name your own salary, you're worth it, my dear.'"[36] The job of business manager required managerial skills, for Sarah supervised a staff of assistants including three seniors, two juniors, and two sophomores.

She became a member of the Delta Gamma fraternity (as it then was called, rather than sorority), recording secretary of the YMCA, and vice president of the college's athletic association. In the latter capacity she was a member of a committee whose task was to study whether intercollegiate athletics would be more beneficial to the college and its students than its intense intramural program. The committee's unanimous answer was no. The athletic association then passed a motion unanimously opposing Goucher's participation in intercollegiate athletics. To do otherwise would have surely changed the democratic atmosphere at Goucher, for only the best athletes would be permitted to play on the intercollegiate teams. Far more important to the college was the development of well-rounded women.[37]

Individual classes not only fielded their own athletic intramural teams; they also put on their own class plays. In Sarah's class production of *Sherwood Forest* she played the role of Much. For a senior class production of *Macbeth* in 1917 she took the part of a murderer. Students made their own costumes. In another production, *A Thousand Years Ago*, she was one of three assistant stage managers. In such plays the female students assumed all parts, including those for men.

When her old Western High School held a college day during Sarah's junior year she was one of four alumni who returned to speak there. Sarah's topic, one she had learned well through experience, was "Student Activities Other Than Curricular."[38]

Despite the frequent and sometimes vigorous activities in which the students regularly participated, there was an air of traditional domesticity at Goucher. The practice of knitting, for instance, was so prevalent that many students even knit during their professors' lectures. One student decried this practice in a letter to the school newspaper, pointing out that it was disastrous to the lecturer working so hard to impart knowledge.[39]

Generally, students' ambitions for future careers seemed modest by today's standards. Most of them intended to be teachers; a few planned to be secretaries; a few others to be social workers and librarians. Even so, the number of Goucher students majoring in science was nearly twice the national average. Sarah chose to major in biology; she minored in mathematics and took Latin for three years, doing very well in all her courses. But, like so many Goucher students, she accepted the likelihood that she would become a teacher.[40] Already she was getting some practice, earning forty dollars a month as a part-time playground teacher in the Baltimore public schools.[41]

Suffrage continued to be a major concern of the students as well as of the nation. Goucher sponsored its own chapter of the College Equal Suffrage League. In April 1916 a leading feminist and brilliant speaker, Beatrice Forbes-Robertson-Hale, addressed a meeting sponsored by the organization, leaving an impression on Sarah's receptive mind.

Sarah, however, was too preoccupied with college life to be looking very far outward at this stage. By her junior year she had accepted and appreciated the traditional distinctions among the classes of Goucher, in which freshmen treated upperclassmen with deference, and seniors especially held a position of privilege. In a call for the continuation of such measures, she wrote a "Point of View" essay in the college magazine *Kalends*, observing, "We are fast getting away from little courtesies which were formerly paid the Seniors." The possibility for members of the various classes to mingle at Goucher, though, was one of the best things about the college, she thought.[42] Yet, there were clear signs of individualism in Sarah. She resigned on principle from an honorary society, Red Strings, because she believed some nominations were being influenced by pull rather than by merit.[43] Over the years, her memories of Red Strings mellowed. More than fifty years later, speaking to a Goucher alumni group, she recalled fondly the thrill of seeing who would be tapped for Red Strings on the last night of step-singing.[44]

During Sarah's years there Goucher made great advances toward its financial well-being. In 1913 its officials successfully completed an endowment drive to pay off mounting debts that had threatened the stability of the college. In the fall of Sarah's senior year, college officials mounted another fund-raising campaign, and by spring slightly more than a million dollars already had been gathered. A new chapel with a ten-thousand-dollar organ was opened in her junior year, permitting students to attend services on their own campus instead of next door at the First Methodist Church. For the chapel's inaugural service the student body entered by class in order of seniority, with all seniors, juniors, and sophomores wearing caps and gowns but the freshmen not yet privileged to wear academic regalia. The student newspaper quoted Dr. Guth as urging his students to "find out whither they were going and to seek out a straight line to that goal and to keep to that line as far as possible."[45]

By graduation, Sarah had earned a remarkable reputation for determination, hard work, and scholarship. She was one of only nine students selected for the Senior Society. Her senior photograph in the college yearbook shows an attractive, pleasant-looking young woman with her hair pulled back tightly in a bun. She chose as her motto one to which she would adhere the rest of her life: "Early to bed and early to rise makes a man healthy, wealthy and wise," although she would have insisted that "or woman" be included. The yearbook description of "Sally," as she was then called, said she definitely followed Ben Franklin's maxim. "We know this is true, she retires at six and arises at two. And healthy—just look at her basket-ball fame; both hockey and swimming have won her a name. While as for her wisdom, she rivals the sharks and shines in the classroom as well as in marks. She says she's not wealthy, and maybe it's true, but if she needs money, she knows what to do."[46]

On June 5, 1917, Goucher College had its twenty-sixth annual commencement exercise at Baltimore's Lyric Theater. Students marched into the ceremony behind class banners and stood until the graduating seniors and faculty had taken their places on the platform. "America, the Beautiful" was sung, and the president of Oberlin College, Henry Churchill King, gave an address on the topic "Reverence for Personality." Sarah was recognized at the ceremony for two attributes that would mark the rest of her life—athleticism and scholarship. She was one of just three seniors to be awarded a sweater for her athletic prowess, and she was also elected to Phi Beta Kappa.[47]

She would remember her years at Goucher with great fondness. "I have many nostalgic memories," she said half a century later. "There were plenty of good times—basketball, hockey, tennis, swimming, glee club, plays, and weekly teas in the fraternity alcoves. Most cherished were the Spring boat rides. And then there was Commencement Week with its Freshman lantern chain, nightly stepsinging, and Sophomore daisy chain."[48] Most important, though, was the institution's pioneer spirit. The idea that women were the intellectual equals of men and that academic standards for men and women should be the same was still novel and refreshing. "The major aim of the college," Hughes realized only later, "was to prepare the student for a full life—to open the windows of the mind, to encourage exploration and a receptive attitude to new ideas, and to welcome and accept responsibility." The students themselves absorbed but did not fully appreciate the faith of the college's founders and their vision of education.[49]

As the young graduates pondered their futures, events in troubled Europe dominated the news. Two months earlier Congress had approved Woodrow Wilson's call to declare war on Germany and to make the world safe for democracy, and it had authorized the Selective Service Act to require American men between the ages of twenty-one and thirty to register for the draft. A month earlier Nicholas II had abdicated as czar of Russia, and Vladimir Lenin had arrived in Petrograd in a sealed railroad car. War news overshadowed other events in nearby Washington, D.C., but of interest to young women of Sarah's age and sensibilities was the arrest of four women for picketing outside the White House in behalf of suffrage.

• • • • •

Sarah was ready to embark upon a teaching career, but a crisis at home provided an entirely new challenge for the promising Miss Tilghman. Her mother was ill, but summer had arrived and there were thirty tenants at the boardinghouse and three employees who needed supervision. Unpaid bills were piling up. A mortgage payment was due. Sarah took over her mother's chores, doing everything—going to the market twice a week, cooking, dishwashing, and sweeping. "It was the most difficult job I ever had," she later said, "a nightmare." But she was successful at it, and with the arrival of fall she left the boardinghouse and departed for the first real job of her life.[50]

The position she had accepted was as a teacher in her mother's home state of North Carolina at the sort of institution that by now was familiar and comfortable for her—Salem College and Academy, an all-women's boarding school for both high school and college students. The setting, however, was opposite to the dense urban environment in which she had spent her life. The school was located in Winston-Salem, about thirty miles from the Blue Ridge Mountains in a tobacco-growing region. A historic and prestigious institution, Salem College and Academy had been founded in 1772 by Moravians, a Protestant denomination whose followers believed in simplicity in worship, individual freedom, and disciplined Christian living. It was the oldest school in the nation dedicated to the education of women. Sarah Tilghman's position primarily involved teaching high school physics, chemistry, and general science, but she also taught biology to the college students. As a beginning teacher, she earned a salary of six hundred dollars a year plus "maintenance," or room and board.[51]

Little is known about Tilghman's experiences there beyond the fact that she remained for two years. Years later, when the Federal Bureau of Investigation conducted a background check upon her nomination as a federal judge, an agent located the retired treasurer of the college, who vaguely remembered her. She could recall her only as "an intelligent and very competent instructor."[52] Later, Sarah Tilghman, by then Sarah T. Hughes, would recall these two years at Salem College and Academy as the most frustrating of her life. She lacked the patience required for teaching; opportunities for advancement seemed limited; and there was a haunting fear—she told an interviewer years later—that if she remained there she might become a stereotypical old maid teacher.[53] Moreover, her competitive nature undoubtedly required a more open field if she were to satisfy her yearning for measurable accomplishments. One may suppose that—as different as this North

Carolina setting might have been from what she was accustomed to—all-female institutions were too familiar for her naturally adventurous spirit. A more interesting and challenging world outside beckoned.

Resigning at the end of her second year, she returned to the comfort of Baltimore and home, still uncertain about what that new world might be. She enrolled briefly at Johns Hopkins University to take a graduate course in zoology, then quickly realized this was not what she wanted either. After one week she quit. A far more exciting possibility had dawned on her that could offer a far larger canvas for her potential—law school.

It was, she later said, "the only other thing that I could think of." Evidently, though, the idea had been percolating in her head for some time. She had a cousin, about seven years older, who had graduated from the University of Virginia Law School. When Sarah was a very young girl, he had been her hero. "And so I wanted to follow in his footsteps. I decided that I would study law."[54] On another occasion she would say she decided to go to law school because she knew it would be an avenue for running for political office, an ambition she said she had felt since childhood.[55]

How would she finance it? Where would she enroll? The George Washington University Law School in Washington, D.C., was a convenient choice. There, students could choose either a morning or an evening class schedule, graduating either way in three years. Women and men had been admitted on an equal basis at GWU's Law School since 1914, when the board reversed a policy adopted in 1883 stating that legal training for women was not required by any public want. In 1916 Marion Clark had become the first woman to graduate.[56]

All that remained for Tilghman to study law there, aside from being admitted, was finding a job that would support her. She submitted applications with the U.S. Patent Office and with the Washington, D.C., police department. The first offer came from the police department to be a "Class 1" female officer. She quickly accepted it at an annual salary of approximately sixteen hundred dollars, more than twice what she had been earning at Salem.[57]

Progressive police departments such as that of Washington, D.C., had begun to hire female officers, not to perform the same duties as men, but to work in a preventive fashion with wayward young women and girls.[58] The Women's Bureau had become a part of the District of Columbia police department during World War I. Tilghman reported for work on September

30, 1919, as one of twenty-one female officers. Each "copette" was a college graduate, a trained nurse, or an experienced social worker.[59] The duties on Sarah's daytime shift centered around patrolling areas where female runaways and young prostitutes might be found, especially the magnificent new Union Station near the Capitol building. She also patrolled dance halls, moving-picture houses, restaurants, and skating rinks. A large part of her work involved the investigation of cases involving women and children. In her job Tilghman carried neither pistol nor whistle; nor did she wear a uniform. The idea in this progressive concept was not to punish but to rehabilitate. Female offenders were placed in a house of detention for their brief detainments, a facility designed to resemble anything but a jail. Girls and women were interviewed in depth, given mental and physical examinations, treated for venereal diseases if necessary, and assessed so that an intelligent recommendation could be made to the court for their disposition. Recreational and educational opportunities were offered, and supervisors sought to change offenders' attitudes so that they could reenter society as productive citizens.[60]

Tilghman's experience here formed an outlook that would endure for her lifetime. Years later, as a state district judge with special domestic and juvenile responsibilities, she would be committed to these same values, observing repeatedly that juvenile delinquency was caused not by personal choice but by failure of parents to supervise and provide a proper environment. She would carry the same concept to her work as a federal district judge in one of her most celebrated cases.

The Women's Bureau provided room and board for Tilghman and other female officers. She lived at 1737 T Street NW, rooming with her police partner, Carol Bliss Whiteford. Years later Whiteford recalled her roommate as being different from most young women she had known. She was not "chatty," and she displayed little interest in domestic activities. She imposed high standards on herself as well as on others. With so much time spent at the police station and in local courts, both young women realized that up to this point they had led sheltered lives. Now, for the first time, they were thrust into a world of complex problems. The results for those caught in these webs often were devastating, for they were entangled in situations in which their own initiatives often were hopelessly inadequate.[61]

Money was in short supply for this beginning officer, as was evident in a letter Sarah wrote to her brother, Richard. "At present, I have exactly $26. Tomorrow I have to pay ½ month's board $22 and I owe my law school tuition for this month $15 and a bill at a store for $6.95. Where oh where does that money go?" Despite her financial situation, she found herself compelled at times to assist the desperate people she encountered in her police duties. The $6.95 bill was an example. She had charged that amount at a store to help buy a coat for a needy young woman with the understanding that her husband would reimburse her. "Husband skipped," she wrote, "and I am in the hole for $6.95—more than I can save in 2 months." [62]

Sarah's interesting job caught the attention of her hometown newspaper, the *Evening Sun*, which carried a story about her under the headline "Goucher Girl Policewoman in Washington." The story quoted her extensively, and in it she explained that she had been drawn to the police force because she preferred to "study human nature" instead of inanimate things. Miss Tilghman's "penetrating eyes and sound knowledge of sociological problems reveal the matured judgment of an educated and well-poised woman," the writer, Gertrude Leimbach, noted. Yet, in physical appearance she resembled a girl of not more than eighteen years of age. Sarah explained her work:

> It must not be forgotten that the old conception of catching criminals constituting the sole duty of members of the police force does not apply to the female officer of the law. We are engaged in a phase of social service—our primary aim is constructive work, not detective work. We carry neither pistols nor blackjacks—those whom we must apprehend are made to feel that we are their friends and well-wishers and not their enemies. Professor Thomas, at Goucher College, always impressed upon us that we could learn more through studying people than we could through studying things. That is why I joined the women's police force of Washington—it gave me the opportunity of studying human nature as it is. Instead of as it is partially portrayed in books. Then, too, I am studying law in connection with my work, and I find that my contact with life in all its phases is invaluable to me in that connection. [63]

Her experience taught her that girls went wrong invariably because of a lack of parental authority and discipline. She believed that their morals, as many were beginning to attest in these first years of the Jazz Age, were "very much looser" than formerly, not because of increased depravity but because of the absence of supervision by their mothers. Such young girls were not branded as outcasts by the Women's Bureau but were taught "the beauty of high-minded womanhood, and the duty that every woman owes to society and to the race." It was a lesson Sarah Tilghman would never forget.[64]

One of Tilghman's most interesting assignments was an early one unrelated to her usual duties. She was sent to monitor one of the regular demonstrations being held outside the White House by women suffragettes.[65] One of the demonstrators Hughes may have exchanged glances with was a young woman with whom she later would have much in common, Burnita Shelton Matthews, a 1919 GWU Law School graduate who in 1949 would be named to a federal district judgeship by Harry S. Truman, the first woman to gain such an appointment. (Sarah would be the second.) In years to come Matthews and Sarah Tilghman Hughes would also share a common frustration that they both sought to correct through legislation—the continued exclusion of women from juries.

Suffrage for women, after a struggle of eight decades, was a year away, and in Tilghman's first year in Washington, D.C., both congressional houses passed resolutions to submit a constitutional amendment to the states for approval. In August 1920, the measure would be ratified as the Nineteenth Amendment. It served as a signal to many women's organizations that their lengthy struggle for equality had been won. Tilghman, as a battler who had missed direct involvement in the suffrage movement, would recognize it as only a small, first step toward equality.

The nation's capital, so near to Baltimore but so different in atmosphere, was an endlessly fascinating place for someone with Sarah Tilghman's natural instincts for battle. Here was an arena for all sorts of exciting and competing issues—women's suffrage, the League of Nations, Attorney General A. Mitchell Palmer's Red Scare raids, Democrats versus Republicans, internationalists versus isolationists, and on and on. The city's unique landscape was charming in another way with its handsome government buildings, monuments, statues of heroes, and broad avenues with great vistas. Even then, two decades into the twentieth century, small parties of American Indians dressed in their colorful native costumes could sometimes be seen walking up and down the streets, peering into the government buildings, viewing the White House and Capitol with awe, and wandering into the trinket shops of Pennsylvania Avenue as they explored the "Great White Father's" city.[66]

* * * * *

With a stimulating job and a reasonable salary secured, Tilghman completed her goal by enrolling as a full-time evening student at GWU's Law School on October 19, 1919. Three years' study was required for the LL.B. degree (until 1898 only two years' study had been required). Enrolling with Tilghman was an overflow first-year class of 374 students, many of them women. First-year classes—common law, contracts, equity, personal property, real property, and torts—taught by six full-time professors and fifteen part-time professors and lecturers, provided a dramatic shift in subject for her.[67] So crowded were the classes that the next year the university purchased a new building for the Law School, the old brownstone and brick headquarters building of the U.S. Department of Justice at McPherson Square. In this building a special women's room was designated, furnished attractively as a retreat for female students, who by 1921 amounted to a surprising 15 percent of the total enrollment of 896.[68] The bloom of suffrage had boosted female enrollment, but only briefly, for the number of women studying law would decline over the next several decades.

Miss Tilghman immediately plunged into a full round of law school activities. Her energy, ambition, and talents quickly propelled her into the leading circle of students in the school. Her job as a Washington, D.C., policewoman seemed to be no hindrance to extracurricular activities. She became one of sixty-four members of the Women's Legal Club, dedicated to the "promotion of a high standard of professional ethics and the preparation of women students for a full and worthy participation in the American system of self-government." In her second year she was elected the club's secretary, and in her third year she became its president. She also joined Kappa Beta Pi, a women's legal fraternity, and a host of other organizations. For all three years of study she belonged to the Law School senate. She was elected vice president as a second-year student and president in her final year.[69]

One of her favorite activities—and one that would remain so throughout her life—was debate. She served on the Debating Council and was a member of the Columbian Debating Society. In her senior year she was one of ten members of the debating fraternity, Delta Sigma Rho. Separate debate teams existed for women and men, although they also combined efforts for coeducational competition. For a year she was manager of the women's debate team, and in at least two intercollegiate debates she took the affirmative for the subject "Resolved, That the United States should recognize the soviet government of Russia." Her team won by unanimous decision on both occasions. After another debate held against West Virginia at the public library, Tilghman's photograph appeared in a local newspaper with three other female members of the team. Their debate subject was whether or not state legislatures should create industrial courts similar to one in Kansas.[70]

The young woman was making a vivid impression in Washington, not just at the Law School, but through her police work as well. Her combined qualities of short stature and aggressive demeanor made her a familiar figure in the city as she patrolled the streets checking on and giving assistance to delinquent children and young women. A law school classmate, Thomas Hudson McKee, attested a dozen years afterward that "her genius for administration and her zeal for social improvement" soon made her "the most attractive and well-known social worker and police official in Washington."[71]

Now, for the first time in her life, she had occasion to interact regularly with members of the opposite sex. One of the first young men to become a close friend was Lawrence Brooks Hays from Arkansas. The two of them discovered much in common in their developing views on economic and social justice as they prepared themselves for debate competitions. In their conversations, Hays later recalled, they often discussed how the political system might be used to help solve the problems of the less fortunate members of society, whom Sarah was seeing on a daily basis in her police work. When Hays at one point informed his friend that he was considering abandoning his studies of law and the possibility of a political career in favor of becoming a Baptist minister, Tilghman was convinced this would be a mistake, and she contacted a Lutheran minister in Baltimore, John G. Fleck, to counsel Hays. Fleck did not attempt to change Hays's mind, but he helped him to understand the spiritual and moral possibilities available in a political career. In his autobiography, *Politics Is My Parish*, Hays credited Fleck and Sarah for his decision to continue with his study of law and a political career.[72] Hays would become a long-time Democratic congressman from Arkansas, serving from 1943 to 1958, then serving as a special adviser to President John F. Kennedy. His interest in religion continued, though, and he eventually won election as president of the Southern Baptist Association. Hays's wit and lively personality were suggested by his oft-repeated quote: "Back of every achievement is a proud wife and a surprised mother-in-law." The friendship between Tilghman and Hays would continue throughout their careers.

The 1920 election pitting U.S. senator Warren G. Harding against fellow Ohioan James M. Cox provided grist for lengthy discussions among Tilghman, Hays, and other students. For Tilghman and other women students, it was their first opportunity to vote—the Nineteenth Amendment had been ratified only in August. The election served as a national referendum for whether or not the United States should join the League of Nations. Tilghman cast her first presidential ballot for the Democrat Cox, the candidate who favored the League of Nations.

Besides Hays, Tilghman encountered another young male classmate in her freshman year with whom she developed a more personal relationship—George Ernest Hughes Jr. from Texas. Hughes had been born in a log cabin in East Texas near the small town of Palestine. At Palestine High School he became president of his senior class and captain of the football, basketball, and debating teams. Upon graduation he attended the University of Texas. Service with the National Guard took him to the Mexican border during the troubles with Pancho Villa in 1916, and during World War I he went overseas with the Fortieth Infantry Division. He was discharged from the army in October 1919 at Camp Pike, Arkansas. From there he promptly went to the nation's capital to enroll as a first-year law student at GWU at the same time as Tilghman. He was four years older and far more knowledgeable of the outside world than she, and he was rugged, handsome, and smart. Tilghman found him intriguing and appealing. He became an outstanding lineman for the GWU football team in those days when law students were eligible to compete. Like Tilghman, he found a job to support himself during law school, working as a clerk for the Department of Treasury.[73]

Hughes was a contrast to Tilghman in temperament. He was quieter, more conservative, and, unlike Tilghman and her friend Hays, not fascinated by the often vitriolic give-and-take of the political world. But, as Tilghman would recall later, he was "very good looking, and he talked very 'Southern.'" Proud of his Texas roots, he joined other southern students in a club that bore the playful title the Ancient, Independent and Effervescent Order of the Yellow Dog. The two served together in the Law School senate all three years at GWU. They began to play tennis together and took canoe outings on the Potomac River. By their senior year the couple had declared their love for one another and made the decision to marry—even before graduation.[74]

They determined to have the ceremony performed quickly and quietly, and they succeeded. Their marriage took place on March 13, 1922, after they had furtively acquired a marriage license at the courthouse. The event did not go unnoticed. "Yesterday," a news story related, "the bride was in the courthouse about four times, and each time dodged some of her fellow workers. Finally seeing the coast clear the bridegroom got the license and the couple were married by the Rev. M. Leo Rippey." The simple event was deemed worthy of news coverage because Sarah was described as the "littlest, but one of the most efficient policewomen" on the force. The article appeared under the headline "Policewoman a Bride" and was subtitled "Miss Sarah Tilghman Weds G. E. Hughes in Law Romance." Friends were not surprised, the story related, because for several months "Sarah has been wearing a rather absent look."[75]

Secretive though they had been about their wedding, they afterward sent notices to friends, including the dean of the Law School, Merton L. Ferson, who responded: "[I was] pleased, indeed, to receive the announcement of your marriage, although it contained no information that was news to me." In expressing his warmest congratulations, the dean had "no misgivings as to the future success and happiness of the new firm."[76]

The couple's meager financial resources kept the number of notices sent to a minimum. Sarah's own mother somehow did not make their list. Sarah's brother received an announcement, though, and Sarah asked him to forward his invitation to her. "I didn't have enough to send her one too," she explained. Sarah and her mother had grown apart. While Sarah always would describe her mother as the greatest influence on her life, the closeness they had enjoyed in the early years was not destined to continue until more than a decade later, when, now widowed, Mrs. Tilghman moved to Dallas to live with her daughter and son-in-law.[77]

The couple found time for a brief honeymoon in Richmond, Virginia. From there the new Mrs. Hughes sent a card to her brother, Richard, signing it "Mrs. George E. Hughes." (Years later, Richard's daughter would state her belief that this quite likely was the only time her aunt Sarah—so committed to equality for women—ever signed her name that way!)[78] On the third day the young newlyweds discovered their room was costing nine dollars a day—more than they had anticipated—and they lacked enough money to pay their bill. George's desperate telegram to a fraternity brother brought funds for their rescue, and the couple returned to their work and classes.[79]

They settled briefly at 1732 P Street, NW, and made an important decision about their futures. A law professor assured the couple they could make a living wherever they chose to go, so they would move to George's native state of Texas upon graduation and open a law firm. This would cost money they did not have. To help save funds they took a dramatic step. They would give up their apartment in favor of a primitive sort of tent-cabin that Hughes's fraternity, Phi Sigma Kappa, owned in the woods across the Potomac. Living there would be far less expensive than their room—in fact, free. They moved to the site for the last couple of months preceding their June graduation. A canoe solved the problem of crossing the Potomac. Each morning they rowed across the river to the campus, and each afternoon they rowed back to their tent. "It was the last care-free existence of my life," Sarah later said. Life was busy, though, as well as spare. "We've been on the go every minute, and how we get our lessons done is more than I can see but we do usually manage to get them," she wrote to her brother.[80]

On graduation day, June 7, 1922, Sarah Tilghman Hughes could be proud of her achievements. Under her picture in the university's yearbook, *The Cherry Tree*, there were seven lines of memberships and accomplishments, more than anyone else in her graduating class. She had served as president of the Law School senate, and in a day when grading standards were severe, her overall academic average was 80.7. She had performed well as a police officer, too, having been promoted during her three years from Class 1 to Class 3 status.[81]

Now the moment for the newlyweds' great adventure had arrived—the beginning of their law careers in Texas in the fast-growing city of Dallas. Although for many years their choice of Texas was described as jointly made, four decades later Sarah would put a slightly different coloring to it: "He would have nothing else but to return to Texas and that suited me just fine."[82]

2 ～

Settling Down in Dallas

The place Sarah and George Hughes chose to launch their law careers, Dallas, was a vigorous, fast-growing northeast Texas city with a population of about 160,000. It was less than half the size of Baltimore or Washington, D.C. Many of its residents were new city-dwellers, fresh from the farms of surrounding black lands that in this decade were producing more than one-third of the nation's cotton crop. It was a city with aggressive leaders, committed to progress, led at the top by a cadre of bankers, department store moguls, and utility company executives. Less involved in the city's inner workings but an important peripheral group were would-be oil tycoons who were raising money in town and prospecting in nearby regions. Even though the sensational East Texas discovery of 1930 was eight years away, the petroleum industry already was important to Dallas; the tallest building in town, the twenty-nine story Magnolia Building, had been completed in 1921 and named for its oil company tenant. Dallas's growth and obvious potential for future prosperity was attracting large numbers of lawyers besides the Hugheses. In the first six years of the 1920s, membership in the Dallas Bar Association would more than triple, increasing from 127 members to 428.[1]

Before they could get to Dallas, though, Sarah and George Hughes needed enough money to buy two train tickets. It would be helpful, as well, they reasoned, if at least one of them had a job when they got there. Living in the fraternity cabin across the Potomac had helped them save on rent, but not enough. Sarah suggested, half seriously, they might hitch-hike or hop freight trains to get to Texas. Or, she joked, perhaps they could row their canoe to Dallas. A better idea was to sell the canoe, which they did, for forty-five dollars.[2]

Their search for work began long-distance from Washington. George, as an army veteran, easily found a position with the Dallas regional office of the U.S. Veterans Bureau. This was the beginning of a long career, for with the exception of a brief hiatus when he did manage to work in the same law firm as his wife, he would spend forty-three years with the Veterans Bureau and its successor, the Veterans Administration, before retiring at the age of seventy in 1962.

George went first to Dallas, reporting to his new job in September. Sarah remained behind to continue her work as a police officer until she could find a position in Dallas by mail. Her letters of applications to about twenty law firms failed to elicit any responses.[3]

By December they had accumulated enough money for Sarah to quit her police job and join her husband. The couple moved into a rooming house in the northeast section of town at 5627 Victor Street. Not having a kitchen, they took many of their meals at a United Cigar store counter. They started accumulating necessary household items by saving coupons. Their first purchases were an electric iron and a set of water glasses.[4]

Sarah daily rode the streetcar downtown to look in person for a job with law firms. In the past, persistence always had paid off for her, but this time persistence seemed not to be enough. "I went from top to bottom of every building, offering my services to every law firm in Dallas," she wrote to her brother, Richard Haughton, or "Haughtie." "It just seems like there are too many handicaps in the law profession for me. I'm too young, a woman and unknown in Dallas. Whether I will overcome those handicaps or not I do not know." It was one of the few times in her life that she was so thoroughly discouraged.[5]

She paid an early visit to William Hawley Atwell, a stalwart Republican who had just been nominated by President Warren G. Harding to be the new U.S. district judge for the Northern District of Texas. President Harding's sister had worked with Sarah Hughes on the Washington, D.C., police force, and she had encouraged Sarah to call on Atwell. Atwell was destined to serve on the federal bench until 1954, his career noted for his conservatism. When Hughes visited him, however, his predilections were those of a progressive Republican. The year before, he had challenged the constitutionality of a restrictive city of Dallas ordinance prohibiting African Americans from living in neighborhoods specified for whites. And eight years earlier he had befriended the first woman to practice law in Dallas, Lillian D. Aveilhe, by providing her office space. Atwell gave Hughes a cordial reception, but he had no job for her.[6]

Despite the difficulty, Sarah T. Hughes was not single-handedly attempting to break the gender barrier in Dallas. When Lillian D. Aveilhe had appeared in a local courtroom in 1914, the sight was so startling that it caused a stampede of curious courthouse employees, hangers-on, and other attorneys to see how she performed in what heretofore had been a man's world.[7] Soon afterward, Aveilhe disappeared from view. By the early 1920s, though, a half dozen or so other women lawyers were practicing in Dallas. They were inevitably denied affiliation with the major law firms, although ironically, many of them had become interested in legal careers only after working in those same firms as secretaries or stenographers.

Sometime in 1923, Hughes finally achieved a modest breakthrough. A small firm, Priest, Herndon and Ledbetter, offered her rent-free space in the anteroom, vacant because of a departed receptionist/secretary. Andrew J. Priest, the principal partner, also promised to refer some cases to the fledgling attorney, presumably in return for her services as a receptionist. In Hughes's law school studies the emphasis had been on common law. With statutory law prevalent in Texas, she found that a considerable amount of extra studying was necessary as she prepared to begin her career. In her first case, heard in a justice of the peace court, she represented a client seeking to collect an outstanding note, and she was pleased to win a judgment. Her practice began to grow when other lawyers with whom she had interviewed in her job search and who remembered her also began to make referrals to her.[8]

Hughes knew what she must do to make a name for herself in Dallas. She began joining and becoming active in women's organizations—the service-oriented Zonta Club, the Business and Professional Women's Club, the Dallas Women's Political League, the League of Women Voters, the YWCA, Dallas College Club, and the American Association of University Women. She appears to have become treasurer or perhaps secretary for the Dallas Joint Legislative Council as early as 1925, for a small account book in her possession bears that organization's name. She soon used the account book to keep track of her own expenses, listing in 1926 and 1927 payments of five or ten dollars to the Dallas Council of Mothers, Council of Jewish Women, League of Women Voters, Federation of Women's Clubs, Business and Professional Women, and the Woman's Christian Temperance Union.[9] She also was admitted to the Dallas Bar Association, an organization overwhelmingly male but essential to her professional career. (This bar association had admitted its first woman member, Helen Viglini, in December 1920.) With so few female lawyers in town, Hughes and the other women were something of a novelty. Their mere existence attracted attention. Speaking engagements, especially to women's groups, began to be offered, and Hughes accepted them.

Probably her most important early connection was with the Zonta Club, which had organized in Dallas in 1924 with several of the city's other female lawyers, such as Sarah Menezes and Hattie L. Henenberg, as members. All three would serve as president within the next fifteen years, but Hughes—although newer to the city than both—was the first to do so. As president from 1929 to 1931 "Sally" Hughes, as she continued to be known, initiated a monthly letter to the membership that evolved into a permanent and regular bulletin. She would continue to be active in Zonta into the 1960s.[10]

Her connection with Andrew Priest was especially valuable. A few years earlier, in 1919, Priest had started his own law school in Dallas, the Jefferson School of Law, with just three students. This sideline venture, done at first on a part-time basis, continued to grow and prosper during the next decade. By 1930 Jefferson would have its own three-story building downtown as well as a branch in Fort Worth, thirty miles to the west. Jefferson even fielded football and baseball teams, and it had not only a law school but also specialized programs in its School of Commerce and Accounts and School of Secretarial Training. Priest, increasingly impressed by Hughes, called her into service at Jefferson as a part-time instructor for the evening classes. She also was designated secretary of the school.[11]

On February 1, 1925, Dallas's *Daily Times Herald* published a lengthy article profiling eight local prominent women attorneys who were part of an avant-garde movement defying the axiom that a woman's place is in the home. One of the eight was Sarah T. Hughes. "A 'lady lawyer' is one of the most business-like persons on earth," the author of the article stated. These Dallas women were disproving those skeptics who predicted dire consequences with the admission of women to the bar. They were proof that women could function at a level equal or superior to their male counterparts, and they seemed especially to excel in closing arguments. It was being realized that some women preferred a female attorney just as many preferred a female physician.

The newspaper article served as a presumably complete listing of the city's female attorneys, who were labeled as the women's division of the Dallas bar. Many of them already boasted significant achievements. The most noted was Edith Eunice Therrell Wilmans, admitted to the bar in 1918. In 1922 she became the first woman in the state's history to be elected to the Texas Legislature. Instead of running for re-election to the House in 1924, she had campaigned without success for the governorship. She would repeat an unsuccessful gubernatorial race in 1926 before fading from public view. Her sister, Helen Viglini, was admitted to the bar in June 1919. District Attorney Maury Hughes had appointed her as the first woman to serve as an assistant district attorney in Dallas County. In 1920 she became the first female member of the Dallas Bar Association. (Helen Viglini would continue to practice law in Dallas until her retirement in 1963.) Grace N. Fitzgerald learned the law while working in the Dallas office of the U.S. referee in bankruptcy. She established her own practice in 1920 after being admitted to the bar in 1918. She told the newspaper she yearned for the day when women would not seem conspicuous in their appearances in court. Sarah Cory Menezes attended law school at the University of Kansas, and in the year the *Times Herald* article appeared, she became the first woman appointed as an assistant U.S. attorney for the Northern District of Texas. Two of the women portrayed, Isabelle Albright and Hollie B. Martin, were graduates of the Jefferson Law School. Hattie Leah Henenberg began studying law while she was a stenographer for a Dallas attorney and through courses at the Dallas YMCA's evening law school. In 1924 she was appointed director of the Dallas Bar Association's new free legal aid bureau. One month before the newspaper article appeared, Governor Pat Neff had appointed Henenberg as one of three members of his all-female special supreme court after every male justice disqualified himself from a case because each was a member of a fraternal organization, Woodmen of the World, a party in the pending suit. (The governor's original appointments had included Edith Wilmans, but she was disqualified when it was realized she lacked the mandatory six years' experience as an attorney.)[12]

Sarah T. Hughes was the last of the women portrayed. After a brief description of her background, the newspaper article said she had secured "a firm foundation and an understanding of criminal law." Yet she told the reporter she did not prefer criminal law. "There is enough in the civil courts to keep me busy." (Years later as a federal district judge, Hughes would claim a distinct preference for criminal law.)[13]

By the time the *Times Herald* article appeared, Hughes's name already had been added to Priest's firm. It was now Priest, Herndon & Hughes. Encouraged by his wife's success and acceptance, George Hughes quit his job with the U.S. Veterans Bureau and joined his wife's law firm himself. Finally, the couple achieved their goal to practice law together. But the move proved to be overambitious. After about two years George Hughes returned to the regular paycheck offered by the Veterans Bureau.[14] By then the couple's finances had improved enough for them to leave the rooming house on Victor Street in favor of a garage apartment at 3700 Dartmouth Avenue, where they would live for the next six years.

Baltimore seemed a long way off, but Sarah was reminded sadly of the family she had left behind when on October 21, 1925, word came that her father had died. Three days later James Cooke Tilghman, age sixty-five, was buried at the Loudon Park Cemetery in a private ceremony. Funeral services were held at the home of his sister. There is no evidence that Sarah was able to attend.[15]

Sarah T. Hughes's law office was in the Dallas County State Bank Building at Main and Lamar streets, a busy location promoted as "Where All the Cars Pass." From her fourth-floor window she was dismayed and surprised one evening to see a parade of masked men marching down Main Street. "All those white-sheeted people wearing masks and marching down the street was really something to see," she remembered nearly fifty years later, describing her first encounter with the Ku Klux Klan. "We immediately decided that we wanted none of it, so that in the first election after we arrived . . . I supported the candidates who were anti-Klan." She and George saw more than one such parade in their first years in Dallas, for the Klan was marching regularly on city streets and in small surrounding county towns. She and George also learned that the couple who were their landlords on Victor Street belonged to the Klan.[16]

The Klan in Texas had become almost overnight a powerful political force after the organization's reincarnation in Atlanta following World War I. Its concept of patriotism, morality, native Americanism, and fundamentalist Christianity appealed to large numbers of men in small towns throughout the South and Midwest and especially in Texas. In 1922 its strength accounted for the victorious U.S. Senate campaign of Earle M. Mayfield, an acknowledged Klansman himself, who defeated former governor James E. Ferguson. Many enlightened individuals recognized the dangers of the Klan's myopic views, and ferocious debates arose as the organization cut a wide swath through society. These debates dominated county and statewide elections in Texas in 1924, with candidates taking pro or con positions on the Klan.

To oppose the Klan in Dallas in the early 1920s, as Hughes decided to do, was a risky proposition. During these few years the Klan ruled city and county politics. Dallas Klan No. 66, with thirteen thousand or more members at its peak in 1924, was said to be the largest klavern in the nation. The Klan boasted in the spring of 1922 that in Dallas it had abducted and flogged sixty-four transgressors as punishment for alleged misbehavior. Some of the city's leading ministers commented favorably on Klan activities. Membership included some of Dallas's most influential men. Many Dallas police officers, including the police commissioner, were Klansmen. In the 1922 county election, the district attorney, sheriff, and a district judge campaigned openly as Klan members and were elected. Klan-endorsed candidates captured the other courthouse offices, too. In the 1923 Dallas municipal elections, Klan-endorsed candidates swept the slate. That fall, at the State Fair of Texas in Dallas, a special Ku Klux Klan Day attracted huge numbers of Klansmen from throughout the South and Midwest.

The *Dallas Morning News* opposed the Klan in a vigorous editorial crusade, but it did so at a high cost. The Klan, in retribution, boycotted the *News*, severely threatening the newspaper's economic well-being and causing it to sell its sister newspaper, the *Galveston News*, to raise money. Stung by the backlash from so many readers and advertisers who opposed its crusade against the Klan, the *News* was forced ultimately to pull back from its editorial position.[17]

In joining the opposition to the Klan, Sarah T. Hughes aligned herself with the minority viewpoint, holding that this hooded organization threatened civil liberties and democratic society. As a lawyer, she focused her attention on the race for district attorney, in which the Klan was the key issue. The incumbent, Shelby S. Cox, had emerged from obscurity in 1922 to capture the office on the strength of his Klan membership. His opponent for reelection in 1924 was Cavin Muse, who centered his campaign on an anti-Klan message. Hughes became one of the most active members of the women's group formed to support him, the Women-for-Muse District Attorney Club. She was chairman of an event at which several hundred women rallied at the downtown Jefferson Hotel to support Muse and three statewide anti-Klan candidates—Miriam "Ma" Ferguson, who was running for governor (opposing a Dallas Klansman, district judge Felix Robertson), Dallasite Barry Miller for lieutenant governor, and Dan Moody for attorney general. The meeting, while sponsored by and intended for women, also attracted a number of men, who slipped in after the session was underway to hear the speakers. Each speaker reiterated the theme that the campaign had been reduced to a single issue: the Klan. Hughes visited at least one Dallas County town, Carrollton, to organize another Women-for-Muse District Attorney Club. She was the key speaker for Muse at a suburban Oak Cliff rally, and at another rally she introduced the chairman of the Dallas County Democratic Executive Committee.[18]

Throughout the state the results of the 1924 election suggested diminished power for the Klan. Running on a strong anti-Klan campaign, Miriam A. Ferguson won the gubernatorial election over district judge Felix Robertson, of Dallas, after dissension split the statewide ranks of the Klan. Also, Dan Moody was elected attorney general. However, the Klan's power in Dallas held fast. Shelby Cox won a second term as district attorney after a runoff with Muse. Even though Robertson lost the state, he easily carried Dallas County in the runoff, by a 22,155 to 16,494 margin.[19]

The election of Miriam Ferguson as the first female governor in Texas's history was not the sort of victory that brought a great deal of cheer to proponents of women's rights. A shy woman without any government experience, she campaigned as a surrogate for her husband, James E. Ferguson, who took to the stump with her. James Ferguson's earlier service as governor, 1914-17, had been shortened when the Texas Legislature impeached, convicted, and removed him from office. One of the strongest proponents for his removal had been the Texas Equal Suffrage Association, which viewed him as an opponent of women's suffrage. Prohibited from running again for office, Ferguson had simply offered his wife as an alternative. "Two governors for the price of one," was one of the campaign slogans. Upon her election, he set up a desk beside hers in the Capitol building.

Klansmen or Klan-anointed officials continued to hold sway at Dallas City Hall as well as at the courthouse, but their strength did not discourage the dynamo from Baltimore. With the spring 1925 municipal elections approaching, she gave a spirited address in opposition to them. The occasion was a Dallas Women's Political League meeting, summarized by a newspaper headline as "Women Plan to Beat Klan in City Election." Hughes and two other women speakers urged both Republicans and Democrats to set aside their differences to defeat this common enemy in the upcoming municipal elections. "Women must get busy right now and not wait until the campaign gets hot and the issues beclouded," she told league members. Hughes managed to work into her comments another issue of growing importance to her—the need for women to "make their weight felt as never before and force recognition on an equal basis with men."[20] Debate about Klan influence at city hall never materialized as a hot issue in this election, though, and voters returned to municipal offices the same candidates who two years earlier had won election with Klan endorsements. Even so, Klan membership rolls were beginning to decline rapidly, and the organization's power was destined to disappear almost as quickly as it had arisen. Still, Dallas Klan No. 66 maintained an office in Dallas as late as 1929.

For two consecutive elections Hughes had been on the losing side in local races. As a person committed to liberal beliefs, she had become politically active in a town dominated by an opposite political outlook.[21]

Speaking in public was no problem for Sarah T. Hughes. In fact, she relished it. She enjoyed getting out and meeting as many people as possible and making a wide circle of acquaintances. Her willingness to accept speaking engagements—and her ability to carry them off with such verve—was beginning to project her into prominence as one of the foremost women lawyers in town. Women's groups especially turned to the few female lawyers in town for their programs. Usually, the speakers were asked to discuss topics connected with the law, but that wasn't always the case. As Hughes observed, "If the clubs can find no other speaker we are supposed to be familiar with almost everything." She worked up speeches on subjects as varied as Clara Barton, Robert E. Lee, and the socially minded woman's obligation to society in government.[21]

As she spoke to audiences about the law, she began developing her own ideas about the nature of her profession. Law, she concluded, was "the common sense of the race." Accordingly, she believed common sense was the most important trait for any lawyer. This was not something that could be learned at any university. As to the business of learning, she emphasized that it should "make itself plain to the unlearned." The highest wisdom used the simplest language. Law that appealed to the "common sense of everybody" could never fail.[23]

Hughes's short stature and youth continued to generate attention. "Oh! I expected to see a much larger and older woman," was one of the remarks that frequently greeted her. She sensed disappointment. "They expected a woman lawyer to radiate dignity, largeness, and ability[,] and it is really difficult to come up to expectations when I have to stretch so as to reach five feet and one half inch and to joggle the scales around a little to make them go up to 105 lbs.," Hughes said.[24]

She was not seeking to specialize in her law practice. "Young lawyers can't have specialties," she observed. She primarily handled civil cases, frequently appearing in court, and enjoyed appellate work. Her practice was earning her about a thousand dollars a year—less than her policeman's salary. She would continue to earn approximately this amount into the mid-1930s, when she became a state district judge.[25]

The sympathy with which she viewed the less fortunate members of society as victims of circumstances was evident in defending a black man charged with transportation and possession of liquor. Police found twenty-four quarts of whiskey in his car upon stopping him on the highway in the winter. He claimed he suffered from rheumatism, and he needed the whiskey as medicine because of the aggravation of picking cotton bolls on the cold, wet ground. "Of course," Hughes acknowledged in a speech, "he had enough to have lasted him about ten years, taken as a medicine, yet I worked myself up to the point of absolutely believing him and thinking it would be a terrible injustice to convict him." It was testimony to Hughes's own enthusiasm on her client's behalf that caused the jury, too, to accept his story and acquit him.[26]

One of the most pleasant aspects for her in the practice of law was that it prompted her to associate with business and professional men and women. Hughes continued to expand her membership in such organizations as the Open Forum, Travelers Aid, and the Dallas College Club.

The legal profession also seemed to offer a natural entrée into politics, a subject of growing fascination for Hughes. In the 1928 presidential election she campaigned for the New Yorker Al Smith, whose Catholic religion and antiprohibition views prompted many Texas voters to abandon their traditional support of the Democratic ticket in favor of the Republican Herbert Hoover. Hughes, however, enthusiastically supported the Democratic nominee and participated in a presidential campaign for the first time by making speeches in Smith's behalf. On several occasions she shared the speakers' platform with a fellow Smith supporter and Texas politician with whom she would maintain a lifelong friendship—Representative Sam Rayburn, of Bonham. Hughes's appearance on the platform on these occasions generally came as a surprise, since she held no elected position herself, but she quickly became a crowd-pleaser at towns on all sides of Dallas. "He would speak and I would speak and that would be the way it was done and then we would go up to somewhere else and do the same thing," she said later. Rayburn later recalled that "the people came to see us, but they stayed to listen to her."[27]

There remained some novelty about seeing a woman speaking on such occasions. At one political rally at the public square in Lancaster, just south of Dallas, a minister who followed Hughes on the platform declared he would "take the pants off that woman." Informed of the threat, Hughes clenched her fists and confronted the preacher. "I'd like to see you try it!"[28]

"The thrill of being in a fight and the joy of possible victory are too much for me, and I always participate," she said in 1929 about her political involvement. To this point she had campaigned only for others, but the thought of running for office herself already had taken hold. "Always I have the feeling that if I could be elected to just anything, even public weighter [sic], which is the smallest job I can think of, I would be thrilled to have won," she said. "[But] the wonder of it would always be how I had possibly persuaded enough people to vote for me."[29]

She had not long to wait for her wish. At the beginning of the Depression decade, Sarah T. Hughes was approaching her thirty-fourth birthday. She professed on many later occasions that she and George had decided they would have no children. She was more interested in advancing her career; he was happy to support her and content to remain offstage. Less gregarious by nature, he also was more conservative in his political views. Sarah, established now in her profession and experienced at speaking out for other politicians before large crowds, was ready to make her own entry into politics. No one person or group suggested that she seek election. "I encouraged myself to run," she said.[30]

Later she would say she had been thinking about running for office from the moment she and George had moved to Dallas. "It was just a question of being here long enough and feeling as if I knew enough people to run." All her speech-making had been a form of preparation for a political campaign, not to mention her work toward the election of other Democrats. Her immediate decision to become a candidate herself came in 1930 when John E. Davis of Mesquite, an incumbent and one of five at-large Texas Legislature representatives from Dallas County, decided to seek the office of state treasurer rather than run for reelection. Hughes was not the only person to see an opportunity here; so did four other candidates who also filed for the open seat, Place 3, as Democratic candidates. It never occurred to her she might lose. However, she was by no means the favorite.[31]

The Republican Herbert Hoover sat uneasily in the White House. The ebullient mood of the 1920s had ended suddenly in the great stock market crash of 1929. Hoover and Congress hesitantly explored ways to steady the nation's faltering economy. While the Depression brought hard times to much of the nation, Texas suffered less than the more industrialized states. The state's economy was helped in 1930 by the discovery in East Texas of what was up to that point the richest oil field in history. The battle over the Klan had subsided as the organization faded away. The U.S. senator the Klan called its own, Earle Mayfield, lost in 1928 to Tom Connally. The Texas Legislature, dominated by representatives from rural areas, met only in odd-numbered years. After a single term in office Miriam A. Ferguson had been succeeded as governor by the youthful Dan Moody.

After only eight years in Dallas, Hughes's qualifications to represent her chosen city in the state legislature were impressive. Aside from membership in numerous organizations, she promoted herself as "a Southern woman and an honor graduate of Goucher College and the Law School of George Washington University." Her ties to so many women's organizations and her heavy speaking schedule were of special benefit. She was president of the Zonta Club, which eagerly endorsed her candidacy.[32] And she already had firsthand experience as a political campaigner for local, state, and national candidates.

One of her opponents in the countywide race was Helen M. Viglini, the first woman admitted to the Dallas Bar Association, a former Dallas County assistant district attorney, and the sister of Edith Wilmans, the first woman in Texas history to be elected to the legislature. Wilmans, also a Dallas attorney, had been elected in 1922 with the backing of the Klan.[33] Hughes, of course, was well acquainted with both sisters. Prior to entering the race, Viglini, recognizing Hughes's experience and unaware that Hughes soon would declare for the same office, had visited her to ask her opinion about her chances for election. Hughes frankly replied that with a foreign-sounding name she could not win voter approval. Viglini ignored her advice, filed for the office, and soon learned that Hughes herself would be one of her opponents.[34]

Viglini, a widow and mother of several children, assumed a domestic posture in the race—the opposite of Hughes's professional image. Viglini said she was "old-fashioned enough to believe a woman's first duty is to her husband, home and children," a backhanded criticism of her opponent. She could not blame anyone for refusing to vote for a woman who neglected either of these to run for office. "But since I am a widow and have raised my children," she said, "I feel that I can with a clear conscience ask the privilege of representing my county in the legislature."[35]

A more formidable opponent was D. C. Bell, a colorful plain-talker who admitted to taking an occasional drink, favored legalized betting on horse races (prohibited in Texas since 1909), and wanted the prohibition laws "humanized." Bell, like Hughes, had campaigned in 1928 for Al Smith. In describing Bell, a newspaper reporter noted that he "kept hitching his trousers a notch higher with each appearance, and getting more and more incensed over church domination of politics and the high price of bootleg liquor." His direct and unsophisticated approach appealed to many voters.[36]

Hughes's own candidacy was far more professional than Viglini's or Bell's or the two other candidates'. Realizing that her gender alone would lose her a certain number of votes, she determined to work that much harder to make up the difference. She prepared a careful news release describing her platform and enclosed with it an attractive one-column portrait of herself. She purchased newspaper space for a series of one-column advertisements. Even so, her total costs for the campaign did not exceed the legal limit of three hundred dollars.[37]

She opposed legalized racetrack gambling in Texas, stood against any attempt to interfere with the free public school system, wanted Prohibition to continue, favored economy in government, and urged a redistribution of taxes to relieve small homeowners and farmers. "In Sarah T. Hughes," her advertisement stated, "Dallas county will have a representative who will owe no debt to any corporation and who will honestly, courageously and diligently safeguard the interests of the great masses of our citizenship."[38]

More intriguing were her comments on how she could provide food for Texans in these Depression years. "If I had 7,000 acres of ground and 2,500 men from the prison I could raise enough black-eyed peas to feed all the people of Texas," she said. There would be no opportunity as a member of the legislature to achieve anything of the sort, and Hughes had no idea that such a thing could be attempted, much less done, but "it sounded good and people just loved it," she later laughed, recalling her campaign nearly four decades later. "I really didn't have any platform; I just talked," she said.[39]

Neither did she have a campaign headquarters or a campaign manager. It was a one-person campaign. George sat on the sidelines and nodded his approval as Sarah went in person to the offices of the four daily newspapers (the *Dallas Morning News*, the *Daily Times Herald*, the *Dallas Journal*, and the *Dallas Dispatch*) to deliver her news releases. She also visited the offices of the smaller newspapers in various county towns.[40]

In the days of the infancy of radio and before television, political advertisements in newspapers were especially important but secondary to campaigning on a face-to-face basis. Political rallies were held almost nightly in auditoriums, on street corners, in parks, and in the squares of small towns. Voters could make direct comparisons of the candidates by seeing them in action. Politicians made endless visits to office buildings, factories, warehouses, firehouses, police stations, and other places. And the business of shaking countless hands on downtown streets and passing out campaign literature was no less essential.

Sometimes Hughes's aggressive demeanor backfired. When she shook hands with one woman in an office building and asked if she would vote for her, the woman surprised her by saying she would not. Why not? Hughes asked. "Because you shake hands too hard," the woman said.[41]

At the political rallies Hughes made it her practice to arrive early so she could mix with the crowd, shake as many hands as possible, and introduce herself individually to those in attendance. She stayed late for the same purpose. When it was her turn to speak—five minutes or so per candidate—she made a dynamic impression with energy that seemed about to burst from her small and youthful frame. There was no sound amplification at any of the locations. Her clear, piercing voice served her well. As the two women candidates in the same race—unusual itself—she and Helen Viglini found themselves pitted against one another. Viglini argued that her female opponent, unlike herself, was not a true southerner because she was born in Maryland. Hughes corrected her—indeed, she said, she was a real southerner.[42] "I dug up all my ancestors to prove that I was a Southerner," she later recalled. "There was a sheriff in Oklahoma that was a Tilghman, and there was a general in the Confederate army from Alabama. I knew that all my people who have the name are related in some way, so they all became my relatives." By the end of the campaign she believed she had been accepted as "a Texan—true."[43]

In their campaign appearances the two women made a striking contrast. Viglini tended to be more formal and less comfortable. Hughes moved to the edge of the platform to get as close to the voters as possible. She was the more striking speaker. "Sarah T. Hughes . . . continues to captivate her audiences by her enthusiasm and earnestness," reported the suburban *Oak Cliff Tribune*. "When she is introduced listeners who have been inattentive and listless immediately become quiet and attentive."[44] Other newspaper accounts acknowledged that the two women's presentations at political rallies generated the most interest. "The novelty of a woman seeking public office and speaking from the same platform on the same equality as men, apparently has not worn off," opined one newspaper reporter. "When the two women spoke the crowd gathered closer around the stand and gave rapt attention."[45]

The rigors of the campaign required Hughes to think out her own positions on current issues in more depth than before. Later, she readily classified herself as a liberal, but in these days the easy categorizations between liberal and conservative that would eventually become so important in Texas and the rest of the nation had not yet become established. Some of her comments reflected basic positions that would remain with her throughout her life. This was especially true in her frequent observations that the state tax system should be overhauled to give a break to the small homeowner and farmer. She also favored establishing a civil service system for government employees in order to raise the standard of efficiency.

She took a strong position favoring fiscal responsibility and economy in the federal government and opposing any increase in taxes, a stance that later would be identified primarily as a conservative tenet. Extravagance in government, she proclaimed, had become "the most vital issue" of the legislative campaign. "The cost of government has increased forty times during the last thirty-five years," she said, a circumstance that would mean a corresponding increase in the burden of taxation on the people. "If taxes continue to increase in the next twenty-five years as they have in the past twenty-five, it will mean nothing more or less than government suicide."[46] She contrasted Texas Legislature appropriations of two million dollars in 1896 to eighty-four million in 1928. "This is a serious proposition." Reorganization of the State Department (of Texas) on a "business basis" should be given primary consideration, she said.[47]

Her theme of eliminating excessive expenditures carried over into the private sector. Waste also was causing severe losses in business, she believed. With Dallas becoming a great industrial center, there should be a voluntary and cooperative policy whereby businessmen, industrial executives, and engineers could come together to discuss ways to eliminate waste in the city's industries, she stated.[48]

Hughes's knowledge of police work gave her confidence in discussing the situation in Texas. The Texas penal system, she believed, should be industrialized so foodstuffs and other essentials could be produced and the prisons made self-sufficient. She also recommended legislation providing for a state department of criminal investigation so a centralized, modern system of identification and record-keeping could be instituted. Such a department would include a network of branches set up throughout the state, all of them reporting directly to a central office in Austin. "The cost of setting up and administering such a department would be inconsequential as compared to the annual crime bill in Texas," she said.

Her comments on such weighty matters contrasted sharply to those of her colorful but popular opponent, D. C. Bell, who emphasized in his campaign the need to legalize pari-mutuel betting at horse races and legalization of boxing. The *Dallas Dispatch* labeled him an "anti-prohibitionist." He freely acknowledged that he occasionally took a drink, "the last one being in February," and his mind would dictate to him when he would take the next drink. But when that time came it would be "drug store whiskey and by a doctor's prescription," which, he stated in a newspaper advertisement, is permitted and regulated under the law.[49]

As the July 1930 election approached it was evident that Hughes's membership and participation in so many women's groups was a great advantage. Many of the women's organizations held receptions for her. Yet, she did not seek to be a special-interest candidate; she tried to appeal equally to all voters, male and female.

In an editorial in her behalf the Carrollton newspaper said her candidacy was one of the "bright spots" in an otherwise humdrum political season. Her campaign stood out as a "refreshing relief" to those conducted so frequently on unimportant issues that merely caught the popular fancy. "In all her speeches she holds the attention of her audience by her earnestness and enthusiasm," the newspaper commented, and she discussed issues of real import in "a simple but forceful manner."[50]

Perhaps the most favorable newspaper account of Hughes's campaign appeared on July 3:

> The earnest face, the clear voice, which sends well-turned phrases into the voters' ears; each three minute exhortation a plea not for personal support but for the consideration of vital problems of government. This is Mrs. Hughes—young, and not without charm, she is the modern woman in public affairs. There is nothing of the feminist about her. One lawyer said of her, "She thinks like a man. She's as levelheaded as any lawyer in town."[51]

On the eve of the election Hughes told the *Daily Times Herald* there was "no doubt whatever" that she would reach the runoff and she would be elected to the legislature in the general election. The newspaper apologized for inadvertently omitting her name from a sample ballot, commenting that she had "won a niche among the women lawyers" in Dallas.[52]

Election results proved Hughes to be a prophet. Votes among the five candidates were well distributed, but Hughes finished second to Bell. With his failure to achieve a majority, she was in the runoff, scheduled a month later. The crusty gentleman, having spent only sixty dollars on his campaign, received 9,402 ballots. Hughes followed him with 8,482. Helen Viglini was third with 5,558, followed by Alton Stewart with 5,176 votes, and Henry Jurgens with 3,611.[53]

The two women together had drawn more than 13,000 votes, a strong indication that voters were willing to cast their ballots for female candidates. Odds for Hughes to win the August 23 runoff looked good. Henry Jurgens, who had come in last but with a respectable 3,611 votes, gave his endorsement to her at once.[54]

Early in August, Democrats at their Dallas County convention were confronted by another issue—whether or not to require their chosen delegates to the state convention to support all Democratic nominees in the fall general election. The issue sprang from the fact that many Democrats in 1928 had supported the Republican Hoover instead of Al Smith. At the meeting in the city hall auditorium, Maury Hughes insisted the delegates selected must vow to support all Democratic nominees. When the majority of the convention members declined to join in such a pledge, Hughes led a group out of the city hall auditorium and into a corporation courtroom, where they selected their own rump delegation.[55] Such debates would become familiar in the years ahead for Texas Democrats. For Sarah T. Hughes, there would be no debate in such matters—she always supported the Democratic ticket.

Hughes chose her birthday, August 2, to launch her runoff campaign, choosing Mesquite, the small town east of Dallas where the previous state representative from Place 3, John E. Davis, lived. She solicited and received endorsements from many of Dallas's leading attorneys (including four past or future presidents of the Dallas Bar Association), who placed their names on an advertisement in which she emphasized economy in government as one of her priorities. Perhaps it was a compliment to her political skills that among those attorneys publicly endorsing her were Shelby S. Cox, the former Klansman district attorney whom she had opposed six years earlier, and Dr. A. C. Parker, the former Cyclops of the Dallas Ku Klux Klan.[56]

Later she announced the endorsement of two more prominent Dallas attorneys: Thomas B. Love, state senator, and the venerable Barry Miller, three-time lieutenant governor of the state and an unsuccessful candidate for governor who had failed to make the runoff.[57]

She declared early that she would base her runoff campaign on her unequivocal opposition to racetrack gambling and her support of Prohibition laws, positions that would place her squarely opposite her opponent. Soon, though, she began emphasizing the need to eliminate extravagance in government, to initiate prison reforms, and to improve law enforcement.[58]

On the morning before the August 23 election, the *Dallas Morning News*, in capsule summaries of all the candidates, gave a glowing description of Hughes: "Phi Beta Kappa. Liberal of the quiet but efficacious sort. President of a service club. Secretary of a law school. Law instructor. Fearless and practical." Her work on the Washington, D.C., police force was cited as a plus, and she was described as a person with "well-defined ideas who knows how to put them across." A hallmark of her campaign was her belief that the rising costs of government were destroying individual initiatives. Another lawyer, a man, was quoted as saying, "She's the most level-headed woman in town." The newspaper portrayed Bell in far less flattering terms. He was a man who "knows politicians high and low." His most outstanding ideas during the campaign were on Prohibition and horse racing. He denied being a "wet" but admitted to taking an occasional drink. He was the most outspoken candidate in the runoff.[59]

When the votes were tallied in the August runoff, Hughes was the victor with 18,867 votes to Bell's 16,086. "I am grateful to the voters of Dallas County for the confidence they have shown in me and I appreciate the assistance of my friends in the campaign," she said. "My desire is to be faithful to the trust reposed in me." Winning the general election in November against Republican opponent E. C. Harpold was a foregone conclusion in this one-party county in a one-party state. She defeated him by an overwhelming margin, 9,153 to 1,298.[60]

Hughes said she would be going to Austin in January with an open mind, realizing that as an "infant legislator" she would have a lot to learn. She had no bills to propose, and she was pledged to no special interests. She would support certain principles, she said, such as economy in administration and prison reform.

Neither did she have a desire to foist the "woman's viewpoint" on either the legislature or the people of the state. "To my way of thinking, there is no 'woman's' or 'man's' viewpoint, broadly speaking. A person's mind is either progressively or conservatively tuned, whether that person is man or woman. For goodness' sake, I don't want to be the kind of female in public affairs of whom they say, 'isn't that just like a woman!'" A newspaper article said she would go to Austin "with no pet bills and no program of reform, no women's rights and no feminine angle to sponsor."[61]

She would go, however, with a handsome new leather briefcase that Zonta Club members gave her when honoring her with a send-off party and roasting her with "silly insults" at a Sunday party just before she departed for the capital the first week of January 1931.[62]

With her in the 42nd Legislature would be three other women. Hughes said she had no intention of joining a female coalition, though. "I'm in the Legislature as an individual and not as a woman," she said.[63]

The Texas Legislature would convene with a new governor taking office—Ross S. Sterling, former chairman of the highway commission and the anointed choice of outgoing governor Dan Moody. Sterling had promised "a business administration . . . by a successful business man." However, the problems awaiting were manifest: taxes in arrears, state income off sharply, and expenditures as high as ever.[64]

~3

Political Immersion

When Sarah T. Hughes went to Austin in January 1931 to begin her duties as a neophyte legislator, the nation was entering a perilous new era. No more abrupt economic break had ever occurred in American history than the dramatic transformation from prosperity and optimism in the 1920s to depression and gloom in the 1930s. In the White House, Herbert Hoover, elected as the nominee of "the party of prosperity," was becoming an object of contempt. His government programs to cope with declines in industrial production and the subsequent pay cuts, layoffs, and joblessness were timid and ineffective. Accumulations of flimsy shanties sheltering the unemployed and homeless across the nation were designated derisively as Hoovervilles.

Democrats in the nation's capital had no better alternatives for the deteriorating situation. In fact, many of them criticized Hoover's federal initiatives as irresponsible. Sarah T. Hughes herself had campaigned against extravagance in government, calling it "the most vital issue" of the day.[1]

Neither did the various factions of the Democratic Party in Texas present clear-cut alternative solutions to problems of the Depression. Fergusonism,* Prohibition, and personalities dominated public discussion, not ideology. In the 1928 presidential election many Democratic Texas voters had deserted their party's own Al Smith, a Catholic, in favor of Hoover, who smashed tradition by carrying the Democratic state. The breakthrough would be short-lived; the Republican Party would not emerge as a force in local and Texas politics for several decades.

---

* "Fergusonism" was an unsympathetic reference to the controversial, off-and-on gubernatorial tenures of James E. Ferguson and his wife, Miriam A. Ferguson, that extended over two decades. James E. Ferguson was elected in 1914 and 1916. In 1917 he was impeached and removed from office. In 1924, Ferguson was unable to run for office again, so his wife, Miriam (Ma), campaigned as his surrogate and was elected to a single term as the second female governor in the nation. She was elected to another term in 1932. When not in office, James Ferguson usually was a factor to be considered in all Texas politics. Charges against the Fergusons ranged from misapplication of public funds, to acceptance of kickbacks in return for road contracts, to irregularities in the granting of pardons to prisoners.

Clearer political choices lay just ahead in both the nation and the state. They would be defined by the transition of the Democrats under Franklin Roosevelt into the party of the New Deal, the party that believed the federal government should assume greater responsibility for the welfare of individual citizens, the party that concluded that federal expenditures were a way to prime the economy's pump, and the party that was forming a powerful coalition of labor, urban residents, and minorities.

Just as the nation and its political landscape were in transition, so was Texas. Ranching and farming interests had dominated the economy for years, but the discovery of oil at Spindletop in 1901 had introduced a new industrial age to the state. That transition was underlined and heightened in 1930 when C. M. (Dad) Joiner brought in an even more prolific oil field in East Texas. His Daisy Bradford No. 3 in Rusk County disproved experts and showed that immense amounts of oil lay under that area. No enterprise in the state now had more impact than the petroleum industry.

The Democratic Party continued the domination in Texas that had begun with the end of Reconstruction. However, not all Texas Democrats would support Franklin Roosevelt's New Deal. During the 1930s and 1940s two clearly defined wings, separated by their positions on Roosevelt's social welfare programs, emerged within the party. One contingent, eventually identified as the liberal or loyalist wing, supported the national party's transition under Roosevelt toward federalism. Another powerful element in the party, as was true throughout the South, fought against federal expansion and for states' rights. These two elements in Texas would vie for political preeminence, prompting sharp internecine struggles that were especially vivid in primary elections. Sarah T. Hughes, during what would be three elected terms in the state legislature, developed a life-long and unwavering commitment to the liberal wing of the party.

The Texas Legislature met only in odd-numbered years, reflecting the deep-seated distrust of government existing when the state constitution was adopted in 1876, just after Reconstruction. The constitution itself revealed the power of the frugal and independent-minded ranchers and farmers. Their influence created a design for state government intended to be lean in all respects, including limitations on the authority of the governor.

In certain respects, though, the 42nd legislative session represented the beginning of an era for Texas lawmakers in which the leash had been loosened, if only just a bit. Voters in 1930 had approved a constitutional amendment that let the legislature meet twice as long as previously—120 days for the regular session instead of 60. Pay for individual members also had been doubled from five to ten dollars daily for the first 120 days and five dollars for each day thereafter in called sessions. Each member also received a small mileage allowance for travel plus a hundred dollars for postage, telegrams, and telephone calls.

Austin, the state's capital, was located at the edge of the Hill Country on a site selected in 1839 by Republic of Texas president Mirabeau B. Lamar. The huge, granite capitol building, completed in 1888 and modeled after the nation's capitol, faced straight down Congress Avenue toward the Colorado River. Austin normally was enlivened by only two major entities, University of Texas students and state of Texas employees; however, during the odd-year legislative sessions the town took on an entirely different dimension. Transformed by the influx of lawmakers, it sprang suddenly to life, becoming what has been described as the city of Three Bs (beefsteak, bourbon, and blondes). Politicians, lobbyists, staff members, and social companions filled the hotels and bars as talk of politics and deal-making wafted through the haze of cigarette smoke and the tinkling of glasses.[2]

Serving in the legislature with Hughes in this predominantly man's world were four other women—three representatives and a senator. Two of the representatives, Helen Moore of Texas City and Frances Rountree of Bryan, had replaced husbands who had died in office. The other woman in the House was Mrs. N. R. Strong of Slocum.* Elected to the Senate as its only female was Margie Elizabeth Neal, in the midst of four terms as the first woman to serve in that body. The four women in the House for the 41st session would be among only six women to serve in that body throughout the 1930s. Hughes would be the only one of the four House members to be reelected.[3] She was the youngest of her female contemporaries; at thirty-four she was the youngest of the handful of females yet to serve in the legislature.

The new governor, Ross S. Sterling of Houston, had been elected over twelve other candidates, winning a runoff against Miriam A. Ferguson, who

---

* Although most women in public life at this time customarily identified themselves through their husbands' names, Sarah T. Hughes always used her own given name.

had been out of office since losing her bid for a second term in 1927 to Dan Moody. In the attorney general's office, beginning his first term, was James V. Allred of Wichita Falls, a future governor destined to play an important role in Hughes's career.

The legislature convened on January 13, 1931, as the members took the oath of office en masse, swearing among other things that they had "not fought a duel with deadly weapons." The first important order of business was to elect a Speaker of the House. In the first speech of this first day, Fred Minor of Denton was nominated. In the second speech of this first day, freshman representative Sarah T. Hughes, unwilling to postpone her maiden speech any later than her first minutes on the job, seconded his nomination.

She had met Minor on two previous occasions, once when he, as chairman of the judiciary committee, discussed with her a proposed bill, and another time in regard to a legal matter. Minor was, Hughes told the legislators, an able lawyer and a member of a distinguished law firm in Denton. "When Mr. Minor speaks, his word is law," she said. "During the next two years the members of the Forty-Second Legislature will also say that Fred Minor's word is law." Three other briefer seconding speeches followed, and then Minor was elected unanimously. Freshman legislator Hughes had made an impressive beginning.[4]

On the next day outgoing governor Moody, in his farewell message, told Hughes and her fellow legislators that their actions would "touch every field of human endeavor and affect every enterprise and business in which people engage." They should forget partisan bitterness and unite in a "patriotic and unselfish program" for substantial accomplishment.[5]

A week later came the inauguration of Ross S. Sterling, who in his speech seemed unconcerned about the Depression and its possible impact on the Lone Star State. "Texas has fared better than other parts of the nation; and as far as Texas is concerned, we know the depression is merely temporary," he declared.[6] As the Depression developed, its effects soon became a material focus of the 42nd Session of the legislature. Just ahead lay a marked deterioration of the Texas economy as prices of both cotton and oil plummeted, banks closed, and declining state revenues caused huge deficits.

As evidenced by her early maiden speech, Sarah T. Hughes was not the sort of person to sit back and interminably contemplate a situation. She immedi-

ately immersed herself in legislative activities. She served on three committees—the state eleemosynary and reformatory institutions, education, and
judiciary—all of which reflected her experience and interests. Before the 42nd
legislative session would complete its work nearly two years later, she would
be recognized as one of its leading figures.

Before taking office, Hughes had told friends she planned to go to Austin
with no particular agenda except becoming a good legislator. Thomas B.
Love, a former Speaker of the House, outgoing state senator, and good
friend, advised a different approach. Go there with the idea of immediately
"getting into the fray," he told her. It would not take long for her to catch on
to the routine, he said. Her first-day speech in behalf of Minor, given without the aid of amplification but heard throughout the chamber because of her
loud, clear voice, indicated her ready acceptance of his advice. His advice was
reinforced when she realized she preferred a faster pace. The cumbersome
process of forming committees and the painstakingly slow pace of legislation
made her impatient.[7]

During the regular session, lasting until May 23, Hughes introduced thirteen bills. Seven of them became law. Many of the bills she introduced
reflected interests she would retain throughout her life. Her first successful
effort, House Bill 75, streamlined procedural matters for paupers in appealing rulings in the state courts. While she had pointedly proclaimed an intent
to avoid stereotyping herself as a woman acting as a woman, she sponsored a
great deal of legislation in this first session and throughout the remainder of
her legislative career that dealt with women's issues. One Texas law that would
irritate her for years was a demeaning requirement intended to protect
women's rights but instead acknowledged women's assumed weakness. This
was the requirement in the sale of homesteads that a married woman make
separate acknowledgment, out of her husband's presence, that he was not
coercing her into the sale. Hughes's bill repealing this law earned a favorable
report from the judiciary committee but went nowhere else.[8] She also introduced three other bills related to women, but these failed to get out of
committee. Each of them would have limited the number of hours women
could work in factories, workshops, mercantile establishments, hotels,
theaters, barber shops, and other enterprises. Hughes's later viewpoints led
her to conclude that legislation that presumes women need special protection
is actually harmful to them. Her work in advancing women's rights throughout the remainder of her career would reflect her more considered belief, in

line with forward-thinking feminists such as Alice Paul, that the proper course of action is to remove such barriers so that women can have the same opportunities.[9]

Her police experience in Washington, D.C., in placing delinquent girls in a "house of detention" for rehabilitation probably inspired her to introduce legislation authorizing Dallas County to issue bonds to "establish, own and operate a parental home and school for the care and training of dependent and delinquent youth." The bill was cosponsored by the other four members of the Dallas delegation. It passed, but not until years later, under Hughes's continued prodding, would a juvenile home be constructed in Dallas County.[10] Another bill, offered by Hughes alone and also signed into law, called for legal guardians to pay for the support and maintenance of their children who were placed in certain state institutions and schools.[11]

Another of her efforts on behalf of juveniles was intended to award good scholarship for schoolchildren in Texas and to promote patriotism. Hughes proposed a thousand dollars in prizes through the Texas Library and Historical Commission for the three best essays on the life of Jane Long, "the Mother of Texas." It failed to get out of committee.[12]

Hughes successfully introduced a bill suggested by the Dallas Bar Association providing a way to finance a county law library. For many years, every effort to create this much-needed library had failed because of inadequate funding. House Bill 992, supported by every Dallas County representative, permanently solved that problem by authorizing collection of a fifty-cent fee from every proceeding in a Dallas County court. The library that was established proved in years to come to be an important addition to the Dallas legal community. Less than a dozen years after its opening, the library had more than twenty thousand volumes.[13]

The Dallas County delegation also worked together on other bills relevant to their community, especially the Trinity River Navigation Bill, intended to make the river a navigable waterway. This elusive dream, one that had tantalized the city since it had been founded in 1841, was not destined to be realized.

In the hectic last two weeks of the regular session Hughes demonstrated her quick mastery of the labyrinthine world of the legislature by introducing and pushing through to passage a bill that toughened compulsory school attendance laws for children between the ages of seven and fifteen in Dallas County. It superseded the less restrictive state law requiring compulsory attendance between eight and fourteen. She introduced the bill, H.B. 1054, on May 11, gained approval from the education committee on May 13, persuaded the House to omit the normal printing of the bill to save time, successfully moved for the suspension of the constitutional rule requiring bills to be read three days before passage, and saw House ratification on the same day. Senate approval came on May 21.[14]

With her slight stature, her bobbed hair, her energy, and her youthfulness, Hughes made a vivid impression. At first glance she appeared to be entirely out of place in this male-dominated environment. Early in the session, before everyone had come to know her, she sought out a fellow representative whom she had not yet met to ask about a certain point in a bill he had sponsored. He answered her courteously, but his lifted eyebrow showed his puzzlement. Why was this young lady asking such a question?

"Oh, I see! Your mother's a member, isn't she?"
"My mother a member?" was her bewildered response.
"Why, yes, aren't you Mrs. Sarah Hughes' little girl?" he questioned.
"Sarah Hughes' little girl! I'm Sarah Hughes!" was the vexed cry of the baffled new legislator.[15]

There would be plenty of time for everyone in the 42nd Legislature to get to know Sarah T. Hughes. After the regular session ended on May 23, 1931, Governor Sterling would call four additional sessions of about one month each, the last one concluding on November 10, 1934. By the time of final adjournment, nearly two years had passed since the body first convened.

This hectic Austin schedule left Hughes little time for a private life or for her law practice back in Dallas. The normal routine during sessions was for Sarah to stay in a rooming house or hotel and return to Dallas on weekends to be with her husband. At the end of the 1920s the couple had purchased a two-bedroom house of their own at 3816 Normandy Avenue in Highland Park, not far from downtown Dallas but in a separate municipality. It would remain their home for the rest of their lives.

George Hughes's work with the federal government required him to avoid politics. He had no regrets about that, for he preferred to stay at home away from the limelight in which his wife thrived. Throughout the couple's married life he would approve of Sarah's political activism, but he wanted no part of it himself other than entertaining guests at home or other routine socializing. He must have held his aggressive wife in a measure of pride and awe as she maneuvered her way with growing skills through the rough world of Austin politics.

It was assumed in these days that a wife automatically cooked all the meals in a household. With his own wife gone so much, the question of just how George Hughes handled that situation was a matter of some interest. A newspaper feature sought to answer the question under the headline: "Lawmaker's Husband Turns Cook; Finds 'Batching It' Is Real Fun." A photograph of Hughes at the sink, wearing an apron and washing dishes, accompanied the story. His favorite menus, the story related, included brook trout, lamb and mushroom sauté, grapefruit salad, spinach, and baked potatoes. "It is generally agreed by his friends that nobody can make better waffles than he can," the story continued, pointing out that he cooked more than just special dishes. "He cooks entire meals often—and likes it."[16] George's prowess in the kitchen would continue throughout their marriage. As for Sarah, a newspaper article summed up her position: "Mrs. Hughes states that politics is her vocation, but she is interested in her home and can cook very acceptably, when she has a good recipe."[17]

After the regular session ended Hughes had time to spend time with her constituents and friends in Dallas. Having completed her term as president of Zonta in 1931, for the next year she became treasurer, an office to which she was reelected for 1932-33. A special event for Hughes and all Zontians occurred in June 1931, when she and other club members greeted the female aviator Amelia Earhart, who flew into Dallas on a borrowed "windmill" airplane, having wrecked her own "autogiro" when she tried to avoid flying into a crowd greeting her in San Angelo.[18]

The governor's prerogative to call the legislature into special session had become an expected routine. At the expiration of the 42nd Legislature's regular session, it was clear that the state was in a situation spiraling downward. The prices of oil and cotton, so critical to the economy, had tumbled precipitously; taxes were in arrears; state expenditures remained high. In first calling the lawmakers back into session on July 14, 1931, Governor Sterling chose to focus on the conservation and development of natural resources. There was, he said in his summons, "a deplorable condition in Texas on account of the great waste of our natural resources, particularly of oil and gas."[19]

What to do about it was another matter, and if Sterling hoped the state legislature could provide remedies, he was mistaken. The immediate problem centered around the increasingly prolific East Texas fields. With huge amounts of oil being pumped in this ever-expanding region, the price of oil had fallen lower and lower, finally reaching eight cents a barrel. Yet, independents especially wanted to push their fields to the maximum production at any price. The Texas Railroad Commission, the regulatory agency for such matters, tried to place strict limits on the production of oil, but many operators simply ignored them. Others sought to tie up the restrictions by challenging them in the courts.

Finally, in August, Governor Sterling declared martial law in four East Texas counties and called out the Texas National Guard to enforce the regulations. A three-judge federal panel ruled in February that the governor had exceeded his authority. Eventually, the production of illegal oil declined, and the courts upheld the proration plan.

There was little the legislature could do in this situation, but Hughes cosponsored a bill that would have brought some order to the congested oil fields. Rather than permitting each individual to drill his or her own well (frequently different owners had wells side by side), the bill called for shared units in which only one well in an area might be drilled on behalf of several owners, with each receiving a proportional share of the oil. The bill died in committee.[20]

The second called session dealt with falling cotton prices, a matter affecting far more Texans than the dip in oil prices. By late summer 1931 Texas farmers were selling their cotton for as little as five and a half cents a pound. In an effort to bring up the prices, Governor Sterling recommended to the legislators that they pass a bill to reduce cotton acreage in the state by 50 percent in the next year. Hughes voted in favor of the legislation, but before the bill could take effect, the courts ruled in February 1932 that it was unconstitutional because of the "inherent and constitutional right of the citizen to use his property as he chooses."[21]

Before the governor summoned the 42nd Legislature back into its third session in August 1932, elections had to be held for the 43rd Legislature (not to begin until January 1933). Hughes's intentions were undeniable. She would campaign for reelection. Six opponents lined up against her in the Democratic primary in July, including her previous foe and fellow attorney Helen Viglini. Hughes won more than three times as many votes as her nearest challenger, G. P. Sears, and in the August runoff she more than doubled his total, 22,058 to 10,587. Her margin of victory was greater than that of any candidate for public office in the county. Her work in Austin clearly had been appreciated.[22]

In the third called session, August 30-September 21, 1932, Hughes achieved a success she always considered her greatest legislative accomplishment. It was a remarkable feat of skill and courage against considerable odds. The issue pitted Hughes against the state's big landholders and oil companies over proposed legislation dubbed the West Texas land bills. From it she emerged as a progressive or liberal who was not afraid to oppose powerful special interests.

The issue, a complicated one, concerned ownership of royalties from mineral rights on vast amounts of public lands specified to benefit the Permanent School Fund. The Relinquishment Act of 1919 had been interpreted as directing that fifteen-sixteenths of the mineral proceeds on these lands should go to the surface owners, among them large ranchers in West Texas, and the remaining one-sixteenth to the state's Permanent School Fund. In an act that signaled the beginning of his long and prominent career as the leader of Texas liberals, Ralph Yarborough, a new assistant attorney general with responsibility for the Permanent School Fund, challenged this division of mineral royalties. He argued that it was contrary to the actual intent of the Relinquishment Act, unfair to the state, and harmful to the welfare of children for generations to come because it deprived them of school revenues. With the approval of Attorney General James V. Allred, Yarborough obtained a state supreme court ruling confirming his opinion that the lion's share of mineral royalties belonged to the state and its school fund, not to the surface owners.[23] The disappointed landowners, encouraged and supported by the oil companies, sought legislation to nullify the supreme court decision.

In September 1932, several legislative bills were introduced to achieve this purpose. One was proposed to permit those who already had bought surface land from the state to purchase now the mineral rights to their properties at a nominal tenth of the original sales price. In return, the state's Permanent School Fund would be given one-sixteenth of the royalties.[24] Another convoluted bill, introduced by Senator Clint Small of Amarillo, proposed an arrangement whereby the state could reclaim lands on which the interest had not been paid, then give back priority of purchase to the previous owner. The new contract would specify the fifteen-sixteenth and one-sixteenth arrangement, with the bulk of royalties again going to the owner.[25]

Yarborough, determined to continue his court battle in the legislature, began searching for a liberal-minded legislator who would oppose the landowners and oil companies and fight the proposed legislation. He approached former classmates of the University of Texas Law School who were now in the legislature, but they were hesitant to oppose such powerful interests in what seemed destined to be a losing battle. One suggested that Yarborough talk to Hughes. Hughes listened but was reluctant to adopt it as a crusade until Yarborough presented the issue as one that pitted "the poor little school children against the large oil companies." Armed with this perspective, she agreed to take up the cudgel in the legislature.[26]

In mid-September the House began consideration of Senator Small's bill, S.B. 25, already approved in the Senate and recommended for passage by the House Committee on Public Lands and Land Office. Few would have anticipated its defeat in debate at this point before the full House, but Hughes, supported by R. J. (Bob) Long of Wichita Falls and Clarence Farmer of Fort Worth, mounted an intensive battle against S.B. 25 and a companion piece of legislation, S.B. 26.

"Who does this benefit?" she asked rhetorically. "Oil companies solely. At whose expense? School children and taxpayers. . . . [The bill] should be entitled—An act to enrich oil companies at the expense of the school children of the state."[27] In desiring to populate the state, Texas had given away vast parts of its original public domain by selling the bulk of its school lands at far below actual value, she said. The minerals underneath were worth many times the price paid for the surface land, and she argued that it would be scandalous for the state to give schoolchildren a mere one-sixteenth of these royalties instead of the bulk that rightfully belonged to them. What the proposed legislation amounted to, she emphasized, was a "constitutional steal."[28]

> If validating means taking the birthright from Texas and its school children, call it validating if you will, but I prefer the shorter word, and I repeat that what is proposed is a constitutional steal. On one side we are faced with 10,000 ranchers to whom we are asked to do justice. On the other, there are 6,000,000, including the school children, to whom we should not do an injustice.[29]

Hughes's fiery and direct words placed fresh perspective on the matter for many legislators. She offered an amendment to alter S.B. 25 radically by making it conform to the supreme court ruling won by Yarborough. "If this bill is not amended, if it passes like this, [it] will relieve oil companies and lose to the schoolchildren these millions of dollars," she argued. She listed the oil companies it would benefit by name—Empire, Humble, and Shell. Her remarks were persuasive; her amendment was adopted by a vote of sixty-eight to fifty-four. The contested bills then died, as she preferred, when a motion to suspend the rules for final passage failed to receive the necessary four-fifths vote. Several other attempts at similar legislation also failed to pass under Hughes's relentless assault.[30]

Hughes had proved herself a skilled strategist in parliamentary procedures and a persuasive debater on an important issue involving some of the most influential interests in the state. Newspaper accounts of the legislative battle brought her a statewide reputation as a liberal crusader. "The incident illustrates the value of returning to Austin again and again Representatives who will show initiative, courage and concern for the public welfare. Representative Hughes has done well," editorialized the *Dallas Morning News*.[31]

More than thirty years later, Ralph Yarborough, by then a U.S. senator who had supported Hughes's successful quest to be a federal judge, wrote a congratulatory note in which he reminded her of her "brave and courageous fights for the Permanent School Funds of Texas." He recalled having searched in vain to find someone to assist him in the legislature until finally Hughes listened to the facts and took a stand based on principle. "Courageously and with great ability and resolution, you fought the measures through to a successful conclusion."[32]

In the fourth and final called session of the legislature, summoned to explore again the question of oil and gas matters, Hughes introduced no bills. But she joined the entire body in extending congratulations to the newly elected president and vice president of the United States, Franklin Delano Roosevelt of New York and John Nance Garner of Texas.[33]

By the time the 43rd Legislature began its regular session in January 1933, Sarah T. Hughes, although having served only one previous term, could feel like a veteran. She came back as the only remaining female in the House, the other three having been overwhelmingly defeated. Margie Neal also returned to the Senate, once more the sole woman in that body. Outgoing governor Sterling, in reviewing the work of the previous legislature, called the previous two years the most turbulent, economically, that the state had experienced since Reconstruction. "Hurled from the heights of prosperity into the depths of an unprecedented depression, the State has suffered an ordeal unlike anything that ever before befell this fair Commonwealth." There had been a "sharp and tremendous falling off of revenues." He had vetoed many spending bills, but government expenditures remained as high as ever. A projected deficit of five million to seven million dollars loomed. The 43rd Legislature must either find new revenues or retrench, he said.[34]

Governor Sterling's successor, Miriam A. Ferguson, was no stranger to the capitol building. "Ma" Ferguson had been returned to office for a second term after a hiatus of six years. In her campaign she and her husband had blamed Sterling for the state treasury deficits. Her victory in the Democratic primary runoff was by a margin of fewer than four thousand votes out of nearly a million cast. Sterling, upset by his loss and the Fergusons' attacks on him, defied custom by leaving Austin before the inauguration took place, declining even the tradition of marking a passage in the Bible for his successor.[35] Miriam Ferguson's opening address to the legislature took the same tone, as Sterling's farewell address but in far more lyrical terms. During the past two years, she said, the people of Texas and other states had been "cast hither and thither upon the angry waves of financial distress and destructive depression. Upon every hand we hear, now, the wail of the orphan, the cry of distress, the murmur of discontent, and the protest of the unemployed."[36]

Replacing Fred Minor this session as Speaker of the House was returning legislator Coke Stevenson of Junction. The conservative rancher-attorney was not someone with whom Hughes found herself in sympathy. "I was on the opposite side of everything that he wanted to do," she later said.[37] A freshman legislator from Godley, Robert B. Anderson, nominated the candidate who lost to Stevenson. In this and in other matters, Hughes and Anderson found much to agree on. They would sponsor a number of bills together in this session. Anderson, who had been elected to the legislature on the same day he graduated from the University of Texas Law School, was beginning a career that two decades later would see him become secretary of the treasury under Dwight Eisenhower.

Hughes, already especially visible as the only woman representative, seemed omnipresent during the regular session of the 43rd Legislature and the four called sessions that followed into November 1934. Of the 960 bills introduced in the House during the regular session, Hughes's name is listed in the *House Journal* index on 46 of them. Her bills touched on a wide range of topics: pipeline easements, salaries of county officials, procedural matters in court appeals, changes in the criminal code, a definition of "practicing law," removal of exemptions for admissions to the bar, receipt of federal funds from the Reconstruction Finance Corporation, procedures for a state convention in acting on proposed amendments to the U.S. Constitution, and others.

Hughes's concentration on legislative matters was interrupted when word came on March 22, 1933, that her mother had died. Elizabeth Haughton Tilghman had moved to Dallas to live with her daughter six years earlier after her husband's death. Elizabeth's health had been failing for several months before she died unexpectedly at the Hughes home on Normandy Avenue. Hughes was granted an excused absence for two days, Thursday and Friday, then she returned Monday for the resumption of legislative business. The House passed a resolution in memory of Elizabeth Tilghman on March 23.[38]

Under the looming shadow of the state deficit and bold newspaper headlines about the deteriorating situation, there was much to do in Austin. Two basic alternatives presented themselves: (1) reducing state expenditures or (2) imposing additional taxes. Governor Ferguson favored a sales tax. Hughes had a different idea—a state income tax placed on individuals and corporations. The sales tax was straightforward but was criticized as unfair to individuals with lower incomes; the income tax was seen as a liberal measure with progressive features that favored lower-income individuals.

After Ferguson's tax bill died in early April 1933, Hughes's bill (H.B. 282), signed by eleven others (none from Dallas), came up for consideration a week later. It provided exemptions of one thousand dollars for single individuals, two thousand for married couples, and two hundred for each dependent. Thereafter, the tax would be 1 percent for the first thousand dollars, increasing to a maximum of 7 percent for each thousand dollars over eleven thousand. Corporations would pay 1 percent for the first thousand dollars of income and 6 percent for income over six thousand dollars.

There existed—as has continued to be the case into the twenty-first century—great resistance by Texans to a state income tax. Yet, in these hard times many legislators were willing to consider various approaches to raising money. Hughes estimated that her tax would produce about twelve million dollars annually. Its exemptions, she contended, would exclude individuals who could not afford to pay the tax. Pipeline, oil, and sulfur companies had ample resources to pay the tax, she said. She won a favorable report from the Revenue and Taxation Committee, managed to get the bill taken up out of regular order for discussion in the House, and successfully fought off several amendments to it. In its final form the bill levied a tax of 1 percent on the first thousand dollars of income over the amount of exemptions, raised from two thousand to twenty-five hundred dollars. Corporations would be taxed at 2 percent on the first thousand dollars and up to 6 percent on income in excess of six thousand dollars.

An opponent in the legislature labeled Hughes's proposed income tax as a "vote-catching" idealistic measure that "would wreck Texas business." Hughes countered: "If you don't raise money by this bill, you will have a sales tax rammed down your throat. The newspapers have criticized me introducing this bill, but I'm not afraid to go before the people of Dallas County on the one issue that I shifted the burden of taxation."[39]

Hughes could feel political winds of liberalism blowing behind her as she pushed for her bill's passage before the House. "Andrew Mellon and Herbert Hoover favor the sales tax. Franklin Roosevelt [favors] an income tax. Are you going to follow Andrew Mellon and Hoover or are you going to follow Franklin Roosevelt?" she asked. "Do you represent the vested interests or the common people of Texas?" The bill passed, seventy to fifty-five.[40]

In the more conservative Senate, arguments centering around the bill's harmful impact on business prevailed, and Hughes's income tax proposal died, never again to resurface as a serious possibility. Hughes, however, once again had earned praise for her courage in tackling a tough issue. It reinforced her reputation as one whose political ideology reflected progressive or liberal causes. In years to come, her success in pushing such a bill through the House in conservative Texas would be viewed with amazement, especially considering opposition in Dallas to her position.

None of her fellow Dallas delegates had joined her in the income-tax bill, and it was evident that Hughes was exposing herself to substantial political risk. As the *Dallas Dispatch* observed, she could "count on the fingers of one hand all the people in this district who want to pay an income tax." In her reelection campaign, the newspaper noted, she had told voters she favored "rigid economy." Sponsorship of an income tax violated that pledge. "Economy, retrenchment, is what the people want, not more taxes," the editorial concluded.[41] The *Daily* [Dallas] *Times Herald*** also pointed to contradictions from her campaign statements. Her proposed income-tax bill would hit hardest in larger cities where industries are situated and where salaries are higher, the newspaper observed. "Yet Mrs. Hughes is supposed to represent Dallas."[42] On the editorial page of the *Dallas Journal* political cartoonist Jack Patton depicted a woman (Hughes) in a burglar's mask, fleeing with stolen goods taken from a beaten man ("Texas"). Just around the corner waiting for the burglar was a policeman ("Senate"), with billy club in hand, ready to apprehend the culprit. One of Hughes's former supporters sent her a copy of this editorial cartoon, noting: "This is how your friends feel who voted for you. We can't pay our taxes now. Are you crazy?"[43]

Still, her boldness in sponsoring the income tax bill cast her in a new and often favorable light on a stage far broader than Dallas County. The *Austin American-Statesman*, although noting the bill had "many defects," commended her and predicted a bright future. "Now wise ones say she may come to the senate two years hence as the successor of the Honorable George Purl [of Dallas]."[44] The legislative correspondent for the *Fort Worth Press* placed Sarah T. Hughes first on his list of representatives who would be "ten times as good" as any of the present senators. He wrote: "The name of Sarah Hughes of Dallas leads all the rest. The lone woman member came close to being the best man of the lot."[45]

Sarah's alma mater, Goucher College, was proudly taking note of her accomplishments. A profile in the May 1933 issue of the *Goucher Alumnae Quarterly* characterized her in glowing terms. "It is her personality and intellect that have won for her not only recognition in her district but over the entire State." As for her political philosophy, she had "definitely aligned herself with the liberal forces" and was on record as freely advocating such social legislation as unemployment insurance, old-age pensions, minimum hour and wage laws, and the redistribution of wealth. In summarizing her actions on the West Texas land bills, the article noted that "almost single-handedly" in two days of hectic debate with veteran solons of the House, she had defeated the bill and saved the state's schools millions of dollars. "So

---

* On September 13, 1954, the *Daily Times Herald* would change its name to the *Dallas Times Herald*.

signal was her victory that she received commendatory editorials and press reports from newspapers all over the state, and even from some that had theretofore favored the bill." All this, the article said, from a youthful-looking female who weighed "hardly a hundred pounds."

Her battle with the West Texas land bills lingered. Surfacing once again this session was another bill favoring the landowners and oil companies, this time in another format. Once again Hughes jumped to the forefront in opposing it. H.B. 218 would grant a twenty-year extension to landowners and oil companies for revenues they owed the state. Hughes once again tacked on a substitute amendment, this one eliminating the extension for the oil companies. "If my opposition to this bill means defeat of all my political ambitions, I shall gladly go down to defeat. I shall cheerfully be a martyr to the cause of the school children," she said. "I am willing to give the landowners an extension, but not the oil companies who are able to pay. This amendment I have offered is a test of whom the legislature represents. If you represent the oil companies, vote against it, if you represent the people and the school children, vote for it." Her substitute amendment carried, seventy-five to forty-eight, and the effect of the bill was negated.[46]

Nor had the possibility of a sales tax been removed. In an effort to forestall it Hughes wrote a critical column for the *Daily Times Herald* in August 1933. She wanted to show the "injustice and unfairness" of a tax that was being promoted by the rich and by legislators who represented two railroads, a steel company, a sulfur company, two public utilities, and three oil companies. An income tax would be fairer, she believed. "Taxes should be paid in proportion to ability to pay, and if 20 per cent of the people own 80 per cent of its wealth, it is only fair and just that they should pay and should continue to pay, 80 per cent of the taxes." She decried the increasing concentration of wealth in private hands, noting that while in 1921 there had been only six individuals in the nation admitting to incomes of more than one million dollars a year, in 1929 there were thirty-six. A sales tax would shift the burden from those best able to pay to those least able.[47]

Hughes had hit her stride. She seemed to fear no one. She could be counted on to summarize issues in a direct, plain-spoken manner that left no question as to how she stood. When a bill to remit the interest and penalties on delinquent taxes was offered by Representative W. E. Pope of Corpus Christi, she pointedly observed before the House that he was doing it for personal gain. Pope owed the state $2,392 in penalties and interest and $8,000 more in taxes, she said, amounts accumulating since 1928. A newspaper account described her: "Mrs. Sarah T. Hughes . . . stood on tip-toe at a house microphone. A wisp of bobbed hair fell across her forehead. With lashing tongue she discussed the merits of the bill." She pointed out that another representative who favored the bill was occupying a suite of rooms at a downtown hotel. "Why didn't he live in a boarding house room?" Sarah demanded. (Sarah herself alternated between rooming houses, of which there were plenty in Austin, or sometimes she shared hotel rooms with the chief clerk of the House, Louise Snow Phinney.)[48]

In a debate over an unequal distribution of automobile license fees that seemed to favor rural over urban areas, she sounded much like a fiery evangelist. "Oh, you outnumber us 5 to 1 and we know you can put this over on us if you want to. But what you are doing is highway robbery. It's legalized hijacking. If you want to steal from us, go to it, but when you go home tonight, get down on your knees and pray to God to forgive you for your theft." As she predicted, her comments in this instance did not persuade; the bill passed.[49]

When Governor Miriam Ferguson sought legislation that would permit her to reorganize and personally dominate the new Texas Relief Commission, created largely to handle the federal funds beginning to come into the state, the governor encountered a buzz saw in the House—Sarah T. Hughes. To reorganize the commission now just after the federal government had recognized it as the authorized agent for receiving and dispensing Civil Works Administration funds, Hughes contended, might jeopardize that arrangement. A day of "stormy, bitter debate" saw Hughes emerge as the opposition leader. "Are we going to tear it up and all the county relief boards too at the whim of the governor? I don't think we will. Are we going to do it just because she and he [Jim Ferguson] want a new commission? I don't think we will." She was right; the House voted against the Ferguson plan, eighty-four to fifty-three.[50]

About this time in 1933 a young University of Texas journalism student, Claudia Alta Taylor, who was to be courted by and wed the next year to congressional aide Lyndon Baines Johnson, had lunch with the fiery young legislator whose name was becoming so well known around Austin. They met adjacent to the University of Texas campus at a café on Guadalupe Street ("the Drag") where political dialogue flourished. Four decades later, Lady Bird Johnson recalled being deeply impressed by this "ardent and learned woman who was already somewhat of a trailblazer in Texas law and politics." Lady Bird remembered thinking of Hughes at the time: "Gee, it's wonderful that this woman who knows so much and talks so well is a member of the legislature. I was very proud of her."[51] Not until nearly three decades later would the two women resume their relationship and see it grow much closer.

Hughes, having proved herself more than equal to the men in the legislature, could feel safe now in speaking out about the inequalities of women under Texas law without fear of being stamped as a legislator interested only in things related to women. When a self-congratulatory speaker in the House droned on and on about legal rights granted to women in Texas, Sarah charged to the microphone. "It's a lot of bunk about women in Texas having rights. They don't even get a square deal."[52]

She was especially concerned over the ineligibility of women in Texas to serve on juries, despite having the right to vote. She coauthored with Helen Moore a proposed constitutional amendment to remedy the situation, but it went nowhere. During the next two decades she would prove to be a relentless advocate for an amendment to permit women to serve. Not until 1954 would this right be granted in Texas, and no one worked harder for it or came to be more closely identified with the cause than Hughes.

She had become, as time allowed, increasingly active in an organization in Dallas dedicated to the betterment of women, the Business and Professional Women's Club. Attending a district meeting in Tyler, she delivered a speech entitled "The Legal Status of Women in Texas." She provided a long list of inequities in need of remedy. For the rest of her life she would seek to correct them. She spoke of such anomalies as when a woman in Texas married, she retained her real and personal property but could not sell that property without her husband's consent or without gaining permission from a court. To secure a lien or the right to improve this property, she would first have to get her husband's signature of approval. Revenue from such property became community property, but the husband controlled the returns. When a woman in Texas married, Hughes said, she became "to some extent the same as a minor or non compus mentis."[53]

If she was earning a reputation as a liberal maverick in the legislature, Hughes was careful to pay homage to the special culture of her adopted state. Her effort in the previous session to reward schoolchildren for the best essays on Jane Long, "the mother of Texas," had failed. Now, she sponsored along with her Dallas County colleagues a bill to give uniformity to salutes to the Texas flag and to describe the flag clearly so that all renditions of it would be standardized concerning such matters as the precise placement of the star. The bill, H.B. 575, found acceptance in the Senate and became law.

She also became the leading champion in the House for funding the Texas Centennial Exposition, conceived to commemorate the state's independence from Mexico in 1836. A world exposition had been planned for years, and after a spirited competition with San Antonio and Houston to be the host city, Dallas had been designated as the site. With deadlines drawing closer to begin construction and to initiate other complicated arrangements for the mammoth event, the legislature now seemed remarkably reluctant to allot needed funds. The proposed five-million-dollar appropriations bill raised eyebrows, but some concerns went deeper than that. Resentment lingered among many who claimed that Dallas, a place that did not even exist at the time of the Texas revolution, did not deserve such an honor. Historic San Antonio with its Alamo and Houston with its proximity to the San Jacinto battlefield were more logical sites, it was argued belatedly but with a certain logic. "If Dallas wants a fair, let it pay for it," protested one legislator.[54]

The initial effort to pass a five-million-dollar appropriations bill had failed in the 43rd Legislature's third called session. Now, with panic beginning to set in, Governor Ferguson convened the fourth called session in October 1934 to consider, with a handful of other items, appropriations for the Centennial. Senator George Purl of Dallas worked an appropriations bill through several barriers in the Senate, but in the House more serious trouble arose. A representative from Somervell County offered a resolution to prohibit any legislative appropriation for the Centennial. He recommended that the exposition in Dallas be funded by private sources. For much of a week in November 1934, the House debated the issue, with harsh words directed toward Dallas as an entirely inappropriate site.[55]

Hughes took the lead among her Dallas County colleagues in supporting the appropriations bill and convincing the House to suspend legislative rules that were on the verge of preventing its consideration. In her impassioned remarks she appealed to the spirit of the pioneers, who despite formidable obstacles had created the Republic of Texas. "There was a panic in 1819," she said, "but that didn't stop Moses Austin. He went right ahead with his plans to colonize Texas. It's true Dallas has no Alamo; it has no San Jacinto; but it does have the same spirit that prompted Austin, Houston, and Travis." At least ten million people would attend a Texas Centennial and they would spend at least a hundred million dollars, an amount, she argued, that would drive the Depression out of Texas.[56] Her spirited remarks drew rare applause in the House as the members voted to suspend their rules and consider the bill. It also won for her the gratitude of Dallas's most powerful businessmen, who had worked so diligently to win the right to host the Centennial.

The *Dallas Dispatch* cheered her success, labeling her the Joan of Arc of the Texas Centennial. "More of that sort of spirit, the spirit which the diminutive woman legislator shows when she gets into her fighting clothes, will make a complete success of the celebration which is causing so much of politicking in Austin."[57] As it happened, despite her persuasive remarks, the legislative session died before final approval of the appropriations bill. But the tide had been turned, and the 44th Legislature, convening in January 1935, approved a reduced appropriation of three million dollars in May.[58] (The Texas Centennial Exposition would be held from June to December 1936, attracting 6.3 million visitors, bringing worldwide attention, and forever changing the image of Dallas and Texas for much of the world.)

Another battle that would bring widespread attention to Sarah T. Hughes lay just ahead. In what for her was an unusual twist, she went to great lengths to oppose an important aspect of a pet project of the president she admired, Franklin Delano Roosevelt.

In these early exploratory days of the New Deal, the Interior Department under Harold Ickes was interested in funding large-scale water projects that would develop hydroelectric power, control floods, and create jobs. An earmarked project of this nature was to harness the Colorado River, an endeavor undertaken earlier by the Samuell Insull interests in Chicago but abruptly halted with the sudden collapse of Insull's gigantic but paper-thin network of utilities across the nation. Insull's Texas project, the George W. Hamilton Dam (soon to be renamed Buchanan Dam in honor of Congressman James P. "Buck" Buchanan) in Central Texas, now lay dormant. Receivership of this failed project went to a former state senator, Alvin J. Wirtz, who enlisted Ralph W. Morrison of San Antonio to organize the Colorado River Company to finance completion of the dam. Two attempts, engineered by Wirtz to secure federal loans for this work from the Reconstruction Finance Corporation and the Public Works Administration, had failed for various reasons. Still, there was an acknowledged need for flood control, hydroelectric power, and jobs. While Wirtz continued to work in both Texas and Washington to gain support, Congressman Buchanan used his influence in the White House.[59]

The story is told that in a visit with President Roosevelt, Buchanan told him, "Mr. President, I want a birthday present." "What do you want, Buck?" the president replied. "My dam," Buchanan said. "Well then, I guess we'd better give it to you, Buck," the president is said to have replied, picking up the telephone and giving orders to that effect to Secretary of the Interior Ickes.[60]

In Austin, legislative efforts engineered by Wirtz concentrated on the creation of a state agency that would purchase the interests of the Colorado River Company and then receive a $4.5 million loan from the Public Works Administration. Ickes's legal counsel, Henry T. Hunt, and a reclamation engineer spent several days in the state capitol helping draft the appropriate legislation, giving it the stamp of certain New Deal authority and impressing most legislators with the prospective federal largesse. What attracted Hughes's attention—but evidently no one else's—was the fact that the proposed buyout of the Colorado River Company would include an immediate payment of $3.2 million to Morrison and associates. Morrison, a Democrat, had contributed a hundred thousand dollars to Roosevelt's campaign, the second largest sum given, and Hughes believed he was getting an immediate and largely undeserved payoff for that contribution.[61]

She expressed her indignation on the floor of the House, creating a buzz as she outlined this information, which seemed to surprise her fellow members. A *Chicago Tribune* newspaper reporter, Philip Kinsley, sent to Austin by his anti-New Dealer publisher, Colonel Robert McCormick, gave a series of critical reports on the pending legislation. He portrayed it as an expensive adventure in river control and power-making similar to the Tennessee Valley Authority. His heroine was Hughes. "Slight and girlish, yet strong of voice, earnest in manner, keen in debate, she faced the big room filled with lolling, bored, shirt-sleeved legislators," he wrote. This "slender little woman" had lifted the curtain a bit upon the "back room manipulations of the New Dealers." Hughes said that if Morrison were the great patriot and Democrat he should be, he would turn the property over free of charge to the state of Texas. "He is a multimillionaire and he should be glad to do this for the United States. After all, we are the people who are putting money into this. We are the people of the United States."[62]

Two days later as the called session reached the last hours of the final day, a joint House-Senate committee of ten, including Hughes as a member, appeared ready to report the bill out for a vote. Waiting impatiently, with majorities in both houses evidently ready to approve it, were Congressman Buchanan and Henry T. Hunt, the New Deal lawyer who had helped frame the bill (or "dictate" it, as Kinsley wrote in the *Tribune*). Hughes needed two more votes from House committee members to avoid sending out the bill for a vote and certain passage. The *Chicago Tribune* described the dramatic scene: "Olan Van Zandt, blind member from Tioga, had his pen raised ready to sign the conference report once, but she [Hughes] called him aside and talked him out of that. Will Scott of Sweetwater, a farmer who was wavering, was also persuaded by Mrs. Hughes to leave the committee room." Seven of the ten members voted to send out the bill, but that was not enough. The bill thus died at 2 A.M. and the legislature's special session ended. "A woman, a blind man, and a farmer, then were the ones who finally defeated a measure said in debate to be desired by the President himself," summed up Kinsley in the *Tribune*.[63]

The *Dallas Dispatch* said Hughes had exposed the legislation as a "pork barrel" so "flagrant" that it had attracted the faraway attention of the *Chicago Tribune*. But the *Austin American* charged that "one obdurate and two uncertain members" had killed legislation that might have brought more relief to workers of Texas than a six-million-dollar bond issue.[64]

Another special session loomed just ahead with the Colorado River proposal certain to be on Governor Ferguson's agenda. Hughes began advance crusading against the bill, this time at a higher level—the president of the United States. She wrote directly to Franklin Roosevelt, advising that "more than a possibility" of a small national scandal existed if the legislation passed. "I know that you want a real Public Authority created with no possibility of its getting into private hands, and I do not believe you want any one man to become enriched at the expense of the government," she wrote. She believed she had eliminated the possibility of a single individual becoming "enriched," but now she was concerned about the possibility of private rather than public ownership. "I hope that I am not asking too much of you to look into the matter and advise me in regard to the project," she concluded.[65] The president did not respond.

She sent the same letter to Secretary Ickes of the Interior Department. "I want to see a real Public Authority created, with no possibility of its getting into private hands," she wrote. "In addition, I want to be sure the project is free from graft and scandal. I know that this is also your point of view." She asked him to "make an investigation and verify the facts I have stated."[66]

During the fourth called session of the legislature, October 12 to November 10, 1934, other forces opposing the bill coalesced. These included the West Texas ranchers and their chambers of commerce, insistent about retaining their water rights in the upper third of the Colorado River watershed. They were joined by smaller public utility companies who believed the state should not be part of a river authority. Finally, however, a water rights amendment satisfied the West Texas ranchers. The Lower Colorado River Authority Bill (LCRA) was passed, and Morrison would still get a commission of $1.6 million.[67]

The battle was not over, though, for the river authority still needed the loan from the PWA. Hughes now mounted a campaign to persuade federal officials not to recognize the authority. In mid-November, desperate to have her story heard, she "crashed the gates" at a meeting of the American Petroleum Institute where Ickes was the speaker and sat in the front row (alongside the governor's husband, former governor Jim Ferguson) in hopes of buttonholing Ickes directly. She persuaded the executive vice president of the API to introduce her to him, and Ickes agreed to give her five minutes of his time in his hotel room. "I did most of the talking, attempting to get over in five minutes the actual situation," she wrote to a fellow representative, Weaver Moore of Harris County, an ally in the battle. Ickes told her he had no knowledge of many of these matters, but he asked Hughes to write to him with more details.[68]

This she did, beginning a series of exchanges unsatisfactory to her. "My position for some time," Ickes wrote, "has been that it is up to the State of Texas to pass whatever legislation may seem appropriate to it. I don't think I can properly interfere in such a matter."[69]

In January 1935, with the 44th Legislature in session and Hughes now beginning her third term as a legislator, she attempted again to deprive Morrison of his commission with the "No Commission Amendment Bill." Hughes urged Ickes to advise the legislature that this amendment would not adversely impact the federal government's commitment to the Lower Colorado River Authority. Ickes replied in a telegram to Hughes and two of her colleagues, Sidney Latham and Weaver Moore: "Regret I cannot reply to you except in general terms but my position is that I have no desire to influence Texas Legislature."[70]

Hughes, disappointed, advised him wryly that the No Commission Amendment Bill had been killed the previous night in committee. "Having no information from you, [the committee] took at face value the information from Mr. Buchanan that the Amendment would kill the Bill. I regret very much that you felt that you could not make any statement . . . especially in view of the fact that a man in your office, Mr. Hunt, was the cause of the Amendment being defeated at the previous session."[71]

Ickes did not express to Hughes his own concerns about the project. He did not tell her he was asking Hunt to head a three-man advisory committee to conduct an extensive examination on the financial and legal status and engineering feasibility of the half-completed Buchanan Dam. Hunt's detailed and favorable report, completed in May 1935, led to the immediate approval of a twenty-million-dollar PWA allotment to the Lower Colorado River Authority. In years to come the LCRA would become a huge, multipurpose public agency, generating hydroelectricity from six dams on the lower Colorado to supply electricity to Texans in fifty-three counties and providing water supplies, recreational facilities, wastewater services, and other services to a vast area.[72]

As for Morrison's financial windfall that Hughes had so vehemently opposed, disbursement of the initial funds to the LCRA provided a settlement of $2.2 million, divided among Morrison, Alvin Wirtz, and Morrison's son-in-law, C. G. Malott, who had worked on the project. Wirtz and Morrison sought in vain to have Malott appointed head of the LCRA, but the new board declined to do so because of political and personal considerations.[73] Wirtz was appointed legal counsel for the LCRA, and he became the legal representative for the new construction company that completed Buchanan Dam—Brown & Root. In his work toward establishing it and gaining federal funds, Wirtz had come to know Congressman Richard Kleberg's young secretary, Lyndon B. Johnson. Johnson proved to be invaluable to Wirtz through the Washington contacts he already was making. Their relationship continued to deepen when, upon Buchanan's death in 1937, Johnson succeeded Buchanan and adopted the LCRA as a pet project of his own. Later, Johnson would look to Wirtz as his most important mentor. "Alvin Wirtz was my dearest friend, my most trusted counselor," he said. "From him . . . I gained a glimpse of what greatness there is in the human race."[74]

Later, Hughes would never refer to her efforts to unravel the LCRA at its beginning, preferring, perhaps, not to remind the New Dealers with whom she would associate herself through the years of her position. In addition to Lyndon B. Johnson's close association with the LCRA, Ralph Yarborough served on its first board of directors. Strictly speaking, though, her opposition was not an inconsistency. She favored the concept of the project. Her primary opposition had been to what she believed was an undeserved reward going to an individual of substantial means as payment for a campaign contribution. This was consistent with viewpoints she would maintain throughout her career.

In the summer of 1934, Sarah T. Hughes faced reelection for her third term. The attention she had attracted through her sponsorship of a state income tax bill had brought to the surface several opponents who thought her unpopular stance made her vulnerable. One of the opponents was Edith Wilmans, the attorney who had become the first female elected to the state legislature in 1922. It had been Wilmans's sister, Helen Viglini, whom Hughes had defeated along with other opponents in both 1930 and 1932.[75]

Many voters undoubtedly felt the same as the *Dallas Journal*, though. Although the newspaper had opposed Hughes's proposed state income tax, it recognized her as "a useful and courageous" representative. "[The *Journal*] would rather take Mrs. Hughes and run its chances of defeating new taxation then [*sic*] to take Mrs. Wilmans on *The Journal's* own platform."[76]

Wilmans was only one of five other candidates who opposed Hughes in the July Democratic primary. As it turned out, this pioneer legislator, first elected with the support of the then powerful Ku Klux Klan, posed no threat. The Klan's power in Dallas and elsewhere had evaporated. Other aspects of Wilmans's life also had changed since then. She had divorced her first husband, married a Chicagoan and moved there, divorced him, and returned to Dallas. In the July primary she finished fifth in the six-person race. First primary returns showed Hughes with 8,890 votes, almost as many as the other five candidates combined but not enough to avoid a runoff in August against the second-place finisher, Sam Hanna.[77]

Hanna conducted a spirited campaign, attacking Hughes. He reproduced in a newspaper advertisement a letter she had sent to Governor Miriam Ferguson asking her to extend a ninety-day furlough she had given a man convicted of murder and imprisoned. Hughes had told the governor the man's wife was in need of his assistance and he had conducted himself properly while on furlough. Hanna promised not to use his own influence as a state representative to secure paroles and furloughs for "murderers, bank robbers and other dangerous criminals." In the final joint debate of the campaign, Hanna spoke last, finishing with a zinger. At the conclusion he summed up by saying, "Slap her in the face and send her back to the kitchen." The crowd, as Sarah later said, "simply went wild." To see a woman candidate handled so irreverently rather than deferentially somehow brought great satisfaction. In the August 25 runoff, held while the legislature was in its third called session, Hughes won by a margin of some seventeen hundred votes out of thirty-seven thousand cast.[78]

A month later, in September 1934, in the midst of Hughes's struggle against the LCRA, the nine newspaper reporters who covered the House conducted a poll among themselves. Who was the "most valuable" of the 154 members of the House? Their unanimous choice was Sarah T. Hughes.[79]

4 ~

Breaking Barriers

In January 1935, two months shy of his thirty-sixth birthday, James V. Allred, the "fighting district attorney," moved into the Governor's Mansion. During the two terms he would serve as governor, he would be acclaimed as the most progressive Texas chief executive of the era. In this lawyer-politician from Wichita Falls, who had earned his nickname for battling the Ku Klux Klan, Sarah T. Hughes found a kindred spirit, both politically and personally. She had campaigned enthusiastically for him in his earlier race for attorney general as well as for the gubernatorial election. His willingness to confront vested interests, his skills as a colorful public speaker, his desire to allot more funds for education, his belief in regulating public utilities, his enthusiasm for New Deal programs, and his youthful zeal endeared him to Hughes.

In the several days prior to the convening of the 44th Legislature, Hughes joined forces with Allred to ensure the election of his choice, Robert W. Calvert, as Speaker of the House. Calvert was a young politician in the early stages of a career that would bring him to the post of chief justice of the Texas Supreme Court. For Allred or any governor to have a sympathetic ally as Speaker was one of the most important factors for success. To this point in the state's history, custom had dictated that a Speaker served only one term in office. Thus, it was assumed that the Speaker for the last session, conservative Coke Stevenson, would follow tradition and return to his regular seat in the House, opening the way for the governor's choice, Calvert, to succeed him. A strong contingent of conservative legislators, though, implored Stevenson to ignore tradition and seek a second term as Speaker. Buoyed by this encouragement and resenting the implied pressure from Allred that he should step aside, Stevenson agreed to be a candidate for reelection. This prospect dismayed Hughes, not only because she was a friend and political ally of both Allred and Calvert, but because Stevenson was a man who opposed everything she favored.

A fiery contest loomed as liberals and conservatives took sides. Hughes arrived in Austin several days early to campaign for Calvert among the undecided. Calvert supporters set up headquarters in the Stephen F. Austin Hotel; those for Stevenson camped out just around the corner at the Driskill Hotel. Jim Ferguson, disappointed because his candidate for governor had lost to Allred, continued to try to exert his influence in the capital by lobbying for Stevenson. The contest came to be viewed as a battle not so much between Calvert and Stevenson as between the new liberal governor Allred and the old political machine of Jim Ferguson. On the day of the election, Hughes made a resounding speech for Calvert, lambasting Ferguson's manipulative, behind-the-scenes efforts and charging that through him powerful lobbyists were seeking to control the House. When the vote was tallied, incoming governor Allred had suffered his first loss. Stevenson won with eighty votes over Calvert's sixty-eight. Among the Dallas delegation, only Hughes had supported Calvert.[1]

Ferguson, stung by Hughes's criticisms of him on the floor of the House, now counterattacked in his political organ, the *Ferguson Forum*. He derided "little Sarah Hughes, the precocious political female," for having taken every opportunity to "tear into me and dig up all the political animosities of the past." He followed his initial blast with a second, prolonged diatribe, "The Lady Lawmaker from Dallas." Never had Hughes experienced such a public scolding as this. For as long as civilization had lasted, Ferguson wrote, women had shared in the glory and achievements of their particular generations. Many had played important parts in the affairs of government, bringing their "feminine personalities" to the political forefront with judgment, vision, and understanding not shared equally by the masculine sex. Almost without exception, he wrote, these women had personified the feminine qualities of mind and heart that had "blessed the sex since God gave Eve to Adam, more than six thousand years ago." Similarly, he wrote, many women in Texas had helped shape the political destiny of the state with unchallenged patriotism, courage, and ability. "The Honorable Sarah T. Hughes of Dallas, unfortunately, does not exemplify this type of gentle, dignified, quiet womanhood which has so effectively and creditably held its place in the new field accorded by the granting of suffrage," he wrote. Instead, she had proceeded on the theory that "noise can take the place of knowledge and assertions substitute for facts." In her speech for Calvert and against himself, Ferguson described her as having tossed her head, stamped her feet, and bandied words with the best of the worst sort of male politician. "She is ready to enter any contest or debate with a gusto and reckless disregard for truth which would do justice to the most hardened ward-heeler in New York's East Side slums," he continued. "But in the qualities on which her sex must always depend for supremacy in the unequal contest with men—poise, accuracy and gentleness—the Honorable Sarah is sadly lacking." What Hughes needed, he said, was a reversion to the "characteristics and qualities universally demanded of women, whether they grace drawing rooms, decorate business offices or adorn legislative halls."[2]

This lengthy attack failed to give Hughes the slightest pause. In fact, it was a testimony to her abilities in the rough and tumble world of Texas politics. Now at the height of her powers as a legislator, confident and afraid of no one, she was ready to join the progressive new governor in his efforts to bring more New Deal programs to Texas. She also was continuing with her lobbying effort against the Lower Colorado River Authority, concentrating now on persuading Secretary of the Interior Ickes to take her side. Certain to emerge again in this legislative session would be an effort to impose a sales tax upon the state's residents. Ready to fight it was Sarah Hughes, still disappointed in her failure to prevail with her income-tax proposal. Miriam Ferguson, in her farewell speech to the legislature early in January, urged the sales tax as the best way to overcome a state deficit of nearly twenty-one million dollars.[3] Hughes already had been alert to that possibility. Three weeks earlier in Austin she argued against it before the legislative tax survey committee. Her fiery debate there with Senator Tom Holbrook of Galveston appeared to be a precursor to the coming session.[4]

In his first speech as governor, Allred told a joint session of the House and Senate that the state's most pressing need was not the imposition of a sales tax but the "restoration of jobs for the idle." With some 250,000 families in Texas on relief rolls, he urged the issuing of relief bonds totaling twenty million dollars and the establishment of old-age pensions.[5]

The challenges before the 44th Legislature were formidable. Hughes was expected to be in the thick of the struggle, amidst a divided leadership, to cope with the ravages of the Depression. She would be a staunch ally for Allred and a thorn for Stevenson.

As the legislature convened on January 8, the *Austin American* chose to highlight Hughes in an editorial profile:

> She made a marvelous record in preceding legislatures. She is thoroughly independent. Those who know her best say that she never takes orders

from political bosses, kings of the lobby or unvested interests, but goes her way as a servant of the people. . . . She will be in the picture for two years—a lawmaker during the Centennial roundup of all the people who glory in the past of Texas and have an abiding faith in its future.[6]

Fortune had something else in mind. A conflict of a different type presented itself to Hughes, one that would abruptly and permanently change the direction of the rest of her public life. In the spirit of combativeness, unwilling to back away from a fight, she gladly undertook this new challenge, not fully realizing the long-term impact it would have on her career. The episode started after Governor Allred, in one of his first acts, appointed William M. Taylor of Dallas to the Supreme Court Commission of Appeals, leaving vacant Taylor's seat on the 14th District Court. District judges in Texas normally were elected, but when vacancies occurred the governor had the power of appointment until voters could select their choice at the next election. District judges had four-year terms; reelection was often no problem for the incumbent; and the annual salary of six thousand dollars was good pay. A clamor immediately arose among Dallas lawyers to be Taylor's replacement. A news story listed nine aspirants by name. One of them—which one is not known—asked Hughes to speak on his behalf with her good friend, Governor Allred. She agreed to do so.[7]

Hughes found the governor less than enthusiastic about the man's nomination. His unspoken reason was that he had another candidate in mind—Sarah T. Hughes herself. The president of the Dallas Democratic Women's Luncheon Club, Mrs. Harold Abrams, who had campaigned with Hughes for Allred, had placed Hughes's name before the governor. Mrs. Abrams realized that a unique opportunity had arisen to advance the cause for women in Texas. No other woman in the state's history had received a permanent appointment as district judge. Surely no other woman in the state's history had been so well-qualified, nor had the moment ever been so opportune for that to take place. Hughes seemed ideally situated to break this gender barrier.[8]

News stories describing Hughes as a dark horse candidate came as a "complete surprise" to her. However, the idea of becoming judge, although she had not before considered it, seemed appealing. It was a different sort of challenge, and Sarah Hughes always appreciated a challenge. It was reported that Allred might be hesitant to appoint her because he needed her support in the House as a trusted and effective ally. Yet, he recognized the debt he owed for her crusade on behalf of Calvert for Speaker as well as for her work toward his own election. Supporters urging Hughes's appointment observed that passing her up for the nomination because he needed her would be a sorry way to display his appreciation. Walter C. Hornaday, political writer for the *Dallas Journal*, insisted that her appointment would be a smart move, both politically and practically. Her appointment would enhance Allred's strength among women all over the state, and it would eliminate inevitable hard feelings if he had to choose from one of the several capable men candidates. Additionally, Hornaday wrote, Hughes was more than qualified for the appointment, and for Allred to name the first woman in the state's history as district judge would bring honor to him. Whatever the outcome, Hughes undoubtedly would continue to be as loyal as ever to Allred, but perhaps not as "spiritedly and full-heartedly" as before. "After all," Hornaday wrote, "district judgeships paying $6,000 a year and good for four years do not fall in the laps of either men or women every day, not to mention the honor involved, particularly that of being the first woman to be named to such a post in Texas."[9]

With William M. Taylor vacating his judgeship on Friday, February 1, and assuming his new office that day in Austin, the issue grew more complex. A number of lawyers in Dallas declared that the state constitution forbade the governor from making appointments from the House membership. Hughes, curious herself about this legal issue, visited the new attorney general, William McCraw of Dallas, who had directed a staff member to research the matter. His conclusion that such an appointment would be legal settled that matter in Hughes's own mind.[10]

Privately, Allred already had made up his mind to appoint Hughes, but "senatorial courtesy" held that the governor clear such appointments through the senator from the appointee's district. That person was blustery Claud Westerfeld, in his first term as senator from Dallas County. Allred learned that Westerfeld would absolutely oppose Hughes's appointment. Knowing this, Allred asked his assistant, Edward A. Clark, to contact Hughes and apprise her of the situation's complexity.[11] "[Clark] called me in my hotel room," Hughes later said, "and told me that the governor was going to appoint me but that my own senator [Westerfeld] . . . was going to oppose my nomination. And the governor wanted to know whether or not I wanted the name sent up in view of his opposition." This was the sort of direct challenge Hughes relished. Yes, she wanted the nomination, and she would fight in her own behalf to win confirmation.[12]

The challenge did not promise to be easy. In addition to the senatorial courtesy problem, Senate confirmation would require a two-thirds vote of those present. This was a difficult standard compared with the simple majority needed in the U.S. Senate to approve presidential appointments. Moreover, no one in recent memory, perhaps ever, had been appointed over the objection of that person's own senator.

On the same day Taylor arrived in Austin to assume his new duties, Allred announced his decision to appoint Sarah T. Hughes to the 14th District Court. "I am proud to be the first governor of Texas to appoint a woman to this high position," he said. "Mrs. Hughes is capable, conscientious and courageous."[13] The confirmation process was not expected to be lengthy, for her name reportedly would be submitted to the Senate on Monday, February 4.

The aspect of the news story most prominently displayed and most thoroughly covered, however, was not the novelty of the appointment but the fact that Westerfeld would oppose her. The Dallas senator claimed that the governor had said nothing to him about the appointment despite the tradition of the governor conferring with the senator of the district before taking action. (Just how Allred was able to tell Hughes in advance that Westerfeld would oppose her without having talked to him is open to conjecture.) The custom of senatorial courtesy, Westerfeld said, means the Senate usually rejects nominees opposed by the senator from that district. He hoped his fellow senators would accord him that courtesy.[14]

And then Westerfeld made a biting comment—absolutely counterproductive, as it turned out—that would antagonize Hughes and women throughout the state. "Mrs. Hughes is a married woman and should be at home washing dishes or something else," he snapped. The snappish comment became a flashpoint. Women throughout the state, insulted by the remark, responded by mobilizing on Hughes's behalf with even greater enthusiasm.

Westerfeld further elaborated to newspapers reporters the reasons for his opposition:

Second, her husband draws $300 or more a month from the Federal Government and why give the family $500 or more from the State?

Third, I don't think she is temperamentally fitted for the position. Fourth, I don't think that the Governor should pay his political debts with appointments. Mrs. Hughes was very active during the election of the Speaker of the House for Allred's candidate, Robert W. Calvert of Hillsboro, and now the Governor is simply paying off. I see no reason why the taxpayers, litigants and lawyers of Dallas should have to pay the Governor's political debts and suffer from the appointment.

Fifth, and perhaps the most important, is that the Fourteenth District Court has been presided over by great men. Judge Kenneth Foree was one of the greatest Judges Texas ever had and he was succeeded by another great one, Judge Taylor, who now has gone to the Supreme Court Commission of Appeals. I would like to have another great man, one that Judge Foree himself would approve for that bench.[15]

Hughes, in Dallas the weekend Allred made his announcement, said she would accept the appointment, of course. She would remain in the House until the Senate confirmed her. A brief biographical portrait in the *Dallas Morning News* article told of her upbringing in Baltimore, her undergraduate and law studies, and her marriage to George Hughes. Asked how she had come to Dallas, she said: "I have a Texas husband. He was born in Palestine and Texans always come back to Texas." Her hobbies, she said, were horseback riding, tennis, and gardening. "I'm not a bad cook," she added.[16]

On Saturday morning, the day after Allred's announcement, the Dallas Bar Association met to select a temporary judge for the 14th District Court. Their choice was D. A. Frank, a prominent attorney who next year would become president of the Dallas Bar Association. Some, including the *Daily Times Herald*, interpreted the choice of Frank as a slap at Hughes, believing members just as easily could have chosen her. "The fact that she was not even nominated placed the meeting in the category of a protest or indignation meeting," said one of the attorneys, W. B. Pope.[17]

Clearly, her appointment was controversial, although a day later Dallas attorney Harold Young contended that the choice of Frank as temporary judge was not intended to snub Hughes. She was "highly acceptable to most members of the bar," he said. Still, the comments in the first-day news stories and Westerfeld's opposition made it apparent that confirmation by the Senate was anything but certain.[18]

The clubwomen of Dallas lost no time in mobilizing behind Hughes.

Grace Fitzgerald, one of the city's pioneer women lawyers, a good friend to Hughes, and president of the Dallas Business and Professional Women's Club, took a leading role. On Saturday, a day after the announcement, Fitzgerald, friends of Hughes, and fellow clubwomen began writing letters to women's clubs and local chapters of the Business and Professional Women in more than sixty Texas towns to ask their state senators to support the Hughes's nomination. Fitzgerald also called an "indignation meeting" of the B&PW at the University Club to protest Westerfeld's opposition. The educational chairman of the B&PW told of "militant action" to be taken by groups of women all over the state.[19]

News of Hughes's appointment brought scores of congratulatory telephone calls to her home. The first call on Saturday morning came at 6:30 A.M. at a moment when she said she was at home preparing breakfast for George. "Yes, I do fix breakfast for my husband and dinner, too," she said, omitting what might have been qualifiers of "sometimes" or "occasionally." "And I can and do wash the dishes." After accepting these early calls, Hughes worked on her own behalf most of the day from the office of fellow female attorney Hattie Henenberg and part of the day from her own law office. Telephone pledges of support were pouring in from both men and women. Hughes made her own calls to senators all over the state asking for their support in the confirmation vote.[20]

Westerfeld was digging his heels in deeper. As the debate intensified, he added new reasons to support his opposition to confirmation. He saw Hughes's nomination as a plot by the governor to embarrass him and, since he believed Hughes had little chance of confirmation, a roundabout scheme to secure the ultimate selection of M. R. Irons for the post. Irons was a former law partner of Allred's new secretary of state, Gerald Mann, who had headed Allred's North Texas gubernatorial campaign. Westerfeld's own choice for judge was Edward P. Dougherty. "I may not get Dougherty appointed to the post—I probably won't—but I certainly will fight the confirmation of Mrs. Hughes," Westerfeld said.[21]

Returning to his basic concern, Hughes's gender, Westerfeld said he was opposed especially to married women taking the place of men. Hughes lacked, he insisted, the poise and temperament to serve as judge, referring especially to her unrestrained speeches during the last political campaign. "It is generally recognized that probably 80 per cent of a trial judge's acts are discretionary," he said, "and the average woman is so constituted that she responds to intuition rather than knowledge or aptness in deciding matters needing instant action. The rare exceptions are extremely masculine women."[22]

Hughes coyly expressed bewilderment over Westerfeld's continued opposition. "I have always been friendly to him," she said, "and thought he was a friend of mine."[23] As to his argument that her husband already was earning a good living and she didn't need the job, Hughes said: "I have always thought that judicial offices should be filled by merit, and do not see how the fact that one member of the family has an income has anything to do with qualifications. I did not know it was necessary to select appointees from among paupers."[24]

More telling were her disingenuous personal observations. "The Senator says I should be home washing dishes. He has a most charming wife and if she had been home dishwashing instead of working for him, he couldn't have been elected."[25]

When legislators arrived in Austin on Monday the halls buzzed with speculation about the impending confirmation battle. Hughes, buoyed by the widespread support of women throughout the state, found the day opportune to reintroduce legislation she had offered in her first year. This was her bill to eliminate separate examination for a married woman, out of the presence of her husband, before real property could be conveyed. The statutory requirement was "obsolete and impliedly questions the intelligence of a married woman," she said.[26] As before, though, the proposed bill went nowhere.

The obstreperousness of Westerfeld's comments, now being repeated throughout the nation, made the story even more newsworthy. Newspapers across the state reported his remarks with apparent glee, and wire services sent them throughout the land.

The *Dallas Morning News* pointed out a particular oddity. If Hughes won confirmation, she would preside over a court in which she would not even be eligible to serve as a juror. As Hughes was well aware, statutes stipulated that "the jury in the District Court shall be composed of twelve men." When, as occasionally happened, women were summoned by mistake, they were immediately sent home.[27]

A male fan who listed his name only as "Lester" broke into poetry for the *Fort Worth Press*, extolling Hughes's virtues as "our fighting feminist" and lamenting that her fiery temperament would be subdued into a "bland judicial calm" if the Senate approved her. "Sarah, I hate to see you come to it, But it's a good trick if you do it," he concluded.[28]

An editorial cartoon by Jack Patton in the *Dallas Journal* under the title "Texas Judiciary Scene of the Future" showed a woman judge, recognizable as Hughes, on the bench with a trial in progress. Sitting with her, chewing a court document and pounding the judge's gavel amid a confusion of toys, bottles, and rattler, was a boisterous baby. Off to the side a bratty brother was pulling the tail of a cat. "Junior, keep quiet," the judge admonished as the witness attempted to respond to an attorney's question.[29]

"She ought to be home washing dishes." That was the remark that set the women all over the state on fire, Hughes recalled later. And it was a statement she had recognized immediately as a powerful tool in overcoming Westerfeld's opposition.[30] Over the weekend she happily posed for a *Dallas Morning News* photographer, washing dishes at her kitchen sink and smiling broadly at the camera. A wire service delivered the picture to newspapers in major cities across the country.[31]

By Tuesday, February 5, the day Allred sent his formal nomination to the Senate, the Dallas Business and Professional Women's organization, the Zonta Club, the Altrusa Club, the Dallas College Club, and the American Association of University Women already had passed resolutions and circulated petitions urging Hughes's confirmation. They were using affiliate clubs throughout the state to drum up further support. Men, too, were being contacted and asked to urge her confirmation, and Grace Fitzgerald announced plans to poll Dallas Bar Association members.[32]

On this same day, the attorney general cited two previous opinions holdings that the governor indeed had authority to appoint a member of the House of Representatives to office. Westerfeld refused to accept the opinions as legitimate and vowed to continue arguing that Hughes's appointment was unconstitutional. The barrage of attacks against him from women's groups evidently had taken effect, though, for he stopped basing his public objections against her on the grounds of her gender.[33] Others, though, such as a Culberson County man, continued to object to Allred on this basis. "A woman is always a woman first and Governor or Judge or this or that next," wrote W. R. Hegler. "This Dallas woman may know the Law, she may have unusual ability, but she or no other woman is fit to sit on the bench and judge her fellow man."[34]

In the House of Representatives, a petition favoring Hughes's confirmation began circulating. Before week's end, from 100 to 125 members had affixed their signatures to the document. Robert W. Calvert was one of the delegation who presented the petition to the governor.[35]

"Dallas County is getting tremendous enjoyment out of the roaring blast of Claud Westerfeld," the *Dallas Journal* reported. His only logical complaint against Hughes, the newspaper concluded, was that she was a political payoff for the governor, but "he spoils it . . . by demanding as a matter of senatorial courtesy that he be allowed to dictate the rejection of Mrs. Hughes." Nobody, the newspaper observed, could deny the "mental equipment" of Hughes or that she had made an "excellent legislator." What could be said with certainty, according to the newspaper, was that if Westerfeld succeeded in keeping her off the bench, "the next Senator from Dallas is going to be somebody not named Westerfeld. . . . A fairly good guess is that it will either be Judge Hughes this year or Senator Hughes four years hence."[36]

Before the end of the week the Senate committee on the governor's nominations took up the matter of the Hughes appointment. An attorney from Dallas's largest law firm, Thompson & Knight, advised committee members that he favored her appointment and that he had sent telegrams to several senators to that effect. One senator spoke up. "Well, what does the senior member of the firm think?" Just then the senior member of the firm, William Thompson, who happened to be in the capitol, walked into the room and said, "I'm for her, too." The committee voted eight to one in favor of Hughes, thus sending it to the full Senate for consideration. Voting no was Roy Sanderford of Belton, Miriam Ferguson's floor leader during the last legislative session.[37]

Back in Dallas, Tom C. Gooch of the *Daily Times Herald* sang the praises of "Miss Sallie" in his daily column. She had proved her competency both as a potential judge and as a homemaker, he argued, overstating his rationale to be sure. "As a young wife she did a good job of dishwashing and housekeeping. She not only helped a husband to become a lawyer, but she propped open law books on the kitchen sink and studied the statutes of the land as she wiped the pots and kettles. The result was that she received a law license and graduated from the kitchen." Both as a lawyer and political candidate, he wrote, she "never lost her womanly loveliness nor the feminine touch."[38]

On Monday, February 11, the Senate, in executive session, debated Hughes's appointment. One of the outstanding attorneys in Dallas and the state, Harry P. Lawther, former president of the Dallas Bar Association and recently president of the State Bar of Texas, spoke against her confirmation. His testimony failed to impress most of the committee when the only plausible reason he could list for not supporting her was that she had failed to vote for a bill he had favored at a previous session. Another lawyer, J. Frank Wilson, contested Lawther's claim that the Dallas lawyers did not endorse her. "Yes, I doubt if Mrs. Hughes could obtain the indorsement [*sic*] of 10 percent of the corporation lawyers of Dallas, but of the others she could poll between 25 and 50 percent and that is a large number." She was capable and able and deserved confirmation solely on her ability and qualifications, said Wilson, who would become her political opponent in another decade. A surprise witness in Hughes's behalf was C. F. Cusack—a surprise because in Westerfeld's last campaign he had served as his manager. As it turned out, Cusack was an aspirant for her position as a state representative.[39]

Eyes focused during the debate on the thick-chested Westerfeld with his shaggy white hair and menacing eyebrows. Because the executive session was closed, his words were unrecorded, but eleven years later Westerfeld re-created the scene for writer Wallis M. Reef, gesticulating broadly as he sat at a bench in Dallas near Hughes's courtroom. "Strength has got to rule," he said he had told the senators. "You can measure a man's virility by the length of his whiskers—and women can't sprout them at all. . . . A man with long whiskers is a man of virility, a man who'll fight at the drop of a hat. But women—women belong in the home. They always have and they always will!"[40]

His exaggerated bombast failed to persuade the Senate members. After four hours of debate, they voted twenty-three to seven to confirm the appointment of Sarah T. Hughes as the first woman in the state's history to be a district judge. Only a few formal requirements remained to complete the task, and they were done in about twenty minutes. Allred issued the commission, Secretary of State Gerald Mann signed it, and Hughes took the oath of office before notary public Arlene Wilson. Next day the House members gathered at 11:30 A.M. to hear a final word from their departing colleague, who was introduced by Speaker of the House Stevenson.[41]

In high spirits, she joked about the legislative fights she had been a part of. "You all know how I hate to leave you, but after I got into this fight I just had to win it. . . . We all enjoy fights. That's one thing I have enjoyed about the legislature."[42]

In retrospect, Hughes would realize that what attracted her about her appointment was not an overriding desire to become a judge, for such had not even occurred to her. It was instead the irresistible possibility of triumph against overpowering odds. She could not resist entering the battlefield, and the emergence of such a salty opponent as Westerfeld energized her. What suited her own temperament ideally, she later would recognize and acknowledge, would have been continued service in a legislative body. There, she could debate political issues without restraint and use her considerable powers of persuasion to win her way. The chief clerk of the House of Representatives since 1925, Louise Snow Phinney, summarized Hughes's remarkable aptitude for such work by saying she was "perhaps the nearest to a legislative 'boss' in the last 10 years and also probably the ablest floor leader in that time."[43] On the bench she would find herself cast as an impartial mediator, presiding over the disputes of other people and following the law as recorded. She would be a person largely removed from the rough and tumble world of politics. Even so, for the rest of her life, politics would remain her first love, and she would manage remarkably to serve both as a judge and to involve herself, to the extent that was possible, with the issues of the day.[44] Within her designated role as a state judge, though, she would work hard to succeed, and she did, achieving an outstanding record over twenty-six years of service. Later, as a federal judge in a less constricted legal environment, she would exemplify an age that encouraged judicial activism.

On the day after her Senate confirmation Hughes enjoyed word of another triumph. Her bill to require examinations for all applicants to practice law—no exceptions—was passed to become effective in 1937. Up to this point, graduates of more than a half dozen approved law schools were certified to practice law in Texas without examination. This included the tiny Dallas law school where Hughes had taught, Jefferson, now struggling to survive amid the woes of the Depression. Hughes's bill, encouraged by the Dallas Bar Association, had provoked much debate. Efforts to exempt graduates of the University of Texas, Baylor, and Southern Methodist University from examination requirements failed. Representative W. E. Pope of Corpus Christi (whom Hughes had excoriated for delinquent taxes) argued that the state should simply tear down the University of Texas Law School if it would not recognize its graduates as fit to practice law. Hughes's legislation represented a marked upgrade in standards for legal education and a final blow to such older practices as reading law in an office and then being examined by a friendly judge.[45]

The 14th was the oldest district court in Dallas County. A court with the designation of 14th Independent District Court had served the county since

1854. After the Civil War, it had been presided over by three Republican judges appointed by governors. In 1885 it was created anew by the state legislature as the 14th Judicial District Court. When the new Criminal District Court was established in 1893, the 14th was confined to civil cases. Presiding over the court during its long history had been some of Dallas's most outstanding jurists, including Judge Kenneth Foree, who sat on the bench from 1909 until his death in 1931. The courtroom was located in the massive, Romanesque revival courthouse made of red sandstone and blue granite, completed in early 1893 at the site designated for such purpose by the town's founder, John Neely Bryan. For many decades the building had stood at the center of town. Now, although the center of downtown had moved about half a mile to the east, the courthouse dominated an expanding county government complex. Across the street the Dallas County Criminal Courts Building, completed in 1915, housed the criminal district courts, jail, sheriff's office, and other county offices. Adjacent to the Criminal Courts Building was the new Records Building, opened in 1928.

Hughes lost no time in moving from the legislature to the courthouse. Returning to Dallas by train, she was greeted at Union Terminal by her husband and friends Hattie Henenberg and Margaret Evans. She arrived at the courthouse at 8:55 A.M. the next day, Wednesday, February 13, to begin her duties. A hundred or so friends and supporters already had gathered there as a surprise greeting. Two large floral arrangements lent a celebratory air to the occasion. The presiding judge of the judicial district, Claude McCallum, was on hand to congratulate the new jurist, and two other judges, John Rawlins and Royall R. Watkins, joined the crowd in applauding her.

On the bench in the midst of a trial was the temporary judge, D. A. Frank, who after a brief private session with his replacement, introduced her to the jury and spectators. "Ladies and gentlemen, I have the honor and pleasure to present your new judge, Judge Hughes."

The new judge responded modestly. "There isn't anything I can say that will even begin to express my gratitude. I had no idea I would have all these flowers and that all these people would come out to see me preside. I shall try to be worthy but I know I cannot do half as well as my two predecessors, Judge Taylor and Judge Foree."[46]

Questions from newsmen and photographs followed. Judge Hughes would try to "follow the law and hold reversals to a minimum," and she was certain her male counterparts were doing the same thing. As for keeping lawyers under control in debate, she foresaw no problem. "I've taught school," she pointed out. Her short stature was no concern either. If necessary, she said, she might put some law books on her chair so she could see over the bench. As for the uniqueness of her position as a female, she emphasized her conviction that women should receive no special favors. Nor, however, should they be discriminated against. "I feel women should be permitted to choose their careers the same as men." She acknowledged that "most married women prefer home life," but it was clear she was not one of them.[47]

With a trial already in progress, Judge Hughes decided to sit jointly with temporary judge Frank for its duration. But just before the noon break she accepted her first solo assignment. J. Frank Wilson, who had spoken on her behalf in Austin on Monday, asked her if she would stay during the lunch hour and try a divorce case for his client. "I was really petrified," she said later, but she agreed to do so. "I wouldn't have known, I think, what to do if he had forgotten some of the principal things that needed to have been proved." But after this initial baptism, all fear was lost. (Later, Wilson and Hughes would oppose one another in a 1946 race for Congress. Wilson won, and subsequently he became a district judge at the courthouse himself.)[48]

The *Dallas Dispatch* described Hughes's first day: "She took over her new duties confidently but accepted her honor modestly. At the same time the fact that she had written a new page in legal history of Texas cast no weight on her naturally exuberant spirits. She laughed merrily and smiled graciously with all who approached. Asked how she felt at being the first woman judge, Judge Hughes said happily, 'Just like anything else.'"[49]

A luncheon on Saturday, February 16, signaled the end of one of the most memorable weeks of Hughes's life. The Dallas Zonta Club, presided over by Hughes's attorney friend Sarah Menezes, honored the new judge and their former president with a luncheon at the Baker Hotel's Crystal Ballroom. Attending were prominent leaders in state and local affairs, judges of the local courts, members of the Dallas Bar, and members of men's and women's clubs from throughout the city. Governor Allred was there, too, boasting about "my appointee" and claiming Sarah T. Hughes would "prove to be one of the greatest district judges Texas has ever known."[50]

Other speakers made crowd-pleasing comments. The city editor of the *Dallas Morning News*, Ted Barrett, told of calling Hughes after Westerfeld's dishwashing comment to see if she would pose over her kitchen sink for her newspaper. "Come and get it," she had replied. Now, on this occasion was able to add, "No one likes to wash dishes." Yet another speaker was Mrs. Harold Abrams, who first had suggested Hughes's appointment. It had been her idea, she said, to "seek some recognition for women who have proven their ability."[51]

Upon completing her first jury trial in her second week on the job, jury members presented Judge Hughes with a fountain pen to commemorate the occasion. Perhaps this caused her to realize early the familial connection jurors felt to their presiding judge. She began the practice of sending out Christmas cards to all who had served as jurors in her court. Perhaps more important, the cards acknowledged that Texas judges, facing reelection every four years, were always mindful of opportunities to win votes.[52]

As a competitive person, Hughes felt a need to excel, to gain recognition that would distinguish her from other district judges. The next year she would have to stand for reelection. To hold her position, Hughes would have to win the quick approval of voters. In the legislature, public acclaim could come quickly through newspaper coverage. An incumbent could cite bills introduced, votes cast, speeches made, and a myriad of other activities associated with a legislator's job as reasons for voter support. An incumbent judge enjoyed no such advantage. Most of the cases tried—damage suits, workmen's compensation, divorces, child custody, and the like—were not newsworthy. Even if they were, the judge rarely was the center of attention in the news stories. How, in a judicial campaign, could one cite a measurable, identifiable, competitive edge over an opponent? The answer, Hughes concluded, lay in disposing of a large number of cases and maintaining an up-to-date docket. To do this, she soon developed a system emphasizing pretrial procedures, encouraging out-of-court settlements before coming to trial, and keeping her docket clear.[53]

To prevent accumulations of old cases, Hughes began issuing a general call of the docket every three or four months. On these occasions all cases in which no action had been taken would be set for pretrial or trial. Each Monday the docket was called for those cases set for trial that week. If a plaintiff failed to appear, the case was dismissed. The plaintiff then was given ten days to reinstate the case. If the defendant in a case failed to appear, Judge Hughes granted a default judgment to the plaintiff. In the years to come Hughes gained a reputation as the only judge in the county to keep her docket clear.[54]

To keep time-consuming trials at a minimum, she recognized the value of pretrial procedures, and she became a leading advocate of what soon became a common practice. In these conferences Hughes considered motions, stipulations, or simplifications that might aid in the disposition of cases. They gave her opportunities to narrow the issues and force the attorneys to seriously consider the merits of their cases. A large number of out-of-court settlements resulted from these procedures, and even if settlements did not occur, many time-consuming issues were streamlined.

If a case came to trial, Hughes conducted it in such a manner as to leave no doubt as to who was in charge. She became an active participant. Woe to the attorney whom she deemed guilty of being unprepared or who meandered too far from the central purpose.[55]

In December 1935, when she announced her candidacy to election for a full term on the 14th District Court bench, Hughes was able to cite genuine accomplishments. In her first six months she had conducted 118 jury trials and disposed of 509 nonjury cases. This, she offered, was proof that a woman can dispose of litigation as efficiently as a man. "In this business of being a judge, I use common sense," she said. "Good law is no more subtle than that."[56] A few weeks later a newspaper headline, "Woman Jurist Cleans House," underscored her efficiency. On examining her docket she had found five cases that had been there since 1915. These and others, 273 in all, she dismissed.[57] On her first anniversary on the bench in February, yet another headline told of more good news: "Judge Hughes Ending First Year on Bench without One Reversal." Of seven cases appealed to the 5th Court of Civil Appeals, none had been reversed.[58]

The December announcement that Hughes would campaign for reelection provided the *Daily Times Herald* with good reason to profile the state's first woman jurist after ten months on the bench. The reporter asked her if she had considered running for governor. No, she replied, she had not thought of that, but she would not deny that her ambitions might carry her to such places in the future.

She had discovered she preferred the bench to the practice of law. Even so, politics was nearer her heart than anything. "I love the color, the activity, and the thrust and defense of politics. I realize, of course, that politics offers a precarious career compared with the security of an established profession, or my place on the bench; but the excitement of campaigning or battles in legislative chambers fascinate me," she said.

"I don't care about money—that is, in any considerable amount. I know that will sound foolish to many persons, but I am sincere. I do enjoy public honors and I have an ambition to do something for the state," she said.*[59]

Having a business or professional career for a woman did not necessarily stand as a barrier to washing dishes. Hughes went on:

It depends upon the woman. It hasn't been so with me. We have a home and I take a large interest in it. We eat all our meals there—as a matter of fact, I prepare the meals. I prefer to do that to having a cook prepare a dinner for two. My husband has a flower garden and gives it a lot of his spare time. After business we don't enjoy going to parties or other night gaieties, because I can't work well the next day. A wife who stays at home likes to go out at night and take her husband, who also has to work the next day.

(She did not mention that there was now an electric dishwasher in the house and a daily maid.)[60]

The newspaper reported that Hughes presided over her court from a high swivel chair behind a big mahogany bench. Often she enlivened the formal proceedings with a spontaneous smile or hearty laugh. "Her large head, topped by an unruly bob of thick, chestnut-colored hair, often bends forward to hear arguments or other low-voiced inquiries. She gestures with her right index finger to emphasize her remarks." Recently, she said, a juror had come to her after a trial and told her he had enjoyed his service because she "was the only judge he ever had seen smile." She accepted that as a compliment.[61]

Hughes had been campaigning for reelection through a busy speech-making schedule ever since her appointment. As the state's only woman judge and the most visible district judge in Texas, she was in great demand by the countless civic organizations that needed luncheon or dinner speakers, and she eagerly accepted these engagements. Speech-making would continue to be a major part of her life. During 1935 she spoke to the Zonta Club, the Dallas Retail Credit Men's Association, the Dallas Technical High School

---

* A bill introduced in the legislature in 1936 would have awarded Dallas County district judges an additional fifteen hundred dollars in annual pay, but Speaker of the House Stevenson successfully squelched it.

National Society, the Dallas Agricultural Club, the Junior Chamber of Commerce, and other groups. Occasionally, she ventured outside the county to speak, especially to chapters of the organization that had become and would continue to be her favorite civic activity, the Business and Professional Women's Club. She became a popular speaker at meetings of African Americans, who were becoming more and more politically active in Dallas at this time. She attracted a capacity crowd when she spoke to the all-black Moorland Branch of the YMCA on the subject of "responsibilities of citizenship," and she was the kickoff speaker for a poll tax drive at the same place with the goal of registering ten thousand African American voters.[62]

She lost none of the tartness she had exhibited in the legislature in these talks. Speaking to the Woman's Good Government League and its junior auxiliary in Fort Worth, she gave seven reasons why the Texas Legislature was a "do-nothing institution." She cited three of the principal ones as a "powerless governor," a too-strong lobby, and a "stubbornly conservative Senate which thinks with the corporate interests."[63]

Early in 1936 an opponent, Arthur A. Cocke, announced as a candidate for the 14th District Court. He was a veteran Dallas attorney who had practiced law in the city since 1906 and held degrees from Georgetown University and the University of Chicago. Cocke pointed out that he was the head of a home and a family man with responsibilities, while his opponent, Hughes, was married with no children. She already was well provided for, since her husband, Cocke claimed, "draws a good salary from the public treasury."[64] Such an argument held some credibility in these dark Depression days, when jobs were scarce.

But the lawyers of Dallas approved of how Hughes was handling her duties in the 14th District Court. She solicited them for their endorsements, and they readily responded. By the time of the election Hughes's newspaper advertisements cited endorsements by 584 lawyers, a powerful statement, since the yellow pages of the Dallas telephone directory listed just 619 lawyers.[65]

In her campaigning she managed to reach deeper into her heritage than ever before to find a historical tie to Texas. She liked especially her ties to Oswald Tilghman, the cousin who left a "well-ordered" life in Maryland to join Terry's Texas Rangers to bring law and order into the Lone Star State. As a headline in a newspaper was able to say, "Sally Hughes Traces Her Ancestry to Texas Pioneers."[66]

The fact that she had left her courtroom unadorned with signs of femininity was seen as a plus. Some lawyers had feared that as a woman Hughes would remove all the spittoons from her courtroom, long a staple in the county courts. This had not happened. Lawyers could still chew and spit tobacco in her court. Nor had she placed ruffled curtains at the windows.[67]

One of Hughes's law school classmates, Thomas Hudson McKee, who also had settled in Dallas, wrote in a newspaper column that he believed Hughes would make a good governor as well as a fine judge. "As governor, she would make a most amazing contribution to the science of government and to the reorganization of both society and the state," he said. McKee, that year an unsuccessful candidate for Congress, said Hughes had made "a greater contribution to Dallas, and probably to Texas, than any other one woman who has championed social welfare and economic justice." He cited especially the work she did after a typical day in court. "One finds her in odd hours lecturing in the YMCA to a group of underprivileged young women. Again, as guest speaker before a labor organization composed of under-paid factory workers bent upon improving their plight. Or again as a prime mover in Crime Prevention campaigns." She was motivated, he said, by a feeling that she must contribute something "fine" to her adopted state, and thus pounded away almost twelve hours daily as a "sterling leader in the political, social and civic life of Texas."[68]

The widespread endorsements and compliments for Hughes left little maneuvering room for an opponent. Cocke was no match for her. She easily defeated him in the Democratic primary and then ran as an unopposed candidate in the general election. Voters were pleased to return her to the bench for a full four-year term.

"To be a judge a man or woman, besides being a lawyer, must be interested in politics," Hughes observed not long after the campaign. "There are speeches to make, people to meet, and an organization to build. It requires all these for re-election, and neglect may cost even a good judge his office. To some this part of a judge's life might not be pleasant but to me it is. I like the thrill of the campaign. I like to plan and organize for the race. I like to see the voters, and I like to make speeches."[69]

Hughes's former nemesis, Senator Claud Westerfeld, instead of running for reelection to the state Senate, had sought in this 1936 election to unseat the veteran congressman Hatton Sumners. Westerfeld again had made a miscalculation. Voters rejected him. Never again would he be elected to public office. The manner in which his dishwashing comment had backfired on him would not be forgotten. When people in Texas spoke of political blunders during the next few years, they called it "pulling a Westerfeld."[70]

Having no opponent herself in the general election, Hughes campaigned for the national slate of Franklin D. Roosevelt and his Texan vice president, John Nance Garner. "The economic freedom of the people is at stake," she said. The issue was not a loss of personal freedom from government intervention, as many people were complaining, but one of survival, she told a rally for women in Gregg County in East Texas.[71]

In Cleburne she sought to rationalize the continuing expansion of the federal government's role into daily lives. With increasing urbanization in society, with the gathering of people into large groups, and with the rights of minorities being threatened, "it becomes the duty of government to protect you," she said. "Practically all of our activities are now regulated by government."[72]

In Dallas the effects of the Depression were less severe than in so many parts of the nation. Several large public works projects generated jobs. One was the recent realignment of the Trinity River from its natural course two blocks from the courthouse for placement between two levees as a protection from floods. And now in 1936 a related project across the street from the courthouse saw the completion of the triple underpass at Dealey Plaza, a major rerouting of Dallas's three main streets.

Even more significant was the project Hughes had played such a large part in rescuing from a recalcitrant House in Austin—the Texas Centennial Exposition. This international exposition began on June 6, 1936, after a mammoth construction job at the State Fair grounds and an official opening by President Roosevelt. After it closed its doors on November 29, Dallas and its image would never be the same. The positive publicity generated by the event made the nation mindful of the city as never before.

Hughes's contributions toward its creation were not forgotten. She frequently was targeted by the newspapers for feature photographs at the Centennial. An early photograph depicted her wearing a cowboy hat above the caption "Judge Salutes Centennial." When a prominent visitor, William Jennings Bryan Jr., son of the silver-tongued orator, came, a newspaper photographer captured Hughes greeting him. Yet another photograph showed Hughes being helped into a covered wagon by Mayor George Sergeant for a ride across the Centennial grounds to the livestock for the "christening" of four newborn calves. Hughes, the "Joan of Arc" of the Centennial, now became godmother to one of the calves.[73]

Such high times frequently were contrasted by the stressful cases she presided over every week in her courtroom, especially custody cases involving children. These were the hardest to decide. One of her toughest early cases involved custody of a child given to the care of his grandparents after his mother's death. Four years later the father remarried and sought custody of his son. "I denied the application because I felt it was in the child's best interest to remain with the grandparents," she said, but the decision haunted her.[74]

The divorce cases she heard led her to observe that far too many marriages occurred without thought to permanency. The result often was devastating to many children from the union and also to society, because it seemed to her to be a factor in so many cases of truancy, juvenile delinquency, and crime. Many of the situations reminded her of problems she had encountered doing social work as a policewoman in Washington, D.C., except now the final disposition was hers. She began now to think more deeply about such social problems, and in the years ahead she would eagerly expound her point of view.

5 ～

Extending Boundaries

Judge Sarah T. Hughes had become the most visible and respected woman in the state of Texas. There was no other female public official of equal stature. Her position as a district judge—gained and reaffirmed through election at a time when those of her gender were barred from serving as jurors—was an inspiration for women and women's organizations. Their successful, concerted effort against a male-dominated legislature to win confirmation made women realize they could do even more.

What next for Hughes? Governor? Congress? A state appeals court? The U.S. Supreme Court? All these possibilities were speculated. Talk of the Governor's Mansion was common. A Texas rumor, repeated in a caption under her photograph in a Washington newspaper, had her seeking election to Congress. When the position of chief justice of the state's 5th Court of Civil Appeals opened, the Dallas Central Labor Council urged Governor Allred to appoint her to the post. In 1939 a Dallas man suggested a campaign to persuade President Roosevelt to appoint her to the U.S. Supreme Court.[1]

Honor and accord were visited upon her. The George Washington University Law School conferred upon her the University Alumni Award for Notable Achievement in the Profession of Law. Leadership roles became nearly automatic for her in any civic and political group in which she was a member. Before her 1935 judicial appointment, Hughes already had been president of the Zonta Club, an organization that would continue to be important to her in years to come. In the last years of the 1930s she would become president of the Dallas Democratic Women's Luncheon Club, president of the Dallas Business and Professional Women's Club, and president of the Texas Federation of Business and Professional Women's Clubs. A dozen years later in 1952 she would become national president of the B&PW and afterward would expand her perspective to a worldwide level as vice president of the International Federation of Business and Professional Women's Clubs. From 1940 to 1946 she chaired the Status of Women Committee for the American Association of University Women. When the war years caused a shortage of faculty at the Southern Methodist University Law School, Hughes was called into service as a part-time instructor while maintaining her position as judge. She taught a course on contracts in 1942-43 and one on evidence in 1943-44. As her contribution to the war effort and to the SMU budget, she refused to accept payment. She also declined the university's offer of precious gasoline rationing coupons.[2]

Her position as a judge, she learned, had not removed her from the arena of public affairs. She soon would find herself involved in some searing controversies in which her tart tongue was an advantage. Notwithstanding her extra judicial work, being a judge proved to be an intriguing adventure in itself. When Sheriff Smoot Schmid confiscated 17 illegal gaming tables and 180 slot machines, Hughes ordered him to destroy them all but first to salvage the wooden legs, frames, and glass tops so that carpenters could use them for building tables and furniture at the county-operated Parkland Hospital. This did not seem practical or possible to the veteran sheriff, and he questioned the validity of the judge's order. Before declaring him in contempt of court, Judge Hughes, five feet, one-half inch tall, paid the six-foot-six-inch sheriff a visit. She had him escort her to the confiscated gambling devices, and she showed him precisely what parts he must remove before destroying them. The sheriff backed down and did as ordered.[3]

One day in her courtroom a Mesquite man, testifying in an estate hearing, mentioned the price of his hay, nine dollars a ton. After he finished and left the witness stand, Hughes quickly adjourned court, climbed down from the bench, and hailed the man before he could got out the door. "Hey, how about some hay?" she asked him. She promptly ordered forty bales of hay for the two horses she and George owned and rode on a regular basis.[4]

When she heard a divorce suit involving a Spanish-speaking couple whose attorney, Robert Benavides, also spoke Spanish, Hughes—according to a brief news item—conducted the proceedings in that language. She not only was able to comprehend the testimony, according to the report, she even spoke in Spanish herself as she interjected occasional questions and rulings. She had become a student of Spanish, a language she would continue to study for most of her life. (The news account almost surely exaggerated the extent to which Spanish was used in the proceeding, for Hughes at this point was in the early stage of her studies of the language.)[5]

• • • • •

Hughes's most effective work outside the courtroom—and her favorite launching pad for advancing women's rights—had become the Dallas Business and Professional Women's Club. This organization, commonly referred to as B&PW, was one of a network of thousands of local clubs, all of which linked in a hierarchy to the state, national, and international federations. In B&PW Hughes was surrounded by energetic, accomplished, working women who were determined that winning the right to vote in 1920 was but a beginning in the women's movement for equality across the board. It was through this organization and Zonta that Sarah T. Hughes exerted her influence and directed her efforts toward her next immediate goal, one intended to advance the rights of all women—the right to serve on juries.

The continued exclusion of women from juries nearly three decades after winning the right to vote was a constant reminder, especially for women attorneys, of the secondary status to which their gender continued to be relegated. Many had assumed suffrage would automatically permit women to serve on juries, since jurors were selected from voter registration records, which now included both sexes. In just under half the states this in fact had occurred, but the majority of states continued to exclude women from juries under various rationalizations—the need for mothers to stay home with their children, the difficulty of providing additional facilities for women at the courthouse, and the astonishing assertion that women lacked the willpower to resist arguments made by handsome attorneys. The issue failed to capture the attention of more than just a few women, however.

Texas was one of twenty-five of the forty-eight states excluding women from juries, a number that would gradually be reduced as the years went by. In 1937 the U.S. Congress granted women the right to serve on federal juries, the issue having won the support of the House Committee on the Judiciary, of which Dallas congressman Hatton W. Sumners was chairman.[6] One of the most ardent supporters appearing before Sumner's committee had been Burnita Shelton Matthews, who had graduated from George Washington University Law School in the same year that Hughes entered it and who had written persuasively on the subject.[*] In the Texas Legislature, Hughes's fellow female representative, Helen Moore of Texas City, and Joseph F. Greathouse

---

* Matthews would be appointed by Harry S. Truman in 1949 as the nation's first federal district judge. Hughes in 1961 would be the second.

of Fort Worth had offered legislation in 1935, two months after Hughes resigned to become a judge, calling for a constitutional amendment to permit women to serve on juries. After a favorable report from the Committee on Constitutional Amendments, the bill had disappeared. (Hughes on several occasions would describe herself as a coauthor of the bill, an indication that she had been involved in preparing it before she left the legislature.)[7]

Now, in 1936, under Hughes's leadership, members of both the Dallas B&PW and Zonta attacked the problem of jury discrimination as a problem of misinterpretation. Hughes reasoned that a logical reading of the state constitution already meant that women should be included in the jury pool. Her argument was as follows: since the constitutional provision of freedom of religion for all men had been accepted for years as a generic term that included women too, the same interpretation should apply to the statute (Article 2133) providing that "all men over twenty-one years of age are competent jurors." Why would *men* mean one thing concerning freedom of religion but another thing concerning jurors? A favorable judicial ruling validating this interpretation might be easier to obtain than a constitutional amendment.[8]

Following this line of thought, attorneys Sarah Menezes and Sarah Daniels filed a suit on behalf of Stella Glover, a florist shop operator who like Hughes belonged to both Zonta and B&PW, in Paine L. Bush's 68th District Court. They asked Bush to order Tax Assessor-Collector Ed Cobb, District Clerk George Harwood, County Clerk Ed Steger, and Sheriff Smoot Schmid to place Glover's name and those of all other qualified women in the county in the jury "wheel." No matter how logical the argument might seem, Judge Bush rejected it. The case was appealed to the 5th Court of Appeals, but in December 1938 that court upheld Bush's ruling. The Texas Supreme Court denied an application for a writ of error.[9]

The drive for women jurors was far from over. The Dallas Federation of Women's Clubs endorsed it; the Zonta Club adopted it as a pet project; and Hughes would continue the struggle, especially through her growing role as a leader of B&PW.[10]

In 1937 Hughes became president of the Dallas B&PW, succeeding her friend Grace A. Fitzgerald, who moved on to become president of the statewide federation. At the same time, Hughes—presumably appointed by Fitzgerald—became state chairman of the Special Committee on Women for Jury Service in Texas. In this position she was charged with planning and directing an educational campaign among women and carrying the fight to the Texas Legislature.[11] Those who knew Sarah Hughes realized her committee would do far more than conduct a survey of attitudes and problems and issue a report with recommendations.

"Judge Hughes Leading Demand of Women for Equal Rights on Jury," was the headline for a United Features Syndicate news story. The judge said if necessary she would seek an amendment to the Texas Constitution to win that right. The reporter went a step further by polling Hughes's fellow Dallas judges about their own beliefs on the subject. They merely hemmed and hawed, he wrote. Some were evasive; others had no comment. Some handsome attorneys, though, according to the report, "brushed their lapels and straightened their ties" as they dreamed of women jurors who could be swayed by "good looks or nice compliments." Asked to respond to this possibility, Hughes said that pretty female witnesses who crossed their legs on the stand already swayed men jurors. So what was the difference?[12]

In 1938, now president-elect of the Texas B&PW, Hughes injected the issue into the political arena. She announced plans to have all seventy-six chapters of the state organization poll candidates seeking election to the Texas Legislature about their attitudes. "'We want women on juries,' Judge Hughes grimly commented."[13]

When a resolution for a proposed constitutional amendment again failed to win approval in the legislature, Hughes, now in office as state president of B&PW, published in the organization's newsletter a list showing how all representatives had voted. She told B&PW members they should get together and support for reelection all representatives who had voted favorably on the amendment and urge others to join them. If their representative had not favored the proposed amendment, members should determine the reason.[14]

The subject became Hughes's favorite topic for speeches. As state president in 1939-40, she traveled across Texas speaking to individual clubs about women jurors. "Let us make jury service for women a byword in every community, so that when the Legislature meets in 1941 the submission of the constitutional amendment will be a foregone conclusion," she told the women in Colorado City.[15] She wrote numerous articles on the subject for publication under variations of the phrase "the half citizen." Women, she observed, receive all the benefits of government, including such things as free schools, fire and police protection, and use of highways. But they were only half citizens because they could participate in only one of the two ways the average citizen could fulfill the responsibilities of citizenship—voting and serving on juries.[16]

The struggle was doomed to failure for many years. When the legislature declined to sponsor a statewide vote on the matter, Hughes took the issue to the Dallas Bar Association, seeking to win that organization's support. In a Saturday morning legal clinic held by the bar in April 1943, she told her fellow attorneys Texas was only "half a democracy" because of its prohibition against women jurors. In states where women served on juries, she said, women performed their duties enthusiastically, unlike so many men who commonly sought to avoid jury service. Women with small children at home could be exempted from duty. On the following Saturday, D. A. Frank, who had filled in as temporary judge for the 14th District Court pending Hughes's arrival from the legislature, was given equal time to speak against women jurors. Two weeks later the bar association's constitutional amendment committee rejected Hughes's proposal to support women on juries. When she saw how the wind was blowing, she succeeded in tabling the doomed motion so that the bar association's minutes would not reflect an official position on the matter.[17]

The battle to achieve the right for women to serve on juries in Texas would last much longer than anyone might have suspected. Not until 1954 would it become a reality. No one worked harder than Hughes to achieve that goal, and there would be many ups and downs before that time.

Despite the B&PW's determined work toward this goal, it was by no means its dominant issue. The organization was involved in a wide variety of efforts on behalf of working women and women in general.

The National Federation of B&PW, founded in St. Louis in 1919, was the first national organization for working and professional women. The Dallas chapter, having been organized at the behest of a YWCA official in 1916, predated the national organization. The leading figure in Dallas in these early years and for many years thereafter was Dr. Minnie Lee Maffett, a physician and surgeon, who went to St. Louis in 1919 as a Dallas delegate to found the national federation. On her return, she organized a meeting at the Adolphus Hotel in Dallas to form a statewide organization. She was elected first president of the Texas Federation of the B&PW for 1919-20. From 1939 to 1944 she was president of the National Federation of the B&PW. Hughes's attorney friends, notably Grace N. Fitzgerald, who as local president had forcefully used the club to lobby for Hughes's appointment as judge, and Sarah Menezes also were active.

Hughes had been an active participant in the Dallas B&PW since 1931. With her departure from the legislature and her return to the city on a full-time basis in 1935, her involvement deepened. In 1937 she began a two-year term as president of the Dallas club. At the 1937 state convention in El Paso she gave a report to members entitled "Progress in the Legal Status of Women," outlining once again the need for remedial legislation concerning property rights for women and other such matters. ("If the judge should run for governor on such issues as these she would go further in getting behind her the women's vote in the state than with any other issue she could set up," a newspaper editorial commented.) The next year she attended the national meeting in Atlantic City. At the state conventions in 1938 in Fort Worth and 1939 in Beaumont she was very visible, reporting on steps taken to allow women as jurors, and at the latter meeting she presented a twenty-five-minute program on what was becoming an overall priority, an Equal Rights Amendment for women. On July 1, 1939, Hughes advanced from president of the Dallas club to state president of B&PW, succeeding Grace N. Fitzgerald. Later that summer Dr. Minnie Maffett began her term as president of the national organization, and Fitzgerald became national membership chairman.[18]

Hughes, as president, headed a statewide organization with eighty-seven clubs and 3,475 members. She wrote a monthly column in the B&PW publication, *Texas Business and Professional Woman*, and she traveled over the state to visit local clubs and to attend district meetings, invariably speaking not just on jury service but on other topics such as property rights for women, problems of divorce, juvenile delinquency, and international affairs. In her column, "Your President's Page," she discussed these matters and miscellaneous B&PW affairs. In this column and through her many visits with clubs throughout the state she continued to expand the range of her friendships.[19]

The Texas Centennial had brought Franklin and Eleanor Roosevelt to Dallas in 1936 to open the exposition officially. Two large downtown luncheons, one for men and another for women, feted the presidential couple. Dallas men honored the president at the Adolphus Hotel. Mrs. Roosevelt was guest of honor at an all-women's luncheon across the street at the Baker Hotel. Hughes was thrilled to meet Eleanor Roosevelt, however briefly, at the noon affair. She noted with approval the "simplicity" with which the president's wife dressed—contrasting greatly with the women guests who wore their "best bib and tucker with large hats"—and Mrs. Roosevelt's friendly, down-to-earth manner in addressing the crowd. References to her husband as "Franklin," instead of "the President," were also pleasing. There was no opportunity to meet the president on this visit, but an introduction was not far away.[20]

Only a few months later in early January 1937, Dallas congressman Hatton W. Sumners invited Hughes to attend a White House reception with him in honor of the judiciary. Sumners, chairman of the House Committee on the Judiciary and a Democratic member of Congress since 1912, was widely believed to be in line for the next vacant Supreme Court position. The reception occurred one week prior to Roosevelt's second inauguration (the first to be held in January rather than March).

Hughes made the most of her visit of several days to the Washington area, intertwining social and professional events. She stayed in Bethesda, Maryland, with her former roommate and police officer colleague, Carol Whiteford, now Mrs. Guy B. Early. At Carol Early's home she enjoyed a reunion with friends and acquaintances from her days as a police officer and law student. She spoke to the Kappa Beta Pi fraternity of the George Washington University Law School and was honored at a reception afterward at the Carlton Hotel. At her other alma mater, Goucher College, she spoke at a vocational conference on the subject "women and the law." She also was pleased to visit the U.S. Supreme Court, where on the motion of Sumners she was admitted to practice.[21]

The anticipated high point of the visit was the presidential reception at the White House. Hughes looked forward to meeting and perhaps even chatting with President Roosevelt. "I wondered just how I would introduce myself to the President," she recalled in an oral history interview years later. "I always say I'm Sarah Hughes, but I was anxious for him to know that I was a judge. On the other hand I didn't want to say I'm Judge Sarah Hughes." She had thought it would be a very small reception, including members of the judiciary committee of the House and the Senate, a few specially invited guests, and maybe the federal judiciary in the District of Columbia. To her amazement, when she arrived at the White House with Sumners there were hundreds of guests. Men wore top hats. Seven of the nine U.S. Supreme Court justices were placed with their wives at the head of a long receiving line, with Chief Justice and Mrs. Charles Evans Hughes first. A White House official announced to those in line that gentlemen should precede their lady guests. Sumners accordingly stepped in front of Hughes. The line moved slowly as the president and his wife shook hands with each guest and exchanged brief pleasantries.[22]

At the top of the stairs another White House official announced the name of each person as he or she reached the president. Hughes was still wrestling with the problem of what to call herself when she heard Sumners introduced as "Mr. Sumners" followed quickly by her own introduction as "Mrs. Sumners." She was so startled she had no time to make a correction. She shook hands with the president and Mrs. Roosevelt and then moved along. "So I came all the way to Washington to be introduced to the President as Mrs. Sumners," she lamented. "The only consolation I got was that I was sure that the President knew that there was no Mrs. Sumners [Sumners was not married], but he still didn't know who I was."[23]

After the last guest had been received, the president retired to his private upstairs White House quarters. Eleanor Roosevelt mingled with the guests and watched the dancing in the East Room.[24]

"It was not as thrilling as I would have liked it to have been," Hughes recalled. There was no chance of a cozy little chat with the president. The fact that she met the justices and their wives seemed of little import to her. After Roosevelt had departed early, she said in her oral history, there was nothing for her to do but "partake of a few refreshments and leave."[25]

The president possibly had a motive in mind as he honored the judiciary. Unbeknownst to the guests, stormy times lay just ahead. Less than a month after the gala White House event, Roosevelt announced a controversial proposal that would generate probably the most heated criticism of any he would receive during his many years in the White House—his plan to reorganize the federal judiciary. The "court-packing plan," revealed to Sumners and other key congressional leaders in a White House meeting on February 4, 1937, was a bold initiative to thwart court rulings that in the last year had struck down some of his key New Deal acts as unconstitutional. A shortage of judicial personnel, Roosevelt declared, had caused a backlog in the federal court dockets. He proposed a plan that would permit him to appoint as many as six new justices to the Supreme Court and forty-four new judges to the lower federal tribunals, supplementing federal judges who did not resign or retire after their seventieth birthdays. Opponents quickly saw through his rationalizations and identified the plan as one designed to create a Supreme Court friendlier to New Deal legislation.

Sumners, as chairman of the House Committee on the Judiciary, would be a key ally for the president in winning support for the president's plan. But Sumners, after the White House meeting at which the plans were revealed, joined several of the other congressional leaders in a taxi afterward and said, "Boys, here's where I cash in my chips." He would not support the president's plan. Sumners would gain national attention for breaking with the president, a move that many said cost him an appointment to the Supreme Court.[26]

Many liberals were concerned about the plan. Vice President John Nance Garner did not support it. Conservatives abhorred the idea. Hughes fully supported the president. If she were in Congress she would vote for the reform, she said. The high court was in her estimation "just a political body that should be reformed if it cannot lend a literal interpretation to the Constitution." In fact, she said, the Supreme Court already had been "packed in the past for big business," for before their appointments members were attorneys for large corporations.[27]

Speaking to a B&PW meeting in Marlin, Texas, she declared that unless the justices interpret the Constitution liberally enough to meet the changing needs of our nation, it should be modified by amendment. "The Constitution should not be revered because it is 150 years old, but because it is our government and should be revered only as long as it meets the changing needs."[28]

Sumners bottled up the proposed legislation in his committee, and opposition that would doom the plan rapidly mounted. Ironically, Roosevelt's need for introducing the measure seemed to disappear. In May 1937, the court upheld one of the key programs of the Roosevelt administration, the Social Security Act, and its negative rulings concerning the New Deal halted. Less than six months after Roosevelt had announced his court-packing plan, it was dead. Even so, two and a half years later, Roosevelt had named five new justices to the nine-man court. He would claim he had lost the battle but won the war.

Some decades later, Hughes said in an oral history that while she had favored Roosevelt's plan at the time, in retrospect she realized it to be a bad idea.[29]

Troubles in Europe seemed ominous but far off to many Americans. Direct involvement in the affairs of European nations was out of the question in the mid- to late 1930s. Four congressional neutrality acts between 1935 and 1939 affirmed an official position of noninvolvement for the United States. President Roosevelt was careful in his pronouncements, but as the situation darkened in Europe, concern over the role of the United States gradually began to replace domestic affairs as a national priority.

In 1937, with American neutrality sentiment probably at its peak, Sarah T. Hughes became alarmed about what she perceived to be a growing prowar sentiment. "We must think peace instead of glorifying war," she was quoted as saying in a profile of her in the *Democratic Digest*. She saw the fundamental cause of war as being economic. "So long as the demands of nations that have no colonies and no raw materials are ignored, we will have no peace. Economic boycott of aggressor nations will help temporarily, but in the end the so-called 'have' nations must make some sacrifices to the nations that 'have not,' if peace is to be obtained. It will cost less, in the long run, than a war." Over the past few years, she said, the United States and Great Britain had almost refused to negotiate with these have-not nations—Germany, Japan, and Italy—as they sought needed resources and supplies. The result, she said, could be seen in such hostile actions as Italy's seizure of Ethiopia.[30]

Hughes believed women could have a major impact on the nation's policies in this regard. She urged them to unite to end both war and poverty by informing themselves of the best remedies and then fighting for their adoption. "It is possible for this country to avoid the situation now prevailing in Italy, Germany, and Russia if Americans will turn their attention to bettering the economic situation of the masses," she told the Arlington, Texas, B&PW Club at a banquet.[31]

Military training for high school students through ROTC programs was misguided, she believed. "I can not see any good in school military training," she said. Such programs did no more than inculcate a spirit for war, she argued, aiming her barbs directly at the Dallas high schools. Her pronouncements, as usual, merited newspaper headlines. "Before a peace movement can be completed," she said, "people must think peace and they can not think peace in a uniform."[32]

In October 1938, shortly after the Munich agreement in which Czechoslovakia's Sudetenland was all but ceded to Germany by Great Britain and France, Hitler's forces invaded the territory and took possession. Even so, military preparedness did not seem to be a reasonable response to Hughes.

When plans were announced for an American Legion-sponsored downtown Armistice Day parade in November 1938, featuring every military group in the county—high school ROTC units, National Guardsmen, and

Army and Navy reservists, along with assorted military equipment—Judge Hughes quickly took issue. The parade would be, she complained, no more than a demonstration glorifying war. Positioning Mayor George Sprague and former mayor Joe E. Lawther (by virtue of his having been mayor during World War I) in the parade's lead car made the situation more lamentable to her. Armistice Day should commemorate peace, not war, Hughes argued. "We don't want to emphasize war. We want to emphasize peace. Martial music inspires, hides the horror of war. It tends to make youth feel war is glory. If they are going to show war at all, why don't they show it in its true colors, with its blood and horrors on the battlefields, the rows of poppies in the cemeteries, the weeping mothers at home?" Hughes was supported in her position by Mrs. E. M. Guest, president of the Dallas Council of Parents and Teachers. A newspaper headline described them as peace lovers.[33]

Other women's groups soon joined in the crusade for promoting peace instead of displaying armaments. Mrs. L. M. Marks of the local Committee on the Cause and Cure of War suggested the women sponsor a separate parade glorifying peace.[34]

The chairman of the American Legion parade, Laurence Melton, suggested the women join his parade and express any sentiments they chose. "Judge Hughes is sincere in her beliefs," he said. "And thank God this is America, where we are free to think what we please and give expression to our thoughts. We're interested in the same end that Judge Hughes and the other women are—peace. But ex-soldiers believe that preparedness is the only way to preserve peace."[35]

Disarmed by these accommodating remarks, Hughes and the clubwomen of Dallas finally agreed to take part in the American Legion parade on these terms. In three separate cars they carried their own signs: LET'S WORK FOR UNIVERSAL PEACE, ECONOMIC JUSTICE MAKES FOR PEACE, and DAY BY DAY—EDUCATION. Hughes's Dallas B&PW, of which she was president, was joined by women from the YWCA, WCTU, PTA, Dallas College Club, Federation of Women's Clubs, Federated Council of Clubwomen, Council of Jewish Women, and the Sisterhood of Temple Emanu-El.[36]

A crowd of 150,000 was estimated to be present as the parade moved through the downtown streets. At Main and Lamar streets, though, the continuity of the women's three cars was interrupted when six uninvited cars sponsored by the socialists of Dallas and bearing more militant signs barged into their midst. LET WALL STREET PROTECT ITS OWN INVESTMENTS, LET THE

PEOPLE VOTE ON WAR, and OUR COUNTRY IS IN NO DANGER OF ATTACK were typical of the signs the socialists displayed. Carl Brannin, a Dallas socialist who recently had campaigned unsuccessfully for governor, was the leader of the group. His entourage, he said, had the same right as any other to join the parade. The women were dismayed. The impact of their own antimilitary effort was muted by the more strident and more numerous messages of the socialists.[37]

Hughes's own pacifist views were short-lived. Her notion of yielding territories to have-not nations such as Germany failed to yield peaceful benefits. In March 1939, Hitler, not satisfied with the Sudetenland, marched his troops into Prague, the capital of Czechoslovakia. Now the entire nation was under his control. A few months later on September 1, Germany invaded Poland. All Europe was plunged into world war. Never again did Hughes speak out in opposition to military preparedness. A decade later she would gain national headlines by calling for the drafting of women into the armed services.

Roosevelt, reelected by a solid majority in 1940, saw his victory as a mandate to lead the nation into a new role as the "arsenal of democracy." Hughes began writing and talking with the assumption that the United States ultimately would be involved in the war. In the first two issues of a new magazine, *Today and Tomorrow*, she published a two-part article in the March and April 1941 issues under the title "If Democracy Survives." In combating fascism, she wrote, the nation must avoid totalitarianism and protect free speech. Her article in the *Cotton Ginners' Journal*, May 1942, "Ginners and Civilian Defense," urged increased farm production because of the war. She advised farmers and farmwomen to hold group meetings to find ways of obtaining maximum yields as a way of assisting in the war effort.[38]

In August 1943, a Liberty ship named for Hughes's distant ancestor, the Revolutionary War hero Tench Tilghman, was launched. Perhaps it was this family tie that prompted Hughes to apply to be an officer in the Women's Reserve of the Navy. In her file she included letters of recommendation and the attorney general's opinion that she could continue to fulfill the duties of her judgeship if she joined the WAVES. Her application was rejected because there was no position in the Naval Reserve in which her professional abilities could be adequately used.[39] However, she did serve on the Dallas board that selected the first officer candidates in the city for the Women's Army Auxiliary Corps.[40]

In 1944 Hughes again urged the reelection of Roosevelt. The election, in her opinion, was probably the most momentous one to face the nation in almost a hundred years. New York governor Thomas E. Dewey, FDR's youthful and vigorous opponent, was politically handicapped, Hughes believed, because his experience was confined to the state level.[41] Having already broken in 1940 the unspoken taboo against third presidential terms, American voters returned Roosevelt to the White House in 1944 by an overwhelming margin.

Hughes's personal life, happily and quietly shared with George, gave ballast to her public life. "Neither mannish nor womanish in her work, Mrs. Hughes becomes a woman when she crosses the threshold of her home," a writer described her in a 1938 profile for *Independent Woman*. "The change is not spectacular, but subtle. George Hughes is president of their home and their marriage, and Sarah Hughes, vice president, is glad to have a bulwark to lean upon in her private life."[42] A maid, Mattie Green, had been handling the couple's domestic chores on a daily basis since 1931, relieving the Hugheses of many housekeeping duties and keeping the antique-filled house neat and clean.

George enjoyed cooking, more so than his wife, and he gained a lasting reputation for his skills at bread-making. He continued his career with the Veterans Administration, but in 1938 he was transferred to the Waco office, about a hundred miles south of Dallas. A weekly commute began for him that would last until his return to the Dallas office in 1944. During these years he lived in a hotel in Waco while working and returned to Dallas for weekends.

Together the couple developed a lifelong love for gardening; they were often accompanied in the yard by an aging fox terrier, acquired in the mid-1920s. When a century plant with a flower stalk five feet tall bloomed in their yard, the *Dallas Morning News* printed a photograph of it. They still played some tennis together, but their favorite sport had become horseback riding. They owned two horses, named Peggy and Don Allen, and stabled them nearby so they could make frequent weekend rides, Sarah favoring the English style, usually wearing jodhpurs and a regulation white shirt.[43]

In August 1938, Sarah T. Hughes retrieved an old discarded account book that had been used briefly in the mid-1920s for the financial records of the Dallas Joint Legislative Council. In it she began recording in her unique, tight hand minute details of household and family expenses. Groceries purchased by Mattie Green were listed only by the dollar amounts, but aside from that no specific expenditure was too small to list—stamps, ice, milk, gas, utilities, parking, items of personal hygiene such as toothpaste and the like. At the end of Hughes's own self-proclaimed fiscal year—September through August—she itemized all these expenses under categories such as household, clothing, charity, automobile, gifts, entertainment and clubs, horses, and travel. For the fiscal year 1938-39, the first full year for which she kept records, household expenses amounted to $6,276.80.[44] The meticulous detail of this record-keeping was not a temporary whim. Hughes would continue it until at least late 1956.

As a high-profile person, some of the news articles about Hughes tried to give a more personal view of her. "She is rather unique in this era of hand-painted feminine faces," wrote one reporter. "She has never used mascara nor eye shadow. She doesn't use lipstick in the daytime. And she has never used colored nail polish." When the writer interviewed her, Hughes's face was "well-scrubbed looking, faintly dusted with powder." A single aquama-rine pin shaped like a bluebird adorned her dress at the shoulder line. The judge said she did not approve of much jewelry. As for hats, she wore them only when she felt she had to—which in this era was often. She preferred long sleeves to short ones as a general rule, and she liked "the easy drape" of English-fitted suits. She did not smoke, and she never drank more than a single cocktail.[45]

With a penchant for understatement in dress, it seemed surprising when Judge Hughes agreed to be photographed and quoted in a fashion advertise-ment in the *Dallas Morning News* in January 1938, under the caption "Women Executives O.K. Smart Business Fashions." In this advertisement she was portrayed sitting at her desk in a smart suit and described as a "modern busi-ness woman [who] has no time for idle artificiality nor fussily frivolous costumes." She was said to be thrifty, but one who selected her fashions with an eye to "quality as well as to price."[46]

The editorial stings she suffered because of this advertisement assured that never again would she be tempted to repeat it. The advertisement was described as "cheap publicity" more appropriate for a "torch singer in a beer joint or a hoochie coochie dancer in a night club." By using the high office of a judge for "self aggrandizement," one newspaper editorialized, Hughes lowered the dignity of her position and left the impression that she was not worthy of the public trust.[47]

Hughes's satisfaction with her personal life contrasted sharply with the acrimonious divorce cases over which she presided so frequently in court. In the six civil district courts in Dallas County, divorce suits were the most common cases heard. She began gathering data on divorce and making speeches on the subject.

Two out of three marriages in Dallas County, she found, were ending in divorce. In 1936, a total of 4,928 marriage licenses were issued. In the same year the courts granted 3,349 divorces. She concluded in these prewar Depression years that lack of money was a primary factor for the failure of many marriages. In a two-week period in 1938, the judge found that of the eight divorces she granted in which children were involved, only one family had a decent income.[48]

The inherent difficulties could be seen in the case of one divorced woman with eight children ranging in age from ten months to eighteen years. This mother complained to Governor Allred about Hughes's inability to force her husband to pay the five dollars weekly in child support she had ordered him to do. This single mother complained that Judge Hughes, without children of her own, did not seem to understand the dire nature of her problem. "Every time Mrs. Hughes summons him for non-payment, he plays like he is sick, and she, being inexperienced with crooked men, lets him get by with it." The responsibility of providing for her children rested upon her second eldest son, age sixteen, because her eighteen-year-old son had left home for parts unknown. The younger son was making $1.25 a day, and it took about half of that for him to clothe and feed himself. Other problems she enumerated seemed insolvable. "I understand that you appointed Judge Hughes," she wrote the governor, "and I think it is your place to know just how she is treating the poor people."[49]

There was nothing, of course, for the governor to do. "While you may be assured that this office is deeply sympathetic, I regret there is absolutely nothing that the Governor can do to aid you," Allred's secretary responded to her.[50]

Actually, Hughes was always especially sympathetic to women whose husbands failed to comply with her orders. When in 1938 a divorced father fell $522 behind in making court-ordered payments for his young son, Judge Hughes set a deadline for him. When he ignored her deadline, she had him arrested at his Commerce Street junkyard and ordered him confined to jail every weekend until he caught up by paying a hundred dollars cash and twenty-five dollars monthly toward the support of his minor son. Hughes's action, taken at a time before attention was focused on delinquent fathers, was deemed drastic enough to warrant headlines in the newspapers.[51]

In one case in which a middle-aged woman sought a divorce, Hughes asked her how many times she had been married. Five times, the woman acknowledged. "Are you planning on marrying again—if you get your divorce?" the judge asked. The woman grinned and said, "Well, ma'am, if I can find a man—and get a chance." Hughes said, "Well, in that case you won't get a chance. Divorce not granted. You've been married enough."[52]

Hughes had been alarmed when she learned that the judicial system handled divorce cases "as if they were being rolled out of a roller with no thought or consideration being given them at all." Nor, she lamented, was there a counseling service to assist those couples as they contemplated divorce.[53]

Hughes believed strongly that a special domestic relations court should be established to handle divorce and custody cases rather than merely rotating them from court to court. Such a court would hear juvenile cases, too, then being handled by the county judge rather than a district judge. In 1938 she persuaded her fellow Dallas County district judges to begin a practice that was one step short of a special court—the practice of assigning all domestic relations cases (divorce, custody, juvenile proceedings)—to one particular district court and rotating that court every six months (later, a year). Since the idea was hers, her own court was the first to be so designated, beginning October 31, 1938. Moreover, the designation of her court was said to be appropriate, because her "woman's intuition and sympathetic approach to the problems of estranged couples and children" had established her reputation for wisdom in these matters. It might develop, the *Dallas Dispatch* wrote, that all future domestic cases should be heard in her court.[54]

In the first case she heard under this new plan, Hughes granted a divorce to a department store clerk with two minor children who was earning just $10 to $12 weekly. Hughes ordered the woman's husband, who made $17.50 a week as a gas station attendant, to pay $5 weekly in child support.[55]

The problem of divorce grew with the end of the Depression and the beginning of home-front pressures associated with World War II. Hughes sent queries to court officials in Houston, Los Angeles, Baltimore, New York, and Reno to gather data about divorces in those cities. According to figures she collected, Dallas County had a higher divorce rate than most other cities.

She provided her information to *Dallas Morning News* columnist Richard West, who wrote that "Dallas is fast becoming a Reno—the hottest divorce spot in the nation." Hughes told the writer that a divorce suit was filed for every 71 persons in the county compared with one for every 200 persons in Los Angeles, one for every 469 in Chicago, and one for every 5,112 persons in New York City. The 6,324 divorces filed for 1943 in Dallas County were nearly 2,000 more than in 1941.[56]

In a speech typical of those she made on the subject, she told girls at Dallas Technical High School in downtown Dallas to marry only after determining that they and their husbands would be able to secure sufficient food, shelter, and clothing. Investigate the prospective groom, she said, just as carefully as one investigates a potential business partnership before signing contracts. Assess whether the husband would be a good citizen and a good provider. Marriage should not occur under the age of twenty, she said. Girls who marry at a young age usually stop their schooling at a time when their responsibilities and obligations are increasing. Moreover, between the ages of fifteen and twenty-five, she cautioned, one's tastes change rapidly. In marrying young, both parties take the very great chance that one of the two will develop intellectually more quickly, leaving the other behind. Usually, it was the male who advanced more quickly because of the broadening nature of his contacts in business.[57]

Hasty wartime marriages were particularly troubling to Hughes. War had brought emotional unrest. The problem of marriages entered into too quickly on thirty-day furloughs by couples without long relationships was compounded by the lengthy periods of time the husbands were then gone, periods in which the interests, attitudes, and personalities of both sometimes changed drastically.[58]

In 1943 Hughes, in Chicago for a meeting of the American Bar Association and to speak to the National Association of Women Lawyers, visited and sat on the bench with a veteran divorce judge, Joseph Sabath. The *Chicago Daily News* interviewed Hughes about her own perspectives. She reported that divorces in Texas were up 25 percent during the war and largely because of the war. "Furlough marriages" were a special problem, she observed, because hasty weddings between servicemen on leave and young women did not have a good prognosis for success. The chief sufferers from the resulting broken homes would be children. Homes that had been broken up by the war or war work preventing parents from properly supervising their children were paramount causes for a substantial rise in juvenile delinquency in Dallas, she was certain.[59]

Hughes was firmly convinced that juvenile delinquency was closely related to family problems, particularly divorce. Juvenile delinquency became for her a subject of concern equal to that of divorce. It was not the delinquent child so much as the parents and society in general who should be brought before the court of justice, she believed. When in 1936 the city of Dallas built a replica of Robert E. Lee's home in Arlington, Virginia, at Oak Lawn Park (renamed Robert E. Lee Park), Hughes complained that it would have been better to spend the money for a public park for children in impoverished west Dallas.[60]

"The problem of crime," she said, "is to a large extent a problem of juvenile delinquency." The home environment was critical, and parents must be trained in the importance of the home for character-building. Next as a key element was the school, followed by the community itself. Urbanization, coupled with the disappearance of the farm and small town, required the creation of places for recreational play and opportunities for supervised play. "Records of juvenile courts show that delinquency in most instances results from a failure of one or more of these factors to assume their responsibility to the child."[61]

With the advent of war and the absence of so many fathers, the problem of juvenile delinquency worsened. Figures Hughes obtained for Dallas County showed an increase in juvenile delinquency of 11.5 percent between the first full year of war, 1942, and the previous year. And the first ten months of 1943 showed a further increase of a whopping 55 percent over the same period in 1942. The reasons for this, she was convinced, sprang from the turmoil of wartime. Many fathers were in the armed forces; some fathers had left home to work in the war industry in another city; many families had been relocated to new communities; housing was scarce and often inadequate; many mothers now were working and away from their children; inadequate recreational facilities sent many children overflowing into the streets.

"Even adults are restless and emotionally upset," she said.

There is a large increase in divorce cases throughout the country and certainly this adult restlessness influences the lives of the children. They [the children] are torn by so many desires—to be old enough to get into the fight is the wish of many. To go to school or to work must be decided. For years preceding the war we kept our boys and girls children. Work was scarce and we didn't want them in the labor market. Now with high wages and the shortage in manpower, there is a temptation to leave school and go to work.[62]

With large numbers of women joining the work force to replace men who had departed for military service, Hughes had an opportunity to reassess from this wartime perspective her beliefs about working women and their obligations to family. This came through her capacity as volunteer chairman of the local Office of Civilian Defense Committee on Service to Children. She became concerned about the Dallas County Juvenile Department hearing more and more complaints about children not attending school because their mothers were at work and could not supervise them. This was disquieting to Hughes. While she would always encourage women to seek the same career opportunities as men, maintaining a strong home life was important to her. For women with children, home life had to take priority, she believed.

The finest contribution a mother could make toward the strength of the nation and its effectiveness, she said, was to give her children "the security of home, individual care and affection." Women without children, though, should take their rightful places in industry and military with all the fervor war demanded. She realized, too, economic necessity made it imperative for many mothers with young children to take jobs outside the home. "But I am genuinely alarmed," she wrote, "at the steadily increasing number of newspaper stories and pictures telling of mothers becoming welders, electricians and the like."[63]

Her committee and other similar groups were convinced, she said, that "whenever possible the nation's best interest could be served by mothers staying at home and devoting their energies to the development of intelligent, honest citizens to live in and to govern the world that will come tomorrow when the military victories have been won."[64]

In the last two years of the war, Hughes decided to do something to correct the deplorable treatment of juvenile offenders in Dallas County. The harshness of Dallas's facilities and policies contrasted sharply with the attitudes she had experienced more than two decades earlier as a police officer in Washington, D.C. She could not forget the emphasis there on rehabilitation. In Dallas, juvenile offenders who were apprehended for whatever reason found themselves placed adjacent to adult inmates on the fifth floor of the county jail, languishing there until their cases could be adjudicated.[65]

The method of her initiative was to address the problem through a series of hard-hitting speeches made to women's groups, luncheon clubs, churches, parent-teacher associations, and civic organizations. In these speeches she campaigned for drastic overhauls of the accommodations for juveniles, beginning with a suggestion of a new two-story addition to the Records Building adjacent to the county jail and advancing to a conviction that an entirely separate facility removed from downtown was needed. She described to her audiences the awful conditions in which juvenile offenders were held and expressed her conviction that their daily exposure to adult offenders could bring only harm, not rehabilitation. When only a few hours after his release from custody a thirteen-year-old boy was caught stealing a car, she cited it as a striking example of the effect of placing a child next to hardened adult criminals.[66]

Her campaign caused great distress among her fellow judges, for the county commissioners she was criticizing controlled the purse strings for the county's courts. Moreover, the supervisory county juvenile board consisted of the eight district judges (including Hughes herself) and the county judge himself, who was the presiding officer of county commissioners. Hughes, undaunted at the possible consequences to her own courtroom, relied on winning public opinion to her point of view.

What she wanted came to be known as the Hughes Plan. Initially a one-person crusade, Hughes's speeches soon prompted women and women's groups to complain and to demand that the county commissioners correct the situation. County judge Al Templeton, who presided over the commissioners, said it simply was not feasible to build a new facility during the war years. Other priorities prevailed. Under pressure, though, while Hughes was out of the city gathering information about the juvenile facilities in St. Louis and Washington, D.C., Templeton and the four county commissioners voted to spend twenty-five thousand dollars to improve the juvenile program.[67]

Returning just a few hours after the vote, Hughes condemned it as little more than a sham. Dallas was far behind the two cities she had visited. In those cities, she found that juvenile offenders had recreational facilities both inside and outside the building. During the daytime they were taken outside to play games. Vocational training was provided. Juveniles in Dallas still would be kept in three "cages," two for white boys and one for Negroes. "The cages are barred on all sides and over the top and have iron beds chained to the bars. Even in the zoo some wild animals are not caged as thoroughly," she said. "The facilities that Dallas has now are encouraging delinquency rather than discouraging it. What I am urging is a home of detention which will serve, not only to detain, but also to provide guidance and training, serving the child's welfare in the best interests of the state."[68]

County Commissioner Frank Buck responded. "The thirty juveniles now in jail, largely from outside the state of Texas, are not little innocent children who could be contaminated by their stay, but are big tough, hardened subjects charged with assault, rape, burglary, safe cracking and the like," he said. Most of the female juveniles had been interned for treatment of venereal disease, he added.[69]

This woman, county judge Templeton said of Hughes, either did not know that America was fighting a big war or was not able to draw lines of demarcation between a child and an experienced juvenile criminal. The special detention home she wanted would cost approximately two hundred thousand dollars, and the county could not afford it, he said, letting loose what a newspaper headline called "a vicious blast at Sarah Hughes."[70]

Hughes countered that in Essex County, New Jersey, the County Probation Service had constructed a separate home for juveniles that cost only thirty thousand dollars. It was located two miles from the business district, and it contained a courtroom, judge's office, separate rooms for all juveniles, playrooms, and playgrounds. Clothing and provisions for all juveniles cost fifty-six thousand dollars annually. That, she said, was half the amount Dallas County spent to fence juveniles behind bars.[71]

Despite Hughes's continued complaints that the commissioners' improvement plan was inadequate, the Dallas County Commissioners Court proceeded by awarding a contract to improve the juvenile quarters in the county jail. Juveniles would continue to be placed in the county jail, but a separate entrance was provided and new spaces were created to keep them away from adult inmates.[72]

Hughes, combative as always, was not content to leave the commissioners court alone. In a speech to the Dallas B&PW she called county government "antiquated and creaking." There should be consideration of combining city and county functions, she said, touching on a point she had to realize was always sensitive to the commissioners court.[73]

Finally, in February 1945, the commissioners court asked the Dallas

Council of Social Agencies to investigate the situation. The Council of Social Agencies opted to create an independent fourteen-member committee of citizens who would take the matter out of what was termed a political squabble and make recommendations. Seven months later Judge Hughes was one of three county officials, including county judge Templeton, who served with three Dallas city councilmen on a joint committee to arrange details for placing a proposed new juvenile home on a bond program to submit to voters. In November 1946, citizens of Dallas voted to approve a million-dollar bond program to build an entirely new facility for the juvenile program. Its plan adhered closely to what Hughes had advocated. Construction of the new quarters, away from downtown Dallas on Harry Hines Boulevard, was not completed until 1951.[74]

～ 6

Dynamo from Dallas

I n 1942 the U.S. Congress considered a proposal by Secretary of Treasury Henry Morgenthau to deny married couples the right to submit separate income tax returns. They would have no option but to file a combined return. To Sarah T. Hughes such a proposal was ridiculous and a backward step for married women. She believed this arrangement would further subjugate them to their husbands' dominance. The plan would discourage couples from marriage, and it would discriminate financially against all married persons. As the House Ways and Means Committee considered the proposal in March 1942, Judge Hughes went to Washington, D.C., to testify against it. Morgenthau's proposal, she argued with aplomb, was unconstitutional, unwise, and un-American. As Texas's acknowledged leading spokesperson against the measure, she was said to literally steal the show. Her appearance brought commendations from virtually every member of the committee. Drew Pearson and Robert S. Allen, in their influential, nationally syndicated political column, wrote that her outstanding performance brought no joy to Hatton W. Sumners, the congressman who represented her district. Their comment was prompted by the committee's chairman, Representative Robert Doughton of North Carolina, who told Hughes: "With no prejudice toward any sitting members, I would like to say that a person with your intelligence would do very well in Congress. Have you ever thought of running?"

Judge Hughes glanced at the sitting member to whom Doughton referred, Sumners, and winked. "I've been trying to get Mr. Sumners to step aside and let me run for several years, but he won't get out of my way."

Sumners, sixty-seven years of age and now one of President Roosevelt's foes, blushed. He had no comeback. But he was not ready to retire.[1]

To Hughes, the idea of running for Congress was intensely appealing. It had been a dim notion since her days as a law student, when she had engaged in public policy discussions with Brooks Hays. Her great success in the Texas

Legislature made it seem not at all unreasonable. Her record as a pioneer woman jurist, outstanding by any account, and her continued work in energizing women to expand their opportunities, brought her even further recognition. Her chances for success in a congressional race seemed good. The problem, of course, was Sumners. Dallas voters had returned him to office time and time again since he first went to Washington in 1912. Just how long must she wait for his retirement?

As it turned out, if Sarah T. Hughes had any notion of challenging Sumners in the 1944 election, she would be obliged to postpone it. An event occurred that for the first time in her life cast aspersions on her exemplary reputation and thrust her into a battle she did not want—one to preserve her good name. This new development in her life arose over an allegation that she was one of thirty-four citizens, many of them prominent, arrested by police in a gambling raid at a downtown hotel.

Dallas was not a city where crime or corruption flourished; yet, petty vices—if not officially sanctioned—were permitted when they were discreetly conducted. Authorities had loosened their enforcement of laws against gambling, liquor, and prostitution during the 1936 Texas Centennial because it was deemed necessary for the entertainment of thousands of visitors. Afterward, the reins had not been tightened. As regular games sponsored by gambling kingpins such as Benny Binion prospered, law enforcement officials either looked the other way or occasionally imposed nominal fines. One ongoing operation was held in an upstairs suite at the Jefferson Hotel, across the street from the train station, one block from the old red courthouse, where Judge Hughes presided over the 14th District Court.

On the evening of July 31, 1943, one of Hughes's colleagues, district judge Claude McCallum of the 101st District Court, was in the Jefferson Hotel lobby when he happened to become aware of the gambling operation upstairs. When a hotel employee informed him that the gambling was safe from police harassment, the judge became irate. He immediately called Dallas City Manager V. R. Smitham to complain and to allege that Smitham did not have the guts to close down this illegal game. Smitham advised the judge to wait around the hotel lobby for a few minutes and see for himself. The city manager, under whose authority the Police Department worked, called the desk sergeant on duty and ordered him to raid the gambling den.

The desk sergeant, uncertain, checked with the night police chief, Lieutenant O. P. Wright, who then telephoned the city manager himself and obtained confirmation to proceed.[2]

Behind doors with peepholes drilled to preview those approaching was an elaborate gambling setup with lounge and bar as well as gambling rooms. Thirty-five well-dressed persons, including fourteen women, were shooting craps, betting at roulette wheels, playing cards, and involved with various other gambling activities when at 11 P.M. Lieutenant Wright and two officers brandishing at least one shotgun burst into the room. All of the gamblers were arrested. Because of the large number arrested, other officers were summoned immediately to help escort them to the city jail, where they were booked, fined, and released. Many of the arrested individuals were prominent. A number of them were from the oil industry, and some were known well enough to be recognized by Lieutenant Wright. As those under arrest were being processed at the scene, Lieutenant Wright said one woman whom he did not recognize approached him and introduced herself as Judge Sarah Hughes. He did not question her identity, but when the arrested individuals gave their names at the city jail the same woman listed her name as Mary Martin, the popular singer and actress from Weatherford, Texas. This obviously false identification was not challenged. Dallas police frequently permitted prominent persons arrested in gambling raids to give phony names. The woman "Mary Martin" was not further questioned.[3]

Front-page news stories the next day described the event as "one of the biggest raids . . . in several months." The articles did not identify by name those arrested, nor did they identify them in the days to follow except for the two men charged as operators (Jerry Rosenberg and Johnny Andrews). The stories reported that among the swank crowd were two district judges. Gossip concerning their identities dominated courthouse conversations on Monday. District judge W. L. (Jack) Thornton admitted to being one of the two arrested, and speculation about the second one, fevered by rumors circulating about the woman who supposedly first said she was Sarah T. Hughes, then Mary Martin, naturally centered on Hughes herself.[4]

When a local minister, the Reverend Luther Peak, radio commentator and author of a paid newspaper column sponsored by his Central Baptist Church, received a private letter, he detailed the episode about "Sarah Hughes" and "Mary Martin." Accepting the story as factual, he wrote a series of columns excoriating Judge Hughes and Jack Thornton for so blatantly defying the law. They had rendered themselves unfit, he declared, for public office. Peak challenged law enforcement officials, the district attorney, the local ministry, and the citizens of Dallas not to "meekly accept a whitewash, a cover-up and a camouflage" of the affair. He called upon the Dallas Bar Association to appoint a committee to investigate the matter and make its findings known, upon the grand jury to probe the situation, upon the ministry of Dallas to hold a special meeting to discuss the situation, and upon the daily newspapers to make editorial comment.[5]

At first Judge Hughes remained silent, not bothering to deny the charges. She had not been identified by name in the regular press accounts, and she no doubt believed that a denial would call further attention to her possible guilt. Finally, as rumors continued to circulate, she decided to attempt to clear her name. Six days after the arrests she went to Lieutenant Wright's home and introduced herself to him to prove she was not the woman who had identified herself that night as Sarah Hughes. Next day, as a further precaution, Wright visited Hughes's courtroom and confirmed for himself that Judge Hughes was the person who had called upon him at his home, not the person who had identified herself on the night of the raid as Sarah Hughes. At the request of A. J. Thus, acting city of Dallas attorney Wright signed a statement briefly stating that the woman who had identified herself as Sarah Hughes was actually someone else. His statement absolving Hughes was published in the newspaper on August 8 under the headline, "Judge Hughes Not Present in Game Room, Says Raider."[6]

Rev. Peak, challenged as well by Hughes, replied that he wanted to be absolutely fair, and he offered to her his column space to tell her side of the story. Accepting his offer, she explained in the column that on the evening of the raid she had had dinner at home with her husband and two friends, Mr. and Mrs. Charles S. McCombs. "[We] spent the entire evening in the back yard. Our friends left at a few minutes before eleven and Mr. Hughes and I retired. I remained at my home, 3816 Normandy, from Saturday before dinner until Sunday morning after breakfast."[7]

News of the gambling raid prompted an outpouring of sympathetic letters to Hughes from old friends, some of whom assumed she had been caught in the raid. Few Brewster, judge of the Texas Commission of Appeals, was one who wrote. Hughes responded: "Your words of consolation were deeply appreciated. At first I was amused to hear I was in a gambling raid at a time when actually I was in my own back yard trying to keep cool. However, by the end of the week I had been reminded so many times that I was at the Jefferson Hotel the night of July 31st I began to wonder just where I had been. Anyway, the story grew and grew until it could no longer be laughed off. . . . I'm glad the Bar has finally appointed a committee—that is, if they will do and say something—and I believe they will. At least the alibi and mistaken identity defense have both proceeded to the point where I can again think the story is a joke." [8]

The committee to which Hughes referred was appointed by James L. Lipscomb, president of the Dallas Bar Association. He had formed the committee, he explained, "in justice to her [Sarah T. Hughes] and in justice to District Judges who were not involved in that raid." [9]

Meanwhile, Hughes realized more directly the negative impact of the news stories on her reputation when her engagement to speak to the Women's Society of Christian Service at the downtown First Methodist Church was canceled. "In all my years of speaking, this is the first time I have had an engagement canceled," she responded. She could not help but wonder if the cancellation had occurred because of the "false and malicious rumor" that had been circulated about her. "If such rumors are credited with truth and if a reputation built upon years of community service can be completely disregarded, then Christian Service means little. With such reports current, I would think church women would go out of the way to defend and explode such unfounded rumors, rather than by their action give countenance to them." [10]

Another disquieting cancellation came from the First Baptist Church. Her planned talk before a men's group there was canceled, the embarrassed chairman tried to explain, because a new member of the class had engaged her to speak without realizing that the affair was stag. [11]

Before the month of August ended, the bar committee completed its investigation and declared that Hughes had not been present at the Jefferson Hotel. A touch of ambiguity remained, though, when the report stated that committee members had been "unable to determine the truth or falsity" of many other rumors. The nature of these rumors was not stated. [12] The committee's findings justified Hughes in declaring that she had been "completely exonerated." Judge Ocie Speer of Austin, noting the committee report, asked whether the verdict was a "Scotch verdict" of "not proven, or the more comprehensive one of not guilty." Hughes replied, "I am glad to advise that the verdict of the Bar Investigation committee was 'not guilty.' " [13]

The *Daily Times Herald* concurred. "This should end the matter," it reported in an editorial. "Judge Hughes stands exonerated. The Bar Association investigation has confirmed the reputation that she enjoys among her fellow citizens."[14] The *Dallas Morning News* agreed, saying that the report had exonerated Hughes of any involvement in the gambling raid.[15]

Two years after the gambling raid, a deputy county clerk, Maudie I. Walling, told writer Wallis Reef, gathering information for a feature story on Hughes, that she was the person who gave the name "Mary Martin" at the police station. She said Lieutenant Wright had mistaken another woman as Judge Hughes and that he had made an erroneous statement to bystanders that this woman was Judge Sarah Hughes.[16] Walling wrote a long letter to Hughes, reaffirming what she had told Reef and saying the gambling accusation, instead of hurting her politically, "may be the very thing which (in a round about way) will send you to Washington."[17]

Two months after the gambling stories had created such a stir, Hughes, with her reputation redeemed, could think once more of her political future. Speculation appeared in print that she would be a candidate for Congress, opposing Sumners in 1944. Perhaps in light of the negative publicity from the gambling raid, she chose instead to run for reelection as judge. Her attorney friend J. Frank Wilson campaigned against Sumners in the Democratic primary. In her own announcement for reelection Hughes said she had heard more than twelve thousand civil cases since her appointment and now carried the endorsement of 80 percent of Dallas lawyers. Her uppermost thought, she said, had been to be "fair and impartial on the bench, to conduct the business of the court with dispatch yet with thoroughness, and to see to it that my decisions reflect true justice."[18]

She enjoyed and was intrigued by the use of radio in her campaign. The script for one such radio commercial, possibly narrated by Judge Hughes herself, went as follows:

"LET JUSTICE BE DONE! . . . this you SENSE . . . and EXPERIENCE . . . when you enter Judge Sarah T. Hughes' 14th District Court . . . Dallas.

"'You don't wait months to have a case tried in Judge Hughes' court' . . . say Dallas citizens.

"GREAT DECISIONS, rooted in Justice . . .

"SPEEDY TRIALS
"THESE SAVE YOU TIME . . . and MONEY.
"YOUR vote for Judge Hughes will continue this service in Dallas . . .
"Thank you, very much."[19]

Hughes's opponent, James Guthrie, a former justice of the peace and assistant district attorney, lamely claimed she exaggerated—she had the support of 57.9 percent of Dallas lawyers, not 80 percent.[20] Voters, however, once again returned Hughes to the bench by a substantial margin. She continued to be the only female district judge in the state. Sumners, as expected, defeated J. Frank Wilson in the race for Congress.

Hughes returned to Washington in June 1944 to attend a White House conference, "How Women May Share in Post-War Policy-Making," an event sponsored by four women's groups in response to a challenge by Eleanor Roosevelt, who urged women to take a more active role in public life. Hughes's B&PW friend and colleague Dr. Minnie L. Maffett of Dallas, president of the National Federation of the B&PW, was one of the four women who sent out invitations. Hughes also was invited by virtue of her position as national chairman of the Status of Women Committee of the American Association of University Women. This was a position she held from 1940 to 1946.

Some two hundred women representing seventy-five organizations at the conference voted to take every step within their power to further the active participation of qualified women in positions of responsibility, both national and international. Toward this goal, the conference adopted a blank form for women to use in recommending other women for appointment as members of policy-making bodies. Eleanor Roosevelt, in closing the one-day affair, called it a "first step in setting our house in order that we may be able to do the things that need to be done."[21]

Returning to Texas, Hughes and Dr. Maffett were the leaders in summoning women to the state capital in September 1944 for that second step. They sought to achieve on a state level the same goals as those in Washington. More than two hundred women representing some twenty-five women's organizations attended. Judge Hughes, as the primary speaker for the one-day conference, addressed the crowd from a familiar podium in a familiar place—the hall of the House of Representatives. She said the women were uniting not in a spirit of criticism but "to suggest a list of qualified women whenever there are places in the government available to them." Among the delegates was Texas's first woman governor, Miriam A. Ferguson, now returned to her household chores. The present governor, tradition-bound Coke Stevenson, was viewed as being unsympathetic to the conference. Since Hughes's days with him in the legislature, Stevenson had advanced from Speaker of the House to lieutenant governor and now, since 1941, to governor, showing no interest in advancing the cause of women. "There are no women on many boards because the governor evidently doesn't know the qualified women in this state," Hughes said.[22] To remedy that situation, the delegates departed with the same instructions given in Washington—to compile a list of qualified women to submit to the governor for appointments. They also adopted a resolution to submit to the forthcoming state Democratic convention, calling for the appointment of qualified women to the state's boards and commissions. Within two months Judge Hughes had the list in her possession, and she submitted it with some fanfare to Governor Stevenson—"forcefully," as one newspaper described it. The document contained a cross-indexed list of forty-four Texas women, both Democrats and Republicans, qualified and ready for appointment to state agencies.[23]

Two weeks later, in November 1944, Hughes was back in Washington, this time inspecting juvenile facilities in that city as ammunition for her crusade to have a separate juvenile home built for Dallas and attending a meeting of the directors of the American Association of University Women. But there was another important reason to be in Washington. Judge Hughes paid a publicized courtesy visit to Congressman Sumners to give him early warning of a decision she had made. Whatever his plans concerning the 1946 congressional election, she advised him, she would be a candidate for that office herself. Some years earlier, she reminded him, she had expressed an ambition to succeed him, and the time to attempt it had arrived. Hughes told reporters: "I prefer not to have Mr. Sumners as an opponent, but it is now my intention to run regardless." In a show of cordiality, both Hughes and Sumners agreed it was too early to expect Sumners to commit himself to his plans for the 1946 campaign.[24]

Despite the show of friendliness on the occasion, Sumners and Hughes were at odds in their political philosophies. Early in Roosevelt's administration, Sumners had supported New Deal legislation such as the Agricultural

Adjustment Act and the National Industrial Recovery Act, but after his break with the president over the 1937 court-packing plan, he had dedicated himself to halting the growth of the federal bureaucracy. Hughes, on the other hand, continued to be an enthusiastic supporter of Roosevelt throughout the Depression and into the war years.

With her declaration of candidacy achieved at an early date, Hughes returned once more to her perennial goal of advancing women's rights. Now in 1945 she repeated in Dallas the same basic women's programs held in Washington and Austin. This time, of course, the goal was to encourage greater participation of women in local government. Some three hundred women attended a meeting on the roof garden of the Adolphus Hotel. Under Judge Hughes's direction and following the pattern set in Washington and Austin, each delegate would nominate a qualified woman for appointment to a city or county policy-making board. A roster of all these women would be presented to city and county officials in Dallas. Mayor Woodall Rodgers attended the meeting and offered vague and somewhat puzzling encouragement: "If women can find a way to clear the slums in public office, which men have not yet done; if they influence the unification with the mother city of all her branches, they will have passed the test of statesmanship."[25]

Sarah Menezes, Hughes's long-time friend and pioneer woman lawyer in Dallas, jokingly related at the conference how men serving with her on a Republican Party committee tried to shield her from meetings held in hotel bedrooms or at places where they would be drinking. "That is the excuse men use to exclude women from their meetings," she said.[26]

In truth, Hughes had become alarmed at the inertia of so many women in asserting their rightful place in society, and the speeches she now was making in many cities in Texas and sometimes elsewhere in the nation reflected that. Women's secondary status, she said in a speech to the Alabama Federation of Business and Professional Women's Clubs, was their own fault. And their inertia was harming the nation. As long as the United States continued to use only the male half of its resources, it would not be able to reach its potential, not just in government but throughout society. "Very few women are executives," she said. "Pay scale for women is less than it is for men holding equal positions. Women are still discouraged from taking certain courses and entering certain professions. And they aren't holding enough policy-making posts and participating in government as they should." She contrasted the American situation, where 1 percent of legislative membership was female, with that of the Soviet Union, where 21 percent of membership in the law-making bodies was female, and that of Poland with 9 percent female membership and Japan with 8 percent.[27]

Women could do better, she insisted, and while she did not use herself as an example, in fact, she was a striking example. In February 1945, her photograph appeared in the *Dallas Morning News* as she celebrated her tenth anniversary on the bench. She had not missed a single day because of illness.[28] In those ten years she had not had the privilege of a single woman juror in her courtroom, and changing the state law in that regard continued to be a top priority for her.

Hard times during these war years, with so many men departed for military service, reemphasized the need for women jurors, Hughes said. Not only were men scarcer than ever, many of them used every excuse they could not to serve. Of 450 male jurors called for service in her court in 1945, 327 had legal excuses. Joint resolutions were pending in both houses of the Texas Legislature to place the issue before the voters, but once again they failed.[29]

Related to her crusade for a juvenile home was her mission to save marriages. She drafted a plan to create a county agency where husbands and wives could go for counseling with their marital problems. It would be a way to cheat the divorce courts wherever possible by mending broken homes before they could be destroyed. "There is many a disheartened husband and wife crying their hearts out for someone to tell their troubles to and hear an encouraging suggestion," she said. The government should recognize this important need. "I can think of no new public service that more deserves the expenditure of tax funds than one which will be helpful in lowering our shocking divorce record."[30]

With her eye on an upcoming 1946 congressional campaign and a desire for achieving even greater visibility, Hughes began in April 1945 a fifteen-minute weekly radio report, "Viewing the News," broadcast between 8:45 and 9 A.M. every Saturday on WRR. After opening with a simple "Good morning," she immediately launched into a discussion of the major events of the past week. For each broadcast she prepared a five-page, double-spaced script that emphasized international and national news, included a substantial dose of state news, and occasionally dealt with local events.[31]

In one of her first reports just after the death of President Roosevelt, she described Harry Truman's first address to Congress as "not a remarkable speech." His tone was "rather twangy and flat." But she found a "note of sincerity and determination that was encouraging." Her appreciation for Truman would grow with the passing of years.[32]

She was very much encouraged by the formation of the United Nations, favored federal aid to local school districts despite opposition from two Dallas school board members, approved the rebuilding of Europe, feared the ultimate consequences of the new jet-propelled fighter plane ("such a plane is no cause for thrills"), and agreed with scientists who said the nation's atomic secrets should be shared internationally.[33]

At every opportunity she discussed women's issues: jury service, equal pay, the proposed Equal Rights Amendment, and the need for more women attorneys. Never did she open a broadcast with news about women, but she highlighted instances in which women were excelling at jobs normally handled by men—women truck drivers, for instance.[34]

One of her most interesting broadcasts was her vivid description of Dallas citizens celebrating on VJ Day, the day on which Japan surrendered. She was at a meeting on the second floor of the Baker Hotel with a fine view of the city's premiere intersection, Commerce and Akard streets, and observed the antics repeated in cities throughout the country.

> As I looked out the window, there was a girl being carried on the shoulders of two sailors, a soldier was high on a lamp post, standing on a narrow ledge with knees clamped to the pole, and waving a tiny American flag. As I watched, a girl, worming her way up the street, reached a bottle up to him which he put up to his mouth. It was a gesture of comradeship—he didn't drink much. A sailor, pretty far gone and oblivious to the danger, was embracing two shore patrolmen. . . . Soon feathers began to fall from the windows high up in the Baker and Adolphus [Hotel]. Occasionally the empty pillow cases followed. It was a howling, happy crowd, celebrating the day of days for many. . . . Even the back streets were crowded with automobiles whose horns blared constantly.[35]

One of the features Hughes initiated in 1946 was the "Quiz Kids Current Information Contest," in which high school students from throughout the county competed. When Rayburn Wright of Pleasant Grove High School won the award as the county's best informed student, Judge Hughes drove to his modest frame house to pick him up for a ride downtown to be on her show. Years later, Wright's memory of the occasion was dominated by his recollection of the judge driving a big Buick with "the longest hood I had ever seen."[36]

With Franklin D. Roosevelt dead from a stroke suffered in Georgia, the long war winding down to a close, and the then-undistinguished Harry S. Truman in the Oval Office, Judge Hughes cast her eyes about for her own choice as Roosevelt's successor in the 1948 election. Truman presumably would yield the presidency after serving out FDR's unfinished term. Hughes's own choice, without knowing which political party he preferred, was General Dwight D. Eisenhower. In one of her first radio shows she called upon Eisenhower to lead the nation in peace just as he had led it to military victory in Europe. "There is no other living American in whom the people have greater trust and who can so well bring faith and confidence to the people," she said over the radio. To most Europeans, she said, General Eisenhower epitomized what is best in America, and since Roosevelt's death he had become for them the man who speaks for America. "His prestige, both at home and abroad, is not simply military prestige. He has had to deal with many diplomatic problems and has acted with tact, understanding, and force. No small element of his success is that he is a truly democratic man." The nation had been hungry for the special kind of leadership that Eisenhower seemed to be able to provide.[37]

Besides her radio show, another activity that regularly put her name before the public was a series of book reviews she began in 1945 for the *Daily Times Herald.* The books she reviewed reflected her deep interest in women's issues, politics, labor, and the law and included *Congressional Elections: 1896-1944,* by Cortez A. M. Ewing, *Married Women's Bill of Rights,* by Nathaniel Fishman, *Labor Lawyer,* by Louis Waldman, *The Cotton Mill Worker,* by Herbert J. Lahne, *Women as Force in History,* by Mary Beard, *When You Marry,* by Evelyn M. Duvall and Reuben Hill, and *Brandeis: A Free Man's Life,* by Alpheus Thomas Mason.[38]

As she prepared for a campaign against Sumners, whose intentions still were unknown, Hughes began accumulating information on women in Congress. She was encouraged. She clipped and placed in her files an article entitled "Our Women in Congress," which appeared in the small magazine *Coronet.* Another article she clipped and saved was headlined "Record Number of Women to Serve in Congress," a news story concerning the 84th Congress.

The Library of Congress Legislative Reference Service printed out for her in early 1945 a report entitled "Women in the Congress of the United States."[39]

Eager to get started in the campaign, Hughes accepted an invitation to be the key speaker at a Labor Day picnic in 1945 sponsored by the United Auto Workers (an affiliate of the CIO). The setting was adjacent to a small, spring-fed lake at Kidd Springs Park in a wooded section of Oak Cliff. To this friendly, family audience she delivered a blistering attack against Sumners, ridiculing his conservative record in Washington and comparing it with her own liberal views. The veteran congressman, she said, had failed to recognize that America was changing. His negative attitude toward "reconversion" legislation to soothe the transition from a wartime economy had "exposed the gap between his horse-and-buggy political and economic attitude and the absolute requirements of a changed world." She joked about his comments advocating a return to normalcy after the war. "I presume that means he wants to go back to a prewar condition in which there were eight million unemployed." The federal government, she believed, had a responsibility for guaranteeing full employment such as required by the Murray-Patman Full Employment Bill. She favored provisions for raising unemployment compensation to a maximum of twenty-five dollars weekly for twenty-six weeks, for broadening Social Security legislation to cover farm and domestic labor, for stimulating private construction of housing through special legislation, and for jumping the minimum wage from forty cents an hour to about sixty cents.[40]

The only legislation Sumners had favored, Hughes said, was a bill to limit the president's term to six years. Under such a limitation, the nation would not have had Roosevelt in the war years and it would not have had Woodrow Wilson in the critical years of 1918-19. "And if he [Sumners] would just place that six-year limit on congressional terms, too, we might see that the present Congressmen could have been retired four or five times."[41]

Had Hughes known then that the congressman would decide not to run for reelection, she might have avoided such a direct attack on him. The intemperate nature of her talk made at a labor-sponsored family picnic in an increasingly conservative city would put her on the defensive in the campaign ahead as she sought to fight off accusations that she was a puppet for union bosses. Nor would Sumners forget the attack, and he soon would seize the opportunity for retribution.

A suburban newspaper commentator had early advice for Hughes. "If we might presume to advise Her Honor, we would suggest toning down the next speeches just a bit. Radical ideas are going out of style rapidly in this country right now."[42]

Hughes and Sumners would find themselves together at a banquet just a month later. The occasion was a celebration for a lawyer from Dallas, Tom C. Clark, who had been selected in June 1945 by President Truman to be attorney general of the United States. Clark returned to Texas in October for a round of receptions in his honor. His first stop was Dallas, where the pro-business Dallas Chamber of Commerce and the Dallas Citizens Council, an exclusive organization of business and civic leaders, planned a lavish stag banquet for him. Judge Hughes, as a woman, was not invited and probably was the only prominent public official in town not to receive an invitation. This, for her, would not do; she made a telephone call to request tickets. The planning committee pondered the matter and finally responded. "You may come as a public official, but not as a woman," was its Solomon-like judgment. "I wouldn't think of attending in any other capacity," she said. The next day her invitation, signed by Clark's brother, Dallas attorney Robert L. Clark, arrived in the mail.[43]

Some seven hundred men and one woman—Hughes—attended the party in the grand ballroom of the Adolphus Hotel. One speaker that evening described those present as "the greatest collection of bankers and big business men I ever saw." General Chairman Robert L. Thornton, a prominent Dallas banker and civic leader, singled out Judge Hughes, sitting with her husband, George, and asked her to stand. The crowd, very much aware of her unique presence, rendered applause that newspapers described as "uninhibited." Tom C. Clark stepped down from the head table, where he was sitting with Hatton W. Sumners, to greet her, an instance captured by news photographers. Sumners was overheard muttering, "She's going to run against me."[44]

Two weeks later Sumners announced that after thirty-four years in Washington he would not seek reelection. The federal government had become, he complained, an "instrumentality of favoritism, tyranny, oppression and corruption." Perhaps Hughes's attack on him at the Labor Day picnic had helped convince him he would have faced a difficult campaign. At any rate, he was through with politics.[45]

Hughes, of course, had declared her intentions to run in November 1944. Speculation now mounted regarding other possible challengers for Sumners's office. J. Frank Wilson, who had unsuccessfully opposed Sumners in the 1944 election, seemed certain to be in the race. Another formidable opponent might be William McCraw, the former attorney general of Texas. Other strong potential candidates existed, too. State senator W. C. Graves had his eye on the office. Perhaps the most promising candidate of all, if he chose to run as speculated, would be Robert G. Storey, the Dallas lawyer who had gained prominence as an assistant prosecutor at the war crimes trials at Nuremberg. Still another possibility was Fred (Red) Harris, a navy hero who recently had returned to Dallas to reopen his law office.[46]

Hughes made her official declaration of candidacy on February 24, 1946, issuing a five-page news release prepared by public relations counselor Bernard Brister. The announcement was a straightforward statement of her views concerning the problems of postwar America. It outlined a vigorous role for the federal government. "My platform is simple," she said. "It is a platform of ACTION. I propose to render the same type of service in Congress that I gave in three terms as your Representative in the Texas Legislature, the same type of service that I have given during the last 11 years as District Judge." She favored price controls to battle inflation until a stabilized peace-time economy could develop. Labor disputes should be settled as speedily as possible through collective bargaining. The federal government should offer a conciliation service that in ordinary labor disputes could render cooperative assistance, not compulsion. To relieve the discomfort and suffering resulting from the postwar housing shortage, she favored a bold and comprehensive program in which direct government aid could be used for temporary housing and a program offered for a permanent expansion of the building capacity of private industry. Preference should be given both in building materials and in completed houses for the returned war veterans. The GI Bill of Rights should be strengthened in housing benefits and in helping the veterans recoup lost educational opportunities. More flexible insurance benefits should be provided to veterans, and especially medical care. She announced she would take a leave of absence from the bench beginning March 1 for the campaign. In May she paid a thousand-dollar filing fee with the County Democratic Executive Committee. Attorneys H. B. Sanders and Louis Lefkowitz were named as co-managers of her campaign.[47]

Opportunely, in late April one of Hughes's women's club affiliations brought a dividend. The Zonta Club, of which she had served as president from 1929 to 1931, presented to her an award for rendering "the most outstanding service to the community life of Dallas." The citation for the award summarized her contributions in this way:

> Her quiz kids contest throughout the county awakening students and parents to democracy's need of keeping up with community and world affairs; her efforts in awakening public opinion on problems of divorce and juvenile delinquency; improvement of child labor laws; improvement of citizenship and working status of women and elimination of tax discrimination against community property states; her planning of Dallas' back-to-school drive; her co-ordination of agency activities for the care of children of working mothers and other children without adult supervision; her work to stimulating young people toward achievement by her award for many years to the outstanding girls' debating team of Dallas and her leadership in Girl Scout work.[48]

With the deadline for filing at hand, former attorney general McCraw declared from New York he would not be a candidate. Robert G. Storey had other things in mind and decided not to run; he became dean of the Southern Methodist University Law School. Fred (Red) Harris chose to run for state senator instead of Congress, a race he would win. Those who filed for the office were state senator W. C. Graves; Bill Burrow, a lawyer and veteran; and Preston Pope Reynolds, a lawyer and minister. The favorite of the Dallas business leaders, attorney J. Frank Wilson, had not yet filed. Wilson, who had lost to Sumners in 1944, was the more moderate of the two. In 1942 he had served as president of the Dallas Bar Association, and he was past chairman of the Dallas County Democratic Convention. Hughes, it was readily apparent, was too liberal for business tastes. The businessmen met quietly and pledged a campaign chest as encouragement for Wilson. Thus supported, the man who had spoken up for Hughes during her quest to receive Senate confirmation as a judge and who had tried a divorce case before her on her first day on the bench, paid his filing fee.[49]

Hughes, responding to this behind-scenes maneuvering, issued a statement that further set her at odds with Dallas's most influential businessmen, conservative Democrats known to be an unusually powerful force in the community. The businessmen's political action committee had met, she said, because they realized she was the "people's candidate." They wanted a candidate of their own, choosing who would answer to them. "In their desperation" to defeat her, she said, they had anointed a man who would "go all out for them." Control by pressure groups of business, Hughes emphasized, was as detrimental to Congress as control by a pressure group of labor. "This must be a government for the people and by the people, and all thinking men and women will so agree," she said. "Special interest representation and legislation must cease. I am confident that the people of Dallas will not stand for control of the Dallas Congressman by the PAC of labor or of business."[50]

Hughes unmistakably was the candidate of liberalism. Her bombastic speech at the United Auto Workers picnic at Kidd Springs had left no question about that, if indeed there ever had been one. Her friendly relations with organized labor further opened her to attacks from her conservative opponents. "Any candidate who is backed by an organization such as the Political Action Committee of the CIO must be looked upon with suspicion," Senator Graves, one opponent, commented. "All candidates with Socialistic and Communistic leanings must be defeated," he added, making a potentially devastating allusion she would have to deal with.[51]

Another conservative opponent, the Baptist minister-lawyer Reynolds, was vituperative in castigating Hughes. His scathing remarks, Hughes believed, injected into the campaign a bitterness that had not previously been there.[52]

The Southern Democratic Club, whose conservative members largely were made up of Texas Regulars who had defected from Roosevelt in 1944, sent Judge Hughes a questionnaire and asked her pointblank if she was a "so-called liberal." Yes, she responded, she was a liberal in the sense of being one who advocates progress. Had she supported Roosevelt in all four presidential elections? Yes, she replied, and she had made speeches on his behalf every time. Would she "resist the continuous activity of the federal bureaucracies to take over the functions of the state government"? She replied, "My answer is that depends on whether the local and state governments assume their full responsibility." If not, then the federal government must step in, she said.[53]

Hughes was fearful of veering so far to the left that she would alienate many voters, and in one of her regular campaign advertisements she criticized "unprincipled labor leaders like John L. Lewis," who threatened to get strangleholds on the nation's economy unless curtailed. (Lewis, head of the United Mine Workers, recently had led a devastating forty-five-day coal strike that threatened the postwar economic recovery and infuriated Truman.) "Too long we have talked of the rights of labor and the rights of management. It is time to consider the rights of the public," she said. "I will not go against my convictions to get votes from either management or labor."[54]

One litmus test for candidates was how they stood on extending price controls imposed by the government during the war. The authority of the regulating agency, the Office of Price Administration, was to expire on June 30. President Truman saw the battle against inflation as an important priority in the postwar period, and he urged voters of similar opinion to make their feelings known to Congress so that new legislation could provide a mechanism for holding down prices. Many in Dallas, especially the leading businessmen, were eager for an end to controls so that market forces could dictate prices. Hughes and Stanley Marcus of the exclusive Neiman-Marcus store, both Truman supporters, decided to join forces in support of the president and call a mass meeting of Dallas citizens to demand that Congress enact a tough price-control bill. In early July 1946, some four hundred citizens responded to their call and met at the Automobile Building at Fair Park to hear speeches and to show their support for federal price controls. At that meeting, Marcus vowed that with or without the OPA, his firm would hold its prices. Truman soon could claim a minor victory. On July 25 he signed a watered-down bill—not nearly as broad as he had desired—extending price controls for another year.[55]

The continuing charges that she was a captive of the CIO, a lingering effect of her Labor Day speech, made Hughes feel she must deny it. Responding to a news article stating she had been assured CIO support, she said she had not asked for CIO support, nor did she want it, although she did welcome the support of individual members of labor as well as of management. She did not seek the endorsement of either as a group or that of any other group. "I will be absolutely free in Congress to vote my convictions and I do not wish even the semblance of favoring one group over another.[56] Years later, she acknowledged that while she did have some labor support during the campaign, labor unions were in such disfavor that to admit it would practically doom a candidate.[57]

In a campaign advertisement she declared, "I have not received and will not receive any amount of money from the CIO or any other group. That includes any Political Action Committee of Big Business, which, like various 'pressure-groups,' would like to have a Congressman they can dictate to." The only contributions to her campaign, she said, had been from individuals—one dollar and up—who believed in her integrity and ability to get things done. "For that reason my ads will be small, my radio programs few and short, I won't be able to hire stunts or other vaudeville entertainment."[58]

With the popularity of W. Lee "Pappy" O'Daniel and his hillbilly band, the Light Crust Dough Boys, still a happy memory in Texas, she occasionally did have entertainment at her campaign rallies. Her first campaign appearance in Mesquite was enlivened by the appearance of three teenage musicians—a vocalist and mandolin player, a steel guitar player, and a guitarist. This trio also played in at least one of her radio campaign reports.[59]

She billed herself in her campaign literature as the "Dynamo from Dallas." In a campaign folder she stated: "She never takes orders from political bosses, kings of the lobby, vested or unvested interests, but goes her way as a servant of ALL the people."[60] Her supporters included individuals such as the Reverend Robert Raible, pastor of the First Unitarian Church; Bishop Harry T. Moore, Episcopal Diocese of Dallas; and Mrs. John Hanna, former national YWCA president and former president of the Dallas Council of Church Women.[61]

When votes were counted in the July primary, Hughes held a very slight lead over Wilson, 19,820 to 18,512. A distant third was Burrow, with 8,930; followed by Graves, 6,218; and Reynolds, 2,268. As the *Dallas Morning News* summarized it, "Liberal little Sarah T. Hughes, who billed herself as 'the Dynamo from Dallas,' slugged her way to the top of a bitter contest for Congress Saturday night, and conservative Frank Wilson was just a step behind."[62]

Actually, the prognosis was not good for Hughes, and she recognized that immediately. A runoff was required, and it seemed certain Wilson would pick up most of the votes from the defeated conservative candidates. Hughes, as the only liberal in the race, had already captured that vote. She calculated that a primary victory with a margin of five thousand votes would be required if she were to win the runoff.[63]

With the stakes narrowed and the runoff a month away, the race suddenly became more bitter. Increasingly conservative, Wilson declared immediately that Hughes's alleged ties to the CIO Political Action Committee would be the primary issue, but soon he went several steps further. On the first Monday of the runoff campaign he summarized the race this way: "[It will be] the Communists and the CIO-PAC against the rest of the folks. I want to represent the rest of the folks." Wilson said he had no personal quarrel with Judge Hughes, but he did oppose the "ruthless, left-wing radicals who are supporting her in this race" and the bosses of the CIO's Political Action Committee who were "trying to dictate to the voters what kind of Congressman they should have." He charged that his opponent had never taken a stand against the Fair Employment Practices Commission, had never protested against federal attempts to interfere with state poll tax laws, had never mentioned her thoughts on segregation laws, and had not whispered a single word against socialized medicine. "She has, however, consistently praised the producer-consumer cooperatives which would destroy the small American businessman."[64]

Hatton W. Sumners, having not endorsed any candidate in the wide-open primary, now took his revenge. He declared himself in favor of Wilson, an announcement Hughes later would see as an important factor in the race.[65]

Hughes called herself "a real Democrat." The race, she said, would be "progression against reaction." Hers would be a modest runoff campaign, she said, because she didn't "have the support of the big-business PAC of Dallas." As to Wilson's allegation that the Communists wanted her to win, she said that Democrats standing for reforms had always been falsely labeled as Communists. "As to the charge that I am a Communist, I am not a Communist and never until this campaign have I been called one. It is interesting to note that many other Democrats have been called 'Red' in their day— Thomas Jefferson for his proposals for free education, Texas's great governor, Jim Hogg, for his proposal to create the Railroad Commission, Andrew Jackson, Cleveland, Woodrow Wilson." Frank Wilson was falsely portraying himself as a conservative, she said. "When he ran against Hatton Sumners in 1944 he didn't call himself that. . . . I cannot help but ask if this is the same man who now is calling himself a fighting conservative."[66]

As Wilson continued his criticisms that Hughes was the CIO candidate, a charge she continued to deny, an unexpected development suddenly brought help. Three local labor officials wrote a letter to Wilson and made it public. Wilson's complaints about Hughes's labor support were rendered hollow by the letter. It related how in his own 1944 race against Sumners, Wilson had accepted the secret backing of the CIO and the UAW-CIO at a meeting in his office. The support was to be "quiet, and not public, and above all there would be no endorsement." Now, the three labor officials said it was entirely unfair for Wilson to charge in such scurrilous tones that Hughes was the captive of union support. "Our purpose in writing you this letter, Mr. Wilson, is to put the record straight. The people of Dallas are entitled to know the truth, and should not be misled by false, malicious and unsupported statements."[67]

In his exaggerated rhetoric against Hughes as a liberal, Wilson had correctly assessed the political atmosphere that developed in postwar Dallas and would continue to hold sway far into the future—an unabashed conservatism. In this race Hughes was clearly the liberal—she said so—and Wilson the conservative. The result for Hughes in the August 24 runoff was her first loss ever in a political race. Wilson captured 61 percent of the Dallas County votes, won 102 of 122 precincts, and was elected as the representative of the 5th Congressional District by a count of 37,206 to 23,590, a margin of nearly 14,000 votes.[68] The 1946 elections also marked a change in national voting patterns—for the first time since the Depression, the Republicans carried both houses of Congress.

Hughes, years later, believed she should have been more cautious in her approach. "I guess I learned that I ought not to jump to conclusions. I ought to analyze the situation a little more than I did. But I wanted to run so much that I perhaps didn't find out what the true situation was in Dallas before I announced."[69]

After the election a news story from Washington, D.C., reported it an "open secret" that almost to a man the Texas congressional delegation had favored Wilson. "The conservative-minded Texans didn't care for Judge Hughes's liberal views, but the delegation's attitude toward her was based on one fact—she is a woman." The Texas delegation for years had met for lunch every other Wednesday in the dining room of the Speaker of the House. Not even wives could attend. The Texans preferred to keep it that way.[70]

Men, as usual, dominated this first general election of the postwar period, especially returning veterans from the war. Eager to participate in the democracy they had helped save, they were particularly successful in Dallas County. Voters replaced the female Pearl Smith as county clerk after four terms in office with a returning veteran, Bill Shaw. She, along with Hughes, had given female visibility at the courthouse, but now her former employee, Shaw, back from the army, was elected, beginning a thirty-four-year tenure as district clerk. Smoot Schmid, after seven terms in office as sheriff, lost to an inexperienced former Air Force sergeant, Steve Guthrie. A former major in the army, Will Wilson, won the office of Dallas County district attorney over several candidates, including Hughes's former law partner, Andrew J. Priest.

For the first time in Texas Democratic politics, a sharp rift appeared between liberals and conservatives, a distinction that would persist and grow sharper in coming years. The clearly defined liberal in the Democratic gubernatorial runoff, Homer P. Rainey, lost to the candidate backed by the party conservatives. Rainey had been dismissed in 1944 as president of the University of Texas by the Board of Regents after he had sought to defend professors sympathetic to the New Deal. In the 1946 campaign, espousing a liberal platform, he was attacked as a dangerous radical. Beauford H. Jester, railroad commissioner with moderate viewpoints, gained the support of the conservative, anti-Truman elements in the state party and defeated Rainey by a wide margin.

Disappointed at her loss, Sarah T. Hughes would not seek any office other than reelection to her judgeship for the next twelve years. The schism she felt between herself and the city's business-minded leaders widened; she would not forget their failure to support her in the campaign. Two years afterward she showed her displeasure when two of the city's most important and, as she described them, "dydamic"* leaders approached her and asked her to take on the chairmanship of a committee concerned with welfare. As the incident was related by a *Dallas Morning News* reporter, Hughes leveled her gaze upon them and said coldly, "Two years ago I asked you to help me, and you refused. Now you come asking my help. I'm turning you down. That makes us even, doesn't it? Good day." Then she turned and walked away, leaving them open-mouthed and flabbergasted.[71]

There were for her, though, plenty of other fish to fry. In November 1946, she prepared legislation for Representative-at-Large Preston P. Mangum to introduce on the first day of the 1947 session of the Texas Legislature a constitutional amendment to give women the right to serve on juries.

In conjunction with this legislation, Judge Hughes announced that an extensive campaign to acquaint newly elected members of the state legislature with the subject would begin shortly. Six times previously the legislature had voted down the proposition. Twice it had passed the House, and in 1945 it had failed to win Senate approval by only three votes. Texas now was one of only seventeen states not permitting women to sit on juries.[72]

"Any jury which is to be truly representative should have women on it,"

---

* "Dydamic" was a corruption of *dynamic*, made popular by prominent banker and civic leader Robert L. Thornton, a self-made man who had come from the cotton fields of Ellis County.

Hughes said. "The chief function of a jury is to determine the credibility of witnesses—whether or not they are telling the truth. Women can better tell when another woman is telling the truth about anything." The notion of women jurors had been endorsed by the B&PW, the American Association of University Women, the Congress of Parents and Teachers, and the American League of Women Voters.[73]

The "half-citizen" continued to be a favorite topic for her speeches. Sometimes Hughes would remind audiences that only three classes of people could not serve on Texas juries: criminals, lunatics, and women. More seriously she would sum up that for a jury to function it must represent a cross section of the community. Democracy flourished when the laundry woman and the banker joined with other members of a community to decide a case.[74]

Once again, though, the effort in 1947 to give this right to women failed. A new rationale based on economics rather than on the emotional state of women had emerged: it was argued that the expense of building new jury facilities for women was too much for the taxpayers to undertake.

Disappointment along the same lines also came through a development at Goucher College. Trustees in 1947 elected a man, Dr. Otto Frederick Kraushaar, to succeed another man, Dr. David Allan Robertson, as president. Goucher, an all-women's college, had never had a female president. Hughes, distraught, wrote a letter to the *AAUW Journal* to complain. "When I read in the Goucher Alumnae Quarterly that the new president was a male, I was completely deflated. That Goucher College itself has not graduated a woman qualified to head a woman's college is difficult to believe, but that there are none available in the United States is inconceivable." The emphasis at Goucher should be on giving opportunities to women, she argued, and if Goucher itself would not do so, there seemed little chance for other institutions to overcome prejudice and tradition and give recognition to women. If no woman could be found at the present time to serve as president, she said, the position should have been held open until one could be found.[75]

Despite her complaints in 1947 about Goucher, Hughes believed the institution would be a good college for her niece, Constance Tilghman, who was attending high school in Palm Springs, California. When the time arrived for Constance to select a college, Hughes suggested Southern Methodist University, in Dallas, as another possibility. She invited her to stay with her in Dallas for three weeks in the summer of 1947 prior to her high school senior year to get acquainted with the institution, which was not far from the Hugheses' home on Normandy Avenue. Constance decided to attend SMU, no doubt encouraged by her aunt's offer to live with her and George. She enrolled there in September 1948 and, except for summers, lived with her aunt and uncle through 1950. Constance's father, Richard Tilghman, was in the midst of his own distinguished career as a mechanical engineer with a specialty in steam boilers used on ships.[76]

Constance discovered life in the Hughes household to be quite lively. Always present was a treasured dog and frequently two. Hughes reported to her radio listeners in October 1945 a particular problem concerning Donnie, who spent nights in the backyard, but at 6 A.M. barked to be let inside the house. With clocks being set back for daylight savings time, though, 6 A.M. for Donnie had become 5 A.M. "Every morning at five—which was her old six o'clock, she rouses the house, and the neighbors, too, I'm afraid. If any of you have had the same problem and solved it, I certainly wish you would let me know. I am becoming somewhat desperate, as I don't want to get up at five," Hughes said.[77]

To help Constance make friends when she arrived, Judge Hughes held an open house. The primary guests were a group of Girl Scouts from high school for whom she was the leader. A sherbet and ginger ale punch was served, and Sarah was dismayed when she discovered George had enlivened its content by "spiking" it.[78]

Once when George suspected their long-time maid, Mattie Green, of secretly taking an occasional nip of his gin, he put a padlock on the liquor cabinet door. Mattie, angry, exacted her revenge. When she served the chicken stew that Sarah Hughes requested for dinner that night, it arrived in a large bowl with the bare skeleton of a chicken protruding. Mattie was called to the table for a quiet lecture from Sarah, and then Mattie took the dish back to the kitchen to prepare it properly.[79]

The Hugheses relied very much on Mattie, whom they considered to be a faithful and honest employee. They began paying Social Security for her as soon as it became available. When guests were expected, Sarah and Constance would join Mattie in cleaning the house. And when Mattie divorced—as she did several times—and remarried, it was always Judge Hughes who both saw to the divorce and then performed the next wedding ceremony.[80]

George continued to be a pillar of support, if not directly in the political arena, certainly in the household. When the price of a loaf of bread climbed to fourteen cents, he vowed to do something about it. He began baking bread each Saturday, creating a long-time hobby for himself and winning plaudits from his wife and friends with whom they frequently shared the bread.

George's prowess with baking bread earned him a nickname among employees at the Veterans Administration—"the Biscuitmaker." When George had difficulty finding dill pickles in the stores, he planted cucumber seeds in the family garden and successfully grew them as well as fruits, green beans, corn, okra, potatoes, and other vegetables. Sarah was an eager partner in his gardening endeavors, and they took pride in frequently putting their own home-grown vegetables on their table. Together, the couple took up square dancing, a nice complement to their now long-time hobby of horse-back riding. George Hughes was, Mrs. Hughes declared, "the best husband in the world."[81]

The Hugheses joined St. Matthew's Episcopal Cathedral in 1945. Sitting regularly in the third-row pew every Sunday morning, they were very visible. When in 1956 the church's thespian group, the Cathedral Players, produced "The Solid Gold Cadillac," George played a role as a board member of a corporation.[82]

In his own career at the Veterans Administration, it was George Hughes who was preeminent. Louise Raggio, a lawyer who would become a long-time friend and colleague of Sarah T. Hughes, recalled first meeting her at a picnic held by employees of the Veterans Administration at Flag Pole Hill at White Rock Lake. Raggio was there with her husband, Grier, a new attorney with the Veterans Administration. It was the summer of 1946, and Raggio was intrigued by the sight of a diminutive, energetic woman who was wearing shorts and anklets and very busily handing out cards to the picnickers. "Who's that?" she asked. "That's George's wife. She's running for Congress."[83]

7 ⁓

A National Perspective

er loss to J. Frank Wilson was a huge disappointment in Sarah T. Hughes's political life. She would have thrived in Congress—just as she had in the Texas Legislature—for in such a body her skills as a debater and strategist would have shone. As one of only half a dozen women in the House, she would have become, almost without a doubt, a nationally recognized figure. Her realization of this made the loss especially difficult. For as long as three years afterward, many of her acquaintances believed, the loss caused her to lose some of her customary zest for life.[1]

Wilson, far less engaging or imaginative as an individual than Hughes, would blend quietly into the congressional background during four terms in office, leaving little if any lasting impression of his years of service. Yet, given the landslide nature of his runoff victory in 1946, when voters had the clear choice between his conservatism and her liberalism, there seemed little or no reason for her to try to challenge him again in 1948 or in the years ahead. Dallas's political climate, hospitable to Hughes and her New Deal principles in the 1930s, was changing in this postwar climate. The need for big government, so evident in the Depression and war, seemed for many to be over. A conservative outlook reigned in the business-minded city, an outlook soon to evolve into distrust of federal government totally alien to Hughes's belief that the government should address and seek to ameliorate, if not solve, society's most pressing problems. Persuading Dallas voters to reelect her as a district judge every four years was one thing; winning office as a legislator charged with creating public law was another. Never again would Hughes seek congressional office, but despite any lingering disappointment from 1946, she would not lose her love of politics.

The hardening of lines between liberalism and conservatism, visible in Dallas and Texas in general, lay just ahead for the nation, too, as debates arose over Cold War politics and civil rights. The elections of 1948 in Texas and the nation would prove to be a case in point. The battle in Texas for the U.S.

Senate seat was especially noteworthy, for the incumbent, the once-popular radio announcer and hillbilly singer W. Lee "Pappy" O'Daniel, clearly would be defeated if he chose to run again. Realizing this, he declined to seek reelection. Two formidable challengers quickly emerged: Coke Stevenson, restless after two years away from the governor's office, and Lyndon Baines Johnson, the congressman who had become Franklin Delano Roosevelt's pet during the 1930s. The ensuing race between these two men from rural Texas would become legendary in the state's history, a race that ultimately changed the course of the nation's history.

Sarah T. Hughes knew one of the candidates, Stevenson, well. She had opposed him on many fronts in the legislature; she did not like him.[2] She had never met Lyndon Johnson, although fifteen years earlier she had felt warmly toward his young bride-to-be, Claudia Alta (Lady Bird) Taylor when they had lunch together in Austin. Even without knowing Johnson personally, his close ties to the New Deal and his loyalty as a Democrat were enough to win Hughes's approval. The facts that Johnson had warmly adopted the Lower Colorado River Authority as his project, that its champion Alvin Wirtz had become his mentor, and that its chief contractor, Brown & Root, was his financial supporter did not matter. That brief chapter in Hughes's political life when she opposed the river project was over. She supported Johnson with no hesitation. When an invitation came from Houston to go there and speak to several women's groups on his behalf—her only opportunity to travel out of the city for the campaign—she readily accepted.

She told a Houston reporter she had served four and a half years in the state legislature with Coke Stevenson, and the only speech she ever heard him make was in favor of taking public land away from the schoolchildren. That, she charged, was the only public stand he took in all those years, and his 1948 campaign against Johnson indicated that he had not changed. "What we need is a fearless young thinker who stands for preparedness, peace and progress." Lyndon Johnson, she believed, was that type of man.[3]

When the Democratic primary votes finally were counted, Johnson appeared to have beaten Stevenson by the scant margin of 87 out of 1 million votes cast. A furious legal battle ensued concerning possible voter fraud in South Texas, and it seemed possible Johnson's narrow victory might be overturned.

As Coke Stevenson's lawyers pressed hard to have a federal court throw out disputed and decisive ballots from Duval County, Johnson joined President Harry S. Truman on the Texas leg of his whistle-stop campaign, which would turn the tide in his reelection effort. Truman's uphill battle that year at first seemed destined to fail under the challenge of Thomas E. Dewey. Truman's campaign seemed to have a tone of desperation.

On this four-day September railroad trip to Texas, packed with twenty-four stops and twenty-five speeches, Truman and his entourage were late in arriving at Dallas's Rebel Stadium. Hughes was one of several local Democratic officials who spoke and filled time as the crowd waited. She modeled her impromptu talk on a radio speech she had heard her friend House Speaker Sam Rayburn deliver a few days earlier. His enthusiastic and well-ordered argument on behalf of Truman had made a deep impression on her. Truman already had made stops that day in Austin, Georgetown, Temple, Waco, Hillsboro, Fort Worth, and Grand Prairie before finally arriving in Dallas an hour late. His entourage included Texas governor Beauford Jester and Speaker Rayburn in addition to Lyndon Johnson. Hughes no doubt shook hands with Truman on the platform but had no chance to speak with him at any length. She had met Johnson briefly during his primary campaign when she spoke on his behalf on several occasions but had not become well-acquainted with him. Not until 1960 would she have an opportunity to come to know Johnson personally, although they would correspond frequently and amiably in the 1950s.[4]

Johnson, distressed over the still uncertain outcome of Stevenson's challenge to his narrow primary victory, had shocked White House aide Jonathan Daniels when he joined the Truman campaign train the previous day in San Antonio. He came aboard, Daniels later recalled, "looking like the damnedest tramp I ever saw in my life," not having shaved for at least two days and appearing to be "sick as hell." Truman, on the other hand, was picking up energy on this brief Texas whistle-stop campaign. The enthusiastic crowds buoyed him as he sought desperately to win Texas's twenty-three electoral votes.[5]

His Dallas speech signaled the beginning for Truman of a harsher level of attacks against the Republicans and the GOP-dominated "do-nothing" Congress. The GOP, he charged, was a party "run by the wealthy for the wealthy." At stake in the election, he said, were issues that went to the core of American life. Republicans wanted not unity but surrender, "and I am here to tell you people that I will not surrender." The battle before him, he said, was the toughest political fight in the history of the Democratic Party.[6]

Republicans seemed startled by this harshness. Herbert Brownell Jr.,

Thomas E. Dewey's campaign manager, responded immediately. Truman's talk in Dallas, Brownell said, reached "depths of bitterness which are unusual in American political campaigns." The president in effect endorsed "lynch law" against the Republicans, Brownell said.[7]

The Democratic Party itself was experiencing a split between southern Democrats and liberals in this election year. Many southerners were incensed at Truman's stand earlier in the year in favor of civil rights. He had urged, among other changes, an end to Jim Crow laws in interstate transportation, elimination of the poll tax, and a federal antilynching law. Dallas, as was the case throughout the South, maintained strict segregation in its school system, in its public transportation, in its hotels and restaurants, and its housing patterns. Yet, perhaps in deference to Truman's stated beliefs, the city's usual segregationist policies were dropped for his appearance at Rebel Stadium. African Americans, who constituted about 30 percent of the audience, mingled with whites throughout the stadium and on temporary seats on the playing field. Both blacks and whites enthusiastically cheered the president with one voice.

For Hughes, this exciting day was her closest involvement yet in a presidential campaign. Truman was only the fourth president ever to have visited Dallas. For both Truman and Johnson, good days lay just ahead. A federal court soon ordered Johnson's name to be placed on the ballot for the November 1948 general election, assuring him of a victory in a one-party state. Truman, continuing to pick up support as he blasted away at Republicans, surprised the nation's most sophisticated pollsters by upsetting Dewey and claiming the presidency for a full term, carrying Texas in the process. The effect of both of these victories in Texas was to create an even sharper divide between the conservative and liberal wings of the Democratic Party.

Truman's surprise victory was manifested just afterward in a humorous incident occurring in Judge Hughes's courtroom during her weekly docket call. One of the city's most colorful lawyers, George H. (Bud) Crane, showed up wearing his customary bib overalls but with an astonishing new addition— a miner's cap with a light on the front. Crane, as thorough a Democrat as Hughes was, began to crawl back and forth under the counsel tables in the crowded courtroom. When Judge Hughes reacted to the laughter and finally saw him on his hands and knees, she asked him what he possibly could be doing. Crane replied in his loud and distinctively nasal voice: "I'm looking for a Republican, Judge."[8]

Hughes's feet were planted firmly in the liberal wing. She described herself at the time as one who "embraces the most liberal ideals of the Democratic Party, ardent admirer and avid supporter of Franklin D. Roosevelt, and classes herself as a 'New Deal Liberal.'"[9]

Politics aside, plenty of work remained for Sarah T. Hughes in the area to which she already had devoted so much of her life—women's rights. Her involvement in the Business and Professional Women's Clubs grew even deeper as she progressed from local to state and now to a national level of leadership. In July 1948, she was elected to a two-year term as first vice president of the National Federation when it held its biennial convention in Fort Worth. If all went well, in 1950 she would become president.[10]

The *Christian Science Monitor* profiled the new first vice president as she appeared at the convention, describing her apparel in a manner that later would raise the hackles of progressive women, who pointed out that similar stories about men did not include such details. In fact, though, Hughes's striking appearance on the day of the interview did attract attention. She was dressed in a riding outfit, perhaps deliberately to reinforce visitors' notions of what Texans were expected to look like. She wore "a picturesque broad brimmed hat with a leather strap under her chin, plaid shirt, her bright tie caught with a pin in a Texas Longhorn design, and trim riding breeches."[11]

She had a serious message for the reporter who interviewed her, though. She emphatically urged him to "please say we don't have women jurors in this State, and we should have." The effort to include women as jurors in Texas, she said, would be one of the major projects for the B&PW in the coming year.[12]

Texas remained one of a dwindling number of states—only eleven—continuing to exclude women from jury service. Of Judge Hughes's many concerns about inequalities based on gender, exclusion from jury service was the one she would speak longest and most often about during her career. Her commitment—aside from early legislation she had introduced in Austin, which she declared to have been a mistake—was not to gain special privileges for women but to have them treated as equal to men. This in her mind entailed obligations as well as privileges, a conviction that soon would lead her to contend that women should serve in the military as equal to men in all capacities.

Opinion in Texas seemed slowly to be changing in favor of having women as jurors. When the Texas Legislature convened in early 1949, Hughes was hopeful as she pushed once more for a constitutional amendment. Two Dallas lawmakers, Senator Fred (Red) Harris and Representative Preston Mangum, successfully engineered through both houses the required resolution for a statewide vote. Governor Beauford Jester favored it, too, and he signed the legislation calling for voter approval. The proposed amendment was one of ten to be submitted to the voters on November 8, 1949. Before the election could occur Governor Jester died, but his successor, the far more conservative Allan Shivers, also favored the amendment. A favorable outcome at last seemed likely, and Hughes was receiving much of the credit. News accounts noted that Judge Hughes had pushed the idea from its start in 1935.[13]

As usual, she traveled across the state, speaking and mobilizing women in support of the amendment. In an October speech in Brownwood, before the combined membership of the local B&PW, AAUW, and Delta Kappa Gamma, she outlined a strategy for getting the amendment passed. First, members should publicize her talk as much as possible. Second, they should arrange for radio talks by judges or lawyers who favored the amendment, or they should prepare skits for radio appearances. Third, they could obtain a list of all first voters at the courthouse and send cards to them promoting the amendment. Fourth, on the day before the election, they should place advertisements in the newspapers.[14]

"I think it would be tragic if we were unsuccessful," she said. "I would like to be able to go on to something else. I would just have to have to start over again, but until we can get this over we have to keep on. Not in our lifetime will there be full equality for women."[15]

She placed in a number of newspapers her own advertisement in the format of a letter to the voters. In it she made a personal appeal for voters to approve the amendment so that Texas women could join those in thirty-seven other states where they served on juries. She cited all the arguments she had repeated now for so many years: women make good jurors, women receive the benefits of government and should share in the responsibilities of citizenship, juries rarely are kept overnight and never in civil cases, and women with young children would be excused. She signed the advertisement with her signature.[16]

Dallas Morning News writer Ken Hand devoted a long column to Hughes's crusade. He repeated her comment that in Texas "only lunatics, criminals, the feeble-minded—and women—are excluded from jury service." Even Negroes, he said, had been given the right to serve on juries.[17]

Once again, though, on November 8, 1949, Texas voters rejected the proposed amendment, this time by a margin of 54 percent of the 285,000 ballots cast. They also declined to abolish the poll tax and turned down pay raises for legislators. In all, they passed only two of the proposed ten amendments—one related to district judges serving more than one county and the other permitting the establishment of rural fire prevention districts.[18]

Jury service for women in Texas would continue to be a priority for Sarah T. Hughes. The longer the wait, the more pressing it became. But in these years she was beginning to pay more and more attention to national and even international affairs. Her position as first vice president of the National Federation of Business and Professional Women, as well as her work for the American Association of University Women, prompted her to begin to concentrate on the Equal Rights Amendment. First proposed in 1923 by the National Women's Party, it had been opposed by most other women's organizations whose goals were directed more toward protective legislation than removal of barriers. Since the amendment's introduction, Congress often had considered the measure, but it had languished in various subcommittees. In postwar America, following an era when most protectionist laws for women had been suspended because of labor shortages, possibilities for passage had improved.

In August 1949, Hughes sent letters to the new senator from Texas, Lyndon B. Johnson, and to the senior senator, Tom Connally, urging their support of the amendment. "As you probably know, I have long been interested in the status of women and in removing all legal discriminations against them," she wrote to Johnson. "There are, at this time, many discriminations against women in the laws of the various states. The most effective way of wiping them out is by Constitutional amendment, and I hope very much that you can see your way clear to vote in favor of submitting the amendment to the states for their action."[19]

Johnson soon voted with a two-thirds majority favoring the Senate version of the amendment, but it had been watered down by a rider offered by Senator Carl Hayden of Arizona. Hughes thanked Johnson for his vote but diplomatically explained her objections to the version that had passed. Hayden's rider, adopted by a vote of fifty-one to thirty-one, provided that the proposed constitutional amendment would not "impair any right, benefits, or exemptions now or hereafter conferred by law upon persons of the female sex." The effect of this deferential bow to women, Judge Hughes advised Johnson, was to confuse the meaning of the resolution. "For example," she wrote, "jury service is an 'exemption' conferred by law and this would not be affected by the adoption of the resolution." She wanted the Senate to reconsider the resolution, and she expressed her hope that Johnson would use his "efforts to see that it is submitted as it was introduced and particularly without amendments which would tend to confuse the meaning."[20]

Passage of the ERA—a complicated issue with layers and layers of cultural baggage—now joined jury service for women as a priority for Hughes. Although she still did not know Senator Johnson on a personal basis, her regular correspondence with him in the early 1950s on the subject of the ERA soon had them addressing their letters to one another as Lyndon and Sarah. There would be plenty of time to exchange letters on the subject, for not until 1972 would both houses of Congress pass and submit the proposed amendment to the states for ratification.

Another issue during these years, far larger in the public's mind, was the Cold War. A general fear existed that an outbreak of hostilities in this nuclear age would mean the end of civilization. Avoiding this awful possibility occupied the minds of many. It seemed apparent that something stronger than the new United Nations would be needed to end conflicts between nations and alliances. Thus, a movement sprang up to create a world federal government in which a single international authority would supersede national sovereignties. In the United States the most prominent of these organizations was the United World Federalists, Inc.

By April 1947, the Dallas chapter of the United World Federalists was reported already to have seven hundred members and to be rapidly growing. Among the liberal-minded people of Dallas who joined were Sarah and George Hughes. Sarah became a member of the board of directors for the Dallas chapter. Even the normally passive George Hughes, a World War I veteran, urged an American Legion chapter in Dallas to pass a resolution in favor of the United World Federalists.[21]

Judge Hughes represented these viewpoints on behalf of the United World Federalists in a panel discussion at Southern Methodist University in March 1948, on the question "Can the United Nations survive? Is it the way of peace?" In her opinion, the United Nations, although certainly a step in the right direction, was inadequate to the task. For it to succeed, the organization would need a police force and the ability to make decisions on a majority basis. "It cannot be effective unless it is strengthened," she said.[22]

Two months later, in a commencement speech to the girls of the exclusive Hockaday School in Dallas, Hughes elaborated on her viewpoints. She told the graduates that the nation "must discard the policies of preventive war" and seek the establishment of a "world federation, based on law, with courts to interpret and police to enforce the law." This did not mean relinquishing anything the nation already had. "National sovereignty, which it is contended we would be giving up, is a myth," she said. "Will anyone argue that the U.S. Congress decided on war with Japan? Was it not rather the Japanese war lords who picked Pearl Harbor as the time and place to strike?"[23]

Security among the people of nations, she emphasized, will come only when the sovereignty of the *people* stands above that of the nations. "The shape of this world government is clear. It would have a legislative body to make the laws, courts to decide the disputes and a world police to enforce the law." The alternative to world federation, she said, "is destruction, chaos and the end of civilization as we know it."[24]

Military preparedness in the United States could have its usefulness for Judge Hughes, although this usefulness emerged in an unconventional way. While presiding over juvenile court in September 1948, she encountered a sixteen-year-old youth who was a chronic traffic violator. He had been cited for twenty violations. In looking for a way to rehabilitate him, she gave him two directives. First, she forbade him to drive for the following year. Next, since he would become seventeen the next month, she ordered him to join any branch of the armed forces within sixty days or face further consequences from her.[25]

In November 1949, Goucher College named Hughes one of its fifty best-known graduates. A few months later in June 1950, the college awarded her an honorary doctorate, presenting it in an outdoor graduation ceremony with anthropologist Margaret Mead as the principal speaker. Also honored with a doctorate was a fellow Goucher alumnus, the actress Mildred Dunnock, then starring in Arthur Miller's Broadway success *Death of a Salesman*. Goucher president Otto Kraushaar, whose appointment two years earlier had so distressed Hughes because she had wanted a woman in the presidency, made the presentation. "Just and skillful judge, crusader for humane causes, reformer of the penal institutions of the State of Texas, relentless fighter for the underprivileged, your liberal ideals, unquenchable spirit and signal achievements are a challenge and inspiration to men and women everywhere," he said.[26]

Two months before receiving her honorary degree, Hughes was heartened by President Truman's appointment of the nation's first female U.S. district judge, Burnita Shelton Matthews of Washington, D.C. Matthews's career was remarkably parallel to that of Hughes. Born in Mississippi in 1894, Matthews migrated to the nation's capital and studied law at George Washington University Law School just ahead of Hughes, taking evening classes while working days at the Veterans Administration. During her law school studies she picketed the White House on Sundays on behalf of women's suffrage, a time when Hughes as a policewoman occasionally monitored the picketing. Matthews passed her bar examination in Washington, D.C., in 1920 and entered private practice. Throughout her career she was a dedicated feminist who worked to eradicate protective rights from legislation related to women. Her special mission, however, was in gaining jury service for women, and her work was instrumental in securing that right in federal courts by act of Congress in 1937. She was married but had no children, concentrating instead on her career. Democratic Party faithful India Edwards, who soon would be pushing Hughes for federal appointment, had recommended Matthews to President Truman.

In another pleasing development, President Truman recently had named Hughes's political friend former governor James V. Allred to be U.S. district judge for the South Texas area. (Allred's sister-in-law, Bessie Allred, was Hughes's court reporter.) Encouraged by the appointments of both Matthews and Allred, Hughes decided to do some politicking on her own behalf. Her goal was to receive her own presidential appointment as a U.S. district judge. The two federal judges in Dallas were aging, and their retirement seemed imminent. Judge William Hawley Atwell, a Republican who had been appointed by President Warren G. Harding in 1923 and who Hughes had visited when she first moved to Dallas, was eighty-one. Judge T. Whitfield Davidson, appointed by President Franklin D. Roosevelt in 1936, was seventy-three. While she was in the area to receive her honorary degree from Goucher, Hughes made a series of calls to promote her own candidacy to replace either of these men if one of them retired. The *Daily Times Herald*'s

Washington-based reporter learned of her efforts. With few details and some exaggeration as to the possibility of Hughes's appointment, he wrote, "For the first time in history a woman is a leading candidate for a federal judgeship in Texas." The reporter observed that Hughes had the support of India Edwards, head of the Democratic Party's women's activities. Hughes, it was noted, had been an energetic fighter for giving women important jobs in government.[27]

Two days later, under the *Times Herald's* headline "Hughes Silent on Judgeship," she expressed surprise that the story had appeared. But she would make no further comment "since there is no vacancy at the present time."[28] As it happened, no vacancies were imminent. Atwell would not retire until 1954 at the age of eighty-four, and Davidson would wait until 1965 to retire, by then he would be the oldest federal judge in the nation, at eighty-nine.

On June 25, 1950, Communist North Korea surprised the world by launching a sudden military invasion of democratic South Korea with apparent intentions to overrun the country. President Truman quickly authorized United States military forces under United Nations authority to repel the invasion, using ground troops, a naval blockade of the Korean coast, and air strikes as necessary. The Cold War suddenly had turned hot, and no one could be certain what the ultimate result would be. One week after the invasion and on the eve of the biennial meeting of the National Federation of Business and Professional Women's Clubs, the organization's executive committee, including Hughes, passed a resolution commending Truman for his quick response to the situation in Korea.

With the Korean conflict very much on their minds, 2,545 women registered in San Francisco for the biennial convention of the National Federation of Business and Professional Women. The women, the largest number ever to attend a B&PW convention, heard California governor Earl Warren welcome them at their first session, and he was followed by a response from the B&PW first vice president, Sarah T. Hughes.

As first vice president, Hughes was the sole nominee to assume the presidency. With her long history of local, state, and national leadership roles in the B&PW, she was well prepared to lead a powerful organization now numbering some 160,000 members affiliated with 2,700 clubs throughout the nation and in Hawaii and Alaska.

What was expected to be a routine accession to the office was interrupted by a sudden flare-up, however. Critical comments began to circulate about Hughes's membership in the United World Federalists. Members in some chapters, particularly from the Los Angeles district, saw this as cause to object to her elevation to the presidency. In this era of the Red Scare and so soon after the invasion of South Korea by Communist North Korea, some viewed the world federation movement as part of a subversive communist plot. Hughes's position on the board of directors of the Dallas chapter of the United World Federalists, they charged, had been deliberately kept secret to avoid possible controversy.[29]

Judge Hughes did not deny her belief in world government. "The people in Dallas know that I'm a United World Federalist, but they know it has nothing to do with my objectives," she said. "I grew up with B&PW. I know its objectives and I believe in it. The leaders of this federation can do nothing unless you have confidence in us." Although the movement to deprive her of the presidency had little chance of success, concern about her membership in an organization that was committed to something less than absolute American sovereignty resulted in a short-lived and futile movement to impose a "little loyalty oath" on all candidates for National Federation offices. Hughes and her supporters, forced to respond, obtained a statement from the attorney general's office declaring that the United World Federalist organization was not on a list of subversive organizations. Although unopposed in the election, Hughes received only 871 of the potential 1,315 votes. If she had not already been nominated for the presidency, she believed, her candidacy would have failed because of the controversy.[30]

With the United Nations assuming its active role in the Korean "police action" and with the world federalist movement losing its momentum, Hughes was in the process of switching her primary allegiances. She became an ardent booster of the United Nations; her interest in world federation withered away.

In her San Francisco B&PW acceptance speech, widely reported in the nation's newspapers, Hughes declared the Korean events to be the nation's most serious crisis in five years. Truman's quick action in Korea, she believed in agreement with the National Federation's executive committee, had been what was necessary at this critical time. The United Nations, not armed with sufficient authority in the view of world federalists, now faced its severest test, she said. "The situation calls for all the resources of women as well as men. It offers us our greatest challenge. . . . Let us accept the challenge of the times. Let us take up the responsibilities that will be ours in the crucial days ahead and press forward in order that we may demonstrate that now, as always, women can indeed be a force in history."[31]

In an interview afterward with the *Christian Science Monitor,* she said that women, if united, could be a greater force in directing human events than they ever had been. She expressed hope that B&PW members and women in general would become steadily more cognizant of their responsibility for taking an active part in government. "Women should vote, attach themselves to the party of their choice, go into precinct meetings, and run for office."[32]

Thus began a fast-paced, challenging, and rewarding two-year term as president of the organization, which would see her travel all over the country as well as to London and The Hague to represent the National Federation at international meetings. The organization, now thirty-one years old, was unusually well established. It was, the *San Francisco Examiner* declared, "perhaps the most articulate of the organized groups of American women."[33] Certainly its leadership constituted the cream of American business and professional women, replete with lawyers, accountants, business executives, physicians, and the like. Its membership rolls across the nation, though, reflected a broad range of female workers; almost half of its members were clerical workers attracted to the organization because of its emphasis on career development.

Executive offices for the National Federation of Business and Professional Women's Clubs, Inc., were at 1819 Broadway in New York City, where a staff of more than a dozen, headed by an executive director, worked on a wide range of affairs. Three were assigned to the organization's slick, well-edited magazine, *Independent Woman,* which carried B&PW news and articles of interest to women. A full-time lobbyist resided and worked in Washington, D.C., with the title of director of legislation and capital representative. Another member of the staff was the director of international relations and observer at the United Nations. A huge hierarchy of volunteer leaders stayed busy across the nation. There were six hard-working standing committees, B&PW chairpersons for six national regions, and presidents for every state organization. And of course, the 160,000 members throughout the nation represented a powerful army of women interested in advancing B&PW causes such as the Equal Rights Amendment and jury service for women. The standing committees, to which paid staff members were specifically assigned, indicated the breadth of interests for the organization: Public Affairs, International Relations, Health and Safety, Education and Vocations, Membership, and Program Coordination.

Serving as national officers with Judge Hughes were women from a broad geographical spectrum. First vice president Helen G. Irwin was from Des Moines; second vice president Marguerite Rawalt, from Washington, D.C.; third vice president Elaine C. Barnes, from Tulsa; treasurer Anita Calhoun, from New York City; and recording secretary Eunice Hennessy, from San Francisco. These women, all on the executive committee, met every two months at major cities such as New York, Washington, Chicago, and Boston.

Three weeks after taking office, Hughes made her first visit to Europe. She flew to London with five other B&PW delegates to attend the fifth congress of the international B&PW. The women enjoyed a huge banquet in the historic Guildhall, a prominent landmark in London since 1440. It was said to be the first time ever that the government building had been opened to a women's organization.[34]

While in England, Hughes took time to pursue a recent interest—genealogy. Accompanied by her fellow American B&PW delegates, she went to Snodland, a short train ride southeast of London, in Kent County. It was a small town described by a relative as the one-time seat of the Tilghman family. Sure enough, she saw there the Tilghman coat of arms in the church floor and found entries related to the family in the parish register. The church vicar served tea and cake to the women. No Tilghmans lived in the area any longer, but it was from here that Hughes's ancestor Dr. Richard Tilghman had come to America in 1660, settling on a thousand-acre site named Canterbury Manor, granted to him the previous year by Lord Baltimore. He acquired other property in Maryland, some eighty-two hundred acres in Talbot County alone. His descendants—many of them illustrious, such as George Washington's aide Tench Tilghman—would continue to live in Maryland for many generations to come, leading up to Sarah Tilghman Hughes.[35]

Life was moving unusually fast these days. Just after her return from England, Sarah and George took their annual summer vacation at the Billy Wills ranch near Creede, Colorado, where they fished in streams, square danced, and rode horses along mountain trails. However, their idyllic days there, away from the limelight, were interrupted by an unexpected telephone call from India Edwards, vice chairman of the Democratic National Committee. Edwards had important news. A prestigious federal appointment awaited Hughes.

If she would agree, President Truman was ready to appoint her to the Federal Trade Commission, the powerful five-member body charged with examining unfair trade practices in commerce. Appointments were for seven-year terms. No more than three of the five commissioners could be members of the same political party. The job paid $15,000, a considerable boost over the $10,900 Hughes was earning as a state judge. Edwards not only had recommended Hughes's appointment, she already had cleared it all the way from state Democratic leaders to Congressman J. Frank Wilson to Senators Lyndon B. Johnson and Tom Connally. The only obstacle remaining was Hughes's own permission for the president to place her name in nomination. If she accepted and won Senate confirmation, as expected, she would be only the second woman in history to be appointed to a federal commission, following Federal Communications Commission member Frieda Hennock.[36]

India Edwards urgently emphasized to Hughes the importance of this appointment. The agency was the federal government's principal protector of the consumer, an especially vital function because women did most of the buying for their families. Yet, there had never been a female representative on the FTC.[37]

"I am delighted to get the news," Hughes told the *Daily Times Herald* upon her return from Colorado. "When I receive official notice of the offer, I'll certainly give it serious consideration." One news story said there was little doubt that she would accept the appointment.[38]

She had some personal misgivings to overcome, though. The term being offered was not a full one. She would replace the late Ewin Davis, who had died in office, and her term would expire in 1953 just after the inauguration of a new president. Hughes was now fifty-four years old, and if she took the position she would lose certain state retirement benefits accruing to her as a state judge. Moreover, she believed there was still the possibility of a federal judgeship, declared by the *Times Herald* to be a known ambition of hers.[39]

Even so, Judge Hughes appeared to be leaning toward accepting the appointment. The *Times Herald* reported on September 18 that her nomination was expected within two or three days. Talk circulated openly around the courthouse about who would replace her in the 14th District Court. A spokesman for Governor Allan Shivers said he likely would ask for recommendations from the Dallas Bar Association. President Truman made no personal comment about the pending appointment, although one of his secretaries, Donald Dawson, told the press, "President Truman considers Judge Hughes a fine woman and thinks most highly of her." Finally, just over a week after the news first had broken about the possible new job, Hughes called India Edwards to inform her she did not want the appointment after all. The call, according to one account, was a "last-minute reconsidered decision." The shortness of the term was a deciding factor, but later Judge Hughes would say in an interview that her contacts with federal agencies had been such that she "wouldn't want to be a member of any one of them."[40]

Little more than a week later she was in the national headlines again, this time while she was in Washington, D.C., where it was beginning to seem she was a weekend commuter. During this period of extreme tension in the Korean conflict following the daring Inchon landing behind enemy lines, she took the bold step of advocating that women be drafted into the military on the same basis as men. She made her comments on a network television show, NBC's *American Forum of the Air*, in a debate with Norman Thomas, the perennial socialist candidate for president. In what was described as a fiery argument, she reasoned that war is total, and women should bear arms and be used for any kind of duty for which they were qualified. This included combat. As an interesting sidebar, she pointed out that one of the beneficial results of drafting women would be to permit more fathers to remain at home to look after their children, thus preventing the breakup of as many homes as had occurred during the last war.[41]

The television appearance coincided with her visit to Washington as the featured speaker on October 6 at a strategy committee meeting, called chiefly by the National Federation of B&PW, for women's organizations to plan for full partnership of members in all phases of civil defense and economic and military mobilization. The result of the meeting was the establishment of the Assembly of Women's Organizations for National Security, consisting of the membership of twelve women's organizations.[42]

In her keynote speech Hughes told the women that the most immediate need of the country was to build a strong defense. "Men are being drafted; so, too, should women. As citizens they should share with men the responsibility of defending their country."[43]

The novelty of Hughes's belief in drafting women brought her widespread national news coverage. She was invited to make other national media appearances to discuss the issue on such radio shows as CBS's *The People's Platform* and *We, the People*. With the money given her for appearing on *We, the People*, she established the World Fellowship Fund for the National Federation of B&PW to give financial aid to women from other countries coming to the United States seeking to advance themselves professionally. She invited women from all B&PW Clubs to join her in building up the fund.[44]

Although she had spoken on the need for drafting women within the context of her presidency of the National Federation of the B&PW Clubs, her position had not been sanctioned by the organization. The topic seemed especially pertinent to her, though, and in the April 1951 issue of *Independent Woman* she wrote a column entitled "Women Should Be Drafted" and asked state organizations to consider the matter at their state conventions so the National Federation could take a legitimate official position. In her message, given at a time when United Nations forces in Korea, under General Douglas A. MacArthur, were suffering heavy casualties from Red Chinese forces, she listed for the membership her reasons for supporting the drafting of women.[45]

First, she said, there were practical reasons. A critical need existed for every phase of the national defense program, and there simply were not enough men to meet the requirements. Census figures, she wrote, showed a million fewer young men between the ages of eighteen and twenty-five than there had been in 1941.

Philosophically, she saw no justification for requiring men to serve while permitting women the luxury of deciding for themselves whether or not they should serve. Her reasoning was an extension of her argument for women to serve on juries—women had the rights of citizenship and they should share its responsibilities as well. "It must be a frustrating experience for young women to be told that their brothers' services are needed, but their country can get along very well without them," she wrote. Of course, they could be used as a supplement or auxiliary, but this was hardly adequate. "They know that a supplement or auxiliary is not a full partner. How much better it would be to tell them that they and their brothers will do the job together in the capacities for which they are best fitted."[46]

Hughes's opinions had placed her far in front of the views of most women, and they provided an interesting contrast with her own pacifist views of the late 1930s. Editorials appearing in newspapers invariably opposed her stance, as did people informally surveyed on the street by reporters. "Women should stand for peace," said the dean of women at Southern Methodist University, Lide Spraggins. "There is much that they can do in civilian life, but war in any form has always been disastrous for women."[47]

The subject was explosive, *Independent Woman* observed. It was surrounded by "emotional charges, inaccurate information, social prejudice and political implications." But the organization's board of directors passed a resolution at its July 1951 meeting in Chicago favoring Hughes's position by the unanimous vote of seventy to zero. Drafting both men and women was "more democratic and effective than voluntary enlistment," the resolution declared. It urged federal legislation to provide for the registration of women under the Selective Service Act in a manner similar to that required for men and the drafting of women for military service when it "may be advisable in the interests of humanity."[48]

The intent of the resolution was not to harm family life by taking mothers away from their homes, but rather to strengthen the home by permitting more fathers to stay there. This would be achieved through the proposition that women *without* domestic obligations should be required to serve their country *before* married men and fathers were called to duty. By using more women, military service among men with family responsibilities could be delayed. Thus, home life and the security of children would be enhanced.[49]

While the B&PW's resolutions did not achieve the recommended change in law, in November 1951 the organization was called upon to help recruit seventy-two thousand additional women into the various women's branches of service. Hughes represented the B&PW along with the presidents of the General Federation of Women's Clubs and the American Association of University Women in planning the drive under the auspices of Assistant Secretary of Defense Anna Rosenberg. At the time, just forty-two thousand women were in uniform. In a message to B&PW members, Hughes called upon them to "take the lead in this important work—call the presidents of the larger women's clubs in your community, and lay your plans for accomplishing this important job."[50]

Her goal in these efforts—the achievement of world peace—was no different from what it had been in the late 1930s, when she criticized military training programs in high school as a form of war mongering. She summed up her attitude in a Christmas message to B&PW members in 1951. "Every morning before I go to work," she wrote, "I listen to the Breakfast Club over the American Broadcasting Company network, and I hear Don McNeil [the host] say, 'And now it is prayer time around the breakfast table. For a world united in peace, bow our heads and let us pray.' Those who earnestly join in that prayer each day will come to the belief that war is not inevitable and that eventually we can have peace on earth."[51]

Substantive issues such as the draft were always discussed at the bimonthly National Federation executive committee meetings. Typical was the March 31-April 1, 1951, meeting at the Lexington Hotel in New York City. Several resolutions were passed. One was addressed to the Commission on the Status of Women, soon to assemble for its fifth annual session.[52] It urged the commission to "go forward in its work of securing for women full and equal suffrage, equality before the law, equal pay for equal work, and opportunity for full participation in the public life of each country." Another resolution reaffirmed the National Federation's belief that the best hope for promoting peace was to strengthen the United Nations. Still another resolution passed at the meeting urged the building up of "backward and needful areas of the world through technical assistance and economic development," and it praised the work of Nelson Rockefeller and his "Partners in Progress" report to President Truman. This resolution contained another recommendation. It asked that qualified women be given the opportunity to serve on development missions and that projects be initiated that would prepare women "for full participation in the economic and political life of their countries."[53]

Many women, perhaps most women, were puzzled about the fervor of people like Sarah T. Hughes, who talked so constantly about equality for their sex. It so often was said that women already had achieved full equality with men. "'What more do women want?' many people ask in genuine bewilderment," wrote one of Hughes's B&PW colleagues, Elizabeth Lansing, in *Independent Woman* in April 1952. People who asked such a question, Lansing wrote, were judging the sexes by different standards. "Equality can hardly be said to have arrived when, in a population fifty-one percent female, only a small minority of women reach the national ideal of what constitutes success—leadership—top authority and earned wealth." Women want to be able to develop their abilities in a field where they lie instead of being restricted to where tradition affirms they should lie, she continued. "She wants the avenues to success opened to her by her own efforts in her own behalf, rather than as a result of making herself useful to another. Her demand is not for privilege, but for equality."[54]

Hughes looked at the U.S. Congress in 1951 and saw only eight women serving in the House of Representatives and one lonely female, Margaret Chase Smith, in the Senate. Only a handful of women had chosen the legal profession as a career. The 1940 U.S. Census reported just 4,447 women lawyers in the entire nation, and that number had not grown appreciably a decade later.[55] The snail-like growth rate in terms of numbers of women lawyers was visible to Hughes in her own city. In Dallas in 1925 she had been one of eight women practicing the profession. By 1939 there were only fourteen women attorneys in the city, and by 1956 that number would rise to only twenty-two.[56]

Much of the lack of awareness and discrimination Hughes found was so deeply imbedded in the culture that few thought about it. In her first Christmas message to National Federation of B&PW members, Hughes described one instance typifying prevalent attitudes. The superintendent of one of the Dallas County homes for both boys and girls had told her about a men's service club inviting all the boys of the home—about twenty—to a big Christmas party. Besides the fancy dinner prepared for them, the club passed out numerous gifts such as pen knives, cowboy belts, and such. Girls were excluded from the party. "Can you imagine the heartaches of the girls in the home?" Hughes wrote. "No party and no special gifts! So frequently boys receive attention while girls are overlooked! If only our Business and Professional Women's Club had known, the girls might have had a party too. With a little inquiry we could have known—we just did not think."[57]

For a professional woman who had no children and claimed to have no interest in having any, Hughes was unusually sympathetic to the well-being of children and their home life. Her interest in juveniles and domestic affairs never lagged as she continued to carry out her duties as a district judge. She believed one of the seven district courts in Dallas County should be designated strictly for juvenile and family matters, but the other judges' response was not favorable. She found only one ally among the seven judges in favor of her proposal, and only Hughes herself expressed a willingness to take on the permanent assignment of handling family court matters.[58]

Nor did she lag in paying attention to local B&PW clubs, especially in Texas. On a November 1950 trip to the Rio Grande Valley for a weekend district conference, she suffered an attack of appendicitis and was taken to the hospital in Mercedes. There, she underwent an appendectomy, recovering quickly with no complications. During her brief confinement a steady stream of get well letters, calls, and telegrams descended upon the hospital. So many came that nurses, somewhat puzzled, referred to her as "the popular girl."[59]

At the 1950 convention in San Francisco, B&PW members had voted to endorse the election of early suffragist leader and feminist Susan B. Anthony into the nation's Hall of Fame at New York University. This was accomplished, and the Hall of Fame invited the organization to raise money for an artist to sculpt a portrait bust of Anthony. Donations totaling about eight thousand dollars were gathered for this purpose during Hughes's presidency, and Hughes was the principal speaker at the unveiling of the bust at New York University on May 18, 1952.[60]

The words etched on the tablet beneath Anthony's bust echoed Hughes's sentiments and those of many other women in the B&PW: "The day will come when man will recognize woman as his peer, not only at the fireside but in the councils of the nation. Then will there be the perfect comradeship between the sexes that shall result in the highest development of the race."[61]

As she neared the end of her two-year term as president in the summer of 1952, Hughes returned to a subject so important to her—jury service for women in Texas. During her term she had seen two other states, Oklahoma and Tennessee, remove restrictions against women jurors, primarily because of B&PW initiatives. Now it was time to move forward once more in Texas. Hughes sent a letter to all Texas club presidents announcing plans to form a statewide citizens' committee to pursue that goal. Both men and women would be on the committee, and they would represent different organizations and various regions of the state. Committee members would work toward two goals: (1) securing the necessary votes in the Texas Legislature to submit the proposition to the voters, and (2) educating the public about the merits of jury service by women.[62]

The plan was to involve every community in Texas through the formation of local committees. Each local B&PW president would be asked to submit the names of two of the most influential citizens in her community— man or woman—to serve on the local committee. In her letter to the presidents, Hughes also asked them to interview political candidates in their districts for both the Texas House and Senate, to ascertain their attitudes on the subject. This would be done in face-to-face meetings, with the local B&PW presidents seeking to have representatives from two other organizations accompany them at the interviews. The results of the information gained would be pooled with that of the statewide committee.[63]

The process of introducing bills in the legislature concerning women jurors, winning support in both houses, and then submitting the matter to voters in a statewide referendum was a long and tedious one. This time, however, with the best groundwork to date being laid, chances seemed better than ever for attaining this elusive goal.

In her opening-day remarks as outgoing president of the National Federation in June 1952, Hughes told the delegates in Boston's Symphony Hall that passage of the Equal Rights Amendment must be their first priority. Even with this accomplished, though, still more must be done, she insisted. Women must accept responsibility and actively participate in government. "As we face the future and the tasks that lie before us, I would wish for us the faith in ourselves and zeal for our cause of Susan B. Anthony, Lucretia Mott and Elizabeth Cady Stanton—their courage to overcome tradition and customs and persistence in the face of repeated defeats."[64]

With both political parties meeting later that summer for their 1952 presidential conventions, Judge Hughes sent a telegram from Boston to the leading Democratic and Republican presidential candidates asking their attitudes toward the Equal Rights Amendment. Both parties had endorsed the ERA in their 1944 and 1948 conventions, but the proposition still had not passed Congress. "Will you give us a statement as to whether, if it is again in the platform of your party and if you should be nominated and elected President, you would be willing to urge Congress to submit the amendment to the several states for ratification," she asked. "We should like to read your reply to the 3,000 delegates before adjourning."[65]

A great honor greeted Hughes at the first session of the B&PW convention. The New York State branch of the National Federation, led by its president, Mrs. Dorothy Titchener, submitted a resolution to nominate Hughes at the approaching Democratic National Convention in Chicago as the party's vice-presidential candidate. In a non-partisan spirit, the same honor was accorded U.S. senator Margaret Chase Smith of Maine, a Republican, who would be nominated at the Republican National Convention, also scheduled for Chicago. Smith held the distinction of being the first woman elected to both houses of the U.S. Congress. Beginning in 1940 she served four terms in the

House of Representatives and in 1948 was elected as the first woman to serve in the Senate. The cheering delegates immediately and enthusiastically adopted the resolution proposing the nomination of these two women.

A number of ten-gallon hats suddenly appeared to coincide with the resolution's passage, one of which Titchener presented to Hughes, who quickly signaled her acceptance by tossing her new cowboy hat through a hastily improvised ring. Both hats immediately were circulated among the delegates for contributions toward campaign chests for the candidates. Within ten minutes $1,026.50 was collected, to be divided equally between Hughes and Smith. This amount would be added to a sum of $500 previously provided.[66]

The resolution to seek nominations for the two women was not a spontaneous gesture. It had been planned for months. Statewide B&PW conventions in New York, Ohio, Michigan, Georgia, and Montana already had endorsed the idea.

"I am not so naïve as to think that we are likely to elect a woman for Vice President this year," Hughes said, "but I do think we should get into the arena and start to fight." Even the office of president of the United States should be considered for women at some point, she believed. Women should be copilots and not backseat drivers, she declared. They too long had been willing merely to "stuff letters and lick stamps." (Hughes herself had never been reluctant to perform such chores.) Now it was time for a full partnership with men. "The home is the foundation of our democracy, and no home can be properly conducted by a bachelor. Uncle Sam needs a wife."[67]

Senator Smith, not present at the National Federation convention, sent a telegram expressing her thanks for the action. "You have done me a great honor for which I am most grateful. . . . Go ahead with the nomination. I am highly honored."[68]

Yet another prominent woman had been mentioned as a possibility for vice president on the Democratic ticket. She was India Edwards, who as a member of the Democratic National Committee had urged the appointment of Hughes to the FTC in 1949 and had suggested Burnita Shelton Matthews as a district judge. The prospect of having her friend Judge Hughes as a rival for the vice-presidential nomination, Edwards said, was "just fine."[69]

While Hughes's candidacy admittedly would be symbolic only, her male loyalist colleagues were lukewarm in their comments. Edward (Ned) Fritz, an attorney who was organizer of the Kefauver for President Club in Dallas County, said he would be happy to place her name in nomination if it was satisfactory to Senator Kefauver. Loyalist delegate John "Preacher" Hays, a labor leader, was hesitant. It would be a long jump for women, he said, to reach the vice presidency. They should first seek gubernatorial or congressional offices. A prominent conservative, Wallace Savage, chairman of the Dallas County Democratic Party, said that while he always had favored Hughes in her judicial campaigns, he could not support any candidate in advance for either the presidency or vice presidency.[70]

For the first time in history the 1952 conventions were televised to the entire nation. Thousands of viewers, witnessing a process that until now had seemed remote and mysterious, were mesmerized as they watched ballot after ballot and actually saw on the screen famous politicians who until now had been only names.

The Republicans met first in Chicago, opening their convention on June 8. On the first ballot former general Dwight D. Eisenhower gained the presidential nomination over the conservative senator Robert A. Taft of Ohio. Arrangements had been completed to have Senator Smith nominated for the vice president as planned, but before it could be done a Republican committee met quietly with Eisenhower to ask his own preference. The name of Richard Milhous Nixon of California, who as a member of the House of Un-American Activities had gained national attention through his dogged pursuit of Alger Hiss, topped Eisenhower's list, and it was a choice enthusiastically accepted by the nominating committee. Learning of this, Margaret Chase Smith requested that "in the interests of party unity" her name not be submitted for consideration, and it was not.[71]

Less than a week later the Democrats met, also in Chicago, offering for the television audience more fireworks in a keener competition for the nomination. Despite her intense interest in politics, Sarah T. Hughes had not attended a Democratic National Convention since that impressionable summer in 1912, when she had visited the Baltimore proceedings as a teenager. Not attending had been a deliberate decision, she once explained, for there always had been a rivalry in Texas between factions of the Democratic Party, and she wanted the votes of all in her campaigns for reelection as judge.[72] For this reason, Hughes had refrained from involving herself in the county and state Democratic Party conventions, from which delegates to the national convention were chosen.[73]

In fact, the rivalry between loyalists—or liberals—and conservatives was more intense than ever in Texas. It was exacerbated by the tidelands dispute as to whether off-shore oil rights along the Texas coast should be the property of the federal government or of the state of Texas. President Truman's support of federal ownership had alienated many conservative Democrats in Texas, and it had placed his loyalist supporters in Texas in the difficult position of appearing not to support their own state's interests. Eisenhower, in contrast, favored Texas ownership of the tidelands. His position exerted a powerful incentive for Texas Democrats to support him.

In May 1952, at the State Democratic Convention in San Antonio, the split between loyalist and conservative Democrats in Texas had erupted into an emotional confrontation that would divide the party for decades. At that convention the conservatives, led by Governor Shivers, refused to guarantee that they would support the national Democratic ticket in November. Loyalists, or liberals, vastly outnumbered and furious, stormed out of the convention under the leadership of Maury Maverick. With invectives flying, they promised to challenge the legitimacy of the "Shivercrats" in Chicago and seek to be seated themselves as the official delegates from Texas. As a result, two sets of Texas delegates vied in Chicago for accreditation as the party members gathered.

Hughes at first refused to take sides. When she asked Shivers for his support in her vice-presidential bid, his response was to ask his own question: Who did she support in the fight between the conservatives and the loyalists? When she responded that she preferred not to take sides, Shivers then said he would wait until later to discuss her vice-presidential bid. That night Hughes decided to give her answer—she showed up at Maury Maverick's loyalist caucus. "Hughes Joins Mavericks," read a newspaper headline.[74]

Despite the remoteness of her chances for winning the nomination, as an acknowledged vice-presidential candidate Sarah T. Hughes did not attempt to be coy. On the first day of the convention she held a press conference and handed out her platform with a brief biographical sketch. As one newspaper account summarized: "The little woman jurist was in dead earnest. She said it was time to put a woman on the ticket and that the Democrats would be helped wonderfully if a Texan were chosen." Hughes said she had no preference in the presidential competition, but she believed that the convention should select the vice-presidential candidate rather than the presidential nominee.[75]

At the convention there was other work for Hughes to do besides campaigning, particularly on the Democratic Party platform. On the national level, her views were more in accord with party leaders such as her friend Sam Rayburn, himself no friend of Shivers. She managed to have the wording strengthened on the plans for equal rights and equal pay for women. The original wording concerning pay had been cloudy: "We favor legislation assuring equal pay for equal work regardless of sex." The new wording, pushed successfully by Hughes, was stronger: "We believe in equal pay for equal work regardless of sex, and we urge legislation to make that principle effective." Similarly, the wording of the plank on the Equal Rights Amendment was made more to the point.[76]

Now in an arena that was about as purely political as one could find, Hughes was in her element. She continued to campaign with enthusiasm all the while for her vice-presidential nomination, visiting many of the state delegations to ask the members for their votes. "I don't think I ever had more fun than at the Democratic convention," she said later in an oral history interview. Success was not her measuring stick for this particular race. By the end of the week she had received pledges for two and a half votes.[77]

A vice-presidential candidate could be considered only after the convention had selected a presidential candidate. On the third ballot, the Democratic delegates nominated Adlai E. Stevenson of Illinois to be their candidate after the failed attempts of Estes Kefauver, Richard Russell, and Averill Harriman. On the following day, June 27, vice-presidential nominations were in order. To find a delegate willing to nominate Sarah T. Hughes was one thing; getting recognized for that purpose by the chairman, Sam Rayburn, was another. Rayburn, Hughes's friend, agreed to permit her nomination if she would then withdraw her name. Bernice Kingsbury, a B&PW member from Montana, made the nominating speech for Hughes, and Mrs. William Anderson of Idaho seconded the nomination. Then Rayburn recognized his friend from Texas so that she could to come to the platform to make her comments.

Hughes spoke briefly and effectively, making clear the motives that had inspired her campaign for the vice presidency. Then, as agreed upon, she withdrew her name. Afterward, India Edwards was also nominated for vice president. Edwards also withdrew her name. Finally, the delegates chose Senator John J. Sparkman of Alabama as their vice-presidential candidate.

After a brief demonstration his nomination was accepted by acclamation. With much bigger stories to cover that day, the press gave scant attention to the nominations of Hughes and Edwards.[78]

The presidential campaign that followed, especially in Texas, was marked by acrimony between conservative and liberal Democrats, which came to a head but would endure for years. Governor Allan Shivers, citing the tidelands issue primarily, refused to support his own party's candidate, Stevenson, and threw his support to Eisenhower, creating a permanent breach with Sam Rayburn, who considered Shivers's action to be a betrayal. Other conservative Texas Democrats followed Shivers. The State Democratic Convention reluctantly placed Stevenson's name on the ticket but passed a resolution urging all Texas Democrats to vote for Eisenhower because he favored state ownership of the tidelands.

In Texas, Sarah T. Hughes campaigned unabashedly for the Democratic ticket and viewed with disdain those who would jump to the Republican Party. The tidelands issue was a phony one, she said. Neither Shivers nor any of the other Eisenhower Democrats had attempted to insert a plank into the party's platform regarding it when they had the opportunity to do so in Chicago. Eisenhower, she said, was a confused man on the issue. Moreover, a vote for Ike was a vote for isolationism, for he appeared to be going over to the Old Guard. She was referring to the isolationist, conservative wing of the Republican Party, led by Senator Robert Taft of Ohio.[79]

She was equally forthright on another issue that had become politically sensitive—the controversial campaign by Senator Joseph McCarthy of Wisconsin to purge the government of alleged Communists and Communist sympathizers. As Eisenhower remained reluctant to speak out on the issue of "McCarthyism," Hughes deplored the senator's "ascending influence" in Republican circles. It was not the first time she had attacked McCarthy. In 1951 she protested directly to McCarthy after he bumped Senator Margaret Chase Smith from his special investigating Senate subcommittee because she had opposed his rough-shod tactics in identifying government officials as Communists without proof.[80]

In Texas as well as in the nation, the effort to maintain the twenty-year Democratic control of the White House was fruitless. Eisenhower carried the normally Democratic Lone Star State by more than a hundred thousand votes. Liberal Democrats within the state did not fare well. Ralph Yarborough, Hughes's friend from the 1930s and a recognized liberal, failed in his effort to take the gubernatorial nomination from Shivers. The political future in Texas did not look promising for those Democrats who remained faithful to the more liberal tenets of the national party.

8 ～

A Liberal's Viewpoint

arah T. Hughes had little time for remorse over the Republicans' November 1952 triumph. Only a week afterward, she joined five leading American women for a month-long tour of West Germany on a government exchange program. Hughes went as the representative of the National Federation of Business and Professional Women's Clubs, and the other women were leaders of other influential organizations. Their charge was to visit and interact with newly formed women's groups in West Germany. These organizations, not permitted under Nazi Germany, were in their formative stage in this new postwar society. With their new freedom, women's groups were popping up across the breadth of the land. Among the many established throughout West Germany since 1950 were twenty-one Business and Professional Women's Clubs.[1]

The itinerary, prepared by West Germany's cultural division in the capital city of Bonn, took the women to fourteen cities, from Berlin in the east to Hamburg in the north to Berchtesgaden in the south. As usual, Hughes was a careful observer. She tried to assess the overall progress of German women as well as their new associations and to gather impressions about conditions in general in the divided nation. She was pleased to see German women discussing serious political issues and working toward speedy implementation of the equal rights already proclaimed for them in their new constitution. Women seemed to be unusually active in public affairs. With some chagrin, Hughes noted that more women served in the Bundestag than in the U.S. Congress and that West Germany had more women judges than the United States had.

She found both men and women cheerful and optimistic, pleased to cooperate with the free world, but also eager to reunite their divided nation. The overall success of democratic West Germany seemed evident to Hughes as she noted the great influx of refugees from East Germany and other Eastern European countries—prompted, she declared, by their unhappy experiences under Communism.

This was Hughes's second look at postwar Germany, the first having been her quick detour there during her visit to England in 1950. Now, two years later, she was struck by great progress made in clearing away the ruins and rubble left from the war. Few signs of destruction remained, particularly in Frankfurt and Munich.[2]

Returning to Dallas late on Wednesday, December 10, Judge Hughes was back at work the next morning on her 14th District Court bench. Before resuming her judicial duties, though, she met briefly with local reporters, with whom she always had good relations, and spoke of her journey in glowing terms. Exchange programs such as the one she had just completed, she believed, constituted one of the most important means of establishing world peace.[3]

A surprise awaiting her was an important new government assignment. In her absence the State Department had named her to a position that would underscore her growing interest in international affairs and focus her attention more than ever in that direction. The appointment, extending into 1956, was to the U.S. National Commission for the United Nations Educational, Scientific, and Cultural Organization (UNESCO), a body established by the U.S. Congress to advise the State Department. Judge Hughes was to represent the National Federation of B&PW on the commission, an appointment that in the next year would be broadened with her membership on the executive committee for the National Commission.[4]

In January 1953, soon after her UNESCO appointment, Hughes and a handful of like-minded friends met in a downtown bank auditorium to organize a United Nations support group—the Dallas United Nations Association. The idea to form a local organization had been discussed among this small group in the late fall of 1952 in three separate meetings because of an increasing number of bitter attacks in Dallas against the UN and particularly against UNESCO. Members of the "Minute Women," or individuals connected to the right-wing, H. L. Hunt-sponsored radio show *Facts Forum*, were responsible for many of the attacks. Hughes's appointment to the UNESCO commission likely was the push needed to spur her and her friends to immediate action. Hughes's preference a few years before for a more powerful world federation with coercive powers had yielded to her realization that such was not a practical idea. The UN was now, in Hughes's opinion, the best vehicle for obtaining peace.[5]

Those who met with Hughes at the bank auditorium were people with some influence in the community. All of them shared a faith in the worthiness of the UN. They included the Reverend Luther Holcomb, a Baptist minister, and H. Grady Spruce, an executive with the Dallas YMCA, both of whom were elected vice presidents at the meeting. Hughes, of course, became the organization's first president.[6]

Two others closely involved were special friends of Hughes who earlier had been drawn into her circle of influence. One was Louise B. Raggio, who was elected secretary of the organization. Raggio's friendship with Hughes had grown since 1946, when they first met during Hughes's campaign for Congress. Raggio and her husband, Grier, who worked with George Hughes at the Veterans Administration, were socializing these days with the Hugheses on a regular basis. In their work together now and in years to come, Louise described herself as Tonto and Hughes as the Lone Ranger. A few years later Raggio would become a powerful force in her own right in winning women's rights in Texas through her work as chair of the Texas State Bar's family law section.

Another of the participants in the new organization was a young lawyer also destined to make a name for himself. Oscar Mauzy was placed on the board of directors. A navy veteran and University of Texas Law School graduate, Mauzy later would become a long-time state senator and then an associate justice on the Texas Supreme Court.

The word *temporary* preceded the titles of all involved, because the new organization was not yet recognized as an official unit of the American Association for the United Nations. This designation came four months later when on May 12 accreditation was announced. From the beginning, the new association, with eleven committees formed for special activities, was well organized and ambitious.[7]

There was much work to be done in Dallas, for a thriving anti-UN sentiment had developed in the city. Bitter criticisms were being aired on a regular basis, and the new chapter now began countering them promptly at every opportunity. A committee headed by Cordye Hall sought to respond to each letter critical of the UN that appeared in the two daily newspapers. The speakers bureau, headed by Johnnie Marie Grimes, secretary to the president of Southern Methodist University, sent letters to some five hundred civic, religious, and educational groups announcing the availability of individuals who could give factual talks about the UN and its work. This activity, Hughes believed, was the new organization's most important endeavor.[8]

Hughes herself was perhaps the most frequent speaker. She appeared before women's clubs, service organizations, church groups, and practically anywhere she was invited. In her talks she generally outlined the aims and purposes of the various organizations within the UN, including especially UNESCO. She took care to point out benefits the United States received from membership and expressed her opinion that the only alternative to the UN was war. Although she had given up on her earlier notions about a world federation, she thought that some day after a journey over a long and rough road, peace could be achieved through national disarmament and a world police force.[9] If the United Nations had failed in its nine years to achieve world peace, Americans should not feel discouraged, she told a group in Paris, Texas. After all, the struggle to achieve peace had been going on for hundreds of years.[10]

So persistent were public criticisms in Dallas of the United Nations that UNESCO's staff director, Max McCullough, after a visit during the organization's first year of existence, requested a compilation and analysis of the attacks with a report on what had been done to combat them. A committee headed by Mrs. E. R. Brownscombe responded with a chronological account of the attacks and a listing of the organization's responses.[11]

One of the attacks indicated how deeply the anti-UN movement had penetrated Dallas. It occurred at an unlikely place—a meeting of the Dads' Club of the Lakewood Elementary School. The speaker was Sidney Latham, a vice president of the oil company owned by H. L. Hunt, a particularly energetic anti-UN vocal opponent. After no discussion was permitted following Latham's speech, several fathers insisted that in fairness a positive presentation now should be heard. Their request went to the speakers' bureau. The logical person to respond, Hughes believed, was the Reverend Luther Holcomb, who, in addition to being vice president of the local association, was pastor of the Lakewood Baptist Church in the same neighborhood as the school.

Hughes warned Holcomb that he must be at his sharpest, for Latham was anything but a buffoon. She had served with him in the legislature and found him to be "a clear, logical speaker, with an unusual emotional appeal." Although Holcomb at the time was visiting American troops in Korea on a UN-sanctioned tour, he presumably made the pro-UN response upon his return.[12]

Latham's employer, Hunt, the famous Dallas oilman frequently described at the time as the richest man in the world, was financing an extensive campaign to promote ultraconservative causes and to discredit liberal politics and the United Nations. His sponsored radio program, *Facts Forum*, had gone on the air in 1951, and in 1953 a television version was added. The programs were being heard or seen by as many as five million people a week. Hunt also was generating scores of publications with the same political slant, and he regularly wrote letters to the editors of the daily newspapers espousing his views. One of his political pets was Senator Joseph McCarthy of Wisconsin, whose anticommunist campaign and demands for investigations into the State Department regularly made headlines.[13]

Sometimes the attacks on the United Nations took on absurd dimensions. One that infuriated Hughes involved a trustee election in her neighborhood's Highland Park Independent School District. A newspaper political advertisement on behalf of three candidates declared that they must be elected to the board of education "if we are to guard against . . . the UNESCO plan of education in our schools." No further explanation appeared. Hughes countered with a lengthy letter published in the newspaper, and she wrote individual letters to those whose names appeared on the advertisement. All were prominent people in the community. They included well-known attorneys and civic leaders, a professor at Southwestern Medical School, an insurance executive and future congressman, and the head of the Dallas Crime Commission.[14]

In her letters Hughes declared in exasperation that there was no such thing as a UNESCO plan of education for American school districts, and there was no danger of one ever existing. The purpose of UNESCO, she explained, was to assist countries only at their request, primarily underdeveloped countries. "Such unfounded statements as appeared in the school ad cast suspicion and aroused fear about an organization whose entire program is devoted to the promotion of peace through educational, scientific, and cultural relations of the people of the world," she wrote to those whose names had appeared on the advertisement.[15]

Almost all of those who responded to her letters admitted a lack of knowledge about UNESCO. They had endorsed the individual candidates but had not known that the UNESCO comment would be a part of the advertisement.[16]

Even though the efforts of the Dallas UN Association often seemed entirely defensive, before its first year was over the organization could look back on a large number of successes. At its first luncheon meeting in 1953, attended by 175 persons, Bishop C. Avery Mason of the Dallas Diocese of the Episcopal Church spoke. The mayor of Dallas, R. L. Thornton, issued a special proclamation for UN Week in October. Some sixty-five organizations participated in the latter occasion, an event that included sponsorship of a festival at Fair Park; a speech by Robert G. Storey, dean of the SMU Law School; the display of UN flags at seventy-five business establishments; operation of four information booths in downtown Dallas; and significant news coverage by radio and television stations. "Despite a few recent adverse speeches, I feel we have made progress," Hughes said in summarizing the first-year achievements.[17]

The effort to bring understanding and appreciation for the United Nations received a boost when the Dallas organization entered its third year and Eleanor Roosevelt spoke at a January 1955 meeting. The former first lady was chairman of the board of governors of the American Association for the United Nations. Hughes introduced Mrs. Roosevelt at a news conference at the Press Club of Dallas, and a picture of the two of them together appeared in the *Dallas Morning News*. After the press conference, the Hugheses entertained Mrs. Roosevelt and several friends and associates at their home. It was the first of several occasions in coming years in which Sarah Hughes would entertain Eleanor Roosevelt at her home.[18] On the following day, Mrs. Roosevelt addressed several hundred members and guests of the Dallas UN Association. News coverage was positive, although the *Dallas Morning News* declared in an otherwise favorable editorial that a problem with Mrs. Roosevelt was "her blanket defense of the special agencies of the U.N., some of which have spread socialized programs over the world at our expense." While these agencies were well intended, the newspaper opined, some of them had "fallen into the hands of crackpots."[19]

The anti-UN movement was one aspect of the Red Scare sweeping the nation in the late 1940s and 1950s, especially through the efforts of Senator McCarthy. The effort to uncover Communists and Communist sympathizers in American institutions touched even Judge Hughes, although probably she was never aware of it. In May 1953, an individual reported to the Federal Bureau of Investigation that he had received information that Hughes attended a subversive meeting at a church in Highland Park. The complainant said it was common knowledge that Hughes was socialistic, and he understood the meeting was held either by Communist Party members or by persons leaning that way. The FBI learned that the subversive meeting was actually a public affairs discussion held at the Unitarian Church and quickly dropped the matter.[20]

The power of the far right in Dallas was manifested in the November 1954 congressional elections by the astonishing upset victory of a neophyte Republican candidate who assumed the seat vacated by J. Frank Wilson upon his retirement. The winner, Bruce Alger, became the only Republican congressman in Texas and, because of his surprise victory, instantly became a national figure and a symbol of conservatism in Dallas unmatched by any other Texas city. An ardent opponent of federal government programs, including even the popular school lunch program, Alger consistently urged Congress to withdraw from the United Nations and to terminate relations with the Soviet Union. At first his victory was believed to be a fluke, but Dallas voters would send him to Congress for five terms.

Alger's election in 1954 came at the expense of a conservative Democrat, Wallace Savage, former mayor of Dallas and state chairman of the Democratic Party's Executive Committee. Alger's win foreshadowed the eventual switch of virtually all conservative Democrats to the Republican Party, a phenomenon that would take place not just in Texas but throughout the South. With their mass exodus to the Republican Party still some years away, though, conservative Democrats continued to control the Democratic Party in Texas. Loyalist Democrats continued their struggle under the leadership of Ralph W. Yarborough, the former assistant attorney general of Texas and Hughes's friend from her legislative days in the 1930s. His efforts to move into the Governor's Mansion were thwarted by Allan Shivers in 1952 and 1954 and by Price Daniel in 1956. Finally, in a special election in 1957, Yarborough won Daniel's vacated Senate seat, providing a glimmer of hope and inspiration for the state's struggling liberals.

Hughes enthusiastically supported the loyalist-liberals in their campaigns. Her momentary reluctance to choose sides in the Texas delegation battle in Chicago in 1952, prompted by her candidacy for the vice presidency and her desire for support from all Democratic quarters, was long since forgotten. At a meeting of the Young Democrat Clubs of Texas in Fort Worth in 1954, she said Shivers had "betrayed the Democratic party more than any other person in Texas."[21]

The effort to change Texas law so that women could serve on juries remained one of the major goals in Judge Hughes's life. Texas procrastinated as state after state amended their laws to add women to the jury pools. In 1951 three more states enacted jury service legislation for women, and in 1953 Georgia was added to that list.

Oscar Mauzy, a new attorney in Dallas in 1952, later recalled vividly how Hughes had enlisted him in the cause. At the conclusion of a trial in her court in which he had represented a female plaintiff, Judge Hughes called him into her chambers and asked him his impressions about the trial. Mauzy thought everything had been just fine.

"Did you notice anything unusual?" Hughes asked him.

Mauzy said he had not but added that he was a new lawyer without much experience.

"Didn't it strike you as unusual that your client was a woman, that I'm a woman judge, that you and your opposing counsel were men, and that all twelve jurors were men?" the judge asked him.

Mauzy agreed this was indeed unusual, and he acknowledged its unfairness.

"Well, I want you to do something about it," Hughes told him. The Texas Legislature soon would begin a new session, she informed him, and she wanted him to go to Austin and help to lobby for an amendment. Mauzy accepted the assignment, went to Austin, testified, and became a close associate of Hughes while he developed in coming years into a leading liberal Democratic politician in the county and state.[22]

Results from Hughes's groundwork, initiated as outgoing president of the National Federation of B&PW, became quickly evident. When the Texas Legislature met in January 1953, several bills for the desired constitutional amendment were immediately introduced. Approval by the constitutional amendment committees was quickly won, overwhelming majorities in both the House and Senate agreed to it, and Governor Shivers approved the legislation that would place the matter of women jurors before Texas voters in the November 1954 general election. Judge Hughes, again leading the charge for the amendment, predicted passage by a landslide.[23]

The jury amendment was seventh on a ballot of eleven proposed amendments for voter approval, the largest number in Texas history. The State Bar of Texas, of which Hughes was an active and leading member, was no help, for it took no position. In reviewing the proposed constitutional amendments, the state bar went on record as favoring passage of only number four—the transfer of unused Confederate Pension Fund money to the State Building Fund. "Neither the State Bar of Texas nor the *Texas Bar Journal* [its official journal] is advocating passage or rejection of any other amendment," the *Journal* reported a month prior to the election.[24]

This time, though, major newspapers did lend their support. The *Dallas Times Herald* called the failure to have women on juries "a senseless discrimination." Newspaper advertisements by the Texas Citizens Committee for Jury Service for Women urged passage of the amendment. Judge Hughes's name appeared at the top of a listing of fifteen judges who endorsed it in a newspaper advertisement.[25]

Early vote returns from smaller towns and rural Texas, where more conventionally minded voters resided, caused concern, for the jury amendment was clearly in danger of rejection. But the later tallies from metropolitan areas showed urban voters approving the amendment by a wide majority. Their numbers carried the day. Final returns showed the proposal passing by a handsome margin of 57 percent, 237,978 to 175,398. The margin represented a dramatic turnaround from the 1949 election, when voters had rejected the same amendment by a margin of 54 percent.[26] For Sarah T. Hughes the victory was cause for jubilation, the culmination of a struggle she had waged for more than two decades against a discrimination that seemed so patently illogical and unfair. She celebrated by writing an article for *Independent Woman* magazine entitled "Now I Can Throw Away That Speech."[27] In her long career she had spoken or written on no topic more often.

The practical benefits of women jurors quickly became evident. By the end of 1955, 39 percent of the jurors in Judge Hughes's court were females, a percentage no doubt equaled in other state courts. After five years she was able to say she had found little difference between women and men jurors. "They do not ask to be excused any more than men do, and they show the same interest or lack of interest as men do," she wrote to a man in Amarillo who had inquired about discrimination against women. "I should say that there are more women who show an interest in service probably because it is a new experience for them."[28]

A matter of great concern to Hughes continued to be the small number of women attorneys in Dallas and Texas in general. She kept a close watch over new female attorneys entering the Dallas bar, making it a point to meet them. Eventually, she began compiling and regularly updating her personal list of the women lawyers, not a difficult task since as late as 1956 only twenty-two were practicing in Dallas.[29]

Hughes's took a personal interest in the advancement of these women in the profession, encouraging them in many ways. She urged her friend Louise Raggio, a 1952 graduate of the Southern Methodist University Law School, to apply for a position as an assistant district attorney for Dallas County in 1954 at a time when there were no female prosecutors in the office. (Thirty-five years earlier Helen Viglini had become the first woman assistant district attorney in Dallas County, but no female had followed her.) Raggio applied as Hughes recommended, and Hughes successfully persuaded District Attorney Henry Wade to hire her. "Henry hired me to get Sarah off his back," Raggio said. Not long afterward, Raggio recalled, she prosecuted a case before an all-woman jury and obtained a guilty verdict. It was believed to be the first time in the state's history that an all-woman jury returned a guilty verdict.[30]

There remained for Sarah T. Hughes, of course, another matter of even broader potential benefit to women—the much delayed, much debated Equal Rights Amendment to the U.S. Constitution. Before it could be submitted to the states for the necessary three-fourths approval, both the House and Senate had to agree upon the form of the amendment. Now, more than thirty years after it had been introduced in Congress, debate still persisted as to how it should be defined. A basic question was just "how equal" women should be. Should the amendment offer special protection for women in certain jobs requiring night work or heavy lifting, such as contained in the Hayden rider attached to the Senate bill? The most vociferous female proponents of the ERA, including Sarah T. Hughes, wanted equality across the board without such protections. Hughes explained to Congressman Tom Pickett, who represented George Hughes's hometown of Palestine, that such protections frequently were used to discriminate *against* women and prevent them from obtaining certain positions that they otherwise might have.[31]

Now, in January 1952, two years after Hughes had expressed her disappointment to Lyndon B. Johnson when he voted for the Hayden amendment, she continued to try to change his position. Their regular correspondence on the matter, which began in 1949 when Johnson was a newly elected senator, displayed a certain disingenuousness—Hughes pretending that Johnson was naïve on such matters, and Johnson pretending his mind was open. With another vote looming, Hughes as B&PW president urged Johnson to do everything possible to have the Senate consider the ERA at an early date and to make "every effort to see that no crippling amendments are attached to it, such as the Hayden amendment of a previous session."[32]

Johnson thanked her kindly. "I have very much in mind the views of the National Federation of Business and Professional Women's Clubs and you can be sure that I shall do what I can to be helpful," he replied. "Lady Bird joins me in sending you our warm personal regards."[33]

More accommodating in this regard was Hughes's old friend from law school, Brooks Hays, now a Democratic congressman from Arkansas. Hughes implored Hays to support the Equal Rights Amendment without the Hayden rider, and he agreed to be a sponsor for it in the House without the rider. "Your comments influenced me in this decision," he wrote to her.[34]

But it was Johnson, Hughes was keenly aware, who was becoming a powerful force in the Senate and whose support she and other proponents needed. When Congress convened in January 1953, Johnson, after only four years as a senator, was the new Senate minority leader of the Democratic Party. When he once more voted for the Hayden rider, despite Hughes's earlier admonitions, she wrote to him expressing her regret. Lecturing to him again as if he were a schoolboy, she described the discrimination the so-called protective legislation actually caused for women. "For instance, the prohibition against night work is supposed to protect their morals, but actually it discriminates since many skilled jobs, such as that of printers, pay more at night and are more desirable. It is significant that charwomen have never been barred from night work."[35] It was basically the same letter she had sent him in February 1950, thanking him for his support of the ERA but lamenting his acceptance of the Hayden rider and explaining why it was ill-conceived.

The cordiality between the two never lagged, though, as evidenced in a steady stream of letters. Amid pleasantries, Hughes made suggestions on pending legislation, and Johnson responded graciously. The letters exuded warmth suggesting a much closer personal relationship than actually existed. When Johnson thanked Hughes for her advice about congressional appropriations for UNESCO, he concluded: "How is everything down your way. I hope fine and be sure to let me know if I can do anything to be of assistance from up here."[36] When Hughes visited Hawaii in the spring of 1953, she sent him a chatty letter detailing her impressions and urging that statehood be granted. Johnson found her comments most interesting. He noted her statement that the islands were ready for statehood but advised that no action was being taken now. (Many southern Democrats opposed statehood for Hawaii; not until 1959 would it be granted.)[37] When Johnson, now Senate majority leader, suffered a highly publicized heart attack in July 1955, Hughes sent an encouraging letter with an admonition to prolong his stay at his Hill Country ranch so that he could be assured of a full recovery. Johnson thanked her for being so sweet and thoughtful and said she was "absolutely right about the ranch and the Pedernales being the perfect site for a recuperation." Her remarks about his value to the country, he said, were flattering. "If I were just half as good as all that, I would be gratified."[38]

Despite the warmth of their correspondence and their later friendship, Hughes later said she did not become personally acquainted with Johnson until the 1960 presidential campaign, a rather surprising situation given their involvement in Texas politics over the same years. "I was for him and followed his political career, but actually being a friend I can't say that we were acquainted," she told historian Joe B. Frantz when he interviewed her in 1968 for the LBJ Library Oral History Collection.[39]

In summarizing Sarah T. Hughes's reputation, a national magazine in 1954 described her as being well known throughout Texas for her work in promoting understanding of the United Nations and for her efforts to obtain service on juries for women. Her appointment nearly two decades earlier as the first woman district judge in the state, the ensuing controversy over it, and the uniqueness of her gender in the judiciary had long since ceased to be defining elements of her career. Still, the post office occasionally delivered mail to her addressed simply as "Woman Judge, Dallas."[40]

Approaching her sixtieth birthday, Hughes's daily life centered on her judgeship. Each day she reported to her 14th District Court on the fourth floor of the massive red and gray granite courthouse, filling a city block that long since had ceased to be the center of town. On the same floor were three other district courts. Four more were on the second floor. In July 1955, the county commissioners moved all eight of these courts to the newer, air-conditioned County Records Building across the street. A delay had occurred in obtaining the furniture and fixtures for the new quarters, and Judge Hughes refused to transfer her operations there until all was in place. A newspaper article described her as sitting in her old courtroom with the thermometer at ninety-seven degrees, again defying the commissioners by being obstinate. When finally she moved to her new quarters, she decorated the walls with old political cartoons depicting her 1935 struggle to win appointment and chiding her for her militant campaigns for women. There were also certificates and plaques bestowed on her for her contributions to the community and profession. She estimated she had heard some twenty-eight thousand cases in her old courtroom, an astonishing figure compiled over twenty years' service.[41]

Each day the judge counted on the companionship and assistance of her personal secretary, Gwen Graul, a dynamic divorcee and single mother of three sons. Graul had begun working for Hughes in 1940. To reach Judge Hughes, one had to go through Graul. Their relationship went beyond the office, for it had developed into a close friendship. Graul was and would continue to be an essential part of Hughes's life, often buying clothes for her and taking care of many personal needs. She would remain with the judge for forty years in a relationship ending only with Graul's death in 1980. She, like the judge, was an affable yet direct person who knew her way around the courthouse, having started there as a file clerk following her divorce in the 1930s. Graul's father, Ed Cobb, was a powerful figure at the courthouse. He held office from 1930 to 1934 as the county's tax assessor and from 1934 to 1947 as the tax assessor-collector when the two offices were combined. One day in 1940, Cobb had stopped Hughes on the street outside the courthouse and told her he wanted his daughter to work in her court. He would discuss it with District Clerk Pearl Smith, who assigned clerks to the courts. Graul soon reported to work. She was an atrocious typist and could not take short-hand, but it soon developed that she knew how to run an office and would take nonsense from no one. Sarah T. Hughes liked a woman like that.[42]

Throughout their lives George and Sarah Hughes were creatures of habit, maintaining the same daily routines and friends for years. In the years of the Eisenhower presidency they continued to enjoy gardening, especially growing vegetables. A faithful gardener, Robert Dean tended to the lawn and shrubbery for many years, just as his wife, Lillian Dean, who replaced Mattie Green, took care of basic cooking chores, despite George's well-known culinary skills.

Furnishings in their home on Normandy Avenue were modest. A 1958 inventory of items, presumably taken for insurance purposes, described such pieces as a walnut coffee table purchased in 1926 for thirty dollars, a chair bought in 1929 for thirty dollars, a piano and bench purchased in 1940 for four hundred dollars, a dictionary stand bought in 1941 for fifteen dollars, and miscellaneous jewelry including three watches worth sixty dollars, four rings, one set of cuff links, two pins and brooches, and three necklaces.[43]

The couple enjoyed vacations together at the ranch near Creede, Colorado, where they met annually with a regular group of vacationers. Sarah Hughes seemed unpretentious in that setting, a friend remembered, although she inevitably held center stage and commanded respect and curiosity from those around her. As this friend recalled, she had no small-talk vocabulary but always proved herself to be a "versatile, quick and often humorous conversationalist."[44]

Her work with B&PW went on unabated. In 1956 she became first vice president for the International Federation of B&PW. In the same year the Dallas chapter honored her with a special award for her work in promoting women in the professions. Her membership and participation in the Zonta Club also continued.

In late 1957 the urge to step outside this routine and run for elective office again appealed to Sarah T. Hughes. The political climate in Dallas, she knew, made it virtually hopeless for her to repeat a bid for Congress with any hope of success. She had passed up a good opportunity to do so in 1954, when incumbent J. Frank Wilson declined to seek reelection. While her well-known liberalism may have deterred her from seeking other elected offices, it had not been a negative factor in her successful judicial campaigns. Dallas's conservative establishment accepted her, and members of the Dallas Bar Association recognized her outstanding performance on the bench, endorsing her for reelection without fail. Although so many in Dallas voted Republican in the 1952 and 1956 presidential elections and had chosen a Republican as their congressman, all elected officials at the courthouse continued to be Democrats.

After more than two decades of exemplary service, Hughes concluded that promotion to the Texas Supreme Court seemed reasonable and possible. The court consisted of a chief justice and eight associate justices, all elected for overlapping six-year terms. Two seats were up for election in 1958. Hughes quietly made a careful and deliberate calculation. One position had no incumbent, but Justice Robert W. Hamilton of El Paso, on the appeals court, already had announced for it, and he appeared to be a strong candidate for election. The other position, Place Four, was held by a short-time incumbent, Joe R. Greenhill Sr., who had just been appointed in September 1957 by Governor Price Daniel as a reward for having served as his campaign manager in his 1956 gubernatorial victory over Ralph Yarborough. To Hughes this position seemed to offer her best chance for winning.[45]

Some probably construed Hughes's decision to run against Greenhill as part of the effort by Texas loyalists to undo the political machinery of the "Shivercrats," those Democrats who with Allan Shivers had supported Eisenhower instead of Stevenson. Greenhill's sponsor, Daniel, was a leading figure in this group. Another possible incentive was that if successful, Hughes would become the first elected woman member of the Texas Supreme Court. While women judges still were rare in the late 1950s, the possibility of a female on the Texas Supreme Court no longer seemed shocking. Neither partisanship nor women's rights were incentives for Hughes in this instance. The matter was far simpler. She later reflected that her decision came because she had never been one to be satisfied with the job she had. "I always wanted to have a better job, and it seemed to me an appropriate time to run for the Supreme Court."[46]

Her announcement would wait, though. Having made her decision privately, Hughes embarked upon an energetic plan designed to put her name before Texas voters prior to the campaign. Before running for Congress in 1946, she had begun a weekly radio program in Dallas. Now, with a statewide election looming, she turned to a topic on which she was an expert—juvenile delinquency. She prepared a series of articles and taped recordings expounding her views on the subject. These she submitted in early 1958 to newspapers and radio stations across the state. Publicity gained in this way would be nonpartisan—and it would be free. In an accompanying editor's note she identified herself as a judge who had handled more than twenty-five thousand juvenile and family relations cases and an even greater number of civil cases. Family law, she noted, was "probably the most important phase of the law."[47]

She took care to present the approximately fifteen articles in a polished format, having them prepared as mats that could be printed exactly as submitted with no need for typesetting or even headlines. Newspapers could choose either a short or a long version. The short series linked her photograph to brief comments on the subject. The long series provided more elaboration and was accompanied by a photograph of Hughes that could be placed wherever the editor preferred. She offered radio stations three different versions, with spots lasting one minute, three minutes, or five minutes. Recordings were sent only to those station managers who indicated an interest from query letters.[48]

Those who ran the series, either in print or over the airwaves, found them to be timely and instructive for their readers and listeners. In the series Hughes elaborated on her long-held views on juvenile delinquency and domestic affairs. One of her most important points was her insistence that facilities and personnel for rehabilitating juveniles in counties throughout the state were inadequate. "Many counties have no probation or parole officers. In some instances small boys 10 to 13 are sent to Gatesville [where a state juvenile delinquency facility was located] because [the] county has no facilities for handling them." Any community that permitted a ten-year-old child to be committed to Gatesville was failing in its responsibility to youngsters, she maintained.

The articles emphasized the value of developing a sense of personal worth for young people. Although Hughes saw no single factor as causing juvenile delinquency, in her opinion the most important cause was the failure of many youths to have a sense of their own significance. This feeling of inadequacy, she felt, often started them on the road to delinquency as a misguided means of achieving attention. Invariably at the root of this problem of self-image, she felt, was an improper home life and environment. Parents needed to nurture in their children a feeling of self-importance, a sense of belonging, and a recognition that they were important elements in the family.

Good parents set high standards for their children through their own actions by displaying "right attitudes, high moral and ethical standards, and religious faith." Hughes cited her own upbringing as a model. "Among the happiest memories of my childhood are the times I spent with my parents," she recalled. "There were the bonfires my father and I had from the leaves we raked together, and the Sunday picnics, and walks in the spring. They are among my fondest recollections."

In this decade of the 1950s the media had discovered the problem of juvenile delinquency. The subject was gaining widespread attention as never before in the press and in movies. Some alarmed individuals were calling for tougher laws, but Hughes thought these notions were misguided.

"Treating young offenders like criminals isn't the answer," she emphasized. It had been tried before in Texas with little success. Until 1856 children in Texas had been subject to the death penalty; until 1907 they could be confined to the Texas penitentiary with hardened criminals. And Hughes could remember all too well her own battle in Dallas County to segregate juvenile offenders from adult prisoners in the county jail. Understanding of the problem, early intervention, and rehabilitation were the proper responses.[49]

As always, her belief was that the principal reason for incarceration—not just for juveniles, but for adult criminals, too—was to rehabilitate. "What they [juvenile delinquents] need is training and education and a different slant on life. Many of them come from broken homes or from homes that have no appreciation for education or community involvement." These qualities and perspectives, she believed, should be taught to juveniles as well as to adult offenders in a special school or institution. "There's no use in just sending them there to confine them. They should come out better citizens than when they went in. You can't do that by harsh methods. It has to be by understanding and counseling," she said in her oral history years later.[50]

Although these articles were tied to Hughes's forthcoming announcement as a candidate for the Texas Supreme Court, her interest in the subject was long-standing and genuine. She had spoken and written on the subject for years, and she would continue to do so in the future. Not long after the series, in 1960 she would prepare a more formal presentation entitled "Handling of Juvenile Delinquents in Texas" for the *Texas Law Review*.[51] A year after that she would speak on the subject to the annual conference of the Texas Study of Secondary Education. Her talk, "The Unfortunate One Per Cent—Our Responsibility," was published by the organization as a research paper.[52]

The 1958 series of articles was well received by newspapers in smaller towns, which often were eager to fill space inexpensively with relevant material. Less successful were Hughes's efforts to place the articles in bigger newspapers. However, the overall results led her to conclude that she got an amazing amount of free publicity. "I knew that I was campaigning," she said. "I wouldn't have done all that work if it hadn't been campaigning."[53]

A radio station manager in New Braunfels, in rejecting the proffered radio talks, said his station in the past had carried her programs and found them very satisfactory. "However," he wrote, "it is my understanding that Judge Hughes is a declared candidate for a political office; and in as much as

I have that understanding, I do not believe it would be entirely in the public interest to broadcast Judge Hughes spots, as they would have a political advertising value to her candidacy and we are not in the advertising business." After the political races were over, he said, he would be interested in running "anything that Judge Hughes might be backing as we are ardent admirers of hers." Hughes hoped all station managers would not be so politically aware. Her official declaration of candidacy was three weeks away.[54]

Before the series was released in early 1958, supporters among Hughes's network had begun making preliminary inquiries in principal cities and counties throughout Texas to identify potential campaign managers. These actions meant that her plans to run for office could not be kept secret indefinitely. *Dallas Times Herald* political writer Bob Hollingsworth surmised in a column in late December 1957 that Judge Hughes was likely to challenge Joe Greenhill for his seat on the state supreme court.[55]

Two weeks later Hughes acknowledged that she indeed was contemplating a race for that position. "I am considering it. But I have not fully made up my mind," she said. Her lack of effort to discourage supporters from making inquiries throughout the state on her behalf was cited as a positive indication she would be a candidate.[56]

On Saturday, April 19, 1958, three months before the Democratic primary election was to be held, Sarah T. Hughes sent news releases and photographs to newspapers, radio, and television stations throughout the state announcing her candidacy. After more than two decades on the 14th District Court bench, during which time she had enjoyed the endorsement of the Dallas Bar Association and had been reelected six times (three without opposition), she said she was ready for this step.

"I believe my 23 years on the bench, seeking out and applying the law, have materially increased my ability to serve on the Supreme Court and earnestly hope the voters of Texas will consider my record worthy of support for this higher job," she said in her announcement. "I will apply diligence and fairness to the Supreme Court cases." She pointed to the fact that she kept current her docket in the 14th District Court and tried contested cases without undue delay.[57]

She faced the usual problem of a judicial candidate's need to create voter awareness—political labels had little to do with one's capabilities as a judge.

Nor could a candidate suggest how he or she might be expected to rule in disputes. A judicial candidate ostensibly could do little more than point to experience and qualifications.

Hughes prepared a color, fold-over pamphlet declaring that "Justice in Texas . . . Demands the promotion of JUDGE SARAH T. HUGHES to the TEXAS SUPREME COURT." Five special qualifications were cited: She was "an outstanding jurist, learned in the law . . . qualified by education and experience . . . [possessed] intellect, courage and administrative ability . . . [had] legislative experience . . . [and had received] community and professional recognition." On the inside appeared a notation that she was the first woman candidate for the Texas Supreme Court.[58]

In her last race for reelection as district judge, the Dallas Bar Association had endorsed her by more than two to one. Sixty-nine percent of the voters had favored her. Endorsement by the Dallas Bar could be anticipated once more with the same positive results at the poll. Notwithstanding her high public profile in other matters across the state, Hughes's active participation in the Dallas Bar Association and her committee work with the State Bar of Texas had brought her wide acquaintanceship with attorneys and judges throughout the state. Her chairmanship of the state bar's judicial section was helpful in this regard. She sent an early letter to every lawyer in the state advising that she would challenge Greenhill. Greenhill himself was anything but a neophyte in state politics or in judicial work. In addition to having served as Daniel's campaign manager, he was an Austin insider, a former assistant attorney general in Texas, and a one-time briefing clerk for the Texas Supreme Court. He was generally popular and well-liked.

Hughes commenced an energetic campaign that took her all over the state, from small towns in East Texas to cities along the lower Rio Grande Valley and from large cities such as Amarillo in the Panhandle to San Antonio in Central Texas and to Houston in the southeast. Much of her travel, especially to the small towns, was by car.

> The first thing that I'd do when I'd go to a small town was to go around [to] the newspaper. I had a printed interview which I'd give the editor, a copy accompanied by a photograph, and I would suggest to him that he put it in the paper. They always did, and I never had any trouble about that. Sometimes I would go around to the radio station, and almost always they would interview me.[59]

The campaign, as was true in most judicial races, lacked fireworks, but sometimes neither the situations nor the questions encountered were routine. When Hughes arrived at the Galveston daily newspaper for a scheduled interview, she found union printers picketing the building over a labor dispute. Although the interview would have resulted in good publicity, she declined to cross the line. Asked in El Paso whether she believed cameras should be permitted in the courtroom—a growing issue between the judiciary and the press—she said the decision should be left to the individual judge. However, if cameras did not interfere with the normal courtroom procedure, she believed they should be permitted. At a Rotary Club meeting in Sulphur Springs, the question of the United Nations came up, and she reaffirmed her belief that it was the world's best hope for peace. While in Brownsville in the Rio Grande Valley, she encountered her one-time benefactor, the former governor James V. Allred, now a U.S. district judge. Allred introduced her to the jury over which he was presiding and to a number of lawyers who came into his chambers. Hughes thought he seemed partial to her.[60]

Although the campaign was the most ambitious one Hughes had ever undertaken because it required extensive statewide travel, the contest never reached the level of intensity she experienced in her 1946 congressional race. Not once did she encounter her opponent on the campaign trail. The closest she came was in Vernon, where she appeared on the same platform with Greenhill's wife.[61]

Differences in the two contestants' political views were not readily apparent. "Of course, the lawyers knew that I was a liberal," Hughes later said, "but they have always said that when I get on the bench that that made no difference at all." The Democrats of Texas, a new organization of liberal Democrats, helped considerably, particularly in Houston, where a well-known liberal, Frankie Randolph, led the way. Labor unions printed small signs on Hughes's behalf, and in Henderson County, an attorney who later became a prominent federal judge, Wayne Justice, worked hard for her.[62]

Hardly ever mentioned, and never brought up as an issue, was the fact that for the first time a woman was seeking a seat on the Texas Supreme Court. This amounted to a double-edged sword, for the controversy over a woman being a judge in 1935 had been helpful because it rallied women's groups to her cause. Now, twenty-three years later, the intense dedication to putting her in office because she was a woman was missing. Of great help were Hughes's friends in the B&PW Clubs all around the state. Many of them entertained her with receptions and dinners when she came to their towns.

Hughes wanted an endorsement by the Texas Federation of B&PW. Behind the scenes, she lobbied hard to get it. Another leader in B&PW, Hermine Tobolowsky, a rising star in the battle for women's rights who later would gain fame as the mother of the Texas Equal Rights Amendment, believed an endorsement was improper for an organization whose members were both Democrats and Republicans. The two hard-nosed women clashed.

Tobolowsky, a graduate of the University of Texas Law School and twenty-five years younger than Hughes, had moved to Dallas from San Antonio in 1951 upon marrying a retail clothing store executive. She began working as a solo practitioner and plunged into volunteer work, her first major effort involving the crusade so dear to Hughes—winning the right for women to serve on juries. In 1957 she made an appearance in Austin before the Texas Legislature to argue on behalf of legislation that Hughes had strongly favored for many years—the right for women to sign deeds or handle property sales without the consent of their husbands. As a fellow member with Hughes in the B&PW, her drive and determination quickly put her in leadership roles. She was legal counsel for the National Federation of B&PW and was in line to become president of the Texas Federation in 1959.[63]

Now, though, in her position as chairwoman of the Texas Federation of B&PW's Women in Government Committee, she believed clubs and state federations had no right to endorse women for appointive and elective offices, not even Sarah T. Hughes. Tobolowsky told state president Claudia G. Hazlewood of Midland that while individual clubs should encourage women to participate in affairs of government, should make lists of qualified women to submit to appropriate government agencies, and should encourage the membership as *individuals* to support women of their choice, they should not officially endorse particular candidates.[64]

Individual members of B&PW, she pointed out, had diversified political opinions. Some were Republicans; some were Democrats. It would not be fair to require a B&PW member to support a candidate offered by a political party not of her own choice. The Texas Federation's board of directors had discussed this matter in August, she said, and they had concluded that official endorsement of a particular candidate would seem to require members either to follow the directive or to leave the organization. A widespread exodus of members conceivably could occur.[65]

Hughes argued otherwise. She cited the number of the page of the *Handbook of Federation Procedure* stating that "on the basis of women's eminent fitness, the Federation and its affiliated clubs may endorse and work for the election and appointment of qualified women for local, state, national and international offices, boards and commissions, who at the time of endorsement believe in and practice the principles and policies of our federation." This national policy, Hughes said, should override Tobolowsky's view. "If Texas and the local clubs took such position it would certainly weaken our position with reference to getting women appointed or elected," Hughes wrote.[66]

The sensible thing to do, Hughes argued, was to have Democrats work for the election of Democrats and Republicans for the Republicans. Hazlewood was distressed as to the proper course. "We have an apparent paradox," she wrote, and to Hughes's dismay left the matter as it was.[67] And while Hughes enjoyed the unofficial support of many club members, she failed to have the benefit of widespread, organized B&PW campaigns on her behalf, as had proved so effective in 1935.

While not offering an official endorsement, the Texas Federation of B&PW found another way to honor Hughes two months before the primary election. A newly created Sarah T. Hughes Women in Government Award was presented at the annual meeting in Lubbock to the club having done the most to promote the participation of women in government.[68]

In June, one month before the election, another major disappointment occurred. For the first time in any of her judicial races, Hughes failed to win the endorsement of her own Dallas Bar Association. She had expected to gain its backing, but the poll by bar members, announced in newspapers by the bar association's judicial committee, gave Greenhill 419 votes and Hughes 315.

"The substantial local majority for Greenhill," according to an editorial in the *Dallas Morning News*, "was obviously a tribute to his efficiency in service." But it also reflected, the newspaper wrote, "considerable lawyer skepticism over Judge Hughes's overliberal tinge in Texas politics." It would not be an overstatement, the newspaper declared, to say that Greenhill was the choice of conservatives and Hughes the choice of liberals.[69]

More damaging but perhaps less stinging than the Dallas Bar's vote was the statewide poll conducted by the State Bar of Texas endorsing Greenhill. State bar members, who had begun taking the poll in 1952 and announcing the results to the public as their assessment of the fitness of judicial candidates, favored Greenhill, 5,844 to 1,727.[70] The failure of both the state and local bar associations to endorse Hughes seemed to be a political statement reflecting the growing conservatism of Dallas and the state as well as the changing nature of the legal profession. Rather than having general practices, more and more attorneys were representing specialized business interests and working out of increasingly large law firms with corporations as clients.

In seeking to define her own niche, Hughes began appealing more directly to liberal elements in her speeches. "Mine is a people's court," she said. "I am close to the people and have an understanding of their problems. Nobody on the present Supreme Court has this experienced understanding of the law in relation to the people themselves." The Texas forefathers had been wise, she said, in writing into the constitution the provision that judges should be elected by the people rather than by any special group.[71]

When the Democrats of Texas, a group of liberals, met in Austin two weeks prior to the primary election, Hughes sat on the platform along with new U.S. senator Ralph Yarborough, who had cheered the state's liberal Democrats the previous year by winning the Senate seat vacated by Price Daniel. News reports said that the fifteen hundred delegates from throughout the state gave the biggest ovations to Yarborough, now seeking a six-year term over oilman Bill Blakley; to Henry B. Gonzalez, campaigning for the governorship over Price Daniel; and to Sarah T. Hughes.[72]

Newspaper editorials overwhelmingly endorsed Greenhill. "When a man is serving on the Supreme Court of Texas and is doing his work well, it is expected that he will make a good man to succeed himself on the bench," wrote the *Dallas Morning News* in an editorial that struck a typical theme.[73] Without any pressing issues in the race and with newspapers throughout the state invariably favoring conservative Democrats, there seemed little reason to oppose the incumbent Greenhill, short though his tenure had been.

It also was likely that her reputation as a liberal, which now had superseded her nonpartisan fame as the state's first female district judge, was a factor in the negative editorials. The *San Angelo Times* referred to her "trouncing" in the state bar poll as evidence of "substantial lawyer skepticism of her over-liberal tinge in Texas politics." The *Greenville Herald Banner* described her as one who "has long been a local liberal[,] even an 'overliberal.'"[74] The word *overliberal*, appearing in both of these editorials, seemed to owe its origin to the earlier *Dallas Morning News* editorial.

Nevertheless, for a while early returns in the July 27 election had Hughes ahead. But in the end, voters returned Greenhill to office by a margin of less than fifteen thousand votes out of more than a million cast. The outcome, 580,994 to 566,807, was far closer than most observers had anticipated.

"Her good showing may prompt the judge to try for another statewide office at some future date," concluded "Weathervane," an unsigned column in the *Dallas Morning News*. A columnist in another newspaper wrote that Hughes's showing provided the biggest surprise of the election. "I didn't think she'd come within a country mile of Judge Greenhill's vote," he wrote. Another writer credited the nearness of the election to the women of Texas. "They almost elected her," he wrote.[75]

Afterward, though, Hughes expressed her disappointment about the failure of the Texas Federation of B&PW to endorse her because of Tobolowsky's position. She told her friend Louise Raggio that this had cost her the election.[76]

And while Hughes had expected to win when she first announced for the office, she was not entirely displeased with the race itself. "I did everything that I could to be elected," she said, "and I had no regrets about it at all." The campaigning, once again, had been enjoyable, and she did not spend any money that she did not have. "It was worthwhile as far as the fun that I got out of it," she said eleven years later in an oral history interview.[77]

She spent $28,934.14 on the campaign. More than half of that amount, $16,000, was her own money. Her biggest benefactor was Oscar Mauzy, who contributed $1,000. Greenhill had a far bigger campaign budget, reporting expenditures of $48,149.82.[78]

Election returns showed that despite the Dallas Bar Association's negative poll, Hughes carried Dallas County as well as Tarrant, Harris, El Paso, Jefferson, and Wichita counties, the Rio Grande Valley, and much of East Texas. However, Austin voters in Travis County and San Antonio voters in Bexar County were heavily against her, as were voters in the Panhandle and Lubbock.[79]

Although Hughes had not pushed political ideology as an issue for voters to consider, the *Dallas Morning News* blamed her loss on voters' perception of her as "a liberal-labor-loyalist political leader."[80] She did not agree with this assessment, believing that liberal-conservative factionalism may have been a "slight factor" but not a major one. She thought she had erred in choosing to run against Greenhill instead of Hamilton. Greenhill, she realized, was "qualified and he had been a good judge."[81]

For those in the "liberal-labor-loyalist" camp, only one bright spot resulted from the primary election. Ralph Yarborough was returned to the Senate seat he had held since the special election the previous year. Gonzalez, the liberal gubernatorial candidate, was swamped by Price Daniel. The war between liberals and conservatives in the state's Democratic Party continued.

~9

Campaigning for the Federal Bench

Sarah T. Hughes and Sam Rayburn shared a common bond—unqualified devotion to the Democratic Party. The majority of Texans jumped ship in 1928 to vote for Herbert Hoover instead of the Democrat, but Catholic, anti-Prohibitionist, Tammany-connected New Yorker Al Smith. Hughes, just getting her feet wet in politics, and Rayburn, already a veteran congressman, campaigned enthusiastically together for Smith in Tyler and Canton in East Texas and in McKinney in North Texas.[1] When twenty-four years later, Texas Democrats abandoned Adlai Stevenson over the Texas tidelands issue in favor of Republican Dwight Eisenhower, Hughes and Rayburn again steadfastly and publicly supported the Democratic national ticket. And they did so again in 1956 when the majority of Texans once more cast their votes for Eisenhower instead of Stevenson.

Three times, then, Hughes and Rayburn to their dismay had seen Texans forsake their traditional Democratic roots for a Republican presidential candidate. In 1960, there was a good chance it would happen again.

Lyndon B. Johnson, having been denied at the summer convention the privilege of serving as his party's presidential candidate, surprised even his closest friends by accepting Senator John F. Kennedy's bid to be his vice-presidential nominee. Whether Johnson's place on the ticket would ensure a Democratic victory throughout the South was uncertain, nor was it assured that his presence would return Texas voters to the Democratic camp. If the Democrats were to reclaim the White House in November, though, Texas's twenty-four electoral votes were desperately needed. For this to happen, more votes must be won in Texas's metropolitan areas.

In this regard an assignment fell to Hughes to play a leading role in the presidential campaign in Dallas County, one evidently recommended by her old friend, Rayburn. The actual summons came from State Democratic Party headquarters in Austin. A comment she made about it eight years later in an oral history interview suggested the intensity of her commitment to the

Democratic Party: "Actually the person who contacted me—I hate to say it now because he's a Republican—was Will Wilson." (Wilson later had become a Republican.)[2]

Hughes was one of a triumvirate of party stalwarts expected to lead Dallas County voters back into the Democratic camp. Their task was not an easy one, for voters not only had rejected Stevenson twice but also had continued to send the Republican Bruce Alger to Congress. Given equal billing with Hughes as cochairman was Carl Phinney. They both reported to the manager of the Dallas County campaign, Barefoot Sanders.[3] Hughes was well acquainted with both men. Sanders, an attorney who had known Hughes for years, had served in the Texas House of Representatives from 1952 to 1958. At the age of thirty-five, he was a rising star among the state's loyalists. Between Hughes and Sanders there was special connection. H. B. Sanders, Barefoot's father, had served as Hughes's cochairman for her 1946 congressional campaign. Hughes also had a long relationship with Phinney, a Dallas attorney, World War II infantry hero, and commanding general of the 36th Infantry Division of the Texas National Guard. Her friendship with Phinney and his wife, Louise Snow Phinney, dated to her service in the Texas Legislature, when Louise was the chief clerk, and she and Louise sometimes shared a hotel room in Austin. Phinney's appointment was generally understood to be a gesture toward conservative Democrats; Hughes appealed to the liberal wing; and Sanders bridged the gap between the two.

There was much to be done. Hughes, thrilled to be involved in what she loved best, pitched in enthusiastically at all levels—planning events, making speeches, and even addressing envelopes and stuffing campaign literature into them. Hughes said: "I even went so far as to put out stickers on people's cars. I did anything and everything that was necessary to get the votes. I tried to get money—did get some." At the State Fair of Texas in October she donned a red, white, and blue outfit and passed out leaflets. Her friend and secretary, Gwen Graul, helped her with much of the clerical work. In her speeches Hughes, at least in her own mind, avoided negative attacks ("all my speeches emphasized the positive things that would be done by a Democratic administration"). Before a large audience of the Council of Jewish Women, she debated with Bruce Alger over the merits of Kennedy and Nixon. "She was out front and very glad to be out front," Sanders later recalled in describing her activities as cochairman, and she did so without neglecting her judicial duties.[4]

All campaign activities in the county fell under the supervision of Sanders,

Hughes, and Phinney, and there were some noteworthy ones. An early event was in helping the Democratic Women's Committee sponsor a reception for two of John F. Kennedy's sisters and his sister-in-law, Ethel Kennedy, at the Adolphus Hotel. Hughes, working with Barefoot Sanders's wife, Jan, had been concerned that the city's predominant Republicanism might cause a slim turnout. The two women scouted the city for a reception site that would not swallow the crowd. Finally, with some trepidation, they chose the grand ball-room at the Adolphus Hotel. They were delighted when the crowds turned out to be so large and enthusiastic that the police had to hold them back from the platform to safeguard the Kennedy women. On another occasion Sam Rayburn visited the Dallas suburb of Duncanville to speak at a large event, sharing the podium once again with Hughes and keeping intact their record of campaigning together for every Democratic presidential nominee since Al Smith.[5]

The biggest event for the campaign committee occurred on September 13, when the two candidates themselves, John F. Kennedy and Lyndon B. Johnson, came to Dallas on their barnstorming tour of Texas. With them was a star-studded list: Speaker of the House Sam Rayburn, Kennedy's sister Patricia Kennedy Lawford, Lady Bird Johnson, and prominent Texas politicians including Gerald Mann, the state campaign director whom Hughes had met when he was Governor Allred's secretary of state.

This brief Texas tour was especially eventful. A compelling issue before the nation was whether a Catholic could be elected president, a subject Kennedy decided to confront in Houston in a nationally televised address. He arrived in Houston on the evening of Monday, September 12, having made earlier stops that day in El Paso, Lubbock, and San Antonio. Kennedy made his much-awaited appearance before a large gathering of skeptical Baptist ministers in the Rice Hotel. His adroitness in handling the matter before a national television audience, it soon would be acknowledged, removed the issue of his religion as a factor in the campaign. Now, the morning after, the Texas tour resumed in Fort Worth with both candidates appearing before an enthusiastic crowd at a downtown park.

The Dallas itinerary began with the departure from Fort Worth, where Hughes and Sanders joined Kennedy and Johnson for the thirty-mile ride to Dallas in an open-top limousine. Hughes, thrilled to be meeting Kennedy and enjoying her exposure to Johnson, squeezed in between them in the back seat. Sanders sat in front with the driver. It was the first time Hughes had met

Kennedy, and it was her best opportunity up to that point for a visit with Johnson. Although she had met Johnson briefly in 1948 in Dallas during the Truman whistle-stop campaign and had corresponded with him regularly in recent years, she had not developed a personal relationship with him. The ride with Johnson and Kennedy would signal the beginning of a much closer friendship. She would reflect on the automobile ride with Kennedy and Johnson as "one of the most exciting experiences I ever had and one which I will never forget." [6]

Conditions for conversation were not optimal, though. Kennedy, tired from so many speeches and with more to come, tried to save his voice by not talking at all. He listened, though. Hughes told him the liberal Democrats in Dallas County were much better organized than previously, and she was very optimistic about the election. (In this regard, the committee had established an ambitious "get-out-the-vote" plan with precinct chairmen that extended even to assigning a worker to canvass the neighbors on every residential block.) Brief stops and impromptu talks were made in Arlington and Grand Prairie. Supporters lined the congested highway for a glimpse of the candidates. In Grand Prairie, Hughes was amused to see a woman attempt to take Kennedy's handkerchief from his pocket. Kennedy instinctively covered it with his hand, then reached over and pulled Johnson's handkerchief from his pocket to give her. At this same stop, Kennedy reluctantly and briefly put on a western hat presented to him, then quickly took it off.[7]

Hughes later said what she remembered most about their time together was a comment Johnson made to Kennedy somewhere along the way. "Now if you want to appoint a woman to an office, here's one that's pretty good," he said.[8] It was a back-handed compliment, no doubt, but Hughes did not take umbrage.

On the downtown streets of Dallas, en route to Memorial Coliseum, where the main rally was to be held, huge and enthusiastic crowds slowed the motorcade to a crawl and sometimes to a complete stop. "The crowds were simply enormous," Hughes later said. Kennedy seemed energized, speaking and shaking hands with bystanders who crowded next to the convertible. Progress was so slow that at one point Hughes saw Johnson's staff member Liz Carpenter jump out of the press car just behind, run into a department store, and purchase a new shirt for her boss, all in time to get back into the car before it could leave her behind.[9]

At one point Johnson turned to Sanders and asked him to get an estimate from police about the size of the crowd, wanting to contrast it favorably with that of the previous day, when Richard Nixon had been in town. He was pleased at what he later learned. Police Chief Jesse Curry estimated the street crowds at 175,000, considerably more than the estimated 100,000 who had cheered Nixon.[10] At Memorial Coliseum some 9,500 enthusiastic supporters greeted Kennedy and Johnson, the same number that had welcomed Nixon at the same location.

Nearly two months later, four days before the November election, Lyndon and Lady Bird Johnson returned to Dallas to be honored at a Democratic Party luncheon at the Adolphus Hotel. All Dallas County Democratic office-holders—legislators and courthouse officials largely—were invited. Only a few of them accepted the invitation, indicative of their lack of enthusiasm for the Kennedy-Johnson ticket. Rank-and-file Democrats, though, enthusiastically responded, and the luncheon crowd was huge—eighteen hundred persons. As it turned out, this presumably routine affair created more national headlines than the September visit by both Democratic candidates.[11]

That morning, conservative congressman Bruce Alger summoned his well-dressed "Alger Girls" downtown, ostensibly to pin Nixon buttons on pedestrians. By noon they and other right-wing Republican supporters, many of them bearing anti-LBJ pickets, congregated at the intersection of Commerce and Akard streets, where they knew Johnson would appear. They spilled into the lobbies of the Baker and Adolphus hotels. When Johnson and Lady Bird came down from their rooms at the Baker, they were surprised to find themselves surrounded by a crowd of hostile demonstrators, who showered insults and epithets on them. Barefoot Sanders, there to escort the Johnsons across the street to the Adolphus, where Sarah Hughes and the luncheon crowd waited, suggested a detour to a side door to avoid more demonstrators on the streets and in the Adolphus lobby. Johnson declined the offer. The hectic scene continued outside on Commerce Street, where Alger, standing tall and looking haughty, displayed a sign, LBJ SOLD OUT TO YANKEE SOCIAL-ISTS. One sign said simply, "LBJ TRAITOR." One person thrust a sign, DOWN WITH LADY BIRD, in front of Mrs. Johnson, whose hair was mussed up by the crowd and who later said the demonstration was her most frightening moment in politics. At one point Johnson paused, evidently ready to say something. One of the demonstrators preempted him by shouting, "Louder and funnier, Lyndon." Another man called out, "He never said anything in his life." The frantic scene continued into the lobby of the Adolphus, where John Tower, the GOP candidate for Johnson's Senate seat, tried to confront him in an impromptu debate in the midst of this rabid crowd.[12]

A reporter described the situation as being the "nearest thing to an uncontrollable mob" in Dallas since the wilder days of the Texas-Oklahoma pregame football activities. At one point, police officers endeavored to clear a path through the demonstrators, but Johnson would have none of it. "If the time has come when I can't walk through the lobby of a hotel in Dallas with my lady without a police escort, I want to know it," he said.[13]

In the grand ballroom, Hughes and the crowd of eighteen hundred supporters, unaware of the turmoil, awaited the honored couple's arrival. "We just thought they were delayed," she said. Sanders believed if those at the luncheon had been aware of the melee downstairs and had stepped into the lobby themselves, there would have been a mob fight of enormous proportions. His wife, Jan Sanders, having learned of the contretemps outside, feared the demonstrators would invade the banquet room and create chaos there, too. Finally the Johnsons managed to work their way through the crowd and arrive in the banquet room. Hughes, sitting not far away at the head table, heard them relate what had taken place. "Mrs. Johnson was somewhat upset, but Mr. Johnson was quite calm," Hughes recalled. In fact, his composure was such that he delivered a ringing speech, described by Jan Sanders as one of the most memorable campaign speeches she had ever heard.[14]

After the luncheon Hughes and Jan Sanders arrived early at the site of the afternoon Johnson event, Wynnewood shopping center in Oak Cliff, fearful that some of the downtown demonstrators might appear there. To set a positive, upbeat tone that would contrast with the shocking downtown scene, the two women mounted the platform and entertained the waiting crowd by dancing the Charleston to the accompaniment of a Dixieland band. As it turned out, there were no troublemakers here, and a large enthusiastic crowd greeted the Johnsons.[15]

The emotional noontime demonstration, headlined across the nation, was shocking both in its intensity and in the fact that it had been directed at two unusually prominent fellow Texans. Many believed the hostility created a backlash against the Republicans. As early as the next day some were crediting it as turning the tide in Texas for the Kennedy-Johnson ticket. "Demos

Claim GOP's Jeers to Help LBJ," read a headline in the *Dallas Times Herald*. Johnson himself, in calmly confronting a threatening mob of Texans, was portrayed across the nation in a new, more favorable light. Liberals and intellectuals from the East Coast who had viewed him disdainfully as a crude, anti-intellectual cowboy, now realized he had a new dimension they could appreciate: He, too, they saw, was despised by the right-wingers.[16]

Four days later, the nation's voters made their decision. They sent Kennedy to the White House by the slimmest of margins, giving him 49.7 percent of the votes compared with 49.6 for Nixon. Texas voters returned to the Democratic Party, favoring the Kennedy-Johnson ticket by a margin of 46,233 out of about 2.3 million total votes. Dallas County remained in the Republican camp, its voters casting about 60 percent of their ballots for Nixon. They also returned Republican Bruce Alger to Congress for his fourth term and elected for the first time a Republican as county commissioner. Hughes, having watched the election returns at home that night with George, was encouraged. "I thought that we helped to win Texas for Kennedy by the strenuous campaign that we put on in Dallas County even though we lost Dallas County," she said.[17]

With a Democratic administration now ahead, Hughes's thoughts returned to the idea she had first entertained in 1949 after Harry S. Truman had been elected—her experience and her faithful work in the Democratic Party might lead to presidential appointment as a federal judge. Such a lifetime appointment was highly prestigious and ordinarily a matter of patronage. Hughes had no thought of waiting around until the idea occurred to someone else; she would propose her own candidacy.

Her campaign began with the assistance of friends, whom she undoubtedly tipped off and encouraged to write letters on her behalf. One of the first was former state district judge and future fellow U.S. district judge William M. (Mac) Taylor Jr., at the time in private practice. (Hughes had an interesting link to Taylor; her appointment to the bench in 1935 had been to fill the vacancy created when Taylor's father resigned as judge of the 14th District Court. Five years after Hughes went on the federal bench, Mac Taylor would join her when Lyndon B. Johnson named him a federal judge.) Taylor sent identical letters to Vice President Johnson and Senator Yarborough on December 15, 1960, urging Hughes's appointment if another federal judgeship was created for the Northern District of Texas, which he believed likely with the election of Kennedy and Johnson. Her skills as a judge, he wrote, were outstanding in every respect—"one of the finest and ablest Judges before whom I have had the pleasure of appearing . . . has a fine an appellate record as any trial judge in this state. . . . the docket of her court is current." Her goal always was "ultimate justice." Beyond all these factors, he wrote, introducing what would be a common theme in the coming drive, she is an avowed Democrat in a community in which "to put it mildly—[it] is very difficult for an avowed Democrat. . . . She has fought and bled for the Democratic party, its principles, its tenets, and its candidates, and she has done this stoutly and vigorously and even when her own office was at stake."[18]

As was Hughes's custom, she showed no reluctance in campaigning for the appointment, beginning with a trip to see "Mr. Democrat," Sam Rayburn, in his hometown of Bonham, two hours northeast of Dallas. Over the Christmas holidays she drove there with a long-time Texas Democrat, Bill Kittrell, to ask Rayburn for his support.[19] Rayburn, relaxing in his bachelor home amid "old and comfortable" furniture, readily agreed to help his old friend gain the appointment. As Speaker of the House he would have no direct involvement, but his influence and power concerning all matters in the capitol were well known.[20]

Next, Hughes turned directly to another friend whom she had known almost as long as Rayburn and who could lend special assistance—Ralph Yarborough. As the state's sole Democratic U.S. senator and a member of the body that would confirm judicial appointments, Yarborough would be the designated individual to exercise patronage privileges. Learning that he would stop over at Dallas Love Field Airport while en route to Washington for the opening session of Congress, Hughes drove there to tell him between flights that she wanted to be a federal judge. Yarborough enthusiastically agreed to support her and said he would speak to the president and attorney general about it.[21]

Hughes also worked another angle. She encouraged other friends to begin a letter-writing campaign on her behalf to Yarborough and Johnson as well as Senator James O. Eastland of Mississippi, chairman of the Senate Judiciary Committee. The letter writers often turned over to Hughes the responses they received from these key individuals. Johnson told J. Hart Willis he did not expect to participate in the selection, since he would be vice president, and the responsibility of selecting judges would rest with the

Democratic senators from Texas. "Nevertheless, I am glad to have your recommendation here, and will certainly bear it in mind in the event I am asked about the matter." Willis sent a copy of Johnson's response to Hughes, displaying great perception in his own appended comment: "I believe we may count on Lyndon and [I] feel they will ask his suggestions."[22]

Word of a possible appointment inevitably leaked to the press. On Christmas Day, 1960, a story in the *Dallas Morning News* quoted "reliable Democratic sources" as saying that right now Judge Hughes was the favorite for appointment to a new federal court Congress was expected to authorize early in the next session for the Northern District of Texas. Her strongest competitor in the behind-the-scenes rope-pulling was said to be a fellow judge, Claude Williams of the 160th District Court. A third Dallas County courthouse official, District Attorney Henry Wade, was identified as a dark horse who had been saying privately he "wouldn't mind a crack at the job." Hughes, interviewed by the newspaper reporter, said she had had no contact from anyone about the job. Would she take it if offered? she was asked. "Surely," she replied.[23]

A month later Hughes went to Washington, D.C., with a group of Texas Democratic loyalists to witness the inauguration of John F. Kennedy. Never before had she attended an inauguration. This one would be remembered almost as much for the bitterly cold weather as for the event itself. On the night before the ceremony, Hughes and her companions, Mike and Betty McKool, Dallas liberal-loyalist stalwarts, tried to buy woolen underwear for the next day, but the department stores were sold out. The next day, with six inches of snow on the ground, Hughes nearly froze as she watched the ceremony outside the Capitol Building from a reserved section. One of the men in her party, Wayne Justice (later a federal judge in Texas himself), lent Hughes his scarf so she could wrap it around her head. Hughes and those around her bought and placed newspapers on the snow in hopes of keeping the cold from their feet. In these frigid circumstances under a bright sun Hughes heard the nation's thirty-fifth president declare, "The torch has been passed to a new generation of Americans," and to implore his fellow Americans, "Ask not what your country can do for you—ask what you can do for your country." She was excited to hear these stirring words from a person she very much admired.[24]

Because of the extreme cold, the McKools had decided to stay in their rooms and watch the inauguration on television. Sarah returned to the small hotel she shared with them, shivering, and the McKools worked hard to warm her up, covering her with blankets and massaging her icy feet for an hour.[25]

That night, though, Hughes braved the weather once more to attend one of the presidential balls, where she received, along with other guests, a medallion for her charm bracelet. She kept it the rest of her life as one of her most cherished possessions. She shook hands at the gala with the new vice president, Lyndon B. Johnson, but missed seeing President Kennedy.[26]

During her stay in the nation's capital Hughes found time to talk to two important men about her future aspirations—Walter Jenkins and George C. McGhee. Jenkins had been a key staff member for Lyndon Johnson since 1939. McGhee, recently living in Dallas, had years of experience in the Department of State and soon would serve on Kennedy's Policy Planning Council and later as undersecretary for Political Affairs. With Jenkins she mentioned only the judgeship. With McGhee, she explored another idea she mentioned to no one else—an ambassadorship.[27]

Back in Texas, Sarah T. Hughes wrote letters four days after the inauguration to President Kennedy, Vice President Johnson, and presidential assistants Lawrence F. O'Brien and John Bailey. She announced her desire to have "an appointment in the present administration."[28]

In presenting her case, she pointed to service dating as far back as campaigning for Al Smith in 1928 and speaking from the same platform as Sam Rayburn in East Texas towns. "I have actively worked for every Democratic presidential nominee since that time," she said, "and at the National Democratic Convention in 1952 my name was placed in nomination for Vice President of the United States." Her twenty-six years' experience as judge of the 14th District Court of Texas, she believed, qualified her for a federal judgeship. There presently was no vacancy for a federal district judge in the Northern District of Texas, she pointed out, but she expected Congress in all probability to add an extra judgeship in the immediate future (in fact it added two). A need existed in the Northern District, for there had not been an additional judge since 1922 even though the population in the district had grown sixfold.[29]

She provided more explanation for her interest in an ambassadorship. "While I have not been in the foreign service, I have had contacts with UN

Agencies and with many peoples of other countries," she wrote. She listed her three years' experience on the executive committee of the UNESCO National Commission, her representation of the International Federation of Business and Professional Women's Clubs at two sessions of the Status of Women Commission, one in New York and the other in Buenos Aires in the spring of 1960. She had made eight trips to foreign countries, and through opportunities provided by the Business and Professional Women's Clubs she had visited with the people of those countries and learned about their institutions. "I recognize the need for our representative abroad to understand the problems of the countries to which they are accredited, learn the language, and know the people."[30]

Johnson replied: "I don't know to what extent I will be consulted on these appointments, but it will be a pleasure to use every opportunity I have to insure that your experience, your willingness, and your qualifications are given the highest consideration."[31]

Hughes had done her homework concerning a possible judgeship. When President Kennedy assumed office, there were eleven vacancies in the federal courts. A tremendous backlog had piled up in federal courts across the nation, and four months after Kennedy's inauguration the passage of the Omnibus Judgeship Act meant that his administration was charged with the responsibility of appointing more than a hundred federal judges. No president ever had been confronted with such a massive task. As a practical matter, despite Article III of the Constitution, as Assistant Attorney General Joe Dolan commented, the judges were to be appointed in effect by the Democratic senators of the relevant states, by and with the advice and consent of the president rather than the other way around.[32]

In the case of Texas, that relevant senator was Ralph W. Yarborough, but the former senior Democratic senator, Lyndon B. Johnson, did not think it fair to be suddenly excluded from patronage privileges just because he had become vice president. This, among other things, would complicate the situation for Sarah T. Hughes. And while the names of prospective federal judges would come largely through the senators, it was the Justice Department that checked their backgrounds and presented the nominees to the president. Deputy Attorney General Byron R. White was given the job of overseeing this entire process. During the first two years of the Kennedy administration, an average of one judge a week was to be sent to the Senate for confirmation.

Hughes's interest in an ambassadorship no doubt had been piqued by her spring trip to Buenos Aires, which she attended in her capacity as UN chairman for the International Federation of B&PW. At that meeting, the fourteenth session of the UN Commission on the Status of Women, Hughes had spoken on behalf of the B&PW on her favorite topic, political rights for women, before delegates from countries around the world. Her interest in the sessions was so keen that she took sixty-one pages of handwritten notes on a stenographer's notepad.[33]

She followed a slightly different route in pursuing the ambassadorship, continuing to use McGhee, recently appointed to Kennedy's Policy Planning Council, as her primary contact. McGhee informed her that after their initial discussion, he had spoken on her behalf with Yarborough, Johnson, Rayburn, and Chester Bowles. "It is not always easy to find out who makes the final decisions in these matters," McGhee wrote to her. "However, I will continue to do all I can to see that you receive something along the lines you desire."[34]

When her law school friend, Brooks Hays, was appointed assistant secretary of state, she sent him a congratulatory note and said she hoped to see him in Washington. Once she was there in February, she primarily wanted to meet Secretary of State Dean Rusk but had to settle for Undersecretary of State Chester Bowles. Afterward, she reminded him to remember her as a candidate for future ambassadorial appointments or commissions of the United Nations. "While I fully realize the importance of the Judiciary, twenty-six years as a District Judge is a long time, and I would really like the opportunity to serve in what I now consider an even greater field," she wrote. She reminded him that in addition to George McGhee she was a good friend of another member of his staff—Brooks Hays.[35]

In Washington she continued to work both possibilities, meeting with Hy Raskin at the Democratic National Headquarters and Ramsey Clark of the attorney general's office. Clark, a Texan serving as head of the Lands Division, was the son of Supreme Court Justice Tom C. Clark, and he later would become attorney general himself. Evidently Hughes confined her comments about the judgeship to Raskin and Clark, for in her letters of appreciation she mentioned only that. Clark offered to set up a meeting for her with Attorney General Robert F. Kennedy at some point in the future when the time seemed right. "I'll be ready any time you feel it is advisable, and will also appreciate it if you will let me know of any developments which would be helpful," she told Clark.[36]

Clark was counseling patience to Hughes, not an easy attribute for her.

In mid-April he repeated his advice in a telephone call. "Your assurances always make me feel better," she wrote afterward. "I admit that doing nothing frustrates me, so if there is anything at all that should be done, please let me know." She reminded him that her birthday, August 2, was approaching. She would be sixty-five, and for that reason any delay concerned her. "I feel fortunate in having you in the Attorney General's Office, otherwise my chances might have already gone out the window. I shall always be grateful to you for what you have already done."[37]

In fact, it was impossible for Hughes to follow Clark's advice to do nothing. After her conversation with Clark and undoubtedly at her encouragement, a new spate of letters went out from Democratic friends such as Joe Pool, Cordye Hall, Mike McKool, Charles O. Galvin, and Oscar Mauzy recommending her for the judgeship. Multiple copies often were sent to the president, Johnson, Rayburn, Robert F. Kennedy, and Yarborough.[38]

These letters emphasized the point especially important to loyalist Democrats and first raised by William M. Taylor Jr.: While other Democrats had either abandoned the party or kept quiet during the 1960 campaign—not to mention 1952 and 1956—Hughes had worked faithfully and ardently for the Democratic presidential nominees. For President Kennedy now to choose a lukewarm Democrat instead of Hughes would betray the loyalists who had had the courage to support him at considerable political risk. Joe Pool, congressional candidate who had been defeated in his 1960 bid against Bruce Alger, summarized this point of view in strongly worded telegrams to President Kennedy, Vice President Johnson, Speaker of the House Rayburn, Attorney General Robert F. Kennedy, and Senator Yarborough:

> I know who led the fight for the Democrats in Dallas. District Judge Sarah Hughes worked day and night for President Kennedy, Vice President Johnson, myself, and the Democratic ticket. We suffered personal abuse and ridicule to stand up for our convictions. . . . Judge Hughes who has been the best district judge in Dallas for 26 years should be appointed to bolster the morale of the working Democrats. Please investigate and see who those were who did the work and who those were who only gave lip service.[39]

Oscar Mauzy wrote to Yarborough in similar fashion. Denying a judgeship to Hughes he said "would be the worst thing that could happen" to the morale of loyal Democrats in Dallas County. For many years she had stood as the rallying point for all loyal Democrats, never wavering in her support of the party. "To refuse to reward her for such loyalty would discourage many hundreds of our precinct workers from further activity in behalf of the Democratic Party and its nominees." Mauzy also denied rumors planted, he alleged, by "some of Judge Hughes's enemies" that she no longer wanted a federal judgeship because she preferred to campaign again in 1962 for the Texas Supreme Court. Mauzy said he had talked to Hughes about this matter, and there was no truth to it. "This is just another attempt to create a smoke screen to pave the way for a 'compromise candidate,'" he wrote.[40]

Meanwhile, it soon developed that perhaps the most important obstacle was the one Hughes had mentioned to Ramsey Clark—her age. At sixty-four, she was older than American Bar Association guidelines for appointment to a lifetime federal judgeship. An important aspect of the nomination process for federal judges, in place since 1946, was a review of candidates by the ABA's Standing Committee on the Federal Judiciary. While no administration was bound to follow ABA recommendations, that influential organization's stamp of approval was much desired. The attorney general, the president's brother Robert Kennedy (who was thirty-five years old), had expressed his determination to abide by ABA findings.

Hughes's chances brightened when in May Congress passed the Omnibus Judge Act of 1961, authorizing seventy-three new judgeships throughout the nation. The Kennedy administration was faced with filling these new judgeships as well as existing vacancies, a total of more than a hundred.

She returned to Washington in early May to make her case, hoping to see Robert F. Kennedy. These were busy times for the administration, though, and Robert Kennedy was spending so much time at the White House that Deputy Attorney General Byron White was practically running the Justice Department. First, in April, there had been the Bay of Pigs disaster. Now, in May, Freedom Riders were touring the South in desegregated buses, determined against all odds to ensure that federal laws mandating integration of buses were honored. White told a friend he had never worked so hard in his life.[41] With Robert Kennedy unavailable, Hughes managed to see only White and Joseph Dolan. She also visited Sam Rayburn and Walter Jenkins. Afterward, she thanked Cliff Carter of Vice President Johnson's staff for his assistance in arranging her appointments. "At least Mr. Dolan and Mr. White did not think I looked my age, and that was worth the trip," she told Carter. She added, "Please get in touch with me if you have any suggestions. I'll need all the help I can get."[42]

Walter Jenkins sent a note to Vice President Johnson after Hughes's visits. "Sarah Hughes has seen me twice in the last two days. She says Senator Yarborough and Speaker Rayburn have both told the Attorney General they think an exception should be made for age in her case. She says she believes if you would do so too, it would cinch it. I gave her no assurances, but said I would pass the message on to you."[43]

In response, Johnson penned a note to Jenkins. "Tell Ramsey Clark I hope they can make an exception for her because she is very deserving and outstanding."[44] Ralph Yarborough was less tentative in his favorable responses to those writing in Hughes's behalf. "You may rest assured that I shall do everything I can to bring about her appointment," he wrote to Mike McKool on May 10.[45]

Fearing that the ABA's age limitation might cause the Justice Department to prevent President Kennedy from even seeing Hughes's name as a candidate, Otto B. Mullinax, a Dallas labor lawyer, wrote directly to presidential adviser Arthur Schlesinger Jr. to circumvent that possibility. As to Hughes's age, he pointed out that she was in excellent health, and she had been absent for illness less than two weeks in twenty-six years.[46]

Schlesinger forwarded Mullinax's letter to White, who was overseeing the nominations. White, who had known John F. Kennedy since the 1930s and had bonded with Robert F. Kennedy, seemed in his response to sound a death knell for Hughes's appointment. "The American Bar Association Committee on the Judiciary has informed us that they will not report as qualified any candidate who has reached his or her 64th birthday and the Department of Justice had adopted a policy of not recommending for appointment persons who have reached their 64th birthday. This policy applies to appointments to both the District Court and the Courts of Appeal." When he met with Hughes, he said, she had argued most eloquently that she should be the exception that proves the rule. Without saying so, he did not appear to agree.[47]

In early July an opportunity arose for Hughes to see Lyndon Johnson personally and argue her case when he spoke to the annual meeting of the State Bar of Texas in Fort Worth. Having made arrangements through Johnson's aide Cliff Carter, Hughes went to Johnson's suite in the Texas Hotel to ask again for his support. Somewhat awkwardly, she found among those present in the room another prominent claimant for the judicial appointment, Henry Wade, Dallas County's district attorney who had lost to Alger in the 1956 congressional campaign. Wade's record as district attorney over the past ten years was exemplary, and although he had not been as outspoken as Hughes in his support of the national ticket, he had been faithful to the party, and he was more acceptable to the Dallas business community. Moreover, his father had been a staunch supporter year after year of Sam Rayburn, including service as his campaign manager in Rockwall County, where Henry was reared.[48]

This was Hughes's first occasion to see Johnson since her brief encounter with him at the inauguration. Despite the difficulty in communicating with the vice president in the presence of Wade and others, Hughes said although he didn't give her "a definite promise," she "certainly came away with the feeling" that Johnson would support her. Later, when she contacted both Walter Jenkins and Cliff Carter, she "knew definitely that he was [for her]."[49]

Meanwhile, Hughes's good friend and campaign associate Barefoot Sanders received an appointment as U.S. attorney for the Northern District of Texas and was sworn in on July 24. The four new federal judgeships authorized by Congress for Texas, two of them for the Northern District, still remained vacant. The delay was caused by a behind-the-scenes battle over patronage between Johnson and Yarborough. While Johnson no longer enjoyed the direct patronage rights he had held as the state's senior Democratic senator, President Kennedy, as a courtesy, had offered him veto authority over Texas appointments. Yarborough, as Texas's only Democratic senator (Republican John Tower had won Johnson's vacated Senate seat in a special election), was offended at yielding any of the privileges normally afforded his position, and a feud ensued. President Kennedy finally broke the deadlock by declaring that Johnson and Yarborough each could nominate two of the four federal judges for Texas. At the direction of Robert Kennedy, Ramsey Clark was designated to work out the problem and to bring back the names of four judicial appointees. On a visit to Dallas, Clark advised Hughes he soon would arrange this meeting between the two in Washington to resolve the issue.[50]

To Robert Kennedy, and particularly to Byron R. White, the ABA's position that Hughes would not be qualified for the position because of her age remained the primary obstacle. White, known as "Whizzer" during his spectacular college football days as a running back at Colorado University in the 1930s and during his brief professional football career, was second in command at the Department of Justice as deputy attorney general and less than a year away from appointment as an associate justice of the Supreme Court. According to Clark, it was White, "a hard-headed, aggressive purist," who was the real roadblock to Hughes's appointment. He opposed her for no reason other than her age. The problem was complicated for him by pending recommendations of several other judicial candidates who were as old as or older than Hughes but less qualified. To make an exception for Hughes would take away his easy excuse for rejecting them. The appointment of Wade, who was not disliked by Johnson, Yarborough, or Rayburn, would be the simplest avenue to take.[51]

Still uncertain as to what might happen, Sarah and George took their usual vacation to the Billy Wills ranch in Creede, Colorado, from July 15 to August 4. Hughes advised Clark where she would be just in case anything developed. A week after their return to Dallas, having heard nothing new, a succession of seemingly authoritative but ultimately confusing stories appeared in the Dallas newspapers.[52]

The reports, all with unidentified sources, began on Friday, August 11, when John Mashek, Washington correspondent of the *Dallas Morning News*, wrote that Sarah Hughes may be close to appointment. According to reliable sources, both the vice president and Senator Yarborough had agreed upon her, and this was tantamount to appointment. The only stumbling block remaining, Mashek wrote, was her age.[53]

Scooped on this major story, the afternoon *Dallas Times Herald* could do no better the next day than to locate Yarborough at Dallas Love Field on a stopover en route to El Paso. Yarborough could confirm nothing. Despite his own very early and unswerving support of Hughes, because of her age she remained as far as he knew a dark-horse candidate.[54]

Sunday morning, though, the situation—as far as the two newspapers were concerned—dramatically changed. Both papers reported that Henry Wade had been chosen over Hughes to be the federal judge for the Northern District of Texas. The *News* story, written by political editor Allen Duckworth, cited a source close to the Kennedy administration as its authority. Wade's support had come, it was said by Duckworth's anonymous source, from Speaker Rayburn, whose ties to the Wade family were "long-time, personal and political."[55] The *Times Herald* story was written by Margaret Mayer, a veteran Austin-based reporter who had been close to Johnson, who based her information on "reliable" sources in the Texas capitol. Agreement

on Wade between Johnson and Yarborough, she wrote, "reportedly elimi-
nates Judge Sarah Hughes as a candidate."[56]

So confident were the news stories concerning Wade's pending appointment that all speculation was removed. It was a foregone conclusion, the
Times Herald wrote in a follow-up story concentrating on Wade's likely
successor as district attorney. An editorial in the *News* carried the headline
"Judge Wade." The newspaper concluded he "should make a good judge."[57]
Hughes was convinced her chances had ended. Johnson evidently had
informed her already that the Kennedy administration refused to yield on the
issue of her age. She conceded in a letter to Johnson on the day after the
Sunday news stories appeared:

> I am sure that what was in the Sunday papers about the federal judge-
> ships is correct and that we are at the end of the road.
>
> I want you to know that I appreciate all you did in my behalf. While
> I had hoped the age limit would be waived, apparently the Attorney
> General was adamant. I do understand the situation he faced with refer-
> ence to other appointments.
>
> Perhaps after all the present appointments are filled he will be will-
> ing to make an exception in case of another vacancy in the Northern
> District.[58]

She wrote a similar letter to Ramsey Clark on the same day. "You have
been wonderful, and I will always remember your efforts in my behalf. Thank
you. From now I turn to other fields—probably the Supreme Court—Texas,
not the U.S. There is no age limit for it. Tell Whizzer [Byron R. White] I
understand his problem. He has my sympathy."[59]

To Ralph Yarborough, also on the same day, she wrote: "Perhaps the
future will be brighter. At any rate, at this point I intend to relax and get some
sleep, which is something you need more than I do. Do you realize the other
night when you called me it was 12:30 in Washington and you were still in
your office?"[60] (In Dallas the time was 11:30 P.M.)

Just how the conflicting news stories arose can be speculated upon with
some certainty. Mashek's original story in the *News* probably was based on
information obtained from Johnson or Yarborough, both of whom had
agreed upon Hughes. Mashek had duly recorded the only caveat—the problem of her age. Neither Yarborough nor Johnson at this point knew whether

this obstacle could be surmounted. The Sunday stories proclaiming Wade as the choice probably originated with Johnson, who by now had reluctantly accepted Hughes's rejection by both Kennedy and White. Knowing Wade was acceptable to them, Johnson evidently leaked the news of his almost certain appointment.[61]

Hughes did not know that Wade, on the same day she wrote letters amounting to her concession to him, had a completely different viewpoint about the news stories. Wade, who normally maintained close and friendly relations with the courthouse reporters who covered his office, lost his temper when *Dallas Morning News* reporter Jim Lehrer showed up at his office Monday morning to get his reaction to the Sunday news stories about his almost certain appointment. Wade believed the news stories actually would lead to his downfall. "You guys cost me a federal judgeship," he said, then slammed the door as he retreated into his office to escape Lehrer.[62]

Indeed, Wade's nomination was far from certain. In fact, it began to unravel almost immediately. Hughes, after writing her letters of virtual concession, discussed the matter with several friends. Some of them contacted Johnson, who evidently assured them that the matter was less settled than the news accounts seemed.[63]

One close political ally took an even more aggressive action. Oscar Mauzy had been close to Hughes since that day when he had agreed to help win the right for women to serve on juries and was chosen to be a campaign chairman in her 1958 bid for the Texas Supreme Court. Nearly thirty-nine years later Mauzy, after a prominent public career including a term as an associate justice of the Texas Supreme Court, recalled the interesting and critical steps he took immediately after the news stories about Wade's appointment appeared. After discussions with C. B. Bunkley and W. J. Durham Jr., prominent Dallas African American attorneys who had supported Hughes,[64] the three men decided to make a direct protest to the attorney general. Instead of selecting Hughes, a person who was highly regarded in the African American community for her strong support of civil rights causes, the president was going to select Wade, who had made strong segregationist statements in his losing congressional campaign against Alger in 1956. Wade had seized upon the fact that Alger, reared in Missouri and a Princeton graduate, did not share the prevalent southern obsession for maintaining strict segregation. He attacked Alger for failing to protect the segregation traditions of the South, for favoring gradual integration of public schools, and for "running on the coattails of a member of the NAACP [Vice President Richard Nixon, an honorary NAACP member]." He noted that Alger had refused to join southern Democrats in Congress in pledging to muster every legal option available to oppose the 1954 *Brown v. Topeka* decision.[65]

Mauzy, Durham, and Bunkley felt that neither the president nor the attorney general had known of these proclamations. A problem, of course, for the three men was in gaining access to the proper individuals to give them this information. As it happened, one of Mauzy's close friends in Washington, David Bunn, was also a friend of Byron White's. Bunn agreed to arrange a meeting with White so that the three men could present their information to him.[66] The three Hughes supporters immediately flew to the capital, bringing with them the news stories and advertisements containing Wade's segregationist campaign statements. Robert F. Kennedy, who was present for the meeting, took note of the new information and agreed that the pending announcement confirming Wade's appointment, which Mauzy understood to be imminent, would be delayed indefinitely.[67]

As it soon developed, segregationist views would seem to be no obstacle to the Kennedy administration in its appointment of southern federal judges, perhaps in deference to Senator James Eastland of Mississippi, chairman of the Senate Judiciary Committee, but also because it was difficult to find southern candidates who had not made statements in the past endorsing segregation. The appointment of segregationist W. Harold Cox, Eastland's college roommate, in particular, would prove to be embarrassing. (Cox had been given the ABA's highest rating.) Yet, the information presented about Wade's segregationist viewpoints may have assumed special significance. Within a month the Dallas public schools were to be integrated for the first time, and it was feared segregationists might demonstrate in the same way that had brought harsh headlines to Little Rock, New Orleans, and Houston.

The news stories in Dallas about Wade's forthcoming appointment prompted even more letters from Hughes's supporters, who expressed hopes that the reports were not accurate and continued to write on her behalf. Lyndon B. Johnson replied to them that in the event he was consulted he would keep in mind their comments.[68]

The response of one of White's chief assistants, William A. Geoghegan, infuriated one of the letter writers, for in his acknowledgement he evidently alluded to the views of the *Dallas Morning News*. The letter writer, John E. V. Jasper, fired back caustically and asked Geoghegan to give his letter directly to Kennedy:

It has been the policy of *The Dallas Morning News* [Jasper wrote] to fight against many things Judge Hughes has stood for over a long period of time, particularly her support of the Democratic nominee for the presidency. This newspaper bitterly assailed President Kennedy in practically every issue during his race last year. It has been just as bitter for a long period of time toward Speaker Sam Rayburn. That the Attorney General would do something to gratify *The News* by turning thumbs down on Judge Hughes is indeed ironic. This is feeding a mouth that bites the administration and all those that give their assistance to it.[69]

Suddenly, though, in another reversal, news stories declared Sarah T. Hughes once more the front-runner. On August 28, *Dallas Times Herald* reporter Lonnie Hudkins reported that Judge Hughes "has moved back into contention in the behind-the-scenes race for appointment for federal judge." Hudkins cited a meeting between Sam Rayburn and Robert F. Kennedy as the turning point. "According to sources," Hudkins wrote, "Kennedy wanted to talk to Rayburn about the administration's foreign aid bill and the speaker, reportedly miffed at reports he had sponsored Wade, is said to have discussed the appointment of Hughes." Hudkins wrote that Democratic leaders such as Bill Kittrell (who had accompanied Hughes to Bonham to see Rayburn about her appointment) and India Edwards had besieged Washington with letters supporting Judge Hughes. A significant result of all this, Hudkins reported, was that the Federal Bureau of Investigation over the weekend had begun making the routine checks on Hughes that are normally made on all potential federal appointees.[70]

Hudkins's story was accurate on all counts. The meeting he described between Kennedy and Rayburn later would be recounted as having occurred when the attorney general visited the Speaker's office to inquire why a particular bill, presumably the foreign aid bill, had been frozen in committee. "That bill will pass as soon as Sarah Hughes becomes a federal judge," Rayburn is said to have replied. When Kennedy mentioned the ABA objection to Hughes over her age, his own agreement with that position, and the administration's reluctance to violate the ABA standard, "Mr. Sam" snapped back at the thirty-five-year-old attorney general, "Sonny, in your eyes everybody seems too old."[71]

Ramsey Clark later described with "clear recollection" the pivotal meeting taking place on what he believed was the next morning in the attorney general's office. Johnson and Yarborough, who had worked out their agreement on the four judicial appointments for Texas in their earlier meeting with Clark, were to be present, presumably for a final meeting on them. Clark came early to wait with Kennedy and Byron White for their arrival. Clark, pointedly addressing White, who seemed to be the primary obstacle to Hughes, said he felt pretty strongly in favor of her, and he would like to have just two minutes to state the case for her to Kennedy. "I don't even think I took two minutes," Clark later said in recalling his comments:

> The first was that the rule [concerning age] was arbitrary, and arbitrary rules always cause great losses. If we had had a rule like that as in Justice Holmes [Oliver Wendell Holmes], it would have been just wrong.
>
> Second, if you want to have a firm rule, you ought to have a firm rule that's based on facts. There is a difference between men and women, if you hadn't noticed. Women live longer and all this stuff. And third a gentleman never asks a lady her age.[72]

Clark recalled that Kennedy "just whirled around and said something like, 'Let's do it.'" The decision, he believed, had been made in that instant. White said nothing in protest, but Clark knew he disagreed with his boss. "Poor Byron was thinking, 'How am I going to live with this?'"[73]

A few minutes later Johnson and Yarborough entered the office together, neither knowing that the roadblock preventing Hughes's appointment had just been removed. As Clark recalled, "He [Robert Kennedy] wanted to go for it. He liked Sarah Hughes. She was a strong person."[74]

More important than Clark's arguments, persuasive though they seemed at the time, had been the stubborn insistence of Rayburn. His legendary power on Capitol Hill could not be dismissed easily.

To Johnson, the sudden decision to appoint Hughes seemed a humiliating statement about his loss of power. Recently hailed as one of the nation's most powerful men and a genius as Senate majority leader, he now saw that as vice president he could not exert the same influence as his fellow Texan and long-time mentor, Mr. Sam.

Four years later, when Johnson was president, his conversation with Attorney General Nicholas Katzenbach, recorded by the White House taping system and now available at the LBJ Library, shed light on the matter. Johnson said he had asked the administration to please appoint Sarah Hughes, but he had been assured by Byron White, Robert F. Kennedy, and President Kennedy himself that she could not be named because of her age and the ABA's refusal to endorse her. "So I went to her," Johnson said, "and told her they wouldn't do it." It was after this that Rayburn met with Robert Kennedy. Rayburn recalled for Johnson what he had told Kennedy: "Boy, you don't pee a drop here unless you name Sarah Hughes. You don't get a bill in here." That very evening, Johnson said, Bobby Kennedy told the *Dallas Morning News* that Hughes would be named a federal judge. "By God, Sam Rayburn got her named," Johnson said.[75]

By this time, Johnson had brought forth Henry Wade's name for appointment, and Robert Kennedy would not let him forget it. "I wanted her, and she was my manager, and I had my obligation to her, but Bobby then just razzed the hell out of me at every White House dinner and said I was a four flusher. I came down and recommended her, but when she was named I didn't want her," Johnson told Katzenbach. "Well, I wanted her if I could have had anything to do with naming her, but I turned her down, and she got mad at me, and I went out and got the district attorney [Henry Wade], and we got him ready to name, and then he [Robert Kennedy] went back, and all of them did what they promised me and assured me that couldn't be done, and then it left me hanging out."[76] In a telephone conversation with New York politician Edwin Wiesl Jr., also recorded by the White House secret taping system, Johnson said the affair had "damn near ruined me" and that he "hadn't recovered from it yet."[77]

Katzenbach, in his conversation with Johnson, put yet another twist on Hughes's appointment. The real reason it came about, he insisted, was not because of Rayburn's threat but because President Kennedy was fully aware that Rayburn was ill—destined to die before the year was over—and he wanted to honor his request as a well-deserved courtesy.[78]

Having settled on Hughes, Robert Kennedy promptly advised Joseph F. Dolan, his assistant deputy attorney general, to instruct the FBI to begin the customary background checks on her prior to appointment. This Dolan had done on August 25, and on the same day FBI director J. Edgar Hoover sent an urgent Teletype to offices in Dallas, Baltimore, Chicago, San Antonio, and Washington advising agents to initiate at once a thorough investigation of her background.[79]

At this critical juncture—alerted by Hughes herself who quickly learned the investigation was under way—the president of the National Federation of Business and Professional Women's Clubs, Katherine Peden, sent special delivery messages to all national board members. "YOUR HELP IS NEEDED," she wrote. "Telegrams, letters and personal contacts should be forwarded IMMEDIATELY to President Kennedy and Attorney General Robert Kennedy on Hughes's behalf."[80]

Peden wrote letters herself to the president and attorney general. "The 175,000 members of the National Federation of Business and Professional Women's Clubs strongly support Judge Sarah T. Hughes for appointment as Federal Judge, U.S. District Court, Northern District, State of Texas," she said in her letter to President Kennedy. She sent copies of her correspondence to Hughes, who replied: "The letters are excellent. . . . I am immensely pleased and grateful for the action you have taken and am hopeful of the results." As to the latest news, Hughes said she had "heard some rumors that were favorable, but nothing definite from Washington." The next step for Peden, Hughes advised her, was to call or visit the vice president and Byron White.[81]

Although Hughes and Johnson exchanged several personal notes during this period, discussion about the judgeship was avoided. On August 25 Johnson sent Hughes a warm letter. "Lady Bird and I do not need the calendar to remind us that this is the end of August and a year from the time we were embarking on the great adventure of our lives—the campaign for the Democratic ticket. We cannot possibly pass this milestone without thinking of you." The tours through Texas had been a major factor in the victory, he said, "and we well know how much skill and time you put into making them so."[82]

Two days after Johnson wrote his letter, Hughes sent a telegram to him wishing him the best for his birthday on August 27. Johnson replied: "Birthdays are worth celebrating when they bring me your kind words! . . . You are always tops with us and we hope we'll be seeing you along the Pedernales sometime this fall."[83]

Meanwhile, Peden's urgent message to B&PW members brought almost immediate results. Within two days a cascade of letters and telegrams from officers and members across the nation poured into the presidential office, praising Hughes's leadership of the B&PW, her integrity, her experience as a judge, and other qualities. "[She] is one political officeholder who has never given even lip service to the segregationist philosophy down here," wrote Mrs. Pearl C. Anderson, a leading Dallas African American for whom a public school soon would be named. Many of the letter writers spoke directly to the issue of age. "She was not too old last fall to work diligently and effectively in Dallas so that you could carry the state of Texas, and she is not too old now to serve effectively as a Federal judge," wrote Joseph L. Allen, a professor of social ethics at Southern Methodist University, who also pointed out that she was "enormously younger" than recent federal judges in the district. (He referred to William Hawley Atwell, who had retired as federal judge at the end of 1954 at the age of eighty-five, and to T. Whitfield Davidson, still active at eighty-five.) Lawrence F. O'Brien, on behalf of President Kennedy, responded with the same letter to each person who wrote, thanking them and assuring them that their recommendations would be "weighed in considering the matter."[84]

The FBI investigation was immediate, fast, and thorough, extending from August 25 to September 11. Agents interviewed friends and former friends, neighbors, past employers, lawyers, judges, county officials, political opponents, and others. They explored Hughes's high school days, her work as a police officer in Washington, D.C., her teaching career at Salem Academy and College in North Carolina, her law school days, her service in the Texas Legislature, her pacifist stances in the late 1930s, her alleged arrest in the gambling raid in 1943, her performance as a judge, her political philosophy, her credit ratings, her association with groups such as the World Federalists and NAACP, and more.[85]

An early synopsis of reports sent to Washington on August 31 summarized information gathered in Dallas: "Numerous prominent persons believe applicant not qualified for Federal judgeship because of her age, not believed temperamentally suited, prejudicial on occasions, 'socialist' views, and said to show favoritism. Other prominent individuals consider her qualified and capable judge, and recommend her for responsible Government position."[86]

Governor Price Daniel told the FBI agent he believed it would be a great mistake to waive the age requirements for Hughes but acknowledged she had "made a good State District Court Judge in spite of being a sometimes highly controversial political figure."[87] Hughes's old law partner from the 1920s, E. M. Herndon, had had no contact with her since 1928, but he described her as a good lawyer, a good judge, and fair in her decisions. He had always considered some of her views, though, as too far to the left.[88] Dallas County district clerk Bill Shaw said, "From an ability and legal standpoint, Judge Hughes is probably the most capable of all judges presently presiding in Dallas District and County Courts." She would never win a popularity contest, he said, because she operated a well-disciplined court and sometimes was "extremely firm with attorneys, predominantly men, and 'I believe that some of these men attorneys resent her sharp and cutting tongue.'" Federal district judge T. Whitfield Davidson, with whom Hughes would be a colleague if appointed, said he would "not in any manner" recommend her for appointment. He had known her for some twenty-five years, and he said she was "a temperamental and sometimes prejudiced person in her views." The FBI report paraphrased his views by saying "he has looked on her as being the type of person who championed the cause of socialism."[89] The president of the Dallas Bar Association, Fred T. Porter, was very positive, believing her to be an excellent trial judge whom he had not previously believed to be more than sixty years of age.[90]

An interesting appraisal came from J. Frank Wilson, her 1946 political opponent and since 1954 a close associate as a fellow state district judge. Wilson recalled that after he defeated Hughes in the race for Congress, she had been extremely critical of him and rarely spoke to him. Now, while they were not close personal friends, they maintained cordial relations, even though Wilson described himself as an ultraconservative and Hughes as an ultraliberal, and they did not agree on anything politically. Even so, he believed her political opinions did not influence her courtroom behavior or rulings in any way. He considered her to be a very good lawyer and an outstanding judge.[91]

Any investigation during this period of Cold War tension touched on the subject's loyalty to the country, especially involvement with communist organizations. Hughes's liberal beliefs and extensive contacts with many individuals and organizations had inevitably involved some who had been listed over the years as subversive, although in 1949 she already had been cleared in a "loyalty-type" FBI investigation.[92] Still, further investigations were made, beginning with her antiwar activities in the late 1930s. It was discovered that her name had appeared on an unofficial membership list, generated by a private detective agency, of the American League for Peace and Democracy, a coalition of liberal and left-wing organizations founded in 1933 as the American League against War and Fascism. Member organizations included the American Communist Party, socialist groups, and the National Association for the Advancement of Colored People. Hughes acknowledged that as a peace advocate at the time she had probably given permission for her name to be used in some activity sponsored by the group.[93]

Another touch point for examination came through a tenuous link to the People's Educational and Press Association, an organization created in 1944 in San Antonio when it replaced the Communist Party of Texas upon the party's dissolution. Hughes's name was mentioned as a prospective sponsor for the organization's proposed bookstore. The next year she had written a congratulatory letter to the president of the organization, Dave Carpenter, concerning a paper published by the organization.[94]

In 1954 Hughes had made a talk to the Central Democratic Club in Texas, an event attended by about twenty-two persons at a private residence. Six of those individuals, according to FBI informants, were Communist Party members, including the leader of the Communist Party in Dallas. Hughes, it was acknowledged, seemed not to have known that Communists were at the meeting. A year later, Haven Perkins of St. Louis, a representative of the National Committee to Secure Justice for Morton Sobell, had contacted her and asked her to review the Sobell case. If her opinion was favorable, it was felt she might help the organization by writing letters on Sobell's behalf. Sobell, under a thirty-year sentence for treason, had been convicted in 1951 with Julius and Ethel Rosenberg for stealing and giving atomic bomb secrets to the Soviet Union. There was no evidence that Hughes ever agreed to assist the committee, which the House on Un-American Activities listed in 1957 as a subversive organization.[95]

An existing 1955 report within the Dallas office, "Communist Infiltration of the NAACP," described an NAACP meeting attended among others by Hughes and two Communist Party members. "Inasmuch as the only two Communist Party members present there were Bureau informants, that information is not included in this report," the document stated.[96] Equally tame was the office memorandum generated in 1953 after a person reported to the FBI that Judge Hughes had attended a subversive meeting at an unnamed church that had turned out to be a discussion program held at the Unitarian Church, two blocks from Hughes's house.[97]

Reexamined in the investigation was Hughes's alleged arrest in the gambling raid in 1943 at the Jefferson Hotel. Agents contacted a number of individuals with firsthand knowledge of the event, including the officer who had coordinated the raid. He confirmed that Hughes had not been present and that the mistaken identity probably had resulted because one of the arrested women resembled Judge Hughes.[98]

On September 11, with the investigation completed except for a check of Internal Revenue Service records, agent W. V. Cleveland submitted all the reports to Courtney Evans, the FBI's official liaison with the Justice Department. He sent copies at the same time to Byron White in view of his request to expedite the investigation. As was customary in such reports, the FBI drew no conclusions or submitted evaluations concerning what its agents had found. In his two-page summary, Cleveland repeated almost word-for-word the summary already provided by the Dallas office on August 31, quoted above.[99] There was, in short, no smoking gun. The overall picture emerging of Sarah T. Hughes was one of a vibrant, energetic, direct, and patriotic individual whose multifaceted life exemplified a strong commitment to social progress, liberal ideals, and American democracy and whose strong opinions rubbed some people the wrong way.

Sarah T. Hughes knew of the investigation and its significance, but the general public did not, and she herself could not be assured of the outcome. Supporters continued, then, to send letters to Washington officials, and they frequently forwarded to Hughes the wary responses they received. Johnson and Yarborough preferred not to speculate and declined even in their usual responses to acknowledge their support of Hughes. Yarborough replied in his letters that he would give her name serious consideration. Johnson, similarly laconic, wrote: "In the event I am consulted about this appointment I shall keep in mind what you have written."[100] Senator Lister Hill of Alabama was far more open. He told one of his Alabama constituents that Senator Yarborough had recommended Hughes and that Vice President Johnson and Speaker Rayburn had strongly endorsed her. As for himself, Hill said he would do anything he could on behalf of Hughes.[101]

As word spread in Dallas that Hughes's appointment seemed imminent, a flurry of opposition took place. Logan Ford, a partner in a downtown law firm, encouraged his colleagues to move beyond opposing the appointment and urge denial of her confirmation by the Senate Judiciary Committee. He directed that telegrams sent to its chairman, Senator James Eastland of Mississippi, and to John Tower of Texas should be billed to the firm, and he enclosed in his memo a copy of his own telegrams to Eastland and Tower. "JUDGE HUGHES'S POLITICAL PHILOSOPHY AND JUDICIAL TEMPERAMENT IS FAR TOO LEFT OF CENTER TO MERIT HER CONSIDERATION FOR FEDERAL JUDGESHIP DURING THESE PERILOUS TIMES WHEN THE IDEOLOGIES OF FREE MEN ARE COMPETING FOR SURVIVAL IN THE UNITED STATES AND ELSE-WHERE." He enclosed for their consideration as well a telegram written by another partner, Clarence Guittard (later a state judge): She should be denied confirmation, Guittard wrote, "BECAUSE OF HER AGE AND PERSISTENT VIOLA-TION OF ABA CANON OF JUDICIAL ETHICS NO. 28 AGAINST PARTISAN POLITICS WHILE HOLDING OFFICE AS STATE DISTRICT JUDGE."[102]

Growing support within Dallas, though, also was evident. Mae W. Avrey of Sanger-Harris Department Store prepared and circulated a petition on behalf of Hughes signed by the city's businessmen, which grew to "about a mile long." Hughes was pleased. "It certainly shows that at least some of the business folks of Dallas are for me."[103]

At 3:50 P.M. on the afternoon of Monday, September 25, the telephone rang in Judge Hughes's courtroom. An assistant U.S. attorney general in Washington, perhaps Byron White or Ramsey Clark, notified her that on that day President Kennedy was presenting her name along with three other district judges, three marshals, and four customs collectors in Texas to the Senate for confirmation.[104]

Griff Singer, a reporter for the *Dallas Morning News*, found Hughes beaming at the news that afternoon when he interviewed her. The appointment, only the second of its kind in the nation to go to a woman after Burnita Shelton Matthews's selection by Harry Truman in 1949, fulfilled a dream Hughes said she had held for many years. "But I didn't think I had a chance until the Democrats were put into office this time." A touch of melancholy appeared when Singer asked her about her future in politics. "That is my chief regret. . . . I cannot take an active part in politics. One of my biggest thrills in life has been as a campaigner and a politician. All I can do now is vote. But you can be sure I will do that."[105]

How did she respond to reported opposition from Senator James O.

Eastland, chairman of the Judiciary Committee? It was just a rumor, she said. "I have to know something before I believe it." Would she be able to adjust to the federal bench? A little more formality would be expected, she said, and she would have to don judicial robes. "But I don't see how I could be a state judge 26 years and find the situation much different in the federal court." As to questions concerning her age, she said it was no secret how she stayed in shape. "I always exercise regularly and eat regularly—the proper foods. You might say I have a great enthusiasm for life." At five feet and one-half inch tall and sixty-five years of age, she weighed 115 pounds and swam regularly at the YMCA pool near her house.[106]

When the reporter asked why she thought she had been appointed, she laughed and replied, "Exceptional ability." Then, her eyes twinkling, she added, "Really, wouldn't you call it politics?"[107]

Her feelings were expressed more formally in her letter of thanks to President Kennedy:

> It is difficult for me to express my full appreciation to you for my appointment. . . .
>
> To be a member of the Federal Judiciary is an honor almost every lawyer covets, but it is much more. It is an opportunity to serve my country and a responsibility to use all my abilities to see that justice is done.
>
> It was not only for myself that I wanted the appointment, but also for the loyal Democrats of Texas. For them it will be an encouragement to renew their efforts on behalf of the party.
>
> My only regret is that from now on I will have to put aside active participation in politics, and in 1964 when you come to Texas I will not be able to ride with you in a red convertible from Ft. Worth to Dallas.[108]

Meanwhile, she basked in the glowing tributes that flowed her way. One of the first came from her fellow contender, Henry Wade. "They could not have picked a more loyal Democrat, and I believe you are well qualified and I wish you much success there," he wrote, signing it, "Your Friend." The ideological leader of Texas liberals, Ronnie Dugger, editor of the *Texas Observer*, told her that her appointment was "the most important event for decent values and progress in Texas since Senator Yarborough's election; and exceeds that event in its meaning for the state and its people." Eighteen members and three officers, including the president of the Dallas Building and Trade Council wrote: "We are proud of you for your relentless fight for the rights of the laboring people. You have proved to us your loyalty to the Democratic Party by always making your beliefs known publicly."[109]

Old friends popped up suddenly, including a former law school professor, Henry W. Edgerton, now on the U.S. Court of Appeals, D.C. Circuit. "When you were a student in the George Washington University Law School your presence there was more cheering than you could have suspected to several members of the faculty," he wrote. Another old friend, Irvin S. Taubkin, now promotion director of the *New York Times*, sent his warmest congratulations to the woman he used to know as Sally.[110]

In the order of things, her induction as a federal judge, scheduled for mid-October, would come first. She would begin her duties on the bench even before confirmation—or rejection—by the Senate, and she would do so as only the second woman to be appointed to a federal trial court. Acknowledging that it was presumptuous, she asked Vice President Johnson to give her the oath of office at her induction, a suggestion that soon was squelched as improper by the presiding judge of the Northern District, Joe E. Estes, who would perform that service himself.[111]

U.S. attorney Barefoot Sanders strongly encouraged the vice president to attend the ceremony anyway. In a letter to Johnson's chief aide, Walter Jenkins, he observed that Judge Hughes's appointment had been "generally well received—by lawyers, by women, and most enthusiastically, by party line Democrats (under which heading I group liberals, labor, 'loyalists,' and all those who stood up publicly and also worked in 1960)." Yet, the newspapers had given the responsibility for her nomination to Senator Yarborough. "The Vice President, although not shown as opposed, is not receiving much, if any credit," Sanders wrote. "It seems to me that this situation should be corrected." Johnson could "strike a real blow for Party unity and for the Administration" if he would attend her swearing-in ceremony."[112]

Indeed, Johnson, accompanied by Lady Bird, came for the October 17 ceremony before a packed crowd in Judge Estes's courtroom. Johnson was the most prominent of several speakers. In addition to praising the new federal judge, the vice president criticized the American Bar Association's opposition to her because of age. "Each of her gray hairs would represent wisdom for a troubled and critical period," he said in his laudatory comments. The event truly seemed to be emotional for him. "This is one of the most moving and inspirational experiences that I have had," he said. Also present was Ralph

Yarborough, who called Hughes the "Portia of Texas." It was the job of the Senate, not the ABA, he said, to advise and consent. Yarborough recalled fondly when he had been an assistant attorney general for the state of Texas, charged with representing the permanent school fund of Texas and the University of Texas permanent fund, and how Hughes alone among the legislators had agreed to help him. "She studied it a long time; she led the fight; she was the parliamentarian; the strategist; she was determined; she was dogged; she was brilliant; she was brilliant in debate, and through her arduous work over two or three years, scores of millions of dollars were saved for the permanent school fund of Texas and large sums of money for the University permanent fund."[113]

Paul Carrington, immediate past president of the State Bar of Texas, pointed to many prominent jurists who had come into federal service between the ages of sixty and sixty-five. It was the ABA's function to assess candidates on their judicial capabilities and abilities, not their physical fitness, he said. Hughes had believed it important for the National Federation of Business and Professional Women's Clubs to be represented, too, and at her invitation Dr. Minnie C. Miles of Tuscaloosa, Alabama, spoke on behalf of that organization. Hughes, having been presented with a new gavel, spoke as well, and she spoke candidly, thanking all who had helped her gain the office. The struggle to win appointment, she said, had been the most difficult campaign of any she had undertaken, far more difficult than any campaign for elective office.[114]

Hughes thanked Ralph Yarborough afterward for the criticism he cast at the ABA. "They had it coming to them," she said. The event itself was the most memorable in her life. While the appointment was important to her, she also wanted it for the loyal Democrats of Texas, because it meant so much to them.[115]

A newspaper photograph showed Johnson congratulating the new judge with a kiss. "I suppose you have seen the photo," she wrote to him afterward. "It seems to have had wide coverage. Very nice, I thought." His remarks were perfect, she said. "For once I was glad to have a few grey hairs, though a few are enough."[116]

Not among those present was a notable figure, Sam Rayburn, who had had so much to do with winning the appointment for Sarah T. Hughes and who had been a role model for her through the years. Mr. Sam was only a few blocks away, hospitalized at Baylor University Medical Center with a cancer that had spread throughout his body. Only a few visitors had been permitted in his hospital room. They included President Kennedy, two former presidents—Truman and Eisenhower—and a future president, Lyndon B. Johnson. At the end of October, Rayburn would return to his hometown of Bonham, where he would die on November 16.

On the evening of her induction, Judge Hughes fulfilled a long-standing obligation to speak to the Dallas Alumnae Chapter of Delta Gamma on the thirty-fifth anniversary of that sorority's existence in Dallas. In 1926, she, a Delta Gamma herself, had helped to install a chapter on the campus of Southern Methodist University. Her topic was a familiar one on a subject that remained no less important to her: legal rights for women.[117]

After her induction she went to Washington, D.C., for a briefing from the administrative office for U.S. courts. While she was there, she met with Ramsey Clark, talked on the telephone to Lady Bird Johnson and Walter Jenkins, and for the first time met Attorney General Kennedy. The meetings and conversations gave her added confidence regarding the upcoming Senate confirmation hearings. "Any fears I might have had . . . are gone," she wrote to Johnson afterward. "Your support and the reaction bring me complete assurance."[118]

Not long afterward she sent a request to the vice president. "It would please me very much to have your autographed photograph for my office. After all, I could not be where I am had it not been for you. And I would like to be able to look up from my desk to see you smiling at me." A week later the photograph was in the mail.[119]

On Friday, December 1, she was further heartened by a huge banquet given in her honor at the Baker Hotel by the Dallas Bar Association. Some five hundred lawyers, including judges and political figures such as Senator Yarborough, state bar president William L. Kerr, and former attorney general Gerald Mann, attended and praised her. In her own remarks, Hughes spoke of her admiration for the great tradition of wisdom, courage, integrity, and understanding exhibited throughout history by members of the federal judiciary. Although she would not have the wisdom of John Marshall, Learned Hand, or Oliver Wendell Holmes, she said, she hoped to approach them in integrity and fairness.[120]

With confirmation approaching sometime early in 1962, Hughes was poised to use the assistance of the National Federation of the Business and Professional Women's Clubs to launch a full-scale campaign against the ABA's contention that she was not qualified because of age. Now, though, she believed they should move slowly unless more vigorous opposition developed. It was sufficient, she said, for Katherine Peden and the Mississippi B&PW president to write to Senator Eastland on her behalf.[121]

When in 1931 Sarah T. Hughes had been a freshman legislator, she wasted no time in getting her bearings before acting. On the first day of the legislature's first session she made her maiden speech. When she became a state district judge four years later, she immediately initiated new procedures to keep her docket up-to-date and dispose of more cases than the other judges. Now, in her early work as a federal district judge, though still unconfirmed by the U.S. Senate, she demonstrated the same fearless resolve.

The issues before her as a federal district judge—securities, antitrust, tax, patents, and such—were far more complex than the familiar suits arising out of automobile collisions, divorce, and workmen's compensation that she had heard in the comfortable setting of a state district court. The federal courtroom, located in the combination courthouse-post office building nearly a mile from the county courthouse complex, was far more formal. For the first time Hughes donned judicial robes; for the first time her entry into the courtroom was heralded by the bailiff's admonition for all to rise; for the first time she might consider a civil case one day and a criminal case the next; for the first time she dealt with federal statutes instead of state law; and for the first time she dealt with constitutional issues with broad societal ramifications.

By January she already was the most productive of the three federal judges in Dallas, disposing of more cases that month than the other two judges combined. "Judge Hughes is handling her docket with vigor and dispatch," U.S. attorney Sanders wrote to Vice President Johnson two days before her Senate Judiciary Committee confirmation hearings. Sanders felt certain that the several other months she had served on the federal bench would match her January record for activity. "I know that the lawyers who have business before her like and respect the way she conducts her Court," Sanders wrote. "She is firm and courageous, and, at the same time, gracious and fair. I should say that her outstanding characteristic as a Judge is her excellent judicial temperament—and that is not surprising, in view of her 25 years of experience as a State District Judge."[122]

Hughes was not aware of another potential problem for her confirmation.

Some members of the American Bar Association's Judicial Review Committee, including its chairman, wanted to appear before the Senate committee to oppose her confirmation for a reason other than age. Comments she had made at her induction about the intense campaign waged for her appointment had bothered them, for the ABA frowned on campaigning for federal judgeships. Leon Jaworski of Houston, one of eleven ABA Judicial Review Committee members and a former classmate of hers at George Washington University Law School, stood up for Hughes in the committee meetings and informed Vice President Johnson afterward in a letter about the tension around the issue. His defense of Hughes, Jaworski said, was imperiled by the fact that two or three Dallasites, prominent in the American Bar, were sending a transcript of the proceedings that had "riled up" the chairman and committee. "It was extremely difficult, therefore, for me to gain the Committee's consent to confine the American Bar's objection to her appointment to age solely. . . . It took much persuading on my part to convince them to desist from making an issue of this in the hearing," he said.[123]

Strong support, though, came from the State Bar of Texas's Committee on Federal Judiciary. The committee, having conducted its own investigation as to the "character, qualifications and fitness" of Hughes's to be a U.S. district judge, found her to be well qualified. William L. Kerr, president of the state bar, sent a letter to Senator Eastland to certify the recommendation. "This, of course, means that the State Bar of Texas recommends that Judge Hughes's appointment as United States District Judge be confirmed by the Senate."[124]

As it turned out, Hughes and others were right to be confident. On March 7, 1962, the U.S. Senate Judiciary Committee at last considered her appointment along with those of the three other judges nominated for Texas—Leo Brewster, Adrian Spears, and James Noel. No one from the ABA spoke. A letter stating the organization's position concerning Hughes's age was introduced, but it generated no comment and had no effect. Vice President Johnson, making his first appearance before a Senate committee since leaving that body, said he had never known a "more competent and humane public servant" than Judge Hughes. Senator Yarborough said the ABA had made a "grave mistake in placing age over ability." Senator Edward Long, a Democrat from Missouri, said Hughes looked forty-five, not sixty-five. Morris Harrell, president of the Dallas Bar Association, appearing at Hughes's request, commented that Dallas lawyers considered her an outstanding judge. Given an opportunity to speak for herself, Hughes said she was pleased simply to let her sponsors speak in her behalf.[125]

It was a day to be remembered. The vice president and Senator Yarborough arranged for Hughes and the three other new federal judges in Texas to visit with President John F. Kennedy in the White House. In a formal photograph of the occasion, Hughes stood between Kennedy and Vice President Johnson. On the same eventful day Hughes was happily surprised to receive a spontaneous invitation to go to the Johnson home on Fifty-second Street for a brief celebration. There, she posed in the living room for informal photographs with Johnson and Lady Bird, admiring greatly the view of the garden covered with snow.[126]

Nine days later Senator Yarborough sent a telegram to Hughes: "I am pleased to advise that the United States Senate has just confirmed your nomination by John F. Kennedy president of the United States by unanimous vote to be judge for life for the U.S. District Court for the Northern District in Texas."[127] Vice President Johnson had a staff member call her with the positive news. She responded: "It was wonderful news and I was very glad to have it. Though I never had been worried[,] with the Vice-President behind me it seemed that the final outcome would certainly be favorable."[128]

The confirmation trip, one she had dreaded, turned out to be a memorable occasion. This was due in large part, she said, to Johnson's attentiveness. "I am sure no other appointee has had the red carpet rolled out for them as the four judges from Texas had. From now on the sailing should be smooth."[129]

~ 10

Center of a Maelstrom

Conventional wisdom, at mid-twentieth century, held the age of sixty-five to be a time when a person's physical and mental capabilities began to lag. The delayed rewards of a productive life were now to be enjoyed—retirement, rest, reflection, and grandchildren. Conventional wisdom never held for Sarah T. Hughes. At sixty-five she was launching a new judicial career, one that would place her on the front stage of the cataclysmic event that occurred in Dallas on November 22, 1963. It was a day that would alter the mood and history of a nation, the effects of which for the next few years would plunge Judge Hughes into the emotional and turbulent issues of the late 1960s and the 1970s. Even before then, in her first year on the bench, the first American was killed in Vietnam, man flew into space, the Berlin Wall was erected, and a CIA-sponsored invasion of Cuba was rebuffed.

On becoming a federal judge, Hughes was at the peak of her intellectual power—thinking, writing, and speaking on topics that long had fascinated her. Five days after she had been sworn in as a U.S. district judge for the Northern District of Texas, her article on problems arising with children in conflicted marriages appeared in the *Texas Bar Journal*. A few months later she published another article for the *Journal* favoring a disarmament treaty. She wrote that same year on the use of corporal punishment in schools and on opportunities for refugee girls. In the next handful of years articles appeared under her name on crime and school dropouts, the crisis in the nation's cities, and achieving world peace through world law.[1]

Hughes was proud not just of being a federal judge but especially of the manner in which she had achieved the position. She stood as her own best example in the advice she gave countless women in speeches. They must not sit back and wait for invitations to gain public offices; they must identify and aggressively pursue those offices, just as she had done. She was well aware in her own case that if she had not boldly presented herself for the job, President Kennedy would not have sought her out and asked her to be a federal judge.[2]

At this point in her midsixties, her physical capabilities were hardly diminished from the days when she was the energetic captain of her basketball team at Goucher College. Exercising regularly, eating well-balanced meals, and taking good care of herself in every way were high priorities for her. Swimming was one of her passions, along with bicycle riding in the neighborhood. A new heated pool in her backyard permitted her to swim at home rather than going to the local YMCA pool. She extended her daily swimming regimen in February 1963 to fifty laps a day, falling in step with a new national passion, the fifty-mile walk popularized after President Kennedy had come across a letter from Theodore Roosevelt insisting that marines should be able to hike fifty miles in twenty hours. The *Dallas Morning News* took a picture of her in her pool on a day when the temperature was below freezing.[3]

Nor was Hughes one to brood or suffer periods of depression. Rather than lingering on disappointments, her normal mode was to be upbeat, eager for the challenges of tomorrow. In her political opinions she often seemed angry and unyielding, but her daily demeanor was that of an optimist. Uncertainty was not one of her characteristics, even when undertaking an unfamiliar challenge.

While Sarah was beginning her new federal career, George Hughes was ending his own. Having reached the mandatory retirement age of seventy in 1962 and after a career of forty-three years, he retired from the Veterans Administration's regional office as assistant chief attorney. A reception attended by Senator Ralph Yarborough and members of the Federal Bar Association honored him, and the American Legion presented him with a commendation for having worked so long for the interests of veterans, their widows and orphans.[4] Now, he began to be more active in the Dallas Bar Association, becoming head of its Lawyer Referral Service, and at St. Matthew's Episcopal Cathedral, where he and Sarah had been active members since the end of World War II.

They began to consider a lake house—or, at least, Sarah did. In the spring of 1963 she purchased property, using her name only, at Howell Lake, a small club lake between Tyler and Kilgore, a little more than hundred miles east of Dallas. The property, a hundred-by-hundred-foot lot next to the water, included a four-room cottage with a screened-in porch and a boathouse. Opportunities for weekends at the lake were rare, and four years after buying the property, Sarah decided to sell it, a seemingly never-ending process because she refused to lower her asking price of $12,500, despite the recommendation of her real estate agent. Finally she sold it herself in 1970, sending a $400 check for the commission to her real estate agent, even though Hughes herself had found the buyer.[5]

Owning lake property in her own name may have been a special pleasure because of previous requirements that a married woman in Texas had limited property rights. Such discriminations, even in far smaller matters, continued to irritate her. She was incensed that women were not eligible to become members of American Airlines' Admirals Club. Although Admirals Clubs were no more than special rooms away from the crowded terminals in major airlines where frequent travelers could relax in comfortable chairs with reading materials and refreshments, the exclusion of women seemed cruel and senseless. Several times Hughes wrote to the president of the airlines, C. R. Smith, requesting membership, only to be rebuffed by responses that the Admirals Club was for men only. A breakthrough came in April 1963, when Charles C. Tillinghast Jr., president of Trans World Airlines, informed her she had been elected to TWA's Ambassadors Club (which provided the same services as the Admirals Club). "It will be a pleasure to make use of the facilities of the club," she wrote back, adding that it had "always been a source of irritation" that American Airlines would not permit women in their club.[6]

When American Airlines followed suit and ended its restrictions against women, Hughes wrote again to request membership, reminding Smith she had been rejected several times because of her gender. "While I do not travel as frequently as earlier when president of the National Federation of Business and Professional Women's Clubs, I still travel often and I hope you will look on my application with favor. It would please me very much to have membership in the Admirals Club." A vice president of the airlines responded on behalf of Smith. "It will be my pleasure," he wrote, "to advise our Admissions Committee of your desire for membership." In August 1963, Judge Hughes was notified of her admission. Perhaps most noteworthy about the exchange of letters was the surprisingly supplicatory tone Hughes used concerning a discrimination that undoubtedly had infuriated her for more than a decade.[7]

The political mood in Dallas continued to be unusually conservative if not extremist. Many of the right-wing invectives were appearing in the *Dallas Morning News*, which for several decades had enjoyed status as the leading newspaper in the Southwest under its long-time publisher, George Banner-man Dealey, a man of moderation but a crusader for civic improvements and leader of the difficult battle against the Ku Klux Klan in the 1920s. Dealey had died in 1946, and his son, E. M. "Ted" Dealey, now controlled the news-paper. Under him it developed a right-wing editorial stance reflecting viru-lent anticommunist, antifederal government sentiments. In the fall of 1961, shortly after Sarah T. Hughes's appointment as a federal judge, at the invita-tion of President Kennedy, Dealey attended a luncheon at the White House with other Texas publishers. The occasion was a social one, but in a highly publicized incident Dealey seized the moment to launch an impolite attack against Kennedy's foreign policies. "You and your administration are weak sisters," he admonished the president loudly across the luncheon table. "We need a man on horseback to lead this nation, and many people in Texas and the southwest think that you are riding Caroline's bicycle." The occasion for his blunt attack had seemed inappropriate, but the *News* reported later that 84 percent of more than two thousand communications received from readers expressed approval of Dealey's comments and behavior.[8]

Sarah T. Hughes was among the 16 percent who disapproved, and she wrote to President Kennedy to say so. "Many of us in Dallas do not agree with the statement of Ted Dealy [*sic*] of the Dallas News, purporting to reflect 'grass-roots sentiment' of Texas. We have the utmost confidence in you. We admire your courage, your sincerity and your leadership in dealing with world problems. Perhaps after meeting and hearing Mr. Dealy, you can better understand the reason so many people in Dallas are brainwashed. They read only the Dallas News. Faithfully yours."[9] The president's popular press secre-tary, Pierre Salinger, writing for the president, thanked her for the letter. "The reaction around the luncheon table," he wrote, "was ample evidence that Mr. Dealey was not speaking for any of the other publishers."[10]

Four days later Hughes sent another letter to President Kennedy, this time asking for his autographed picture. "I realize that you have many requests," she said, "but perhaps not too many from a U.S. District Judge, who happens to be a woman." She had been and would continue to be his devoted admirer, she said, and she wrote that despite the Hatch Act (which prohibited political activities for federal employees), she looked forward "to another occasion when I can ride from Fort Worth to Dallas between you and Vice-President Johnson."[11]

On January 31, 1963, Hughes appeared as a guest on a popular local radio talk show, *Commentary.* In the course of the interview she made complimentary statements about the Federal Bureau of Investigation, noting especially her favorable impressions of agents who often testified in her court. Curtis O. Lynum of the Dallas FBI office was listening, and he found such positive comments from a federal judge known for her liberal politics especially refreshing. He sent her a letter of appreciation, which Hughes courteously acknowledged, reemphasizing her favorable opinion of FBI agents. "Every agent with whom I have come into contact has been doing superb work in my estimation," she wrote.[12]

So pleased was Lynum that he sent a copy of Hughes's letter and his own characterization of her laudatory comments on the radio to the director of the FBI, J. Edgar Hoover. Lynum had a recommendation for his superior. "It is respectfully suggested that you may desire to acknowledge Judge Hughes's kind letter."[13]

Hoover replied nine days later. "In connection with your suggestion that I may desire to acknowledge Judge Hughes's letter of February 5th the following information is set out." Hoover then proceeded to summarize at length the severest of the alleged radical or communistic accusations made against Hughes in the recent FBI investigation concerning her judicial appointment. "In view of Judge Hughes's controversial reputation," Hoover concluded, "I do not wish to initiate correspondence with her and you should bear the foregoing information in mind in any future dealings with her. Almost all of the foregoing information is contained in Dallas files and you should have considered it before recommending that I write to her. In the future your recommendations should reflect results of file checks."[14] Lynum surely regretted his simple request.

Outside of politics, many liberal-minded Dallasites such as Sarah T. Hughes found an outlet for their idealism in the Dallas chapter of the United Nations Association, referred to by members as DUNA. Having served as the chapter's first president in 1953, Hughes returned to the presidency in 1962.

If anything, the harsh anti-UN sentiment in the area had grown stronger since her first term nearly a decade earlier. This was illustrated by a legislative bill passed by the Texas Senate making it illegal to fly the United Nations flag on any property owned by the state or owned by any city, county, or political subdivision of the state. With the bill pending House approval in early 1963,

Hughes wrote to Governor John B. Connally, Lyndon B. Johnson's friend and former aide, to encourage his veto if the legislation reached his desk. "This bill is intended to be an attack on the United Nations and disapproval of its accomplishments. . . . To prohibit the flying of this flag would be a poor advertisement for our state." The bill, she said, was evidence "of the efforts of the extreme right to isolate our country and have it withdraw from international organizations." She believed approval would only encourage such individuals in their anti-UN activities and their criticism of the Kennedy administration.[15]

State Representative Howard Green of Fort Worth, speaking on the floor in behalf of the UN, said his position had generated letters from people who were "dangerously extreme" and "emotionally disturbed." Only by the slimmest of margins did the bill fail to pass the House. Although favored there by a majority, it failed to gain the two-thirds vote needed for immediate consideration and did not reemerge before the legislative session ended.[16]

What was needed in Dallas to counter massive propaganda efforts against the UN and its goals, Hughes believed, was a higher profile so that the public could better understand its benefits. Opponents of the UN seemed to have no problem in attracting attention. In the summer of 1962 a number of young and pretty women dressed in white and decorated with red, white, and blue streamers with the words DISARMAMENT? NO distributed petitions on downtown streets declaring that the Geneva disarmament proposal would lead the nation "on a direct path toward world government," amounting to a "surrender of our individual and national sovereignty." Using the DUNA newsletter to alert its members to such efforts, Hughes urged them to be prepared to answer this "propaganda."[17]

In December 1962, she proposed to the Arms Control and Disarmament Agency a conference in Dallas on disarmament. Just three days later she asked George McGhee of the State Department if he could have a film prepared to counteract the effects of an anti-UN, antidisarmament film proposed by a conservative group billing themselves as "80 Women from Texas." In her annual report of activities for DUNA during her term as president, Hughes was able to cite a full and active program of events, including seventy-eight speeches made by members—many by herself—during the year in front of approximately ten thousand people.[18]

Her successor as president in March 1963 was Jack Goren. Hughes became chairman of the board. Goren, a vice president at Neiman-Marcus, soon realized that his new visibility might be a liability as far as some customers were concerned. He found himself reminding those who complained that his work with the United Nations Association had nothing at all to do with his position at Neiman-Marcus.[19] He was not in dangerous waters—the head of his company, Stanley Marcus, also was on DUNA's board of directors. So were other prominent Dallasites, including Raymond Nasher, a developer who already was planning what would become one of the city's finest shopping centers, NorthPark; the Reverend Baxton Bryant, a liberal Baptist minister; Edward B. Winn, an attorney; and Gerald C. Mann, former Texas attorney general, a football hero of Southern Methodist University in the 1930s, and a friend of Hughes since her days in the Texas Legislature.

Each October the Dallas chapter was among those throughout the nation that attempted to educate the public during UN Week. Speeches were made, the UN flag was displayed, and booths were set up to explain the goals of the organization. With anti-UN sentiment increasingly vituperative, board members in Dallas agreed something noteworthy should be sponsored for the 1963 UN Week. What better than a visit and speech by the United States ambassador to the United Nations, Adlai E. Stevenson? Goren, as president of DUNA, issued the invitation.

In August 1963, Stevenson accepted, agreeing to speak on the culminating day of the week-long event, October 24. Arrangements were made for him to appear in Memorial Theater at the Convention Center in downtown Dallas. For added support, the Dallas League of Women Voters agreed to join as cosponsor. Stevenson's speech, "U.S. Foreign Policy and the U.N.," was billed in promotional literature as a "major address."[20] A local station, KRLD-TV, a CBS affiliate, agreed to provide live coverage of the event. In its resolution proclaiming October 18-24 United Nations Week in Dallas, the Dallas City Council urged all citizens to acquaint themselves "with the aims, objectives, and organization of the United Nations toward the desirable end that the United Nations can be implemented and developed as a truly effective instrumentality for preventing war and establishing peace both in these times and in times to come."[21]

Not to be outdone, an ultrarightist group recently formed in Dallas, the National Indignation Convention, prevailed upon an unwitting Governor John Connally to declare "U.S. Day," purposely choosing October 23 for its observance—one day prior to UN Day and Stevenson's address. The organization then booked the same Memorial Theater where Stevenson would speak. The National Indignation Convention (later renamed Conference) had been founded by a thirty-two-year-old man named Frank McGehee, who had become indignant upon hearing that pilots from communistic Yugoslavia were being trained at Perrin Air Force Base in Texas. He and others had met in indignation as the National Indignation Convention to protest loudly, and a number of chapters were formed in other cities. U.S. Day itself had begun a few years earlier as a counter to UN Day by right-wing organizations in Texas, Arizona, and California, designating the day prior to UN Day to emphasize the contrast. As the U.S. Day and UN Day approached, cars were seen in Dallas with signs bearing such slogans as "U.S. DAY OR UNITED NATIONS DAY— THERE MUST BE A CHOICE; YOU CANNOT RIDE BOTH HORSES."[22]

The best-known participant in U.S. Day and one of its organizers was Edwin A. Walker. A native of Texas, the former U.S. Army major general had chosen Dallas as a comfortable haven when he angrily resigned from the military after being criticized widely for inculcating his troops with John Birch Society material. In Dallas he continued to air his views about the dangers of communism and the government's seeming unwillingness to respond to it. He traveled to Mississippi to join the mob demonstrating against the admission of James Meredith into the University of Mississippi; he regularly flew a U.S. flag upside down at his large house on Turtle Creek Boulevard as a sign of distress; and he campaigned unsuccessfully and pathetically on an ultra-rightist platform in the race for Texas governor, finishing last in a field of six.

As the primary speaker on U.S. Day, Walker told the crowd of some fourteen hundred that U.S. district judge Sarah T. Hughes and U.S. attorney Barefoot Sanders were responsible for bringing Adlai Stevenson to Dallas. The audience lustily booed their names. (Judge Hughes, as chairman of the board, had helped make the arrangements, but although Sanders was a member of the organization, he had taken no role in planning the event.) "I'll tell you who started the U.N.," Walker continued. "It was the Communists and Alger Hiss and that crowd."[23] The real battle in the Cold War was being fought inside the United States, Walker said, and it was the United States versus the United Nations. "Tonight we stand on a battleground identified on this stage as U.S. Day—the symbol of our sovereignty. Tomorrow night there will stand here a symbol to the communist conspiracy and its United Nations." Another speaker, a rancher and well-known Texas historian named J. Evetts Haley, won loud applause when he announced he did not want to impeach Chief Justice Earl Warren, he wanted to hang him.[24]

It later would be learned that not everybody in Memorial Theater that night was a right-winger. An interested observer was Lee Harvey Oswald, a young Marxist, former U.S. Marine, and one-time defector to the Soviet Union who six months earlier from a dark alley had fired a rifle shot at the former general as he sat at a desk in his house on Turtle Creek Boulevard, narrowly missing him because the shot was deflected by a window pane.

U.S. Day was only the first of *two* days planned by its leaders, for they intended to continue their activities into the next day to disrupt Stevenson's speech. Quite likely, they were responsible for the handbills anonymously circulated on the city streets the next morning bearing pictures of President Kennedy with the bold words, "Wanted for Treason. This Man is wanted for treasonous activities against the United States." Among the charges listed against him was permitting "known Communists" to work in federal offices and "betraying the Constitution."[25]

The UN Day event—free to all—became almost as much of an affair for right-wing zealots as it was for UN supporters. Those opposing the United Nations arrived early, threw up several pickets outside the building, and carried a handful of anti-UN signs into the auditorium with them. As the time arrived for the program to begin, it became apparent that the crowd of some 1,750 contained perhaps as many foes of the United Nations as supporters. Among those on the platform with Ambassador Stevenson were Hughes, who read the proclamation from President Kennedy declaring UN Day; Jack Goren, president of DUNA; and Stanley Marcus, who introduced Stevenson amid catcalls from the audience.

That the night would be like no other became certain when Stevenson attempted to begin his speech at the rostrum. Frank McGehee of the National Indignation Convention immediately stood up at the front with a bullhorn and demanded that Stevenson answer certain questions before speaking. Many in the crowd shouted at McGehee in an effort to quiet him, and one elderly man tried to push him back to his seat, but with the cheers of his own partisans ringing in his ears, McGehee persisted until finally police removed him from the auditorium. Stevenson, finally, was able to speak, but only amid continuing disturbances. Protestors frequently walked up and down the aisles, many of them carrying miniature American flags upside down as a sign of distress. Deliberate coughing was incessant, as were clicking sounds from hand-held noisemakers and derisive laughter. Midway through the speech a banner high above Stevenson with the words,

"WELCOME ADLAI," was flipped over to display the other side, "U.N.—RED FRONT." It later was learned that the banner had been placed there the previous night.[26]

More picket signs arrived outside during Stevenson's speech, and afterward about 150 demonstrators waited patiently for his departure, which was delayed about forty-five minutes for a reception for the sponsors. When some of the demonstrators spotted Stevenson leaving the auditorium from a side door, they rushed to confront him. Cries of "Communist" and "traitor" were shouted. As Stevenson paused to attempt to reason with one of them, a middle-aged woman, who the night before had attended the U.S. Day event, hit Stevenson on the head with her picket sign; a young man spat on him; and when finally Stanley Marcus jerked Stevenson into the waiting car, the crowd began rocking the automobile. Stevenson was heard to say, "Are these human beings or are these animals?" Marcus prevailed upon the driver to "get the hell out of here." Photographers, both newspaper and television, captured images of the angry scene.[27]

Stevenson was taken to a small reception hosted by Marcus and Robert Storey, former dean of the SMU Law School, at the downtown Chaparral Club, where Hughes, Barefoot and Jan Sanders, and ten or so other supporters joined them for refreshments. To Hughes, Stevenson appeared to be very calm but somewhat astounded by what had happened. Hughes herself was upset by the disruptions.[28]

Dallas, once again, had made ugly national headlines. The national press covered the event with all its sordid details. All three major networks showed footage of the disturbances. ABC's commentator Edward P. Morgan said, "Big D stands for 'disgrace.'" *Time* magazine's coverage came under the headline "A City Disgraced." *Christian Century* blamed the event on the refusal of civic leaders to respond to previous irrational attacks by right-wing extremists, such as that on Lyndon and Lady Bird Johnson, and particularly on the editorial pages of the *Dallas Morning News*. Dallas mayor Earle Cabell, the president of the Chamber of Commerce, and some hundred businessmen representing both Democrats and Republicans sent a telegram of apology to Stevenson. Mayor Cabell asked the city to reject hate groups just as it had finally rejected the Ku Klux Klan in the 1920s.[29]

Hughes sent a telegram to Stevenson, expressing her dismay but emphasizing as well the positive aspects of his appearance. She followed her letter with newspaper clippings describing the evening. Stevenson gracefully agreed that the incident had produced a "net gain for the United Nations and sanity." He told her in his letter he had received hundreds of invitations to return to Dallas, and he would do so gladly, "hopefully to share again the platform— and the applause—with you."[30]

As *Time* had said, though, the city was disgraced. What was even more alarming than Stevenson's ugly reception was the that President John F. Kennedy already was scheduled to visit Dallas on November 22. What would the right-wing elements do to mar his visit? Could Dallas endure the publicity that would occur if a similar event occurred?

Many prominent persons in Dallas believed the trip should be canceled. Hughes dreaded the prospect of what might happen. Adlai Stevenson agreed with some of the leading people in Dallas who wondered whether the president should visit. Barefoot Sanders recommended cancellation as strongly as he could to a presidential advance person, and three days before the Kennedy visit, when Vice President Johnson was in town, Sanders again spoke earnestly with Johnson's aide Cliff Carter just outside Johnson's car, saying, "I really think he shouldn't come. He just shouldn't come." Carter responded by telling Sanders to get into the car. Finding himself next to the vice president, Sanders told Lyndon Johnson the same thing. Johnson replied: "Look, I don't think he should come either, and I've told him that, and John Connally has told him that, too, but by god he's coming and you'd better get behind him." When Stanley Marcus also told the vice president the trip should be canceled, Johnson responded to him in almost precisely the same words he had used with Sanders.[31]

President Kennedy regarded the city's reputation for extremism as a good reason to come, not a reason for avoiding it.[32] For one thing, he believed he needed to come to Texas—and to Dallas—to help settle or at least ameliorate the ugly struggle in the state's Democratic Party between Senator Ralph Yarborough and his liberal supporters and Governor John Connally, increasingly identified with the conservative wing of the party. If some sort of truce could not be achieved, the chances of carrying Texas in the 1964 presidential election would be severely damaged. And that was the primary reason for the visit—to win votes for the upcoming 1964 campaign. Only by the slimmest of margins, 46,223 out of 2.3 million total Texas votes, had the Kennedy-Johnson ticket won the state in 1960. The trip to Texas would include visits to five major cities—Houston, San Antonio, Fort Worth, Dallas, and Austin—capped with a visit to the LBJ Ranch, and it was expected to generate an enormous amount of favorable publicity.

Dissension already was brewing, though, for Governor Connally, as official host for the visit to Texas, had met with Dallas's leading businessmen early in October and asked their assistance in promoting a nonpolitical presidential visit. This, in effect, excluded Senator Yarborough and liberal-loyalist Democrats from meaningful participation in planning the event, for few if any among the businessmen other than Stanley Marcus identified with that wing of the Democratic Party. Dallas's businessmen, with rare exception, were Republicans or conservative Democrats. They held little if any affection for Ralph Yarborough or, for that matter, John F. Kennedy. Even Marcus, a prominent businessman but a loyalist Democrat, found himself excluded from the planning process: "My anti-Kennedy business associates took charge of the whole affair and froze me, a known Kennedy supporter, out of the program."[33]

It was ironic indeed that faithful supporters of Kennedy were given no roles for the visit, a circumstance made even clearer when the powerful organization of downtown businessmen, the Citizens Council, announced after the Stevenson fiasco that it would assume sponsorship of the president's visit to Dallas. This done, the group—intent on a successful visit that would not include ugly demonstrations against the president and further embarrass the city—launched a broad campaign through newspaper articles, television reports, and speeches to educate Dallas citizens as to the critical need for a positive, incident-free reception. News stories thoroughly reported security measures that would be taken. The Dallas City Council adopted a new ordinance designed to protect the president by prohibiting individuals from interfering with lawful assemblies. Police Chief Jesse Curry asked citizens to report any suspicious activities during the presidential visit or to take necessary preventive actions themselves if it appeared someone was planning to commit an act harmful or degrading to the president. Off-duty officers would be called into service on the day of the visit.[34]

But as the date of the visit approached, the city continued to be on edge. Three days before the president's arrival segregationist governor George Wallace of Alabama spoke to the Public Affairs Luncheon Club at the downtown Baker Hotel. In the audience of this predominantly conservative group were H. L. Hunt and former major general Edwin A. Walker. During

Wallace's speech, television cameraman George Phenix approached Walker's table in the middle of the dining area. Walker, irritated, stood up and shoved the cameraman into the laps of other diners, sending chairs, dishes, glasses, and silverware flying. The audience burst into spontaneous applause.[35]

On the morning prior to President Kennedy's arrival, leaflets with mug shots of him and the headline "WANTED FOR TREASON" once again appeared on the city streets. On the morning of his arrival, November 22, the *Dallas Morning News* carried a shocking full-page advertisement surrounded by black borders with twelve rhetorical accusatory questions directed to the president implying he had sold out to the communists. The advertisement was sponsored by the American Fact-Finding Committee, a spontaneously formed group of men that included Joseph P. Grinnan, local coordinator for the Birch Society, Nelson Bunker Hunt, son of H. L. Hunt, and H. R. "Bum" Bright, chairman of the board of a trucking company and later owner of the Dallas Cowboys.

Yet, from the moment they stepped down from *Air Force One* at Love Field after a brief flight from Fort Worth, the president and Mrs. Kennedy were warmly and enthusiastically greeted in Dallas, first by the businessman-dominated reception committee and then by huge crowds of ordinary citizens, who seemed overjoyed to be in their presence. Approximately two hundred thousand Dallasites lined the streets for a glimpse of the presidential couple as they led a motorcade on a circuitous route via downtown Dallas to their destination at the Trade Mart, where a luncheon awaited them. Riding with the president and Jacquelyn Kennedy in their Lincoln convertible were Governor Connally and his wife, Nellie. Two motorcycle officers rode on each side of the presidential convertible. Just behind was a presidential follow-up car bearing eight Secret Service agents and presidential assistants David F. Powers and Kenneth O'Donnell. Next came the vice-presidential car with the Johnsons, Ralph Yarborough, and Special Agent Rufus W. Youngblood. Then came a vice-presidential follow-up car, five cars for other dignitaries including Mayor Earle Cabell of Dallas, three cars for photographers, a bus for White House staff members and others, and two press buses. All along the motorcade route, from Love Field through downtown Dallas, onlookers' jubilant cheers resounded. The few anti-Kennedy pickets seen along the way were rendered virtually impotent by the thousands of Kennedy supporters.

Eagerly awaiting the president's arrival at the Trade Mart among the well-dressed and well-heeled crowd was Sarah T. Hughes, her dress with huge white polka dots adorned with a large corsage. As she entered the building, the women's editor for the *Dallas Times Herald*, Vivian Castleberry, intercepted her for a quick interview. Hughes's comments reemphasized the apprehension of the moment. As Castleberry later said, "I recall vividly that she said three things. One, that it was a great day for Dallas. Second, that she had been gravely concerned about the president visiting Dallas. And third, that she would be glad when he left Dallas."[36]

Hughes had received one of a hundred or so tickets designated for Kennedy's Democratic admirers. Hers had come from Barefoot Sanders, who at the last minute had been given the tickets for distribution among the Democratic faithful. They had been sent to him only after his personal plea to Vice President Johnson on his trip to Dallas three days before the event. Resentment had been boiling among loyalist Democrats who had worked hard for the Kennedy-Johnson ticket but found no way to get inside the Trade Mart to hear the president. They believed it unfair to be frozen out of the luncheon while the city's conservative business elite rubbed shoulders with the president they had opposed. Immediately after Sanders's request to Johnson for tickets, one of the planners had called Sanders and asked him how many he needed. About a hundred, Sanders replied. They were delivered within the hour. Working hurriedly, Sanders and his wife, Jan, had sent out the coveted tickets via special delivery to grassroots Democrats such as Hughes.[37]

Sitting next to Hughes at one of the many long and resplendent tables on the first floor was Jan Sanders. Barefoot Sanders would join them when he arrived on the VIP bus in the presidential motorcade. Hughes's court reporter, Odell Oliver, and Hughes's secretary and friend, Gwen Graul, who also had been given tickets, had less desirable seats on one of the three upstairs balconies overlooking the central court. After lunch, Hughes planned to ride with the Sanderses to Austin, where they would continue to be with the presidential party.

A few people in the balconies or standing around the fringes of the seated diners were monitoring the progress of the motorcade with small transistor radios. At 12:30 P.M. shots rang out at Dealey Plaza, and moments later those people with radios heard unconfirmed reports of the shots, not knowing at first whether anyone had been hit. "You could just see the news as it seeped into the crowd," Jan Sanders said later.[38] Sanders, Hughes, and virtually everyone became alarmed and agitated. People began to cluster in small groups, speculating and worrying about the possibility of an incident too awful for words. No one knew yet that President Kennedy had been shot just as the motorcade was leaving the downtown area; that Governor Connally had been seriously wounded; and that the presidential limousine with its stricken passengers had bypassed the Trade Mart to go directly to Parkland Hospital. The motorcade buses, trailing much farther behind, stopped at the Trade Mart as planned and discharged their passengers, largely journalists, who themselves were bewildered but understood that something terribly wrong had happened at Dealey Plaza. The frantic newsmen scurried to find telephones and to interview one another about what they might have seen when their buses passed by the horrified witnesses and confused scene at Dealey Plaza.

"The press came in and we kept on waiting, and Jan began to get worried," Hughes recalled. "She [Jan] says 'Something has happened,' and I said, 'Oh, no, no, it can't be.'" But Mrs. Sanders was certain. She began to cry even before a shaken Erik Jonsson, president of the sponsoring Citizens Council, came to the podium at 1:01 P.M. to make a cautious announcement.[39]

Speaking slowly, Jonsson said: "There has been a delay in the arrival of the motorcade. There has been a mishap. We do not know the extent of it or the exact nature. We believe from our report we have just received that it is not serious. We hope you will keep your seats. As soon as we have something to tell you, believe me, we'll do it."[40]

Nine minutes after his first announcement, Jonsson, obviously more shaken than before, returned to the podium. He told the crowd he felt a "little bit like the fella on Pearl Harbor day." The president and Governor Connally had been shot, he confirmed. "We do not know how seriously. Our reports are scant, they are difficult to get. We shall tell you as much as we know as soon as we know anything."[41]

Someone in the audience shouted. "Those damn fanatics, why do we have to have them in Dallas?" The shock of the moment was overpowering. It was assumed instantly that right-wingers had carried their protests to the ultimate extreme. The Reverend Luther Holcomb, president of the Dallas Council of Churches, offered a prayer, followed shortly by another prayer from the Reverend William H. Dickinson Jr. of Highland Park Methodist Church.[42]

With her worst fears about the presidential visit now realized and with her friend Jan Sanders next to her in tears, Hughes retained her composure. "She was such a strong, stoic person," Sanders said later in describing these moments. "She was stronger than I was. I cried."[43]

There was nothing for Hughes to do but leave. With Sanders, she walked out to the parking lot to their separate cars. A television cameraman from KDFW-TV in Dallas focused his lens on Hughes outside the Trade Mart as she stopped in her car outside the building and listened carefully as a blond-headed woman, evidently Gwen Graul, bent over at her window to tell her something. Instantly, Hughes was transformed by a shocked, pained expression in which her eyes widened and her mouth opened. It appears to be the moment she learned of the president's mortal injury. The woman—Graul—then walked around the car to take the front passenger seat.[44] Graul and Oliver had ridden to the Trade Mart with Hughes, intending to drive her car back to her house, since she planned to depart for Austin from the Trade Mart with the Sanderses.[45]

"Numbly and hardly realizing what had happened, I drove home," Hughes wrote immediately after the assassination in recalling the traumatic day for the *Washington Post*. "There was no reason to go to court. In the face of the tragedy that had befallen us, all else seemed of little consequence."[46]

Graul and Oliver rode with Hughes to her house, about fifteen minutes away, where they had parked a car for their return to the courthouse. On the way the three women speculated about where the vice president would be sworn in. One of them—Hughes later couldn't recall who—thought rather foolishly in these moments of complete uncertainty that the planned journey to Austin and the LBJ Ranch in the Hill Country might be completed and that Johnson could take the oath of office there. On reflection they agreed it more likely that he would go on to Washington and be sworn in immediately there. "No one even thought that he'd be sworn in in Dallas," she said. When they reached Hughes's home, shortly before 2 P.M., Graul and Oliver departed. Hughes, inside the house, immediately called her court to advise that she was home. She was told that Barefoot Sanders was in the office looking for her. He wanted to speak to her.[47]

"Immediately I heard his familiar voice," Hughes recalled. The vice president wanted her to swear him in. Could she? How soon could she get to Love Field?[48]

The man who would be charged with the assassination, Lee Harvey Oswald, an order-filler at the Texas School Book Depository at Dealey Plaza, had fled the building after the shooting, gone to his rooming house in Oak Cliff, picked up a pistol, and begun walking toward Jefferson Boulevard. Several blocks away, confronted by police officer J. D. Tippit, Oswald shot and killed him, then hurried to the nearby Texas Theater and slipped inside as police sirens sounded. Dallas police officers, alerted to his whereabouts by those who had seen him looking furtive as he hurried down Jefferson Boulevard, arrested him at 1:50 P.M. after a brief struggle. These events were for the moment of secondary importance to Lyndon B. Johnson, Sarah T. Hughes, and those aboard *Air Force One*.

At 1:26 P.M., less than an hour after shots had been fired at Dealey Plaza and shortly after President Kennedy had been declared dead, Lyndon B. Johnson, crouching down in an unmarked police car driven by Police Chief Jesse Curry to avoid a possible second assassination attempt, left Parkland Hospital for Love Field and the presidential airplane. Squeezed into the car with him were U.S. representatives Albert Thomas and Homer Thornberry and Special Agent Rufus Youngblood. In a second unmarked police car behind the Johnson automobile rode Lady Bird Johnson, accompanied by Representative Jack Brooks and Secret Service agents. Some thirty minutes later a casket bearing the slain president's body was loaded onto a hearse at Parkland Hospital. Jacquelyn Kennedy, who had stayed at the hospital, rode in the hearse with the casket to *Air Force One*.

At Love Field, official White House photographer Cecil Stoughton already was recording the tragic history of that day. His images show the casket being loaded onto *Air Force One*, Jacqueline Kennedy walking unaided up the stairway into the airplane, two police officers saluting the casket, and another holding his hat over his heart.

Johnson, already inside *Air Force One*, was pondering the matter of proper accession to the office. Should he take his oath of office in Dallas, or should it be delayed until the return to the nation's capital? He began working the telephone. He called the attorney general, the slain president's brother. "A lot of people down here think I should be sworn in right away," he told Robert Kennedy. "Who could swear me in?" Kennedy, still in shock and disbelief, said he would check it out and get back to him. Johnson made other phone calls to Walter Jenkins and McGeorge Bundy. Then Kennedy was back on the line. Nicholas Katzenbach, the deputy attorney general, had advised him that anyone, even a justice of the peace, could administer the oath. Katzenbach had told Kennedy, "I imagine he'll want Sarah Hughes."[49]

Johnson asked Kennedy about the oath. "You can get the oath," Kennedy said. "There's no problem about the oath, they can locate the oath."[50]

Johnson, who had retreated inside *Air Force One* to a bed in the state-room, dictated brief notes of these telephone conversations to his secretary, Marie Fehmer. Then he told her to get Waddy Bullion. J. W. Bullion, counsel to Lady Bird Johnson for twenty-three years and a prominent Dallas lawyer, was in Shreveport. "Get Sarah Hughes," Johnson now told Fehmer. Hughes's law clerk, John Spinuzzi, picked up the telephone to hear an unidentified voice asking for Sarah Hughes. The judge, he said, was not there; she was at the Trade Mart. After he hung up the telephone immediately rang again. "This is Lyndon Johnson. Find her." And when he located her, she was to contact him immediately at *Air Force One*.[51]

"Try Irv Goldberg," Johnson next told Fehmer. Irving L. Goldberg, a Dallas lawyer and friend since the 1930s, had helped Johnson in his political campaigns. In 1966 he would be appointed by Johnson to the 5th Circuit U.S. Court of Appeals. Goldberg, already home from the Trade Mart, answered the phone, and in discussing the situation with Johnson he stated his belief that Johnson already had become president upon Kennedy's death by virtue of constitutional devolution, even without taking the oath of office. However, he agreed that his succession should be "memorialized by some formality with witnesses"—in other words, a swearing-in ceremony. Sarah Hughes should be the choice, Goldberg thought, explaining that she was "a Democrat, a supporter of yours, a woman, and a fine judge."[52]

"We're trying to get her. You try, too," Johnson said, ending the conversation by urging Goldberg to come right away to Love Field to be with him on *Air Force One*.[53]

Goldberg agreed to help locate Hughes but demurred on coming to Love Field, explaining that Johnson did not need him. Goldberg's search for Judge Hughes consisted of calling Barefoot Sanders at his U.S. attorney's office, directly below her courtroom. Having gotten a ride to his office from the Trade Mart, Sanders was attempting to find a statute under which the president's alleged murderer, already arrested by Dallas police, could be charged. There was no such statute—the assassin was guilty only of a Texas felony. Murder of a president was a state crime, not a federal one. Goldberg told Sanders of his conversation with Johnson. Sanders, who already had been alerted to find Judge Hughes, agreed that she was the best person to swear Johnson in. Now, with the need to find her paramount, he dashed upstairs to her courtroom, thinking she might be there. He arrived just at the moment Hughes called there to advise her office staff that she was home. Sanders took the phone.

"This is Barefoot. The vice president wants you to swear him in as president. Can you do it?"

As logical as that had seemed to Lyndon Johnson, Goldberg, and Sanders, the possibility that she would be the person to swear in the new president evidently had never occurred to Hughes. But she was unruffled. Yes, she could, she said, immediately. "Where do I go?"

"Love Field," Sanders said. "I'll clear you with the Secret Service. How soon do you think you can get there?"

"Ten minutes," she said, "but what about the oath?"

"I'll have it at the airport when you get there," he replied, still uncertain as to where he would find it.

"Don't worry about it. I'll make it up," the judge replied.[54] She got into her car and drove to Love Field.[55]

Hughes later explained her seeming lack of concern about finding the oath. "The essentials of every oath are the same. You have to swear to perform the duties of the office of President of the United States, and to preserve and defend the Constitution of the United States. I was not afraid. I could do it without a formal oath." She had sworn in many people—jurors, public officials, and many young lawyers. They all had to swear to perform the duties of the office and to uphold and preserve the Constitution of the United States. She felt certain that these were the two principal elements of the presidential oath.[56]

Hughes was not the only federal judge in Dallas who could swear in the new president, but she was the best and most logical choice. Of the other two judges, T. Whitfield Davidson, an eighty-seven-year-old cantankerous Democrat, had opposed Johnson politically by seeking to forbid the Democratic Executive Committee from certifying him as the senatorial nominee in 1948, and he had become in his old age something of a curmudgeon. The other, Joe Estes, was an Eisenhower Democrat, appointed by Dwight Eisenhower.[57]

Later, Hughes would say, everybody wanted to know what she was thinking about on that short and solitary drive, just three blocks from her house on Normandy Avenue to Mockingbird Lane and then about a mile down that busy thoroughfare to the entrance to Love Field. "I was thinking first of all that I must not think about Kennedy," she told historian Joe B. Frantz. "I must think about the country going on. . . . And another thing I was thinking about was that I must get there in a hurry because Vice-President Johnson is always in a hurry and wants things done right now and I shouldn't delay. And the other thing that I was thinking about was what the oath of office was, in case Barefoot couldn't find it. I was brash enough to think that I could give the oath without having looked it up."[58]

Johnson had had the presence of mind to tell Malcolm Kilduff, assistant press secretary to Kennedy, to make arrangements for the swearing-in ceremony.[59] Kilduff, who had startled some when he made the first reference to Johnson as "Mr. President," had done as directed. Kilduff forestalled the effort by an anguished brigadier general Godfrey McHugh, Kennedy's Air Force aide, to have *Air Force One* depart immediately; he arranged for three reporters (Charles Roberts of *Newsweek*, Merriman Smith of United Press International, and Sid Davis of Westinghouse) to come inside the airplane to witness the event and to serve as a pool for the other journalists; he directed White House photographer Cecil Stoughton, a captain in the Signal Corps, to take pictures; and he followed Stoughton's suggestion to grab a stenographer's Dictograph—the only recording device available—to make an audio recording of the event.[60]

Jacquelyn Kennedy was in the small bedroom, seated on a bed around the corner from her husband's coffin, still wearing the blood-stained pink suit that had been so striking that day. Johnson, comforting her, had advised her a few minutes earlier that the swearing-in would be held on the airplane before departure. 'I've arranged for a judge—an old friend of mine, Judge Hughes—to come. She'll be here in about an hour. So why don't you lie down and freshen up and everything? We'll leave you alone."[61]

Judge Hughes, en route alone to Love Field, was intercepted by Dallas police officer James Jennings, who had been sent to find and escort her. "We now have information that Judge Sarah Hughes is en route from Parkland to Love to swear President Johnson in," the police dispatcher announced at 2:35 P.M., assuming erroneously that she was coming from Parkland Hospital instead of her house.[62] Jennings, going the opposite direction from Judge Hughes, had recognized her, turned around to accompany her, and now led her in his police car to a side entrance to the airport runway. Other officers were blocking the entrance, "but there was no difficulty," Hughes later said. She was pleased that so many officers recognized her. "They knew me, and I told them I was there to swear in the Vice-President as President."[63]

Goldberg, too, had decided at his wife's encouragement to follow Johnson's request and go to Love Field. They parked their car and walked onto the runway only to be blocked by a police officer. Goldberg explained that the new president had requested him to come, but the officer only stared. Goldberg told his wife it was difficult to convince policemen of anything, and they simply turned and went back home. (The next day, Johnson called from Washington to ask Goldberg where he had been. "Never mind," Goldberg responded.)[64]

For Hughes, the situation had been different. Dallas Police chief Jesse Curry, Secret Service agent John Ready, and Vernon Oneal, the funeral home owner whose hearse had taken the president's body to Love Field from Parkland, were watching for her. It was Oneal who first spotted her, seeing her when her two-door hardtop automobile rounded the *Spirit of Flight* statue at the terminal. "There she is!" he shouted.[65]

A motorcycle officer took up as escort and accompanied Hughes as she drove her own car closer to the airplane parked near Gate 27. She was struck by its magnificent appearance. "It was a beautiful sight, the presidential plane, long and sleek, a blue and two white stripes running the length of the plane with the words, 'The United States of America,' on the blue stripe," she later recalled. "It seemed to exemplify the strength and courage of our country."[66]

Police chief Curry met Hughes at the ramp with the aircraft commander, Colonel James Swindal, who presented her in turn to Major General Chester (Ted) Clifton, military aide to the president. Someone told her Barefoot Sanders wanted her to call him. "I knew that Barefoot had the oath by then," Hughes recalled later, "but I said, 'Well, I know what the oath is!'" As she proceeded up the ramp someone else mentioned the oath. She replied, "I don't need the oath of office, I know what to say."[67] But the exact wording had been found. Nicholas Katzenbach in Washington had realized that the oath appeared in the U.S. Constitution. He had called *Air Force One* and dictated it to Marie Fehmer.[68] Now someone presented Hughes with the oath, typed neatly by Fehmer on a small piece of stationery.[69]

Hughes, still in the dress with the huge polka dots she had worn to the luncheon, followed Clifton through the airplane's foresections—communications, forward galley, crews' quarters, and the press and staff area—before entering the state room at the midpoint of the airplane. There, the ceremony awaited her.

Sarah T. Hughes stepped inside the crowded, hot, stuffy, and uncomfortable room—packed because Johnson had wanted as many people as possible to witness the event. Hughes, seeing Johnson and Lady Bird, embraced each of them without saying anything. An embrace seemed to her the "best way to give expression to my feeling of grief for them, and for all of us," she said later.[70] Johnson said, "Mrs. Kennedy wants to be here. We'll wait for her."[71]

Stoughton began taking pictures—the first of twenty-one—as soon as Hughes was in place. Already Johnson had been arranging the elements. "How do you want us? Can you get us all in?" he asked Stoughton. "We'll get as many people in here as possible," Johnson said, sending Jack Valenti, Rufus Youngblood, Emory Roberts, and Lem Johns into the staff area to summon others. Johnson followed just behind them and announced, "If anybody wants to join in in the swearing-in ceremony, I would be happy and proud to have you."[72]

Finally, twenty-seven individuals squeezed inside a space designed for ten. Kennedy's traumatized aides, knowing only that their president had been slain on the streets of Dallas, generally assumed he had been the victim of right-wing extremists. Many were reluctant to be included in the swearing-in ceremony, even as spectators. Their feelings of revulsion included not only the city and the state of Texas but also Lyndon B. Johnson as the foremost representative of the state. Some of them were irritated that Lyndon B. Johnson already had taken charge of the situation, delaying the departure for Washington at a time when they were eager to leave. Some were not pleased that Johnson had ordered his and Lady Bird Johnson's luggage removed from the adjacent back-up airplane and placed in *Air Force One* for the return flight.[73]

Nevertheless, several Kennedy aides were in the room to witness the ceremony—Larry O'Brien, Evelyn Lincoln, Pamela Tenure, and Kilduff. Many of Johnson's own aides were now aboard and in the state rooms, too, including Liz Carpenter and the newly anointed Bill Moyers and Jack Valenti. Texas congressman Albert Thomas was there, as was police chief Curry.

"We'll wait for Mrs. Kennedy. I want her here," Johnson told Hughes, then asked that someone bring her. "Just a minute. I'm going to get her," he said, and at that moment Jacquelyn Kennedy walked in.[74]

To Hughes, the bereaved widow, whom she had never met, exhibited clear evidence of her great grief but nevertheless was composed and calm. At that moment she exemplified to Hughes the courage the country needed to carry on. Johnson leaned over to the ashen-faced Mrs. Kennedy and introduced Hughes to her as a U.S. judge appointed by her husband. Hughes acknowledged the introduction by quietly saying to Mrs. Kennedy, "I loved him very much."[75]

In these brief moments Congressman Albert Thomas embraced Mrs. Kennedy. Dallas Police chief Curry told her the Dallas Police Department had done everything it could to protect the president. Johnson took her by the hand and said, "This is the saddest moment of my life."[76]

Towering above all others, Johnson asked Lady Bird to stand on his right and Mrs. Kennedy on his left. Stoughton, all too aware of the significance of his photograph, gave quick instructions to the principals to make minor adjustments. He perched on a sofa behind Judge Hughes, who was clutching the presidential oath. Malcolm Kilduff, kneeling low, held the Dictaphone in front of the judge, ready to activate it. Someone asked, "What about a Bible?"

Sergeant Joseph Ayres, the steward on the airplane crew, said President Kennedy kept his personal Bible under a table between the two beds in his cabin. Ayres went to get it (actually a prayer missal) then handed it to Larry O'Brien, special assistant to Kennedy.[77]

"Just a minute, Judge," O'Brien said, interrupting and handing her the book he described as a Catholic Bible. Hughes hesitated. The book was, she saw, a small volume with a soft leather cover. The fact that it was described as a Catholic Bible comforted her, and the pleasant thought entered her mind that President Kennedy might have been reading it on the trip. On the front was a gold cross. On the inside cover were sewn the initials JFK.[78]

Kilduff pressed the record button on the Dictaphone and extended the microphone in front of him; Hughes held the missal in front of her. Johnson placed his large left hand on it, lifted his right hand, and repeated the oath after Hughes, who at this moment became the first woman in the nation's history to swear in a president. "I do solemnly swear that I will perform the duties of President of the United States to the best of my ability and defend, protect, and preserve the Constitution of the United States." Hughes administered the oath in short phrases, consciously thinking that under tense circumstances people do not do well at remembering long ones. Johnson repeated the phrases after her, slowly and reverently. And at the conclusion Hughes added another phrase that did not appear on the oath itself, "So help me God." It seemed to her that the phrase needed to be said. With the twenty-eight-second ceremony over, the president leaned over, kissed Mrs. Kennedy gently, and then kissed his wife.[79]

Historian William Manchester, author of *The Death of a President*, wrote that Sarah T. Hughes uttered the first few words of the oath nervously, her voice quavering and her body shaking all over. If so, the audio recording does not reflect it, for she is heard in a firm, unhesitating voice.[80]

Stoughton, standing behind the judge, sweating profusely in the hot cabin, had suffered a momentary shock when he first triggered his camera. It had not worked. He had jiggled the film advance lever until he finally heard a click. As he worked, interchanging his Hasselblad with an Alpa Reflex camera, he was struck by the utter silence around him, save for the speaking of the oath itself.[81]

Immediately afterward, Hughes put her arm around the president. "We're all behind you," she said. Johnson, sinking into a chair, told Lem Johns, "Now let's get this plane back to Washington."[82] Hughes, police chief Curry, Westinghouse reporter Sid Davis, and photographer Stoughton quickly left the aircraft. On her way out Hughes handed the prayer missal to someone she did not know, who asked her, "Don't you want to keep it?" Hughes replied, "No, it doesn't belong to me."[83]

As the four stepped off *Air Force One*, Ralph Yarborough was just arriving, too late for the ceremony but in time to see Hughes departing and to hear her recount for him the ceremony just concluded. Yarborough was struck by the calmness with which she narrated those dramatic moments. At 2:47 P.M. the airplane lifted off the runway. Hughes drove home alone, having in these brief moments performed a service that would render her a historic figure for the ages.[84]

At home, she immediately found herself an object of intense interest. Reporters from the national and local media conducted telephone interviews. All three networks filmed her. Vivian Castleberry of the *Dallas Times Herald*, who had interviewed her earlier at the Trade Mart, called and asked her to recapture the moments on *Air Force One*. "It's no big deal," Hughes told her, "he was my friend, they called and asked me to come and I went."[85] Ronnie Dugger, editor of the *Texas Observer* and a free-lance writer for the *Washington Post*, asked her to write an article for the *Post* describing her experiences that day, which she agreed to do. Its publication two days later in the Sunday edition provided the only instant summary of the momentous event written by a participant.[86]

Upon leaving *Air Force One*, police chief Curry went to the downtown police station, where the accused murderer already was denying that he had anything at all to do with the assassination.

Photographer Stoughton normally would have stayed with the president. He would remain the White House photographer under Johnson. But on this day the nation and the world awaited his pictures. To expedite their transmission, he went to the Associated Press's Dallas office, where photographers processed his film as quickly as possible. With prints of the selected black-and-white image ready, both AP and United Press International simultaneously transmitted the photograph to thousands of clients across the globe.[87]

The picture, reproduced immediately in newspapers for millions of readers throughout the world, affirmed that after a shocking, horrible assassination, an orderly, ceremonial transition assured the proper continuity of the most powerful elected office of the most powerful nation in the world. The stark images of the principals summed up the terrible tension of that day in a way that could never be forgotten. Towering above all others in the crowded stateroom was the dominating personage of Lyndon B. Johnson, his left hand on the missal and his right hand uplifted. He was looking directly into the eyes of U.S. district judge Sarah T. Hughes, and it was to her that he swore to preserve and protect the Constitution of the United States, "so help me God."

11

Judicial Activist

arah T. Hughes's vivid description of the events on *Air Force One*, published in the *Washington Post*, provided the earliest written account of this historic occasion by any of the key participants. Alfred Friendly, the newspaper's managing editor, quickly recognized the significance of Hughes's narrative and praised her for it. "As an editor, let me tell you how expert and moving I thought it was. We are in your debt, as are all of our readers who, through you, were a part of history in the making."[1] Distributed in newspapers across the world through the *Post*'s syndication network, the judge's description reinforced for millions of people the historic photograph they already had seen depicting the ceremony.

In addition to communicating to a mass audience through her article for the *Post*, within a week Hughes wrote personally to those principals intimately involved in the tragic events. In her letter to Jacquelyn Kennedy she emphasized the country's love for her late husband. Mrs. Kennedy's secretary, Nancy Tuckerman, responded in a letter with a black border imprinted with the name "Mrs. John F. Kennedy." Mrs. Kennedy was touched by Judge Hughes's letter and most appreciative of her thoughtfulness.[2]

To Mrs. J. D. Tippit, widow of the Dallas police officer Oswald shot and killed, Hughes wrote: "In this your hour of tragedy, I join all of the citizens of Dallas and this Country as well, in sending you my heartfelt sympathy. Your husband gave his life for his country and in his courage you may have great pride."[3]

To Lyndon B. Johnson, she wrote: "Dear Mr. President: In the days to come my thoughts will be much with you. Your task is tremendous, but with God's help and the efforts of all of us the burden may be lightened. As I sped toward the airport last Friday, I had only one thought—to do the job assigned to me. Since then I have realized the honor you conferred upon me and I am appreciative. With esteem, I am Very respectfully yours." And then she added a postscript: "After this letter was written we heard your marvelous and moving address to Congress. Congratulations."[4]

Lady Bird Johnson, who in the aftermath of the assassination was to become much closer to Hughes, wrote a brief response a few days later. "Dear Sarah. It was a nightmare day, but Lyndon and I will always be grateful you were there. With love, Lady Bird."[5]

Two weeks later, Hughes heard from the president himself. "Thank you so much for your warm letter," he wrote. "There were other Judges that were available to swear me in on that sad day in November, but I wanted you to do this for me for a *very special* reason." In the margin he appended a handwritten note: "You were it." She would always be welcome at his office when she was in Washington, he said, signing the letter, "Sincerely, Lyndon."[6]

The attention thrust upon Hughes because of her role in the national tragedy would dwarf the recognition she had received over many decades for all the many accomplishments she had worked so diligently to achieve. Overnight, her name and image became known to millions of people across the globe. Complimentary letters from across the nation and the world began arriving. Such adulation at first seemed odd to her and even a bit irritating. In her mind, she had merely done a job that day. She had answered a call to public service in her capacity as a federal district judge. It was not an accomplishment she had achieved through hard work. The simple act of administering the oath had not been difficult. The praise seemed out of proportion to the deed.

Asked six years after the assassination to name her most thrilling accomplishment, Hughes failed even to mention the swearing-in ceremony. In her most extensive oral history, she said her biggest thrill was getting elected to the Texas Legislature with hardly any money through a "person-to-person campaign." Next came her appointment as a federal judge—"something else that I felt that I had done myself." She explained, "I get thrills out of doing what I want to do." Someone else had summoned her to administer the oath. Her own initiative had no bearing on it; it was not something she had accomplished.[7]

Well-deserved awards and special recognition had been a regular part of Judge Hughes's life, but in the next few years they multiplied at a much faster pace. Honorary doctorates were conferred upon her by Southern Methodist University, Indiana State University, Iowa Wesleyan College, Mary Hardin-Baylor College, and Clarkson College. The board of editors of *Who's Who of American Women* named her the Outstanding Woman of the Year in the field of law. The American Bar Association honored her for service to the legal profession.

Influential persons and organizations touted her for presidential appointment to higher office. The National Federation of the Business and Professional Women's Clubs asked President Johnson to appoint Hughes either to the U.S. Supreme Court or to be secretary of health, education and welfare when a position opened. She had a demonstrated capacity for hard work and straight thinking, the organization stated.[8] The National Association of Women Lawyers endorsed Hughes in a letter to the president for the next available vacancy on the Supreme Court.[9] The push to promote her either to the Supreme Court or the U.S. Court of Appeals for the 5th Circuit continued through the next several years, always without Hughes's encouragement. The president gave no indication that he considered her seriously for such appointments. He had others in mind. He sent Irving Goldberg to the 5th Circuit in 1966. Notably he filled Supreme Court openings with Abe Fortas, whom he had known since 1937, when Fortas was a young official with the Securities and Exchange Commission, and Thurgood Marshall, chief legal counsel for the National Association for the Advancement of Colored People. Marshall had the distinction of being the first African American to serve on the nation's highest court. Had Johnson also chosen Hughes, he could have held the twin distinctions of naming the first woman as well as the first black man to the Supreme Court.

The question lingered as to why it had been Sarah Hughes who was summoned to *Air Force One* on November 22 rather than someone else. Nearly twenty years later Hughes said, "[I would] like to think that I was chosen . . . because he [Johnson] knew me quite well and was fond of me." However, she had realized, this likely was not the case. She had been the logical choice—as Goldberg and Sanders had agreed—because "one of the Judges was a Republican [Estes] and another one [Davidson] had rendered an unfavorable opinion against Lyndon Johnson, and so I was asked to perform the oath."[10]

The president, in a private telephone conversation just over a year after November 22, gave himself full credit for making the choice and described his selection of Hughes with a slightly different twist. Talking to Edwin Wiesl Jr. (a conversation quoted in part in the previous chapter), Johnson said he chose Hughes because she was mad at him for his failure to push harder for her judicial appointment, and he wanted to assuage her anger. Her anger, he said, was prompted because he had accepted the Kennedy administration's rejection of her, assumed he could push her candidacy no further, and then had recommended Henry Wade. "I had her swear me in trying to make up with her a little bit," he said.[11]

Hughes's papers contain no suggestion that she was even aware Johnson had turned to Wade as a nominee, and they give no hint she was angry with Johnson. His support of Wade was never publicized or mentioned in numerous later accounts of the events surrounding Hughes's controversial nomination. At any rate, certainly after November 22, the president and the woman who had sworn him in were bound together as friendly, symbiotic partners. In the months and years ahead, as their relationship grew more personal, each seemed mindful and appreciative of the other.

Shortly after their first exchange of letters following the assassination, Johnson sent the judge an autographed picture of the swearing-in ceremony. Thanking him, Hughes said the expressions on the faces of all, particularly Mrs. Kennedy, reflected the tragic circumstances of the occasion. "I shall treasure the picture as representing a great moment in history and I appreciate your thinking of me."[12]

She took advantage of the opportunity to inform the president about a trip she had taken in December 1963 to Colombia to attend a family law conference sponsored by the United Nations. The president of the Colegio de Abogados de Bolívar informed her that President Kennedy had promised through the American embassy he would send him a bust of Thomas Jefferson. In addition, the college now wanted a bust of Kennedy, whom they had greatly loved. Although Hughes did not request President Johnson's help on the matter, after she gave him this information, he soon advised her that the donation of a bust of Jefferson for the college was "being put into motion." He made no mention of the requested bust of Kennedy.[13]

Johnson's attentiveness caught Hughes off guard. Scheduled to be in Washington, D.C., on February 1, 1964, to speak at the officers' installation of the National Women's Council of Realtors, she had no thought of contacting the president despite his earlier reminder that she was always welcome at the White House. She was surprised when presidential assistant Bill Moyers wrote to tell her the president would like to see her when she was in town.[14]

"It is amazing to me," she wrote back to Moyers, "that the President should note that I would be in the City on that date, and with all that he has to do, still more amazing that he would be willing to take time out to see me if his schedule permits." The visit took place, and afterward Hughes wrote to thank Johnson for being so "very gracious and generous" in seeing her. "I want you to know," she wrote, "that everywhere I find favorable response to your administration—from the taxi-drivers, people I meet on the plane and even friends who voted Republican in 1960." What pleased her even more was what she termed Johnson's master stroke in announcing the appointment of fifty women to high-level posts.[15]

Her hotel room was enhanced on this occasion by a basket of flowers sent by the President and Lady Bird. In a note of thanks to Mrs. Johnson, Hughes had a request. "One thing I wish you could do, which I know is practically impossible, is to slow your husband down just a fraction—we need him."[16]

Feeling far more confident now about her growing relationship with the president, she asked a special favor from him in February. Members of the Tokyo Business and Professional Women's Club soon would be observing their International Night. Could he send them a special greeting from the White House? Yes, he could, and he did.[17]

During these busy times, Sarah and George Hughes did their best to continue enjoying their quiet domestic routine. George, having retired in 1962, was happy in his enlarged role as anchor of the household—taking the lead in cooking, gardening, and making coffee for their early-morning ritual of rising at 5:30 A.M. and reading the morning newspaper together. They had reluctantly given up their enjoyable activity of horseback riding because increasing urban density made it too difficult to stable their horses at a reasonable distance from Highland Park. In their comfortable neighborhood, families tended to settle permanently, and the Hugheses themselves had now lived there for more than three decades. They were on friendly terms with their neighbors, socializing with them at occasional parties, at which politics was not discussed. Few of the neighbors shared the Hugheses' political outlook. The Hugheses enjoyed a Thanksgiving meal each year with their good Republican friends, Hugo and Joy Swan, who lived directly across the street. George always used his domestic skills to carve the turkey.

The husband Sarah Hughes once described as a "pessimist" had never liked politics, even though it was his wife's passion. Perhaps it was just as well that as a federal government employee he had been prohibited from participating in political campaigns. But he always had supported his wife in all her endeavors, generally expressing mild but happy surprise at her accomplishments.[18]

An unfortunate incident dampened George's normally bright spirits during these months. He struck a child who unexpectedly darted in front of his car. The child survived, but the emotional strain on George Hughes was prolonged. A deterioration of his physical health, the extent of which he tried to conceal from his wife because he was reluctant to distract her from her important duties, seemed at first to be a possible result of depression from this accident. But doctors eventually diagnosed his problem as cancer. It had developed at his colon and advanced to his liver. It was impossible to keep this news from his wife.[19] He was admitted to Baylor Hospital in mid-May. When it became clear that George's illness would be fatal, Sarah, in late May 1964, paid $1,890 for two crypts, one for George and one for herself, at Hillcrest Mausoleum, not far from their home on Normandy.[20]

During George's final days in the hospital, Sarah maintained her schedule at court but spent as much time with him as possible, visiting him faithfully each noon hour during breaks from her judicial duties. On the early Monday morning of June 1, 1964, eighteen days after being admitted to the hospital, George Ernest Hughes died at the age of seventy-two. The newspaper obituaries focused on his achievements rather than his link to a famous wife. One story failed even to mention the name of Sarah T. Hughes; the other identified her only in a single sentence. Both obituaries were accompanied by one-column photographs of George Hughes.[21] Funeral services were conducted at St. Matthew's Episcopal Cathedral on June 2.

Lyndon and Lady Bird Johnson sent their condolences in a telegram that arrived on the day of the funeral. "We are also saddened by your loss. The years have taught us what it means to lose those close. Please know our thoughts and prayers are with you."[22]

Sarah T. Hughes, suddenly alone for the first time after forty-two years of marriage, had to learn to cope without the stable presence of her husband. She seemed to manage very well, for even with this significant loss she was not a person to dwell on the past. She was surrounded by friends who could help—Gwen Graul, Barefoot and Jan Sanders, Louise Raggio, and her neighbors Hugo and Joy Swan. On the evening of George's funeral Hughes accepted an invitation from the Sanderses to come to their house for a swim.[23]

Two days after George's funeral, Judge Hughes was back on the bench making headlines with two unusual sentences that caught the attention of the press because of their novelty. Both reflected her usual concern for rehabilitation and her optimism that it could work. First, she considered the case of a man pleading guilty for attempting to pass a forged check. In her usual fashion—working as always under her conviction that improved social conditions were the key to correcting criminal behavior—she tried to identify the root of the defendant's problem by questioning his wife. She learned that the defendant had a drinking problem. "That's his problem, isn't it, drinking?" Hughes asked. The woman agreed. Upon further inquiry Hughes learned that the couple had six children. "You think that's enough?" the judge asked. The woman evidently nodded her agreement. "I think so, too," Hughes said, an observation she often made in such situations. She then placed the thirty-year-old man on probation for three years on the condition that he not become intoxicated.[24]

In the second case a postal worker had removed a hundred dollars from a cash reserve drawer and was caught when he tried later to replace it. The man, she determined, had been having financial difficulties. "I think you have been living beyond your means," she said, sentencing him to two years' probation on this condition: that "[you] not live beyond your means and that what you buy must be for cash."[25]

In both instances, the news story observed, the judge was continuing her practice of attempting to locate lawbreakers' problems and requiring that they meet certain conditions if they were to receive probated sentences. Less than three weeks before George's death she had made headlines when she lectured a long line of defendants against the evils of installment buying and having too many children. She had advised each of the defendants to bring family members, employers, and friends to assist them in telling their stories before sentencing. "You've been plagued by bills all your married life, haven't you?" she asked a substitute mailman who was pleading guilty to stealing money from letters. With his wife sobbing nearby, the man agreed, adding that he owed payments on furniture, food, and transportation. Too many people are buying on the installment plan, Judge Hughes declared. She placed him on three years' probation on condition that he buy nothing else on credit. Another defendant also admitted spending more money than he earned. His pregnant wife stood in the courtroom and said that he had been struggling to provide for her in the same way that her affluent parents had done. Yet, she said, this was not necessary for her. "Is there anything you want me to tell him for you?" Hughes asked the woman. "Tell him I love him," the woman answered. "You can tell him that better," the judge replied. Twice during the sentencing on this day Judge Hughes told defendants they already had enough children for their incomes. Another defendant had been married to one woman but living with another. When the man was unable to explain his actions, Judge Hughes sentenced him to a year in prison. "I think you need to understand we all have to have a sense of responsibility. Your past record indicates you don't."[26]

Only a week after her husband's death Judge Hughes made a ruling that a newspaper suggested "may turn out to be a landmark decision." She sustained a defense motion to suppress police evidence gathered by wiring a microphone into a public telephone booth and intercepting conversations. The defendant, John E. Stone, was accused of handling bets between his Dallas customers and Las Vegas. In a ruling that went against her friend U.S. attorney Barefoot Sanders, who was prosecuting the case, Hughes determined that a "public telephone booth being used by an individual citizen for a private toll call" was protected under the Fourth Amendment, which outlaws illegal searches.[27]

Unlike during her long tenure as a state district judge, when she heard only civil cases, as a federal judge Hughes presided over both criminal and civil cases. She came to prefer the criminal docket. To help her in sentencing offenders, she expected thorough reports from the probation officers. As a result, she developed close working relationships with them. Stiff sentences, she was convinced, would not solve the problem of crime. She had believed since her days as a policewoman that poverty, not personal predisposition, prompted wrongdoing. Individuals could be rehabilitated if their circumstances could be improved. She enjoyed quoting Plato as saying, "Poverty is the mother of crime."[28]

On one occasion she was angered to hear a minister proclaim probation did not work. The next day she went to a probation officer and acquired statistics showing its effectiveness. She used the information to enlighten the minister.[29]

When sentencing criminal defendants Hughes often took on a maternal bearing, showing compassion especially to those who had not had the advantages of society's benefits. As she weighed her decisions, she made comments such as these: "Are you a good worker?" "Will you study for me?" "Are you an addict? If you are, tell me and I will recommend help." "You have good possibilities. But it is largely up to you." "Three children in five years is too many. It is up to you to do something about it."[30]

She opposed capital punishment. "I don't think it deters crime, and occasionally you'll have the wrong person," she said. "And nobody who's white and rich ever gets the death penalty." In May 1965, she wrote to state representative James W. Stroud in Austin to endorse legislation to abolish the death penalty in Texas.[31] The bill failed to pass.

Her reputation for being soft on criminals attracted the attention of the president of the Dallas Crime Commission, John McKee, who began including examples of her supposed leniency in memos to his membership. McKee noted caustically on one occasion that she had granted probation to five different defendants on drug-related cases.[32]

While Hughes mustered more than ample sympathy for defendants whose troubles seemed to be related to unfortunate circumstances—a broken home, addiction, poverty—she had a reputation for being tough on businessmen who profited from fraud or income-tax evasion. A probation officer assigned to her court, recalling the harshness with which she dealt with errant businessmen, said he once saw her sentence the well-to-do president of her own garden club in Highland Park to a year in prison, the maximum, for income tax evasion. She asked him why he had not filed a return, and he said he didn't think he had to because he had made no money that year.[33] On another occasion a high government official was testifying on behalf of a businessman friend who had pleaded guilty to income tax evasion and was awaiting the judge's sentence. When he urged her to take into consideration that his client was a pillar of the community, Hughes bristled. "What do you mean, 'He's a pillar of the community?' This man has just admitted that he cheated the government."[34]

In November 1964, a one-time high-flying businessman who had gained a fortune through fraud, Billie Sol Estes, appeared in her courtroom. Estes was being closely followed by the press because of his alleged previous ties to the Democratic administration. Estes, who had made a fortune in West Texas by falsifying his assets to obtain huge loans, had been free on ten-thousand-dollars bond on the stipulation that he not leave the one hundred counties of the Northern District of Texas. When he violated that agreement by going to Denver on business, he found himself before Hughes. The judge quickly forfeited his bond and ordered him to jail, his first confinement since he had been arrested nearly three years before. She then held another hearing and granted him a new ten-thousand-dollars bond. After two hours behind bars, Estes again was free. The brief incident placed Hughes in the national spotlight.[35]

Although she was appointed to the bench as a Democrat who held definite opinions, Hughes, by most accounts, set aside these political beliefs as a presiding judge. She relied heavily on precedent in her rulings, finding ample legal justification for some rulings that in the late 1960s and 1970s sent ripples of disbelief through much of the Dallas community. Once she familiarized herself with relevant prior decisions, she used a great deal of common sense in deciding cases. As a pragmatist, she desired above all to reach conclusions that would not be overturned on appeal. She wanted to understand the facts, apply the law, and write her opinion as succinctly as possible. Profound discussions of the law did not interest her.[36]

On the bench Judge Hughes was efficient and brusque, a no-nonsense judge who did not tolerate ill-prepared attorneys. She tried to make the most of the court's time, hurrying lawyers along when the pace was too slow to suit her. If a lawyer appeared to be wasting time, she would administer a verbal lashing.

Her impatience was illustrated once at a pretrial conference in her chambers in which both attorneys stipulated certain facts. It was about 2 P.M. when they finished, and Hughes directed the attorneys to draw up the stipulations immediately and return them to her before the afternoon was over. One of the attorneys told her it would be impossible to do that in a couple of hours—it would take him at least a day or two. "I know that, but shoot for today," she said.[37]

Because she maintained tight control over her courtroom and was quick to use her sharp tongue, even distinguished lawyers felt trepidation about appearing before her. Nick Kuntz, as a beginning attorney, recalled walking into her courtroom with John Hauer, a veteran member of his large firm and known as one of the city's most distinguished lawyers, and being surprised at Hauer's apprehension. "It was the only time I ever saw Jack sweat," Kuntz said.[38] Yet, as Kuntz soon learned, many other able attorneys reacted in precisely the same way.

Although Louise Raggio was a good friend to Hughes and a companion to her in many projects, she was not entirely comfortable in her presence. "I often said that I wouldn't mind confessing my sins to God, but I sure wouldn't want to confess them to Sarah Hughes," she commented later. Raggio sensed a much tougher courtroom demeanor in Hughes as she made the transition from state to federal judge. Because a state judge is subject to reelection every four years, alienating attorneys appearing before her could have boomeranged. With a lifetime appointment to the federal bench, such concerns were eliminated.[39]

Raggio believed that at the same time Hughes championed women she was "especially hard on women lawyers," insisting that they maintain higher standards than men. Hughes wanted women to be able to handle all sorts of cases, not just easy ones. In this spirit she deliberately assigned Raggio, who had no experience as a criminal lawyer, to represent four criminal defendants.[40]

Hughes also insisted on a dress code that failed to recognize the changing times. For years she refused to permit women in her courtroom to wear slacks.[41] One day while court was in session, Hughes caught a glimpse of her female law clerk entering the room in a pants suit. She halted the proceedings to tell the shocked clerk to go back home and put on proper clothing. After a few more years, when it became obvious that pants suits were a permanent part of women's fashion, the judge finally accepted such attire. She even reached the point on occasional Fridays when she intended to go straight from court to a favorite weekend getaway, Padre Island, she would discreetly wear slacks beneath her judicial robes.[42]

In complex cases—antitrust, securities, and tax—Hughes, to many, seemed less confident on the bench. Such matters were not a part of her background. She compensated for her own shortcomings by taking voluminous notes, by requiring both pretrial and posttrial briefs, by leaning heavily on her law clerks for research, and by having her law clerks sit in on all hearings. She tried to simplify as much as possible issues before the court and frequently would suggest that the case before her was not as complex as the attorneys proclaimed.[43] What she inevitably preferred, especially in civil cases, was for the parties to settle out of court, and she often would tell the attorneys to so advise their clients.[44]

Once she had grasped the concept of a case, Hughes typically made such comments as these: "Let's move along." "You've already been over that." "That's already been established." Attorneys who sought advice on how best to proceed when appearing before her typically heard such comments as these: "Don't repeat, don't stray, stick to the facts." "On evidence, she sticks to the books." "Don't object just for the sake of objecting just to show you know you can." "Do not try to embarrass another attorney." "Don't lead." "Don't argue with the court. She will change her mind, but you must be convincing. She is confident in herself." "Don't beat around the bush."[45]

She disliked reading lengthy briefs, deeming them a necessary evil, and she advised attorneys to keep them short and to the point. One day an attorney placed a thick brief on her desk. She asked him what it was. When he told her it was a brief, she replied, "I hope you can tell me what is in it because I am not going to read it."[46] In such matters she relied heavily on her law clerks.

Hughes took pride in the amount of work accomplished in her court, just as she had done as a state judge. Each morning she made a list of things she wanted accomplished before the day was over—some were personal (decide what she would eat for dinner), and others were professional (finish a case today). Despite her strong work ethic, she liked to maintain regular hours, and reflecting her identification with labor, she always took short morning and afternoon coffee breaks.[47]

Her busy schedule caused her to begin declining speaking engagements. "It is not possible for me to accept," she said in turning down an invitation to go to Terre Haute, Indiana, to speak to its Business and Professional Women's Club. "I have such an extremely heavy court docket that I rarely accept out-of-city engagements any more."[48]

As a liberal, Hughes admired the Warren Court and its decisions in broadening civil liberties and free speech. She supported the civil rights movement from the beginning. When Martin Luther King Jr. came to Dallas in January 1963 to speak at Fair Park auditorium as part of a voter registration drive, she and Jan Sanders made what was then a courageous show of support. Sponsors of the visit, the city's black pastors, invited members of the Democratic Women of Dallas County to sit on the stage during King's talk, a daring proposition in a city that was still rigidly segregated. While the women's organization pondered this sensitive proposition, Hughes and Sanders retreated to the ladies' restroom to hold their own private caucus. They decided they would accept the offer no matter what. Thus, when King spoke to an auditorium filled largely with black faces, sitting on the stage with the city's black preachers and black politicians were two women with white faces. Outside, pickets demonstrated with signs protesting King's appearance. A rumor circulated that a bomb had been placed in the hall prior to his speech, but the event, attended by some four thousand, went on as scheduled.[49]

In 1968 Hughes was largely responsible for pushing the Episcopal diocese into establishing a new private school for African American children in a deprived area of south Dallas. St. Philip's Episcopal School and Community Center at 1600 Pennsylvania Avenue (the "other" 1600 Pennsylvania Avenue) became one of only two predominantly black Episcopalian schools in the nation. Hughes led the fund-raising drive and chaired the school's first board. Once the school got started, Hughes occasionally would bring food to eat with the students. She volunteered for such chores as simple as changing light bulbs. St. Phillip's went on to become a highly respected institution under long-time director Terry Flowers.[50]

When the Reverend Stephen Swann was seeking support to help found another new private school that became the Episcopal School of Dallas, one of the city's finest, he called on Judge Hughes to make a presentation. Although he did not know her (he was not related to the Swann family who lived across the street from Hughes), she was a fellow Episcopalian, and he expected at least to have an opportunity to explain his goals to her. He was quickly disabused of that notion. No sooner had he introduced himself than the judge drew back and said—as he recalls—"Young man, I know all about you. You're a racist and I won't have anything to do with your school. Good day." Swann was anything but a racist. Judge Hughes's hasty response was set off by a phenomenon of the day that caused her to suspect his motives—the founding of many small private schools that, unlike public schools, could avoid desegregation orders.[51] The incident illustrated a basic characteristic of Hughes: she was so firm in her convictions that outside the courtroom she sometimes made snap judgments that later proved to be in error.

Ernest E. Figari Jr. received a similar reception when Hughes interviewed him in 1964 for a one-year appointment as her law clerk. The judge asked him the expected questions about his background and his studies at the University of Texas Law School, where he was in his final semester, and then shifted to a series of political questions. Whom had he voted for in recent elections? Did he know who the congressional representative was in his hometown? Figari satisfied her with his answers. When she asked if he had ever worked in a political campaign, he replied innocently that he had done so briefly as an undergraduate at Texas A&M. One of his fraternity brothers, he explained, was the son of Jack Cox, the 1962 Republican candidate for governor, and "all of us in the fraternity pitched in to help Mr. Cox."[52]

Any association with Cox, a distinctly conservative Republican, was too much for Judge Hughes. She stood up immediately and to Figari's surprise announced, "This interview is over." She escorted him out the door, and he assumed he had no chance of being hired. Fortunately for Figari, prior to going into the judge's office, he had discussed his undergraduate studies at Texas A&M with Gwen Graul, who viewed the institution with great favor. Two of her own sons had gone to Texas A&M. Learning of Hughes's quick dismissal of Figari, Graul implored her to overlook what she described as his "brief transgression," explaining that he was "politically naïve" and should not be punished for that. Hughes acceded to her secretary. A few days later Figari received a letter—to his surprise—that he was hired. He worked as Judge Hughes's law clerk from July 1964 to August 1965.[53]

Figari, who would become one of Dallas's outstanding trial lawyers, enjoyed his year with Hughes immensely. "It was the most formative experience in my legal career," he said nearly forty years later. He found Hughes to be unusually flexible as a supervisor. She permitted him to sit in on every courtroom proceeding, an invaluable experience. She discouraged him or anyone else in the office from working beyond normal office hours or on weekends. The only time he felt pressure was in preparing a charge for the judge to give to a jury. Occasionally, Figari would be invited to Hughes's home for informal dinner parties. Often her courtroom staff would be there. Assistant district attorneys from Sanders's staff and law professors from Southern Methodist University also were typical guests.[54]

Shortly after Figari left Hughes to begin his own practice, she appointed him to represent a man who was charged for failing to register a sawed-off shotgun; the government commonly made such charges in seeking to identify gamblers, who customarily favored these weapons. In defending the man, Figari argued that the federal government's registration requirement amounted to a violation of his client's right against self-incrimination. Hughes refused to accept this argument, and the defendant was convicted. Her ruling was upheld by the 5th Circuit, but the U.S. Supreme Court accepted Figari's argument and overturned the conviction. Instead of being displeased, Judge Hughes took great satisfaction in this victory by her former clerk, boasting at every opportunity, "My law clerk reversed me."[55]

In the summer of George's death, a two-week cruise, something she would enjoy frequently over the next years, helped Hughes overcome her grief. She and Gwen Graul sailed to South America aboard the *S.S. Argentina*, a luxury liner launched only six years earlier. Her friendship with her long-time secretary grew even closer after George's death, for she relied on her more than ever. They were like sisters, a court official said later in describing their relationship, "although Gwen always knew she [Hughes] was the judge."[56] Hughes, Barefoot Sanders recalled, would "hardly make a move without Gwen." Her influence in persuading the judge to hire Figari despite his political transgression was a clear indication of Graul's standing. She was Hughes's confidante as well as her secretary. Because the petite judge's tiny feet were difficult to fit, Gwen sometimes bought shoes for her in the children's department at Neiman-Marcus. She occasionally also bought clothes there, too, for her friend and employer.[57] When Hughes was out of town, Gwen often took care of her house and pets.

One occasion to look after the house came in July 1964, when President Johnson asked Hughes to come to Washington for dinner. She accepted with pleasure. "Oh, What a Beautiful Evening at the White House," she wrote to him afterward in a thank you letter. "From being escorted to dinner by a handsome young Captain to the climax of a kiss from the President of the United States and everything in between. My surprise and thrill in being invited were matched only by my delight in the occasion itself."[58]

Earlier that month Lyndon Johnson had signed the Civil Rights Act of 1964, the most sweeping civil rights bill in the nation's history, legislation that undoubtedly pleased Hughes. At the Republican Convention in July, Barry Goldwater had been nominated as a GOP presidential candidate who would give voters "a choice, not an echo." At the Gulf of Tonkin, also in the same month of Hughes's visit, North Vietnamese PT boats reportedly had fired on two U.S. destroyers, and the president was preparing to ask for greater authority to retaliate.

In August 1964, Lyndon B. Johnson easily won nomination as the Democratic Party's presidential candidate. Goldwater's uncompromising ideology presented a contrast to Johnson's image of moderation and the liberalism he was exhibiting in the White House, which hearkened back to the New Deal days, when he was a favorite of President Roosevelt. Hughes reported to Johnson that the Democratic campaign was going well even in Republican Dallas County. "But please do not let anyone take the election for granted," she urged him. "The prospect of Goldwater is frightening."[59]

Johnson assured her he was not complacent. "I think you have known me long enough to be certain that I am not one to take the future for granted. This country has a choice on November 3, and I am going to do my best to see that the issues are clearly defined. The people of this land deserve no less."[60]

There was little reason for concern. Johnson's November 1964 victory was a landslide of historic proportions. Hughes was present for Johnson's inauguration on January 20, 1965, on the steps of the nation's capitol, having arrived in the city several days earlier. She visited the Supreme Court to hear opinions handed down, and she was among some five thousand women who attended the Distinguished Ladies Reception at the National Gallery of Art two days before the inauguration. Lady Bird Johnson, standing in a receiving line for the women, was pleased when she saw the judge coming down the line. Hughes watched the inauguration from a close-up preferred seat, arranged for her by the president. This time she was a spectator as Chief Justice Earl Warren administered the oath of office under circumstances dramatically different from those of November 22, 1963. The president's consideration for Hughes on this important occasion was, she told him, "beyond anything I could have imagined." Besides having a preferred seat for the inaugural ceremony, she was given a place in the presidential grandstand for the parade afterward. "[It] was a real thrill, particularly when you took the time to come by and greet me." Johnson's inaugural address, in which he promised a "great society," was—she told him later—"a masterpiece." Aside from his speech, the church services were most memorable for her. "The need for spiritual values was never more apparent. We truly need to take time for our souls to catch up with our bodies. My thoughts and prayers will be with you as you daily seek to achieve the Great Society."[61]

Speculation concerning the president's new appointments for his first elected term in office now appeared in the media. Sarah T. Hughes's name was mentioned for the Circuit Court of the District of Columbia. She had not sought it, but as far as she was concerned this appointment was not out of the question. Instead of communicating directly with the president on the matter, she sent in late November 1964 a candid, handwritten letter to Lady Bird for her to relay to him her availability for any assignment.

> Perhaps you have noticed the mention in various papers and in NewsWeek of the possibility of the President appointing me to some other office, particularly the Circuit Court of the District of Columbia.
>
> I am sure you know I have not asked the President for any other office and I do enjoy my work as a District Judge. But somehow I do not

like to think of anything as permanent and so I wanted him to know that I am interested and would accept whatever he might have in mind for me.

I have complete confidence in his judgment and if he feels that my greatest service is as a District Judge, where contacts with the people are many, I am satisfied.[62]

Lady Bird responded, "You know the high esteem in which Lyndon holds you—the respect for your ability and character, together with that special fondness of feeling that you've both worked the political vineyards striving to serve the people of Texas for many years. I don't know what the needs are nor what his plans are, but I'll make sure that he knows of your letter."[63]

Hughes had no thought of mounting a campaign of any sort for the appointment. The matter was dropped. Nor did there seem to be much chance of an ambassadorial appointment, a possibility that continued to be attractive to her. The remoteness of that possibility seemed to be indicated by a memo White House aide Walter Jenkins sent for reasons unknown to Lady Bird's social secretary, Bess Abell. It put Hughes tenth on a list of names suggested as possible ambassadors to Malaysia.[64]

In the summer of 1965 Hughes returned to Europe, crossing the Atlantic by ocean liner with her neighbors, the Swans, and their grown daughter, Lois. The judge took first-class accommodations on the ocean liner, while the Swanns, who went to Europe every year, took less expensive accommodations. Some interesting people who shared her table on board, she noted, included Frank Lloyd Wright. "The lack of responsibility is wonderful," Hughes wrote to Gwen Graul. "Don't ever have to keep track of money. Lois does that & at the end of the week tells me how much I owe."[65] After landing at Le Havre, they traveled across the continent by car, staying mostly at delightful inns in small towns. Their expansive itinerary included Chartres, Vienna, Turin, Florence, Bologna, Padua, Venice, Munich, Czechoslovakia, and Poland.[66] "Glad to report I have the proper clothes, but too many," she wrote in a joint letter to Gwen and Odell Oliver.[67] It was a lesson she learned well, for in future years she would pride herself on traveling with only a single suitcase and a raincoat. And she would travel often; between 1964 and 1981 she would make nineteen foreign trips.

She came to view these journeys as necessary breaks from the pressures of her duties as a judge, pressures that rarely were visible to her friends and associates. Strenuous exercise—walking, climbing, swimming, and even snorkeling—was always a part of her vacation routine. Hughes left a full record of her trips through her regular letters to Graul, signing them always as "Judge" and often giving detailed descriptions of the meals she ate, the clothes she wore (frequently purchased for her by Graul), and the places she saw.[68]

She preferred vacation sites not unduly commercialized, although her itinerary always was planned in advance and she particularly enjoyed cruises. Sometimes she went with small groups of people on tours organized by the University of Portland in Oregon to such remote places as Rarotonga, Pago Pago, and other South Pacific islands. The place she returned to most often, though, was the small Norwegian town of Tretten in the Lillehammer region, about 120 miles north of Oslo. There, a married couple, Randi and Essen, whom she had come to know well, provided a pleasant base of operations. She first visited Norway in 1967. She returned at least half a dozen times over the next fifteen years.[69]

The fresh air and gorgeous mountain scenery in Norway invigorated her. She took hikes in the daytime and enjoyed wine or cocktails in the evening. She walked for miles and miles—eight, ten, sometimes twelve miles. She described one outing in a letter to Gwen in July 1972, when she was seventy-six years old: "We have done a lot of climbing, 3 to 4 hours a day[,] some over pretty steep ground. I have been rather proud of myself in being able to keep up although sometimes they have to wait for me. We have gone through snow & down precipices & over streams, tiring but extremely rewarding in just being able to do it." That evening, after dinner in the hotel lounge, she danced with her host, Essen. "I love to dance with Essen. While not a fancy dancer he is a good dancer and just suits me."[70]

In the months following the assassination, Dallas was a city in agony. Before President Kennedy's visit it had feared that the zealous right-wing demonstrators who already had done so much to harm the city's image would bring even further, perhaps irreparable, damage. Then, of course, had come the unthinkable tragedy, committed not by a right-wing extremist but by an extremist of another kind—an avowed Marxist and one-time defector to the Soviet Union.

But even if the far right had been guiltless in this event, there was a realization that the political atmosphere of extreme conservatism and intolerance, as evidenced by the nearly violent demonstrations against Lyndon B. Johnson and Adlai Stevenson, needed to be moderated. And while the city's business-man oligarchy endured with patience the often exaggerated, even outlandish criticisms directed from places far away, they and other Dallasites still were sensitive to criticisms from within the community.

Some outspoken individuals were discovering to their own misfortune that they had to pay heavy penalties for expressing sentiments critical of Dallas's political mood. The Reverend William A. Holmes, a Methodist minister, was besieged by death threats and forced to take his family into hiding after he preached a sermon blaming the city's atmosphere for the assas-sination. John Martin Shea, senior vice president for American Petrofina of Texas, found himself under severe attack after he wrote a first-person article for *Look* magazine making similar observations. One day his wife and children found a load of cement in their backyard swimming pool. After pressure from many, including evidently the management of his own company, he resigned. Eleanor Cowan, a fourth-grade teacher, was suspended by the Dallas Inde-pendent School District superintendent when her letter to *Time* magazine was published. In it she said she had seen the seeds of hate planted by the newspapers and many leaders in Dallas. "Don't let anyone fool you. Dallas is as responsible as anyone," she wrote.[71]

Hughes's most publicized comments on the subject, no harsher than those of many others, came in early April 1964, before a group of visiting Latin journalists on a U.S. government-sponsored tour. Hughes was the only nonjournalist on a six-person panel whose purpose was to discuss the assassi-nation. Her comments were printed on the front page of the *Dallas Morning News* under a bold, three-column headline, "Judge Says Dallas 'Climate' Contributed to JFK Slaying." She was quoted as saying: "There was a climate of hate in Dallas that was not evident in any other place. I definitely think that the feeling in Dallas contributed to the fact that Oswald would do this deed here rather than in some other city." The news story paraphrased her as saying that the anti-Kennedy campaign had been manifested long before he had been killed, noting especially the *Dallas Morning News* and its opposition to practically every policy he had proposed.[72]

Such an assessment by an authoritative person, a resident of Dallas who had played such an important part in the events of November 22, was reprinted throughout the nation by wire services to a public still burning with curiosity about the city of Dallas. In an editorial two days after her comments, the *Dallas Morning News* charged that Hughes had no basis for such an assessment. Her damning words, the editorial stated, "have been flashed around the country." She had poured "salt into healing sores" with her indictment. "One is inclined to toss off such comment from afar," the newspaper commented. "But when criticism comes from those who live and gain livelihood here, there is bound to be local resentment." Judge Hughes herself was said to represent an example of tolerance displayed by Dallasites. "This heavily conservative community tolerated her liberal leanings and elected her repeatedly to a district judgeship—not because of her political views but because of her competence." As someone trained in the examination of evidence, the newspaper concluded, she had offered very little evidence to support her point of view.[73]

She had given ammunition to the worst critics of Dallas, and this, to many, was unpardonable. A Republican candidate for the Senate from Texas, Jack Cox, insisted that she and Democratic senator Ralph Yarborough as well should apologize for what he called their irresponsible statements. Yarborough had said a few days earlier that Dallas had become a "citadel of reaction" under the control of an oligarchy.[74]

The criticisms did not deter Hughes. "It could have happened anywhere, but Dallas, I'm sorry to say, has been conditioned by many people who have hate in their hearts and who seem to want to destroy," she said soon afterward.[75] The time had come, she believed, to speak out against the extremism that had been tolerated in the city for so long. Evidence of Dallas's absolutism was clear in the 1960 Lyndon B. Johnson incident in downtown Dallas and in the later demonstration against Adlai Stevenson. "People who participated in these believe they are above the law," she said in a luncheon speech in May 1964 to the Dallas Federal Bar Association. Disrespect for the law could be seen even from eminent people, including the governors of Alabama and Mississippi, and even in Texas governor John B. Connally, who had contributed to the climate by calling a ruling of the U.S. Circuit Court a political decision. Billboards with IMPEACH EARL WARREN, racial violence, and attempts to tamper with juries, she said, were further evidence of a "climate of absolutism and hate which is abroad in the land." Certain people "hate those in high places and charge even presidents with Communist leanings." These people believe they are "possessed with all wisdom and all patriotism."[76]

Many Dallas residents considered such criticisms from a fellow citizen to be little more than treason, and they expressed their disgust to Hughes in spiteful letters. Hughes's law clerk, Ernie Figari, encountered in her filing cabinet an extensive collection of what he said could only be described as hate mail directed to her, astonishing in its virulence. Hughes had quietly preserved the letters. More than ever, Hughes was becoming a pariah in the minds of many conservative citizens who viewed her as a liberal dedicated to tearing down the status quo.[77]

In a letter to a writer from the London School of Economics, she agreed with the statement that "there has been created in Dallas a political atmosphere so highly charged with hatred and potential violence that the assassination of a President fitted the pattern." Stanley Marcus had alluded to that climate as a spirit of absolutism, which, she said, was a more polite phrase.[78]

Marcus was adroit enough to express his viewpoint in a more positive fashion, permitting him to escape the withering criticisms Hughes had to endure. In a full-page advertisement on January 2, 1964, strategically entitled "What's Right with Dallas?" Marcus included positive statements to balance his assessment that the city had suffered from the spirit of absolutism in recent years. Now and in the years ahead, he emphasized, there must be a new mood in which fair play would be accorded for all legitimate differences of opinion.[79]

To a student in New Jersey who asked Hughes how the hatred manifested on November 22 could be eliminated, the judge replied: "The first thing we must do is to realize there is hatred in our country. Until there is this realization, nothing can or will be done about it. To rid this country of hate, it must be replaced with love and concern for our fellow man. . . . This is expressed in doing acts of kindness, promoting understanding and good-will."[80]

One evening at a social event in a private home, Hughes and the executive editor of the *Dallas Times Herald*, Felix McKnight, who had appeared on the panel with her before the Latin American journalists and had taken an opposite point of view, argued heatedly about her assessment of the city's culpability. Their debate went on until midnight, when finally Hughes got up, walked over to him, offered her hand, and said, "Felix, you were good tonight—but wrong. By the way, it's late. Can I catch a ride home with you?"[81]

Even the Dallas establishment, though, realized something must be done to counter the city's widespread reputation for extremism. An obvious target was Congressman Bruce Alger, whose unmitigated conservatism had been highlighted for a decade as representative of Dallas's political mood. Alger's adamant opposition to any federal spending seemed to many city leaders to be the reason Dallas could not get its own much-needed new federal building. Earle Cabell, a conservative businessman who had become increasingly moderate in his political views through his experiences as mayor, resigned that office to campaign as a Democrat against Alger in the 1964 fall election. With the support of the downtown establishment, he upended Alger, went to Washington as a moderate Democrat, and Dallas soon got its federal building—named after Cabell. Cabell's successor as mayor was J. Erik Jonsson, a Republican, president of the Citizens Council and head of Texas Instruments. Jonsson would serve four successful terms as mayor, winning plaudits for his efforts to help the city overcome the trauma from the assassination.

Since much of Dallas donned this new cloak of moderation, the city's right-wing extremism seemed to disappear from view. Hughes reluctantly acknowledged some improvement in the political climate as early as January 1964. "I am not at all sure that the condition has improved to any apparent degree; however, I do see some slight changes."[82]

Headlines in Dallas concerning the assassination began to concentrate on Jack Ruby, the nightclub owner who shot and killed Lee Harvey Oswald in the police station basement. District Attorney Henry Wade lost no time in prosecuting him, taking the lead himself, with the flamboyant "King of Torts" from San Francisco, Melvin Belli, representing Ruby. The trial was held in a criminal district court in the same complex in which Hughes had been a state judge. The presiding judge, Joe B. Brown Sr., declined to grant a change of venue, reasoning that finding a fair-minded jury anywhere in the state would be as difficult as in Dallas.

Judge Brown was besieged with requests for the trial to be televised. Hughes, as a federal district judge, would have no role in such a decision, but she privately expressed her dismay over that possibility. "I know the Judge of that court quite well and he does like publicity," she wrote to a woman in Mississippi. A previous trial in his courtroom of a local nightclub entertainer had "turned out to be almost a farce," she said. She hoped that the Ruby trial could be conducted with more dignity.[83]

In the first week of March 1964, the murder trial of Jack Ruby commenced, without television cameras, although Judge Brown agreed to permit a single pool camera in the courtroom to televise the jury's verdict.

---

* An appeal was filed, and Ruby remained in the county jail during the lengthy process. In October 1966, the Texas Court of Criminal Appeals granted him a new trial, but on January 3, 1967, Ruby died of cancer.

The jury returned that verdict on March 14, 1964: guilty of murder with malice. His punishment: death by execution in the electric chair.*

Dallas struggled as it tried to memorialize the late president Kennedy in a proper way and yet to move beyond the trauma of the assassination. A blue-ribbon committee of local leaders, weighted heavily with prominent businessmen but also including token representatives from labor and minority groups, agreed that a memorial should be built one block from the assassination site just behind the old red courthouse. The prominent Harvard-educated architect Philip C. Johnson, a modernist and proponent of the International Style, known for its lack of adornment, was hired. He presented a proposal notable especially for its simplicity—four plain, disconnected walls, open at the corners and top so visitors could walk inside, be insulated from the traffic on all sides, and look only to the heavens above. The committee accepted Johnson's proposal, but when the design became public in late 1965, Sarah T. Hughes felt obliged to complain.

"I regret that I find myself in disagreement with the present plans," she wrote in identical letters to Dawson Sterling, an insurance executive and chairman of the committee, and to committee member Stanley Marcus. The design is "too abstract for us ordinary human beings who loved and admired him [Kennedy] so extravagantly," she wrote.

> John F. Kennedy was a man of courage, youthful vitality, vision, and warmth—characteristics that people throughout the world admired, and the Memorial should reflect these qualities. . . . The late President's warmth has escaped him [Philip Johnson]. It occurs to me that some thought might be given to the submission of designs by other artists and selection be made from a number. Perhaps three designs could be selected and published in the papers for readers to present their opinions.[84]

An architect friend, Gershon Canaan, joined Hughes in her complaints. He was far more specific in his analysis, which he shared with Hughes as well as with the committee. "This 'Ruin-like,' open square box without any content, constructed of a rough and crude material [concrete] is completely out of line and without the qualities so characteristic of the late President," he wrote to Sterling. It lacked "spiritual idea," proportions, and it created climatic problems within the box from sun radiation. "A fort-like pill box physically hot and spiritually cold will not do in my opinion, and does not fit the nature of the late President."[85]

Stanley Marcus responded to Hughes that he was sorry she didn't see in Philip Johnson's proposal what the committee saw. "We all felt that this simple expression of magnetic force was a great tribute to our late President. Obviously, there are some million possible ways of expressing a memorial, and in the judgment of the committee . . . this was the best and most fitting idea proposed."[86] Sterling also answered her. "We can only hope the finished memorial may prove more appealing in reality to them [critics] than do the drawings."[87]

The memorial was constructed as planned. If the apparent lack of interest in Johnson's structure of millions of visitors to the assassination site in the years that followed is any indication, the memorial turned out to be—just as Hughes believed it would—singularly lacking in popular appeal.

In the summer of 1965 the judge was pleased to be able to help memorialize the late president in another way. Robert Kennedy asked her to be a director of the Kennedy Memorial Book Fund. She agreed to serve, although it was not a position requiring much time or effort on her part.[88]

Hughes was more directly involved in the city's notable reexamination of its soul after the assassination in a program called Goals for Dallas, modeled after the Goals for America program under President Eisenhower. Introduced in November 1964 by new mayor Erik Jonsson, Goals for Dallas involved brainstorming by thousands of Dallasites from all sectors to establish common goals in such areas as local government, design of the city, health and welfare, education, and public safety. Participants were encouraged in a series of meetings to paint "an idyllic picture of what we would like our city to be if money, manpower, and other resources were of little consequences." Sarah T. Hughes attended an initial three-day conference in Salado, in Central Texas, in which ambitious priorities were set, and later a series of meetings throughout the city in which ordinary citizens of all races discussed the goals. Her involvement continued over many years. It was, she said, the most challenging matter of civic endeavor with which she ever had been associated.[89] Goals for Dallas would continue into 1992, involving more than a hundred thousand citizens, and was one of the reasons *Look* magazine declared Dallas an "All-America City" in 1970, an important sign that the city had overcome the stigma of the assassination.

With George gone, the judge held no thought of changing her basic routine and certainly no thought of giving up the house on Normandy Avenue. She intended for life to go on as usual. As the first Thanksgiving without George approached she announced to her neighbors, the Swanns, that she would assume his usual chore of carving their turkey. She arrived on Thanksgiving with the requisite carving equipment and displayed a dogged determination in completing the job, although with less skill than had been customary from George.[90]

This was the time when she took the trouble to change her birth certificate in Maryland. She had been listed at birth only as "Tilghman." Now, in 1966, she amended the certificate to reflect her given name, Sarah, although omitting the middle name her parents had given her, Augusta.[91]

Snapshots in a scrapbook Gwen Graul kept show a small Christmas party "Judge" hosted for Gwen and a handful of friends in 1966 at her house on Normandy Avenue. Hughes, dressed smartly in a turquoise pants suit with a half-apron, is seen carving the turkey, pulling food from the oven, standing beside the organ as a young man plays, and unwrapping gifts alongside the Christmas tree.[92]

She continued to exercise diligently, swimming as usual and now adding yoga to her schedule. She carried on her tradition of riding her bicycle each Fourth of July in the Highland Park parade. Neighbors could see her frequently on Saturday mornings, riding the bike up and down the residential streets, sometimes with Lois Swann, sometimes with a neighborhood child, sometimes with Rena Pederson of the *Dallas Morning News*. Ernie Figari believed she was motivated to be active because her near-rejection as a federal judge on the basis of her age made her conscious of the need to stay fit. Her determination was evident to all at the courthouse, where she always spurned the elevator and walked up the stairs to her third-floor courtroom.[93]

As always, the judge was determined to maintain her intellectual growth. She began writing book reviews in 1968 for the *Wichita Falls Times*, an assignment that permitted her to read new books regularly and with purpose. She would continue her reviews into 1977. Invariably, she chose books of substance that related directly to her own interests and expertise. Typical reviews included the report of the National Commission on the Causes and Prevention of Violence; *The Supreme Court and the Idea of Progress*, by Alexander Bickel; *The Art and Craft of Judging: The Decisions of Learned Hand*, edited by Hershel Shanks; *Hugo Black: The Alabama Years*, by Virginia Van der Veer Hamilton; *Go East, Young Man*, by Supreme Court justice William O. Douglas; *Prophets with Honor: Great Dissenters in the Supreme Court*, by Alan

Barth; *The Lost Art of Cross Examination,* by J. W. Erlich; and *Unbought and Unbossed,* by Shirley Chisholm.[94]

Also in 1968 she began receiving monthly Social Security checks and purchased a new Buick Skylark convertible for $3,866 in cash. Now she had two cars; her second, a 1965 Buick sedan.[95] Her annual salary as a federal judge—thirty thousand dollars in 1966 and forty thousand by 1970—was more than ample. She was a single woman with a lifestyle that, aside from traveling, was modest.

She and Gwen Graul began taking organ lessons together, and she worked harder than ever on her Spanish. Occasionally, to the great consternation of the court reporter, she would feel a need to speak a few phrases in Spanish to a Hispanic witness or defendant.[96]

On many mornings before official court business began, Hughes would practice Spanish with Ed Reyna, one of her favorite probation officers and a native speaker. "Señor Reyna," she would say to him on the telephone, "usted puede venir a mi oficina para hablar in español?" He would come to her office and together they would speak Spanish for about fifteen minutes. "She wasn't great, but she wasn't bad," Reyna recalled years later.[97]

One day she asked Reyna whether he exercised. Not as much as he should, Reyna acknowledged. "Have you ever tried yoga?" she asked him. When he said no, she decided to give him a demonstration. "She came from around her desk and lay down on her back and arched up with her heels and the back of her head," Reyna recalled. "I kind of looked out the door and saw two or three people looking into the office. I felt awfully funny, with a federal judge down on the floor next to me."[98]

As Lyndon Johnson entered his first full term, the White House continued to be a familiar place for the district judge from Texas. In late November 1965, as a panel member at the White House Conference on International Cooperation, she urged the United States to lead the way in assuring women equal rights with men in nations throughout the world.[99] In a single week in March 1966, she attended two White House events. The first was a luncheon attended by a select group of accomplished women, and the next was a White House reception for the judiciary attended by Chief Justice Earl Warren at the time of his seventy-fifth birthday. "[Warren] is a favorite of mine and I was pleased to be able to join in wishing him a happy birthday," she wrote to Lady

Bird. "Visiting with so many friends, including Barefoot and Jan [Sanders], who brought me, added to the pleasure of the evening."[100] Fourteen months later she was again at the White House for a reception for the chief justice, where she had a good time. While she was there, Lady Bird lobbied Hughes on behalf of her beautification program. Hughes promised to write to the two Texas senators and the two Dallas congressmen in support of the program. "I remember your points and I will emphasize them," she promised.[101]

Hughes's good friends Barefoot and Jan Sanders were now living in the nation's capital. Sanders had joined the Justice Department in 1965 as assistant deputy attorney general. He became assistant attorney general the next year, and from 1967 to 1969 he served President Johnson as his legislative counsel.

Very much aware of Hughes's long-term interest in expanded rights for women, President Johnson invited her in 1967 to witness the signing of a bill giving women equal opportunities in the armed services. She also accepted his invitation to spend the night in the White House. "My entire visit was so wonderful—seeing Lynda so happy, meeting Chuck [Robb], renewing a friendship with Oveta [Culp Hobby], being present at a most impressive ceremony and most meaningful to me, just sitting and visiting with you and the President," she wrote to Lady Bird Johnson. "The occasion will always be a memorable one for me."[102]

At the time of her visit in November 1967, the war in Vietnam was going full-scale, with antiwar demonstrations gaining in intensity as they occurred regularly throughout the nation. A week before Hughes's visit, a Roman Catholic priest, Philip Berrigan, was arrested for splattering blood over Selective Service files in Baltimore. Two weeks earlier thousands of antiwar demonstrators clashed with soldiers and federal marshals as they marched on the Pentagon. Some 350 of them, including the novelist Norman Mailer, were arrested. Three weeks before Hughes's visit, folk singer Joan Baez was arrested in Oakland, California, with 118 other antiwar demonstrators at the Selective Service Center. A month after Hughes's visit President Johnson flew to Vietnam and urged the soldiers to ignore the protests they were hearing about in the United States.

As a friend of the president and as member of the federal judiciary, Sarah T. Hughes had no inclination to criticize his handling of the war. She expressed to Lady Bird Johnson her sympathy for his problems. "While there are critics in Texas of the President's Vietnam policies and they make a lot of noise," she wrote in November 1967, "they have no solution and the vast majority are behind him and realize his agony in trying to find a solution."[103]

Her long-held hope that one day international disputes would be settled by law rather than by force gave her no reason to support the war, though. In September 1965, she was among some three thousand jurists and lawyers from 120 nations who went to Washington to attend the three-day World Conference on World Peace through Law. Chief Justice Earl Warren gave the keynote address, and President Johnson attended and spoke. Progress toward international peace had been agonizingly slow, she wrote in an article about the conference, but advances toward that goal were clear. "Through the ages the lawlessness of the jungle has gradually been replaced by order and the peaceful settlement of disputes." In terms reminiscent of the world federation beliefs she had espoused so fervently years before, she wrote, "For world law to be effective there must eventually be national disarmament and a world police force." She expressed this at a time when American troop strength in Vietnam had reached about seventy-five thousand and Johnson had announced plans to send fifty thousand more. Her article was published in both the *Texas Observer* and the *National Business Woman*.[104]

The *Texas Observer*, under the editorship of Ronnie Dugger, was the intellectual voice of liberals in the state and a sharp critic of Johnson because of the Vietnam War and his past ties to the conservative establishment in Texas. The publication was a strong supporter of Sarah T. Hughes. Contributing editors included Larry L. King, whose national reputation as a skilled essayist and playwright still lay ahead, and Willie Morris, soon to become the youngest editor ever for *Harper's Magazine* and later a well-known author. Hughes contributed another article for the magazine entitled "The Crisis in the Cities," which appeared in September 1964. The title referred to an anticipated boom in urban population within the next decades, one that would require a massive program of social services. A year later her *Texas Observer* article "Crime and School Dropouts" emphasized the need to attack the economic difficulties of low-income families.[105]

Dugger thought Hughes should campaign for a statewide office: "I still think we should run you for governor or senator in 1966," he wrote to her in September 1964.[106] The tide seemed to be turning for liberal Democrats in Texas. Hughes's good friends Oscar Mauzy and Mike McKool both were elected to the Texas Senate in 1966 as well as other progressive Democratic candidates across the state. Their impact in the legislature soon would be felt.

While women were not serving in combat in Vietnam, Hughes continued to believe that if men were to be drafted, so should women. "Under our present system of only drafting men, girls and young women are set apart as if they did not exist. . . . The burden of service should be equal and in a country where women are demanding equal opportunity there should be no question about assuming equal responsibility. Women cannot hope to gain rights by asking for privileges not accorded men drafted for military service." Better than drafting young people into the military, she felt, would be universal national service. But if this could not be achieved, then women must be drafted with men.[107] By now, such notions did not seem nearly as far-fetched as when Sarah T. Hughes had advocated them some fifteen years earlier.

After Lyndon Johnson declined to run for reelection in 1968 because he saw no honorable way out of Vietnam, Hughes's views on Vietnam took a sharp negative turn. Johnson was now working on his memoirs at his Hill Country ranch as a private citizen and Richard Nixon sat in the White House. The judge gave her strongest views on the war in 1971 two months after Lt. William Calley had been sentenced to life in prison for his part in the My Lai massacre and nine days before the *New York Times* began publishing the Pentagon Papers. "We are engaged in a senseless war in Vietnam," she told the students, their parents, and their guests in a commencement speech at a prestigious Dallas private school, Greenhill. "For me, the first priority of America today must be peace. Stop this war—unilateral de-escalation if necessary. Put our B-52s on the ground—keep them there." She was pleased at the protests being conducted by the nation's young people. "They are doing something to improve conditions. They were the first to demand an end to the war. They have signed petitions, buttonholed Congressmen, paraded on college campuses and in Washington."[108]

She was pleased, too, with the overall social awareness the younger generation was displaying. "They have joined the Peace Corps and gone to Africa and South America to work to improve the living conditions of people in underdeveloped countries. They have joined Vista and have worked among the poor of this country. They have demanded a greater share in government and in what they are taught in school. They know the problems that confront us and have made a decision to do something about them," she told the Greenhill audience.[109] All this had occurred, she said, "with remarkable suddenness" because of the new generation's "widespread refusal . . . to accept the existing pattern of life and thought merely because it exists." The rationales for their behavior represented in large part points of view she had held all her adult life. A primary reason for the new mood young people were displaying, she told the high school graduates, was their discovery that almost one-fifth of the American people, including minorities, were living in poverty. They also had legitimate concerns that universities and faculties were "not being responsive to the demands of our time and are undertaking activities unrelated to the problems of the community." Finally, there was general disillusion with the performance of the older generation in living up to the ideals of Western civilization and in "failing to adapt to new moral and ethical requirements."[110]

By temperament and by philosophy, Sarah T. Hughes was well suited to the challenges she faced as a district judge in the 1960s and 1970s. During her first few years on the bench, she alone among the three federal district judges then in the city possessed a point of view that would permit her to be comfortable with the changing times and expanded role of the federal courts. Her judicial colleagues in Dallas, Joe E. Estes and T. Whitfield Davidson, with whom she had little in common professionally or personally, reflected a far more conservative outlook on the issues of the day. Estes, who replaced the venerable William Hawley Atwell in 1955, was an Eisenhower appointee who, at least in the minds of some, "embodied the reactionary old guard."[111] Davidson, who began practicing law in 1903 and came to the bench in 1936 as a Roosevelt appointee, was noted for being a staunch defender of states' rights. As the oldest active federal district judge in the nation, his retirement seemed imminent.

A possibility arose in mid-1965 that Hughes might leave these two colleagues through an appointment to the U.S. Court of Appeals, 5th Circuit. Senator Ralph Yarborough, in a letter to President Johnson, placed her on the short list of candidates he believed warranted appointment.[112] In March 1966, Yarborough informed Hughes he had notified Deputy Attorney General Ramsey Clark that she was his preferred appointment to the appeals court and that he had submitted her name to Lyndon Johnson. But when Irving Goldberg's name, not Hughes's, surfaced as the president's nominee, Hughes sent Yarborough a curt acknowledgment for sending her a copy of his recommendation. "However," she said, "it has come to my attention that the name of Irving Goldberg, and not mine, has been referred to the American Bar

Association for appointment to the Fifth Circuit."[113] Despite Yarborough's wishes and his senatorial patronage privileges, it was the president who had the authority to make the appointment to the appeals court, and Johnson wanted his friend Irving Goldberg, who had worked for him in many political campaigns.

Hughes had not sought the position, but as had been the case when her name had surfaced two years earlier for advancement to an appeals court, she almost certainly would have accepted it if offered. Goldberg sailed through the confirmation process in the Senate and joined the 5th Circuit in 1966. Although the appeals court had its headquarters in New Orleans, Goldberg remained in Dallas, maintaining an office in the federal courthouse and post office building with the locally based judges of the Northern District. Soon he would be working alongside Hughes on a very compatible basis.

Another new jurist, also a Johnson appointee, came to the building in 1966 to fill the vacancy caused when Judge Davidson retired in November 1965. He was William (Mac) Taylor Jr. In addition to knowing him well and liking him, Hughes had a special tie to Taylor: she had replaced his father in the 14th District Court in 1935 when he resigned to serve on the Commission of Appeals. Hughes, Taylor, and Gwen Graul formed a most convivial social alliance. Soon, Taylor was picking up Graul every morning at her Lakewood home and giving her a ride to the courthouse.

Born in 1909, Taylor was a graduate of the Southern Methodist University Law School, a former state district judge, and a partner with a large law firm in Dallas at the time President Johnson appointed him. The new federal judge was destined soon to gain considerable attention, and criticism, through court orders he issued that for the first time significantly integrated the Dallas public schools.

To celebrate the appointments of Goldberg and Taylor, these two new and most compatible colleagues, Hughes hosted a cocktail and dinner party in their honor at the Chaparral Club in downtown Dallas. Twenty-four couples, including Senator Ralph Yarborough and his wife, were invited to the affair. One partygoer described the event afterward as having "the magic combination of serious purpose, sentiment and humor."[114]

With these two new judges, both with offices near to her own in the same building, Hughes now was in the company of two jurists who shared her outlook on society and the roles of the judiciary and federal government. All three were Democratic appointees coming to the federal bench at a time of dramatic change. Following the aftermath of the historic *Brown v. Board of*

Education decision in 1954, the 1960s and 1970s witnessed one of the most dynamic legal and social periods in the nation's history. Artificial barriers separating the white and black races began to tumble as the result of the realization that the "separate but equal" concept was unconstitutional, not just in public schools, but also in all public facilities. The civil rights movement, energized through the leadership of Martin Luther King Jr., the Freedom Riders, and massive numbers of demonstrators, challenged state laws across the South. Lyndon B. Johnson's War on Poverty, new social programs, and the Civil Rights Act of 1964 began to shift the balance of power from the official establishment to individuals who for years had seemed to be without power. The boundaries of freedom of expression were tested and expanded in numerous cases related to prior restraint and obscenity. Rights for individuals ranging from prisoners to women were expanded in dramatic fashion.

There was a new judicial freedom for federal courts to intervene on matters previously confined to the state courts. Federal courts traditionally had been reluctant to interject themselves into state proceedings until all appeals, interminable though they frequently were, had been exhausted. However, the ease with which they could do so now was enhanced significantly by the Warren Court in its 1965 decision, *Dombrowski v. Pfister*, which gave federal judges the authority to intervene in important areas, especially concerning the First Amendment, before all possible remedies in the state courts had been heard.

Hughes, a Kennedy appointee, and Goldberg and Taylor, both Johnson appointees, would receive unusual attention when they frequently served as three-judge panels in the latter part of the 1960s and the 1970s in cases related to these societal changes—free speech, equal rights, desegregation, obscenity, privacy, abortion, prisoners' rights, and others—and declared one restrictive state law after another unconstitutional.* With Joe Estes holding senior status, it was Hughes and Taylor who were frequently called to join a 5th Circuit judge on a panel. With Goldberg in the same building in Dallas, he was the practical choice as the representative of the 5th Circuit. When together, the trio—all of whom fit the description of New Deal Democrats—were "probably the most progressive court ever convened in Texas, if not the

---

* Such panels, composed of two district judges and one court of appeals judge, were formed whenever the constitutionality of a state law was challenged. They had been mandated early in the 1900s when Congress decided that individual federal district judges were abusing their powers by striking down too many state laws.

entire United States," said one lawyer who argued cases before them.[115] Their decisions would send shock waves throughout the state. As word spread of their rulings, more and more attorneys who wanted to challenge Texas laws filed their suits in the Northern District of Texas. Liberal lawyers who had avoided the federal courts because they were so conservative now sought them out, particularly in the Northern District.

Europe beckoned Judge Hughes again in July 1967 when she went to Geneva, Switzerland, to attend the World Conference on World Peace through Law, an outgrowth of the meeting she had attended in Washington, D.C., in 1965. She enjoyed visiting with several prominent Dallas lawyers— John N. Jackson, Maurice Purnell, and Robert G. Storey. Storey, a prosecutor at the Nuremberg war crimes trial and former dean of the SMU Law School, was a principal architect of the new organization. "Have really had a most enjoyable time—receptions, boat rides, swimming & a long auto drive," she wrote to Gwen. But one night she had had a terrible dream that the office was a wreck. "I certainly hope it won't look like the dream," she said.[116] Before returning she went north to Copenhagen for two days and to Oslo, Norway, making her first of numerous visits to Norway over the next several years.

Her affection for the Scandinavian countries prompted her in early 1968 to write to her old friend Brooks Hays with an idea. If, as some newspaper stories again were intimating, the president wanted to do something for her, he should know that she had no aspirations to go on the court of appeals. Instead, she wrote, "I would enjoy being an ambassador to one of the Scandanavian [sic] countries!" She was happy in her present work, though, and would "want to fit into any plans the President has in mind for me."[117]

Once again, there was no nibble of interest, but it was at this same time that the State Department's Bureau of Educational and Cultural Affairs awarded Hughes an American Specialist grant for a trip to Mexico. Her assignment was to go to Mexico City, Puebla, Monterrey, and Guadalajara and visit with the president of the Supreme Court of Justice, officials of other higher courts, law schools, and prisons. At several stops she spoke on the American judicial system and on the manner in which the United States was approaching the problem of juvenile delinquency. Her knowledge of Spanish and her sincere interest in the institutions of Mexico made a strong and favorable impression. A report from the American Consulate General in Monterrey to the State Department assessed her this way: "Her naturalness, simplicity, knowledge of her topics, warmth and good humor endeared Judge Hughes to all."[118] A report from the U.S. Embassy in Mexico City to the State Department described her as "one of the [program's] most effective grantees ever . . . due to her already well known reputation as a U.S. Federal Judge as well as her excellent rapport with the Mexicans and her willingness to cooperate in any way with the demands made upon her time."[119]

Hughes enjoyed visiting with law school classes and the Mexico City chapter of the Business and Professional Women's Clubs, but perhaps her most interesting visit was to a prison. She was intrigued by the conjugal rooms for men prisoners, in which they could visit with their wives or girlfriends privately three hours a week. "At least it would keep down homosexuality," she wrote to Gwen in an approving nod of the practice.[120] She bought a bracelet from one of the convicts. "I did not need it, but just wanted to buy something from him," she said. At mealtime she ate the same food as the prisoners, and she was amazed at the expansive menu, which she listed in detail— vegetable and clam soup, fried egg on rice, fish, steak and fried potatoes, beans, pineapple, ice cream, coffee, and "mountains of bread."[121]

She had seen Mexican prison life at its best on this official visit, although she must not have fully appreciated this. "Not even in the United States is there such a perfect penitentiary system as in Mexico," she was reported as saying.[122] Her glowing comments surprised many who had heard so many stories about unfavorable conditions in the Mexican prisons. An American who professed to have special knowledge of the Mexican penal system chastised her severely in a private letter. "With due respect, your Honour, I guess they knew how to pull the wool over your eyes." He proceeded to outline with specific detail the abuses and sometimes awful conditions that seemed to predominate in most Mexican jails and prisons.[123]

In mid-1968 she traveled to Central America. This time she went as part of a State Department-sponsored study group to Nicaragua, Honduras, El Salvador, Costa Rica, and the Canal Zone. Evidently the group visited no prisons.[124]

There were plenty of challenges for Hughes in her own courtroom. The cases she heard during the mid- to late 1960s seemed increasingly to touch upon areas of great concern to her.

Her conviction that individuals accused or convicted of crime should not be denied their constitutional rights—a concern destined to loom even larger in the 1970s in her celebrated Dallas County jail case—was reinforced in the spring of 1964, when she overturned the felony theft conviction of an indigent man, James E. Bush, who thirty-six years earlier had been adjudged insane. The man's request for a psychiatric exam at state expense at the time of his trial in 1961 in Ellis County had been denied. Hughes held that a cursory examination by the county health officer, who lacked specialized training in psychiatry, was insufficient. Refusal of motions by Bush's counsel to commit him to a mental hospital for examination, refusal to provide state funds for employment of a qualified psychiatrist, and failure to make available to the jury evidence as to Bush's sanity after he previously had been adjudged to be insane had denied him his right to a fair trial as guaranteed by the Fourteenth Amendment, she ruled. Hughes said she would grant Bush's petition for a writ of habeas corpus to be released from the confinement he had suffered for three years unless the state retried him within a reasonable time and provided him with adequate psychiatric evaluation at state expense.[125]

State officials decried the decision as expensive and impractical. It amounted, they said, to an encouragement for every indigent defendant in Texas to demand psychiatric evaluation at taxpayers' expense.[126]

Hughes made headlines of a similar nature when she ruled in favor of a man convicted of armed robbery because she deemed he had been represented by ineffective counsel. Connie Ray Caraway had been sentenced in state court to forty years in prison for using a shotgun to take $367 from an attendant at a drive-in grocery store. Evidence showed a woeful defense effort by his court-appointed attorney. The lawyer had visited the defendant only once for fifteen minutes three days before the trial; he did not subpoena any witnesses listed on the back of the indictment; he failed to object to irrelevant and prejudicial testimony and evidence; and he did not attempt to contact Caraway's wife, who might have corroborated his alibi. Hughes ordered the state either to release Caraway from the robbery charge within sixty days or to give him a new trial. Caraway soon pleaded guilty to another charge of attempted armed robbery and was sentenced to ten years in prison.[127]

One of the earliest cases Judge Hughes heard in relation to the relaxation of moral standards regarded the effort by municipalities to censor or classify films. As standards adopted in the industry in the 1930s prohibiting profanity and nudity began collapsing, movements arose in many communities to protect children by classifying films and excluding them from objectionable ones. The case before Judge Hughes, *Interstate Circuit, Inc., v. City of Dallas*, developed in 1965 after a committee of civic leaders headed by Judge Clarence Guittard (who had replaced Hughes at the 14th District Court and who earlier had opposed her confirmation as a federal district judge) wrote an ordinance prohibiting attendance by those under the age of eighteen if, in the judgment of the Dallas Motion Picture Classification Board, it tended to incite or encourage "crime, delinquency, or sexual promiscuity on the part of young persons." Failure to observe the finding of the Dallas Motion Picture Classification Board could result in confiscation of a theater's projection equipment and loss of its permit to exhibit films. Dallas's leading motion picture theater chains sought an injunction against enforcement of the ordinance, arguing that it violated their rights under the First and Fourteenth Amendments.[128]

Hughes found the ordinance's intent to protect youth a reasonable goal. The court had no need, she said, to debate the wisdom of a legislative determination that "certain films can cause a moral deterioration in the young and a resultant tendency towards juvenile delinquency." Such films, she wrote in her opinion, "when presented in a salacious manner are not protected by the First Amendment." However, the provision permitting confiscation of projection equipment and revocation or suspension of a license would also prohibit a theater from showing films deemed appropriate. This provision, she ruled, was overbroad and unconstitutional, and it was so intertwined with the other portions of the ordinance that it became "unenforceable and invalid."[129]

The city of Dallas promptly rewrote the ordinance, but the new one again was challenged, this time in the state courts after the classification board ruled that the movie, *Viva Maria*, an innocuous western, could not be exhibited without the tag line "Not Suitable for Young Persons." The new ordinance was upheld by state courts, but on direct appeal the U.S. Supreme Court overturned it as being too vague.[130] In the next year major film studios attempted to satisfy their critics by inaugurating their own effort at self-regulation by classifying films with such ratings as G (General), PG (Parental Guidance), R (Restricted) and X (Adults Only), the beginning of the system that by the twenty-first century would be a familiar and accepted practice.

One of the most difficult social problems of the 1960s and for years to come—one that intensely concerned Hughes—was the integration of public and private facilities. In *Walker v. Pointer,* a brother and sister contended they were evicted from their all-white apartment in Farmers Branch, a suburb of Dallas, because they had permitted African American friends to visit them there. The apartment manager peremptorily evicted the brother and sister while they were away by entering their apartment, packing their clothes and possessions into boxes and sheets, and hauling them away in a truck. When James Walker returned and attempted to use the telephone, the manager pulled it out of the wall and threw it at him. When Walker and his sister asked to be able to spend one more night, the manager said they could stay without heat and pulled the thermostat from the wall. The manager contended he evicted them because they failed to pay the rent and hosted loud parties, but evidence presented to Hughes proved this to be false. Testimony also established a clear pattern of discrimination at the apartment house in refusing to accept black tenants. The issue of whether the federal court had jurisdiction in this case revolved ultimately around the interpretation of a section of the U.S. Code providing that "all citizens of the United States shall have the same right, in every State and Territory, as is enjoyed by white citizens to inherit, purchase, lease, sell, hold, and convey real and personal property."[131] The question was, Were African Americans included in the reference to all citizens having the same rights as white citizens? In 1936 Hughes had argued that since Texas's constitutional provision of freedom of religion for all men was universally accepted to include women, the phrase opening jury duty to all men over twenty-one years of age similarly should include women as well. Now, using the same logic, she found that "all citizens" automatically encompassed white citizens as well as black. She thus ruled in favor of the Walkers, authorizing both actual and exemplary damages.[132]

More than anything, equality for women was uppermost in Hughes's mind. A federal government accusation that discrimination in pay existed between men and women at a Dallas hospital provided her with an opportunity to preside over what was said to be the first gender-based, wage-discrimination case in North Texas.[133] Secretary of Labor George Shultz brought suit against Brookhaven General Hospital on behalf of eighty female aides who claimed they were paid less than sixteen male orderlies for the same work. In 1967 the male orderlies were earning ten dollars more a month than females; by 1969 the gap had widened to fifty-three dollars per month. Testimony showed both men and women employees fulfilling essentially the same functions. Hughes ruled that the work of female aides and male orderlies required "substantially equal skill, effort and responsibility and was performed under similar working conditions." The occasional performance of duties requiring greater physical exertion did not render jobs unequal if they were otherwise equal. Citing the Equal Pay Act of 1963 and Title VII of the 1964 Civil Rights Act, she ruled that the women were entitled to approximately a hundred thousand dollars in back wages.[134]

Frequently it was Hughes, Taylor, and Goldberg who heard cases involving social issues. They came together in 1967 for the first time as a three-judge court when a community college music teacher challenged the state of Texas's requirement that all state employees take a loyalty oath. Everett M. Gilmore Jr. was a tuba player who contracted with the Dallas County Community College system to give private lessons. When Gilmore was presented with the loyalty oath, he refused to sign, arguing that it abridged his right to free speech and free association. He promptly was fired.

Gilmore took his complaint to the Dallas chapter of the American Civil Liberties Union, which directed him to attorney David Richards, husband of the future governor Ann Richards. Richards filed a suit on behalf of Gilmore, which was assigned to Hughes. Since a state law was being challenged, she arranged with the chief judge of the 5th Circuit for a three-judge panel to be formed. Irving Goldberg was assigned to represent the 5th Circuit, and Taylor joined Hughes in making up the panel. The three judges unanimously concurred in striking down the Texas loyalty oath as overly broad. On appeal to the U.S. Supreme Court, their opinion was upheld. Hughes-Goldberg-Taylor for the first time had struck down a significant Texas law.[135]

Hughes and Goldberg were joined by district judge Halbert O. Woodward in another highly publicized case, this one stemming from a police raid on Brent Stein, publisher of the rabble-rousing counterculture newspaper entitled *Dallas Notes*. In his biweekly underground newspaper Stein, known as Stoney Burns, extolled sex, drugs, and irreverence toward authority. Police raided Stein's house/office—or, in the vernacular of the day, his "crash pad"— in October 1968 and removed two truckloads of newspapers, cameras, equipment, and furniture. Officials charged him under a state statute making illegal the distribution, sale, exhibition, and possession of obscene material. Soon after his release from jail, Stein managed to publish another issue and included his own personal and inflammatory summary of the fifteen "pigs" who had conducted the raid. Police promptly returned to Stein's premises, working under an alleged tip that they would find marijuana there. They found none but once more confiscated many of Stein's belongings.[136]

Stein sought legal assistance from the American Civil Liberties Union, which referred him—as they had done for Gilmore—to David Richards. When Richards filed a suit against the Dallas Police Department to reclaim Stein's property and prevent future harassment, the case was assigned to Judge Hughes. Richards was elated, for, as he later put it, "the Dallas Police were paralyzed at the prospect of having to answer for their misdeeds before the Honorable Sarah T. Hughes—a daunting prospect for most of Dallas officialdom." The city's attitude immediately became cooperative, and at the first hearing the Dallas city attorney agreed to return all the seized goods and stop the raids. Richards later said he and his hippie client then "had a splendid afternoon" sitting on the steps and watching the Dallas police return Stein's belongings to his house.[137]

Richards and Stein next proceeded not only to sue the police for harassment but also to challenge the constitutionality of Texas's obscenity statutes, making it a class-action suit. Defendants included Dallas Police chief Charles Batchelor, District Attorney Henry Wade, and other members of the police department. With a state statute thus being challenged as unconstitutional, Hughes appropriately notified the chief judge of the 5th Circuit, who then assigned Woodward to join Hughes and Goldberg in hearing the case. Hughes, presiding, ruled that the only issue appropriate for the three-judge panel to consider was whether or not the state statute on obscenity was "constitutionally defective on its face." To the dismay and consternation of many, definitions of obscenity in recent years had been widely broadened in a number of Supreme Court cases—including notably the Fanny Hill case in 1975, in which material had to be found "utterly without redeeming social value" to be declared obscene.[138] Having these rulings before them, Hughes and the other two judges found that the Texas definition of obscenity was unconstitutional and that other sections of the law were vague and overbroad.[139]

On appeal, the U.S. Supreme Court ruled that the three-judge panel had gone further than it should have. Although the panel's decision concerning the state obscenity statute was said to be proper, the high court ruled that the plaintiffs needed to show irreparable injury before federal courts could properly interfere with pending state criminal prosecutions. Although the three-judge decision was thus reversed, the Texas Legislature already had rewritten the state obscenity statutes. Stein was able to continue publication of *Notes* without further interference.[140]*

In May 1969, Alvin Leon Buchanan, who twice had been arrested for sodomy with another man in a public restroom, filed suit against Dallas Police chief Charles Batchelor for enforcing state sodomy laws.[141] Hughes, Taylor, and Goldberg were convened to hear the case. They permitted a married couple, Michael and Jannet Gibson, to join the suit as intervenors. The Gibsons claimed that they feared prosecution under the sodomy law (carrying a penalty of from two to fifteen years in prison) for acts committed in the privacy of their home. Although the state of Texas had never charged any married couple with sodomy in their own home, it had the freedom to do so according to the broad wording of the statute. Because of this possibility, the three-judge court declared the state's sodomy law to be "void on its face for unconstitutional overbreadth." Hughes, who wrote the opinion, observed: "Sodomy is not an act which has the approval of the majority of people. In fact, such conduct is probably offensive to the vast majority, but such opinion is not of sufficient reason for the State to encroach upon the liberty of married persons in their private conduct. Absent some demonstrable necessity, matters of taste are to be protected from regulation." Hughes chose not to address in her opinion the question of whether or not sodomy laws outside a marital relationship could be prohibited.[142]

In the eyes of the *Dallas Morning News*, the decision, combined with others such as the relaxation of standards against pornography, would produce "a degenerating effect" on the community. "Filth, smut, permissiveness, and sexual perversion will be encouraged. . . . Immorality has been given additional legal status—if not a semblance of respectability."[143]

The Texas Legislature afterward rewrote the statute to prohibit sodomy by members of the same sex but excluded the husband and wife relationship.

---

* Several years later Dallas police stopped Stein for a traffic violation and noticed a marijuana roach in his car. He was found guilty of a felony for possession of less than one-tenth of an ounce of marijuana and received a sentence of ten years and one day in the state penitentiary. The addition of a single day meant he would not be eligible for probation. Stein served less than a month, for recently elected Texas senators Oscar Mauzy and Mike McKool, both friends of Judge Hughes, had led a drive in the Texas Legislature to reduce penalties for possession of small amounts of marijuana to a misdemeanor. Governor Dolph Briscoe issued pardons for those who had been convicted of felonies on the basis of these small amounts, and Stein was freed.

The constitutionality of a sodomy law restricted in this manner would be upheld by the U.S. Supreme Court in 1986.[144]

Lyndon B. Johnson's War on Poverty and the new federal agencies created as part of it mounted a continuing attack on the problems of the poor. As new approaches to old problems were tried, many issues wound up in the federal courts. One of the agencies spawned by the Office of Economic Opportunity Act was the Dallas Legal Services Project (DLSP). Its basic purpose of extending legal assistance to low-income residents took on a broader mandate in Dallas when the agency began filing a series of aggressive, high-profile class-action lawsuits to overturn state laws and regulations that seemed overly restrictive.

One of the DLSP's earliest class-action suits came in 1968, when the agency sued on behalf of a needy woman who had been denied prenatal care at Parkland Hospital, a public, tax-supported facility, because she had not met county residency requirements. Hughes, Taylor, and Goldberg found the restriction to be an unwarranted classification and discrimination that violated equal protection under the law. Their ruling forced the hospital to open its facilities to a new class of needy individuals who did not have the means to pay for treatment at private facilities.[145]

When in the mid-1970s Sarah T. Hughes filled out a judges' questionnaire for a judicial conference of the United States, she placed *Jefferson v. Hackney* first on her list of her most noteworthy cases. If she intended her listing to be in order of importance, *Jefferson v. Hackney* was a curious choice, for although it dealt with a subject that was intensely interesting to her, it ended in a reversal by the Supreme Court. In this class-action suit with many complicated elements, the Dallas Legal Services Project charged the state's Aid for Dependent Children Program (AFDC) with racial discrimination in its assistance policies. Because AFDC had a large number of minority welfare recipients, Dallas Legal Services contended that the formula had been rigged so that its recipients received less assistance than those in other programs such as aid to the aged and infirm. The case was heard by the familiar three-judge panel of Hughes, Taylor, and Goldberg, who ruled against the plaintiffs on two issues of racial discrimination but found that the state had been in violation of the Social Security Act in failing to raise payments to accommodate cost-of-living increases. On appeal to the U.S. Supreme Court, however, that judgment was reversed. The high court remanded the case to the district court, which then reversed its judgment on the Social Security Act. Appealed once more to the Supreme Court, the plaintiffs again were denied relief on all arguments.[146]

Perhaps no case more clearly illustrated Hughes's commitment to the welfare of children than one in which she was the lone dissenter on a three-judge panel that upheld the constitutionality of Texas law excluding illegitimate children from welfare support and prohibited district attorneys from suing alleged fathers for support. In this case, originating in Hughes's court, she dissented from Homer Thornberry of the 5th Circuit and Robert M. Hill, a new district judge of the Northern District, appointed in 1970 by Richard M. Nixon. Thornberry and Hill held that the woman had no standing to challenge the constitutionality of the statute. Hughes sharply disagreed. Her sense of outrage prompted her to write a dissent that was twice as long as the majority opinion. Such a length, six pages, was a rarity for her.[147]

Traditional arguments that laws discriminating against illegitimate children promote morals, encourage marriages, and deter extramarital sexual relations, she wrote, were not based on fact. Acknowledging that the promotion of morals was a legitimate governmental concern, she doubted that a rule permitting fathers to avoid liability for the support of children born as a result of extramarital relations promoted this purpose. "Rather," she argued, "it would seem to encourage promiscuity as it relieves the father of the duty to support."[148]

She cited a Supreme Court opinion that summarized the unfairness of such laws: "Why should the illegitimate child be denied rights merely because of his birth out of wedlock? He certainly is subject to all the responsibilities of a citizen, including the payment of taxes and conscription under the Selective Service Act. How under our constitutional regime can he be denied correlative rights which other citizens enjoy?"[149]

Texas law, she said, contained no rational basis for a distinction between legitimate and illegitimate children. "The only way in which an illegitimate child can receive support at the present time under Texas laws is for the parents to marry, but the child has no control over this alternative and in this case Richard D. has refused to marry Linda R. S." Had she prevailed in her opinion, she would have declared the Texas law "to be in violation of the Fourteenth Amendment of the U.S. Constitution and would issue a permanent injunction requiring state officials to require parents of illegitimate children to provide support."[150]

Another opportunity to rule on a case involving mothers with illegitimate children proved more satisfying. Hughes, ruling alone rather than as part of a panel, found a bank guilty of sex discrimination because it refused to hire a woman who had illegitimate children. The bank contended it would refuse to hire anyone, male or female, who had illegitimate children. Such a policy placed an unfair burden on women, Hughes concluded, because "it is common knowledge that it is easier to determine if a woman has illegitimate children than men."[151]

She had formed her judgment on such matters on the basis of her lifelong involvement in issues concerning the welfare of women and children. It included her experience in Washington, D.C., as a police officer with social responsibilities, in Austin as a state legislator, and in Dallas as a state judge with frequent jurisdiction over domestic relations issues. But the case that would have the most impact on women throughout the nation was the one in 1970 that dealt with what would become one of society's most controversial issues for the rest of the century and into the next—abortion.

～ 12

Roe v. Wade and More

Throughout her life, in speeches, in articles, and by her own example, Sarah T. Hughes had urged women to reject the secondary status relegated to them by society, to expand their horizons, and to claim their rightful stations in life as equals to men. The most direct paths to these goals, she was certain, were for women to win election to political office, to lobby to remove restrictive laws, to seek appointments to public boards and commissions, and to educate themselves so that they would be prepared to assume at first opportunity prominent positions in government, education, and business. That so few women had responded to this message was for her a continuing disappointment.

When she began practicing law in Dallas in 1922 Hughes was one of fewer than a dozen women attorneys in the city. She and other "lady lawyers," as they frequently were called, had believed that they were the vanguard of an inevitable wave of other women who would infiltrate the professions, government, and business. However, by 1956 only twenty-two women were practicing law in Dallas, just a handful more than in the 1920s, although the city's population had increased about fivefold. When first elected to the legislature in 1930, Hughes was one of four women members in the House. Twenty years later that number had actually declined—there were two women in the House and one in the Senate.

By the end of the 1960s, though, the situation was beginning to change. In Dallas, the number of women attorneys had grown to approximately 150. Similar increases could be seen across the nation as more and more young women were attracted to the law and other professions. In 1969, female enrollment in the nation's law schools had climbed to 6.9 percent; ten years later that number would rise to 31.4 percent. Even further growth lay just ahead.[1] The long-delayed "second feminist wave" finally was at hand.

In June 1969, Iowa Wesleyan College observed the centennial of the first woman's admission to the bar in the United States. Belle Mansfield, an alumnus of Iowa Wesleyan, had been admitted to the state bar in 1869 after "reading law" in a Mount Pleasant, Iowa, law firm. To note this special occasion, Iowa Wesleyan, joined by the National Association of Women, decided to confer an honorary doctorate to a woman who had been a modern-day leader in the legal profession. They chose U.S. district judge Sarah T. Hughes of Dallas, a significant recognition of the work she had done on behalf of women in the profession. Later that summer Hughes solidified her ties to Iowa Wesleyan by becoming a member of the advisory committee on the selection of scholarships for women.[2]

The subject of women and women's rights was becoming a popular area of study in the nation's universities, as new courses were offered and departments of women's studies were created. In the fall of 1969 the nation's first course in Women and the Law was taught at New York University's Law School. In the spring of 1970 a similar course was offered at Yale University. In the fall of 1970 Hughes's alma mater, George Washington University, did the same. Others followed in growing numbers.

The heightened awareness in women's studies was inspired by several developments of the 1960s. In 1963, the same year Congress passed the Equal Pay Act, Betty Friedan's book *The Feminine Mystique* sounded a clarion call for women to challenge the status quo and to advance their own interests. In 1964 the Civil Rights Act's Title VII guaranteed equal opportunity for employment, a potential boon for women. In 1966 Friedan cofounded the National Organization for Women, a group whose activism would make the quieter and more orderly efforts on behalf of women by such groups as the Business and Professional Women's Clubs, important though they were, seem remote and perhaps old-fashioned. By the late 1960s and early 1970s a new breed of women activists, "women's libbers," had arisen. These women had concluded that for the greatest impact they must incorporate high drama into their mission. They took their message to the streets. All the unexpended energy missing since women had won the right to vote in 1920 suddenly was released.

The aggressive tactics of these militant activists caught the nation by surprise. Outside the Miss America pageant in September 1968, television cameras recorded scenes of women who were nothing like the beauty contestants posing inside in bathing suits and uttering platitudes. Angry, shouting demonstrators surrounded the pageant with picket signs and mocked the ceremonies inside by crowning their own version of "Miss America"—a live sheep. Before television cameras the demonstrators gathered up and dramatically dumped into a "freedom trash can" symbols of what they deemed to be past repressions—brassieres, girdles, cosmetics, and high-heeled shoes. A reference to "bra burning" in a news story created a lasting if inaccurate image of the women as bra burners. As similar demonstrations followed over the next months and years, the values extolled by the Miss America candidates at Atlantic City began to lose their credibility as representations of the highest aspirations for womanhood.

U.S. district judge Sarah T. Hughes, now seventy-five years of age, looked on these events with keen interest. She had been an activist, although of a more dignified sort, before most of the new generation of aggressive women was born. The *Dallas Times Herald* sent a reporter to ask what she thought of such developments. She was guarded, although generally encouraged. The movement could "do some good" for women "if they don't kill it by making it a big joke," she said. She certainly was encouraged in "some phases" of the new feminist wave, for she had always disdained timidity. "Women have to be more aggressive than they have been to obtain business, professional and political opportunities," she said. "But I don't favor acting like men. The extreme that some are going to is going to backfire." Indeed, in her estimation it already had contributed to making the women's movement an object of much hilarity.[3]

During her first few years as a federal judge, Hughes reduced the number of speeches she gave, but with the topic of women's rights now more timely than ever, she once more began to accept engagements to speak on the subject. She had lost none of her bite. She ridiculed with relish how the renowned English literary man Samuel Johnson had responded when someone gave him the astonishing news that a woman was preaching. "A woman preaching is like a dog walking on its hind legs," he replied. "It isn't done well, but one is surprised that it is done at all." Another favorite anecdote came from the English legal scholar Blackstone, whom she quoted as having said, "Husband and wife are one and that one is the husband." She also enjoyed enlightening her audiences by reading from the U.S. Supreme Court opinion in 1873 in *Bradwell v. The State* in which an Illinois statute barring women from the practice of law was upheld: "The natural and proper timidity and delicacy which belongs to the female sex evidently unfits it for many of the occupations of civil life."[4]

In her oft-repeated speech entitled "The Status of Women in the United

States since World War II," Hughes lamented the reluctance of women to become involved in public affairs. She buttressed her criticisms with specific details. Since Annie Webb Blanton had been elected state superintendent of education in 1919, Texas had never had another woman superintendent. There had not been another woman governor since the first one, Miriam Ferguson, in 1925 and 1933. (Not until 1991 with Ann Richards would there be another.) There had not been a woman secretary of state since Governor Ferguson's term. Texas had never elected a woman to Congress. No woman had served in a presidential cabinet since Oveta Culp Hobby from 1952 to 1954 under President Eisenhower. In the first year that Hughes served in the Texas Legislature, there had been four women in the House and one in the Senate. In 1971 just one woman served in the Texas House of Representatives and another solitary one in the Senate. Hughes presented specific details about disparities in pay and the lack of representation of women on college faculties and administration. A particularly sore point for her was that at the all-female Texas Women's University the president and all the vice presidents were men.[5]

Recently, she would say, President Nixon had been asked at a press conference what he thought about the status of Negroes. The president had answered eloquently and at length, obviously placing a high priority on the subject. But when a similar query was put to him regarding women, it was followed by laughter all around, and the president responded only perfunctorily because the subject seemed so trivial.[6]

The problems of sex discrimination were deep-rooted, Hughes recognized, because "girls and boys are reared for different roles." At a very early stage, their anticipated roles in society were encouraged by different toys. "Girls are given dolls, doll houses, play-dishes, pots and pans; boys [are given] guns, soldiers, baseballs." High school courses reinforced typecasting—domestic science, cooking, sewing, and child care for girls, and carpentering and machine shop for boys. In college young women were encouraged to become teachers, librarians, home economists, and occupational and physical therapists. If they took business courses, they concentrated on shorthand and typing.[7]

Much of the blame for this predicament, Judge Hughes always pointed out, lay in women themselves. "They are satisfied with their role. They are too humble about their abilities. They are not aggressive enough. They are overcome by inertia." Their attitudes, she said, were frighteningly typified by a female graduate of a university who, when asked what she wanted to do in life, replied, "I would like to be the assistant to a man who is doing something that I really believe in." Hughes pointed in contrast to her own childhood in which her mother convinced her that she could do whatever she wanted to. It had been her mantra since then. "I believed that, and went after what I wanted and ignored possible discriminations."[8]

Two bright lights on the Texas political scene gave Hughes hope when they were elected to the legislature in 1969 as its only two women—Senator Barbara Jordan (the state's first black senator, who soon would achieve national fame as a member of the U.S. Congress) and Frances (Sissy) Farenthold of Corpus Christi. "They shook hands, made speeches, and thus through their own aggressive efforts they got what they wanted," Hughes said. "Women must get into the arena and fight. They cannot be shrinking violets."[9]

Women needed the "zeal of the Negroes." For almost a hundred years African Americans had waited, and then they had become aroused. "You can see the results—they are in the legislature and in Congress. They are mayors, and on the Supreme Court."[10]

In this favorite speech she concluded with what she described as her favorite anecdote. A little boy got up each morning as the clock struck seven. One particular morning the clock didn't stop at seven. It went on and on and on, striking thirteen times. "The little boy jumped out of bed and ran all over the house shouting, 'Get up, get up. It's later than it's ever been.' " The anecdote constituted the essence of her speeches to women's groups—the time was overdue for action.[11]

As the women's movement fomented across the nation, in 1968 Hughes, her friend Louise Raggio, and a handful of other Dallas women attorneys began meeting regularly at the downtown Adolphus Hotel to lay plans for the forthcoming convention of the National Association of Women Lawyers, an organization founded in 1899 that boasted of a long history of advocacy for women in the legal profession. The Dallas women planned a busy program of activities and programs for the three-day meeting that was successfully held in August 1969 in conjunction with the annual meeting of the American Bar Association in Dallas.[12]

Pleased with the work they had done and with the camaraderie they had enjoyed at their regular meetings, the women—with Judge Hughes as their titular leader—decided afterward to continue meeting regularly so that they could exchange information on job opportunities, discuss legislative changes, encourage more female candidates for the judiciary and public offices, and generally advance women's interests. Their informal sessions would continue for years. By 1972 they had created their own letterhead, which read "Committee for Women in Government." Judge Hughes was listed as honorary chairman and Joan Peters as chairman. Members included a number of rising female lawyers in Dallas: Louise Raggio, Edith DeBusk, Sue Goolsby, and Reba Graham Rasor were among them. Their primary activity now was seeking the appointment of women to new courts in Dallas County.[13] Sixteen years after the group had begun meeting, it would evolve into the Dallas Women Lawyers Association, incorporated on May 16, 1984, as a nonprofit organization for women united for their mutual benefit with a goal of elevating the standards of women in the profession.

In 1971 a number of women in Dallas who had been active in women's issues conceived of a permanent organization to achieve their purposes. Meeting at Democratic activist Ann Chud's house, they assumed that Sarah T. Hughes, who was in attendance, would be their president, and they implored her to take that role. She refused, saying that others should lead, but she proceeded without a pause to take charge of the meeting. Since Maura McNiel, who had been active in women's affairs, did not have a full-time job, she would be president, Hughes said. And she handed a pencil to Sandra Tinkham and told her to take notes. "We followed like sheep," recalls Vivian Castleberry, and the women duly elected McNiel as president and Tinkham as secretary of the new organization, Women for Change (later the Women's Center of Dallas). McNiel proved to be an unusually effective, visible, and long-time leader for the organization. Women for Change organized into nine task forces, established a headquarters on the campus of Southern Methodist University, and became a permanent force for the Dallas community.[14]

In October 1971, when the new group held its first public meeting, Hughes was the keynote speaker. "Women have been socialized to marry and have babies," she told the enthusiastic crowd. "Fifty years ago this was a lifetime career, but times have changed. Now a woman has half of her life ahead of her after the children are grown." Her comments were an implicit assumption that a linch-pin for society, in her opinion, continued to be a normal and stable home life. At the second public meeting Gloria Steinem, at the height of her visibility as a feminist leader, attracted an overflow crowd that had to be carried by video to those outside an auditorium on the Southern Methodist University campus.[15]

During these heady times for women, Hughes one evening happened to be at a social occasion when she overheard the chief executive of the city's largest bank, Republic, after a few drinks, tell someone, "No, we don't have any women vice presidents at the bank, and as long as I have anything to do with it there won't be." Hughes, furious about the comment, next morning called Louise Raggio: "Louise, go buy some Republic Bank stock." Hughes did the same herself, and she advised Raggio of her strategy. At the next shareholders' meeting they would lodge a protest about the bank's failure to have women officers. As it turned out, Raggio recalled, they were required to wait six months before they could speak at a meeting. Republic Bank officials, perhaps learning of what they planned, appointed two women vice presidents just two days before the shareholders' meeting. Again, Hughes was furious. "She [Hughes] told me to get up at the meeting anyway and brag on them for appointing two women," Raggio said. "So I did. And then she got up after me and gave them fits, saying they needed a woman on the board of directors. Within a year they had one."[16]

Activists such as Betty Friedan considered the repeal of anti-abortion laws as one of the primary objectives of the new women's movement. They viewed these restrictions as a denial of a woman's right to control her own body. In 1969 Friedan and others founded an organization known as the National Association for the Repeal of Abortion Laws (soon to become the National Abortion and Reproductive Rights Action League [NARAL]). At first, the organization's activities consisted of lobbying in states to have the laws repealed and sponsoring grassroots demonstrations.

By late 1969 the organization had concluded that the best way to attack anti-abortion laws was by challenging a state law in a federal court. A ruling there could be appealed to the U.S. Supreme Court. The organization's attorneys decided that the most favorable federal trial court in the nation would be found in the Northern District of Texas, which they and others regarded as the most liberal of the districts in all ten regional federal court circuits. Since the constitutionality of a state law would be at issue, a three-judge court would be convened, and a case filed in the Dallas District of the Northern District almost certainly would mean that one of the three judges on the panel would be the Honorable Sarah T. Hughes, widely known as an advocate for women's rights. While her views on abortion had not been publicly stated, it seemed certain that she would be sympathetic to the issue.[17]

Before NARAL could prepare a challenge, though, a group of young women activists in Austin, Texas, beat them to the courthouse. The Women's Liberation Birth Control Information Center, located across the street from the University of Texas campus, had begun investigating the possibilities of offering referral assistance for women contemplating abortion. They contemplated whether or not such assistance would make them susceptible to charges of violating the law. Two of the center's volunteers casually discussed the issue with Sarah Weddington, a young woman lawyer, when they encountered her at a Saturday morning garage sale. Weddington, intrigued, agreed to study the matter. Unknown to the two, Weddington herself had had a traumatic and secret abortion in Mexico two years earlier. After some discussions in the days that followed, the original question was broadened into a consideration of seeking to overturn the state's abortion laws. It was agreed that a federal lawsuit challenging the constitutionality of the Texas law would have a better chance of success than introducing legislation to repeal the antiabortion statute. Weddington agreed to file the suit.[18]

One of Weddington's law school friends had been Linda Coffee, who had graduated from the University of Texas the year before, in 1968, and recently completed a year-long stint as law clerk for Sarah T. Hughes. Weddington prevailed upon Coffee, now practicing law in Dallas, to join her as co-counsel. In discussing the case they agreed that a pregnant woman would have better standing as plaintiff than the Austin group. Moreover, it would be preferable to find a pregnant woman in Dallas rather than Austin, for, just as NARAL had determined, the Northern District seemed clearly to be the best jurisdiction for a favorable ruling. Both Weddington and Coffee agreed that Hughes would be the ideal judge to hear their challenge. Coffee already had marginal experience in one noteworthy case heard by Hughes concerning a controversial social issue, *Buchanan v. Batchelor*. In that case a three-judge panel that included Hughes had overturned Texas's sodomy laws as unconstitutional. Although Coffee had not been an attorney of record in the case, she had advised and encouraged the plaintiff's attorney, Henry McCluskey, in challenging the Texas statute.[19]

McCluskey, the attorney in the Buchanan case, quickly had a chance to return the favor he owed Coffee. He had been approached by a pregnant young woman, Norma McCorvey, who asked if he could help her arrange an abortion. He told her he could not, but he contacted Coffee to tell her he had found just the sort of woman she and Weddington were seeking. McCorvey, a twenty-two-year-old high school dropout and waitress who already had given birth to two children whom she was not rearing, had concocted a false tale of being raped, which she thought might help her in arranging for an abortion. After Weddington and Coffee met with her, they concluded that because of her apparent instability they needed an additional plaintiff. This they found in Marsha King and David King, a Dallas married couple. Marsha had become involved in abortion discussions through the Women's Alliance at First Unitarian Church on Normandy Avenue, just a few blocks from Hughes's house. A married couple such as the Kings might have good standing as a plaintiff, Weddington and Coffee concluded.[20]

With Weddington in Austin, it fell to Coffee to prepare the legal documents herself. On March 3, 1970, she carried the paperwork to the U.S. district clerk's office at the downtown post office and federal courthouse, paid thirty dollars to cover the fees for two complaints on behalf of Jane Roe (Norma McCorvey) and John Doe and Mary Doe (David and Marsha King), and asked for declaratory judgments holding the Texas abortion statute unconstitutional and for permanent injunctions against its further enforcement. The defendant in both cases was District Attorney Henry Wade, who as district attorney was the officer charged with enforcing the statute in Dallas County. News of the suits spread quickly. Next day both Dallas daily newspapers carried front-page stories about them. Other follow-up stories appeared in the next several days. The *Dallas Times Herald* reported that an estimated three thousand illegal abortions were being performed each year in the city. Their costs ranged from $150 to $3,000.[21]

In an effort to prevent "judge shopping," cases filed in the federal district courts were assigned by a random drawings of cards bearing the initials of all available judges. As it happened, the clerk drew the card with Hughes's initials for *Roe v. Wade* and the card with William "Mac" Taylor's initials for the accompanying case, *Doe v. Wade*. Hughes had been the first choice for Weddington and Coffee, but the drawing of her name was probably even more fortuitous than they knew. Hughes already had a definite though unpublished opinion about abortion, which she acknowledged afterward when asked whether she previously had a private view. She said, "Oh, well, I was in favor of permitting abortion."[22]

Upon seeing news stories about the case, another lawyer in Dallas, Roy Merrill, contacted Coffee for permission to join as an intervenor. Merrill represented a Carrollton physician facing two criminal charges for performing abortions and possible sentences of two to five years in prison. Having a physician as a party to the suit seemed advantageous, and Coffee and Weddington immediately agreed. Merrill, joined by his senior partner Fred Bruner, filed a request with Hughes to accept their client, Dr. James H. Hallford, as an intervenor, and Hughes granted permission.

With the constitutionality of a state statute being challenged, John Brown, chief judge of the 5th Circuit, duly arranged for a three-judge panel to hear both cases. Hughes and Taylor, having been assigned the two cases, were automatic choices for two of the positions. Their close colleague, Goldberg, was named to represent the 5th Circuit. While Hughes knew how she personally felt about abortion, both Taylor and Goldberg said later that they had not given the subject any particular consideration. They had no preconceived notions about it.[23]

The defendant, District Attorney Wade, had no special animus toward abortionists. Later he would say he had no opinion concerning the subject. Except for nonmedical practitioners who had injured women during abortion procedures, his office rarely prosecuted such cases. With more than a hundred assistant district attorneys on his staff, the job of representing his office fell to the chief of his appellate section, John B. Tolle. Meanwhile, since a state statute was involved, Judge Hughes had alerted the Texas attorney general's office. Assistant Attorney General Jay Floyd was delegated to represent the state of Texas.

Hughes advised Tolle, Floyd, Coffee, Merrill, and Bruner to be present for a pretrial meeting in her chambers on April 3, 1970. At that meeting she announced that the two cases would be consolidated into one and that the state of Texas would be an intervenor. She permitted Coffee and Weddington to amend their complaint so that it would become a "class-action" suit on behalf of all women "similarly situated" to "Jane Roe." The full three-judge panel would hold a formal hearing on the case on Friday, May 22, in Judge Hughes's fourth-floor courtroom.

To prepare for the hearing, Hughes assigned her law clerk, Randy Shreve, to augment the briefs being filed by the attorneys with other materials. Shreve contacted Roy Lucas, the lawyer who originally had planned to challenge abortion laws on behalf of NARAL. Lucas was more than happy to oblige; he sent a package of articles and briefs for Hughes's edification.[24]

On the day of the hearing, five pro-choice women bearing pickets demonstrated outside the courthouse. One sign bore the words MY BODY, MY CHOICE, and another said, COMPULSORY PREGNANCY IS A CRUEL AND

UNUSUAL PUNISHMENT.[25] No anti-abortion supporters were visible. The courtroom was packed with pro-choice women, most of them from the Unitarian church. As the federal rule mandated, cameras were forbidden, so television reporters joined their print colleagues with notepads and pen only. At the plaintiffs' table sat Weddington, Coffee, Merrill, and Bruner. At the other able were Tolle and Floyd. Before them sat the three judges, Goldberg, Hughes, and Taylor. With the initial case having been assigned to Hughes, she presided. Since there were no disputed facts, there would be no testimony. Attorneys would simply argue for their interpretations of the law. "Jane Roe"—Norma Jean McCorvey, now eight months pregnant and beyond the point when an abortion would be possible for her—was not present. The "Does," David and Marsha King, were there.

Coffee, Weddington, Bruner, and Merrill divided their time. Coffee spoke first, concentrating on procedural issues and urging that the court grant both declaratory relief—a statement indicating that the Texas abortion statute was unconstitutional—and injunctive relief, a more effective remedy in which the state of Texas would be ordered to stop enforcing the abortion law.

Weddington, a new attorney, had never appeared before a federal court, and she had never argued a contested case in any court. Only twenty-five years of age, she was visibly nervous. As she began to discuss the constitutional issues, her voice quavered noticeably. And then, as Weddington later recalled, "Hughes looked down at me from the bench; she could see how nervous I was. She gave me a reassuring smile and a slight wink, as if to say, 'Don't be nervous. Everything will be fine.'" Weddington would "always be grateful" for that gesture, a gesture that she took not as an indication of how the judge would rule but as that of an older woman lawyer seeking to encourage an inexperienced colleague in an important assignment.[26]

Weddington's comments, by all accounts, were effective. She sought to answer a critical question: When can it be said that life begins? Her response was thoughtful. This was almost impossible to determine, she said, for if one argues that it begins at the moment of conception, why not go further back and say that life is present in every sperm and every ovum. Should birth control be outlawed because it destroys potential life?[27]

Bruner argued that Texas's single exception to the statute, permitting abortion only for "saving the life of the mother," was unconstitutionally vague. Even hospitals and doctors cannot interpret the language of the statute, he argued. The existence of the statute was driving women to illegal abortionists; its elimination would give women the constitutional right to go to a doctor with proper surgical instruments. Merrill spoke briefly, arguing that the wording of the Texas statute placed the burden of proof on the defendant rather than the prosecutor, a violation of due process under the Fifth, Ninth, and Fourteenth amendments.[28]

When the thirty minutes expired, Floyd and Tolle began their arguments. Floyd, speaking first, challenged the right of the plaintiffs to sue. No woman had ever been prosecuted in Texas for having an abortion, so how could Jane Roe claim to have been injured by the law? As for John and Mary Doe, there was no evidence that Mary Doe was even pregnant. Judge Goldberg pointed out that some of the children involved in desegregation cases already had graduated by the time the cases were litigated. Did this mean they had no standing? Judge Hughes joined in: "What would give them standing in a case like this to test the constitutionality of this statute? Apparently you don't think that anybody had standing." Floyd moved on to his argument that life begins at conception, and to destroy an infant in the womb was murder, just as it would be murder to kill a three-month-old infant in the cradle. Goldberg attacked this point of view, asking Floyd if he contended that the state's compelling interest extended to the instant of conception.[29]

"That is correct," Floyd answered.

"I don't see how that's getting you anywhere," Goldberg responded.

Tolle based his arguments on the state's right to make its own decisions in these matters. At whatever stage life begins, he said, it was the state's right to protect it. As to the alleged invasion of a woman's right to privacy, it was his personal opinion and that of the state as well, he believed, that the right of the child to life was a higher priority.[30]

The hearing was over after one hour. Goldberg had dominated with frequent questions and comments. Hughes was less vocal, perhaps because she already knew what she thought about the issue. Taylor, a quiet man by nature, was content to listen. With the arguments over, the trio retired to Hughes's small library for their private deliberations.

For a decision that once confirmed by the Supreme Court would have such a profound impact on American life, that would engender anguished, soul-searching debate and demonstrations for years to come, and that would become a litmus test for federal judicial appointments and often a measure in political races between conservatives and moderates or liberals, the judges' deliberations were surprisingly brief. After talking for less than five minutes, they agreed that the Texas anti-abortion statute was unconstitutional. Goldberg declared years later: "It was actually an easy case for us. The statute we had before us was clearly bad. It made criminal almost any type of abortion by anyone. You cannot tell me that a woman who gets pregnant due to rape cannot have the burden removed from her body." Asked years later if they had deliberated at all, Goldberg seemed defensive in his response. "We deliberated, that I know," he said. "We hadn't made up our minds in advance." The decision, he said, was "almost inevitable."[31]

Hughes, when asked years later if the plaintiffs' presentation had impressed her, said: "No, I don't remember what it was. It [the statute] was just unconstitutional, that's all. It was a privilege for a woman to decide what she wanted to do, and it was an invasion of that privilege." She saw no reason for any law interfering with the relationship of a woman and her doctor.[32]

Since the case had been assigned originally to Hughes's court, the three decided that she should write the opinion. Judge Hughes wanted to enjoin further enforcement of the law, as the plaintiffs had sought, as well as issue a declaratory judgment. Goldberg disagreed. It would be better simply to hold the statute unconstitutional, he argued, because the Supreme Court recently appeared reluctant to uphold federal judges who issued injunctions against the enforcement of state statutes. Issuing an injunction would increase the chances that their decision would be reviewed and reversed. Taylor agreed, and Hughes consented to their point of view.[33]

Hughes disdained long opinions. "I don't like to go in that library," she later explained. "There are some judges that like to write opinions and like to study. I don't. I have never written an opinion that I didn't have to write."[34] Her initial draft, which she circulated to Goldberg and Taylor, was far briefer than Goldberg preferred. Little of the discussion that had occurred in the hearing and almost none of the analysis that typified most appellate opinions were present. Goldberg and his law clerk, Clarice Davis, worked up an extensive list of changes and amplifications for the opinion. "Judge Goldberg wanted to craft the opinion in his normal, scholarly way," Davis recalled later. "He wanted to start at the beginning and have a legal theory supporting the opinion and move from one topic to another in an orderly way, which was his way of writing. Judge Hughes didn't write that way and didn't really think that way. The contrast was especially interesting for me as a young lawyer to see their different approaches despite the fact that they were very close friends and ideologically very close."[35]

Goldberg, knowing that Hughes was normally impatient with writing lengthy opinions, sent Davis to present Hughes with their suggested changes. "When she saw the amount of writing on the paper," Davis said later, "she said, 'That's too much. I won't talk about that much.' And so then I said, 'Let's start with this.' " But it was no use. After less than five minutes the judge said to Davis, "I've worked on this enough," and booted her out unceremoniously.[36]

Goldberg was not surprised when his disappointed law clerk reported to him the results of her meeting. He refused, however, to pursue the matter further with this friendly colleague whom he greatly respected. Later, Goldberg would say that "maybe we should have written more."[37]

On June 17, 1970, less than a month after the hearing, the judges' decision—issued per curiam on behalf of all three judges rather than bearing Hughes's name as the sole author—was announced. As the judges' questions and comments in the hearing had indicated, they relied on the Ninth Amendment, which declares "the enumeration in the Constitution, of certain rights, shall not be construed to deny or disparage others retained by the people." The Texas statute, Hughes wrote, "must be declared unconstitutional because they [Texas abortion laws] deprive single women and married couples of their right, secured by the Ninth Amendment, to choose whether to have children." The court found any number of precedents in which the freedom to choose in the matter of abortions had been held to be a "fundamental" right. Moreover, even if the state had certain legitimate interests, the Texas laws "far outstrip these justifications in their impact by prohibiting *all* abortions except those performed 'for the purpose of saving the life of the mother.' "[38]

In addition to being "unconstitutionally overbroad," the Texas laws were held to be "also unconstitutionally vague." The state's authorization of abortion "for the purpose of saving the life of the mother" left too many questions unanswered. "How *likely* must death be? Must death be certain if the abortion is not performed?"[39]

As to the rejection of the plaintiffs' request for an injunction against enforcement of the laws, the court said: "It is sufficient to state that legislation concerning abortion must address itself to more than a bare negation of that right." The court also declined to grant standing to the plaintiffs John and Mary Doe (David and Marsha King), although by now that point was moot.[40]

News of the decision was prominently displayed and broadcast across the state and the nation. Its immediate consequences were unknown. One thing was certain: since an injunction had not been issued, the decision did not immediately mean that women could begin having legal abortions. Although Henry Wade at first said he would not try any cases until the Supreme Court settled the matter, on the next day he changed his mind. His office would continue to try abortion cases since the court had "specifically refused to enjoin enforcement of the law."[41]

Appeals were made directly to the Supreme Court by both the plaintiff and the defendant. Wade appealed the ruling; Weddington and Coffee appealed the court's failure to issue an injunction. On January 22, 1973, two-and-a-half years after the decision in Dallas, the U.S. Supreme Court upheld the ruling. Abortion was declared legal throughout the nation. It soon would become painfully apparent, though, that the contest over the issue of whether the legalization of abortion is morally correct had just begun.

The growing activism of women and the widespread attention they were creating for their causes was prompting politicians to take notice. In January 1970, two months before the abortion case was filed in Hughes's court, Texas governor Preston Smith, not known for progressive views on women's rights, was inspired to invite about a hundred leading women to organize the Governor's Commission on the Status of Women in Texas. The roster of those invited was heavily sprinkled with journalists, attorneys, businesswomen, and television personalities. Judge Hughes, of course, was an obvious choice to attend. Lady Bird Johnson was a prominent participant. Of those who attended the January 30-31 meeting in Austin, eighteen were from Dallas, more than twice the number sent by larger Houston and far more than any other city.[42]

Governor Smith designated Margaret Brand Smith, a Dallas lawyer and insurance executive, to chair the proceedings, but when she was unable to attend because of illness the honor of replacing her fell quickly to Sarah T. Hughes. On the first evening of the two-day meeting, Governor Smith, wearing his customary polka-dotted tie, spoke. Hughes followed him at the podium and took the initiative to announce her own appointments of Margaret Estes of Longview as vice chair of the commission and Louise B. Raggio, the friend who so frequently had been at Hughes's side, as secretary.[43]

Next morning the women met at the Commodore Perry Hotel and began to outline the work ahead. They heard first from Mr. W. S. Birdwell Jr., appointed in 1967 by Governor John Connally to head his own Governor's Commission on the Status of Women, an ineffective body that operated without permanent staffing and ceased to exist after making its report. The absence of any outcry in 1967 when a man rather than a woman had been chosen to head such a commission indicated how rapidly the mood of women had changed. A male appointment now would have been inconceivable. Birdwell, though, offered important advice to the women, saying they should create not a governor's commission but a *legislative* commission with funding and permanency. Birdwell, an official with the Texas Employment Commission, emphasized the need for women to receive equal pay to men, for counselors in high schools to urge female students to educate themselves for higher levels of employment, and for the women to use the 1964 Civil Rights Act to their advantage. Hughes, in her own comments, emphasized the need for women to utilize existing laws and especially to try to determine if some of the laws discriminating against women might be unconstitutional. The conference ended with the passage of resolutions urging, as Birdwell had suggested, that the commission be funded permanently and adequately.[44]

Governor Smith announced plans to hold the First Annual Governor's Conference on the Status of Women in August. Privately, he called on Hughes for help. He wanted from her a list of women whom she believed would be interested in attending this much bigger meeting, and he asked her for suggestions for workshop topics.[45]

Held on August 28, 1970, at the Terrace Convention Center in Austin, the conference was basically a continuation of the January meeting. About one thousand women attended. Margaret Brand Smith, now recovered from her illness, was able to preside.

Hughes continued to be an important presence, though. Her fiery talk on women as policymakers, a familiar one for her, this time was heard by an audience entirely capable of acting on her suggestions. Hughes told the women that although for years husband, family, school, and the public had discouraged them, they must involve themselves in politics. Moreover, if they were to accomplish their goals, they must change their negative attitudes about themselves. They must think they *are* somebody, and they must think they can *do* something. Their unequal treatment was the fault not just of men but of women, too, she stressed.[46]

While women in 1970 were beginning to advance their causes in the important role as policy makers, Hughes stressed, they had made only "token progress." For Governor Smith, she had specific observations and requests.

The eleven college coordinating boards in Texas had 126 members, she pointed out, and only 8 of them were women. Four of these women were on the board at Texas Woman's University, which was required by state law. Of their own accord, then, governors had appointed only four women. Thirty-nine of these college board members were due to be appointed in the next year, and it seemed to Hughes "only fair the governor should appoint women to at least half of those positions."[47]

In addition, not a single woman was serving on the board of corrections for the Texas penal system, although crime was a subject of vital interest to women, she said. In the next year the governor would have three new appointments to make to this board. Women must be represented, she said, but women must make certain that these and other appointments go only to qualified women, and not to women who "are the wife or daughter of some prominent man."[48]

Judge Hughes stressed as well the need to use federal courts to advance women's causes, an avenue which she felt women had largely left unexplored. She specifically suggested cases involving unequal pay for equal work.[49]

Her central message for the women was the same one that she had repeated time after time over the years. "Women should not wait for their abilities to be recognized. They have to ask for what they want. It is also up to the individual woman to seek the position she wants and not wait for someone else to get it for her."[50]

Among the resolutions passed by the women was an especially significant one offered by Louise Raggio that again followed Birdwell's earlier recommendation. Adopted by a unanimous vote, it proposed legislation creating a statutory commission on the status of women. The job of writing the bill was given to Mary Ann Harvey, a special projects assistant in the Texas Office of Economic Opportunity, but it was a task especially suited to Hughes. At Harvey's request, Hughes advised her on how the bill should be worded and what provisions it should contain.[51]

Next, many of the women began sending letters to legislators urging that they support the creation of a permanent commission, copies of which many felt obliged to send to Hughes. Hughes herself, as always, joined in the letter writing. She also used her influence with friends in the Texas Legislature for sponsorship of the legislation. She prevailed upon her long-time friend Mike McKool, now in the Texas Senate, to introduce the bill there. "I am sure Barbara Jordan and Oscar [Mauzy] will be glad to join you in introducing it.

Senator [Ralph] Hall said he would also do so," she wrote.[52] She prevailed upon state representative Ben "Jumbo" Atwell of Dallas County to sponsor the same legislation in the House.

McKool sent a favorable report to Hughes as soon as the legislature convened in January 1971. "In accordance with your request, on the first day that bills were accepted for introduction, I introduced your bill creating the Commission on Status of Women," he wrote. He had been joined by Mauzy, Hall, and Barbara Jordan as cosponsors, and he had been informed by Atwell that he would carry the Senate bill through the House once it reached there.[53]

When news accounts gave Hughes credit as author of the bill, she declared them "in error," although there was considerable justification for such statements.[54] She offered to appear before a Senate committee if necessary in support of it, although she told McKool, "If you could slip it through without me coming down I will be pleased."[55] This McKool achieved. The bill passed the Senate in February by a vote of 26 to 3 and was taken up by the House of Representatives.[56]

In the House, state representative Frances Farenthold of Corpus Christi, the sole female member of that body, already was working on proposed legislation for women's rights. She wrote to Hughes asking for information or suggestions. Hughes replied, "I have only two suggestions." First, following her conviction that protective legislation was actually injurious to women, she urged repealing the laws limiting women's hours of work and their work at night. Second, she wanted amendments to statutes relating to "denial of right to work because of age" or because of "race, religion, color or national origin" to be broadened to include "sex."[57]

Any thought that the bill creating the permanent Commission on the Status of Women would have clear sailing through the Texas House of Representatives was mistaken. Opponents suddenly arose who charged that such a body would downgrade the role of the homemaker and threaten family life, would unnecessarily enlarge the state bureaucracy, and would not represent the needs of most women. The bill did not pass. (The commission would not become a reality until August 1977, when Governor Dolph Briscoe, a Democrat, established the Texas Commission on the Status of Women by executive order. He created a budget of fifty thousand dollars and a staff so that it could go about its work of distributing information on women, developing policies to foster equal treatment of women in all areas, and coordinating with other state agencies. Only one year later, the commission became embroiled in dissension, and Republican governor William P. Clements dissolved the body in 1979. Eight years later, back in office, Clements reconstituted the Governor's Commission for Women as his first executive order.)[58]

Despite the roadblock encountered in the Senate, in November 1970 many of the same women who had gathered in Austin in August met to form the Texas Women's Political Caucus. Their announced goals were to get more women elected and appointed to public office and to work toward the passage of the Equal Rights Amendment. In the years to come this organization would become an important force in Texas politics. While the organization's endorsed candidate for governor in 1972, Frances Farenthold, lost in her bid for the Democratic nomination, the number of women elected to the legislature jumped to five that same year and continued to grow in coming years. In 1990 one of the organization's members, Ann Richards, would be elected governor of the state.[59]

In November 1969 Martin Frost, a third-year law student at Georgetown University Law School, applied to Sarah T. Hughes for a one-year clerkship. Frost, who had grown up in Fort Worth, had made good grades during his studies at Georgetown University Law School, had published law review articles, and had been involved in other activities expected of outstanding law students. But for Hughes, Frost recalled later about his interview, "only one thing was important—she asked me if I was a Democrat." The answer for Frost was easy, for not only did he already have pronounced Democratic convictions, he also had aspirations to be a future Democratic officeholder. He was able to relate to Hughes's satisfaction his work for the Hubert Humphrey presidential campaign in 1968. A few hours after the interview Judge Hughes called Frost to tell him he had the job.[60]

Although Hughes had just completed presiding over *Roe v. Wade*, the discussions over it had ended when Frost began work. Later, he would say he could not recall hearing the case mentioned during the year he worked for Hughes. As was her wont, the judge was looking ahead, not to the past.[61]

As an aspiring politician, Frost, quiet and studious by nature, immediately developed a close relationship with Hughes. He was a fast, hard worker and politically astute. His earlier experience and training as a journalist (he was a journalism graduate of the University of Missouri and a former reporter for the *Fort Worth Press* and *Congressional Quarterly Weekly Report*) permitted him to write memos quickly and concisely, just as Hughes preferred. His duties as law clerk primarily included handling the "motion practice," that is, studying the motions submitted when a lawsuit was filed and responding to them. Hughes invariably made rulings based on Frost's recommendations. "I just worked without distractions," Frost recalled. "I didn't receive personal telephone calls. I was used to a deadline, and I typed all my own stuff. She liked all of that."[62]

One of the early cases Frost witnessed during his clerkship provided an eye-opening insight into the judge's methods. The case was *United States v. Wichita Falls* (1970), a desegregation suit involving the Wichita Falls Independent School District. Frost drove with Hughes to Wichita Falls to hear the case. "She knew before she went in that she was going to order desegregation," Frost said. She brought all the lawyers and school officials into her chambers and advised them that she was going to order a complicated redrawing of the school boundaries and teacher assignments to desegregate the system. She acknowledged that she did not have sufficient expertise to do this herself. "I would prefer for you in the school administration to draw the new lines in a way that you know will work," she said. "You tell me how you want me to do it, then I'll announce it as my own and I'll take the heat." She would even be happy for them to criticize her freely for the new boundaries. She would accept their criticisms without complaint. The administrators did as requested; Hughes announced their new boundaries as her own; and then the attorneys and administrators, having secretly drawn up the plan themselves, publicly criticized the judge without fear of retribution, thus sparing themselves possible backlash from disgruntled citizens.[63]

As a further means of achieving the desired desegregation, Hughes appointed a community biracial committee to report to her every six months on the progress being made. It was essential, she realized, for committee members to have the highest standing in the community if they were to act effectively. Frost recalled the deliberate way in which Judge Hughes made a key appointment: "She called a man who was, I believe, the former mayor of the city and told him what she was going to do. She needed him to serve on the committee, and she told him she was going to appoint him. He didn't want to serve and insisted that he wouldn't, but she forced him to take the job," Frost said.[64]

Frost would never forget the pride that Hughes took in her work and her special emphasis on moving her court docket faster than the other judges, achieved in part by her strong pressure on attorneys to settle cases out of court. She was also proud of her staff, which included the only African American bailiff in the courthouse, Eddie Crittenden, a former police officer in Terrell.[65]

Frost and the judge were getting along so well that his wife, Halaine, suggested they ask Hughes to be the godmother to their first child, whose birth was forthcoming. Frost was reluctant. "I can't ask a federal judge to be godmother to our daughter," he told his wife. But Halaine insisted. Frost hesitantly agreed, and when he asked the judge she seemed thrilled and expressed great pleasure. After the baby, Alanna, was born, Hughes, who had chosen not to have children of her own, proudly displayed her goddaughter's photograph on her desk.[66]

The judge had one bit of personal advice for Frost. Believing that one could tell a lot about people by the way they shook hands, and being very much aware of Frost's political aspirations, she told him: "Martin, you've got to press the flesh a little harder. You have a mushy handshake."[67]

Years later, in the midst of a distinguished and high-profile career as a senior Democratic leader in Congress, Frost summed up his experiences with the judge in this way: "The most interesting thing I have ever done in my life, including my twenty-four years in Congress, was working as a clerk for Sarah T. Hughes."[68]

As prominent Democratic politicians gathered in Austin in January 1971 to celebrate the inauguration of Texas governor Preston Smith for a second term, the Securities and Exchange Commission filed a suit in Sarah T. Hughes's courtroom that set off the biggest political scandal in Texas for many years. Charged in the initial complaint with using their public office for private gain were former Democratic attorney general Waggoner Carr, former state insurance commissioner John Osorio, and other prominent men. Fifteen individuals in all, including Houston developer Frank Sharp, who was named as the key instigator, and twelve corporations—all either owned or controlled by Sharp—were named in the initial complaint. There had been, the SEC claimed, "fraudulent manipulation of stock prices, trading in unregistered stock, and arranging bank loans and stock trades beneficial to politicians." The potential for even further political scandal could be seen clearly by a close examination of the documents. The SEC charged that in an effort to avoid further regulation by the Federal Deposit Insurance Corporation (FDIC), this group of individuals had attempted to have legislation introduced and passed by the Texas Legislature that would enable state banks to be insured by a state chartered insurance company. "The defendants, in furtherance of this proposed legislation, caused large sums of money to be loaned to certain legislators, legislators' employees, and members of the executive branch."[69]

As expected, in the weeks and months to come the scandal broadened. Criminal complaints filed in other courts entangled Preston Smith; Ben Barnes, the up-and-coming lieutenant governor; Gus Mutscher Jr., the Speaker of the House; W. S. "Bill" Heatly, the chairman of the House Appropriations Committee; Dr. Elmer Baum, the state Democratic chairman; Tommy Shannon, state representative from Fort Worth; and others.

The essence of the SEC's case was that Sharp had made large loans totaling some six hundred thousand dollars to state officials to encourage them to pass legislation favorable to his financial empire. Through his Sharpstown State Bank, he had provided unsecured loans to the legislators and officials to permit them to make large purchases of shares in National Bankers Life Insurance, then quickly sell their holdings with large profits after a special legislative session was called to consider his proposals. What raised the suspicions of the SEC was that the state officials had purchased their shares from the same broker with loans from the same bank and then sold the stock through the same broker within a matter of weeks. Sharp's desired legislation, with the influential support of both Lieutenant Governor Barnes and Speaker of the House Mutscher easily passed in the legislature. Governor Smith, who himself had taken one of the loans from Sharpstown Bank, purchased National Bankers Life stock, summoned the legislature into special session to consider the legislation, and then surprisingly vetoed the two approved bills because he believed they needed further study.[70]

The Sharpstown case involved just the sort of issues that Sarah T. Hughes had felt so passionately about since her days as a crusading legislator in Austin in the early 1930s: corruption in high places involving influential businessmen and politicians more intent on personal gain than serving the people. While the politicians named in the case and in the ensuing cases were all Democrats, they were generally conservative Democrats who identified with the status quo rather than with the liberal outlook favored by Hughes and her political allies.

Judge Hughes recognized immediately the sensational nature of the case and its implications. Telling her clerk Martin Frost that the suit undoubtedly would reach into the highest levels of state government, she decided to make all documents and evidence freely available to the public and press. Recognizing Frost's journalistic background, she delegated him to be her unofficial press representative. She also put him in charge of arranging the enormous amount of documents in an orderly fashion in her library for the convenience of the press.[71]

As anticipated, the city, state, and national media descended onto the Hughes's courtroom to pore over the documents. Knowing just what the reporters needed, Frost worked with them to make sense of the overwhelming amount of paperwork—records, affidavits, written testimony, bank files, checks and letters, and a myriad of other documents—which he had arranged in stacks on tables in the library. With Frost's guidance, reporters were able to avoid being swamped with the deluge of paper and to cross-check one individual's statement against another's. Among the journalists Frost met during this time were a television reporter from Houston, Kay Bailey, destined to become U.S. senator Kay Bailey Hutchison, and a writer from the *Texas Observer*, Molly Ivins, later to become a syndicated columnist and author. The Sharpstown case was reported in dramatic fashion to national audiences through newspaper headlines, news magazine stories, and television accounts.[72]

With such a large number of defendants represented by separate attorneys, all of whom would be maneuvering to protect the interests of their clients, it would be especially important for Hughes to lay down clear guidelines if the courtroom was not to degenerate into chaos. The first test came in February 1971 in a hearing on a temporary injunction against the defendants. Eight sets of lawyers, seated four rows deep behind the prosecutor and defense tables, packed the courtroom. Hughes's reputation as a stern magistrate had spread quickly among the attorneys. On the eve of this first hearing the *Shreveport Times* summarized what the attorneys were saying about her: "Judge Sarah T. Hughes doesn't look big enough to stand up to a little breeze. She is petite and generally affable, a party lover. But any lawyer foolish enough to try to bluster his way past her will be cut down to size quicker than he can turn a law book page."[73] The *Dallas Morning News* opined that "she has an uncanny ability to spot a phony and is quick to let the hot air out of arrogant counsel, be they twice her size or half her age."[74]

Hughes quickly lived up to her reputation for sternness. Her customary determination to hurry proceedings along was emphasized even more because of the possibility of an unusually lengthy case. Attorneys for those several defendants who had entered into consent decrees were not permitted to cross-examine witnesses. Except for the defense, subpoenas could be served only on witnesses within a hundred miles of the Northern District of Texas. When the proceedings began, it was almost immediately clear that she would succeed in her intention to hold a tight rein. Reporters enlivened their stories by using Hughes's pithy comments as she cut lawyers down to size and sped them along. "Judge Hughes in Command," read a headline in the *Dallas Morning News*.[75]

At the end of three days all but eight of the defendants agreed to consent decrees. Without admitting to any wrongdoing, they agreed to desist from further alleged violation of SEC stock regulations. All others, except former attorney general Waggoner Carr, were placed under temporary restraining orders. Hughes found the evidence against Carr, who had been the most newsworthy of the defendants, unconvincing. However, Carr would continue to be a party to the suit when the hearing for a permanent injunction was held.[76]

That hearing came on August 30, 1971. At this point, only five of the individual defendants were actively contesting the charges. Sharp had been given immunity from criminal prosecution in exchange for his testimony. Nevertheless, they were all represented in the crowded courtroom—some by more than one attorney—and the scene bordered on the chaotic. Tables for the attorneys were laid out in two long rows, with eight or nine lawyers in each row. Hughes's determination to maintain order was challenged as never before. Although each attorney would have the right to cross-examine each witness, Judge Hughes established a procedure by which they would take turns with their cross-examinations. "I hope attorneys will not cross-examine just to hear themselves cross-examine," she said as the day began. Then she added, "I have found that sometimes a client is better served if sometimes an attorney doesn't cross-examine at all."[77]

The first witness, an accountant who had been fired as president of one of the indicted companies, South Atlantic Co., was on the stand throughout the first day. The judge's patience long since had grown thin. "This man has been on the stand all day," she said from the bench. "I could sum up the relevancy of his testimony in five sentences. Now we have sixty-nine witnesses to go through in the trial. If all of them take this long, we'll be here until Christmas. Some lawyers like to talk just to hear themselves talk. Now let's move along."[78]

As the first week progressed Hughes ordered the SEC attorneys to "edit their depositions, to shorten their lengthy witnesses list, and to bring the principal defense in the case to the top of the list." When SEC attorney James Sims rose in protest, Hughes curtly responded: "Don't argue with me. Do as I say." [79]

As had been the case in the initial hearing, the judge's impatience was clear to all. Her sharp comments to the attorneys invariably found their way into press accounts of the trial, and her demeanor became one of the major aspects of the news stories.

Finally, on September 16, 1971, the case ended. Hughes granted permanent injunctions to prevent the defendants from selling unregistered stock or "employing any device, scheme, or artifice to defraud." The 5th Circuit Court upheld her rulings.[80]

Despite all the attendant publicity and the widespread hoopla over the Sharpstown case, Hughes's permanent injunctions had little actual impact. They merely ordered the defendants not to do what already was illegal. The judge could have issued the injunctions without benefit of a twelve-day trial. Although she was presiding over a complicated securities case in which her knowledge initially was limited, the issue—corruption in high places involving politicians and heavy-handed businessmen—was one that always had drawn her closest scrutiny.[81]

The publicity generated by the Sharpstown case ensured continuing fallout for many influential Democrats in Texas. Shortly after Hughes's ruling, Speaker of the House Gus Mutscher, state representative Tommy Shannon, and Rush McGinty, an aide to Mutscher, were indicted in a state court for accepting a bribe from Sharp. They were found guilty, and each man was sentenced to five years' probation.

A reform movement in the 1971 legislature composed of both Democrats and Republicans would bring long-lasting changes as its members, dubbed the Dirty Thirty, moved against Speaker of the House Mutscher and the system of favoritism long extant in the legislature. One of the prominent leaders was Frances Farenthold, the Democrat from Corpus Christi, who was making the biggest splash in the House as the most outspoken woman since Sarah T. Hughes in the early 1930s. In 1973 the Texas Legislature passed a series of reform laws that included a requirement that state officials disclose their sources of income, forced candidates to make public more details about their campaign finances, opened up most government records for public scrutiny, expanded the requirements for open meetings, and placed new disclosure regulations on paid lobbyists. Among those many whose political careers the scandal ended, in addition to those indicted or convicted, were Governor Preston Smith and Lieutenant Governor Ben Barnes, both of whom had been tainted by the scandal. Nearly half of all the members of the Texas House were voted out of office or chose not to run in 1972.[82]

The importance of politics in the life of Sarah T. Hughes did not go unrecognized by others. In April 1972 her alma mater Goucher College invited her to be the Political Science Department's first "professional-in-residence." Hughes readily agreed. For the week-long visit, she would live in the Alumnae House, where she had stayed before.

To ensure her comfort, she was asked in advance about her preferences in food. The judge responded: "I like practically everything but some food does not agree with me, so I prefer it plain. I do not, however, eat sweets."[83] Three weeks before she was to begin her visit, she had a question of her own: "How do members of the faculty usually dress for classes? Do any of them wear pant suits or is a dress more appropriate?"[84] Her question suggested that Judge Hughes had by now relaxed the dress code in her own courtroom.

During her week on campus Hughes, always at her best in such an environment, made presentations to classes, visited with students and faculty, answered questions, and shared meals with students. At least one of her presentations, entitled "Women in Law and Politics," was open to the public.[85]

Her stay was a resounding success. "This has been a magnificent and invaluable week," summarized the official host, Dr. Brownlee Sands Corrin of the Department of Political Science. "We are not likely to attain the levels of quality and student responsiveness from and by others who may follow. This does not disturb me. If others approach what we have seen and heard this week from you, we will be well served."[86]

Hughes lobbied strongly and successfully for her successor as the next year's professional-in-residence. Her choice was Frances Farenthold. Besides being a lawyer and an aggressive, outspoken legislator in a male-dominated environment, later that year Farenthold would have something else in common with Hughes: at the 1972 Democratic National Convention she was nominated for vice president, twenty years after Hughes had been similarly honored. Farenthold also campaigned for the Democratic gubernatorial nomination in 1972 but lost to the eventual winner of the general election, Dolph Briscoe. In promoting Farenthold as the professional-in-residence at Goucher, Hughes wrote: "I heartily recommend Frances Farenthold as a second professional-in-residence. I would be glad to write her a letter recommending that she accept the invitation and could do so before your letter." Hughes had a second choice, too: Barbara Jordan, who, like Farenthold, had been a "Dirty Thirty" member of the Texas Legislature. Jordan, a senator in the Texas Legislature, had just been elected to Congress from Houston.[87] Hughes was especially proud of both women. They seemed to have come straight from her own mold.

Sarah Augusta Tilghman, daughter of a
respectable, middle-class Baltimore family, was a
child of the Victorian age, born in 1896.
University of North Texas Archives

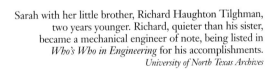

Sarah with her little brother, Richard Haughton Tilghman,
two years younger. Richard, quieter than his sister,
became a mechanical engineer of note, being listed in
Who's Who in Engineering for his accomplishments.
University of North Texas Archives

As a schoolgirl Sarah already had the clear-eyed look
of determination that would be a lifelong hallmark.
Courtesy of Vivian Castleberry

327

Sarah A. Tilghman

Shirley Avenue and Ludwig Lane,
Baltimore, Md.

MAJOR DEPARTMENT—BIOLOGY.

"Early to bed and early to rise makes a man
healthy, wealthy and wise."

In the case of our Sally, we know this is true,
she retires at six and arises at two. And healthy
—just look at her basket-ball fame; both hockey
and swimming have won her a name. While as
for her wisdom, she rivals the sharks and shines
in the classroom as well as in marks. She says
she's not wealthy, and maybe it's true, but if she
needs money, she knows what to do. After
talking all day to a stern business man, she went
off with an "ad" and he called as she ran, "Come
back any day—there's a job for you here,—name
your own salary, you're worth it, my dear."

At Baltimore's all-women Goucher College, Sarah gained a well-deserved reputation as an energetic leader who got things done. This portrait and caption are from the college's yearbook. *Donnybrook Fair yearbook, Goucher College*

As law students at George Washington University Sarah and her new husband, George Hughes, lived in this tent on the Potomac River during the last two months of their senior year so they could save money to move to Texas. *University of North Texas Archives*

In Dallas, Sarah and George briefly shared office space in the mid-1920s in their fledgling law practices. Soon their legal careers would take separate directions. *University of North Texas Archives*

VOTE FOR

SARAH T. HUGHES

CANDIDATE FOR

STATE REPRESENTATIVE

PLACE NO. 3, DALLAS COUNTY

Now held by John E. Davis, who is not a candidate for re-election.

A. B., GOUCHER COLLEGE, LL. B., GEORGE WASHINGTON UNIVERSITY
INSTRUCTOR IN THE JEFFERSON SCHOOL OF LAW, 1926-1930
PRACTICING ATTORNEY, DALLAS COUNTY, 1922-1930

By 1930 Sarah T. Hughes had primed herself for her first political campaign as a candidate for the Texas Legislature. She had this photograph taken to use in her advertising. *Photo courtesy of Vivian Castleberry. Advertisement, University of North Texas Archives*

First as a state legislator, then as a judge, Hughes was accustomed in the 1930s to being the only woman in a room full of men. (The man is unidentified.)
Courtesy of Constance Tilghman Dudley

Immediately after her confirmation by the Texas Senate as a district judge and before returning to Dallas
to begin her duties, Hughes took the oath of office in Austin from notary public Arlene Wilson.
Dallas Historical Society

After her controversial appointment in1935 as Texas's first woman district judge,
Hughes was greeted in her new courtroom in Dallas by the temporary judge, D.A. Frank.
Texas/Dallas History and Archives Division, Dallas Public Library

331

In 1940 Gwen Graul, daughter of Dallas County official Ed Cobb, became Hughes's secretary. She would remain the judge's principal assistant, close friend, and confidante for forty years. *Courtesy of Dolores and J.W. Graul*

During her judgeship, Hughes, shown here in the 1940s, was probably the best known woman in the state of Texas. *Courtesy of Dolores and J.W. Graul*

For many years Sarah vacationed at a ranch in Creede, Colorado, where with George she fished, rode horseback, and enjoyed campfires. *University of North Texas Archives*

Her long involvement with the Business and Professional Women's Clubs led to her presidency of the national federation from 1950 to 1952. *University of North Texas Archives*

"THE EYES OF TEXAS ARE UPON YOU, JUDGE HUGHES!"

1952 BIENNIAL

NATIONAL FEDERATION of BUSINESS and PROFESSIONAL WOMEN'S CLUBS

BANQUET

GEORGIAN ROOM, HOTEL STATLER JULY 2nd, 1952

BOSTON, MASSACHUSETTS

One of Sarah and George Hughes's favorite pastimes was square dancing. They also owned horses and frequently rode. *University of North Texas Archives*

When John F. Kennedy campaigned in Dallas and Fort Worth in 1960, Sarah T. Hughes rode between him and Lyndon B. Johnson in a convertible. Barefoot Sanders, foreground, was the Dallas County campaign manager; Hughes reported to him as co-chairman of the campaign. *Courtesy of Jan Sanders and U.S. District Judge Barefoot Sanders*

At a campaign stop for Lyndon B. Johnson in 1960 at Wynnewood Village in Dallas, Sarah T. Hughes, right, and Jan Sanders entertained the waiting crowd by dancing the Charleston. *Photo by Andy Hanson*

Vice President Lyndon B. Johnson spoke eloquently of Sarah T. Hughes's accomplishments at her induction ceremony as a federal judge in October 1961. Hughes had requested that he give her the oath of office, but Joe E. Estes, presiding judge of the Northern District of Texas, administered it. *Photo by Andy Hanson*

After a positive vote in 1962 by the U.S. Senate, President Kennedy greeted Hughes and the three other new Texas judges in the White House. Left to right, are James Noel, Senator Ralph W. Yarborough, President Kennedy, Hughes, Vice President Lyndon B. Johnson, Adrian Spears, and Leo Brewster. The boy in front is unidentified. *University of North Texas Archives*

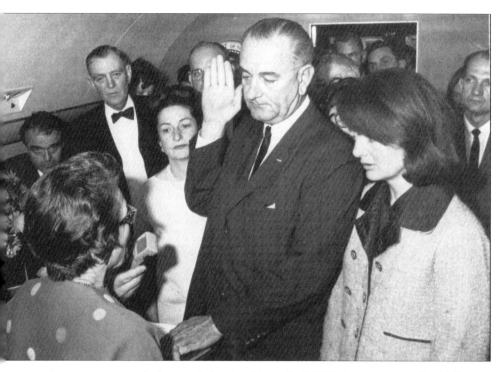

At a moment never to be forgotten in American history, Sarah T. Hughes was summoned to Air Force One on November 22, 1963, to administer the presidential oath of office to Lyndon B. Johnson. *University of North Texas Archives*

Hughes visited with Lyndon and Lady Bird Johnson in their Washington, D.C., home on the day of her Senate confirmation in 1962. They would grow closer in the next years. *University of North Texas Archives*

Although Hughes never had children of her own, she was interested in family life and the well-being of children. Here she greets youngsters after a naturalization ceremony in Wichita Falls. *University of North Texas Archives*

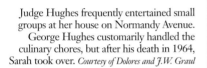

Judge Hughes frequently entertained small groups at her house on Normandy Avenue. George Hughes customarily handled the culinary chores, but after his death in 1964, Sarah took over. *Courtesy of Dolores and J.W. Graul*

Hughes was proud as Texas began to be dotted with women who followed in her footsteps as trailblazers. Here she is with (from left) Julia Scott Reed of the *Dallas Morning News*, the newspaper's first African-American columnist; Chris Miller, Texas's first female state representative from Tarrant County; and Adlene Harrison, who in 1976 became Dallas's first woman mayor. *Courtesy of Vivian Castleberry*

Sarah T. Hughes was always a forceful, animated speaker. She never hesitated to give her point of view on controversial issues. *Photo by Andy Hanson*

Hughes always encouraged young women to follow her into the legal profession, and she began meeting regularly with female Dallas attorneys in the early 1970s. A number of the women in this group became well known throughout Texas, in particular Louise Raggio (sixth from left, starting with Hughes), who rewrote Texas's family law code. *Courtesy of Louise Raggio*

An intimate moment shared with another famous woman, Pearl Mesta, known as "the hostess with the mostest." *Washington Evening Star, courtesy of Vivian Castleberry*

Hughes's close colleague, U.S. District Judge William (Mac) Taylor, shown with her in a 1976 photograph, joined her on three-judge panels for many important decisions, including Roe v. Wade. *Courtesy of Vivian Castleberry*

The accomplishments of Barbara Jordan, who became well known as a Congresswoman, delighted Sarah T. Hughes. She often cited Congresswoman Jordan as an example of what a determined woman could achieve against great odds. In the center is Circuit Judge John R. Brown. *University of North Texas Archives*

Hughes confers with her long-time aide, Gwen Graul, who protected her employer and made certain that the office was tightly run. *Shel Hershorn Collection, Center for American History, University of Texas at Austin*

339

A favorite vacation spot was the Big Bend country of Texas, where Hughes enjoyed a float trip down the Rio Grande. Here she pauses for lunch with fellow camper Sarel Kandell in 1971. *Courtesy of Constance Tilghman Dudley*

Hughes looked back fondly on her undergraduate days at Goucher College. Seen here on a campus visit, she served as the first "professional-in-residence" in political science, and played leadership roles in alumni affairs. *Goucher College Archives*

Foreign travel was a special interest for Hughes, and she made several trips sponsored by the U.S. State Department. On a tour to Mexico in 1968 she visited with legal and penal officials. *University of North Texas Archives*

340

When *People Weekly* profiled Judge Hughes in 1977 during her long jurisdiction of the Dallas County jail case, she demonstrated her yoga exercises for photographer Michael Salas. The magazine ran this photograph full-page. *Photo by Michael Salas*

In 1980, when she was eighty-four, Sarah T. Hughes testified in Washington, D.C., before the House of Representatives' Select Committee on Aging on the topic, "Age Discrimination in the Selection of Federal Judges." *University of North Texas Archives*

This is the last known photograph of Judge Hughes, taken in March 1983 as she holds the daughter of her former law clerk, Joanne Hurtekant. The photograph was made at the nursing home where Hughes spent her last years. *Photo by Joanne Hurtekant*

13 ～

Reforming the Jail

S arah T. Hughes preferred criminal cases. "You're dealing with people," she explained, not things. "There are a lot of civil cases that I don't like—anti-trust cases, patent cases." In her opinion there was nothing duller than a patent case.[1] The people she encountered in criminal cases intrigued her. She enjoyed the challenge of assessing the circumstances under which defendants strayed from the social order and in making recommendations to help them overcome their situations. She considered most defendants (white-collar criminals excepted) to be not innate wrongdoers but people who because of various reasons or circumstances had deviated from accepted norms. From her own probing questions and from information gathered for her by probation officers, Hughes invariably offered pointed advice as she sentenced them, often advising those going to prison to use their confinement in a positive way. Rehabilitation was her goal.

"You feel as if when you're sentencing them that perhaps you can do something for them. I always give them something to hope for," she said. "Some of them . . . will say that they've been born again. If they think they've been born again, I make something of it. I tell them to count on the Lord and put their trust in Him. You're dealing with people. You're hoping that you can get to them and that they will respond to you."[2]

Although the judge's viewpoints were generally shared by penologists, they by no means were held by the general public. Popular opinion conceived of jails and prisons as places where wrongdoers were sent as punishment. It followed that they should be confined in a harsh, no-frills environment.

The conflicting viewpoints between Hughes and popular opinion, especially as reflected by elected county officials, would provide the basis for a legal dispute that would preoccupy Hughes throughout the 1970s. The case would give rise to countless front-page headlines and editorials, prolonged disputes with county officials, and demands by angry citizens that she keep her nose out of local affairs. If the nation was to remember Sarah T. Hughes for giving the presidential oath of office to Lyndon B. Johnson on one of the most traumatic days in American history, Dallas residents would remember her as the aging, scrappy little judge who threatened to shut down the county jail and ordered the building of an expensive new one.

The result of Judge Hughes's persistence and rulings was that Dallas County eventually built a new Criminal Justice Center, which would include a $56.4 million jail, described by Judge Hughes herself as one of the best in the nation, and, as a corollary, a modern $61.5 million criminal courts building. In Judge Hughes's opinion, the case that prompted all this, *Taylor v. Sterrett*, was the most important one she ever tried.[3] The Dallas case would be followed by a wave of other lawsuits concerning violations of minimal standards in county jails, creation of the Texas Commission on Jail Standards, and widespread reformation of jails throughout the state.

The dispute over the Dallas County jail once more reflected the tumultuous times in which society's disenfranchised seemed forever to be challenging and upsetting established authorities. In this case, those who challenged were the lowest of the low—jail inmates. Representing them was the Dallas Legal Services Project, which already was creating consternation among the Dallas establishment. The DLSP's aggressive class-action lawsuits concerning such controversial matters as sodomy, pornography, welfare, and civil rights had created a popular conception of the federally funded body that it was revolutionary in intent, aiming to reorder all of society.

Problems at the Dallas County jail had been long evident, but this would be forgotten in the ensuing controversy. Ironically, the jail's deficiencies did not result from an aged, outmoded facility. The jail was still new, having opened in 1966 on the top six floors of a new and modern twelve-story, white granite government building* across the street from the old red courthouse and one block away from the old jail built in 1914. The new jail had a bed capacity of approximately 1,220. Sheriff James E. (Bill) Decker, who had died in 1970 after twenty-two years as sheriff, had complained before it opened that the jail would be too small. And he was right, for its stated capacity was quickly surpassed by several hundred. Other jails in large Texas counties such

---

* The building was known at the time as the County Government Center but later was given the new name of George L. Allen, Sr., Courts Building in honor of a former African American Dallas city councilman, mayor pro tem, and justice of peace.

as Harris, Bexar, and Tarrant similarly were suffering from overcrowding in this time of rising crime rates.[4]

A flurry of complaints in 1970 originating from a jailhouse lawyer, a former Baptist preacher named Julius Dwaine Perry, and sent through the mail had landed in district judge William (Mac) Taylor's courtroom. Taylor had had no patience with them. He declared them "numerous, frivolous, unfounded and unwarranted." They amounted, he said, to an effort by inmates to "take over the operations of the Dallas County jail through the federal courts." Taylor said that in spite of overcrowded conditions, it was a matter of common knowledge that the Dallas County jail was "one of the best run and operated facilities of its kind."[5]

Judge Taylor was following the tradition of the judiciary in adopting a hands-off attitude regarding prison administration. It was widely held that the courts were poorly equipped to handle such problems. The U.S. Supreme Court had seemed to recognize that the nature of the penal system justified the withdrawal or limitation of many rights and privileges of prisoners, who, in effect, suffered a "civil death" upon conviction and lost their normal rights. In one case it had even been held that convicts might be regarded as "slaves of the state."[6]

Less than two months after her good friend Judge Taylor made his harsh comments, Sarah T. Hughes offered a different perspective. "It was only four or five years ago that the Dallas County Jail was completed," she told members of the Dallas Bar Association in September 1970. "We thought it was adequate. We know that today there are 1,800 prisoners lodged there with accommodations for only 1,200. Men are lying on the floor; they do not have any room for either any type of recreation or of educational facilities."[7]

She saw problems in the overall criminal justice system, too, including outmoded courts with inadequate facilities, too few judges, and "too many lawyers uninterested in the causes of crime and their solution." Her criticisms included law schools that showed too little concern with criminal law. "Their attention is directed toward property rights and the way people make money."[8] She was disdainful of the thousand-year sentences being sought and won by District Attorney Henry Wade's staff in high-profile cases. "Can you think of any relation that a thousand-year sentence bears to any sort of crime?" She quoted a federal prison superintendent who told her that confinement beyond five years has no rehabilitative powers.[9]

In early 1971 the overcrowded jail conditions prompted chief jailer

E. L. Holman to tell the *Times Herald* that he was "sitting on a powder keg, waiting for it to explode." In March 1971 a grand jury reported to a district judge that the "crowded conditions in the jail are deplorable." He urged county authorities to remedy the situation as soon as possible. In September and October 1971 three riots broke out behind bars. The worst, on October 5, lasted three hours before order could be restored. Prisoners used makeshift weapons, smashed windows, and set mattresses on fire while they chanted, "We want justice." One prisoner died, apparently from natural causes, a jailer was hospitalized with a heart attack, and nineteen prisoners were injured.[10]

Responding to the problems, another Dallas County grand jury toured the jail and complimented Sheriff Clarence Jones for a jail that was "clean, free of odor and healthy." The facility was admittedly overcrowded, but the jurors were impressed with the caliber of the jail guards and security measures.[11]

Three weeks after the October 5 riot, Dallas Legal Services, acting on behalf of inmates Joseph Taylor, James Douglas Thompson, John Henry Woods Jr., and all other inmates, filed a thirteen-page complaint alleging both a long list of violations of their rights as protected by the First, Eighth, and Fourteenth amendments of the Constitution and the county's failure to comply with state of Texas laws regarding the operation and supervision of the jail. Overcrowding, lack of basic medical attention, inadequate food, inadequate light and heat, lack of recreational facilities, lack of privacy, danger of beatings, improper solitary cells, and intimidation by "goon squads" made up of fellow prisoners were among their many complaints. Named as defendants were county judge W. L. (Lew) Sterrett and the other four members of Dallas County Commissioners Court, Sheriff Clarence Jones, the chief jailer, and the Dallas County health officer. (The county commissioners and county judge were responsible for providing the facility and the budget for its operation; the sheriff was in charge of supervising the jail.)[12]

Following the usual random method of assigning cases, *Taylor v. Sterrett*, as it happened, went to Judge Hughes. It was, without question, a case to her liking. It was not the criminal case for which she had expressed a preference, but it was even better. It dealt with the important matter of how society should respond to crime and criminals, an issue that always had concerned her. Adding to her familiarity with the subject was her intimate acquaintance with the unique courthouse culture, having spent twenty-six years there. As a state district judge, she had never been reluctant to feud with the county commissioners, even though their budgetary powers directly impacted the operation of her own court. It had been a decade since Hughes had left the county courthouse, but its ways and many of the officials had not changed.

She knew county judge Sterrett, the county government's top administrator, as well as any of the top officials. Sterrett was a one-time farm boy who began his career at the courthouse in the 1930s as a temporary assistant in the county clerk's office. He worked his way up to being elected county judge in 1948, a position that was administrative rather than judicial. Sterrett and the four county commissioners, all of whom composed the commissioners court, seemed at once to recognize the significance of *Taylor v. Sterrett*. In an unusual action they wrote and jointly signed a letter to the Dallas Bar Association asking for that influential body's help. If the inmates' suit is successful, the commissioners wrote, "we will be the subject of harassment, be forced to have legal counsel, unpleasant cross examination and be forced to neglect the duties of their [our] respective offices." The jail, they said, echoing the sentiments of many, can not be run as a "country club nor a debating society." Just what the bar association might do in response to this plea was uncertain, but presumably the commissioners hoped they might exert indirect pressure on Judge Hughes to dismiss the suit or to respond in a minimal way. Judge Sterrett explained the aim of the letter to a reporter in simple terms: "We hope that the bar association can give us a little relief from this harassment."[13]

Perhaps unknown to the commissioners, the Dallas Junior Bar Association, an affiliate of the bar association made up of younger attorneys, already had appointed a committee of its own to investigate the jail. This committee's findings, issued on the same day the commissioners wrote their letter, could not have encouraged the county officials. The junior bar's "jail visitation committee" outlined extensive problems similar to the ones lodged by the inmates.[14]

Less than two weeks after *Taylor v. Sterrett* was filed and before it could be heard, Judge Hughes was obliged to consider her first specific action related to it. Attorneys for the plaintiffs complained that jail officials were censoring inmates' incoming and outgoing mail, even communications with their attorneys and families. Under the policy, prisoners had to present their unsealed mail to a jailer who had the authority to refuse to send forward any letter he found unacceptable. The sheriff's stated purpose was to ensure security and prevent the transmission of contraband.[15]

The issue was touchy. Following the doctrine that prisoners automatically lose many basic rights upon incarceration, there had been a consistent judicial reluctance to apply normal constitutional standards concerning their correspondence. The U.S. Supreme Court had never recognized First Amendment rights for prisoners. In this complaint, then, Sarah T. Hughes was entering new territory, and she did so promptly.[16]

She issued a temporary restraining order requiring Sheriff Clarence Jones, who had succeeded Sheriff Decker, and his agents to cease reading or deleting any written matter and to open mail "only to the extent of determining that said mail does not contain any dangerous or contraband material or objects." Mail between inmates and the courts, prosecuting attorneys, probation and parole officers, governmental agencies, lawyers, and the press was not to be opened at all. Just over a month later the temporary restraining order became permanent.[17]

When the U.S. Court of Appeals for the 5th Circuit finally upheld Hughes's order in 1974, the decision represented, according to legal scholar Barry Paul Hitchings, "the first time that any court has attempted to establish in a single case, clear guidelines on prisoner constitutional rights." It was done, he wrote, with a "boldness which has rarely been seen in the area of prisoner rights litigation." Another legal scholar, Mary Christine Hutton, noted that Hughes's decision carried the constitutional rights of prisoners to free speech beyond previous decisions by the Supreme Court.[18]

In March 1972, with the main hearing still pending, Sheriff Jones took another step deemed punitive to the prisoners. He distributed an order to inmates announcing the forthcoming destruction of all books and magazines that were over three weeks old, an act that presumably would have eliminated the legal documents and books being used by "jailhouse lawyers" such as Duane Perry. Once again, Hughes quickly issued a temporary restraining order to prevent the destruction of these materials. Inmates' reading material—all books, magazines, and newspaper clippings "to which any inmate may either attach a personal importance or evince a desire to retain"—simply had to be kept in good condition "and in a manner that will not create a health or fire hazard."[19] This decision, too, would be affirmed later by the 5th Circuit as a "reasonable provision for the protection of First Amendment rights."[20]

Shortly before the trial was to be heard in May 1972, jailhouse lawyer Perry filed another suit on behalf of all prisoners complaining of inadequate medical services. His similar complaint in 1970 to Judge Taylor had proved fruitless. Hughes, though, accepted it and consolidated it with *Taylor v. Sterrett.*[21]

To prepare for the hearing, Hughes decided in typical fashion to examine the jail herself. On an announced visit, accompanied by attorneys for the plaintiffs and the defendants, she walked up and down the jail corridors, chatted with guards, sampled the food, and counted bunks in the cells and in the hospital ward. She expressed shock over what she saw. "It was in deplorable condition," she said afterward in an oral history interview. Because of overcrowded conditions, several hundred men and women inmates were sleeping on mattresses on the floor. She found the single cells used to confine inmates as punishment to be particularly bad. "They put them there to punish them, and it wasn't big enough for a man to even lie down. There was no place for the toilet facilities except a hole in the middle of the floor; there was a light burning all night long right in his eyes; there was no place for him to take a shower, to wash, or to do anything. . . . Even in the hospital section they didn't have enough beds. Even those people had to be placed on the floor."[22]

She found that the jail inmates had virtually nothing to do for amusement except play dominoes. With many of them being held for several years, Hughes was convinced they often returned to society "worse than when they went in."[23]

On March 17, 1972, the judge sent a notice to "all persons" confined in the Dallas County jail. She summarized the issues in a way that must have sent cheers down the corridors:

> The defendants are charged with having failed to maintain the County Jail in a manner consonant with the United States Constitution and with other federal standards, in that, persons confined in the jail have suffered from inadequate food, inadequate light and heat, a lack of recreational activities, a lack of adequate facilities for conferences with attorneys, a lack of adequate sanitation facilities, a lack of adequate medical attention, a lack of privacy, overcrowding, the danger of beatings, sexual attacks, improper solitary cells, and other forms of intimidation resulting from an inadequate guard system.[24]

As she was soon to learn, she could have augmented her references to the U.S. Constitution and to other federal standards as a basis for action with a surprising fact: the Dallas County jail was in clear violation of the state's own laws. It failed to comply with the minimum standards established by the Texas Legislature and promulgated in Article 5115 of Vernon's Texas Revised Civil Statutes Annotated. In fact, the jail had been in violation of Article 5115 on the day it opened. So, it soon would be realized, were most of the county jails throughout the state.[25]

The trial, heard in mid-May 1972, lasted only a few days. None of the defendants were in the courtroom, and this irritated Hughes. "They just completely ignored me," she said later.[26] Arguing on behalf of the county officials was John B. Tolle, the same assistant district attorney who had represented the state in *Roe v. Wade*. Several prisoners testified. Some of their most compelling testimony described the "cop-out" men from the district attorney's office who had free access to the cells to negotiate plea bargaining directly with the defendants outside the presence of their own counsel. The cop-out men offered defendants deals in which they would serve a certain number of years if they would plead guilty. Dallas Legal Services attorney Robert Byrd pointed out the failure to segregate prisoners in the jail. Those who had not yet been convicted of any crime and might be found innocent were treated the same as convicted felons. Tolle acknowledged overcrowding in the jail, and he saw this as the cause of almost all the problems.[27]

Although Hughes disdained long opinions—she had written only seven pages for *Roe v. Wade*—this case was an exception. In *Taylor v. Sterrett* she wrote eleven pages.

Before she released the document, she called in one of her favorite probation officers, Dennis Shaw, a plain-spoken, experienced former lawman with whom she frequently chatted informally. Eager to hear his impressions, she asked Shaw to sit down and read her opinion. Thirty years later Shaw recalled that it took him about twenty minutes to read the eleven pages. He was astounded. "My God, Judge, they can't do all that," he exclaimed. She responded, "I'll be happy if they can do half of it."[28]

County officials were just as astonished as Shaw. Hughes ordered the Commissioners court and sheriff to institute sweeping changes that seemed at the time nearly impossible to accomplish. Some changes amounted to policy modifications, but others required significant structural changes, difficult if not impossible to achieve at the present facility. The words she chose in describing the shortcomings often were harshly condemnatory.

In her "Memorandum Opinion and Judgment," delivered on June 5, 1972, she provided careful descriptions of the jail, its crowded conditions, an analysis of practices, policies, and procedures, and an assessment of medical facilities. She acknowledged that federal courts "are reluctant to interfere with the internal operations of jails," but the claims made by the plaintiffs did not involve "mere matters of preference or convenience concerning administrative practices." They raised basic questions of constitutionally protected rights. And even though prisoners had "obvious limitations placed on their privileges and rights," they had not lost all their constitutional rights. What was important to her, and this was emphasized in her opinion, was that the county jail facilities failed to meet the state of Texas's own requirements as stipulated in Article 5115, Vernon's Texas Revised Civil Statutes, Annotated.[29]

She gave vivid and specific descriptions of cells that were smaller than required by state law, of the lack of running water and drinking fountains, and of undersized solitary confinement cells with mattresses on the floors and rarely flushed holes in the floor as the only toilet facility. The cells were smaller than the state's statutory requirements (forty square feet for a single-person cell and a minimum of eighteen square feet per prisoner in larger cells). She referred to "the practice of placing the inmate in the cell nude and on bread and water diet" as an example of cruel and unusual punishment.[30]

She observed that the failure to have written rules for inmates' conduct in the jail subjected them to arbitrary punishment from a guard or another inmate known as a corridor boss. In a point that would prove to be particularly difficult in the years ahead, she noted the failure to provide programs or an area for exercise and recreation. Inmates who might remain in jail for several years had no recreational activities other than reading and playing cards or dominoes. They had no exposure to either sunlight or fresh air. Save for the voluntary work done by chaplains, there were no trained counselors for the inmates, and the only opportunity for religious services was when the chaplain entered a "tank" and spoke.[31]

County officials, she wrote, had ignored the rehabilitative role the jail should play in the criminal justice system. "The practice of the jail is totally devoid of any constructive measures which might act on an individual prisoner to influence him to become a contributing member of society," she wrote. "The inmates are relegated to the dehumanizing existence of idle isolation in a cage. The fundamental objective of correctional institutions, that of rehabilitation, has been subordinated to the limited goal of punishment and security." Instead of attempting to influence the lives of the inmates in any positive way, the county was performing "an exclusively custodial function of placing the accused and the convicted into crowded cells and letting them vegetate until their release."[32]

A special concern was the failure to classify and segregate prisoners according to their particular situations. Some inmates were merely awaiting trial because they had no money to post bond; others were serving out brief misdemeanor sentences; many were convicted felons awaiting appeal decisions or transfer to the Texas Department of Corrections; and a number were federal prisoners lodged in the county jail while they awaited their trials. Assignments to cells failed to take these differences into account; they were done strictly by alphabetical order. Pretrial prisoners, in some respects, found themselves in a position worse than that of convicted criminals, for they were not allowed the relative freedom given inmates chosen to be trustees, and they could not engage in the limited educational programs accorded convicted criminals (instituted only after the filing of the lawsuit in October 1971). "The obvious conclusion," the judge wrote, "was that these technically innocent individuals suffer worse punishment in the jail than the convicted in the penitentiary."[33]

Judge Hughes supported her ruling by reprinting extensively from Article 5115 of Vernon's Texas Revised Civil Statutes Annotated under sections entitled "Suitable Segregation," "Suitable Security and Safety," and "Suitable Sanitation and Health." Violation of these standards was not at issue, for it was a fact. "The defendants have been quite candid in their admission that the county does not provide facilities which conform to article 5115," she wrote. She cited numerous federal precedents giving her authority to act, especially *Holt v. Sarver,* a federal case in which the entire Arkansas prison system, largely because of the absence of training and rehabilitation programs, was found to be in violation of the Eighth Amendment forbidding cruel and unusual punishment. She cited Warren E. Burger, chief justice of the U.S. Supreme Court, in saying that recreation is a necessary concomitant with education in prisons.[34]

The judge said that both the correctional programs and facilities of the Dallas County jail were in "desperate need of upgrading and expansion." Dallas County had shown "complete indifference to its responsibility to attempt rehabilitation of those offenders charged to its care." The old attitude of confining the accused and the convicted behind bars as inexpensively as possible would have to change. She ruled in her first point that the commissioners be enjoined from further violations of Article 5115, and she directed them immediately to provide sufficient cells and tanks to accommodate a number of inmates equal to the largest number in the Dallas County jail during 1972 in any one day; solitary cells of not less than forty square feet with a bunk, water closet, and a combination drinking fountain and lavatory; increased capacity of the hospital ward with bunks provided for all patients; and padded cells with hammocks for insane persons. No one would be placed in a solitary cell unless it was provided with a bunk, water closet, and a combination fountain and lavatory. Recognizing the difficulty of achieving these requirements because of the crowded conditions and limited space, she suggested that the former jail be renovated and that the women's floor in the present jail be redesigned to accommodate both male and female inmates. As to the daunting word *immediately*, she interpreted this to be six months.[35]

One of the more difficult requirements, considering that the jail was enclosed on the top floors of the County Government Center, was her order that the commissioners court provide for prisoners an outdoor area for exercise and a rehabilitative program of recreation. A temporary arrangement, she thought, might be to remodel the roof of the building and arrange for outdoor activities there.[36]

Aside from the facilities themselves, she had other directives. One was to provide enough jail guards for security so that the practice of using inmates for assistance could stop—in other words, no more corridor bosses. She repeated and included in her order the directive about stopping mail censorship and prohibiting guards from destroying reading matter belonging to inmates. She directed the sheriff to establish a new policy for prisoners relating to rules of conduct and to communicate this information to the inmates so that they could appreciate what kind of conduct would subject them to discipline. The practice of permitting cop-out men from the district attorney's office to have free access to the inmates was forbidden except with the consent or request of the inmates. A classification system was to be established to segregate pretrial detainees from convicted inmates. Employees and inmates who handled food in the kitchen must be examined by a licensed physician to detect the presence of communicable diseases.[37]

In her concluding paragraph, an ominous one, Hughes wrote that "while this opinion closes this case it may be reopened within a reasonable time on application of the plaintiffs contending that Defendants are not making a diligent, good faith effort to comply with the order of this Court."[38]

Three days after issuing her order, she told the *Times Herald* that by putting people in the jail the county was "promoting crime rather than reducing it." She had been shocked by the conditions she had seen on her tour of the jail, and she said she would hope that the majority of citizens would be similarly shocked if they could see it.[39]

Not long before she was assigned the jail case, Hughes had heard a sermon one Sunday morning by her minister, the Reverend C. Preston Wiles of St. Matthew's Episcopal Cathedral. Dr. Wiles, who had a doctorate in criminology from Duke University, spoke earnestly of the need to emphasize rehabilitation in incarceration rather than punishment, deploring conditions at the Dallas County jail. After the sermon, Hughes approached him and expressed her shared sentiments. She often sent people to jail or prison, she told him, and she was very concerned about the problem. Shortly after rendering her opinion, she saw Dr. Wiles at church and accepted his congratulations. "I thought you'd be pleased," she said.[40]

"Resistance High to Housecleaning of County Jail," read a headline in the *Dallas Morning News.* The initial reaction, according to many, was that Judge Sarah T. Hughes was out of line. Why should an appointive federal judge be able to tell an elected county sheriff how to run his jail? The ruling contained not a hint of where the necessary funds for making the changes could be obtained. Some county officials acknowledged, though, that the judge had them over the proverbial barrel, because their jail clearly was in violation of state law. And if this was the case for one of the newest county jails in the state, then hundreds of other jails also must be out of compliance. The repercussions seemed immense. Indeed, as the next months and years proved, this was the case.[41]

County officials immediately announced their intention to appeal the decision. Commissioner John Whittington urged that the appeal be based on the separation of governmental powers. County judge Lew Sterrett expressed a hope that the Texas Legislature would enact a law requiring prisoners whose cases were on appeal to be transferred to the state penitentiary system. District Attorney Henry Wade suggested that lawmakers could amend the statutes so that the Dallas County jail would no longer be out of compliance. Sheriff Clarence Jones believed that a regional jail would eventually take care of the situation, but such a facility would be at least five years away.[42]

The *Dallas Morning News* attempted to explain the widespread dissatisfaction with Hughes's opinion in an editorial:

> The idea of applying scarce tax funds to upgrade the living conditions for jail inmates provokes the public to anger and disgust. . . . It has been alarming to observe the courts, supposedly the arbiters of justice, spending so much time and effort defending the interests of the predators while so little attention is given to the rights and safety of those who are preyed upon by the criminal. . . . It is understandable that the public cannot work up much sympathy for an armed robber who refuses to enter his cell until he meets with officials about the transfer of his law books.

Yet, the newspaper observed, the painful conclusion was that if the jail fell below minimum standards required by law, changes must be made to meet those standards.[43]

"Judge Hughes was around this courthouse long enough to know our problems," Sterrett said. And in a clever comment perhaps designed to complicate the issue for those with humanitarian impulses, he added: "The jail hasn't been a high priority item as caring for the poor and the young. We couldn't possibly provide the funds for the jail without cutting services to these people."[44]

One day after Hughes's ruling, James Douglas Thompson, one of the three prison plaintiffs, was reportedly placed in an undersized solitary confinement cell despite the order that such cells were not to be used unless they contained at least forty square feet and were provided with a bunk, water closet, and a combination drinking fountain and lavatory. Dallas Legal Services Project attorneys quickly called the violation to the judge's attention. She immediately reaffirmed her requirement that the sheriff and the chief jailer, Carl Rowland, not put prisoners in solitary confinement cells that did not meet state requirements, and she ordered them to come to her court and tell her why they should not be punished for contempt of court. Lamely, they contended they were unaware the order had taken effect. The judge said she would give them the benefit of the doubt and not hold them in contempt. But the message was clear: the next time could be different.[45]

Three weeks after her June 5, 1972, decision Judge Hughes climbed into the Dallas Press Club's "hot seat," a regular feature in which reporters grilled newsmakers in a free-wheeling exchange. Her decision, she said, undoubtedly with a wink, "seems to have stirred up somewhat of a hornet's nest on the other side of town." Charges that she wanted to turn the jail into a country club were ridiculous, she said. She never had any doubt but that the Dallas county commissioners could find the money to make the reforms. "They get it for everything else," she said. "All I did was tell the Commissioners Court to abide by the state law," noting that commissioners courts all over the state also were not in compliance with the law. Asked why her own assessment of the jail's condition differed so markedly from that of the earlier and positive grand jury report, she said, "The grand jury only found that the jail was clean. I agree with that. And they found that the food was good. And I agree with that."[46]

During the grilling by reporters she naturally was asked about other matters, too, and her responses were just as direct. She believed that Frances Farenthold lost her bid to become governor only because the women of Texas failed to endorse her and work toward her election. And even though Farenthold had not been elected, she could claim credit for cleaning out the state government after the Sharpstown case. Hughes predicted that a woman would shortly be appointed to the U.S. Supreme Court. Finally, although she was now seventy-five years of age, Hughes said she had no plans to retire despite certain rumors. "I don't feel I'll ever retire," she said.[47]

A month later, Sterrett, who had emerged as the most outspoken opponent of Hughes's jail case decision, took the same hot seat at the Press Club. Noted for his forthright comments—just the opposite from those of Hughes, because his inevitably came from a hard-nosed, conservative point of view— he lashed out at both the Dallas Legal Services Project and the federal courts for interfering with the jail operations. The Dallas County jail is "one of the best jails in America," he claimed. "If the criminals don't like our quarters, let them move elsewhere."[48]

Two weeks later the county judge and all four county commissioners offered a startling proposition to Sheriff Clarence Jones. If he would defy Hughes's order concerning mail censorship, they would go to jail with him on a contempt charge.[49] The sheriff declined their offer.

Sarah T. Hughes, always firm in her convictions, had an unusually high threshold for public criticism. She would not be intimidated or deterred from the task before her. In this struggle, she held the upper hand. As was clear from the beginning, her ambitious order could not be met in the six months she specified, nor could it be met in a year, or even a few years. But she held to her opinion and would continue for the next seven years to oversee the work of the sheriff and the county commissioners as they attempted to satisfy her order. Standing behind Hughes was the U.S. Court of Appeals, 5th Circuit, which with rare exception approved of her supervision of the case. They inevitably ruled in her favor on appeals from the county. One of the early exceptions dealt with her order prohibiting persons from seeing inmates without the consent or request of the prisoner. The court of appeals held that order to be too broad because it "might be interpreted to eliminate visits from official investigators engaged in efforts to solve crimes or to perform other legitimate duties."[50]

Many changes Hughes had ordered (cessation of mail censorship, elimination of corridor bosses, a halt to cop-out men, and the like) dealt in policy without involving structural changes to the jail facility. Sheriff Jones began to implement these without significant protest. More difficult to achieve were the requirements for recreational activities and minimal cell sizes. With the six-month deadline for compliance approaching, on January 5, 1973, the county commissioners requested a stay, and a court of appeals panel of judges saw little alternative but to grant it.[51]

County commissioners, admittedly facing a difficult situation, allotted $125,000 for a comprehensive study on how to implement Hughes's long-range requirements. A particularly tough problem was complying with the judge's order to provide an outdoor area for exercise and a rehabilitative program of recreation. How could an outdoor recreational facility be created for prisoners whose cells were on the top floors of a government building that had courtrooms and offices below? The judge also had advised the creation of quarters for chapel services and educational programs. The county commissioners devised a compromise plan they hoped she would accept as an immediate solution—the installation of television sets for commercial reception and a closed circuit for special programs. Without leaving their cells or tanks, inmates could be led through in-place exercises via closed circuit. Religious and educational programs also could be broadcast. Commercial programming might keep inmates preoccupied and reduce the inevitable tensions that arise when large numbers of inmates are confined in a small space. Although Judge Hughes had mentioned nothing of television in her order, county officials learned that commercial television in other correctional facilities had had a positive effect, improving morale and reducing the number of altercations.[52]

Judge Hughes approved the plan as a short-term substitute for a recreational area. Later, she would look back at it with some pride: "One of the first things that we did was put in a TV. It was color TV, and a good many people on the outside objected. They said, 'We don't have color TV! Why should the prisoners have color TV?' "[53] The plan brought even more dividends than expected. She noted them in penciled comments made to herself sometime in 1974, probably during or after a jail visit: "Sick calls lessen . . . fewer violations of rules, less violence & abuse of other inmates." Another benefit was the jail officials' ability to check on the prisoners more effectively with the closed-circuit television monitors.[54] These were points she would put to good use in her speeches.

As county commissioners complained about the costs involved and reluctantly arranged for improvements and changes, Hughes willingly bore the brunt of public criticism. She understood that the commissioners were politicians who needed to satisfy their constituents. With her lifetime appointment, she had no such concerns. She paid close attention to the case, overseeing and scrutinizing progress and making occasional visits to jail. She required the commissioners court to submit regular progress reports as they improved conditions. After each report Hughes would issue an order outlining their progress and suggest the next course of action. Many of her suggestions went beyond her original 1972 order. She expressed a keen interest in offering inmates a yoga exercise program being broadcast on KERA-TV, Dallas's public television station. Medical care was improved and dental care introduced. Eyeglasses began to be provided. A pretrial release program and a night magistrate's program were initiated. Educational programs began, permitting prisoners to obtain high school equivalency degrees. When Judge Hughes attended their first graduation in 1975 the inmates gave her a standing ovation. Students from Southern Methodist University began visiting the jail to teach prisoners on a variety of topics, including laws related to custody of children and worthless checks.[55]

Still, it seemed apparent that a new jail must be built if compliance with the law was to be met. The idea of a bond issue to provide funds for a new jail arose at a June 1975 meeting between Judge Hughes and Sheriff Jones. The sheriff liked the idea, but public support would have to be won. According to notes of the meeting, both Sheriff Jones and Judge Hughes were uneasy about placing a bond issue before the voters, but they also "felt that it should be called as soon as possible because of inflation."[56]

It was not a new idea. As early as September 1970, Dallas County commissioners had considered the possibility of a new regional jail, built with federal assistance, that could serve all cities and counties of the North Texas area. The notion had gone no further than discussion. In her original June 5, 1972, court order, Judge Hughes had envisioned a new regional jail as a possible answer to the problems. Now, on June 23, 1975, following her meeting with the sheriff, Hughes told the commissioners court that a bond program to finance a new jail should be their first priority.[57]

Four months later, with the jail population continuing to grow, county commissioner David Pickett acknowledged that a new jail would have to be built. "But people aren't going to spend $50 million on a new jail right now," he said. "The average citizen doesn't give a flip about a new prison." Hughes, however, threatened to close the jail unless something was done to avoid having prisoners sleep on the floors.[58] At one point in 1976 the constantly fluctuating jail population had reached a high of 1,940. With the numbers at 1,744 in early September, jail director Tom Craig called it an emergency situation. Aside from having space for the inmates, a major problem was in hiring enough deputies to oversee them. "My men are worn out," Craig said. The situation created a breach between Sheriff Jones and the commissioners. When Jones requested funds to hire 130 additional jailers, county auditor George Smith advised the commissioners court that there was no money to pay for them. The gulf between the two parties became evident at a hearing before Judge Hughes on September 29, 1976, when the separate attorneys representing the sheriff and county commissioners chose to sit on opposite sides of the courtroom. "I do think there is a disagreement between the sheriff and commissioners court, but I'd like to see them sitting together," the judge said. They quickly complied.[59]

Even the *Dallas Morning News,* so severely critical of the judge for interfering in local affairs, noted that if the county were to adhere to accepted national standards there would be room in the Dallas County jail for only 363 prisoners.[60] An unsatisfactory effort to relieve the situation had begun in the spring of 1976 through the rehabilitation of the old Woodlawn Hospital (previously Parkland), in the nearby Oak Lawn area, as a minimum security jail for those convicted of misdemeanor crimes and as the base for a pretrial release program. But problem after problem occurred, including a protest from Adlene Harrison, the acting mayor of Dallas, who said the jail would jeopardize the revitalization of the neighborhood. Protests also arose from neighborhood homeowners' groups. By December 1976, only about thirty inmates had been housed at Woodlawn. A disappointed Hughes ordered that a hundred additional inmates serving misdemeanor offenses be put there.[61]

It was clear that at some point a new jail must be built, and it most likely would be a regional jail—that is, one that would eliminate the need for the city of Dallas to operate its temporary holding facility at the police station and would also serve all the towns in the county. An architect had completed a study of such a facility on April 7, 1975. Dallas County public works director C. Judson Shook Jr. and representatives of the city of Dallas had begun afterward to search for possible sites. By the spring of 1977 they had identified some forty possible locations. Still, the political climate for passage of a bond issue to finance such an expensive project seemed uncertain.[62]

With no end in sight to the overall problems at the jail, Hughes appointed—at Dallas County's expense—a "special master" with full authority to inspect the facilities, question prisoners and employees, and examine records. He was Charles Campbell, who had recently retired as warden of the federal correctional institution in neighboring Fort Worth. In her order and charge to Campbell, Judge Hughes expressed concern about the overcrowded condition and security of the downtown jail, the underuse of Woodlawn, activities carried on in all areas of the jail, and "little progress being made in providing expanded quarters."[63] Campbell's report, given to Hughes on April 14, 1977, included twenty-five wide-ranging recommendations as varied as jail design, training of officers and supervisors, and relations among inmates.[64]

Less than a week later, Sheriff Carl Thomas, who had been elected to succeed Clarence Jones, reported distressing news. Some inmates were still sleeping on the floor.[65]

Shortly afterward came a sudden escalation in the simmering controversy. On April 27, 1977, an impatient Hughes issued a "scorching condemnation of inaction" on the part of the Dallas County Commissioners Court. She ordered the commissioners to build a new jail and to be quick about it. They must, within two months—by July 15, 1977—select a site, sign contracts to purchase the land, and adopt a plan for both jail and court facilities. A second deadline, July 15, 1979, was issued for completion of the new building. If the commissioners failed to meet her first deadline, already rapidly approaching, she would immediately close the jail to any new inmates."[66]

The sting of her ultimatum was diminished somewhat by the further progress city and county officials had made toward a new regional jail. They had already scheduled for December 14, 1977, a bond election to build a new criminal justice center with jail, courtrooms, and related offices. Some $36 million of the $189 million bond program would be allotted to the justice center. Whether such a program would pass, though, was by no means a certainty.

That was not, as Judge Hughes explained in her order, a concern of hers. Failure of voters to endorse the bond issue would not be an excuse. "It is here pointed out," she said, "that a lack of funds is not sufficient excuse for not proceeding with constructing a new facility." Thus far, she said, there had only been talk of a new jail. "No site has been selected, nor have any plans for a facility been adopted. A date for a bond issue has been agreed on, but, so far as the court knows, little has been done to make the public aware of the county's needs." She believed the bond election had no chance of passing unless an extensive program was mounted in its behalf.[67]

Although the order to build a new jail overshadowed her other orders, Hughes included other important directives. She ordered the sheriff to increase the capacity at Woodlawn so it could accommodate from 200 to 250 inmates and to provide those inmates with at least one hour per week of outdoor exercise. Beginning on May 2, the sheriff was directed not to accept any inmates beyond the capacity of the main jail and Woodlawn. The commissioners court was directed to provide sufficient deputy sheriffs for the security of the jail and for county patrol. The sheriff was directed to furnish sufficient deputies to fully implement the exercise and closed-circuit television programs. The sheriff was directed to improve mail-handling procedures so that letters to prisoners' lawyers and the courts were not inadvertently opened. The commissioners court was ordered to expand the pretrial release program and to furnish adequate facilities for visiting between inmates and their families.[68]

Particularly interesting—and objectionable to many—was yet another requirement. Complaints about cold food had been numerous, so Judge Hughes ordered that sufficient hot food carts be obtained to serve hot meals on every floor of the jail. Later, she would chuckle about this. "Well, I admit that doesn't have much to do with the overcrowding of the jail or the way that the jails should be constructed under the statute, but it has a great deal to do with the happiness of the prisoners. You know, if you don't have anything to do, the thing you think most of is food, and if your food isn't hot, you don't like it."[69]

One inmate who wrote discovered that the judge had no intention of solving every minor irritant. He complained that because he was located far from the kitchen, the ice in his tea was melted and the tea too weak by the time it got to him. Hughes responded directly by letter to him. "Why not try coffee. I like it and you probably will, too." The direct complaints to her became so numerous she soon issued a memo telling inmates to quit writing to her. They should communicate with their attorneys, she said, for it was improper for her to respond to them.[70]

The deadline she had imposed for the new jail presented a significant problem for the county commissioners and especially for public works director Shook. Even if voters were to approve the bond election, Shook said, past experience indicated it would be at least ninety days before the funds would be available. "If that's the case this time, I would only have 16 months to design and construct a new jail. Practically speaking, it can't be done." The entire project was the most complicated thing he had ever seen. Coordination would be required with the sheriff, the bar association, the judges, the Texas Commissioner on Jail Standards, the federal court, and others. "I'd be surprised if we got it designed in a year after we get the money. I doubt if we even will get started on the design until March 1978 and probably won't finish the design until March 1979. That will leave us four months to build it, and I think it will take at least two years to build." Even if the building already were designed, Shook still did not think there would be enough time to do it.[71]

Less than a week after Hughes's order, the commissioners directed Earl Luna, the attorney they had hired to represent them, to appeal the order to the 5th Circuit. Luna prepared two separate versions for their adoption—a short one merely authorizing him to appeal the decision, and a longer one indicating that no matter what the result of their appeal, the commissioners had "no intention of slowing down the planning and the work that the County is doing on the Criminal Justice Center." Commissioners unanimously adopted the longer version since it reflected, they said, their actual plan.[72]

Less than three weeks before the July 15, 1977, deadline, the commissioners were presented with three final choices as the site for the new jail. One was a three-block downtown area immediately south of the County Government Center, a site that would be convenient to the courts and tied in with the rest of the courthouse complex. Another was just across the Trinity River at the site of the old minor league baseball stadium, where there was ample space for future enlargements. The third was a nineteen-acre site at Industrial and Commerce streets, west of the courthouse complex and separated by Dealey Plaza, a railroad track, and Stemmons Freeway. At their June 27, 1977, meeting, the commissioners selected the downtown site over the old baseball field by a divided 3-2 vote.[73]

Even with this forward step, as the July 15, 1977, deadline approached, it became apparent the commissioners could not comply with the judge's order. Accordingly, Judge Hughes shocked them and the community when she announced the jail would be closed to new inmates beginning at 1 A.M. on Friday, July 22. Consternation reigned. Four days prior to the shutdown, she met in her chambers with the sheriff, county commissioners, and the Dallas police chief. Despite their importunities, she refused to retract her order, although she said she might reconsider if the commissioners could complete the purchase of the downtown property by Friday. Realizing the impossibility of this, they asked her what they should do with new prisoners. She replied, "You all don't worry about it, just turn them loose."[74]

Her seemingly flippant comment had purpose. "I knew that would get them moving," she explained afterward.[75] To Commissioner Jim Jackson her decision was unbelievable. Commissioner Jim Tyson, who had been elected to commissioners court with the backing of labor, complained that her order might allow felons to run free on the streets.[76] Her decision, opined the *Dallas Morning News*, was "unusually harsh."[77]

A *Dallas Morning News* columnist, William Murchison, lambasted Judge Hughes for not having "confined herself to enforcing the law." His fiery column attracted a rebuttal from the president-elect of the Dallas Bar Association, Robert Thomas, who wrote that it was "the responsibility of the Bar Association to speak out when the media unfairly and unjustly attack the judges and the courts." Murchison's column, he said, was "an unjust and improper attack" on Judge Sarah T. Hughes. She had written no new laws; she had merely directed the county officials to comply with Article 5115 of the Texas Civil Statutes, Thomas pointed out. Murchison's "unfair and sarcastic article reflects a prejudice which is not in accord with either the law or the facts, and seriously damages the prospects for the passage of the forthcoming bond issue for a Criminal Justice Facility which is so badly needed for Dallas County." Stanley Marcus congratulated Thomas for his letter. "As a citizen I am most appreciative of the fact that you set the record straight. Charles O. Galvin, dean of the SMU Law School, sent a similar note of approval to Thomas for his "very well done statement."[78]

On the same day they learned of Judge Hughes's uncompromising stand, county commissioners went into an executive session with Sheriff Carl Thomas. What would they do? The immediate, temporary solution was to authorize the sheriff to enter into contracts with neighboring counties to take in overflow prisoners.[79]

The downtown site selected by the commissioners in a split 3-2 vote was not embraced by the public or by important organizations, as was patently clear at the commissioners' meeting on July 18, 1977. Dallas mayor Bob Folsom appeared before the commissioners with a unanimous resolution from City Council members opposing the site. Robert Thomas advised the commissioners that the downtown site's proximity to the courthouse was not important to lawyers. They wanted a site that could be expanded, the Commerce Street-Industrial Boulevard location. Rick Harrison, president of the Criminal Bar Association, also threw his organization's support to the Commerce-Industrial site. Afterward, the North Dallas Chamber of Commerce passed a resolution on July 20, 1977, urging the commissioners to rescind their vote and the judge to extend her deadline so a better location could be found. Judge Hughes herself also favored the Commerce-Industrial site. Acknowledging that it was not her job to select the site, Hughes observed that the smaller downtown location would make it difficult to provide the outdoor recreation areas that she had mandated and state and federal guidelines required.[80]

With these not-so-subtle nudges, the county commissioners abruptly reconsidered, switching their preferred location to Commerce and Industrial. When they were able to tell the judge this news on the eve of her 1 A.M. July 22 deadline, she was very pleased and agreed to delay her order to close the jail to new inmates until 1 A.M. Tuesday, July 26. At this time she would expect to see architectural drawings for the new jail and a "piece of paper" showing how the new site would be paid for.[81]

At their meeting on the eve of the next deadline, the commissioners satisfied the judge with the progress they had made, although problems in clearing up the title because of easements had delayed the signing of a contract. Hughes granted another reprieve, until August 7. When that deadline arrived, the contract to purchase the last section of the land had been signed. Judge Hughes lifted her order to close the jail indefinitely, repeating her warning to the commissioners that they must purchase the land regardless of whether voters approved the upcoming bond issue.[82]

The county commissioners, having been forced to act by a district judge who held all the high cards, received another blow just four days before Hughes's deadline when they learned they were to receive no help from the new Texas Commission on Jail Standards. The Texas Legislature had created the commission after the rash of lawsuits, following the lead of the Dallas case, making it clear that county jails throughout Texas were not in compliance with the state law. Sarah T. Hughes had been dubious about the commission. She could not help but wonder if it had been created simply as a means of granting variances from the requirements of Article 5115.[83]

She need not have worried. By August 1977, officials in eighty Texas counties had started or were making plans to begin construction on new county jails as a result of regulations issued by the Commission on Jail Standards. (And Dallas County by now was one of seven urban Texas counties under federal court orders because of their jails.) The Dallas County Commissioners Court had presented the Commission on Jail Standards with more than 110 requests for exemptions from Article 5115 that would permit the county to operate with the existing jail until a new one could be built. The response was not at all what they had anticipated. After a ten-hour meeting with county officials, the commission ordered them to eliminate 432 bunks, or 22.6 percent of them, from the overcrowded jail, giving them six months to do so. This would require major internal remodeling that went beyond Judge Hughes's own orders. In a comment that by now should have sounded familiar to the commissioners, the chairman of the Commission on Jail Standards, James Greenwood III of Houston, reminded them they had been aware for six years that their jail was overcrowded and still they had not complied with the law. "Before [the decision] we were in pretty good shape. Now, we're not in so good of a shape," observed county public works director C. Judson Shook Jr.[84]

The *Dallas Morning News* editorialized, "So Dallas County is now at the mercy of both a federal judge and a state agency." Earl Luna, attorney for the commissioners, said the state agency was considerably tougher than Judge Hughes on space requirements.[85]

The latest round of battles Sarah T. Hughes had fought with the Dallas County commissioners once again had put her in the national spotlight. The angle of the news stories was compelling—a feisty female judge, eighty-one years old, had stamped her foot down on some tough county politicians who normally cut their deals in back rooms. *People*, the magazine with a gigantic circulation, whose mission was to find and spotlight interesting people, published a two-page spread highlighting the judge in its September 26, 1977, issue. It included a full-page photograph of Hughes standing on her head in a yoga position. "If I could do this for half an hour a day, I'd lose all my gray hair and wrinkles," she was quoted in the caption as saying. The upside-down pressure exaggerated the lines on her face and made the veins on her arms stand out. She was old, but evidently as fit as could be. The article summarized the battle over the jail and portrayed her as a "diminutive, leathery figure awash in the somber robes of her office." Although identified as a "firm champion" of the women's movement, she was not inclined to discuss for the magazine the obstacles she had faced in her own career. "It all depends on whether you're willing to work hard enough to get what you want, not what stands in your way. I never wanted to be a *woman* lawyer. I wanted to be a lawyer." She was still driving her own car, taking bicycle rides, and swimming every day in her pool. She tolerated no talk of retirement. "I'm going to live to be 100," she vowed.[86]

The commissioners, moving with greater haste than ever, moved up the date of the bond election from December 13 to November 8. It would be the biggest bond issue ever offered by the county—$215 million. The jail proposal was found in Proposition 4, which asked voters to approve $56.7 million for a criminal justice center including a new jail, sixteen felony courtrooms, offices for the district attorney, sheriff, county clerk, law library, grand jury room, and parking lots. Proposition 5 asked for even more, $110 million for Dallas County bridge and road projects. The bond proposal also contained funds for the purchase and renovation of the old Texas School Book Depository, the building from which Lee Harvey Oswald had fired shots, to be used as a county government facility. Voters also would be asked to select an at-large candidate for the Dallas City Council and for approval of seven constitutional amendments.

Dallas County residents were advised that they would face an increase in taxes to pay for the new jail unless Proposition 4 passed. Hughes took the side of the commissioners, announcing her support of the bond issue. Meanwhile, she believed the Dallas County jail had become one of the best jails in the country, citing the closed-circuit television system, the relieving of overcrowding, an increase in the medical attention given inmates, rehabilitative programs, and the opening of the minimum security facility at Woodlawn.[87]

Even the *Dallas Morning News* enthusiastically supported the bond issue. An editorial in late September opined: "Judge Hughes has been on sound legal ground throughout the jail litigation." In October the newspaper editorialized that a "yes" for the jail proposition would be a "rededication of voters" to the principles of supporting law and order.[88]

If Hughes had appeared to many citizens as an overbearing federal judge interfering in local affairs, the Dallas County Commissioners Court was held by many to be an inept body of hack politicians who refused to move county government into the modern age. Both images caused great pessimism about voter approval of a bond issue for a new jail. One foreboding fact was that Dallas's powerful downtown business leadership—the so-called oligarchy represented by the unofficial Citizens Council—had declined to put its muscle or money behind the bond issue. A prominent attorney who had successfully chaired the city of Dallas's $149 million bond program two years earlier turned down a request to head the county bond program. Instead, a Republican businessman, Russell Perry, and the Democratic attorney for commissioners court, Earl Luna, were named codirectors of the drive. Only $30,000 was raised to sell the program instead of the $150,000 some had predicted would be needed.[89]

Realizing the difficulties before them and painfully aware of the necessity of voter approval, the four county commissioners—Roy Orr, Jim Tyson, Jim Jackson, and David Pickett—and county judge John Whittington (who by now had replaced the retired Sterrett), public works director C. Judson Shook, campaign treasurer Rudy Day, and co-campaign directors Perry and Luna began a hectic round of speech-making. Each made up to six talks a day before service clubs, school groups, churches, political organizations, and employee groups. "I never campaigned as hard for myself as I did this bond program," said Commissioner Tyson.[90]

They emphasized three themes: (1) Voting for the bond propositions should not be construed as a vote for or against the commissioners court.

(2) Judge Hughes had been following the law in her decisions in the jail case and had cooperated with the commissioners court. And (3), the question was not whether a new jail would be built but whether it would be financed through long-term bonds or a huge tax increase.[91]

The surprising result on election day, November 8, was approval of Proposition 4 by a two-to-one margin. More than seventy thousand voters had cast ballots, and they gave a larger margin of approval to the new jail than to Proposition 5 (for roads and bridges). Having been rejected by the city's establishment, which traditionally had played such important roles in winning voter support of bond programs, the county officials had concentrated their campaign on what they called the little people. The *Dallas Morning News* story summarized Commissioners Orr and Jackson's description of the victory as one in which the voters said they did not want a "few people in a smoke-filled room downtown controlling county government."[92]

A month later, seeing early plans for the new jail, Judge Sarah T. Hughes was generally pleased. As the *Times Herald* observed, "The quiet, agreeable voices in Judge Hughes' courtroom are music to our tired ears."[93] Still, she was not ready to let loose. In a new order issued immediately afterward she complained that exercise areas still had not been provided in the present jail despite a previous order requiring the remodeling of Woodlawn to accommodate women and thereby create room for an exercise area in the main jail.[94]

Six months later, upon seeing more complete plans at the county architect's office for the new county jail, Sarah T. Hughes again was pleased. "This is probably the happiest I've ever seen Judge Hughes over what we're doing with the new jail and you know there have been times when she was not very happy," said Earl Luna. The plans included an outside recreation area.[95]

In March 1979 the judge took a noon break from a criminal fraud trial to have lunch with inmates at the Woodlawn Minimum Security Jail. Pleased with what she found, on her return she could not resist telling the jury about the fine menu from which prisoners had a choice of fish, chicken, or stew as their entrées. She glowed with approval, too, over the inmates' garden and the onions that already were growing. Because of her characterization of the jail as a pleasant place to be, irate defense attorneys requested a mistrial. Judge Hughes promptly denied the request. "I don't think anybody would get the idea that it's that nice," she said.[96]

● ● ● ● ●

Throughout the seven years of the jail case, county commissioners had appealed many of the judge's orders. Decisions by the 5th Circuit took as long as two years or more. With few exceptions, Hughes's orders had been upheld, and the U.S. Supreme Court had refused to review the appeals. Particularly important had been her May 1977 order requiring the Dallas County Commissioners Court to build a new jail. That order, too, had been appealed. During its pendency, commissioners had bought land for the new jail and criminal court center, voters had approved a bond issue, and workers had begun digging the foundation for the new ten-story jail at Industrial and Commerce.

On August 16, 1979, the 5th Circuit finally rendered a decision concerning Hughes's order concerning a new jail. According to the court's opinion, she had exceeded her authority. Her directive to build a jail had gone beyond the scope of her original 1972 order to bring it into compliance with state regulations. The appeals court used careful language in its reversal, coupling it with praise of Sarah T. Hughes for the work she had done. "The District Judge deserves the commendation of this court and of the Dallas Community for her vigilance in ensuring that the county obey her 1977 judgment. We are convinced, however, that the district court's role in the process of improving Dallas Jails is now complete." In short, the judge must now relinquish her authority over the case.[97]

Perhaps surprisingly, there were no shouts of glee in Dallas when this decision was rendered. Nor were there complaints from Judge Hughes. No parties expressed any regret over the current construction of a new jail. Work on it would continue. "This does not change our obligations to furnish jail facilities, and we will proceed to build a new jail," said new Dallas County judge Garry Weber. The *Dallas Morning News* published an editorial: "With completion of the new facility, Dallas County will have one of the best jails in the nation. If that goal is reached, much of the credit must be given to Judge Hughes."[98]

C. Judson Shook, county public works director, said: "Probably what a lot of people have not perceived is that Judge Hughes and the county had evolved into a working team. We are going to miss her counsel on this business. It's like we will be missing our coach. But as far as the game, it will go on just like it always has."[99]

Interviewed just after the Appeals Court decision, Hughes said she had no objections to the ruling, but she would miss dealing with the case. "I enjoyed it," she said. "I did a great deal of work on the jail, and I had hoped to do more." She had done, she said, as much as she could under the circumstances.[100]

A week after the appeals court decision, Hughes was interviewed by a professor at North Texas State University to add a final chapter to the ongoing oral history with her that had begun in 1969. Hughes viewed the appeals court decision with equanimity. She looked back with pride on *Taylor v. Sterrett* as the most important case that she had tried. Under her jurisdiction the jail had become, she believed, "one of the best jails in the whole United States." In the beginning, she said, the commissioners court, and especially Judge Sterrett, had been angry and had attempted to ignore her. "But over the years," she said, "they have become quite cooperative, and finally I would say they were willing to cooperate in everything." They were guilty, finally, only of procrastination. "Unless you require your own children to do things, even though they know they might get a whipping, they will procrastinate and not do them. Well, that's the same way with the commissioners and the sheriff. They need a little pushing now, and that's what I was doing with them."[101]

Three years later on December 10, 1982, in a public ceremony, the new facility was opened as "the first jail in this area to comply fully with authorized jail standards." It had been designed for "maximum ease of operation, visibility of prisoners, and safety." The jail contained no steel bars—bulletproof glass was used for security. Each of the nine inmate floors contained twelve eight-cell units built around a recreation area. Visitation rooms on each floor eliminated security problems associated with moving prisoners to other floors for visitation. A fully equipped infirmary virtually eliminated the need to transport prisoners to the public hospital for treatment. The dedicatory program, distributed to all in attendance, echoed words that might have come from Hughes, but did not.

> Modern penology experts now know that if a jail is to work effectively it must not only provide for the best possible security but must also help prevent problems associated with detention of prisoners. Recreation facilities, for instance, greatly reduce the possibilities of prisoner fighting or rioting. In addition, they provide an acceptable, workable method of rewarding good behavior and punishing bad. Far from coddling prisoners, such activities as sports, games and television help control prisoners and improve the chances of successful rehabilitation.[102]

Two ironies marked the occasion. The name of the federal judge who had used her power to force construction of the modern facility in the face of widespread dissent was omitted from the program. Perhaps even more ironic, county commissioners named their new building the W. L. (Lew) Sterrett Justice Center, in honor of the long-time county judge who had so much opposed the federal judge's efforts to create a modern Dallas County jail.

Seven years later a handsome new eleven-story criminal courts building was completed next door to the new jail. It contained all the criminal courts in Dallas and offices for the sheriff's department, district attorney, and other county agencies. It was named the Crowley Criminal Courts Building, in honor of a later county judge, Frank Crowley.

To most everyone in Dallas, though, the new jail and the criminal courts building were recognized as the handiwork of one person—U.S. district judge Sarah T. Hughes. At one of her birthdays, a framed picture of the jail was playfully presented to the judge by her courtroom staff. Across the building they had added a mock sign: HUGHES HILTON.[103]

14

A Life Fulfilled

At the midpoint of the jail case, on August 4, 1975, two days after her seventy-ninth birthday and while she was on vacation in Norway, the *Dallas Times Herald* published on its front page a surprising banner headline: "Sarah T. Hughes retires as federal judge." The story, written by federal courthouse reporter Ruth Eyre, correctly stated that Hughes had requested and received "senior status," effective that day. To the layperson, as well as to the headline writer, this sounded very much like retiring. This status did not mean, however—and certainly in Hughes's case it did not mean—that she was ending her career as a federal judge. Senior status, awarded after years of service, would permit her to select the cases she wanted to hear. In requesting senior status, she had written, "I will retain and try all the cases presently on my docket, and will from time to time take additional hearings and trials." This would be true in the future as she maintained her busy schedule, concentrating solely on the criminal docket and continuing to hold jurisdiction over the jail case.[1]

Perhaps most important, Hughes's assumption of senior status meant that a new federal judge would be appointed to the Northern District of Texas. This would bring much-needed assistance to the beleaguered federal judges, whose case loads were becoming increasingly clogged. Besides Judge Hughes and William (Mac) Taylor Jr., who was the presiding judge of the Northern District, the Dallas area had three other district judges, Robert Hill, Robert Porter, and Joe Estes, who already had taken senior status. The logjam was such that Taylor had requested in July three new federal judges for the Northern District. The prospect of getting at least one additional judge, according to Taylor, was one of the primary reasons Hughes had taken senior status.[2]

Hughes was vacationing in Norway at the time her request was granted. "I'm very interested to see what happens and the publicity," she wrote to Gwen Graul on August 5. When she learned the emphasis in news stories had been on her "retirement," she wrote again to Gwen: "Really, it doesn't surprise me that people think I've retired. After all, there are no businesses or professions that I know of where you can take senior status."[3]

Gerald Ford's occupancy of the White House had given Hughes pause before she requested senior status, for Ford, a Republican, would be responsible for filling the opening. He undoubtedly would select a Republican. Hughes, according to a speculative news story in the *Dallas Morning News* without named sources, had considered this carefully. The writer, Carl Freund, said Hughes let it be known she would take senior status only if the individual nominated to succeed her was satisfactory. The individual with the inside track for appointment, according to Freund, was Patrick Higginbotham, a remarkably youthful thirty-seven-year-old who recently had been appointed a special federal prosecutor in a high-profile case involving an Austin lobbyist. Other possibilities included the U.S. attorney for the Northern District, Frank McCown, who lived in Fort Worth, Bill Hamilton of Dallas, and Richard Lee Brown, also of Fort Worth.[4]

Despite Freund's story, as evidenced in a letter to Graul, Hughes had no assurances about whom Republican senator John Tower of Texas would recommend. Having learned from Graul of the several candidates mentioned in the story, Hughes asked Graul which of them she would prefer. Then the judge answered her own question. She was "not too crazy" about McCown. "Actually, none sound too good to me," she said.[5]

Higginbotham was nominated for the judgeship, and when he took office later in 1975 he became the youngest federal judge in the nation. In 1982 President Ronald Reagan would appoint him to the U.S. Court of Appeals, 5th Circuit.

A year later Hughes told reporters she had no intention of ever retiring. She had always been unusually active, whether playing on the basketball team at Goucher or riding horseback or square dancing or swimming or doing yoga. Now, as questions about her possible retirement occasionally surfaced, she redoubled her efforts at staying physically fit. At the age of eighty she was swimming thirty laps each evening in her pool.[6] No longer did she walk up the stairs to her courtroom, but that was because her courtroom was now on the sixteenth floor of the new Earle Cabell Federal Building instead of the third floor of the old post office and courts building.

Hughes was, according to a writer who interviewed her after her she had turned eighty, "one of those special people who has somehow moved beyond biological time." Her back was "as straight as a dancer's, her eyes are clear, and her voice has a strength that reaches out to seize her listener." Yet, there was no denying the years: "The lines on her face are a part of her beauty—like a piece of fine sculpture chiseled from the strongest stone."[7]

Anne Snider, a grade-school girl who had lived next door to the famous judge all her life, wrote a paper about her neighbor in 1973 as a school assignment. "On some weekend mornings she and I go bike-riding. Occasionally in the summer she lets my family and me go swimming in her pool." She described her neighbor as a woman with "short brownish grey hair" who wore glasses and was small. The judge usually wore pants at home, but when she went to work she "wears a nice dress."[8]

Routine had become Hughes's watchword. A college student who delivered the *Dallas Morning News* to her recalled years later that in the summer of 1970 the judge waited at her door early each morning to greet him and say a kind word before getting on her bicycle for a ride around the nearby Highland Park High School.[9] In 1976 a reporter who interviewed her reported this schedule: She arose each morning at 6:15 A.M. and read the *Dallas Morning News*. Ten minutes of yoga followed, and then came thirty minutes' study of Spanish. By now her part-time maid would have arrived. The maid's first duty was to prepare for the judge a breakfast of one egg, toast, tea, and fruit. For dinner the menu was almost as predictable: meat or fish, two vegetables, and a salad. Exercise and diet—those were the keys to her vitality, the judge believed, and this was why she was able to try just as many cases as she always had, even after having taken senior status in 1975. The den in which Hughes spent most of her time at home was filled with large plants. It looked out on the swimming pool, behind which she kept a small garden with onions, tomatoes, asparagus, and other vegetables.[10]

On three occasions during the 1970s Hughes consented to have her handwriting analyzed. The first time, in 1974, was in response to a request by an Irving, Texas, graphologist, who intended to publish the results in a trade journal. Knowing who her subject was simplified her analysis, but some of her comments were insightful.

> Possibly her willingness to become acquainted with all kinds of people, to become involved with all kinds of situations, to relish all kinds of experiences may be her way of trying to be more fair, as though she says to herself, "Who am I to judge if I don't know first-hand what life's all about, if I don't go there and observe the sights, sounds, smells, flavors, 'vibrations' or life in the raw?"[11]

Four years later two other graphologists, one from Cheyenne, Wyoming, and another from the Dallas suburb of Richardson, did analyses. "She is very decisive and will rarely change her mind," the Cheyenne graphologist, wrote. "Strong willed, determined and mildly pugnacious."[12]

Hughes, always disdainful of extravagance, never had been overly concerned about making money. The required reports she filed throughout the 1970s concerning extrajudicial income listed no remuneration for any extrajudicial work such as writing, lecturing, or teaching. Her salary as a judge, raised to $40,000 annually beginning in 1970, was augmented that year with $13,426 from investments, pensions, and interest-bearing accounts (the majority of which, $10,000, came from her Texas State Retirement program). This income was more than sufficient for her needs, giving her plenty of resources for extensive international travel and regular contributions to charities. A regular recipient of her largesse was a scholarship fund for Southern Methodist University Law School. She often stated a preference that scholarships awarded from her contributions be based on both merit and financial need. "I would prefer that it be a woman student that is intelligent and has need for money," she advised Dean A. J. Thomas in 1980 when she sent her a thousand-dollar check. It was the same admonition she had given a year earlier when she had sent another thousand-dollar check for the fund.[13]

A law clerk who worked with her in 1980 and 1981, Joanne Hurtekant, was privy to her checking account. "She had no financial sense, as far as I could tell," Hurtekant later said. She kept a ridiculously high balance in her checking account and had no time for figuring out how her money could work for her. Hughes knew that her salary and state retirement funds were more than enough to take care of all her needs, and she didn't worry about the rest. She was, in Hurtekant's opinion, a soft touch for charities.[14]

Special honors continued to be a regular part of Hughes's life. In 1975, in the midst of the jail case that was earning her so many detractors, she was given an award for distinguished professional leadership and service to the Dallas community, and in the following year the Women's Center of Dallas nominated her for the Rockefeller Public Service Award, citing in detail the work she had done to reform the Dallas County jail.[15]

The issue that Hughes had campaigned so fervently for throughout her life but that had failed to capture the public's attention—women's rights—by the 1970s had become one of the liveliest topics in the national dialogue. Hughes was no less interested in the subject than ever, but women with far more strident voices and a flair for publicity now dominated public discussions.

Although these voices captured headlines and generated followers, the most meaningful advances benefiting women came from changing the law. Hughes's good friend and colleague, Louise B. Raggio, had become one of the most powerful forces in the state for effecting such changes. Raggio's service as chairwoman of the Family Law Section of the State Bar of Texas from 1965 to 1967 and her leadership of the Drafting Committee for the Family Code from 1966 to 1975 were especially meaningful in this regard.

"We used to say if you're a minor, a mentally incompetent person, a felon, or a married woman, you have no rights in Texas," Raggio later joked. Her first step toward correcting this state of affairs came in 1967, when the legislature adopted her handiwork, the Texas Marital Property Act. This act at last gave married women in Texas the right to conduct business and control property in their own name without having to gain the consent of their husbands. Some said it brought Texas into the twentieth century.[16]

Next, as chairwoman of the state bar's Family Code Committee, Raggio spearheaded an overhaul of the family code statutes, pulling together and streamlining various state statutes concerning marriage, custody, family, adoption, and divorce. Contradictory or antiquated statutes were eliminated. The achievement was hailed as the first unified domestic relations law code in the world, standing as a model for many others. According to Raggio it would not have been successful without a grant of seventeen thousand dollars for funding from the Hoblitzelle Foundation in Dallas, for which Sarah T. Hughes, a member of the foundation's board, was largely responsible.[17]

When the Texas Legislature enacted the comprehensive legislation in entirety, Raggio rushed to tell the news to her mentor, Hughes. "When I told her, she couldn't believe it," Raggio remembered. "She said, 'No, you must be mistaken. Those kind of changes will take many, many years.'"[18] Hughes's incredulity was understandable. She had worked for two decades on such a seemingly simple matter as permitting women to serve as jurors.

Raggio's own distinguished career would take her to other prominent positions, including service as chairwoman of the Family Law Section of the American Bar Association and election in 1979 as the first female director of the State Bar of Texas in its hundred-year history. Numerous other honors followed, including election to the Texas Women's Hall of Fame.

Another colleague of Hughes's, although not such a close friend, also gained acclaim in the decade of the 1970s for her work in advancing the rights of women. This was Hermine Tobolowsky, an attorney who like Hughes had become deeply involved with the Texas Federation of Business and Professional Women's Clubs. Their difference in opinion concerning B&PW political endorsements was overshadowed by their joint commitment to the women's movement. In 1957 Tobolowsky had gone to Austin on behalf of the Texas B&PW to lobby for a bill that would permit married women to control property separately from their husbands. Unsuccessful and angered by the negative, amused reactions of some of the lawmakers, she vowed to win its ultimate passage. She and several other B&PW women stumped the state on its behalf, and beginning in 1959 she and the organization were able to get more comprehensive legislation introduced in the legislature as the Texas Equal Legal Rights Amendment. Year after year the amendment failed legislative approval, but finally in 1971, four years after Raggio's new Marital Property Act had been adopted, the measure was approved by the legislature and presented to voters. Ratification by the state's voters came in November 1972 after an intensive campaign by the Texas B&PW and other organizations. The amendment was a worthy complement to Raggio's work in rewriting the Family Code. Tobolowsky would become known as the mother of the Texas Equal Rights Amendment.[19]

Hughes's participation in these crusades was limited because of her federal judgeship, but she continued to support the movement as she could. When an unsuccessful movement arose to rescind Texas's own ratification of the Twenty-seventh Amendment, the Equal Rights Amendment to the U.S. Constitution, she wrote countless letters to the state's politicians.[20] Her commitment to encouraging female attorneys seemed boundless. She continued her practice of maintaining a typewritten list of all the women lawyers in Dallas. By October 1973 she had the names of 160 women attorneys, almost twice the number appearing on her previous undated list. She encouraged women to strive for elective or appointive offices. Invariably, those who were elected or appointed to public office received congratulatory letters and encouragement from her. When Charlye O. Farris, who twenty years earlier had been the first African American woman in Texas to pass the bar exam, was appointed a special district judge in Wichita County in 1973, Hughes sent her a congratulatory letter with a challenge. "This is a beginning, but I certainly hope your career will not end there. Remember my desire for you to go into politics and you can make it if you make up your mind to do so."[21]

It was customary for Hughes to work behind the scenes for promising women. She prevailed upon Brooks Hays to recommend SMU economics professor Barbara B. Reagan to President Jimmy Carter as regional director of the Dallas Office of Health, Education and Welfare. In his ensuing letter to the president, Hays said he was inspired to make the nomination "by a phone call from Judge Sarah T. Hughes of Dallas, one of my classmates in the Law School of George Washington University." Reagan, though, did not get the nomination.[22]

The new and aggressive Texas Women's Political Caucus, the organization founded in 1971 in Austin, had captured the spotlight from the Texas B&PW as the organization most responsible for pushing women's rights. Its members, who now referred to themselves as feminists, were mindful and appreciative of Hughes's pioneer work and her continued presence as a force in the movement. Hughes served on the organization's 1975-76 advisory committee. Sarah Weddington, upon whom Hughes was pinning much hope for future political leadership, was named in 1973 by the organization as its first annual Woman of the Year. By 1979 Weddington was working in the White House as special assistant to President Jimmy Carter. Hughes believed that upon Weddington's return to Texas she would in all probability run for some major office.[23]

Another of Hughes's young political protégés was Regina Montoya, who served as the judge's law clerk from June 1979 to August 1980. She took Montoya to Democratic luncheons in downtown hotels, introduced her to politicians, and encouraged her to run for office, which she later did. It seemed to Montoya, who followed Hughes's advice and began a career in Democratic politics, that the judge was acting on a deep conviction that she had an obligation to ensure that women continued to seek election to public office.[24]

Goucher College remained one of Hughes's primary concerns. The college moved in 1954 from the central Baltimore site, so familiar to Hughes, to a scenic 287-acre campus in suburban Towson, on the north side of the city. Hughes's anger over the failure of an all-women's institution to have a female president ended in 1973 when President Marvin M. Perry Jr. resigned. Rhoda Dorsey, an American history professor who began her career at Goucher as an instructor and had become vice president in 1968, was named acting president. Hughes immediately launched a letter-writing campaign to remove the word *acting* from Dorsey's title. She sent letters to Goucher's chairman of the board and to every member of the search committee urging Dorsey's selection as permanent president. To Dorsey, she wrote: "It is my fervent hope that you will be selected for permanent appointment." A year later, in April 1974, Dorsey was named the first woman president at Goucher in its eighty-eight-year history.[25]

With Dorsey as president, Hughes's ties to Goucher grew even closer and her financial contributions more significant. In 1978 she substantially increased her annual gift, pledging twenty-five thousand dollars, directed to the Field Political Center, destined later to be the primary beneficiary of Hughes's estate and named in her honor as the Sarah T. Hughes Field Political Center.* Founded in the 1950s, the center sought to facilitate student exposure to and involvement in governmental and political affairs in the Baltimore and Washington, D.C., areas. In the fall of 1980 Hughes assumed for Goucher the leadership of the alumni fund-raising drive. Remembering her major in biology, that year she pledged twenty-five thousand dollars for a biology lab.[26]

"It has been demonstrated once again that your impact on Goucher never ceases," the college's vice president for development, Patricia P. Purcell, wrote to Hughes in January 1980. The official had just received a letter from a woman notifying Goucher that she had added the college to her will. A letter this benefactor had received from Hughes in 1963, when Hughes had headed Goucher's bequest campaign, had prompted her action. It was amazing, Purcell told Hughes.[27]

In the spring of 1979 Goucher's senior class voted to ask Hughes to be their commencement speaker. "This is something I have wanted for years," she told the college president when informed of her selection. She would not accept an honorarium.[28]

Her speech on May 27, 1979, to the 208 graduates was, Dorsey told her afterward, "everything I hoped it would be . . . energetic, clear, candid and inspiring." And it seemed to be even more meaningful to Dorsey. "I want to say how much I valued your seasoned advice which was as helpful to me as it could be to the youngest of the undergraduates. People in responsibility need to hear plain talking; it is a help and also a consolation and so your words were to me."[29]

For the next graduation, 1980, Hughes recommended the person who was looming so high on her personal list of outstanding women—Sarah

---

* Hughes bequeathed her house on Normandy Avenue to the Department of Political Science. The value of the house when the will was filed on December 29, 1987, was $681,500.

Weddington. Dorsey agreed right away and extended a formal invitation to Weddington at her office at the White House. Weddington, however, was already booked to speak at another graduation exercise in North Carolina and had to decline.[30]

In the same year Hughes spoke at Goucher, the Baltimore Public Schools gave her a signal honor. She was selected as one of the all-time top sixty graduates of the school system. The honor placed her in the company of some other accomplished Baltimoreans, including H. L. Mencken, Thurgood Marshall, Stuart Symington, Mildred Dunnock (a fellow graduate with Hughes of Western High School), Al Kaline, Russell Baker, and Garry Moore.[31]

Besides her interest in Goucher, Hughes continued to remember her ties to the George Washington University School of Law. In 1975 she served as president of the North Texas Alumni of GWU. One special event of the year was a dinner to honor her fellow graduate Brooks Hays, held at the home of another GWU graduate and friend of Hughes's, Mike McKool.[32]

Sarah T. Hughes enjoyed near-legendary status. She was famous for her tough-mindedness, and stories circulated in legal circles showing her uniqueness or sometimes her idiosyncrasies as a judge. Perhaps the story most often repeated came from her court reporter from 1977 into 1980, Carl Black Sr.:

Judge Hughes was sentencing a man one day for stealing a truckload of chickens. She asked him why he stole the chickens in the first place. He said, "Your Honor, I kept them at my home all weekend before I decided to steal them." Whereupon the Judge began to scold him about keeping those poor chickens on the truck at his house all weekend without food and water. The man said, "Your Honor—" Judge Hughes told the man to be quiet until she had finished. He interrupted her a couple of more times and got the same reply. "Young man, be quiet until I finish and then I will let you speak." She went on and on about how cruel it was to keep the chickens all weekend on the truck. She remarked that she had seen chicken trucks with crates stacked high and it was cruel enough on the highway, but to let them set all weekend stationary was a very cruel thing to do. After she had finished, she said, "Young man, what did you wish to say to me?" The defendant replied, "Judge, I was just trying to tell you the chickens were frozen."[33]

In the late 1970s a woman defendant appeared before the judge for sentencing. Part of her problem, the judge seemed to believe, was the difficulty she faced in providing for her several children. Hughes told the woman one of the conditions of the probation she was granting her was that she not have any more children. As they walked out of the courtroom, Black noticed the judge grinning and asked her why. "Carl," she said, "you know I can't make that a condition of her probation, but she doesn't know it."[34]

Defendants often would tell the judge before sentencing that they now had found God in their lives. The judge sometimes would ask those who made such claims whether they truly had found God or were just saying that in hopes that she would give them a lighter sentence. Sometimes in sentencing she would quote the Bible herself, and occasionally she would call on her marshal, Norman Parker, to cite an appropriate verse. When a tax protestor appeared before her on one occasion, for instance, she turned to Parker and asked him to quote the verse in the Bible about rendering unto Caesar what was Caesar's.[35]

The judge's interest in politics was undiminished throughout her life, as was her partisanship, but on one occasion the partisanship faltered. A few days before a general election in the late 1970s, she came into her court reporter's office and said, "Carl, I am going to do something I have never done before. I am going to vote for a Republican." Black realized she must be talking about her neighbor, Jack Hampton, a candidate for a district judgeship. "Judge, are you going to vote for Jack?" he asked. She replied, "Yes, but he is a good boy."[36]

Hughes continued to miss politics, as she affirmed in a note to Ralph Yarborough in 1974. "I love politics & only drawback about being a fed judge is that I'm not supposed to participate. Even now I would enjoy the campaign trail." She urged Yarborough, who had lost to Lloyd Bentsen Jr. in the 1970 Democratic primary, to continue to be active. "You have been a leader so long of the liberals in Texas & all look to you for guidance & leadership."[37]

She was especially pleased in 1979 when President Jimmy Carter appointed Barefoot Sanders, her long-time friend and Democratic political ally, to join her as a federal judge in the Northern District of Texas. On many occasions Hughes had said that if she had had a son it would have been Sanders. Hughes and Sanders once more became close working associates, this time in the new Earle Cabell Federal Building rather than the old post office and courthouse building. Sanders, after leaving the White House as legislative counsel to President Johnson, had been in private practice as a partner with the politically powerful Dallas firm of Clark, West, Keller, Sanders and Butler.

Although Hughes normally was gracious and thoughtful, sometimes she seemed unaware that her tendency toward plain speaking might seem abrasive. In a casual moment with one of her favorite probation officers, Dennis Shaw, she said, "Dennis, do you know you use the worst grammar I ever heard?" Shaw was taken aback for only a moment. He replied, "Judge, did you understand what I was saying?" She acknowledged she had. "Isn't that all that matters?" he asked. "I didn't let 'em run over me," he said years later in relating the incident.[38]

On another occasion, when conducting a criminal trial, she called a recess for a half day because Bill Sanderson, the assistant U.S. attorney, went to the hospital to be with his wife for the birth of their baby. He returned for the afternoon session, and as the proceedings began Hughes asked about his wife and baby. What name had they given their child? "Lisa," Sanderson replied. The judge quickly responded. "Oh, good. I have a dog named Lisa." Her comment was greeted with total silence in the courtroom. Hughes, noting the awkwardness of the moment, quickly added, "I love my dog."[39]

Inevitably, Hughes had one or two small dogs as favorite household pets. When speaking to them, she referred to herself as "Momsie." When she was away on vacation she sometimes would send postcards addressed to her dogs.[40]

When Hughes's niece, Constance, and her husband, Ken Youngs, once met her at the San Francisco airport to drive her from one terminal to another, they brought along their one-year-old son, David, of whom they were inordinately proud and whom Hughes had never seen. They also brought their Chihuahua dog. Hughes commented approvingly on how well-behaved their dog was, but said nothing about their baby.[41]

On other occasions Hughes could show unusual sensitivity. Carl Black remembered her as a wonderful employer who spoke harshly to him only once. He had asked her a couple of times without a definite answer whether court would be in session on the day he hoped to attend a court reporters' convention in Seattle. Finally he asked her, "May I go?" She replied sharply, "Yes, you can." Next morning Black heard a tap on his office door. "She came in and sat there and she said, 'Carl, I want to ask you to forgive me for the way I talked to you yesterday. I didn't mean to be harsh.'"

Later that day, Gwen Graul asked Black if she had apologized. "I told her to," Graul said.[42]

Her thoughts these days about national affairs were reflected in a questionnaire she filled out for *U.S. News & World Report's* seventh annual survey of national leadership. She listed the major issues ahead of the nation in the 1980s as (not in order) energy development, environmental protection, unemployment, the curbing of nuclear weapons, relations with Third World countries, world population growth, energy conservation, health cost controls, the future of Social Security, ethics in politics, rights for women and minorities, violent crime, government growth and spending, containment of the Soviet Union, and avoiding war. Her choices for the most influential citizens in national decision-making were, in order, President Jimmy Carter, Paul Volcker (chairman of the Federal Reserve Board), Warren E. Burger, Rosalynn Carter, and Katharine Graham. She ranked President Jimmy Carter as best candidate for the upcoming presidential election. She considered Senator Edward M. Kennedy and California governor Edmund G. Brown Jr. to be mediocre possibilities.[43]

In this age of rising crime rates, Hughes had developed a pessimistic outlook on what lay ahead. In a Sunday magazine newspaper supplement under the headline, "Judge Sarah T. Hughes on Crime and Justice: A Supercity under Siege," her plain statement, "I am afraid to walk outside at night alone," was emphasized. She believed the year 2000, twenty years away, would be a "twenty-first century mess" if trends continued. "Today, I am afraid to walk outside. In twenty years I wouldn't dream of it." She predicted crime in the streets, the homes, the highways, and in every place where Dallasites—and presumably all urban residents in metropolitan cities—would dwell in large numbers. "The larger a city gets and the more crowded it is, the more crimes are committed. And Dallas is going to get bigger and bigger. I think that narcotics will have increased, as well as white-collar crimes, embezzlement and the failure to pay income tax. Also, the kidnapping of children, and even of older people, and continued raping and killing as well."[44]

Her own theory of how police should operate, she said, differed from that of most people. "I think that the police shoot too quickly. In England, for instance, they don't even carry a gun. And when I was a policewoman in

Washington, we didn't carry guns. Here, they draw their guns at the least provocation."[45]

If guns were not banned by the year 2000, she believed Dallas residents would be more widely armed, and murders would increase drastically. This would be especially true in the home environment if family life continued to be eroded by divorce and family problems. "When I was a child, I thought it was awful to have a divorce. Now there are almost as many divorces in Dallas County as there are marriages."[46]

Judge Hughes's reputation for being unusually harsh with white-collar criminal defendants had become widely acknowledged. It stood in distinct contrast to her alleged softness with less ordinary criminals, a belief emphasized by her apparent sympathy for inmates in the county jail. Since taking senior status in 1975, the judge had heard virtually nothing but criminal cases. Consequently, most people in the jurisdiction who failed to file income tax returns were being tried in her court. As the presiding judge over many tax protestor cases, Hughes became a target of their ire. In 1978 a Dallas draftsman whom she had sentenced to a year in prison for failure to pay his income tax filed suit against her in her old 14th District Court asking twenty-five thousand dollars in actual damages and ten thousand in punitive damages. She had violated, it alleged, his common law right to a jury trial and his right to be heard by an impartial judge. The unsuccessful suit was followed a week later by similarly failed suits by two other individuals.[47]

In November 1979 a married couple from Richardson, Texas, was tried in Hughes's court for willfully failing to file income tax returns for 1974, 1975, and 1976. During their lengthy trial—conducted with considerable displays of emotion on the part of the defendants and their attorneys—the courtroom was packed with tax protest sympathizers, evidently monitoring the trial to record evidence of unfairness by Judge Hughes. Concurrently, a support group called the Ad Hoc Committee to Investigate the Federal Grand Jury initiated a petition to have Hughes removed from office by impeachment because she was "biased and prejudiced" in tax cases.[48]

During the first week of the trial U.S. marshal Clint Peoples revealed that death threats against Hughes had been anonymously circulated. As a precaution, three deputy marshals were assigned to her courtroom rather than the customary one. The U.S. attorney's office began an investigation into the possibility that the threats were related to the criminal trials for tax evaders in Hughes's court and the impeachment petition. The founder of the Ad Hoc Committee to Investigate the Federal Grand Jury denied any responsibility for the threats. The judge herself had not known of the threats until Peoples informed her, and she scoffed at the notion that she was in any kind of danger. The source of the threats was never learned, and the impeachment effort against her died aborning.[49]

One of the things that gave Hughes most satisfaction was foreign travel. She had taken her first trips to Great Britain, Germany, Eastern Europe, and South America to attend conferences on government-sponsored programs. Now she traveled for pleasure, and advancing years failed to diminish her enjoyment or her rigorous routine. On a return to Norway in August 1975, she was pleased to find that her customary hotel had built an indoor swimming pool. On her first full day there the seventy-nine-year-old jurist swam before breakfast, walked for two-and-a-half hours after breakfast, and went swimming again in the afternoon. "I really feel like a different person," she wrote to Graul. A week later she had increased her walking to four-and-a-half hours, which she found to be "really too far."[50]

Her most ambitious trip came at the end of 1975, when she traveled with Jennelle Moorhead to the South Pacific, her second trip there. Moorhead had organized many of Hughes's previous trips in her capacity with the University of Portland's Continuing Education Program, including the earlier visit to the South Pacific, but this time the two of them went alone. The itinerary for their trip, which began in mid-November 1975 and lasted until January 6, 1976, centered at first on the islands of French Polynesia—Bora Bora, Papeete, Rarotonga, and others—the Samoan Islands, and Australia. The judge seemed to enjoy meeting and interacting with the natives, even attending church services on one of the islands where the "toothless, barefooted & tieless" preacher spoke no English.[51]

The first part of the 1975-76 tour was a two-week stay at the adult-oriented Club Med facility at Moorea. "Here we are at Club Med settled in a thatched roof cottage with comfortable bed & a well equipped bathroom," she wrote to Graul. The atmosphere was completely informal, with most people wearing swimming suits throughout the day, and the food was rich and plentiful. "There are sports galore—tennis, jogging, yoga, snorkeling, scuba diving, picnic[k]ing, sailing, trips to islands, a glass-bottom boat trip, etc. etc." Yoga exercises were conducted each day at 7:30 A.M. and 5 P.M., and the judge was an eager participant. She also took snorkeling lessons.[52]

Her traveling companion and roommate, Moorhead, proved at first to be especially compatible. "Jennelle spoils me like you do & I love it," Hughes wrote to Graul. "Fixes coffee in the morning, drinks at night, tea during the day & any meal we have in the room. Isn't that luxury for me?"[53] Two weeks later, though, she was beginning to tire of Jennelle's more sedentary nature. "I wish someone was here that I could do things with. Jennelle neither swims, snorkels, or likes to go out in the canoe, nor does she like horse races," Hughes wrote. What Jennelle liked to do was walk on the beach and hunt for shells. "Another thing [,] I have never seen so much stuff as Jennelle brings with her. If you don't have something, pills for all kinds of ailments & I've needed some of them to jewelry & anything else you could think of. She also collects—bags, paper clips, coat hangers she finds, plastic sacks, etc." Besides all that, her suitcases were too big, said Hughes, who prided herself on her ability to travel with the barest of essentials.[54]

Her complaints were short-lived and probably not intimated in any way to Moorhead. The two were compatible for the remainder of the trip, and it would not be the last vacation they took together, for Hughes returned to the South Pacific and Club Med with Moorhead and a small group in 1980.[55]

During this trip and on other trips Hughes relied heavily on Lois Swan Jones and Gwen Graul to take care of her dogs, watch over her house, and occasionally drive her car so the battery wouldn't run down. Her closeness to Gwen was evident to all. Regina Montoya, her law clerk, was impressed at their partnership in handling the court's business. "When you worked for the judge you were sort of working for both of them," she recalled. Occasionally, they would fuss at one another good-naturedly. The judge liked to save her tea bags to use again, and Gwen would throw them away. "Who threw away my tea bags?" the judge would complain, knowing full well who had done it. The fact that Gwen had reared three boys by herself and that Hughes had never had children gave them entirely different perspectives in terms of children and family. Graul often regaled listeners with stories about the judge. "They had weathered a lot together," Montoya said.[56]

Hughes, not given to sentimentality, rarely if ever expressed the depth of her feelings toward her secretary and friend of thirty-five years. When Hughes departed on her lengthy 1975-76 journey, realizing she would be away for nearly two months over the holiday season, her feelings toward Graul almost bubbled over, and she had to contain her emotions as she said good-bye. Several thousand miles away, though, sitting in her thatched-roof cottage, Hughes ended a long letter to her by squeezing in at the bottom of the page an uncharacteristically affectionate closing: "When I left Saturday I really felt like choking up, because you see I love you." And then, as if embarrassed by her own sudden sentimentality, she ended the letter abruptly with her usual closing, "Judge."[57]

A month later, Hughes wrote that the trip had given her time to "think some things through & to realize a few things." For one thing, she wrote, "I do not want to be away from you so long. You are very dear & very close to me. I remember the day your father [Dallas County tax assessor-collector Ed Cobb] met me on the street outside the courthouse & told me he wanted you to work in my court & he was going to see Pearl [district clerk Pearl Smith] about it. That was 35 years ago & over the years we have become closer & closer." Hughes extended an offer for Graul: "I really want you to go on the next trip with me & let me pay for it & you select the place. I would prefer the summer, but anytime you choose & any place will please me."[58] (Not until the summer of 1978 did they take their trip together. Their destination, evidently Gwen's choice, was a cruise on the Black Sea and the Greek Islands on the Royal Viking Line.)[59]

Another thing Hughes had realized, she wrote to Graul, was that "I *cannot* work as I have. It is absolutely necessary to slow down. Going at such a fast pace undoubtedly has been the cause of my troubles."[60]

Despite her ongoing efforts to stay physically fit, Hughes was beginning to be plagued by physical problems. The troubles she mentioned in her letter to Graul referred to occasional fainting spells that she had begun to experience and that were very frightening to her and her friends. Carl Black Sr. knew of two instances in which she had fainted—once on the bench and another time at a beauty parlor. When she fainted on the bench she awoke to find concerned lawyers and others hovering over her. "Well, what are you looking at?" she snapped and then went on with her work.[61] On another occasion she had just returned from dinner at a restaurant with her neighbor Lois Swan Jones, when she collapsed as she got out of the car. Jones struggled in vain to lift the judge's totally inert body. Finally, another neighbor, Jack Hampton, the Republican who had earned her vote, arrived and was able to carry her into the house, where she revived without benefit of paramedics.[62]

There were other episodes, too, and although Hughes did not like to call attention to them, they concerned her. In a letter to Graul from the South

Pacific in December 1975, she wrote: "You'll be glad to know that I have had no indication of fainting. As a matter of fact, I've lost my fear of the possibility out here. I am more & more coming to the belief that you are correct & it is not what I eat but the stress that causes me to pass out."[63]

Graul's daughter-in-law, Dolores Graul, a nurse, remembers that doctors believed the fainting spells were a result of the "dumping syndrome," a phrase she had never heard of despite her medical experience. The dumping syndrome is defined by one medical dictionary as a "group of symptoms that occur when food or liquid enters the small intestine too rapidly."[64] As her comment to Graul suggested, Hughes evidently did not agree with this diagnosis.

By January 1977, when Regina Montoya became Hughes's law clerk, the fainting episodes had ended. Montoya noted how conscientious the judge was in taking a daily aspirin as a blood thinner to ward off the problem. Despite these problems, from outward appearances, Hughes continued to be as vigorous as ever. Her daily swimming routine was still intact. And she was still driving herself, although, as Montoya recalled, she frequently gave the curbs along Turtle Creek Boulevard a serious workout.[65]

However, the situation worsened in 1980, when two more serious episodes occurred. At a small party at Judge Irving Goldberg's house, Hughes suddenly lost consciousness at the dinner table, not breathing at all. Jan Sanders, who had been trained in CPR, managed through mouth-to-mouth resuscitation to get her breathing again before paramedics arrived. Despite the obvious serious nature of the incident, Hughes adamantly refused to go to the hospital. "She didn't want a fuss," Sanders recalled.[66]

But the same thing happened on Friday, February 22, 1980, at a reception for the judges of the Northern District of Texas, held at the Dallas Country Club. When Hughes collapsed this time, Judge Goldberg, who had seen Jan Sanders revive her at his house, shouted, "Jan knows what to do." Sanders vaulted over the table to reach her. She appeared lifeless. "She was gone as far as I could tell," Sanders said. Paramedics were called as Sanders began mouth-to-mouth resuscitation, and when they arrived to take over Hughes still was unconscious. When they finally revived her, though, she became almost instantly alert and insisted once more on not being taken to the hospital. None of the distinguished guests could convince her to do otherwise. Gwen Graul went home with her to spend the night as a precaution. Jan Sanders later was given a certificate by the American Heart Association to acknowledge the prompt action that had saved the judge's life.[67]

On the following Monday, Hughes was hospitalized at Presbyterian Hospital and learned that she had an irregular heartbeat. Doctors implanted a pacemaker with good results. Amid renewed speculation that her retirement finally was imminent, Hughes, now eighty-three, announced instead that she would return to the bench less than a week after the surgery.[68]

Life, less certain than ever for the still peppery judge, was further complicated by continuing difficulties with her hearing and her eyesight. At one point she tried to handle both problems at once by purchasing a new pair of glasses with concealed hearing aids in the earpieces. Only Gwen Graul was supposed to know of this new strategy. During a criminal trial the judge's hearing aid began buzzing loudly, and she desperately but unsuccessfully sought to adjust the volume without calling attention to it. Finally, the defendant's attorney arose and asked, "Judge, what is that buzzing?" Hughes insisted she did not hear a buzzing. She leaned over to her court reporter, Carl Black Sr., and whispered, "Carl, do you hear a buzzing?" Black, who had been tipped off by Graul about the new hearing aid, replied quietly, "No, ma'am."[69]

Hughes would not permit such problems to deter her from her regular schedule. In July 1980, four months after her pacemaker had been installed, she was in Scandinavia for a vacation.[70]

Gwen Graul, eighteen years younger than her friend and employer, was having health problems of her own—emphysema, brought on by smoking for many years. By 1980, at the age of sixty-eight, she was under a doctor's care and taking regular breathing treatments. Despite Hughes's earnest remonstrations, she could not or would not break the habit of smoking. On the morning of Friday, October 18, 1980, when Judge William (Mac) Taylor Jr. stopped by Gwen's Lakewood home to give her a ride to work, as had been his regular practice for some years, she failed to come to the door. Alarmed, Taylor went to the back of the house to investigate. Peering inside, he could see Graul, collapsed on the floor at her breathing machine. She was dead, having suffered a massive heart attack.[71]

The news was quickly relayed to Hughes's office. Hughes was already on the bench, hearing guilty pleas and meting out sentences. Joanne Hurtekant, Hughes's law clerk, was called out of the courtroom and given the news. "I didn't know how or when to tell the judge," she said, "so I went to Judge Sanders's chambers and told him." Sanders sent a note to Hughes on the bench, asking her to see him, and Hurtekant observed him as "ever so gently [he] told her the sad news." Hughes looked stricken for a moment, became "very stoic," and then returned to the bench. She finished the docket without even taking a recess.[72]

Gwendolyn Cobb Graul, survived by three sons and eight grandchildren, had been secretary to Judge Hughes for forty years. "I don't know what I will do without her," Judge Hughes told the *Dallas Morning News*. "I've depended on her for many, many years—not only here but at home as well."[73]

Joanne Hurtekant, with whom Hughes had developed a close relationship, gave Hughes a ride to the funeral services at Restland Memorial Chapel. At the graveside ceremony, Graul's three sons, their wives, and eight grandchildren filled the few chairs that had been set up for the family to hear the minister's closing remarks immediately prior to burial. Nonfamily members, as was customary, stood. There was no chair for Hughes. Instead of standing with the others she—an eighty-three-year-old federal judge wearing her finest clothing—simply sat down on the ground. She whispered to Hurtekant a Chinese proverb to the effect that it is better to sit than to stand.[74]

Graul's death left an emotional void in Hughes's life. After the funeral services Hurtekant drove Hughes along scenic Turtle Creek Boulevard toward her home. She would never forget the poignancy of their conversation. Hughes asked her law clerk if she thought Gwen could hear them as they talked. "When I said yes it seemed to relieve her," Hurtekant recalled. She also wanted to know what Hurtekant thought about life after death. "Then she told me that Gwen had called her every Saturday and Sunday morning at 9:00 A.M., and would I mind calling her that weekend. I realized for the first time how personally alone she was, and that she was afraid that she would die or be very ill and not be found quickly. I continued to call her every weekend until a stroke put her in the hospital and finally a nursing home."[75]

Hughes had another request. Would Hurtekant mind coming over to her house the next afternoon, a Sunday, to have a little sherry with her? Hurtekant agreed to do so, and in the next few years as Hughes's eyesight further weakened, Hurtekant would visit her at her home regularly, read to her, and watch television with her, especially a local public television show hosted by Regina Montoya called *Nuestra Días*.[76]

Graul's death made Judge Hughes more conscious than ever of her own mortality. Having intended for Graul to be the executor for her estate, she now had to make other plans. She walked across the street and asked her neighbor and friend Lois Swan Jones to be the executor. Jones said she would be honored. Jones was surprised when on the very next day Hughes returned with documents giving her power of attorney and adding her name to her checking and savings accounts. These tasks completed, Hughes crafted in her own handwriting a new will. She dated it November 5, 1980, six weeks after Graul's death. The six-page document was signed only by Hughes with no witnesses listed. This would be the will eventually probated upon her death.* A month later in December, she departed with Jennelle Moorhead and a few others for the South Pacific, staying again at a Club Med facility as a base for further excursions.[77]

In August 1981, Hurtekant and Regina Montoya decided to honor the judge with a surprise party at the Mansion Hotel in Dallas in honor of her eighty-fifth birthday. It was a Sunday brunch to be attended by as many of Hughes's former law clerks as could come. Two days before the party Hughes's vision suddenly became markedly blurred. Hurtekant took the judge to her ophthalmologist. He gave her the distressing news that her optic nerve was irreparably damaged, probably having occurred during a mini-stroke. Hughes was devastated at the news.[78]

As she drove the disconsolate judge home, Hurtekant decided that Hughes did not need any more surprises that weekend, so she told her about the party on Sunday. "I made the right choice," Hurtekant recalled. Although she could not see well enough at the party to recognize all the clerks from her

---

* The will provided that her personal papers, including the photograph signed by President Johnson of her administering the oath of office to him on *Air Force One*, would go to North Texas State University. This seemed to be recognition of the interest the institution had shown her in its lengthy oral history with her. To the National Federation of Business and Professional Women's Clubs she bequeathed two thousand dollars, an autographed photograph of President Kennedy, and honorary degrees from three colleges or universities. To her godchild, Alanna Frost, she left two thousand dollars and her opal, amethyst, and diamond ring. To her nephew, B. F. Broyles Jr., and her niece Betty Broyles, she left five thousand dollars each. To another niece, Coni [Constance] Tilghman Dudley, she left twenty thousand dollars and miscellaneous personal properties, including silver, jewelry, paintings, furniture, and household effects not otherwise specified. She left another ten thousand dollars to another niece, Sunny Tilghman, to be held in trust by Sunny's sister, Coni. To Sarah Ruiz Diaz of Honduras, who had been named after her, she left two thousand dollars. She left five thousand dollars to the Southern Methodist University Law School Scholarship Fund, "preference being given to women students." To George Washington University she bequeathed ten thousand dollars for the George E. Hughes Fund for Faculty Research. She also left two thousand dollars "or as much of said amount as is necessary" to be used for the care of "any dogs I may have at the time of my death." To Lois Swan Jones she left fifteen thousand dollars and her choice of any household items not specifically bequeathed. The portion of her estate with the greatest monetary value, her house, valued at $681,500 when the will was probated in December 1987, she left to Goucher College's Department of Political Science and its "program of practical training and education in government and politics." Sarah Tilghman Hughes will. No. 85-1707-P3, filed December 29, 1987, Probate Office, Dallas County Clerk.

table, Hughes asked Hurtekant to whisper to her their names. "She then proceeded to roast each one of them, and had all of us in tears from laughing. She was regal in her delivery." One of the former law clerks who attended was Martin Frost, now a U.S. congressman, who once more listened to Hughes good-naturedly tell him and the audience that to succeed in politics he must develop a firmer handshake.[79]

The deterioration of her vision prompted Hughes in this month of her eighty-fifth birthday to decide to hear no more trials. She would limit herself to arraignments, sentencing, and probation revocations. She had planned that summer to take a Viking Star cruise from Naples, Italy, to Copenhagen but, probably because of her growing health problems, canceled the trip. In December 1981, however, she took a cruise, sailing from Fort Lauderdale, Florida, to San Francisco, paying $6,086 for a single outside cabin on a Viking Star ship. It was the last cruise she would ever take.[80]

Because of her hearing and eyesight problems, Hughes's fellow judges began to be concerned about her capacity to deal properly with the intricacies of her job. Nor could she drive. The judge's new secretary, Sherry Hightower, now picked her up for work each morning and drove her home in the afternoon. On the morning of May 7, 1982, Hightower found Hughes unable to get out of bed, having evidently suffered another mini-stroke. She summoned help and had the judge taken to Presbyterian Hospital, where an even more devastating stroke occurred that same day. The stroke nearly proved fatal, but a determined team of physicians worked diligently and successfully to save their famous patient's life.[81]

The judge's public life was over. She would never return to her home. For the rest of her life, she would be cared for in a hospital or nursing home, too weak to sit up or get into a chair without help. For one who had prided herself on being so active, the transformation in her physical condition was dramatic and heartbreaking to her friends.

Lois Swan Jones, to whom Hughes had given the power of attorney, arranged for a team of nurses to give her special care. After some time Hughes had enough strength to acknowledge and to respond to visitors, and ___ feisty in her customary way to her law clerk, Joanne Hurtekant, ___rly visits. When Hurtekant told the judge that she was preg-___rst child, Hughes replied: "Now why'd you go and do that?"

Then, perhaps realizing the harshness of her comment, she softened and told Hurtekant something she had never been on record as having said before. It contradicted all her previous remarks on the subject. It had been George's wish, she said, not hers, that they not have children. "This was the most surprising thing she ever said to me," Hurtekant later said.[82]

Hughes's secretary continued for several months to respond on the judge's behalf to the random letters that still arrived regularly from throughout the nation, as they had increasingly since 1963, many asking for her recollections of the events of November 22 and some from young women seeking career advice. "Judge Hughes has been very ill and in the hospital since the first of May," Hightower wrote in September to one such letter writer. "It is doubtful she will ever return to public life."[83]

When doctors permitted, Jones had Hughes transferred to the Meadow Green Nursing Home, just a few blocks from the hospital. Joanne Hurtekant visited her there in March 1983, bringing with her the baby she had told Hughes about a few months before. Hughes was able to sit up in a bedside chair and hold her former law clerk's daughter, Kate. A photo taken by Hurtekant, perhaps the last one of Hughes, shows her gazing down at the baby with no discernible emotion. (See the photo section.)

Betty Cadwell, who had been hired to be with Hughes at the hospital, continued as the judge's chief caregiver. Hughes's minister, the Reverend C. Preston Wiles of St. Matthew's Episcopal, found Cadwell to be "a wonderful, very caring nurse who was very, very unusual in the good care she gave her." Other nurses were hired so that the judge would have someone with her at all times, even through the night. This would be the place Sarah T. Hughes would live for the last nearly three years of her life, doing so in privacy and, because of heavy sedation, often with little awareness of her surroundings or visitors.[84]

When Louise Raggio, the great friend who had stood by Hughes's side and carried her mantle so faithfully and so successfully in the struggle for women's rights, visited her, the judge was barely able to acknowledge her presence. However, she managed to say to Raggio in mild reproval: "You never ran for public office." It was the last comment she would ever be able to make to her. Raggio would recall it with fondness as an example of Hughes's life-long determination to have women campaign for public offices.[85]

Before her stroke Hughes had begun to read only large-print editions of books, and now she could not read at all. Her care-giver, Betty Cadwell, read to her. "She loved to have us read political biographies to her," Cadwell said. "We would read four hours a day."[86]

Only a handful of people were authorized to visit her—Jones, Hurtekant, Raggio, Jan and Barefoot Sanders, Regina Montoya, Constance Dudley, her nephew, B. F. Broyles Jr. and his wife, Patsy, and the Reverend Wiles, her minister, among them. Wiles visited her regularly during these difficult years. He described the bedridden Hughes as being "very, very stoic." Wiles sat next to her bedside and read from the book of Psalms. "That was her favorite. It was very comforting to her. She didn't want people to see her in that condition, and they safeguarded her from public scrutiny. She could open her eyes and she could see me."[87]

Nighttime seemed to be worse. She was restless and vocal, involuntarily complaining so loudly that greater sedation was required to keep her quiet.[88]

Most of those who visited her departed with a great sense of depression. Their efforts to communicate seemed ineffective. Their visits, which seemed to have no positive effect on the judge, became less and less frequent. When her niece Constance Tilghman Dudley came to Dallas to visit her, she found that after her medication was decreased Hughes was able to carry on a conversation, but she "was distant and had no interest in what was going on in the world."[89] Louise Raggio recalls her own mixed emotions when one of the judge's nurses once told her they had managed to pull her through a health crisis. Death seemed preferable to her present condition. Jan Sanders, seeing the distressing circumstances of life for Hughes during these agonizing times, anguished over whether she had done the right thing in administering CPR and saving Hughes's life.[90]

In early 1985 Hughes's deterioration became even more severe, and on February 12, 1985, she was returned to Presbyterian Hospital. When Constance Dudley visited she found her aunt on a feeding tube and unable to talk. At 9:30 P.M. on Tuesday, April 24, Sarah T. Hughes quietly died, her faithful nurse Betty Cadwell at her side. Cadwell said that "never once in those three years that she was ill did I ever hear her complain or express any regrets about her life." Hughes's minister, the Reverend Wiles, saw her a day or so before death. "She was slipping away. She died very peacefully," he said.[91]

Even after three years away from public view, in death Hughes once more was the subject of banner headlines. "Judge Sarah T. Hughes Dead at 88," read the huge page-one headline in the *Dallas Times Herald*. She was described as a "women's movement pioneer."[92] News stories gave full accounts of her life and accomplishments.

Hundreds attended her funeral services at St. Matthew's Episcopal Cathedral and heard the Reverend Wiles deliver the eulogies. Her body was placed in a crypt next to that of her husband, George, in the Hillcrest Memorial Park and Mausoleums, a dozen feet from that of Sheriff Bill Decker, her long-time associate at the county courthouse.

On the same day of her death another noted politician and former jurist died. He was Senator Sam Ervin of North Carolina, who gained national attention while presiding over the Watergate hearings that led to President Nixon's resignation. The *Dallas Times Herald* linked him with Hughes in its editorial, "Ervin and Hughes: 2 giants."[93]

"Indomitable Sarah" was the headline for the editorial in the *Dallas Morning News*, the newspaper whose conservative philosophy had run counter to Hughes's for so many years. The newspaper generously summarized the judge's many accomplishments at the same time that it acknowledged her critics. "Even her detractors can agree that one of the things that made Judge Hughes distinctive, and, yes, admirable, was that you always knew where she stood. She stood firm. She leaves a tall legacy in consequence of a remarkable career."[94]

Lady Bird Johnson said she had known and admired Sarah T. Hughes since her days at the University of Texas, when she saw her in action as a Texas legislator. Martin Frost, the former law clerk who had become a congressman and whose daughter was Hughes's goddaughter, declared, "Had she been 10 years younger, I am convinced she would have been the first woman on the U.S. Supreme Court."[95]

Hughes's long-time friend and colleague Judge Barefoot Sanders saw her as the embodiment of "pure determination," who even in her eighties was rising each morning at dawn and adhering to a strict regimen of exercise, diet, and yoga.[96] Rena Pederson of the *Dallas Morning News* recalled that at the end of an exhausting day on a float trip down the Rio Grande in rugged Big Bend, the guide told Pederson and the others that "the most amazing person he had ever guided was an elderly lady from Dallas." The woman had canoed all day and then beat everyone to the top of a mountain that evening. Who was she? Pederson asked. A federal judge named Sarah T. Hughes, the guide replied.[97]

More than physical prowess, though, Sarah T. Hughes was a woman of intellectual vigor. Her views, always firmly stated, sometimes startled or alienated those who were less daring. But, convinced of the rightness of her positions and buttressed by her strong character, she never wavered from expressing them. Although she sometimes made snap judgments in her everyday conversations, on substantive issues the passage of time generally confirmed the legitimacy of her viewpoints.

There was an aura of immediacy around Hughes's personality and her political and social convictions. To delay was to waste time. Her deliberate model was a quote from Tolstoy, which she had copied by hand and kept at her side as a constant reminder. "There is only one time that is important. *Now!* It is the most important time because it is the <u>only</u> time when we have any power." [98]

Contrary to the image she frequently projected through her outspokenness, in her domestic life Judge Hughes was a model of conservative values. She lived in the same modest house for more than five decades; she preferred quiet evenings at home to late-night parties; she worried and spoke frequently about the harm of divorce and its impact on children; and she was loyal to the same friends for many years.

More than anything else the American public would remember Sarah T. Hughes for her dramatic appearance aboard *Air Force One* to give the oath of office to Lyndon B. Johnson as president—she was the first woman ever to do so—on one of the most traumatic days in American history. Women and people who lived in Texas tended to recognize her for her spirited work over many decades in behalf of women's rights. Residents in her home city of Dallas saw her as an outspoken crusader who was eager to challenge the conservative political establishment. Underlying these images was a lifelong list of accomplishments: her service as a fiery, headline-making Texas legislator during the Depression, her controversial appointment as the first female district judge in the state and her battle for confirmation, her long and ultimately successful campaign to win the right for women to serve on juries in Texas, her bid for the vice-presidential nomination of the Democratic Party, her insistence on creating a special juvenile home in Dallas County to separate youths from adult offenders, her struggle against great odds to win appointment as a federal district judge, her important role in the *Roe v. Wade* decision, which marked an important cultural and political dividing line for the nation, and her unyielding resolve in forcing Dallas County to face up to its responsibilities in caring for its jail inmates.

She was proud of all these things, and she would have been proud to know that the Federal Bar Association in 2002 annc creation of the Sarah T. Hughes Civil Rights Award to be given a̱ ꙍally to the member who best exemplified her spirit and her legacy of devoted service and leadership in the cause of equality. Almost forty years earlier, in 1964, the president of the Federal Bar Association, Ramsey Clark, had presented her with the association's first Outstanding Woman Jurist Award.

Her work made a difference in the lives of millions of people. Probably, though, she would have been proudest of the fact that she had lived to see the day when so many other women had taken to heart the impassioned speech she had made so often: "Women ought to get indignant. Women must demand the right to be first-class citizens. This country—the world—needs them in government, business, schools and churches for high-level decision-making. Women are our country's greatest unused resource. And it is the responsibility of all of us to see that that resource is put to work." [99]

⁓ Afterword

A Towering Leader and Intellect

Sarah T. Hughes as remembered by Sarah Weddington

Sarah T. Hughes was a towering leader and intellect.

To those who didn't know her, that might seem a curious statement to make about a tiny woman who was slender and barely five feet tall. But to anyone who knew her, it rings with truth.

I knew her in a variety of contexts. I greatly admire who she was and what she accomplished. I was not named for her, but I was always proud that I had the same first name. I followed her leadership regarding women's issues. I followed her path and became a lawyer. I followed her path in politics and was elected to the Texas State House of Representatives. The case *Roe v. Wade*, which I filed with my co-counsel, Linda Coffee, was first tried before her and two other judges in her Dallas courtroom. Their decision laid the foundation for the right to privacy American women have today. To me, Sarah T. Hughes was a larger-than-life woman who set the pace for others to follow.

When did I first know of Judge Hughes? What were the circumstances when I first met her? The first question I can answer with certainty; not so the second. I have searched my memory with increasing frustration to find that nugget, but it remains elusive.

My lawyer friend Diane Dwight of Spicewood, Texas, and I have the same first memory of Judge Hughes: watching the November 22, 1963, coverage of the assassination of President John F. Kennedy and seeing the scene of Lyndon B. Johnson being sworn in by a woman holding a Bible. Diane remembers asking her father, "Daddy, who is that woman?" His response: "That woman is a federal judge named Sarah T. Hughes." For us, and I'd bet for millions of others, that was our first introduction to a woman lawyer.

My introduction to Sarah T. Hughes via TV that day occurred while I was at work. I was working part-time for Dr. B. H. Ailts, an allergist, while attending McMurry College (now McMurry University) in Abilene, Texas. Indelibly etched in my memory is sitting in the receptionist's chair, greeting patients as they arrived, opening and closing a glass partition to the waiting room as appropriate, pulling patient files for the doctor, and answering the phone. Suddenly I was aware of a commotion of excited conversation; when I looked, the eyes of the overflow crowd in the waiting room were glued to the TV. I opened the partition to find out what was going on and first learned of the assassination. The office staff, including the doctor, ended up crowded around the TV with the patients.

There she was: a woman dwarfed by the height and bulk of Lyndon Baines Johnson. At that moment, the eyes of the nation were focused on those two people, Sarah T. Hughes and LBJ. She was the one who ensured the constitutionally mandated transfer of power as she swore the vice president in as president, and it was her action that reassured the nation that we were not adrift and leaderless. My guess is the event of that moment was seen throughout the world.

The position and importance of Sarah T. Hughes were like a thunderbolt for young women like me. It was a time in West Texas and elsewhere when women trying to plan their futures were told that the appropriate careers for them were nursing, secretarial work, and teaching. As a college junior in 1963, I thought my destiny was, in part, to help eighth-grade students love the literary classic *Beowulf.* Then suddenly I was introduced to a woman who was a lawyer and a judge. The curtain opened to the possibilities of a whole new path. I finished my degree in English and speech, in secondary education, but immediately moved to Austin to work in the January 1965 legislative session and to start law school in June. I had never personally known a woman lawyer, but I had seen Sarah T. Hughes. I knew that path was a possibility for me.

Learning more about Sarah T. Hughes was part of my experience of working in the Capitol. My work assignment was in the office of Enrolling and Engrossing (E&E). In that office each legislative matter was typed and the typing proofed to be sure that it was absolutely accurate and exactly what the legislature had done. Part of the time I was in a pool of typists, and part of the time I was at a big table of readers. The year 1965 predated the era of computers; it was a time when legislative typists had to type an original and nine perfect carbons; one mistake meant the typist had to start over and continue until a perfect document was produced.

When I wasn't needed in E&E, I could be found watching the legislative proceedings from a balcony seat on the House side of the Capitol. I was appalled at the conduct of those on the floor; they propped their shoes or boots on their desks, wandered around not paying attention, and talked loudly even while someone was speaking at the podium. By the end of the session my awe of the legislative process had vanished, and instead I was thinking that perhaps I could do at least some parts of the job as well as—I hoped better than—those I was watching.

That experience also opened my eyes to how few women were legislators. In the House of Representatives there was one woman: Maude Isaacks of El Paso. And in the Senate there was one woman: Neville Coleson of Grimes County. But as I explored the Capitol Building I found the photos of the few women who had previously served. Sarah T. Hughes was in the composite photographs for the 1931, 1933, and 1935 sessions.

The composite photographs are huge framed posters showing a photo of each member of the House of Representatives and each statewide elected official. One poster exists for each legislative session, and they are hung chronologically in the Capitol halls. Today, in 2003, the same composites I looked at in 1965 are still seen by Capitol visitors. The composites with Judge Hughes now can be found in the far-west hallway of the "ground floor," or basement, under the House side. In 1931 her photo shows a short-haired woman who looks especially young and somewhat timid. Four female House members, including Hughes, are shown. Hughes can be seen in the far-right column, fifth from the bottom. The 1933 composite features Hughes still with short hair but appearing more serious. I wondered if this change in appearance had occurred because she was then the only female member of the House. Another female elected official pictured is Miriam Amanda "Ma" Ferguson, the governor. Hughes is found in the far-left column, sixth from the bottom.

By 1935, her photo looks much more mature and confident. She is one of two women pictured; she is now positioned in the top left-hand corner of the members' photos. I can remember wondering what had happened to her during those years from 1931 to 1935 to produce the changes in her photos; I imagined that her experience had included tough legislative battles, some won and some lost. My awareness of her as a judge from the assassination coverage was enhanced by the image of her as a legislator, and I started to wonder whether someday, after I had my law degree, I too might be able to win my way to sit in one of those huge leather swivel rockers reserved for House members.

The 1965 legislative session ended in May. The next month I became a student at the University of Texas School of Law, where I continued, fall, winter, spring, and summer, until I graduated in August 1967. Today about 50 percent of law students are women; in my class there were only a handful. One of them, Kay Bailey Hutchison, now represents Texas in the U.S. Senate.

The women's lounge at the Law School was the scene of frequent conversation about searches for employment and the frustrations in the difficulty of being a woman looking for a job in the legal field. My classmate Linda Coffee wanted to work for a judge. There were conversations about her application to Judge Hughes, her interviews, and her success in getting a job offer. If it is possible to walk on clouds, Linda did the day she accepted the offer. I remember feeling jealous. Linda was on law review and I wasn't; Linda had applied and I hadn't. It would have been a special thrill for me to work for Judge Hughes.

Instead I worked for a law professor and later for the city of Fort Worth attorney's office. Still later my husband, Ron Weddington, and I established a law office to try *Roe v. Wade*. However, my path intersected that of Judge Hughes many times in the years after law school, in regard to activities involving both law and women's issues. She was very active in a woman's organization called the National Federation of Business and Professional Women's Clubs (B&PW); in fact, she served as its national president for 1951-52. She was also active in the American Association for University Women (AAUW). I often went to their meetings and was a frequent speaker, especially for local club meetings around Texas and state conventions.

Judge Hughes was a pioneer in effecting change for women. In one of her most important successes, she was a leader in the movement to allow women to serve on juries. Bobbie Hernandez, a B&PW member, remembers hearing Judge Hughes in a speech describe how, after she became a state district court judge (in 1935), she looked at the jury members and saw a jury box containing only men. "We're going to change that," she thought—and it was accomplished. By 1954 Texas jury boxes held both men and women jurors.

Following in the footsteps of leaders like Hughes, women of my generation were learning that politics and government are important mechanisms for creating change for women. Hughes wanted more women to run for office and to participate in government, and in 1957 she conceived a Women in Government Award, which B&PW gave annually. It is now called the Judge Sarah T. Hughes Women in Government Award. In 1972 when I was exploring the possibility of running for a seat in the state legislature, I turned to Sarah Hughes for advice. She was generous with her time and walked me through the steps to political office and also talked about the plusses and the minuses of public service. In reading this book, I learned far more than she ever shared about the sexist comments that had been made about her as a candidate and as an official. Instead she talked extensively about what could be accomplished to help women via elected office.

The idea of running for office appealed to me. I saw so many policies and attitudes about women that I felt needed change. When I was in high school, women were allowed to play only half-court basketball. Half of our team was on each end of the court; we were not allowed to cross the center line. Also, women were required to throw the ball to a teammate after two dribbles. I can remember arguing that women should be allowed to run full court, as men were, and being told that was impossible. The reason? "All that jiggling and bounding and rebounding might hurt women's innards." That seemed ridiculous then, and now we know it was ridiculous. Women now run full court and play in a professional basketball league. In my secondary education classes I had been told that pregnant public school teachers in Texas had to quit or they would be fired. There was no discussion about the wisdom of that policy; instead, the discussion focused on the ethical obligations of the pregnant teacher and whether she should tell her principal as soon as she knew she was pregnant or whether she could wait until the principal figured it out. I thought women could walk, talk, teach, and be pregnant all at the same time. Now we know that pregnant women can continue to work effectively.

We also wanted to change credit policy. After finishing law school, I applied for a credit card. The man behind the desk told me that I had to get my husband's signature for them to process the application. I explained, in my best new-lawyer voice, that my husband, Ron, had come to Austin after completing military service, that I would be putting him through law school, that I was already a lawyer, and that I hoped someday he would have substantial earnings, but aside from his GI benefits I earned all of our family income. The man explained he really didn't care, that I had to get Ron's signature or he would not issue a credit card to me. I was incensed and wanted to change that for myself and other women.

These were the kinds legislative issues that I talked to Judge Hughes about. She was a very down-to-earth person, and her advice was practical. I still remember the advice Sarah T. Hughes gave to me. She suggested doing solid research on the issues and finding the best way to explain the situation. She also taught me the importance of patience, explaining that it often takes several sessions to get a bill passed. The focus throughout the process must be on building the substance of the case for the long haul and garnering the necessary political and legislative support to get the bill passed. She went on to say that determination and persistence were absolutely necessary.

Judge Hughes was often a coach for people she felt had potential. For example, Dorothy Innerarity, the woman who was the volunteer lobbyist for B&PW, remembers being involved in a B&PW convention-floor effort to get the group to endorse a legislative effort for women. She remembers Judge Hughes saying to her, "Speak up, Dorothy. Otherwise you won't win the votes you need."

The biggest issue for women during this time was attempting to pass the Equal Legal Rights Amendment (ELRA), an amendment to the Texas Constitution guaranteeing equal rights for women. Another focus was preparation to get Texas to endorse the Equal Rights Amendment (ERA) to the U.S. Constitution as soon as Congress submitted it to the states. There were heated debates at various women's meetings about wording and tactics.

Judge Hughes was informed and outspoken on both of these issues. Dorothy Innerarity remembers that the two titans of those debates were Judge Hughes and Hermine Tobolowsky, also a Dallas lawyer. The two women didn't always see eye-to-eye on how best to proceed. Innerarity describes a B&PW state convention at which one of them would jump up with a parliamentary maneuver and then the other would do the same from a different perspective. For those in attendance at the meeting, it was like watching a ping-pong game as the two evenly matched, knowledgeable, and determined adversaries vied for points.

The year 1972 was especially exciting. The ELRA was adopted by Texas voters and added to the state constitution. Texas ratified the national ERA. And I won election as a state representative, becoming the first woman to represent Austin-Travis County in the state legislature. During the 1973, 1975 and 1977 sessions, a great deal of progress for women occurred: the Equal Credit Bill passed, a bill protecting pregnant public school teachers passed, and a bill reforming criminal laws involving rape passed.

Although I sought advice from Judge Hughes about issues such as these, there was one matter I never talked to the judge about: reforming the Texas anti-abortion laws. Prior to running for election I was lobbying the Texas legislature to change those laws. However, there were cases pending in other states regarding similar state statutes, and I felt it would be inappropriate to talk to a sitting judge about the issue. Later I was glad that I had refrained from having that conversation. Judge Hughes played a critical role in the judicial consideration of the constitutionality of the Texas anti-abortion statutes.

Sarah T. Hughes had been appointed as a United States federal judge in 1961 by President John F. Kennedy. She is well known for decisions about a variety of issues, as this book you are reading points out. While she was always a devoted and serious federal judge, she never lost her spunk and never lost her willingness to do the unexpected, such as standing on her head in a yoga pose for a *People* magazine photo. She was legendary among B&PW and AAUW women for her determination to stay fit. In addition to yoga, she swam and, according to Innerarity, continued to be a mountain climber as she advanced in age.

As indicated above, Judge Hughes had a pivotal role in the litigation known as *Roe v. Wade*. The case involved the Texas anti-abortion law, which basically provided that all abortion procedures were illegal except those necessary to protect the life of the woman. That law led to many horror stories of women who sought back-alley abortions or tried self-abortion.

In 1969, I was approached by a group of women in Austin and asked to help answer a legal question. The group was trying, first, to tell women how to avoid pregnancy. But sometimes a woman essentially said, "I'm already pregnant. Where can I go to have an abortion?" The group said they had gathered information about the best and worst illegal places and also information about abortion providers in states where the procedure was already legal, such as California and New York. Their question was whether it would be safe for them to tell reporters about the group and the information they had gathered and whether they could be prosecuted as accomplices to the crime of abortion if they did so.

I did not know the answer, but I told them I would go to the law library and look it up. That trip to the library was the beginning of *Roe v. Wade*, the case in which the U.S. Supreme Court declared the Texas anti-abortion statutes unconstitutional. In the intervening years, people have often asked me how I became involved in the case. When I was writing *A Question of Choice*, a book about the case, I asked a woman from the original Austin group why they had come to me. She explained that there were two reasons. First, they wanted a woman attorney, and I was the only one in Austin they had ever heard of. (Judge Hughes was in Dallas, and by then she was on the bench.) Second, she said they needed someone who would agree to do the case free of charge, and I was willing to do that. Frankly I did not realize that the case would be *the* U.S. Supreme Court case; I thought it would be a way of helping push another case to the Supreme Court. The Supreme Court often accepts a case when many cases involving the same issue are pending around the country.

Soon after I started working on the possible case I called my former classmate Linda Coffee. Linda offered to help, and soon we were researching the case and preparing to begin the legal challenge. On March 3, 1970, the case was filed in Dallas.

Two and a half months later, Linda and I were seated at a long wooden table, preparing to present our arguments to Judge William M. Taylor of Dallas and Judge Sarah Hughes, both of the federal district, and Judge Irving L. Goldberg, of the federal circuit.

I was more nervous than I had ever been. I was twenty-five years old. I had never argued a contested case; my legal experience was limited to uncontested divorce cases, wills for people with few assets, and an adoption for my uncle and his wife. I certainly had never appeared before federal judges. I was grateful that Linda Coffee was the first person to stand to make a presentation.

When my turn came and I began to speak, my voice quavered. Hughes looked down at me from the bench; she must have noted how nervous I was. She gave me a reassuring smile and a slight wink, as if to say, "Calm down. Everything will be fine." I will always be grateful for that gesture. I did not interpret it as an indication of how she would rule in the case. Rather, I took it as an older woman lawyer remembering what it was like when she was starting out. My nerves calmed, and I moved into my part of the presentation with a stronger, surer voice.

Linda called me on June 17 to tell me that the three-judge court had released its decision. It declared the Texas law unconstitutional but refused to issue an injunction telling the Dallas DA Henry Wade to stop prosecuting doctors. Newspapers all over the country carried stories about the decision. I remember one in particular: the *Houston Post* ran a story that ended with the comment, "If their day in court proves anything, it certainly proves that genteel Southern ladies can indeed be very good lawyers."

The three-judge panel's decision was appealed to the U.S. Supreme Court. When that Court agreed to hear the case, I knew that I had to apply for admission to the Supreme Court bar in order to argue before that body. I had to pick two (as I remember it) attorneys to recommend me to the Court. It was an easy decision. Sarah Hughes was the one who pioneered the way to involvement in politics, to widening the world of opportunities for women, to election to the Texas House of Representatives, and to so much more.

I called Judge Hughes to ask if she would be the primary person to recommend me for admission. She said yes. The framed copy of my certificate of admission to the U.S. Supreme Court bears the signature of E. Robert Seaver, the clerk of the Court, but the two names prominently displayed are Sarah Weddington and Judge Sarah T. Hughes.

On January 22, 1973, the Supreme Court issued its opinion, holding that the U.S. Constitution guarantees to women a right of privacy that includes the decision of whether to continue or terminate a pregnancy.

Today the names of a handful of cases are known to almost every individual in the United States and to many around the world; one of those is *Roe v. Wade*. The work of Sarah T. Hughes as a member of the three-judge panel continues to reverberate through that now-famous decision. Her words have had a fundamental impact on the rights of women for over thirty years.

The biggest surprise for me is that the abortion controversy continues as such a hot topic in political and civic life. I thought by now it would generally be accepted that it is inappropriate for government to determine for a woman how she will respond to an unwanted pregnancy. Instead, the opponents of abortion are making huge inroads, primarily through actions of the Bush administration and various state legislatures, toward restricting the availability of abortion procedures. Violence against doctors and clinics in which abortions are performed has had a chilling effect on providers. Other obstacles are growing as well.

The U.S. Supreme Court seems divided five to four, with at least five of the justices unwilling to overturn *Roe v. Wade*. However, there are many rumors about specific justices who might retire. The U.S. president is the one who makes the appointment to fill any such vacancy, and the U.S. Senate must confirm the appointment. It is frightening for me to contemplate the fate of *Roe* if our current president has the opportunity to make such an appointment.

Each time I look across my office at the framed certificate allowing me to argue before the Supreme Court, I see the name of Sarah T. Hughes. I am constantly reminded of who she was and what she accomplished. I often think of the role model that she was for many.

When she died, Judge Hughes gave money to establish a Sarah Tilghman Hughes Field Politics Center at Goucher College, her alma mater. The center finances internships, sponsors visits to the campus by those involved in politics, and supports a Sarah Hughes Award for Public Service. In 1987, Rhoda M. Dorsey, then president of Goucher, called and asked me to speak at the inaugural ceremonies. One of the regrets of my life is that I couldn't accept that invitation because of a prior scheduling commitment.

I am grateful to Darwin Payne, the author of this book, for writing about Judge Hughes. I learned a great deal from reading his words, and I know this volume will allow many others to know more about her, and that, I'm confident, will result in many others admiring her and what she stood for. She was a tiny woman, but, far more important, she was a towering leader and intellect.

Acknowledgments

his book owes its origin to Al Ellis, who as a trustee and past president of the Dallas Bar Foundation conceived of it as a worthy project for recognizing one of the Dallas Bar Association's most distinguished members, the late Sarah T. Hughes. Foundation board members agreed with Ellis, funding for research and writing was shared by the Foundation and the Foundation Fellows. I was pleased to be asked to write the book. Barbara Bratton, Dallas Bar Foundation executive director, and Ellis assembled a distinguished group of Dallas lawyers, many of whom had known Judge Hughes, to serve as an editorial committee. Upon completion of each chapter, committee members and I met for lunch at the Dallas Bar Association's headquarters, at the Belo Mansion, and enjoyed good meals and conversation while discussing my work.

All committee members, including Ellis as chairman, offered invaluable services. U.S. district judge Barefoot Sanders had known Hughes since boyhood. His professional career and hers were intertwined in many ways. Judge Sanders was extremely knowledgeable not only about Hughes and her legal career but also about Dallas, state, and national politics, and he was willing to share such knowledge with me at every turn.

Louise Raggio, one of the city's most distinguished attorneys, worked closely with Hughes on many endeavors, and she and her husband had been close friends with Hughes. Ms. Raggio was always on call as I pondered various aspects of Judge Hughes's career. Aurora Madrigal and Elizabeth Lang-Miers exemplified the accomplished female attorneys encouraged by Judge Hughes for so many years, and they were helpful and faithful members of the committee. Charles Galvin, retired dean of the Southern Methodist University Law School, was personally acquainted with Judge Hughes, and his insights into her personality and career were very helpful. Another former dean of the Southern Methodist University Law School, Paul Rogers, did not know Hughes, but he certainly knew about her, and his sound advice was always appreciated. Walter N. (Nick) Kuntz practiced law in Hughes's court and had vivid memories of her. Lee Simpson, who had clerked for Judge Irving Goldberg of the 5th Circuit when he was a colleague of Hughes, was especially helpful with his knowledge and his careful reading of the manuscript. Larry Newman had important memories of his associations with Judge Hughes at the Dallas Bar Association, and L. A. Bedford Jr. practiced law before her and was especially knowledgeable about her work in the African American community. I am indebted to Spencer C. Relyea for his editorial assistance on this project and on a previous one. Barbara Bratton was unfailingly helpful, efficient, and cordial in her capacity as coordinator of our meetings.

Judge Hughes left her papers to the University of North Texas, where they have been carefully cataloged and maintained by archivist Richard L. Himmel in a location named for her, the Sarah T. Hughes Reading Room. Himmel and his assistant, Perri Hamilton, were unusually helpful in my many visits to the archives. The Hughes papers are voluminous, and the researcher is fortunate that a most helpful index is available as a guide.

Archivists and staff members at other libraries also were helpful. They include Sydney Roby, Goucher College; Lyle Slovik and David Anderson, George Washington University; Carol Roark and the staff at the Texas/Dallas History and Archives Division at the J. Erik Jonsson Central Public Library in Dallas; Jimm Foster, St. Matthew's Episcopal Cathedral; Bob Tissing, Lyndon B. Johnson Library at the University of Texas at Austin; T. Matthew DeWaelsche, Texas State Archives; Steven Williams, Center for American History at the University of Texas at Austin; June Payne, John Fitzgerald Kennedy Library in Boston; H. G. Dulaney, Sam Rayburn Library, Bonham, Texas. The Enoch Pratt Free Library in Baltimore was a pleasant work station with much useful information related to early Baltimore and Hughes's early life there.

A very special thank you is due my e-mail friend, Constance Tilghman Dudley, Sarah T. Hughes's niece. Ms. Dudley provided many important details about her aunt. Lois Swan Jones, who lived across the street from Hughes and was the executor of her estate, was another excellent source of personal information. Susanne Starling lent me the tape recording of an oral history she did with Judge Hughes concerning her first political campaign in Dallas County in 1930.

A large number of individuals who worked with Judge Hughes favored me with interviews and documents. Dolores Graul, daughter-in-law of Hughes's close friend and assistant Gwen Graul, stands out in this respect, and I am grateful to her husband as well, J. W. Graul. Vivian Castleberry, author and former editor at the *Dallas Times Herald*, provided me with her recollections of Hughes and also with her impressive file of materials and photographs. Vivian has been unfailingly helpful and friendly to me over the years.

Others who helped me with interviews or other communications include: the late Oscar Mauzy, the late Stanley Marcus, Betty McKool, Jan Sanders, Jim Lehrer, the Honorable Martin Frost, Dallas County Commissioner Jim Jackson, Ronnie Dugger, John Spinuzzi, Ernest E. Figari Jr., Ed Reyna, John Mashek, Phyllis Macon, Joanne Hurtekant, Regina Montoya, Clarice Davis, Dennis Shaw, the Reverend C. Preston Wiles, Frances James, Lee Cullum, Carl Black Sr., Rena Pederson, Patt Borom, the Reverend Steve Swann, and Michael Collins.

Andy Hanson called to my attention and provided several photographs he took of Judge Hughes when he was a photographer at the *Dallas Times Herald*. Murray Smither located an early catalog of the Dallas County Law Library that provided me with missing information. Max Holland read several chapters and gave me helpful advice.

Some of my graduate students in the Master of Liberal Arts program at Southern Methodist University assisted me with research. I am particularly indebted to David M. Hudson, who helped me find my way through Hughes's legal decisions with an impressive piece of research, "The Federal Judicial Career of Sarah T. Hughes." Phyllis Glickman's paper, "Women Attorneys of Dallas from 1914 to 1954," was helpful. A husband and wife team, David and Cari Hooper, copied all the clippings concerning Sarah T. Hughes at the J. Erik Jonsson Central Dallas Public Library. A Stanford University Law School student (by now a graduate), Kaycie Czelusta, graciously shared with me the paper she wrote on Judge Hughes.

Several colleagues with whom I have been involved in the past two years in the study of Dallas history for the new Old Red Museum of Dallas County History & Culture were helpful: Thomas H. Smith, Michael V. Hazel, Jacquelyn McElhaney, Donald Payton, Robert Fairbanks, Alan Olson, and Sam Childers. Rachel Roberts of the Dallas Historical Society was helpful, as always, as has been my association with that organization.

How pleasing it was to work with Keith Gregory and Kathryn Lang of the SMU Press in bringing this creation to reality. I am grateful for their sage advice and their enthusiasm, and also for the good work of George Ann

Ratchford. I owe a large debt to Paul Rogers for initiating conversations leading to the publishing arrangement with SMU Press. My copy editor, Robin Whitaker, displayed a masterful knowledge of stylistic matters. Her careful reading of the manuscript saved me a large number of gaffes, although, of course, I bear responsibility for all those remaining.

Family members by now surely are weary from having to hear about this project. I am grateful for their patience as well as their interest: my wife, Phyllis Payne; daughters, Sarah and Hannah; sons, Mark and Scott, and their wives, Kristin and Brandy; and grandson, Parker Darwin Payne. My sisters, June Payne Marco and Sally Payne Estes, and Sally's husband, Robert J. Estes III, as always, have cheered me on.

～ Notes

Prologue

1. Quoted by Regina Montoya, in "Judge Sarah Hughes: A Retrospective," *Goucher Quarterly*, Summer 1987, 12-14.
2. *Dallas Times Herald*, Apr. 24, 1985.

Chapter 1, Dynamo from Baltimore

1. "An Exhibit: The Tilghman Family in the War of Independence, The Historical Society of Talbot County, Easton, Maryland, September 30-November 4, 1972," a booklet in Folder 2, Box 92, the Judge Sarah T. Hughes Collection, University of North Texas Archives (hereafter the Hughes Collection will be cited as STH); and Sarah T. Hughes to Benjamin Chew Tilghman, Aug. 28, 1950, Folder 1, Box 1901, STH. Charles Wilson Peale painted a portrait of Tench Tilghman, and his image along with that of Washington and others may be seen in John Trumbull's painting, *Capture of the Hessians at Trenton, December 26, 1776*, Yale University Art Gallery. In World War II a Liberty ship was christened in Tilghman's name (*Baltimore Evening Sun*, Aug. 21, 1943).
2. Stephen Frederick Tillman's genealogy of the family, prepared on March 1, 1962, was made available to me by Sarah T. Hughes's niece Constance Tilghman Dudley. Other details are in "Features of Matthew Tilghman," *Baltimore Sun*, June 12, 1971, as cited by Opal Howard Allread in "Sarah T. Hughes: A Case Study in Judicial Decision-Making," Ph.D. dissertation, University of Oklahoma, 1987, 12.
3. Dickson J. Preston, *Talbot County: A History* (Centreville, Md.: Tidewater Publisher, 1983), 217; Allread, "Sarah T. Hughes," 13.
4. He appears in the 1880 U.S. Census, Nineteenth Ward, Precinct 7, Baltimore, Maryland, Family History Library Film 1254504, NA Film number T9-0504, p. 178B, as a "coal dealer." Baltimore City directories list his occupation later as a clerk without further indication. Family members later were never certain about what kind of clerk he was.
5. Allread, "Sarah T. Hughes," 14; church records from St. Paul's Episcopal Church, Edenton, North Carolina, as supplied to Constance Dudley by Eleizabeth B. Moore.
6. Folder 1, Box 1896, STH.
7. The document requesting a change is dated May 17, 1966. This document states that her father was born in Bueto, Maryland, rather than Baltimore, contrary to the original certificate.
8. In late 2000 the house still stood, showing evidence of recently having been a small grocery store, but was boarded up and apparently unoccupied, as was the case for almost all of the now-dilapidated row houses on the street.
9. Meredith Janvier, *Baltimore in the Eighties and Nineties* (Baltimore: H. G. Roebuck and Son, 1933), 24, 98, 103.
10. Wallace M. Reef, "Dallas Dynamo," undated typescript, Folder 6, Box 1901, STH.
11. The scrapbook is in Folder 2, Box 1908, STH.
12. Allread, "Sarah T. Hughes," 14; Reef, "Dallas Dynamo," STH.
13. Gary Shultz, "Judge Sarah T. Hughes Is Dead at 88," *Dallas Times Herald*, Apr. 24, 1985.
14. Allread, "Sarah T. Hughes," 14.
15. Notes from an undated interview with Sarah T. Hughes by Vivian Castleberry, Vivian Castleberry Papers.
16. Reef, "Dallas Dynamo," STH.
17. Scrapbook, Folder 2, Box 1908, STH.

18. *Baltimore Evening Sun*, Feb. 4, 1944.
19. Scrapbook, Folder 2, Box 1908, STH.
20. Ibid.
21. Ibid.
22. Reef, "Dallas Dynamo," STH.
23. Kristi Throne Strickland, "Sarah Tilghman Hughes: Activist for Women's Causes," M.A. thesis, Tarleton State University, Texas Women's University, Denton, Texas, 1989, 17.
24. Commencement address at Mountain View College, May 18, 1973, Folder 10, Box 1897, STH.
25. Vivian Castleberry interview with Sarah T. Hughes.
26. Speech to Cleveland alumni of Goucher College, undated typescript, Folder 10, Box 1925, STH.
27. Ibid.
28. Francis F. Beirne, *The Amiable Baltimoreans* (New York: E. P. Dutton, 1951), 167.
29. Reef, "Dallas Dynamo," STH.
30. *Donnybrook Fair*, Goucher College yearbook, 1917.
31. *Goucher College Weekly*, Oct. 12, 1916.
32. *Donnybrook Fair*, 1917.
33. Speech to Cleveland alumni of Goucher College, Folder 10, Box 1925, STH.
34. Ibid.
35. Ibid.
36. *Donnybrook Fair*, 1918.
37. *Goucher College Weekly*, May 18, 1916.
38. Ibid., Apr. 13, 1916.
39. Ibid., Mar. 22, 1917.
40. Ibid., Apr. 13, 1916; Vivian Castleberry interview with Sarah T. Hughes.
41. "Judges Questionnaire," prepared by Sarah T. Hughes for Judicial Conference of United States, 1976, Folder 4, Box 1901, STH; speech to Cleveland alumni of Goucher College, Folder 10, Box 1925, STH.
42. *Goucher College Weekly*, Apr. 13, 1916.
43. Reef, "Dallas Dynamo," STH.
44. Speech to Cleveland alumni of Goucher College, Folder 10, Box 1925, STH.
45. *Goucher College Weekly*, Mar. 15, 1917, Oct. 12, 1916.
46. *Donnybrook Fair*, 1918.
47. *Goucher College Weekly*, June 9, 1917.
48. Speech to Cleveland alumni of Goucher College, Folder 10, Box 1925, STH.
49. Ibid.
50. Reef, "Dallas Dynamo," STH.
51. "Judges Questionnaire," Folder 4, Box 1901, STH.
52. U.S. Department of Justice, FBI, Sarah T. Hughes, File No. 77-88126: Charlotte, N.C., Office, Field Office File 77-5217, Aug. 31, 1961, a document that I obtained under the Freedom of Information and Privacy Acts, Sarah T. Hughes, File Number 77-88126.
53. Allread, "Sarah T. Hughes," 19.
54. Fred Gantt, "Interview with Judge Sarah T. Hughes," University of North Texas, Oral History Collection, Number 27, Jan. 15, 1969, 2, STH.
55. "Sarah T. Hughes: Campaigning in Dallas County," an oral history interview by Suzanne Starling, Sept. 1, 1979, courtesy of Suzanne Starling, Dallas, Tex.
56. *From Strength to Strength: A Pictorial History of the George Washington University, 1821-1996* (Washington, D.C.: George Washington University, n.d.), 88-89.
57. Allread, "Sarah T. Hughes," 17; "Judges Questionnaire," Folder 4, Box 1901, STH; U.S. Department of Justice, FBI, Sarah T. Hughes, File No. 77-88126: Washington, D.C., Office, Field Office File No. 77-72382, Sept. 1, 1961; STH to Haughton Tilghman, n.d., letter in Constance Tilghman Dudley Papers.
58. Raymond B. Fosdick, *American Police Systems* (New York: Century Co., 1920), 376.
59. Carol Whiteford, "The Policewoman," *Western Oxford*, undated clipping sent to me by George Drearley, son of Ms. Whiteford.
60. Allread, "Sarah T. Hughes," 21.
61. J. Marilyn Dye, "The Accidental Feminist: A Biography of Sarah T. Hughes," undergraduate honor paper submitted at the University of Texas at Dallas for degree of bachelor of arts, May 1997, 17.
62. STH to Haughton Tilghman, n.d. [spring 1922], letter in Constance Tilghman Dudley Papers.

63. "Goucher Girl Policewoman in Washington," *Baltimore Evening Sun*, n.d., Constance Tilghman Dudley Papers.
64. Ibid.
65. Dye, "The Accidental Feminist," 20.
66. Robert Shackleton, *The Book of Washington* (Philadelphia: Penn Publishing Co., 1922), 115.
67. *The Cherry Tree*, 1920, yearbook for the George Washington University; GWU Bulletin, June 1921.
68. GWU Bulletin, Mar. 1921.
69. *The Cherry Tree*, 1922.
70. Ibid.; undated clipping, Folder 7, Box 1900, STH.
71. Newspaper column, "Tomorrow," by Thomas Hudson McKee, bearing only the date 1935, Scrapbook no. 2, Oversize Box 1908, STH.
72. Brooks Hays, *Politics Is My Parish* (Baton Rouge: Louisiana State University Press, 1981), 46-47; Reef, "Dallas Dynamo," STH.
73. *The Cherry Tree*, 1922.
74. Ibid.; Vivian Castleberry interview with Sarah T. Hughes; Allread, "Sarah T. Hughes," 23.
75. "Policewoman a Bride," undated clipping [Mar. 14, 1922], Folder 7, Box 1900, STH.
76. Merton L. Ferson to Mr. and Mrs. George E. Hughes, Apr. 19, 1922, in scrapbook, Folder 2, Box 1908, STH.
77. STH to Haughton Tilghman, n.d. [spring 1922], letter in Constance Tilghman Dudley Papers.
78. Constance Tilghman Dudley remarks made at the dedication of the Sarah T. Hughes Reading Room at the University of North Texas, video, "Dedication Program, September 6, 1996," University of North Texas Archives, Denton.
79. Reef, "Dallas Dynamo," STH.
80. Vivian Castleberry interview with Sarah T. Hughes; STH to Haughton Tilghman, n.d. [spring 1922], letter in Constance Tilghman Dudley Papers.
81. *The Cherry Tree*, 1922; U.S. Department of Justice, FBI, Sarah T. Hughes, File No. 77-88126: Washington, D.C., Office, Field Office File No. 77-72382, Sept. 1, 1961.
82. STH to Ralph Levering Kirk, Nov. 27, 1963, Folder 2, Box 1892, STH.

Chapter 2, Settling Down in Dallas

1. Minutes, Dallas Bar Association, Apr. 3, 1920, and Jan. 8, 1927.
2. Castleberry interview with Sarah T. Hughes, Vivian Castleberry Papers.
3. Ibid.; Reef, "Dallas Dynamo," STH; Gantt, "Interview with Judge Sarah T. Hughes," Jan. 15, 1969, 2, STH.
4. Reef, "Dallas Dynamo" STH.
5. Vivian Castleberry Papers. STH's letter to her brother is quoted in Allread, "Sarah T. Hughes," 31.
6. Darwin Payne, *As Old As Dallas Itself: A History of the Lawyers of Dallas, the Dallas Bar Associations, and the City They Helped Build* (Dallas: Three Forks Press, 1999), 126, 134; Gantt, "Interview with Judge Sarah T. Hughes," Apr. 11, 1969, 30, STH.
7. *Daily* [Dallas] *Times Herald*, Dec. 27, 1914.
8. Undated, untitled typescript for talk by Sarah T. Hughes, evidently 1929, in Box 1898, Folder 6, STH; Gantt, "Interview with Judge Sarah T. Hughes," Jan. 15, 1969, 5, STH.
9. The account book, provided to me by Constance Tilghman Dudley, appears to be one used by STH for the Dallas Joint Legislative Council. Early entries are in another person's handwriting. Hughes's own personal entries begin in 1923. Membership in various organizations is cited in numerous news clippings concerning Hughes's candidacy.
10. "Zonta Club of Dallas, 1924-1961," a typescript history of the organization, Texas/Dallas History and Archives, Dallas Public Library, lists Hughes's activities in the club.
11. Payne, *As Old As Dallas Itself*, 147-49. The Depression and competition from the Southern Methodist University Law School brought the demise of Jefferson in the 1930s. When Hughes was elected in 1930 to the Texas legislature it was said that she had taught at Jefferson for five years.
12. *Daily Times Herald*, Feb. 1, 1925; Payne, *As Old As Dallas Itself*, 126-30. Frances Hexamer, another woman lawyer admitted to the Dallas Bar early on, was omitted from the article. Hexamer had read law with a Dallas firm before being admitted to practice in 1918.
13. *Daily Times Herald*, Feb. 1, 1925. Jefferson Law School was recognized in 1930 by the Texas Supreme Court as one of four approved law schools in the state, a distinction that meant that Jefferson's graduates were automatically granted a license to practice law without having to take a bar examination.

By 1931 the school had forty-nine senior students, twenty-one of them in the Law School. Jefferson's enrollment declined during the Depression, and it was submerged into the SMU School of Law.

14. *Daily Times Herald*, Aug. 14, 1924. Hughes's departure from the Veterans Bureau might have coincided with a reorganization that ended its status as a district office.

15. A very brief obituary appears in the *Baltimore Sun*, Oct. 23, 1925, as quoted in an e-mail from Constance Tilghman Dudley to me, June 20, 2002.

16. Allread, "Sarah T. Hughes," 33; Gantt, "Interview with Judge Sarah T. Hughes," Jan. 15, 1969, 5-6, STH.

17. Darwin Payne, *Big D: Triumphs and Troubles of an American Supercity in the 20th Century*, rev. ed. (Dallas: Three Forks Publishing Co., 2000), 87, 94, 99-100, 103-5.

18. "Women Gather in AntiKlan Rally," undated clipping [1924], Box 1900, Folder 8, STH; *Daily Times Herald*, Aug. 20 and 22, 1924.

19. Payne, *Big D*, 108; *Daily Times Herald*, Aug. 23, 1924. Norman D. Brown's *Hood, Bonnet, and Little Brown Jug: Texas Politics, 1921-1928* (College Station: Texas A&M University Press, 1984) provides an insightful look into the Klan's influence in the state.

20. "Women Plan to Beat Klan in City Election," Folder 8, Box 1900, STH.

21. Payne, *Big D*, 109.

22. Undated typescript, Box 1898, undated clipping [1924] Folder 6, STH.

23. Ibid.

24. Ibid.

25. "Judges Questionnaire," STH.

26. Ibid.; and undated transcript, Box 1898, Folder 6, STH.

27. Anthony Champagne, oral history interview with Sarah T. Hughes, Feb. 5, 1980, Sam Rayburn Library, Bonham, Texas; and Reef, "Dallas Dynamo," STH.

28. Reef, "Dallas Dynamo," STH.

29. Undated typescript, Box 1898, Folder 6, STH.

30. Suzanne Starling, "Sarah T. Hughes: Campaigning in Dallas County," oral history interview, Sept. 1, 1979.

31. Interview with Sarah T. Hughes, May 22, 1974, cited in Allread, "Sarah T. Hughes," 35; Gantt, "Interview with Judge Sarah T. Hughes," Jan. 15, 1969, 9, STH.

32. Political advertisement, Folder 6, Box 1941, STH.

33. In this election Klan or Klan-endorsed candidates captured all major elected offices at the courthouse. In 1924 and 1926 Edith Wilmans unsuccessfully campaigned for governor, and in 1929, now widowed, she married a Chicago man and moved there, soon to return to Dallas after a divorce.

34. Starling, "Sarah T. Hughes: Campaigning in Dallas County."

35. Undated clipping, Folder 6, Box 1941, STH.

36. Ibid.

37. Newspaper clippings from this 1930 campaign are found in a scrapbook in Folder 6, Box 1941, STH. The three hundred dollars she spent on the campaign is cited in a typescript, "Her Honor the Judge: Sarah Tilghman Hughes," Folder 6, Box 1901, STH.

38. Advertisement in Folder 6, Box 1941, STH.

39. Starling, "Sarah T. Hughes: Campaigning in Dallas County."

40. Ibid.

41. Ibid.

42. "Fewer Laws Are Promised by Candidates," clipping in Folder 6, Box 1941, STH.

43. Dye, "The Accidental Feminist," 33-34.

44. "Sarah T. Hughes Wins Applause in Speeches," *Oak Cliff Tribune*, July 18, 1930, Folder 6, Box 1941, STH.

45. "Fire Lacking in Talks of Candidates," undated clipping, ibid.

46. "Mrs. Hughes Raps Extravagance in Government," ibid.

47. "Expenses as Issue," ibid.

48. "Useless Waste Causes Severe Business Loss," ibid.

49. Undated newspaper advertisement, ibid.

50. "Sarah T. Hughes for Representative," undated, ibid.

51. Undated clipping, ibid.

52. "Candidate's Name Omitted by Error, Is Still in Race," *Daily Times Herald*, undated clipping, ibid.

53. July 31, 1930, untitled newspaper, ibid.

54. Ibid.

55. *Daily Times Herald*, Aug. 2, 1930.
56. Undated advertisement, Folder 6, Box 1941, STH.
57. Undated newspaper article, ibid.
58. *Daily Times Herald*, Aug. 17, 1930.
59. *Dallas Morning News*, Aug. 22, 1930.
60. Ibid.
61. Undated newspaper story, Folder 6, Box 1941, STH.
62. "Zonta Club of Dallas, 1924-1961," p. 10, Texas/Dallas History and Archives, Dallas Public Library.
63. Ibid.
64. Rupert N. Richardson et al., *Texas: The Lone Star State*, 5th ed. (Englewood Cliffs, N.J.: Prentice Hall, 1988), 372.

Chapter 3, Political Immersion

1. "Mrs. Sarah Hughes Raps Extravagance in Government," undated clipping, Folder 6, Box 1941, STH.
2. Robert A. Caro, *The Years of Lyndon Johnson: Means of Ascent* (London: Bodley Head, 1990), 158.
3. Nancy Baker Jones and Ruthe Winegarten, *Capitol Women: Texas Female Legislators, 1923-1999* (Austin: University of Texas Press, 2000), 39, 81-82, 89-91, 93, and 95.
4. State of Texas Legislature, *House Journal*, 42nd Legislature, Regular Session, Jan. 13, 1931, to Apr. 14, 1931, vol. 1: 4.
5. Ibid., 16.
6. Ibid., 85.
7. Gantt, "Interview with Judge Sarah T. Hughes," Jan. 15, 1969, 18-19, STH.
8. H.B. 305, State of Texas Legislature, *House Journal*, 42nd Legislature, Regular Session, Jan. 13, 1931, to Apr. 14, 1931, vol. 1: 211.
9. H.B. 616 , H.B. 690, and H.B. 691, ibid., 321 and 395; Gantt, "Interview with Judge Sarah T. Hughes," Jan. 15, 1969, 24, STH.
10. H.B. 820, State of Texas Legislature, *House Journal*, 42nd Legislature, Regular Session, Jan. 13, 1931, to Apr. 14, 1931, vol. 1: 681.
11. H.B. 955, ibid., 776.
12. H.B. 901, ibid., 751. Jane Long (1798-1880) was recognized as the "Mother of Texas," because she was the first Caucasian settler in Texas to bear a child.
13. H.B. 992, State of Texas Legislature, *House Journal*, 42nd Legislature, Regular Session, Jan. 13, 1931, to Apr. 14, 1931, vol. 1: 980; "Historical," *Catalogue of Dallas County Law Library*, January, 1944, courtesy of Murray Smither.
14. State of Texas Legislature, *House Journal*, 42nd Legislature, Regular Session, Apr. 14, 1931, to May 23, 1931, vol. 2: 1972, 2011, 2026, 2093-94, 2114, 2115, 2148, 2409.
15. Carolyn Holmes Moses, "Miss Sally, Texas' District Judge," *Independent Woman*, April 1938, 107.
16. Undated newspaper clipping [early 1930s], Scrapbook no. 2, Oversize Box 1908, STH.
17. Undated clipping from *Dallas Journal* [1933], Scrapbook no. 2, STH.
18. "Zonta Club of Dallas, 1924-1961," 12, Texas/Dallas History and Archives, Dallas Public Library.
19. State of Texas Legislature, *House Journal*, 42nd Legislature, First Called Session, July 14, 1931, to Aug. 19, 1931, 2.
20. H.B. 35, ibid., 409.
21. H.B. 7, State of Texas Legislature, *House Journal*, 42nd Legislature, First Called Session, July 14, 1931, to Aug. 19, 1931; Seth S. McKay and Odie B. Faulk, *Texas after Spindletop* (Austin: Steck-Vaughn Co., 1965), 128.
22. *Dallas Morning News*, July 23, 1932, Aug. 28, 1932.
23. *Green v. Robison*, 8 S.W. 2d, 655 (1928); Allread, "Sarah T. Hughes," 42-43.
24. [Sarah T. Hughes], "Statement Opposing House Bill No. 220," Folder 11, Box 1943, STH.
25. S.B. 25, *Senate Journal*, 42nd Legislature, Third Called Session, 1932, 57.
26. Interview with Ralph Yarborough, May 3, 1974, as cited in Allread, "Sarah T. Hughes," 43.
27. Notes for West Texas land speech on legal pad, Folder 11, Box 1943, STH.
28. Typescript, "Statement Opposing House Bill No. 220," ibid.
29. "Dallas Woman Victorious in House Battle," *Dallas Morning News*, Sept. 16, 1932, as quoted by Allread, "Sarah T. Hughes," 44.
30. Notes for West Texas land speech, Folder 11, Box 1943, STH; Allread, "Sarah T. Hughes," 44-45.
31. Clipping from the *Dallas Morning News*, October, 1932, Scrapbook no. 2, STH.

32. Ralph Yarborough to Sarah T. Hughes, Sept. 29, 1961, Folder 11, Box 1893, STH. By 1989 the Permanent School Fund was valued at more than $8 billion; its interest provided a dividend of $620 million.
33. State of Texas Legislature, *House Journal*, 42nd Legislature, Third and Fourth Called Sessions, Aug. 30, 1932, and Nov. 3, 1932, 30.
34. Message to the State of Texas Legislature, *House Journal*, 43rd Legislature, Regular Session, Jan. 10, 1933, to Apr. 19, 1933, vol. 1: 19.
35. Ouida Ferguson Nalle, *The Fergusons of Texas or "Two Governors for the Price of One"* (San Antonio: Naylor Co., 1946), 220.
36. Ibid., 102.
37. Sarah T. Hughes Oral History, Interview I, Oct. 7, 1968, by Joe B. Frantz, transcript, Internet copy, LBJ Library.
38. State of Texas Legislature, *House Journal*, 43rd Legislature, Jan. 10, 1933, to Apr. 19, 1933, vol. 1: 1017, 1025; Constance Tilghman Dudley to me via e-mail, May 4, 2001; "Sarah T. Hughes' Mother Succumbs; Services Friday," *Daily Times Herald*, Mar. 23, 1933.
39. "Income Tax Argued," *Austin American-Statesman*, Apr. 11, 1933; and "Attempt to Kill Income Tax Bill Beaten in House," *Dallas Morning News*, Apr. 11, 1933; both quoted in Allread, "Sarah T. Hughes," 48.
40. "Income Tax Bill Passes House," *Austin American-Statesman*, Apr. 28, 1933, quoted in Allread, "Sarah T. Hughes," 49.
41. "People Want No New Taxes," clipping, Feb. [n.d.], 1933, *Dallas Dispatch*, Scrapbook no. 2, STH.
42. Undated clipping, *Daily Times Herald*, Scrapbook no. 2, STH.
43. Undated clipping, *Dallas Journal*, Scrapbook no. 2, STH.
44. "Texas and the Income Tax," *Austin American-Statesman*," May 20, 1933, Scrapbook no. 2, STH.
45. Roscoe Fleming, "Extra! Correspondent Picks New Texas Senate," clipping, *Fort Worth Press*, June 1933, Scrapbook no. 2, STH.
46. H.B. 218, State of Texas Legislature, *House Journal*, 43rd Legislature, Jan. 10, 1933, to Apr. 19, 1933, vol. 1: 820-21; "West Texas Land Bill Opponents Win First Round," *Dallas Morning News*, Mar. 14, 1933, and "Hughes Amendment to West Texas Land Bill Would Exempt Oil Companies from Benefit," *Fort Worth Press*, Mar. 14, 1933, as cited in Allread, "Sarah T. Hughes," 50.
47. "The Sales Tax," *Daily Times Herald*, Aug. 30, 1933, Scrapbook no. 2, STH.
48. "Sarah Hughes Stands on Tip-Toe Before 'Mike' and Flays Rep. Pope," *Dallas Dispatch*, Sept. 14, 1934, Scrapbook no. 2, STH; interview with Louise Phinney Caldwell, Mar. 7, 2001.
49. Clipping, "Car Licenses Cut by House," [*Fort Worth Press*, n.d.], Scrapbook no. 2, STH.
50. Undated clipping, Scrapbook no. 2, STH.
51. "Her Honor the Judge: Sarah Tilghman Hughes," typescript, Folder 6, Box 1901, STH.
52. Clipping, *Fort Worth Press*, Apr. 18, 1934, ibid.
53. Untitled clipping from a Tyler newspaper, December 1932, ibid.
54. Kenneth B. Ragsdale, *The Year America Discovered Texas: Centennial '36* (College Station: Texas A&M University Press, 1987), 66.
55. Ibid., 65-67.
56. "Plea by Hughes Turns Tide in Lower Chamber," *Dallas Journal*, Nov. 8, 1934, Scrapbook no. 2, STH.
57. "Sarah as Joan of Arc," *Dallas Dispatch*, Nov. 8, 1934, Scrapbook no. 2, STH.
58. Ragsdale, *The Year America Discovered Texas*, 73.
59. A full discussion of this project may be found in John A. Adams Jr.'s *Damming the Colorado: The Rise of the Lower Colorado River Authority, 1933-1939* (College Station: Texas A&M University Press, 1990), 24-42.
60. Robert A. Caro, *The Years of Lyndon Johnson: The Path to Power* (New York: Vintage Books, 1983), 378. Caro cites the source of the story as Thomas C. Ferguson, a Lower Colorado River Authority board member.
61. Statement by George J. Leahy, Chairman of the National Job Saving and Investment Protection Bureau for the Coal Industry, Sept. 27, [1934], Folder 4, Box 1941, STH.
62. "U.S. about to Embark on a 'TVA' in Texas," *Chicago Tribune*, Sept. 24, 1934, clipping in Folder 5, Box 1941, STH.
63. "Woman Helps to Kill Texas River Projects," Sept. 27, 1934, ibid.
64. "Remember Alamo and Don't Forget Teapot Dome," *Dallas Dispatch*, Oct. 15, 1934; and "Colorado Bill Killed As Session Closes," *Austin American*, Sept. 26, 1934; both ibid.
65. Oct. 3, 1934, Folder 2, Box 1941, STH.

66. Ibid.
67. Adams, *Damming the Colorado*, 38; Hughes to Harold Ickes, Nov. 5, 1934, Folder 2, Box 1944, STH.
68. Nov. 14, 1934, Folder 2, Box 1941, STH.
69. Jan. 3, 1935, ibid.
70. To Hughes, Sidney Latham and Weaver Moore, Jan. 30, 1935, ibid.
71. Hughes to Ickes, Jan. 30, 1935, ibid.
72. Adams, *Damming the Colorado*, 40-41; Ron Tyler, editor-in-chief, *The New Handbook of Texas*, vol. 6 (Austin: Texas State Historical Association, 1996). 313.
73. Adams, *Damming the Colorado*, 46-47.
74. *Austin American*, June 16, 1952, as quoted by Caro, *The Path to Power*, 373.
75. Clipping, "Mrs. Wilmans Returns," *Dallas Journal* [1934], Scrapbook no. 2, STH.
76. Ibid.
77. Vivian Anderson Castleberry, *Daughters of Dallas: A History of Dallas through the Voices and Deeds of Its Women* (Dallas: Odenwald Press, 1944), 255; *Dallas Morning News*, July 29, 1934.
78. *Dallas Morning News*, Aug. 21 and 23, 1934; Gant, "Interview with Sarah T. Hughes," Jan. 15, 1969, 14, STH.
79. "Rep. Sarah Hughes Is Selected by Scribes as 'Most Valuable' House Solon; Holbrook Named in Senate," *Houston Chronicle*, Sept. 30, 1934, Scrapbook no. 2, STH.

Chapter 4, Breaking Barriers

1. Caro, *Means of Ascent*, 163-64; Gantt, "Interview with Judge Sarah T. Hughes," Feb. 7, 1969, 13-14, STH; "The Lady Lawmaker from Dallas," *Ferguson Forum*, Jan. 1935, Scrapbook no. 2, Oversize Box 1908, STH.
2. "The Lady Lawmaker from Dallas," *Ferguson Forum*, Jan. 1935.
3. State of Texas Legislature, *House Journal*, 44th Legislature, Regular Session, Jan. 8, 1935, to Apr. 16, 1935, vol. 1: 14-15.
4. Clipping, "Sarah Hughes Attacks Sales Tax Proposal," *Dallas Morning News*, Dec. 17, 1934, Scrapbook no. 2, STH.
5. State of Texas Legislature, *House Journal*, 44th Legislature, Regular Session, Jan. 8, 1935, to Apr. 16, 1935, vol. 1: 106.
6. Clipping, "Two Women Lawmakers under Big Dome," *Austin American*, January 1935, Scrapbook no. 2, STH.
7. Gantt, "Interview with Judge Sarah T. Hughes," Feb. 7, 1969, 17, STH.
8. "Decade 2, 1934-44," typescript fragment from history of Dallas Zonta Club, file on STH, Vivian Castleberry Papers; "Club Women of Dallas Seek Appointment of Mrs. Hughes as Judge," *Dallas Journal*, Feb. 1, 1935, and "Sarah Hughes Is Boomed for Judge's Post," *Daily Times Herald*, [Jan. 30, 1935], clippings in Scrapbook no. 2, STH.
9. "Will Sarah Hughes Be Appointed Judge?" *Dallas Evening Journal*, clipping in Sarah T. Hughes file, Texas/Dallas History and Archives, Dallas Public Library; Gantt, "Interview with Judge Sarah T. Hughes," Feb. 7, 1969, 17, STH.
10. Gantt, "Interview with Judge Sarah T. Hughes," Feb. 7, 1969, 18, STH.
11. Hughes told Fred Gantt in an oral history interview that Clark was Allred's secretary of state. However, he was not appointed to that position until 1937. As Allred's assistant Clark was in the early days of a prominent political career that would include serving as legal counsel to Lyndon B. Johnson and ambassador to Australia.
12. Gantt, "Interview with Judge Sarah T. Hughes," Feb. 7, 1969, 18, STH.
13. "D. A. Frank Named to Bench Vacancy after Woman Is Appointed," *Daily Times Herald*, Feb. 2, 1935.
14. "Sarah T. Hughes Appointed Judge of District Court," *Dallas Morning News*, Feb. 2, 1935.
15. Ibid.
16. Ibid.
17. "D. A. Frank Named to Bench Vacancy After Woman Is Appointed," *Daily Times Herald*, Feb. 2, 1935.
18. "Woman Judge Choice Given Wide Support," *Daily Times Herald*, Feb. 3, 1935.
19. Ibid.; and "Women Rally in Support of Sarah Hughes," *Daily Times Herald*, Feb. 4, 1935.
20. "Friends to Fight for Judgeship," *Dallas Journal*, undated clipping [Feb. 2, 1935?] in Scrapbook no. 2, STH.
21. "Sarah T. Hughes Appointed Judge of District Court," *Dallas Morning News*, Feb. 2, 1935.
22. "Westerfeld Claim of Ineligibility Is Refuted by Ruling," *Dallas Morning News*, Feb. 5, 1935.

23. "Woman Judge Choice Given Wide Support," *Daily Times Herald*, Feb. 3, 1935.
24. "Friends to Fight for Judgeship," *Dallas Journal*, undated clipping [Feb. 2, 1935], Scrapbook no. 2, STH.
25. "Women Swarm to Support Mrs. Hughes's Appointment," *Dallas Morning News*, Feb. 3, 1935.
26. "Women Rally In Support of Sarah Hughes," *Dallas Morning News*, Feb. 4, 1935.
27. "May Serve as Judge over Court in Which Could Not Be Juror," *Dallas Morning News*, Feb. 2, 1935.
28. "The Daily Nosegay," *Fort Worth Press*, Feb. 2, 1935.
29. "Texas Judiciary Scene of the Future," *Dallas Journal*, undated clipping, Scrapbook no. 2, STH.
30. Gantt, "Interview with Judge Sarah T. Hughes," Feb. 7, 1969, 18, STH.
31. The picture accompanies the story "Women Swarm to Support Mrs. Hughes's Appointment," *Dallas Morning News*, Feb. 3, 1935.
32. "Woman to Ask Bar's Aid for Sarah Hughes," *Dallas Morning News*, Feb. 5, 1935.
33. "Mrs. Hughes's Name Is Sent to Senate for Seat on Bench," *Dallas Morning News*, Feb. 6, 1935, clipping Scrapbook no. 2, STH.
34. W. R. Hegler to Allred, Feb. 5, 1935, "Judicial Appointments, Judge Sarah T. Hughes, Dallas District Court 1935," Records of Gov. James V. Allred, 1985/024-16, Texas State Archives.
35. Ibid.
36. Clipping, *Dallas Journal*, Feb. 4, 1935, Scrapbook no. 2, STH.
37. Gantt, "Interview with Judge Sarah T. Hughes," Feb. 7, 1969, 18, STH; "Sarah Hughes Faces Senate Floor Fight," *Daily Times Herald*, Feb. 8, 1935.
38. "Miss Sallie—Judge," *Daily Times Herald*, Feb. 3, 1935.
39. Julian Capers Jr., "Nobody's Business," undated clipping, Scrapbook no. 2; and typescript entitled "Excerpts from Clippings in the *Dallas Morning News* on Public Life of Sarah T. Hughes," Folder 7, Box 1900; both in STH.
40. Reef, "Dallas Dynamo," STH. In the interview Westerfeld said he was ready to withdraw his objections to Hughes. "Sarah has made good as a judge—very good," he said.
41. "Mrs. Hughes Is Given New Oath," *Fort Worth Press*, Feb. 12, 1935; and "Mrs. Hughes Waves Farewell as Vote in Senate Comes Out," *Austin American*, Feb. 13, 1935; both clippings in Scrapbook no. 2, STH. Those voting for Hughes were Senators Blackert, Burns, Cotton, Davis, DeBerry, Duggan, Fellbaum, Hill, Hopkins, Hornsby, Martin, Moore, Neal, Oneal, Pace, Poage, Rawlings, Redditt, Regan, Shivers, Stone, Van Zandt, and Woodruff. Those opposed were Beck, Collie, Holbrook, Sanderford, Small, Sulak, and Westerfeld. Hughston was absent.
42. Ibid.
43. Undated clipping, *Dallas Dispatch*, Scrapbook no. 2, STH.
44. Gantt, "Interview with Judge Sarah T. Hughes," Feb. 7, 1969, 20, STH.
45. "Sarah's Bill to Test Lawyers Engrossed," *Dallas Dispatch*, Feb. 12, 1935, clipping, Scrapbook no. 2, STH.
46. "Judge Hughes Takes Bench in Simple Ceremony; Feels about 'As Usual,'" *Dallas Dispatch*, Feb. 13, 1935, clipping in Scrapbook no. 2, STH.
47. "Woman Judge Takes Job on Dallas Bench; Has No 'Pet Policies,'" *Dallas Morning News*, Feb. 14, 1935.
48. Gantt, "Interview with Judge Sarah T. Hughes," Feb. 7, 1969, 21, STH.
49. "Judge Sarah Hughes Takes Bench in Simple Ceremony; Feels about 'As Usual,'" *Dallas Dispatch*, Feb. 13, 1935, clipping, Scrapbook no. 2, STH.
50. "Decade 2, 1934-44," typescript fragment from history of Dallas Zonta Club, file on STH, Vivian Castleberry Papers.
51. Ibid.
52. Typescript entitled "Excerpts from Clippings in the *Dallas Morning News* on Public Life of Sarah T. Hughes," Folder 7, Box 1900; and Henry Relf Lee to STH, Aug. 8, 1975; both in Folder 6, Box 1893, STH.
53. Allread, "Sarah T. Hughes," 60-62.
54. Ibid., 62.
55. Ibid., 66-68.
56. "Will Seek Bench Again, Says Judge Sarah Hughes as First Year Nearly Up," *Daily Times Herald*, Dec. 2, 1935, Scrapbook no. 2, STH.
57. "Woman Jurist Cleans House," undated [1936] newspaper clipping, Scrapbook no. 2, STH.
58. Undated newspaper clipping, February 1936, Scrapbook no. 2, STH.
59. "Will Seek Bench Again," *Daily Times Herald*, Dec. 2, 1935.

60. Ibid.
61. Ibid.
62. Entries in Scrapbook no. 2, STH; "Judge Hughes Speaks to a Large Crowd," *Dallas Express*, May 11, 1935.
63. "Dallas Woman Jurist Speaks," July [n.d.] 1935, *Fort Worth Star-Telegram*, Scrapbook no. 2, STH.
64. Undated political advertisement for Cocke and newspaper clipping, Jan. 23, 1936, Scrapbook no. 2, STH.
65. Undated newspaper advertisement, Scrapbook no. 2, STH.
66. "Sally Hughes Traces Her Ancestry to Texas Pioneers," undated newspaper clipping [1936], Scrapbook no. 2, STH.
67. Undated newspaper clipping, Scrapbook no. 2, STH.
68. Undated newspaper column entitled "Tomorrow," 1935, Scrapbook no. 2, STH.
69. Sarah Tilghman Hughes, "A Daniel Come to Judgment: First Woman in Texas," *Anchora of Delta Gamma*, January 1937, 158-60.
70. Moses, "Miss Sally, Texas' District Judge," 118.
71. "Solid Support of Dem Ticket Urged at Gregg Rally," undated newspaper clipping, Scrapbook no. 2, STH.
72. "Woman Judge Is Class Speaker for Home Graduates," undated Cleburne newspaper, May 1935, Scrapbook no. 2, STH.
73. Photos, Scrapbook no. 2, STH.
74. "Jurist Decries Divorce Cases with Children," undated newspaper clipping, 1935, Scrapbook no. 2, STH.

Chapter 5, Extending Boundaries

1. Caption for photograph of Hughes in the *Washington Herald*, Aug. 5, 1937; "John Rawlins, Sarah Hughes May Get Seat," undated clipping; "Woman Is Backed by Labor Council for Appeals Post," undated clipping; *Daily Times Herald*, Mar. 23, 1939; all in Scrapbook no. 2, Oversize Box 1908, STH.
2. Charles Galvin, former dean of the SMU Law School, was told of Hughes's decision not to accept pay or gasoline coupons by the dean who employed her, Charles Potts.
3. "Judge, Smoot End Destruction Row," *Dallas Dispatch*, Aug. 21, 1939; and *Daily Times Herald* photograph with caption, "Her Honor Shows Sheriff How to Carry Out Court Order," Aug. 21, 1939; both in Scrapbook no. 2, STH.
4. "Judge Sarah Hughes Stops Court to Buy Hay at Bargain Price," *Austin American*, Dec. 1, 1938, Scrapbook no. 2, STH.
5. "Divorce Proceedings Conducted in Spanish," undated clipping, Scrapbook no. 2, STH.
6. "Hearing before Subcommittee No. 1 of the Committee on the Judiciary House of Representatives, Seventy-fifth Congress, First Session on H.R. 3409," Mar. 3, 1937, Folder 2, Box 1943, STH.
7. State of Texas Legislature, House Joint Resolution No. 49, *House Journal*, 44th Legislature, Regular Session, Jan. 8, 1935, to Apr. 16, 1935, vol. 1: 1378 and 96. One such reference to her co-sponsorship is in a quotation from her appearing in her obituary in the *Dallas Times Herald*, Apr. 24, 1985. There she was quoted as having previously said about her legislative service, "I was co-author of a bill to give women the right to serve on juries."
8. "Judge Hughes Quotes Law to Uphold Women's Jury Rights," undated clipping, Scrapbook no. 2, STH.
9. *Glover v. Cobb et al.*, 123 S.W. 2d, 794 (1938); Sarah T. Hughes, "The Half-Citizen," *Legal Chatter: A Monthly Legal Magazine*, May 1939, 31-34.
10. "Zonta Club of Dallas, 1924-1961," Texas/Dallas History and Archives, Dallas Public Library.
11. *Texas Business and Professional Woman*, July 1939, Folder 2, Box 1918, STH.
12. "Judge Hughes Leading Demand of Women for Equal Rights on Jury," untitled clipping, Scrapbook no. 2, STH.
13. Undated article, June 28, 1938, Scrapbook no. 2, STH.
14. "How Does Your Representative Stand on Jury Service," *Texas Business and Professional Woman*, June-July, 1940, Folder 3, Box 1917, STH.
15. Folder 1, Box 1918, STH, contains the Colorado City speech and many others. More on the subject in Boxes 1896, 1917, and 1908.
16. Among the articles are the previously cited "The Half-Citizen," 31-34, and "The Half-Citizen in This

Democracy," *Texas Parent-Teacher*, Jan. 1941, 10-11; "Jury Service for Women," *Emancipator: An Independent Forward-looking Monthly*, Jan. 1943, 10-12; and "The Half-Citizen," *Kappa Beta Pi Quarterly*, Oct. 1943, 118-19. All of these are in Folder 8, Box 1896, STH.

17. Payne, *As Old as Dallas Itself*, 192-93.
18. Programs for these meetings are in Folder 9, Box 1917; undated clipping of newspaper editorial, "Women's Rights," Scrapbook no. 2; both in STH.
19. "The Texas Federation Becomes of Age," *Texas Business and Professional Woman*, May 1940, Scrapbook no. 2, STH.
20. Gantt, "Interview with Judge Sarah T. Hughes," Feb. 7, 1969, 24, STH.
21. Miscellaneous clippings in Scrapbook no. 2, STH.
22. Undated clipping, "Supreme Court Justices Attend State Reception," Scrapbook no. 2, STH.
23. Gantt, "Interview with Judge Sarah T. Hughes," Feb. 7, 1969, 23, STH.
24. Undated clipping, Scrapbook no. 2, STH.
25. *Dallas Morning News*, Jan. 12, 1937, ibid.; Gantt, "Interview with Judge Sarah T. Hughes," Feb. 7, 1969, 24, STH.
26. William E. Leuchtenburg, *Franklin D. Roosevelt and the New Deal, 1932-1940* (New York: Harper & Row Publishers, 1963), 232-34; Payne, *As Old as Dallas Itself*, 176.
27. "Woman Judge Would Change Supreme Court," undated newspaper clipping in Scrapbook no. 2, STH.
28. "Dallas Judge Expresses Views on Constitution," undated newspaper clipping, ibid.
29. Gantt, "Interview with Sarah T. Hughes," Feb. 7, 1969, 27, STH.
30. Ann Gough Hunter, "Two Portias Preside over Southern Justice," *Democratic Digest*, Nov. 1937; and undated clipping, "ROTC Simply Putting War Spirit in Students, Charges Judge Hughes," Scrapbook no. 2, STH.
31. *Fort Worth Star-Telegram*, Mar. 23 [1938], Scrapbook no. 2, STH.
32. "ROTC Simply Putting War Spirit in Students, Charges Judge Hughes," Scrapbook no. 2, STH.
33. "Peace Lovers Protest Legion's Armistice Preparedness Parade," *Dallas Morning News*, Nov. 2, 1938, Scrapbook no. 2, STH.
34. "Legion Plans Parade although Women Talk Rival Peace March," *Dallas Morning News*, Nov. 3, 1938, Scrapbook no. 2, STH.
35. Ibid.
36. Ibid.
37. Ibid.
38. "If Democracy Survives," *Today and Tomorrow*, Mar. 1941, 19, and Apr. 1941, 8; "Ginners and Civilian Defense," *Cotton Ginners Journal*, May 1942, 9-10; both in Folder 8, Box 1896, STH.
39. N. V. Bird, chief of Navy Personnel, Washington, D.C., to Hughes, Mar. 9, 1944, as cited by Allread, "Sarah T. Hughes," 83.
40. "Tench Tilghman to Be Launched," *Baltimore Evening Sun*, Aug. 21, 1943, Folder 1, Box 1901, STH.
41. Hughes speech entitled "Roosevelt," dated 1944, Folder 22, Box 1897, STH.
42. Moses, "Miss Sally, Texas' District Judge," 107.
43. "Dallas Judge Expresses Views on Constitution," undated newspaper clipping in Scrapbook no. 2, STH.
44. The three account books, dating from 1938 to the end of 1956, were given to me by Constance Tilghman Dudley.
45. Rozanne Berghane, "Dallas Fashion Personalities," *Dallas Morning News*, undated clipping [1939], Scrapbook no. 2, STH.
46. The advertisement appeared on Jan. 16, 1938, Scrapbook no. 2, STH.
47. *Bryan Eagle*, Feb. 1, 1938, Scrapbook no. 2, STH.
48. "Two Out of Three Marriages in Dallas End in Divorce," *Dallas Morning News*, undated clipping [1938], Scrapbook no. 2, STH.
49. Mrs. Josephine Scoma to Governor James V. Allred, May 29, 1937, General Correspondence, June 1937/024-6, Records of Gov. James V. Allred, Texas State Archives.
50. George Clarke to Mrs. Josephine Scoma, June 1, 1937, Records of Gov. James V. Allred, Texas State Archives.
51. "Fails to Pay Child Support; Goes to Jail," *Fort Worth Star-Telegram*, June 11, 1938, Scrapbook no. 2, STH.
52. "Value Received No Concern of Divorce Court," undated clipping, Scrapbook no. 2, STH.
53. Gantt, "Interview with Judge Sarah T. Hughes," Feb. 7, 1969, 26, STH.

54. *Dallas Dispatch*, Oct. 13, 1938, Scrapbook no. 2, STH.
55. "New Domestic Court Grants First Divorce," *Daily Times Herald*, Oct. 31, 1938, Scrapbook no. 2, STH.
56. Letters to these officials are in Folder 2, Box 1966, STH. West's column, "Dallas' Rising Divorce Rate Sets Pace for Rest of U.S.," Apr. 2, 1944, is in Scrapbook no. 2, STH.
57. "Don't Be Ruled Only by Heart in Picking Mate, Judge Advises," unidentified newspaper, undated clipping, Scrapbook no. 2, STH.
58. Ibid.
59. *Chicago Daily News*, Sept. 12, 1943, Scrapbook no. 2, STH.
60. "West Dallas Children's Park Needed More Than Lee's Home Replica, Judge Hughes, Claims," *Dallas Morning News*, Dec. 31, 1938, Scrapbook no. 2, STH.
61. Sarah T. Hughes, "Character Education versus Juvenile Delinquency," *Texas Parent Teachers Magazine*, undated, Folder 3, Box 1896, STH.
62. "Juvenile Delinquency," an undated typescript [probably 1943], Folder 5, Box 1967, STH.
63. "First Duty of Mother Is to Children," *Dallas Morning News*, Jan. 25, 1943, Scrapbook no. 2, STH.
64. Ibid.
65. "Juvenile Delinquency," Folder 5, Box 1967, STH.
66. "'Dydamic' Label Fits Sarah Hughes," *Dallas Morning News*, May 29, 1949; Allread, "Sarah T. Hughes," 86-87.
67. "Templeton Fires Vicious Blast at Sarah Hughes," *Dallas Morning News*, [1944], Scrapbook no. 2, STH.
68. *Dallas Morning News*, Nov. 21, 1944, Scrapbook no. 2, STH.
69. Ibid.
70. "Templeton Fires Vicious Blast at Sarah Hughes," *Dallas Morning News*, [1944], Scrapbook no. 2, STH.
71. "Youth Home Called Real County Issue," *Dallas Morning News*, Feb. 12, 1945, Scrapbook no. 2, STH.
72. "Templeton Fires Vicious Blast at Sarah Hughes," *Dallas Morning News*, [1944], Scrapbook no. 2, STH.
73. Undated clipping, *Daily Times Herald*, Nov. 22, [probably 1944], Folder 8, Box 1900, STH.
74. "City, County Move to Include Welfare Building in Plan Vote," *Dallas Morning News*, Oct. 25, 1945, Scrapbook no. 2, STH; "Social Agencies Name Committee to Study Delinquency Problem," *Dallas Morning News*, Feb. 20, 1945.

Chapter 6, Dynamo from Dallas

1. "Strong Argument of Dallas Woman Judge against Joint Tax Return Impresses Body," *Houston Chronicle*, Mar. 26, 1942; and Drew Pearson and Robert S. Allen, "Washington Merry-Go-Round," *Dallas Morning News*, Apr. 18, 1942; both clippings in Scrapbook no. 2, Oversize Box 1908, STH.
2. U.S. Department of Justice, FBI, Sarah T. Hughes File No. 77-88126: Dallas Office, Field Office File 77-4705, Aug. 31, 1961; "Hearings Set for Two Men Taken in Gambling Raid," *Dallas Morning News*, Aug. 3, 1943.
3. Ibid.; and letter from Maudie I. Walling to Wallis Reef, Oct. 8, 1945, Folder 12, Box 1891, STH.
4. Numerous news clippings about this event are found in Folder 12, Box 1891, STH; and interviews conducted by the FBI years later when Hughes was under consideration for a federal judgeship are in U.S. Department of Justice, FBI, Sarah T. Hughes, File No. 77-88126: Dallas Office, Field Office File 77-4705, Aug. 31, 1961.
5. Peak's columns, most of them undated, are in Folder 12, Box 1891, STH.
6. "Judge Hughes Not Present in Game Room, Says Raider," Aug. 8, 1943, *Dallas Morning News*, Folder 12, Box 1891, STH.
7. Hughes to Peak, Aug. 27, 1943, Folder 12, Box 1891, STH. Peak reprinted Hughes's letter in his column on Sept. 4, 1943.
8. Hughes to Brewster, Aug. 14, 1943, Folder 12, Box 1881, STH.
9. Lipscomb to Julius Runge, Aug. 10, 1943, ibid.
10. Hughes to Dr. Angie Smith, Sept. 3, 1943, ibid.
11. Roy A. Skinner to Hughes, Sept. 9, 1943, ibid.
12. Typescript of committee report, entitled "Mr. President and Members of the Dallas Bar Association," September 1943, ibid.
13. Hughes to Mrs. Mabel Bennett, Sept. 20, 1943; Speer to Hughes, Sept. 30, 1943; and Hughes to Speer, Oct. 4, 1943; all ibid.

14. Sept. 17, 1943, clipping, ibid.
15. "Judge Exonerated In Bar Inquiry," *Dallas Morning News*, undated clipping, ibid.
16. Walling to Reef, Oct. 8, 1945, ibid.
17. Walling to Hughes, [1945], ibid.
18. Typewritten announcement for candidacy, 1944, Folder 2, Box 1970, STH.
19. Undated newspaper advertisement, ibid.
20. Undated newspaper advertisement by Guthrie, ibid.
21. "Women Ask Place in Peace Councils," *New York Times*, June 15, 1944.
22. "Stevenson Is Criticized by Judge Hughes," *Daily Times Herald*, Sept. 8, 1944.
23. "44 Women Merit State Posts, Judge Hughes Tells Stevenson," *Dallas Morning News*, Oct. 31, 1944.
24. "Sarah Hughes to Run for Congress in 1946, *Dallas Morning News*, Nov. 17, 1944.
25. Undated newspaper clipping, probably Jan. 21, 1945, Scrapbook no. 2, STH.
26. Ibid.
27. May 1945, clipping from unidentified Alabama newspaper, Scrapbook no. 3, Oversize Box 1908, STH.
28. *Dallas Morning News*, Feb. 18, 1945, Scrapbook no. 2, STH.
29. "Womanpower Given as Solution to Jury Lack by Judge Hughes," *Dallas Morning News*, Mar. 25, 1945, Scrapbook no. 2, STH. See also an unpublished manuscript by Elizabeth R. Rabe, "Full Citizenship Alone Will Suffice: Judge Sarah T. Hughes Takes the Stand," Feb. 28, 1996, a paper prepared for student competition on National History Day, Junior Division, a copy of which was supplied to me by the Honorable Barefoot Sanders, U.S. district judge.
30. *Daily Times Herald*, Aug. 29, 1945, Scrapbook no. 2, STH.
31. A collection of Hughes's radio scripts, beginning Apr. 21, 1945, and ending Nov. 17, 1945, Gwen Graul Papers.
32. "Radio Program—April 21, 1945—8:45 a.m.," ibid.
33. Scripts for Apr. 28, May 5, May 19, Aug. 4, and Oct. 20, 1945, ibid.
34. Scripts for May 12, July 28, and Aug. 11, 1945, ibid.
35. Script for Aug. 18, 1945, ibid.
36. *Carrollton Chronicle*, May 25, 1945, clipping, Folder 7, Box 1900, STH.; interview with Rayburn Wright, June 20, 2001.
37. *White Rocker*, May 19, 1945, Folder 9, Box 1941, STH.
38. "The Story of Sarah T. Hughes, Folder 8, Box 1941, STH.
39. These articles and reports are in Folder 15, Box 1943, STH.
40. "Judge Hughes Says Sumner Behind Times," *Daily Times Herald*, Sept. 4, 1945, Scrapbook no. 2, STH.
41. Ibid.
42. DeForrest Kline, "Political Power," *Oak Cliff Tribune*, Feb. 22, 1946, as quoted by Allread, "Sarah T. Hughes," 96.
43. Reef, "Dallas Dynamo," STH; and undated clipping [Oct. 1945], *Dallas Morning News*, Folder 22, Box 1897, STH.
44. Reef, "Dallas Dynamo," STH.
45. Ibid.
46. "Mrs. Sarah Hughes Announces Her Candidacy for Congress," *Dallas Morning News*, Feb. 24, 1946, Scrapbook no. 2, STH.
47. *Dallas Morning News*, May 12, 1946, ibid.
48. *Dallas Morning News*, Apr. 21, 1946, ibid.
49. *Dallas Morning News*, May 12, 1946, ibid.
50. Ibid.
51. Ibid.
52. Gantt, "Interview with Judge Sarah T. Hughes," Feb. 28, 1969, 21, STH.
53. "Judge Calls Herself F.R. Liberal," *Dallas Morning News*, June [n.d.] 1946, Folder 9, Box 1941, STH.
54. "Hughes Attacks Strike Leaders," undated advertisement, Folder 11, Box 1941, STH.
55. "Views Clash at Rally for OPA Controls," *Dallas Morning News*, undated clipping, Scrapbook no. 2, STH; Harry S. Truman, *Year of Decisions* (Garden City, N.Y., 1955), 491.
56. Allread, "Sarah T. Hughes," 95.
57. Gantt, "Interview with Judge Sarah T. Hughes," Feb. 28, 1969, 20, STH.
58. "The Public Is Entitled to Know," advertisement, *Dallas Morning News*, June 10, 1946.
59. "Candidates for Congress May Debate," *Daily Times Herald*, Scrapbook no. 2, STH.
60. "The Story of Sarah T. Hughes," Folder 8, Box 1941, STH.

61. Advertisement, "Judge Sarah T. Hughes, the Real Democrat for Congress," untitled clipping, Aug. 16, 1946, Scrapbook no. 2, STH.
62. "Hughes Ahead for Congress," *Dallas Morning News*, July 28, 1946, Scrapbook no. 2, STH.
63. Allread, "Sarah T. Hughes," 96.
64. Undated clippings, *Dallas Morning News*, 1946, "Wilson Picks PAC as Issue," and "Wilson Says He'll Debate Mrs. Hughes," Scrapbook no. 2, STH.
65. Allread, "Sarah T. Hughes," 96.
66. "Hughes Says False Label Given Reform," *Daily Times Herald*, Scrapbook no. 2, STH.
67. "Candidates for Congress May Debate," *Daily Times Herald*, undated clipping, Scrapbook no. 2, STH.
68. "Wilson Wins Congress Race," *Dallas Morning News*, Aug. 25, 1946, Scrapbook no. 2, STH.
69. Gantt, "Interview with Judge Sarah T. Hughes," Feb. 28, 1969, 12, STH.
70. "Texas Delegation Opposed Hughes," Aug. 27, 1946, *Dallas Morning News*.
71. "'Dydamic' Label Fits Sarah Hughes," May 29, 1949, *Dallas Morning News*.
72. "Women Revive Jury Bid," Nov. 15, 1946, *Dallas Morning News*.
73. Ibid.
74. Ken Hand, "Offhand," *Dallas Morning News*, Feb. 17, 1949, Scrapbook no. 3, STH; Rabe, "Full Citizenship Alone Will Suffice," 8.
75. *AAUW Journal*, Oct. 27, 1947, clipping in Folder 1, Box 1896, STH.
76. Constance Tilghman Dudley to me, e-mail, Aug. 28, 2003.
77. "Radio Program WRR 10/6/45, 8:45 to 9 a.m., Sarah T. Hughes," Gwen Graul Papers.
78. Constance Tilghman Dudley to me, e-mail, Aug. 12, 2001.
79. Ibid.
80. Ibid.
81. "Only Woman Judge in Texas Has Busy . . ." *Christian Science Monitor*, [July 1948], clipping, Scrapbook no. 3, STH.
82. Family Card for the Hughes, St. Matthew's Episcopal Cathedral, and *Dallas Morning News*, June 1, 1956, clipping in Folder 7, Box 1900, STH. Frances James of Dallas recalled the Hugheses sitting behind her family in the third-row pew during the 1940s and hearing Sarah Hughes frequently telling her how it good it made her feel to see the James family together in church. James, personal communication, May 17, 2001.
83. Interview with Louise Raggio, Aug. 25, 2000.

Chapter 7, A National Perspective

1. "'Dydamic' Label Fits Sarah Hughes," *Dallas Morning News*, May 29, 1949.
2. Gantt, "Interview with Judge Sarah T. Hughes," Feb. 28, 1969, 11, STH.
3. "Mrs. Sarah Hughes to Help Lyndon Johnson," *Houston Post*, Aug. [n.d.], 1948, clipping in Scrapbook no. 3, Oversize Box 1908, STH.
4. Gantt, "Interview with Judge Sarah T. Hughes," Feb. 28, 1969, 11, 13, STH.
5. Sarah T. Hughes Oral History, Interview I, Oct. 7, 1968, by Joe B. Frantz, Transcript, Internet copy, LBJ Library; Caro, *Means of Ascent*, 373; David McCullough, *Truman* (New York: Simon & Schuster, 1992), 675-77.
6. "Live Up to Talk of Unity, Truman Dares GOP Here," *Dallas Morning News*, Sept. 28, 1948; McCullough, *Truman*, 677.
7. "Republicans View Speech as 'Shocking,'" *Dallas Morning News*, Sept. 29, 1948.
8. John L. (Jack) Hauer, *Finest Kind! A Memorable Half Century of Dallas Lawyers (plus a Few from Out-of-Town)* (Dallas: Dallas Bar Foundation, n.d.), 4.
9. Sarah T. Hughes résumé, "Sarah T. Hughes, 14th District Court of Texas," clippings file, Texas/Dallas History and Archives, Dallas Public Library.
10. *Daily Times Herald*, July 10, 1948, Scrapbook no. 3, STH.
11. *Christian Science Monitor*, July [n.d.], 1948, Scrapbook no. 3, STH.
12. Ibid.
13. Undated clipping [1949], *Dallas Morning News*, Scrapbook no. 3, STH.
14. "Judge Sarah Hughes Speaks on 'Jury Service For Women,'" *Brownwood Bulletin*, Oct. 17, 1949, Scrapbook no. 3, STH.
15. Ibid.
16. Various clippings, Scrapbook no. 3, STH.

17. "Offhand," *Dallas Morning News*, Feb. 1, 1949, clipping in Scrapbook no. 3, STH.
18. Returns are from "Constitutional Amendments Submitted, 1949," *Texas Almanac and State Industrial Guide, 1952-53*, 490.
19. Aug. 5, 1949, Folder 1, Box 1942, STH.
20. Feb. 2, 1950, ibid.
21. U.S. Department of Justice, FBI, Sarah T. Hughes, File No. 77-88126: Dallas Office, Field Office File 77-4705, Aug. 31, 1961.
22. "Town Meeting for Peace," *Dallas Morning News*, Mar. 28, 1948, clipping in Scrapbook no. 3, STH.
23. Typescript for commencement speech at Hockaday School, May 31, 1948, Folder 6, Box 1897, STH.
24. Ibid.
25. *Dallas Morning News*, Sept. 17, 1948, Scrapbook no. 3, STH.
26. *Baltimore Evening Sun*, Nov. 10, 1949, clipping, and commencement program, Scrapbook no. 3, STH.
27. "Woman Jurist Seeks Federal Judgeship," *Daily Times Herald*, June 11, 1950, clipping in Scrapbook no. 3, STH.
28. "Hughes Silent on Judgeship," June 13, 1950, clipping in Scrapbook no. 3, STH.
29. Undated clipping, Scrapbook no. 3, STH.
30. "World Government Backer to Head BPW," *Los Angeles Examiner*, July 5, 1950, clipping in Scrapbook no. 3, STH; *New York Times*, Aug. 24, 1953, as cited by James W. Riddlesperger Jr., "Sarah T. Hughes: Biography of a Federal District Judge," M.A. thesis, North Texas State University, 1980, 24; Allread, "Sarah T. Hughes," 89.
31. Her remarks are recorded in Frances Maule, "Hightide," *Independent Woman*," Sept. 1950, 258-63.
32. *Christian Science Monitor*, July 8, 1950, clipping, Scrapbook no. 3, STH.
33. Quoted by Maule, "Hightide," 260.
34. *Daily Times Herald*, Aug. 16, 1950, clipping in Scrapbook no. 3, STH.
35. "Judge Hughes Visits Ancestors' Village," Aug. 1, 1950, clipping in Scrapbook no. 3, STH; Benjamin Chew Tilghman to STH, July 29, 1950, and STH to Benjamin Chew, Aug. 28, 1950, Folder 1, Box 1901, STH; Hughes's handwritten notes entitled "Ancestral Records of Colonial Dames," p. 514, Folder 2, Box 1901, STH.
36. Allread, "Sarah T. Hughes," 97; "Truman Offers Sarah Position on FTC," and "FTC Nomination on Judge Hughes Due in Few Days," Sept. 17 and 18, 1950, *Daily Times Herald*, clippings in Scrapbook no. 3, STH.
37. *Daily Times Herald*, Sept. 18, 1950, clipping, Scrapbook no. 3, STH.
38. "Truman Offers Sarah Hughes Position on FTC," *Daily Times Herald*, Sept. 17, 1950; *Dallas Morning News*, Sept. 19, 1950, clipping, Scrapbook no. 3, STH.
39. "Judge Hughes Spurns Offer to Serve FTC," *Daily Times Herald*, Sept. 24, 1950.
40. Ibid.; "FTC Nomination on Judge Hughes Due in Few Days," *Daily Times Herald*, Sept. 18, 1950, clipping in Scrapbook no. 3, STH; and *Dallas Morning News*, Oct. 24, 1971, as quoted in Allread, "Sarah T. Hughes," 97.
41. "Judge Hughes Declines FTC Offer," *Independent Woman*, Nov. 1950, 359; "Women's Draft Advocated," *Dallas Morning News*, Oct. 8, 1950; and *New York Herald Tribune* clipping, Oct. 9, 1950; both in Scrapbook no. 3, STH.
42. "They All Had Their Say," *Independent Woman*, Sept. 1951, 251.
43. Ibid.
44. "Judge Sarah T. Hughes World Fellowship Fund Launched for Participation by All Clubs," *Independent Woman*, Mar. 1951, 83.
45. "Women Should Be Drafted," *Independent Woman*, Apr. 1951, 113.
46. Ibid.
47. *Dallas Morning News*, Nov. 17, 1951, clipping, Scrapbook no. 3, STH.
48. "Our Stand on Registration and Draft of Women," *Independent Woman*, Oct. 1951, 295.
49. Ibid.
50. "Our National President Asks Every Club to Help in November Drive to Recruit Women for Armed Services," *Independent Woman*, Nov. 1951, 333.
51. "On Earth Peace—Good Will to Men," *Independent Woman*, Dec. 1951, inside cover.
52. In January 1970, nearly two decades later, Texas governor Preston Smith appointed a statewide body with similar goals. Hughes would be a key figure in this group, the Governor's Commission on the Status of Women in Texas.
53. Information describing the meeting is in Folder 3, Box 1914, STH.

54. Elizabeth Lansing, "What More Do Women Want?" *Independent Woman*, Apr. 1952, 97, 123.
55. "Her Honor—the Judge," *Independent Woman*, Jan. 1951, 31.
56. Payne, *As Old as Dallas Itself*, 127, 275.
57. Untitled column, *Independent Woman*, Dec. 1950, inside front cover.
58. *Daily Times Herald*, Sept. 25, 1951, clipping, Scrapbook no. 3, STH.
59. Clippings from *Dallas Morning News* and unidentified San Antonio newspaper, both dated Nov. 1950, Scrapbook no. 3, STH.
60. "Judge Hughes to Participate in Dedication Ceremonies Honoring Susan B. Anthony at Hall of Fame, May 19," *Independent Woman*, Mar. 1952, 87; "Toward Full Citizenship," *Independent Woman*, Sept. 1952, 262.
61. "Toward Full Citizenship," *Independent Woman*.
62. "They All Had Their Say," *Independent Woman*, Sept. 1951, 251; and "Women's Jury Service," *Independent Woman*, July 1952, 211.
63. "Women's Jury Service," *Independent Woman*.
64. "Toward Full Citizenship," *Independent Woman*, 262.
65. "Top Candidates Questioned on Equal Rights," *New York Herald Tribune*, July 2, 1952, clipping in Scrapbook no. 3, STH.
66. "Their Hats Were in the Ring," *Independent Woman*, Aug. 1952, 226.
67. Ibid.; "Sarah Hughes Endorsed for Veep Post," *Dallas Morning News*, July 1, 1952; "Co-Pilot Roles for Women Urged in National Politics," *Boston Sunday Globe*, June 29, 1952, clipping in Scrapbook no. 3, STH.
68. "Their Hats Were in the Ring," *Independent Woman*, 226.
69. Ibid.
70. "Support Given Hughes for Vice-Presidency," *Daily Times Herald*, July 2, 1952.
71. "Their Hats Were in the Ring," *Independent Woman*, 226.
72. Sarah T. Hughes Oral History, Interview I, by Frantz, LBJ Library.
73. Gantt, "Interview with Judge Sarah T. Hughes," Feb. 28, 1969, 11, STH.
74. "Hughes Joins Mavericks," *Daily Times Herald*, July 22, 1952.
75. "Sarah Hughes Opens Battle for V-P Nod," *Dallas Morning News*, July 20, 1952.
76. "BPW Action on the Political Front," *Independent Woman*, Sept. 1952, 260.
77. Sarah T. Hughes Oral History, Interview I, by Frantz, LBJ Library.
78. "BPW Action on the Political Front," *Independent Woman*, 260; "Sparkman Chosen by Democrats as Running Mate for Stevenson," *New York Times*, July 27, 1952. Some contemporary news accounts declared that Sarah T. Hughes, whose nomination was followed closely by that of India Edwards, was the first woman ever nominated for vice president by one of the two major parties. These reports were erroneous. The first woman was nominated for that office in 1924 by the Democrats. She was Mrs. Leroy Springs of South Carolina. See Robert S. LaForte and Richard L. Himmel, "Sarah T. Hughes, John Kennedy and the Johnson Inaugural, 1963," *East Texas Historical Journal* 27, no. 2 (1989): 35.
79. "Judge Hughes Calls Tidelands 'Phony,' " *Houston Post*, Oct. 5, 1952, clipping in Scrapbook no. 3, STH.
80. Ibid.; and "Judge Sarah T. Hughes Blasts Sen. McCarthy," *Fort Worth Press*, Feb. 12, 1951, clipping in Scrapbook no. 3, STH.

Chapter 8, A Liberal's Viewpoint

1. "Judge Hughes Reports on Trip to Germany," *Dallas Morning News*, Dec. 12, 1952.
2. Traveling companions with Hughes were Mrs. Winfield W. Riefler of the National League of Women Voters; Dr. Dorothy Ferebee, president of the National Council of Negro Women, Inc.; Mary Donlon, American Women's Association; Mrs. Oscar A. Ahlgren, president of the General Federation of Women's Clubs; and Mrs. Stuart Brown of the Council of World Affairs.
3. "Judge Hughes Reports on Trip to Germany," *Dallas Morning News*, Dec. 12, 1952.
4. "Sarah Hughes Named to UNESCO Post," *Dallas Morning News*, Nov. 19, 1952; STH to Ray Murphy, Feb. 11, 1955, Folder 14, Box 1934, STH.
5. Gantt, "Interview with Judge Sarah T. Hughes," Mar. 21, 1969, 12, STH; interview with Louise Raggio, Dec. 11, 2001; "How We Organized the Dallas U.N. Association," undated typescript written presumably by Hughes, Folder 1, Box 1923, STH.
6. Untitled typewritten notes, Folder 6, Box 1922, STH.

7. Ibid. By-laws declared the organization's purpose as promoting an understanding of the United Nations and winning support for its objectives. Special committees were formed: UN Week, speakers bureau, special events, finance, radio, membership, study groups, publicity, evaluation, research, and legislation program.

8. "Dallas United Nations Association: Annual Report May 1954," Folder 13, STH.

9. Hughes, "World Peace through World Law," *National Business Woman*, Nov. 1965, 14-16.

10. *Paris News* (Texas), Dec. 6, 1954, as cited by Allread, "Sarah T. Hughes," 90.

11. "Dallas United Nations Association: Annual Report May 1954," Folder 13, Box 22, STH.

12. Hughes to Holcomb, Oct. 27, 1953, Folder 1, STH.

13. Ardis Burst, *The Three Families of H. L. Hunt* (New York: Weidenfeld & Nicolson, 1988), 35-37.

14. Hughes's letter to the editor appears in the *Dallas Morning News*, May 4, 1953, a clipping of which is in Folder 1, Box 22, STH.

15. Ibid.

16. The responses to Hughes's letters are Folder 1, Box 22, STH.

17. Hughes to Rev. Luther Holcomb, Oct. 27, 1953, Folder 1, Box 22, STH.

18. Interview with Louise Raggio, Mar. 3, 2001.

19. "More Patience Needed with United Nations," *Dallas Morning News*, Jan. 11, 1955.

20. U.S. Department of Justice, FBI, Sarah T. Hughes, File No. 77-88126: Dallas Office, Field Office File 77-4705, Aug. 31, 1961, a document obtained by me in a Freedom of Information request. The identity of the complainant was deleted from the file.

21. "Young Democrats Map Fight against Shivers," *Dallas Morning News*, July 12, 1954, clipping in Scrapbook no. 3, Oversize Box 1908, STH.

22. Interview with Oscar Mauzy, June 15, 2000.

23. *Daily Times Herald*, Aug. 1, 1954, clipping in Scrapbook no. 3, STH.

24. "Proposed Constitutional Amendments," *Texas Bar Journal* (Oct. 22, 1954): 580.

25. "Women Jurors," *Dallas Times Herald*, Nov. 1, 1954; advertisement, "Dallas Judges Endorse Jury Service for WOMEN," *Dallas Morning News*, Nov. 1, 1954.

26. Final tabulations for the election appeared in newspaper editions of Nov. 4, 1954.

27. Sarah T. Hughes, "Now I Can Throw Away That Speech," *Independent Woman*, Feb. 1955, 63-64.

28. Political Files, Folders 2 and 7, Box 1943, STH, as cited by Rabe, "Full Citizenship Alone Will Suffice"; STH to Bill G. Cox, Nov. 16, 1959, Folder 4, Box 1933, STH.

29. Payne, *As Old as Dallas Itself*, 275.

30. *Dallas Times Herald*, Aug. 3, 1969, and Louise B. Raggio letter to the editor, *Texas Bar Journal* (Feb. 1998): 110; both cited in Payne, *As Old as Dallas Itself*, 276; Castleberry, *Daughters of Dallas*, 376.

31. STH to Tom Pickett, Jan. 10, 1952, Folder 1, Box 1942, STH.

32. STH to Johnson, Jan. 10, 1952, Folder 1, Box 1942, STH.

33. Johnson to STH, Jan. 14, 1952, ibid.

34. Hays to Hughes, Feb. 28, 1956, ibid.

35. STH to Johnson, Nov. 12, 1953, ibid.

36. Johnson to STH, May 21, 1953, Senate Papers, 1949-61, Masters, Folder 128, Box 90, LBJ Library.

37. Johnson to STH, June 6, 1953, ibid.

38. Johnson to STH, Oct. 5, 1955, ibid..

39. Sarah T. Hughes Oral History, Interview I, by Frantz, LBJ Library.

40. Summary of article from *Charm Magazine*, Oct. 1954, attached to résumé, "Sarah T. Hughes, 14th District Court of Texas," clippings file, Texas/Dallas History and Archives, Dallas Public Library.

41. *Dallas Morning News*, July 15 and 19, 1955; "Her Specialty: Blazing Trails," *Dallas Times Herald*, Nov. 6, 1957.

42. STH to Graul, Dec. 16, 1975, Gwen Graul Papers.

43. "Inventory of the Contents of the Home," 1958, Folder 4, Box 1895, STH.

44. Typewritten recollection by Ruth Spurlock, Artificial Collection, STH.

45. Gantt, "Interview with Judge Sarah T. Hughes," Mar. 21, 1969, 3, STH.

46. Ibid., 2.

47. Ibid., 4.

48. Ibid.

49. The series and clippings from newspapers that published the articles may be found in Scrapbook no. 5, Oversize Box 1908, STH.

50. Gantt, "Interview with Judge Sarah T. Hughes," Mar. 21, 1969, 6, STH.

51. Sarah T. Hughes, "Handling of Juvenile Delinquents in Texas," *Texas Law Review* (1960): 290-302.

52. Sarah T. Hughes, "The Unfortunate One Per Cent—Our Responsibility," Research Study Number 27, Seventeenth Annual Spring Conference of the Texas Study of Secondary Education, Jan. 1959.

53. Gantt, "Interview with Judge Sarah T. Hughes," Mar. 21, 1969, 5, STH.

54. F. T. Wilson to Carolyn H. Moses (who sent out cards in Hughes's behalf), Mar. 28, 1958, Folder 4, Box 1967, STH.

55. "Reporter's Notebook," Dec. 26, 1957, Scrapbook no. 3, STH.

56. "Judge Hughes Eyes Race for Higher Court," *Dallas Morning News*, Jan. 12, 1958.

57. "Dist. Judge Seeks High Court Post," *Dallas Morning News*, Apr. 20, 1958; "Sarah Hughes Seeking Place on High Court," *Dallas Times Herald*, Apr. 27, 1958.

58. Sarah T. Hughes campaign pamphlet, clippings file, Texas/Dallas History and Archives, Dallas Public Library.

59. Gantt, "Interview with Judge Sarah T. Hughes," Mar. 21, 1969, 4, STH.

60. Ibid., 5, 7; untitled, undated El Paso newspaper clipping, [Jan. 1958], and *Sulphur Springs News-Telegram*, Mar. 20, 1958, Scrapbook no. 3, STH.

61. Gantt, "Interview with Judge Sarah T. Hughes," Mar. 21, 1969, 7, STH.

62. Ibid., 8-9.

63. Tobolowsky entry, in *New Handbook of Texas*, vol. 6, 512; Castleberry, *Daughters of Dallas*, 357-58.

64. Tobolowsky's letter is quoted by Claudia G. Hazlewood in a letter to Sarah Hughes on Jan. 20, 1958 [she misdated it as 1957], Folder 1, Box 1917, STH.

65. Ibid.

66. The *Handbook of Federation Procedure* policy is quoted by Hughes in her letter to Claudia G. Hazlewood, Dec. 30, 1957, Folder 1, Box 1917, STH.

67. Hazlewood to Lillie May Hurst, Jan. 25, 1958; and Hughes to Hazlewood, Feb. 20, 1958; both in Folder 1, Box 1917, STH.

68. Folder 4, Box 1918, STH.

69. "The Dallas Bar Vote," *Dallas Morning News*, June 5, 1958.

70. "Justice Greenhill Favored by Lawyers," *Dallas Morning News*, June 18, 1958.

71. *Irving News*, June 2, 1958, clipping in Scrapbook no. 5, STH.

72. *Dallas Times Herald*, June 1, 1958, clipping in Scrapbook no. 5, STH.

73. Undated editorial, *Dallas Morning News*, [June 1958], Scrapbook no. 5, STH.

74. *San Angelo Times*, June 22, 1958, and *Greenville Herald Banner*, July 1, 1958, cited by Allread, "Sarah T. Hughes," 101-2.

75. "Weathervane," *Dallas Morning News*, July [n.d.], 1958; and Robert W. Akers, "It's Like This," undated newspaper clipping. Akers's column attributed the comment about women almost electing Hughes to Ed Van Zandt of the *Journal*. These clippings are in Scrapbook no. 5, STH.

76. Interview with Louise Raggio, Mar. 3, 2001.

77. Gantt, "Interview with Judge Sarah T. Hughes," Mar. 21, 1969, 10, STH.

78. Associated Press news story as reported in Wichita Falls newspaper, June 29, 1958, a clipping of which is in Scrapbook no. 5, STH; Gantt, "Interview with Judge Sarah T. Hughes," Mar. 21, 1969, 8, STH; Secretary of State Campaign Finance Reports, Joe Greenhill and Sarah T. Hughes files, 1958, Texas State Archives.

79. Gantt, "Interview with Judge Sarah T. Hughes," Mar. 21, 1969, 9-10, STH.

80. *Dallas Morning News*, July 28, 1958, as cited by Allread, "Sarah T. Hughes," 102.

81. Gantt, "Interview with Judge Sarah T. Hughes," Mar. 21, 1969, 8, STH.

Chapter 9, Campaigning for the Federal Bench

1. Transcript for proceedings of Hughes's induction ceremony, reprinted in Gantt, "Interview with Judge Sarah T. Hughes," Apr. 11, 1969, 29, STH; Anthony Champagne, "Interview with Sarah T. Hughes," Feb. 5, 1980, oral history, Sam Rayburn Library, Bonham, Texas.

2. Sarah T. Hughes Oral History, Interview I, by Frantz, 4, LBJ Library. Will Wilson was a long-time Democratic Party mainstay, former district attorney of Dallas County, and former attorney general of the state of Texas, and he was one of many conservative Democrats who switched their allegiance to the Republican Party. Barefoot Sanders recalled that his assignment as chairman of the Dallas County campaign had come directly from Sam Rayburn, and although Hughes was called by Wilson, Sanders assumed that Rayburn had been responsible for Hughes's appointment as well.

3. Harold Barefoot Sanders Jr. began using his middle name when running for a student body office at the

University of Texas just after World War II and using an image of bare feet as an attention-getter. He was successful, and he forever after became known by that name.

4. Sarah T. Hughes Oral History, Interview I, by Frantz, LBJ Library, 4, 7; *Dallas Times Herald*, Sept. 1, 1960; Interview with the Honorable Barefoot Sanders, Jan. 23, 2002; interview with Betty McKool, Jan. 28, 2002.
5. Sarah T. Hughes Oral History, Interview I, by Frantz, LBJ Library, 6; Gantt, "Interview with Judge Sarah T. Hughes," Mar. 21, 1969, 21-23, STH; Champagne, "Interview with Judge Sarah Hughes," Sam Rayburn Library.
6. STH to Senator Ralph Yarborough, Mar. 15, 1965, Folder 12, Box 1893, STH.
7. Sarah T. Hughes Oral History, Interview I, by Frantz, 5, LBJ Library; and U.S. Department of Justice, FBI, Sarah T. Hughes, File Number 77-88126: Dallas Office, Field Office File 77-4705, Aug. 31, 1961.
8. Gantt, "Interview with Judge Sarah T. Hughes," Mar. 21, 1969, 20, STH. Hughes later remembered the comment in a slightly different and more awkward way: "Now here is a woman you should appoint when you have the opportunity to some position." This appears in Sarah T. Hughes Oral History, Interview I, by Frantz, LBJ Library, 5.
9. Sarah T. Hughes Oral History, Interview I, by Frantz, LBJ Library, 5.
10. *Dallas Times Herald*, Sept. 13, 1960; interview with Barefoot Sanders, Jan. 23, 2002.
11. Interview with Barefoot Sanders, Jan. 23, 2002.
12. A special provision by the Texas Legislature had permitted Lyndon B. Johnson's name to appear both as a candidate for the Senate and as the Democratic vice-presidential candidate. If he had lost as vice president but retained a majority vote for the Senate, he would have retained his Senate seat.
13. Payne, *Big D*, 349-50.
14. Interview with Barefoot Sanders, Jan. 23, 2002; Gantt, "Interview with Judge Sarah T. Hughes," Mar. 21, 1969, 23, STH; interview with Jan Sanders, Apr. 26, 2002.
15. Sarah T. Hughes Oral History, Interview I, by Frantz, LBJ Library, 6; interview with Barefoot Sanders, Jan. 23, 2002; Gantt, "Interview with Judge Sarah T. Hughes," Mar. 21, 1969, 21, STH; interview with Jan Sanders, Apr. 26, 2002.
16. Rowland Evans and Robert Novak, *Lyndon B. Johnson: The Exercise of Power* (New York: New American Library, 1966), 302.
17. Gantt, "Interview with Judge Sarah T. Hughes," Mar. 21, 1969, 26, STH.
18. William M. Taylor Jr. in identical letters to Ralph Yarborough and Lyndon B. Johnson, Dec. 13, 1960, Folder 1, Box 1893, STH.
19. Champagne, "Interview with Judge Sarah T. Hughes," Sam Rayburn Library. L. E. Dilley of Dallas was mistaken when he wrote to Ralph Yarborough on June 1, 1961, and said Hughes was there with Barefoot Sanders. He evidently mistook Kittrell for Sanders. "They did not tell me what their mission was, but I felt like she was asking Mr. Sam for his help in getting a Federal Judge's appointment." Dilley's letter is in Folder 3, Box 1944, STH.
20. Champagne, "Interview with Judge Sarah T. Hughes," Sam Rayburn Library.
21. Sarah T. Hughes Oral History, Interview I, by Frantz, 8, LBJ Library. Gantt, "Interview with Judge Sarah T. Hughes," Apr. 11, 1969, 1, STH.
22. Lyndon B. Johnson to J. Hart Willis, Jan. 6, 1961, Folder 2, Box 1944, STH.
23. "Loyalist Favored for Post," *Dallas Morning News*, Dec. 25, 1960.
24. Gantt, "Interview with Judge Sarah T. Hughes," Mar. 21, 1969, 28-29, STH.
25. Interview with Betty McKool, Jan. 28, 2002.
26. Gantt, "Interview with Sarah T. Hughes," Mar. 21, 1969, 29, STH.
27. Hughes to Johnson, Jan. 25, 1961, White House Social Files, Alpha File, Box 978, LBJ Library.
28. Ibid.
29. Gantt, "Interview with Judge Sarah T. Hughes," Apr. 11, 1969, 10, STH.
30. Hughes to Johnson, Jan. 25, 1961, White House Social Files, Alpha File, Box 978, LBJ Library. The trip to Buenos Aires mentioned by Hughes is described by her in an article she wrote for the *National Business Woman*, June 1960, entitled "Buenos Aires Meeting on Status of Women."
31. Johnson to STH, Jan. 27, 1961, Vice Presidential Papers, 1961-63, Master File Index, 1961, Folder 128, LBJ Library.
32. Dennis J. Hutchinson, *The Man Who Once Was Whizzer White: A Judicial Portrait of Justice Byron R. White* (New York: Free Press, 1998), 268.
33. An untitled typewritten transcript of her speech and the handwritten notes are in Folder 4, Box 1934, STH.

34. McGhee to STH, Feb. 4, 1961, Folder 2, Box 1944, STH.
35. STH to Brooks Hays, Feb. 20, 1961; to George McGhee, Feb. 20, 1961; and to Chester Bowles, Feb. 27, 1961; all ibid.
36. STH to Hy Raskin, Feb. 27, 1961; and to Ramsey Clark, Feb. 28, 1961; both ibid.
37. STH to Ramsey Clark, Apr. 14, 1961, ibid.
38. Copies of many of the letters and responses to them are in Folder 2, Box 1944, STH.
39. An undated telegram Joe Pool sent to President Kennedy, Vice President Johnson, Attorney General Robert F. Kennedy, Speaker of the House Sam Rayburn, and Senator Ralph Yarborough, ibid.
40. Oscar Mauzy to Ralph Yarborough, Apr. 21, 1961, ibid.
41. Hutchinson, *The Man Who Once Was Whizzer White*, 271.
42. STH to Cliff Carter, May 5, 1961, Vice Presidential Papers, 1961-63, Box 129, "Confirmations-Texas-Judgeships-Northern District/Hughes, Sarah T.," LBJ Library.
43. Jenkins to Lyndon B. Johnson, May 6, 1961, ibid.
44. Undated [early May 1961], ibid.
45. Yarborough to McKool, May 10, 1961, Folder 3, Box 1944, STH.
46. Mullinax to Schlesinger, May 25, 1961, ibid. Mullinax's letter and those of many others writing in Hughes's behalf were sent to Hughes for her own files.
47. White to Mullinax, June 9, 1961, ibid.
48. Sarah T. Hughes Oral History, Interview I, by Frantz, 9, LBJ Library; STH to Cliff Carter, July 10, 1961, Folder 4, Box 1944, STH.
49. Sarah T. Hughes Oral History, Interview I, by Frantz, 9, LBJ Library.
50. Victor S. Navasky, *Kennedy Justice* (New York: Atheneum, 1971), 297; interview with Sen. Ralph Yarborough, Mar. 5, 1974, cited by Allread, "Sarah T. Hughes," 105.
51. Oral History Interview with Ramsey Clark, July 7, 1970, 22, by Larry Hackman, for the Robert F. Kennedy Oral History Program of the JFK Library.
52. STH to Ramsey Clark, July 10, 1961, Folder 3, Box 1944, STH.
53. "Judge Hughes Eyed for Federal Post," *Dallas Morning News*, Aug. 11, 1961.
54. "Senator Says Age May Hurt Hughes," *Dallas Times Herald*, Aug. 12, 1961.
55. "Kennedy Plans to Appoint Wade to Federal Judgeship," *Dallas Morning News*, Aug. 13, 1961.
56. "Wade Said Due U.S. Judgeship," *Dallas Times Herald*, Aug. 13, 1961.
57. "Jim Bowie May Get DA's Post," *Dallas Times Herald*, Aug. 15, 1961; "Judge Wade," *Dallas Morning News*, Aug. 15, 1961.
58. STH to Lyndon B. Johnson, Aug. 14, 1961, Folder 4, Box 1944, STH.
59. STH to Ramsey Clark, Aug. 14, 1961, ibid.
60. STH to Ralph Yarborough, Aug. 14, 1961, ibid.
61. John Mashek, interviewed by telephone on Feb. 14, 2002, could remember forty-one years after the episode only that Hughes had been the front-runner all along.
62. E-mail from Jim Lehrer to me, July 30, 2002.
63. Gantt, "Interview with Judge Sarah T. Hughes," Apr. 11, 1969, 3, STH.
64. Especially noteworthy was their representation of the NAACP in *Smith v. Allwright* (1944), in which the U.S. Supreme Court nullified the all-white Democratic primaries prevalent in the South as unconstitutional.
65. Interview with Oscar Mauzy, June 15, 2000; Payne, *Big D*, 325.
66. Mauzy identified his friend David Bunn as a Texan who lived in Denver, Colorado, and who had worked with Mauzy in the Young Democrats for America.
67. Interview with Oscar Mauzy, June 15, 2000.
68. Copies of these letters and Johnson's responses may be seen in Folder 4, Box 1944, STH.
69. John E. V. Jasper to William A. Geoghegan, Aug. 23, 1961, ibid.
70. "Support Gain Seen for Judge Hughes," *Dallas Times Herald*, Aug. 28, 1961. Rayburn's alleged support of Henry Wade likely stemmed from the fact that Wade's father, an attorney, regularly had served as Rayburn's campaign manager in Rockwall County, which was in his congressional district. This fact, Oscar Mauzy believed, certainly required Rayburn not to be hostile toward Wade's possible appointment.
71. Arthur M. Schlesinger Jr., *Robert Kennedy and His Times*, I (Boston: Houghton Mifflin Co., 1978), 390, and Alfred Steinberg, *Sam Rayburn: A Biography* (New York: Hawthorn Books, Inc., 1975), 338. In their book, *Lyndon B. Johnson: The Exercise of Power* (New York: New American Library, 1966), Rowland Evans and Robert Novak related that Johnson, having been rebuffed when he first proposed Sarah T. Hughes to the attorney general, because of her age, became perturbed when he

learned that Rayburn's comment evidently had far greater impact. He, as vice president, had been turned down, but the Speaker's opinion was decisive. Johnson felt that the whole affair hurt his reputation both in Washington and in Texas by showing his lack of influence, according to the authors.

72. Oral History Interview with Ramsey Clark, 22, JFK Library.
73. Ibid.
74. Ibid.
75. Conversation with Nicholas Katzenbach, Feb. 5, 1965, Tape WH6502.01, Recordings of Conversations and Meetings, Recordings of Telephone Conversations, White House Series, LBJ Library.
76. Ibid.
77. Telephone conversation with Edwin Wiesl Jr., Jan. 11, 1965, Tape WH6501.02, Recordings of Conversations and Meetings, Recordings of Telephone Conversations, White House Series, LBJ Library.
78. Conversation with Katzenbach, Feb. 5, 1965, Tape WH6502.01, LBJ Library.
79. U.S. Department of Justice, FBI, Sarah T. Hughes, File No. 77-88126: "Memorandum for Mr. Hoover, Director, Federal Bureau of Investigation," from Joseph F. Dolan, n.d.; and Teletype from "Director FBI" to "SACS" in Dallas, Baltimore, Chicago, San Antonio, Washington Field, Aug. 25, 1961.
80. Peden to Board of Directors, Aug. 28, 1961, Folder 4, Box 1944, STH.
81. Peden to STH, Aug. 31, 1961, and STH to Peden, Aug. 31, 1961, ibid. Peden to the President, Aug. 28, 1961, White House Central Name Files, Box 1289, JFK Library.
82. Lyndon B. Johnson to STH, Aug. 25, 1961, Folder 4, Box 1944, STH.
83. Johnson to STH, Aug. 31, 1961, ibid.
84. Mrs. Pearl C. Anderson to the President, Aug. 29, 1961; and Joseph L. Allen to the President, Aug. 29, 1961. Copies of these and other letters and O'Brien's responses are in the White House Central Name Files, Box 1289, JFK Library.
85. U.S. Department of Justice, FBI, Sarah T. Hughes, File No. 77-88126, passim; copies of these reports were obtained through the Freedom of Information and Privacy Acts.
86. Dallas Office, Field Office File 77-4705, Aug. 31, 1961, ibid.
87. Dallas Office, Field Office File 77-4777, ibid.
88. Dallas Office, Field Office File 77-4705, ibid.
89. Ibid.
90. Dallas Office, Field Office File 77-4705, Sept. 6, 1961, ibid.
91. Dallas Office, Field Office File 77-4705, Aug. 29, 1961, ibid.
92. Director FBI to SAC, Dallas Office, Aug. 28, 1961, ibid.
93. Dallas Office, Field Office File 77-4705, Aug. 31, 1961, ibid.
94. Ibid.
95. Ibid.
96. Ibid.
97. Ibid.
98. Ibid.
99. U.S. Department of Justice, FBI, Sarah T. Hughes, File No. 77-88126: W. V. Cleveland to [Courtney] Evans, Sept. 11, 1961, reproduced in the reports obtained by the author cited above as File No. 77-88126.
100. Yarborough to Myrtle M. Hembree, Sept. 1, 1961; and Johnson to Myrtle M. Hembree, Sept. 1, 1961; both in Folder 5, Box 1944, STH.
101. Senator Lister Hill to Dr. Minnie C. Miles, Sept. 12, 1961, Folder 6, Box 1944, STH.
102. Memo from Logan Ford to firm members, Sept. 13, 1961, Folder 7, Box 1944, STH.
103. Mae W. Avery to STH, Sept. 20, 1961; and STH to Avery, Sept. 21, 1961; both ibid.
104. "Dream Finally Fulfilled," *Dallas Morning News*, Sept. 26, 1961.
105. Ibid.
106. Ibid.
107. Ibid.
108. STH to John F. Kennedy, Sept. 29, 1961, White House Social Files, Alpha File, Box 978, LBJ Library.
109. Wade to STH, Sept. 27, 1961, Folder 4; Dugger to STH, Sept. 23, 1961, Folder 2; and A. J. Christian et al., Folder 3; all in Box 1893, STH.
110. Edgerton to STH, Oct. 3, 1961, Folder 6; Taubkin to Hughes, Oct. 19, 1961, Folder 9; both in Box 1893, STH.

111. STH to Lyndon B. Johnson, Oct. 10, 1961, Vice Presidential Papers, 1961-63, Box 129, "Confirmations-Texas-Judgeships-Northern District/Hughes, Sarah T.," LBJ Library.
112. Barefoot Sanders to Walter Jenkins, Oct. 5, 1961, ibid.
113. A transcript of the proceedings is reprinted in Gantt's oral history interview with Judge Hughes, Apr. 11, 1969, 8-33, STH. Yarborough's comments are on page 18.
114. Gantt, "Interview with Judge Sarah T. Hughes," Apr. 11, 1969, 30.
115. STH to Ralph Yarborough, Oct. 25, 1961, Folder 11, Box 1893, STH.
116. STH to Johnson, Oct. 23, 1961, Folder 8, Box 1944, STH.
117. "Legal Rights for Women," *Dallas Morning News*, Dec. 15, 1961.
118. STH to Johnson, Oct. 23, 1961, Folder 8, Box 1944, STH.
119. STH to Johnson, Nov. 14, 1961, ibid.; LBJ to STH, Nov. 21, 1961, Box 1891, STH.
120. "Judge Hughes Feted by Lawyers, Judges," *Dallas Morning News*, Dec. 2, 1961.
121. STH to Ruby G. Sills, Oct. 23, 1961; and STH to Katherine Peden, Oct. 23, 1961; both in Folder 8, Box 1944, STH.
122. Sanders to Johnson, Mar. 5, 1962, Box 129, "Confirmations-Texas-Judgeships-Northern District/Hughes, Sarah T.," Vice Presidential Papers, 1961-63, LBJ Library.
123. Two letters detail these events. One is found in Folder 10, Box 1944, STH, with Jaworski's name, that of the recipient, and the date neatly clipped out, but the contents make his identity clear. Jaworski wrote a nearly identical letter to Vice President Johnson on Mar. 22, 1962, in Box 129, "Confirmations-Texas-Judgeships-Northern District/Hughes, Sarah T.," Vice Presidential Papers, 1961-63, LBJ Library.
124. Kerr to Eastland, March 1, 1962, Folder 10, Box 1893, STH.
125. "Body Ignores ABA on Hughes Protest," *Dallas Morning News*, March 8, 1962; Gantt, "Interview with Judge Sarah T. Hughes," Apr. 11, 1969, 5, STH.
126. STH to Lady Bird Johnson, Mar. 8 and Mar. 22, 1962, Folder 7, Box 1891, STH.
127. Yarborough to STH, Mar. 8, 1962, Folder 11, Box 1893, STH.
128. STH to Lyndon B. Johnson, Mar. 16, 1962, Folder 14, Box 1891, STH.
129. STH to Johnson, Mar. 8 and Mar. 16, 1962, ibid.

Chapter 10, Center of a Maelstrom

1. "Problems Concerning Children Arising from Conflict in Marriage," *Texas Bar Journal* (Oct. 22, 1961): 925-26, 100-102; "Against Resolution Opposing Disarmament" (with John N. Jackson), *Texas Bar Journal* (Sept. 22, 1962): 755, 817-18; "Legal Aspects of Corporal Punishment in the Schools," *Delta Kappa Gamma Bulletin* spring 1962, 36-41; "For Refugee Girls: New Opportunity," *National Business Women*, Sept. 1962, 8. Although Jackson is cited as co-author for the article on disarmament, Hughes wrote it, and then sent it to him for editing.
2. Allread, "Sarah T. Hughes," 108.
3. *Dallas Morning News*, Feb. 13, 1963; Hughes to Lloyd Godley, Dec. 18, 1963, Folder 4, Box 1893, STH.
4. Undated clipping [1962], *Dallas Times Herald*, Oversize Box 1908, STH.
5. Various items in Folders 7 and 8, Box 1895, STH, describe the property. Hughes refused for three years to lower her asking price to $10,500.
6. Charles C. Tillinghast Jr. to STH, Apr. 29, 1963; and STH to Tillinghast, May 9, 1963; both in Folder 13, Box 1933, STH.
7. A series of letters concerning this matter are in Folder 1, Box 1910, STH, including one to Smith, July 19, 1963, C. R. Spears to STH, July 26, 1963, and Spears to STH, Aug. 9, 1963.
8. William Manchester, *The Death of a President, November 20-25, 1963* (New York: Harper & Row, 1967), 48-49; Arthur M. Schlesinger Jr., *A Thousand Days: John F. Kennedy in the White House* (Boston: Houghton Mifflin Co., 1965), 752.
9. STH to John F. Kennedy, Oct. 30, 1961, Folder 6, Box 1891, STH.
10. Salinger to STH, Nov. 14, 1961, ibid.
11. STH to John F. Kennedy, Nov. 14, 1961, ibid.
12. U.S. Department of Justice, FBI, Sarah T. Hughes, File No. 77-88126: Sarah T. Hughes to Curtis O. Lynum, Feb. 5, 1963, File 77-88126-35.
13. U.S. Department of Justice, FBI, Sarah T. Hughes, File No. 77-88126: Curtis O. Lynum to "Director FBI," Feb. 6, 1963.
14. U.S. Department of Justice, FBI, Sarah T. Hughes, File No. 77-88126: "Director FBI" to SAC, Dallas, Feb. 15, 1963.

15. STH to John B. Connally, May 9, 1963, STH; H.B. 230, State of Texas Legislature, *Senate Journal*, 58th Legislature, Regular Session, 1919-20.
16. Green's speech is reprinted in State of Texas Legislature, *House Journal*, 58th Legislature, Regular Session, 1919-20; the vote against suspending the rules so that the bill could be considered immediately is reported in the *House Journal* on page 2257.
17. *Dallas United Nations Association News Bulletin*, July 1962, Folder 2, Box 1923, STH.
18. STH to Jerome H. Spingarn, Dec. 14, 1962; and STH to George McGhee, Dec. 17, 1962; both in Folder 1, Box 1896, STH; "Annual Report—Dallas United Nations Association, by Judge Sarah T. Hughes, March 27, 1963," *Dallas United Nations Association News Bulletin*, May 1963, Folder 3, Box 1923, STH.
19. Jack Goren to Charles Meeks, Aug. 9, 1963, Folder 2, Box 1922, STH.
20. "Dallas United Nations Week," *Dallas United Nations Association News Bulletin*, Oct. 1963, Folder 3, Box 1923, STH.
21. The wording of the proclamation is in Folder 2, Box 1922, STH.
22. Warren Leslie, *Dallas Public and Private: Aspects of an American City* (New York: Grossman Publishers, 1964), 190.
23. "Walker Sees U.N. Threat," *Dallas Times Herald*, Oct. 24, 1963; "Walker Says U.S. Main Battleground," *Dallas Morning News*, Oct. 24, 1963.
24. Ibid.
25. Ibid.
26. The events are described in newspaper accounts of the day and in many other accounts, including Leslie, *Dallas Public and Private*, 193-97; Payne, *Big D*, 353-57; and Stanley Marcus, *Minding the Store: A Memoir* (Boston: Little, Brown, 1974), 250-51. As a reporter for the *Dallas Times Herald*, I was present for this event and also saw the demonstrators' confrontation with Stevenson during and after the event.
27. Interview with Stanley Marcus, Sept. 26, 2001; Leslie, *Dallas Public and Private*, 196.
28. Gantt, "Interview with Judge Sarah T. Hughes," Mar. 21, 1969, 16, STH; interview with Barefoot Sanders, Feb. 24, 2002; Jack Goren, DUNA Annual Report for 1963, Folder 13, Box 1922, STH.
29. "Mayor Asks City to Reject Hate Group," *Dallas Times Herald*, Oct. 27, 1963; *Time*, Nov. 1, 1963; *Christian Century*, Nov. 20, 1963.
30. Adlai E. Stevenson to STH, Nov. 11, 1963, Folder 14, Box 1933, STH.
31. Walter Johnson, ed., *The Papers of Adlai E. Stevenson: Ambassador to the United Nations, 1961-65*, vol. 8 (Boston: Little, Brown, 1979), 460; Marcus, *Minding the Store*, 255; Manchester, *The Death of a President*, 39; interview with Barefoot Sanders, Feb. 24, 2002.
32. Theodore C. Sorensen, *Kennedy* (New York: Harper & Row, 1965), 750.
33. Marcus, *Minding the Store*, 254.
34. Payne, *Big D*, 359-60.
35. Ibid., 360.
36. Laura Hlavach and Darwin Payne, eds., *Reporting the Kennedy Assassination: Journalists Who Were There Recall Their Experiences* (Dallas: Three Forks Press, 1996), 55.
37. Interview with Barefoot Sanders, May 24, 2002.
38. Telephone interview with Jan Sanders, Apr. 26, 2002.
39. "Sarah T. Hughes Oral History, Interview I," by Frantz, 15-16, LBJ Library; Payne, *Big D*, 363.
40. The event, recorded on Nov. 22, 1963, is on video in the KDFW-TV Collection, Sixth Floor Museum at Dealey Plaza.
41. Videotape, Nov. 22, 1963, KDFW-TV Collection, Sixth Floor Museum at Dealey Plaza.
42. Ibid.; *Dallas Morning News*, Nov. 23, 1963; "Twenty Years Later," from a special section in the *Dallas Morning News*, Nov. 20, 1983.
43. Telephone interview with Jan Sanders, Apr. 26, 2002.
44. Videotape, Nov. 22, 1963, KDFW-TV Collection, Sixth Floor Museum at Dealey Plaza. In an oral history she gave five years later Hughes recalled the incident in a different way. She said that as she, Oliver, and Graul walked out of the Trade Mart together, someone in a car stopped and told them that the president had died. But as she also said, she was numb and "hardly realizing" what was happening.
45. Sarah T. Hughes Oral History, Interview I, by Frantz, 16, LBJ Library.
46. Hughes, "The President Is Sworn In," undated clipping of the reprint of the original *Washington Post* article appearing in the *Dallas Times Herald*, Vivian Castleberry Papers.
47. Sarah T. Hughes Oral History, Interview I, by Frantz, 18, LBJ Library.

48. Hughes, "The President Is Sworn In," Vivian Castleberry Papers.
49. Manchester, *The Death of a President*, 271.
50. Ibid., 269-72.
51. Ibid., 272; telephone interview with John Spinuzzi, Apr. 16, 2002. Spinuzzi could not recall whether the first caller was male or female, but he supposed later that it must have been Mary Fehmer.
52. Lawrence J. Vilardo and Howard W. Gutman, "The Honorable Irving L. Goldberg: A Place in History," *SMU Law Review* (Sept.-Oct. 1995), 3.
53. Goldberg, in being interviewed by his former law clerks Lawrence I. Vilardo and Howard W. Gutman, did not indicate that Johnson said he was already trying to reach Hughes. William Manchester concluded in *The Death of a President* (page 273) that Johnson already had set in motion an effort to find her.
54. Interview with Barefoot Sanders, May 24, 2002.
55. Sarah T. Hughes Oral History, Interview I, by Frantz, 19, LBJ Library; interview with Barefoot Sanders, Feb. 24, 2002. In these details I have generally followed oral histories provided by Sarah T. Hughes to Fred Gantt (cited above) and to Joe B. Frantz for the LBJ Library (cited above), the interview with Barefoot Sanders on Feb. 24, 2002, and the narrative developed by William Manchester in *The Death of a President*, 269-72. In his own memoirs Lyndon B. Johnson said Hughes called him on *Air Force One* as requested. "I explained the situation and told her that we would send a car for her immediately. She replied that she could get to the airfield faster in her own and would be there in ten minutes." Hughes, in her own first-person account written immediately afterward for the *Washington Post*, does not say that she talked to the president. This would be a strange omission for her if, indeed, she had. It seems likely that Johnson, in the midst of a series of telephone calls, may have incorrectly thought that he had talked directly to Hughes. His version appears in *The Vantage Point: Perspectives of the Presidency, 1963-1969* (New York: Holt, Rinehart, and Winston, 1971), 14.
56. Sarah T. Hughes Oral History, Interview I, by Frantz, 18, LBJ Library.
57. Ibid., 17.
58. Ibid., 18.
59. Ibid., 311-12.
60. Ibid., 315.
61. Ibid., 317.
62. Manchester, *The Death of a President*, 274.
63. Interview with James Jennings, March 15, 2002; Hughes, "The President Is Sworn In," Vivian Castleberry Papers; Sarah T. Hughes Oral History, Interview I, by Frantz, 19, LBJ Library.
64. Vilardo and Gutman, "The Honorable Irving L. Goldberg," 4.
65. Manchester, *The Death of a President*, 320.
66. Hughes, "The President Is Sworn In," Vivian Castleberry Papers.
67. Sarah T. Hughes Oral History, Interview I, by Frantz, 19, LBJ Library.
68. Manchester, *The Death of a President*, 275.
69. Ibid., 320.
70. Hughes, "The President Is Sworn In," Vivian Castleberry Papers.
71. Sarah T. Hughes Oral History, Interview, I, by Frantz, 19, LBJ Papers.
72. Manchester, *The Death of a President*, 320-21.
73. Ibid., 321, 312-13.
74. Ibid., 322.
75. Hughes, "The President Is Sworn In," Vivian Castleberry Papers.
76. Manchester, *The Death of a President*, 323.
77. Ibid., 324.
78. Ibid., Sarah T. Hughes Oral History, Interview I, by Frantz, 19, LBJ Library; John B. Mayo Jr., *Bulletin from Dallas: The President Is Dead* (New York: Exposition Press, 1967), 36; *Washington Post*, Nov. 24, 1963.
79. Hughes, "The President Is Sworn In," Vivian Castleberry Papers.
80. Manchester, *The Death of a President*, 324.
81. Ibid., 325.
82. Mayo, *Bulletin from Dallas*, 36.
83. Sarah T. Hughes Oral History, Interview I, by Frantz, 20, LBJ Library.
84. Yarborough to STH, Mar. 8, 1965, Folder 12, Box 1893, STH; Manchester, *The Death of a President*, 326.
85. Hlavach and Payne, eds., *Reporting the Kennedy Assassination*, 55.

86. Sarah T. Hughes Oral History, Interview I, by Frantz, 21, LBJ Library.
87. Hlavach and Payne, eds., *Reporting the Kennedy Assassination*, 16.

Chapter 11, Judicial Activist

1. Friendly to STH, Nov. 26, 1963, Folder 1, Box 1892, STH.
2. Nancy Tuckerman to STH, Feb. 17, 1964, Folder 5, Box 1893, STH.
3. STH to Mrs. J. D. Tippit, Nov. 26, 1963, Folder 1, Box 1892, STH.
4. STH to Lyndon B. Johnson, Nov. 27, 1963, Folder 15, Box 1891, STH.
5. Mrs. Lyndon B. Johnson to STH, Dec. 2, 1963, Folder 13, STH.
6. Johnson to STH, Dec. 11, 1963, ibid.
7. Gantt, "Interview with Judge Sarah T. Hughes," May 27, 1969, 29, STH.
8. Signature on second page of this letter is missing, but it is on the letterhead of the National Federation of Business and Professional Women's Clubs, Inc., and, dated Feb. 19, 1964. Office Files of John Macy, Box 275, "Sarah T. Hughes," LBJ Library.
9. Catherine Anagnost to Lyndon Johnson, Apr. 28, 1964, ibid.
10. STH to Roger Stavis, March 8, 1982, Folder 9, Box 1891, STH.
11. Lyndon B. Johnson telephone conversation with Edwin Wiesl Jr. of New York, Jan. 11, 1965, Recordings of Conversations and Meetings, Recordings of Telephone Conversations, White House Series, Tape 6501.02, LBJ Library.
12. STH to Johnson, Dec. 16, 1963, Folder 15, Box 1891, STH. The photograph is now a part of the Sarah T. Hughes Papers at the University of North Texas.
13. STH to Johnson, Dec. 16, 1963; and Johnson to STH, Jan. 31, 1964; both in Folder 15, Box 1891, STH.
14. Bill Moyers to STH, Jan. 13, 1964, ibid.
15. STH to Bill Moyers, Jan. 15, 1964; and STH to Lyndon B. Johnson, Feb. 3, 1964; both ibid.
16. STH to Lady Bird Johnson, Feb. 2, 1964, White House Social Files, Alpha File, Box 978, LBJ Library.
17. STH to Lyndon B. Johnson, Feb. 3, 1964, Folder 15, Box 1891, STH.
18. "Judge Sarah Hughes: A Life of Law and Order," *Dallas Times Herald Sunday Magazine*, Oct. 3, 1976.
19. Interview with Louise Raggio, Apr. 24, 2001.
20. George E. Hughes's death record, Texas Bureau of Vital Statistics, No. 35204; D. C. Edwards, Hillcrest Mausoleum, to STH, May 26, 1964, Folder 3, Box 1895, STH.
21. "George E. Hughes Succumbs at 72," *Dallas Times Herald*, June 1, 1964; and "George E. Hughes, 72, Veteran Attorney, Dies," *Dallas Morning News*, June 2, 1964. The obituary in the *Times Herald* states only that Hughes was survived by "his wife," without identifying her. The obituary in the *Morning News* said that George E. Hughes "was the husband of Federal Judge Sarah T. Hughes."
22. Telegram, June 2, 1964, White House Social Files, Alpha File, Box 978, LBJ Library.
23. Interview with Barefoot Sanders, Jan. 23, 2002.
24. "Man Given Probated Term, Ordered Not to Get Drunk," *Dallas Morning News*, June 5, 1964.
25. Ibid.
26. "Judge Hughes Lectures on Installment Buying," *Dallas Morning News*, May 13, 1964.
27. "Phone Booth 'Bug' Evidence Voided," *Dallas Times Herald*, June 9, 1964; *United States v. Stone*, 232 F. Supp. 396 (1964).
28. Commencement address at Greenhill School, June 4, 1971, Folder 5, Box 1897, STH.
29. Interview with U.S. probation officer Al Havenstrite, July 21, 1975.
30. Allread, "Sarah T. Hughes," 180-81.
31. Mark Seal, "Judge Sarah T. Hughes on Crime and Justice: A Supercity under Siege," *Scene*, magazine supplement to the *Dallas Morning News*, Dec. 30, 1979; STH to the Honorable James W. Stroud, May 14, 1965, Folder 12, Box 1944, STH.
32. Undated "Mail Report," Folder 24, Box 114, J. Erik Jonsson Collection, DeGolyer Library, Southern Methodist University.
33. Interview with Dennis Shaw, Mar. 4, 2002.
34. "SEC Case May Be Judge Hughes's Sternest Test," *Dallas Morning News*, Feb. 7, 1971.
35. *Louisville Courier-Journal*, Nov. 24, 1964, Folder 8, Box 1970, STH.
36. Allread, "Sarah T. Hughes," 122-23.
37. The incident was observed by Opal Howard Allread at a pretrial conference on July 23, 1975. It is described in her dissertation, "Sarah T. Hughes," 127.
38. Interview with Nick Kuntz, Mar. 3, 2001.

39. Interview with Louise Raggio, Aug. 30, 2001.
40. Ibid., Mar. 3, 2001.
41. U.S. district judge Barefoot Sanders, who served as U.S. attorney from 1961 to 1965, said the judge would not permit pants suits to be worn. Interview on Mar. 3, 2001.
42. Interview with Phyllis Macon, Aug. 2, 2002.
43. Allread, "Sarah T. Hughes," 124.
44. Ibid., 125.
45. Ibid., 128.
46. Ibid., 124.
47. Ibid., 129.
48. STH to Marge J. Godfrey, [n.d.], Folder 10, Box 1970, STH.
49. Telephone interview with Jan Sanders, Apr. 26, 2002; "4,000 Cheers [sic] King's Civil Rights Speech," *Dallas Express*, Jan. 12, 1963.
50. "A Cherished Chance," *Dallas Morning News*, June 22, 1986; interview with Terry Flowers, Mar. 7, 2003.
51. This anecdote was related to the author by the Reverend Stephen Swann, Mar. 19, 2001.
52. Interview with Ernest E. Figari, Jr., July 25, 2002.
53. Ibid.
54. Ibid.
55. Ibid. The case was *Miles Edward Haynes v. United States*, 88 S.Ct. 722 (1968).
56. American Express statement, July 30, 1964, in Folder 14, Box 1894, STH; interview with John Spinuzzi, July 18, 2002; interview with Ed Reyna, a probation officer, Mar. 4, 2002.
57. Interview with Phyllis Macon, July 31, 2002.
58. STH to Lyndon B. Johnson, July 28, 1964, White House Social Files, Alpha File, Box 978, LBJ Library.
59. STH to Lyndon B. Johnson, Sept. 30, 1964, ibid.
60. Johnson to STH, Oct. 6, 1964, ibid.
61. Lady Bird Johnson, *White House Diary* (New York: Holt, Rinehart and Winston, 1980), 222; "Judge Looks In on High Court," *Dallas Times Herald*, Jan. 19, 1965; STH to Johnson, Jan. 25, 1965, Folder 16, Box 1891, STH.
62. STH to Lady Bird Johnson, Nov. 26, 1964, White House Social Files, Alpha File, Box 978, LBJ Library.
63. Lady Bird Johnson to STH, Dec. 8, 1964, ibid.
64. Jenkins to Bess Abell, July 3, 1964, WHCF Name File "Sarah Hughes," Box 459, LBJ Library.
65. STH to Gwen Graul, [n.d., June 1965], Gwen Graul Papers.
66. Ibid., July 9, 1965.
67. STH to Gwen Graul and Odell Oliver, June 25, [1965], Gwen Graul Papers.
68. The letters are in the Gwen Graul Papers.
69. The couple are referred to in Hughes's letters as Randi and Essen, and there is no record of their surnames. Hughes seems to have alternated between staying at a hotel and at their home, but always she socialized with them and their friends.
70. STH to Gwen Graul, July 22, 1972, Gwen Graul Papers.
71. Payne, *Big D*, 365-66.
72. "Judge Says Dallas 'Climate' Contributed to JFK Slaying," *Dallas Morning News*, Apr. 4, 1964.
73. "No Mean City," *Dallas Morning News*, Apr. 9, 1964.
74. "Cox Raps Senator and Judge," *Dallas Morning News*, Apr. 8, 1964.
75. Schlesinger, *A Thousand Days*, 1027 fn.
76. "Judge Hughes Renews Claim of 'Extremism,'" *Dallas Times Herald*, May 6, 1964.
77. Interview with Ernest E. Figari Jr., July 25, 2002.
78. STH to Tom B. Caldwell, Jan. 16, 1964, Folder 5, Box 1893, STH.
79. "What's Right with Dallas?" *Dallas Morning News*, Jan. 2, 1964.
80. STH to Linda Sweigard, Jan. 7, 1964, Folder 5, Box 1893, STH.
81. Dye, "The Accidental Feminist," 28.
82. STH to Tom B. Caldwell, Jan. 16, 1964, Folder 5, Box 1893, STH.
83. STH to Mrs. Lucy Someville Howorth, Dec. 17, 1963, Folder 4, Box 1893, STH.
84. STH to Stanley Marcus, Dec. 15, 1965, Folder 5, Box 1893, STH. (The same letter was sent to W. Dawson Sterling.)
85. Canaan to Dawson Sterling, Dec. 20, 1965, Folder 5, Box 1893, STH.

86. Marcus to STH, Dec. 20, 1965, Folder 5, Box 1893, STH.
87. Sterling to STH, Dec. 22, 1965, ibid.
88. Robert F. Kennedy to STH, July 16, 1965, ibid.
89. Gantt, "Interview with Judge Sarah T. Hughes," May 16, 1969, 25, STH.
90. Interview with Lois Swan Jones, June 8, 2002.
91. Folder 1, Box 1895, STH.
92. Scrapbook, Gwen Graul Papers.
93. Interview with Ernest E. Figari Jr., July 25, 2002; interview with Clarice Davis, Sept. 19, 2002.
94. Folder 2, Box 1896, STH.
95. Folders 5 and 11, Box 1894, STH.
95. Interview with Phyllis Macon, July 31, 2002.
97. Interview with Ed Reyna, Mar. 4, 2002.
98. Ibid.
99. "U.S. Urged to Lead on Women's Rights," *Dallas Morning News*, Dec. 1, 1965.
100. STH to Lady Bird Johnson, Mar. 24, 1966, White House Social Files, Alpha File, Box 978, LBJ Library.
101. STH to Lady Bird Johnson, May 13, 1967, ibid.
102. STH to Lady Bird Johnson, Nov. 8, 1967, ibid.
103. STH to Lady Bird Johnson, May 13, 1967, ibid.
104. "World Peace through World Law," *Texas Observer*, Oct. 15, 1965, 5; also in *National Business Woman*, Nov. 1965, 14-16.
105. Sept. 18, 1964, 1-2, and Oct. 15, 1965, 3-4.
106. Dugger to STH, Sept. 18, 1964, Folder 4, Box 1933, STH.
107. "Should Women Be Left Behind?" typescript, Folder 3, Box 1896, STH.
108. Typewritten commencement address, Greenhill School, June 4, 1971, Folder 5, Box 1897, STH.
109. Ibid.
110. Ibid.
111. David Richards, *Once upon a Time in Texas: A Liberal in the Lone Star State* (Austin: University of Texas Press, 2002), 90.
112. Yarborough to Lyndon Johnson, May 18, 1965, Folder 12, Box 1893, STH. Others on his list included Judge Ben Connally, L. N. D. (Nat) Wells, Judge Homer Thornberry, and Fagan Dickson.
113. Yarborough to STH, Mar. 17, 1966; Yarborough to Lyndon Johnson, Mar. 21, 1966; and STH to Yarborough, Apr. 12, 1966; all in Folder 12, Box 1893, STH.
114. "Rae" to STH, Aug. 27, 1966, Folder 10, Box 1891, STH.
115. Richards, *Once upon a Time in Texas*, 60.
116. STH to Gwen Graul, [July 14, 1967], Gwen Graul Papers.
117. Brooks Hays quotes her letter in a memo to President Lyndon Johnson, Feb. 15, 1968, White House Social Files, Alpha File, Box 978, LBJ Library.
118. Comments quoted by Elizabeth Brinton, Department of State, Bureau of Educational and Cultural Affairs, in a letter to STH, Feb. 7, 1969, Folder 3, Box 1902, STH.
119. Ibid.
120. STH to Gwen Graul, [n.d., 1968], Gwen Graul Papers.
121. Ibid.
122. "Galahad" to STH, Jan. 6, 1968, Folder 1, Box 1902, STH.
123. Ibid.
124. STH to Elizabeth Brinton, Jan. 27, 1969, Folder 3, Box 1902, STH.
125. *Bush v. McCollum*, 231 F. Supp. 560 (1964).
126. "Judge Backs Mental Test," *Dallas Morning News*, May 28, 1964.
127. [Month illegible] 14, 1969, *Dallas Morning News*, Sarah T. Hughes clippings file, Texas/Dallas History and Archives, Dallas Public Library.
128. *Interstate Circuit, Inc., et al. v. City of Dallas*, 247 F. Supp. 906 (1965); "Ordinance on Movies Enacted," *Dallas Morning News*, Apr. 6, 1965.
129. *Interstate Circuit, Inc., et al. v. City of Dallas* 247 F. Supp. 906 (1965).
130. *Interstate Circuit, Inc., v. City of Dallas*, 390 U.S. 676 (1967).
131. 42 U.S.C.A. § 1982.
132. *Walker v. Pointer*, 394 F. Supp. 56 (1969).
133. "Hospital Ordered to End Discriminatory Pay Scale," *Dallas Morning News*, Oct. 9, 1969.
134. *Shultz v. Brookhaven General Hospital*, 305 F. Supp. 424 (1969).

135. *Gilmore v. James*, 274 F. Supp. 75 (1967).
136. *Stein v. Batchelor*, 300 F. Supp., 602 (1969).
137. Richards, *Once upon a Time in Texas*, 68.
138. *Roth v. United States*, 354 U.S. 476 (1957); *Memoirs of a Woman of Pleasure v. Massachusetts*, 383 U.S. 413 (1975).
139. *Stein v. Batchelor*, 300 F. Supp. 602 (1969).
140. *Dyson v. Stein*, 401 U.S. 200 (1971); Richards, *Once upon a Time in Texas*, 72-73.
141. *Buchanan v. Batchelor*, 308 F. Supp. 729 (1970).
142. Ibid.
143. "Homosexuals and the Law," *Dallas Morning News*, Jan. 23, 1970.
144. *Bowers v. Hardwick*, 478 U.S. 186 (1986).
145. *Suggs v. Parkland*, No. CA3-2486 (N.D. Tex. 1969).
146. *Jefferson v. Hackney*, 406 U.S. 535 (1972). The judges' questionnaire is in Folder 4, Box 1901, STH.
147. *Linda R. S. v. Richard D. and the State of Texas*, 355 F. Supp. 804 (1971).
148. Ibid.
149. She was citing *Levy v. Louisiana*, 391 U.S. 68 (1968).
150. *Linda R. S. v. Richard D. and the State of Texas*, 355 F. Supp. 804 (1971).
151. *Dallas v. American National Bank*, N. CA3-4312B (N.D. Tex. 1971); *Dallas Morning News*, Nov. 18, 1971.

Chapter 12, Roe v. Wade and More

1. "Women Have Their Day in Court—as Lawyers," *U.S. News & World Report*, Nov. 17, 1980, 86-87.
2. Franklin H. Littell to STH, Feb. 18, 1969; and Louis A. Haselmayer to STH, Aug. 22, 1969; both in Folder 17, Box 1929, STH.
3. "Jurist Backs Libs: Judge Hughes Says Movement No Joke," *Dallas Times Herald*, Sept. 1, 1970.
4. Undated speech [circa 1970] entitled "The Status of Women in the United States since World War II," Folder 14, Box 1917, STH. The anecdotes are found in this speech and numerous others in her papers. Her citation from *Bradwell v. The State* is found under that heading in 83 *U.S. Reports* 130.
5. "The Status of Women in the United States since World War II," Folder 14, Box 1917, STH.
6. Ibid.
7. Ibid.
8. Ibid.
9. Ibid.
10. Ibid.
11. Ibid.
12. Dallas Women Lawyers Association Web site, last modified March 22, 2002, http://dallaswomen-lawyers.org/content.htm.
13. Letters from the committee are found in Folder 16, Box 1943, STH.
14. Castleberry, *Daughters of Dallas*, 356; interview with Vivian Castleberry, Mar. 3, 2003.
15. Castleberry, *Daughters of Dallas*, 356, 363.
16. Interview with Louise Raggio, Mar. 3, 2001.
17. David J. Garrow, *Liberty and Sexuality: The Right to Privacy and the Making of Roe v. Wade* (New York: Macmillan, 1994), 386-87; "Reproductive Rights Action League," Women in American History by Encyclopedia Brittanica, Oct. 13, 2002, http://search.eb.com/ women/articles/National Abortion and Reproductive Rights Action.
18. Garrow, *Liberty and Sexuality*, 393-97.
19. Ibid., 398-99, 401.
20. Ibid., 401-5.
21. Ibid., 406; *Dallas Times Herald*, Mar. 3, 5, 6, 8, and 9, 1970; and *Dallas Morning News*, Mar. 4, 1970.
22. Garrow, *Liberty and Sexuality*, 440.
23. Ibid.
24. Ibid.
25. Marian Faux, *Roe v. Wade: The Untold Story of the Landmark Supreme Court Decision That Made Abortion Legal* (New York: New American Library, 1988), 131.
26. Sarah Weddington, *A Question of Choice* (New York: G. P. Putnam's Sons, 1992), 64.
27. Faux, *Roe v. Wade*, 139.
28. Ibid., 140-41.

29. Ibid., 147.
30. Ibid., 150; Weddington, *A Question of Choice*, 46.
31. Faux, *Roe v. Wade*, 161; Garrow, *Liberty and Sexuality*, 451.
32. Garrow, *Liberty and Sexuality*, 451.
33. Ibid., 450.
34. Ibid., 451.
35. Interview with Clarice Davis, Sept. 19, 2002.
36. Ibid.; and Garrow, *Liberty and Sexuality*, 450-51.
37. Garrow, *Liberty and Sexuality*, 453.
38. *Roe v. Wade*, 314 F. Supp. 1217 (1970).
39. Ibid.
40. Ibid.
41. "U.S. Jurist Panel Rules Texas Abortion Law Void," *Dallas Morning News*, June 18, 1970; and "Appeal Promised in Abortion Ruling," *Dallas Times Herald*, June 18, 1970.
42. A roster of those attending is in Folder 11, Box 1933, STH.
43. Louis B. Raggio, "Report of Meetings of Governor's Commission on the Status of Women," typewritten document, Folder 8, Box 1933, STH.
44. Ibid.
45. Governor Preston Smith to STH, July 16, 1970, Folder 6, Box 1933, STH.
46. Handwritten notes for Hughes's talk are in Folder 8, Box 1933, STH. See also newspaper clipping, "Jurist Backs Libs: Judge Hughes Says Movement No Joke," *Dallas Times Herald*, Sept. 1, 1970.
47. "Jurist Backs Libs: Judge Hughes Says Movement No Joke," *Dallas Times Herald*, Sept. 1, 1970.
48. Ibid.
49. Ibid.
50. Ibid.
51. STH to Mary Ann Harvey, Oct. 12, 1970; and Harvey to STH, Oct. 15, 1970; both in Folder 6, Box 1933, STH.
52. STH to Mike McKool, Jan. 12, 1971, ibid.
53. Mike McKool to STH, Jan. 14, 1971, ibid.
54. STH to Mrs. Lila Cockrell, Jan. 15, 1971, ibid.
55. STH to Mike McKool, Jan. 15, 1971, ibid.
56. McKool to Ben Atwell, with a copy to STH, Feb. 25, 1971, ibid.
57. Frances Farenthold to STH, Feb. 24, 1971; and STH to Farenthold, March 2, 1971; both ibid.
58. "Governor's Commission for Women," The Handbook of Texas Online, http://www.tsha.utexas.edu/handbook/online/articles/view/GG/mdg5.html. Last amended Oct. 1, 2002.
59. "Texas Women's Political Caucus," *The New Handbook of Texas*, vol. 6, ed. Ron Tyler (Austin: Texas State Historical Association, 1996), 448-49.
60. Interview with the Honorable Martin Frost, Aug. 22, 2002.
61. Ibid.
62. Ibid.
63. Ibid.
64. Interview with Martin Frost, Aug. 22, 2002.
65. Ibid.
66. Ibid.
67. Regina Montoya, "Judge Sarah Hughes: A Retrospective," *Goucher Quarterly*, summer 1987, 12-14.
68. Ibid.
69. *Securities & Exch. Com'n. v. National Bankers Life Co.*, 324 F. Supp. 189 (1971). Individual defendants in the original suit, in addition to Sharp, Osorio, and Carr, were J. Quincy Adams, Donald S. Akins, Andy Byram, James Farha, Michael F. Ling, H. E. McCain, Phillip I. Proctor, and William B. Strange Jr. of Dallas; Joseph P. Novotny and Sam Stock of Houston; Tom Max Thomas of Austin; and David Hoover of Austin, Dallas and Houston. Corporations, in addition to National Bankers Life Insurance Co., were Master Control, Inc., Olympic Life Insurance Co., Nashwood Corp., FLAP, Inc., South Atlantic Co., Sharpstown Realty Co., Oak Forest Realty Co., Oak Forest Investment Co., Sharpstown State Bank, Dallas Bank and Trust Co., and City Bank and Trust Co.
70. A good summary of the case is found in "Sharpstown Stock-Fraud Scandal," *New Handbook of Texas*, vol. 5, ed. Tyler, pp. 997-98. More extensive information is found in Sam Kinch Jr. and Ben Procter, *Texas under a Cloud: Story of the Texas Stock Fraud Scandal* (Austin: Jenkins Publishing Co., 1972);

David M. Hudson, "The Federal Judicial Career of Sarah T. Hughes," an independent research project for the Master of Liberal Arts program, Southern Methodist University, Aug. 15, 2002; and Kaycie Czelusta, "Grace under Pressure: Judge Sarah T. Hughes and the Cases That Shook Texas," a paper written for the Women in the Legal Profession program, Stanford University Law School, Apr. 5, 2002.

71. Interview with Martin Frost, Aug. 22, 2002.
72. Ibid.
73. *Shreveport Times*, Feb. 7, 1971, as cited by Allread, "Sarah T. Hughes," 186.
74. Feb. 7, 1972.
75. Feb. 10, 1971.
76. *Securities & Exch. Com'n. v. National Bankers Life Ins. Co.*, 324 F. Supp. 189 (1971).
77. "Judge Seeks Faster Pace," *Dallas Morning News*, Aug. 31, 1971.
78. Ibid.
79. As quoted by Czelusta, "Grace under Pressure," 12.
80. *Securities and Exch. Com'n. v. National Bankers Life Ins. Co.*, 324 F. Supp. 189 (1971), 448 F. 2d 652 (1971), and 334 F. Supp. 444 (1971).
81. Allread, "Sarah T. Hughes," 189.
82. "Sharpstown Stock-Fraud Scandal," *New Handbook of Texas*, vol. 5, ed. Tyler, 997-98.
83. STH to Dr. Brownlee Sands Currin, Apr. 12, 1972, Folder 16, Box 1925, STH.
84. STH to Dr. Brownlee Sands Currin, Sept. 7, 1972, ibid.
85. Dr. Brownlee Sands Corrin to STH, Aug. 28, 1972, ibid.
86. Dr. Brownlee Sands Corrin to STH, Oct. 6, 1972, ibid.
87. STH to Corrin, Mar. 5, 1972, ibid.

Chapter 13, Reforming the Jail

1. Ronald E. Marcello, Sarah T. Hughes interview, Aug. 23, 1979, Oral History Collection, No. 489, University of North Texas, 19, STH.
2. Ibid., 19-20.
3. Ibid., 4; *Taylor v. Sterrett*, 344 F. Supp. 411 (1972), 499 F. 2d 367 (1974), and 600 F. 2d 1135 (5th Cir. 1979).
4. "Dallas County Jail Isn't Only One in State Overcrowded," *Dallas Morning News*, May 15, 1970.
5. "Jailhouse Lawyer Deals Decker Fits," July 22, 1970, *Dallas Morning News;* and "Judge Taylor Slams Prisoners," July 28, 1970, *Dallas Morning News.*
6. Barry Paul Hitchings, "Taylor v. Sterrett," *St. Mary's Law Journal* 8 (1976): 582. The Supreme Court decision cited by Hitchings is *Price v. Johnson*, 334 U.S. 266, 285 (1948). The case in which prisoners were said to be "slaves of the state" was *Ruffin v. Commonwealth*, 62 Va. (21 Gratt) 790, 796 (1871).
7. Hughes's speech was entitled "Law and Society—Where Do We Go from Here?" A copy of the Sept. 11, 1970, speech is in Folder 20, Box 1897, STH.
8. Ibid.
9. Ibid.
10. These events are summarized in "Appeal Hinted over Jail Order," *Dallas Times Herald*, June 6, 1972. See also "Revolt by Prisoners Is Put Down," *Dallas Morning News*, Sept. 22, 1971; and "Got Jail Back, Going to Keep It," *Dallas Times Herald*, Oct. 5, 1971.
11. "Jail Passes Grand Jury Inspection," *Dallas Times Herald*, Nov. 8, 1971.
12. "County Jail Probe Sought," *Dallas Times Herald*, Oct. 27, 1971; *Taylor v. Sterrett*, 344 F. Supp. 422 (1972).
13. "Sterrett Asks Help . . ." *Dallas Morning News*, Oct. 29, 1971.
14. ". . . After New Jail Blast," *Dallas Morning News*, Oct. 29, 1971.
15. *Taylor v. Sterrett*, 344 F. Supp. 411 (1972).
16. Hitchings, "Taylor v. Sterrett," 582-83.
17. Temporary Restraining Order, *Joseph Taylor et al. vs. W. L. Sterrett et al.*, CA-3-5220-B, Nov. 5, 1971, and CA-3-5220-C, Dec. 9, 1971.
18. The Fifth Circuit's affirmation is *Taylor v. Sterrett*, 532 F. 2d 462 (5th Cir. 1976). The legal scholars cited are Hitchings in "Taylor v. Sterrett," cited above, and Mary Christine Hutton, "Prisoners Rights: Constitutional Restriction on Censorship of Prisoners' Mail," *Washburn Law Journal* 16 (1977): 535-42.

19. "Judge Issues Injunction on Destroying Reading," *Dallas Morning News*, Apr. 1, 1972; *Taylor v. Sterrett*, 344 F. Supp. 411 (1972).
20. *Taylor v. Sterrett*, 499 F. 2d 367 (1974).
21. *Taylor v. Sterrett*, 344 F. Supp. 411 (1972).
22. Marcello, Sarah T. Hughes interview, 5, STH.
23. "Judge Hughes Backing County Bond Election, Says Jail Is Too Small," *Dallas Times Herald*, Sept. 22, 1977.
24. "Notice to All Persons Confined in the Dallas County Jail," CA-35220-B, filed on Mar. 17, 1972, Folder 10, Box 1952, STH.
25. *Taylor v. Sterrett*, 344 F. Supp. 411 (1972).
26. Marcello, Sarah T. Hughes interview, 7, STH.
27. "DA's Staff to Testify in Jail Case," *Dallas Morning News*, May 22, 1972; "Jail Improvement Decision Awaited," *Dallas Times Herald*, May 23, 1972.
28. Interview with Dennis Shaw, Mar. 4, 2002.
29. *Taylor v. Sterrett*, 344 F. Supp. 411 (1972).
30. Ibid.
31. Ibid.
32. Ibid.
33. Ibid.
34. *Taylor v. Sterrett*, 344 F. Supp. 411 (1972).
35. Ibid.
36. Ibid.
37. Ibid.
38. Ibid.
39. "Jail Fails Test Imposed by Law," *Dallas Times Herald*, June 8, 1972.
40. Telephone interview with the Reverend C. Preston Wiles, Nov. 18, 2002, who recounted the incident; and e-mail to the author from Lee Cullum, Nov. 1, 2002, who heard Dr. Wiles describe the incident at Sarah T. Hughes's funeral service.
41. *Dallas Morning News*, June 8, 1972.
42. "County to Seek Ruling Appeal," *Dallas Morning News*, June 7, 1972.
43. "Painful Conclusion," *Dallas Morning News*, June 13, 1972.
44. "County to Seek Stay in Jail Case," *Dallas Morning News*, June 10, 1972.
45. "Sheriff Facing Contempt Action," *Dallas Morning News*, June 6, 1972; and "County to Seek Ruling Appeal," *Dallas Morning News*, June 7, 1972.
46. "Judge Hughes Stands by Decision on Jail," *Dallas Times Herald*, June 29, 1972; and "Jail Law Clear, Judge Hughes Says," *Dallas Morning News*, June 29, 1972.
47. Ibid.
48. "Sterrett Says Jail One of Best," *Dallas Times Herald*, July 27, 1972.
49. "Commissioners Urge Censorship Defiance," *Dallas Morning News*, Aug. 15, 1972.
50. *Taylor v. Sterrett*, 499 F. 2d 367 (1974).
51. STH to John R. Brown, U.S. Circuit Court of Appeals, Mar. 28, 1974, Folder 1, Box 1952, STH.
52. "Jail Plan Sent to Judge," *Dallas Morning News*, Oct. 1, 1974.
53. Marcello, Sarah T. Hughes interview, 10, STH.
54. Ibid.; and "1974 Results of TV," Folder 9, Box 1952, STH.
55. Allread, "Sarah T. Hughes," 197; "Notes of Meeting with Judge Sarah T. Hughes," June 3, 1975, 12:30-1:30 P.M., Dallas County Sheriff's Department, Folder 9, Box 1952, STH.
56. "Notes of Meeting with Judge Sarah T. Hughes," ibid.
57. "County Mulls Regional Jail, Fund Source," *Dallas Times Herald*, Sept. 4, 1970; *Taylor v. Sterrett*, 600 F. 2d 1135 (5th Cir. 1979), as cited by Allread, "Sarah T. Hughes," 197.
58. "Overcrowding at Dallas County Jail," *Dallas Times Herald*, Oct. 20, 1975.
59. "Auditor Says Officials Doubt Jail Guard Needed," *Dallas Morning News*, Sept. 30, 1976.
60. "Jail Emergency Cited," *Dallas Morning News*, Sept. 4, 1976; and "County Jail Security," *Dallas Morning News*, Sept. 8, 1976.
61. "Officials Doubtful They Can Make Deadline on Jail Order," *Dallas Morning News*, Dec. 4, 1976.
62. "County Plans to Appeal Jail Order," *Dallas Times Herald*, Apr. 29, 1977.
63. "'Master' Tours Woodlawn," *Dallas Morning News*, Feb. 9, 1977.
64. Allread, "Sarah T. Hughes," 197-98.

65. "Deadline Set July 15 for Action on Jail," *Dallas Times Herald*, Apr. 28, 1977.
66. Ibid., and "County Plans to Appeal Jail Order," *Dallas Times Herald*, Apr. 29, 1977.
67. *Taylor v. Sterrett*, 600 F. 2d 1135 (5th Cir. 1979); and "Deadline Set July 15 for Action on Jail," *Dallas Times Herald*, Apr. 28, 1977.
68. *Taylor v. Sterrett*, 600 F. 2d 1135 (5th Cir. 1979).
69. Marcello, Sarah T. Hughes interview, STH.
70. The incident was recalled by U.S. district judge Barefoot Sanders, on Sept. 6, 1996, at the dedication program for the Sarah T. Hughes Reading Room, University of North Texas, Folder 10, Box 1954, STH.
71. "County Plans to Appeal Jail Order," *Dallas Times Herald*, Apr. 29, 1977.
72. Proceedings, Dallas County Commissioners Court, May 2, 1977.
73. After the 3-2 vote the commissioners cast another ballot in an effort to make it unanimous. This time the downtown site carried by a 4-0 vote with one abstention. Proceedings, Dallas County Commissioners Court, June 27, 1977.
74. "County to Ask Legislature for Jail Site Funds," *Dallas Morning News*, July 20, 1977.
75. "In Dallas, Judge Sarah Hughes Will Be Remembered for a Lot More Than Swearing in LBJ," *People Weekly*, Sept. 26, 1977, clipping courtesy of Phyllis Macon.
76. "Judge Hughes Closing Jail to New Prisoners," *Dallas Times Herald*, July 19, 1977.
77. "A Harsh Move," *Dallas Morning News*, July 20, 1977.
78. Letter to the editor, *Dallas Morning News*, Aug. 12, 1977; copies of the Marcus letter (Aug. 22, 1977) and the Galvin letter (Aug. 23, 1977) are in Folder 5, Box 1952, STH.
79. "County to Ask Legislature for Jail Site Funds," *Dallas Morning News*, July 20, 1977.
80. Proceedings, Dallas County Commissioners Court, July 18, 1977; resolution in Folder 9, Box 1956, STH; and "Judge Bans New Inmates," *Dallas Morning News*, July 19, 1977.
81. "Judge Hughes Delays Order on County Jail," *Dallas Morning News*, July 22, 1977.
82. "Hughes Lifts Orders Barring Inmates," *Dallas Morning News*, Aug. 9, 1977.
83. STH to Mattox, May 30, 1975, Folder 3, Box 1952, STH.
84. "County Ordered to Cut 22.6% of Its Jail Bunks," *Dallas Times Herald*, Aug. 3, 1977; and "Other Counties Contending with New Jail Standards," *Dallas Morning News*, Aug. 3, 1977. The Texas Commission on Jail Standards was composed of nine members, appointed for six-year terms, and an executive director.
85. "More Jail Woes," *Dallas Morning News*, Oct. 1, 1977.
86. "In Dallas, Judge Sarah Hughes Will Be Remembered for a Lot More Than Swearing in LBJ," *People Weekly*, Sept. 26, 1977, 30-31.
87. "Judge Hughes Backing County Bond Election, Says Jail Is Too Small," *Dallas Times Herald*, Sept. 22, 1977.
88. "Judge and the Jail," *Dallas Morning News*, Sept. 22, 1977; and "County Jail Bonds," *Dallas Morning News*, Oct. 9, 1977.
89. "Bond Backers Beat the Odds," *Dallas Morning News*, Nov. 10, 1977; and "The Selling of the Bond Issue: It Took More Than Just Luck," *Dallas Times Herald*, Nov. 10, 1977.
90. "The Selling of the Bond Issue: It Took More Than Just Luck," *Dallas Times Herald*, Nov. 10, 1977.
91. Ibid.
92. "Bond Backers Beat the Odds," *Dallas Morning News*, Nov. 10, 1977.
93. "Rare Sweetness and Light," *Dallas Times Herald*, Dec. 6, 1977.
94. "Jail Order Reinforced by Hughes," *Dallas Times Herald*, Jan. 31, 1979.
95. "Luna Says Judge Hughes Pleased by Plans for County's New Jail," *Dallas Times Herald*, May 5, 1978.
96. Interview with Michael Collins, Mar. 27, 2003; "Judge Hughes Takes Break from Trial with Visit to Jail," *Dallas Times Herald*, Mar. 10, 1979.
97. *Taylor v. Sterrett*, 600 F. 2d 1135 (1979).
98. "Still a Job to Do," *Dallas Morning News*, Aug. 19, 1979.
99. "Court Ends Judge Hughes's Jail Authority," *Dallas Morning News*, Aug. 17, 1979.
100. "Judge Has No Regrets on Ruling," *Dallas Morning News*, Aug. 21, 1979.
101. Marcello, Sarah T. Hughes interview, 7, STH.
102. "Dedication of the Lew Sterrett Justice Center," Dec. 16, 1982, located in the Texas/Dallas History and Archives, Dallas Public Library.
103. Interview with Dennis Shaw, Mar. 4, 2002.

Chapter 14, A Life Fulfilled

1. "Sarah T. Hughes Retires as Federal Judge," *Dallas Times Herald*, Aug. 4, 1975; and "Judge Hughes Leaves Post," *Dallas Morning News*, Aug. 5, 1975.
2. "Sarah T. Hughes Retires as Federal Judge," *Dallas Times Herald*, Aug. 4, 1975.
3. STH to Gwen Graul, Aug. 5 and Aug. 6, 1975, Gwen Graul Papers.
4. "Patrick Higginbotham Leading Candidate for Hughes Replacement," *Dallas Morning News*, Aug. 5, 1975.
5. STH to Gwen Graul, Aug. 13, 1975, Gwen Graul Papers.
6. "Judge Sarah Hughes: A Life of Law and Order," *Dallas Times Herald Sunday Magazine*, Oct. 3, 1976, 14; "In Dallas, Judge Sarah Hughes Will Be Remembered for a Lot More Than Swearing in LBJ," *People Weekly*, Sept. 26, 1977, 30-31.
7. "Judge Sarah Hughes: A Life of Law and Order," *Sunday* magazine, *Dallas Times Herald*, Oct. 3, 1976, 14.
8. Ann Snider's language paper for the Armstrong School, Feb. 27, 1973, Folder 6, Box 1901, STH.
9. An e-mail message from David Becker to Rena Pederson, May 21, 2001.
10. Ibid.; and "Judge Sarah Hughes: A Life of Law and Order," *Dallas Times Herald Sunday Magazine*, Oct. 3, 1976, 14.
11. Barbara Halsey to STH, Mar. 6, 1974, Folder 3, Box 1901, STH.
12. Analysis by Sharon P. Barton, Aug. 19, 1978. The third analysis by the Richardson woman, Mary Harrison, was dated June 6, 1978. Both are in Folder 3, Box 1901, STH.
13. STH letter to law school, June 5, 1979; and STH to Dean A. J. Thomas, Apr. 1, 1980; both letters in Folder 14, Box 1894, STH; "Public Report of Extra Judicial Income," Mar. 23, 1971, Folder 3, Box 1894, STH.
14. Comments by Joanne Hurtekant at the dedication ceremony for the Sarah T. Hughes Reading Room at the University of North Texas, Sept. 6, 1996, Artificial Collection, STH.
15. Harvey Sanford to STH, June 11, 1975, Folder 1, Box 1891, STH; and "Nomination of Judge Sarah T. Hughes for the 1976 Rockefeller Public Service Award," submitted by the Women's Center of Dallas, Vivian Castleberry Papers.
16. Quoted in Elizabeth Vrato, *The Counselors: Conversations with 18 Courageous Women Who Have Changed the World* (Philadelphia: Running Press, 2002), 44.
17. Raggio gave this credit to Hughes in comments she made at the dedication ceremony for the Sarah T. Hughes Reading Room at the University of North Texas, Sept. 6, 1996. The Hoblitzelle Foundation, based in Dallas, specialized in grants for education, social services, and cultural and civic activities.
18. Interview with Louise B. Raggio, Oct. 23, 1999.
19. Castleberry, *Daughters of Dallas*, 358-59; entry on Hermine Dalkowitz Tobolowsky in *New Handbook of Texas*, vol. 6, ed. Tyler, 512; "Texas Equal Rights Amendment," The Handbook of Texas Online, http://www.tsha.utexas.edu/handbook/online/articles/view/TT/mlt2.html, last revised Dec. 12, 2002.
20. Copies of the letters are in Folder 1, Box 1942, STH.
21. STH to Charlye O. Farris, Sept. 4, 1973, Folder 16, Box 1943, STH. The typewritten lists of women lawyers in Dallas are also in this folder.
22. Hays to President Jimmy Carter, Apr. 21, 1977, a copy of which is in Folder 14, Box 1943, STH.
23. Marcello, Sarah T. Hughes interview, 16-17, STH; Jane Macon and Martha Smiley, Texas Women's Political Caucus, to STH, Nov. 30, 1976; and Newsletter no. 1 from Texas Women's Political Caucus; both in Folder 12, Box 1933, STH.
24. Interview with Regina Montoya, Jan. 9, 2003. Montoya served as assistant to the president and director of the Office of Intergovernmental Affairs during the Clinton administration, was the U.S. representative to the 53rd session of the General Assembly of the United Nations, and was an unsuccessful challenger in the 5th Congressional District race in 2000 against incumbent Pete Sessions.
25. Copies of the letters to committee members and the chairman of the board are in Folder 7, Box 1925, STH. The letter from STH to Dorsey, July 23, 1973, is also there.
26. Rhoda M. Dorsey to STH, Dec. 14, 1978; and Pat Purcell to STH, Nov. 26, 1980; both in Folder 8, Box 1925, STH.
27. Purcell to STH, Jan. 17, 1980, ibid.
28. STH to Rhoda Dorsey, Nov. 1, 1978, Folder 7, Box 1925, STH.

29. Dorsey to STH, June 5, 1979, Folder 8, Box 1925, STH.
30. Dorsey to STH, Feb. 19, 1980; and Sarah Weddington to STH, Feb. 28, 1980; both ibid.
31. Baltimore Public Schools news release, Folder 16, Box 1925, STH.
32. A copy of the invitation, sent out by Hughes, is in Folder 3, Box 1925, STH.
33. Comments by Carl Black Sr. at the dedication ceremony for the Sarah T. Hughes Reading Room at the University of North Texas, Sept. 6, 1996, Artificial Collection, STH.
34. Interview with Carl Black Sr., Jan. 2, 2003.
35. Ibid.
36. Comments by Carl Black Sr., dedication ceremony, Sept. 6, 1996, Artificial Collection, STH.
37. The handwritten note evidently served as the basis for a typewritten response to Yarborough's letter to Hughes, Aug. 27, 1974, Folder 14, Box 1893, STH.
38. Interview with Dennis Shaw, Apr. 4, 2002.
39. Comments by Carl Black Sr., dedication ceremony, Sept. 6, 1996, Artificial Collection, STH.
40. E-mail from Constance Dudley to me, Nov. 25, 2002.
41. Ibid.
42. Interview with Carl Black Sr., Jan. 2, 2003.
43. "Who Runs America?" was the title of the questionnaire. Hughes's copy of her responses is in Folder 8, Box 1943, STH.
44. Mark Seal, "Judge Sarah T. Hughes on Crime and Justice: A Supercity under Siege," *Scene*, magazine supplement to the *Dallas Morning News*, Dec. 30, 1979.
45. Ibid.
46. Ibid.
47. "Tax Protesters File Suit against Judge Hughes," *Dallas Times Herald*, July 13, 1978.
48. "Judge Hughes's Life Threatened," *Dallas Morning News*, Nov. 21, 1979; and "Ad Hoc Panel Clarified," *Dallas Morning News*, Nov. 22, 1979.
49. Ibid.; and "U.S. Attorney's Office Probing Threats against Judge Hughes," *Dallas Times Herald*, Nov. 21, 1979.
50. *Dallas Times Herald*, Aug. 9 and 16, 1975.
51. *Dallas Times Herald*, Nov. 30, 1975.
52. *Dallas Times Herald*, Nov. 17, 1975.
53. *Dallas Times Herald*, Nov. 30, 1975.
54. *Dallas Times Herald*, Dec. 16, 1975.
55. Information concerning this 1980 trip is in Folder 8, Box 1903, STH.
56. Interview with Regina Montoya, Jan. 9, 2003.
57. STH to Gwen Graul, Nov. 17, 1975, Gwen Graul Papers.
58. STH to Gwen Graul, Dec. 16, 1975, ibid.
59. Brochures and miscellaneous information concerning this cruise are in Folders 1 and 2, Box 1903, STH.
60. STH to Gwen Graul, Dec. 16, 1975, Gwen Graul Papers.
61. "Indomitable Sarah," *Dallas Morning News*, Apr. 25, 2003.
62. Interview with Lois Swan Jones, June 20, 2002.
63. STH to Gwen Graul, [Dec. 1975], Gwen Graul Papers.
64. From the "On-line Medical Dictionary," http://cancerweb.ncl.ac.uk/cgi-bin/omd?query=dumping &action=Search+OMD.
65. Interviews with Carl Black Sr., Jan. 2, 2003, and Regina Montoya, Jan. 9, 2003.
66. Interview with Jan Sanders, Apr. 26, 2002.
67. Ibid.
68. "Judge Hughes Not Quitting Bench Yet," *Dallas Morning News*, Mar. 4, 1980; interview with Dolores Graul, Dec. 17, 2002.
69. Comments by Carl Black Sr., dedication ceremony, Sept. 6, 1996, Artificial Collection, STH.
70. Documents concerning these trips are in Folders 7, 8, and 9, Box 1903, STH.
71. Interviews with Lois Swan Jones, June 20, 2002, and Dolores Graul, Dec. 17, 2002; "Aide to Judge Dies at House," *Dallas Morning News*, Oct. 18, 1980.
72. Comments by Joanne Hurtekant, dedication ceremony, Sept. 6, 1996, Artificial Collection, STH; "Aide to Judge Dies at Home," *Dallas Morning News*, Oct. 18, 1980.
73. "Aide to Judge Dies at Home," *Dallas Morning News*, Oct. 18, 1980.
74. Interview with Joanne Hurtekant, Jan. 17, 2003.

75. Comments by Joanne Hurtekant, dedication ceremony, Sept. 6, 1996, Artificial Collection, STH.
76. Ibid.
77. Documents in Folder 8, Box 1893, STH.
78. Comments by Joanne Hurtekant, dedication ceremony, Sept. 6, 1996, Artificial Collection, STH.
79. Ibid.; and interview with Regina Montoya, Jan. 9, 2003.
80. "Judge Sarah T. Hughes Dies," *Dallas Morning News*, Apr. 25, 1985; documents in Folders 8 and 9, Box 1903, STH.
81. E-mail from Constance Tilghman Dudley to me, Jan. 20, 2003; "Judge Sarah T. Hughes Dies," *Dallas Morning News*, Apr. 25, 1985; interview with Carl Black Sr., Jan. 2, 2003.
82. Comments by Joanne Hurtekant, dedication ceremony, Sept. 6, 1996, Artificial Collection, STH.
83. Sherry Hightower to William Butts, Sept. 2, 1982, Folder 9, Box 1891, STH.
84. Interview with C. Preston Wiles, Nov. 18, 2002; interview with Lois Swan Jones, June 20, 2002.
85. Interview with Louise Raggio, Oct. 23, 1999.
86. "Judge Sarah T. Hughes Dies," *Dallas Morning News*, Apr. 25, 1985.
87. Interview with C. Preston Wiles, Nov. 18, 2002.
88. E-mail from Constance Tilghman Dudley to me, Jan. 20, 2003.
89. Ibid.
90. Interviews with Louise Raggio, Oct. 23, 1999, and Jan Sanders, Apr. 26, 1902.
91. "Judge Sarah T. Hughes Dies," *Dallas Morning News*, Apr. 25, 1985; interview with C. Preston Wiles, Nov. 18, 2002.
92. Apr. 24, 1985.
93. Ibid.
94. Apr. 25,1985.
95. "Judge Sarah T. Hughes Dead at 88," *Dallas Times Herald*, Apr. 24, 1985.
96. "Judge Sarah T. Hughes Dies," *Dallas Morning News*, Apr. 25, 1985.
97. Interview with Rena Pederson, June 1, 2001.
98. Card with quote in Hughes's handwriting provided to author by Constance Tilghman Dudley.
99. "Judge Sarah T. Hughes Dead at 88," *Dallas Times Herald*, Apr. 24, 1985.

Bibliography

Manuscript Collections, Oral Histories, and Personal Collections

Castleberry, Vivian. Papers. Courtesy of Vivan Castleberry. Private collection. Dallas, Texas.

Champagne, Anthony. "Interview with Sarah T. Hughes." Feb. 5, 1980. Oral history interview. Sam Rayburn Library, Bonham, Texas.

Dallas Bar Association. Minutes.

Dudley, Constance Tilghman. Papers. Courtesy of Constance Tilghman Dudley. Private collection. Mt. Pleasant, North Carolina.

Graul, Gwen. Papers. Courtesy of Dolores and J. W. Graul. Private collection. Dallas, Texas.

Hughes, The Judge Sarah T. Collection (STH). University of North Texas Archives. Denton, Texas.
    Artificial Collection (documents related to the opening of the Sarah T. Hughes Reading Room).
    Gantt, Fred. "Interview with Judge Sarah T. Hughes." 1969. Oral History Collection, No. 27.
    Marcello, Ronald E. Sarah T. Hughes interview. Aug. 23, 1979. Oral History Collection, No. 489.
    Scrapbooks. Miscellaneous news clippings.

John Fitzgerald Kennedy (JFK) Library, Boston, Massachusetts.
    White House Central Names Files.
    Robert F. Kennedy Papers.
    Nicholas D. Katzenbach Papers.
    Joseph Dolan Oral History Interview (for the JFK Oral History Program).
    Burke Marshall Oral History Interview (for the JFK Oral History Program).
    Charles Roberts Oral History Interview (for the JFK Oral History Program).
    Ramsey Clark Oral History Interview (for the RFK Oral History Program). By Larry Hackman. July 7, 1970.

Jonsson, J. Erik. Collection. DeGolyer Library. Southern Methodist University.

KDFW-TV Collection. Videotape of Nov. 22, 1963, events. Sixth Floor Museum at Dealey Plaza. Dallas, Texas.

Lyndon Baines Johnson (LBJ) Presidential Library. University of Texas at Austin.
    Office Files of John Macy, Box 275, "Sarah T. Hughes."
    Recordings of Conversations and Meetings, Recordings of Telephone Conversations, White House Series. (Nicholas Katzenbach, Feb. 5, 1965; Edwin Wiesl Jr., Jan. 11, 1965).
    Sarah T. Hughes Oral History, Interview I, by Joe B. Frantz. Oct. 7, 1968. Transcript.
    Senate Papers. 1949-61.
    Vice-Presidential Papers. 1961-63.
    White House Social Files. 1963-68.

Minutes, Dallas Bar Association. Dallas, Texas.

Starling, Suzanne. "Sarah T. Hughes: Campaigning in Dallas County." Sept. 1, 1979. Oral history interview. Dallas, Texas.

Texas/Dallas History and Archives, Dallas Public Library.
    "Dedication of the Lew Sterrett Justice Center." Dec. 16, 1982.
    "Zonta Club of Dallas, 1924-1961." Typescript history of the organization, n.d.
    Sarah T. Hughes, résumé. [1950?]. "Sarah T. Hughes, 14th District Court of Texas" clippings file.

Texas State Archives, Austin, Texas.
    Secretary of State Campaign Finance Reports, Joe Greenhill and Sarah T. Hughes, 1958.
    Records of Gov. James V. Allred. 1985/024-16.

Research Papers, Theses, and Dissertations

Allread, Opal Howard. "Sarah T. Hughes: A Case Study in Judicial Decision-Making." Ph.D. dissertation, University of Oklahoma, 1987.

Brown, Kristi A. "Judge Sarah T. Hughes." Seminar paper, Master of Liberal Arts program, Southern Methodist University, Dec. 2, 1991.

Czelusta, Kaycie. "Grace under Pressure: Judge Sarah T. Hughes and the Cases That Shook Texas." Women in the Legal Profession Program, Stanford University Law School, Apr. 5, 2002.

Dye, J. Marilyn. "The Accidental Feminist: A Biography of Sarah T. Hughes." Undergraduate honors paper, University of Texas at Dallas for degree of bachelor of arts, May 1997.

Glickman, Phyllis K. "Women Attorneys of Dallas from 1914 to 1954." Seminar paper, Master of Liberal Arts program, Southern Methodist University, Nov. 29, 1997.

Hudson, David M. "The Federal Judicial Career of Sarah T. Hughes." Independent research project, Master of Liberal Arts program, Southern Methodist University, Aug. 15, 2002.

Rabe, Elizabeth R. "Full Citizenship Alone Will Suffice: Judge Sarah T. Hughes Takes the Stand." Paper prepared for National History Day, Junior Division, 1996. Copy provided by the Honorable Barefoot Sanders, U.S. district judge.

Riddlesperger, James W., Jr. "Sarah T. Hughes: Biography of a Federal District Judge." M.A. thesis, North Texas State University, 1980.

Strickland, Kristi Throne. "Sarah Tilghman Hughes: Activist for Women's Causes." M.A. thesis, Tarleton State University, Texas Women's University, Denton, Texas, 1989.

Wingo, Harvey. "A Modification & Updating of a Brief History of S.M.U. Law School. Originally Written by Professor Joseph W. McKnight for Publication in *The Brief*, summer 1978." Privately held document. N.d.

Government Documents

U.S. Department of Justice, Federal Bureau of Investigation (FBI). Sarah T. Hughes, File Number 77-88126. Collection of documents obtained by the author by request under the Freedom of Information and Privacy Acts.

State of Texas Legislature. *House Journal.* 1931-35.

State of Texas Legislature. *Senate Journal.* 1931-35.

Proceedings, Dallas County Commissioners Court. 1977 consulted.

Secondary Sources: Books, Magazines, Journals

Adams, John A., Jr. *Damming the Colorado: The Rise of the Lower Colorado River Authority, 1933-1939.* College Station: Texas A&M University Press, 1990.

Beirne, Francis F. *The Amiable Baltimoreans.* New York: E. P. Dutton, 1951.

Brown, Norman D. *Hood, Bonnet, and Little Brown Jug: Texas Politics, 1921-1928.* College Station: Texas A&M University Press, 1984.

Burst, Ardis. *The Three Families of H. L. Hunt.* New York: Weidenfeld & Nicolson, 1988.

Cabaniss, Charles D. (Chuck). *United States Attorney for the Northern District of Texas . . . from Saddlebag to Brief Case.* Dallas: Office of United States Attorney, Northern District of Texas, 1989.

Caro, Robert A. *The Years of Lyndon Johnson: The Path to Power.* New York: Vintage Books, 1983.

——. *The Years of Lyndon Johnson: Means of Ascent.* London: Bodley Head, 1990.

Castleberry, Vivian Anderson. *Daughters of Dallas: A History of Dallas through the Voices and Deeds of Its Women.* Dallas: Odenwald Press, 1994.

Champagne, Anthony. *Congressman Sam Rayburn.* New Brunswick: Rutgers University Press, 1984.

Cox, Patrick. *Ralph W. Yarborough, the People's Senator.* Austin: University of Texas Press, 2001.

Crawford, Ann Fears, and Crystal Sasse Ragsdale. *Women in Texas.* Burnet: Eakin Press, 1987.

"A Daniel Come to Judgment: First Woman in Texas." *Anchora of Delta Gamma,* Jan. 1937.

Evans, Rowland, and Robert Novak. *Lyndon B. Johnson: The Exercise of Power.* New York: New American Library, 1966.

Faulk, Odie B. *Texas after Spindletop.* Austin: Steck-Vaughn Co., 1965.

Faux, Marian. *Roe v. Wade: The Untold Story of the Landmark Supreme Court Decision That Made Abortion Legal.* New York: New American Library, 1988.

Fosdick, Raymond B. *American Police Systems*. New York: Century Co., 1920.
From Strength to Strength: A Pictorial History of the George Washington University, 1821-1996. Washington, D.C.: George Washington University, n.d.
Garrow, David J. *Liberty and Sexuality: The Right to Privacy and the Making of Roe v. Wade*. New York: Macmillan, 1994.
Gooch, Tom. *That's All for Today: Selected Writings of Tom Gooch*. Edited by Decherd Turner. Dallas: Southern Methodist University Press, 1955.
Hauer, John L. (Jack). *Finest Kind! A Memorable Half Century of Dallas Lawyers (plus a Few from Out-of-Town)*. Dallas: Dallas Bar Foundation, n.d.
Hays, Brooks. *Politics Is My Parish*. Baton Rouge: Louisiana State University Press, 1981.
Hitchings, Barry Paul. "Taylor v. Sterrett." *St. Mary's Law Journal* 8 (1976).
Hlavach, Laura, and Darwin Payne, eds. *Reporting the Kennedy Assassination: Journalists Who Were There Recall Their Experiences*. Dallas: Three Forks Press, 1996.
Hunter, Ann Gough. "Two Portias Preside over Southern Justice." *Democratic Digest*, Nov. 1937.
Hutchinson, Dennis J. *The Man Who Once Was Whizzer White: A Judicial Portrait of Justice Byron R. White*. New York: Free Press, 1998.
Hutton, Mary Christine. "Prisoners Rights: Constitutional Restriction on Censorship of Prisoners' Mail." *Washburn Law Journal* 16 (1977).
"In Dallas, Judge Sarah Hughes Will Be Remembered for a Lot More Than Swearing in LBJ." *People Weekly*, Sept. 26, 1977.
Janvier, Meredith. *Baltimore in the Eighties and Nineties*. Baltimore: H. G. Roebuck and Son, 1933.
Johnson, Lady Bird. *White House Diary*. New York: Holt, Rinehart and Winston, 1980.
Johnson, Lydon B. *The Vantage Point: Perspectives of the Presidency, 1963-1969*. New York: Holt, Rinehart, and Winston, 1971.
Johnson, Walter, ed. *The Papers of Adlai E. Stevenson: Ambassador to the United Nations, 1961-65*, vol. 8. Boston: Little, Brown, 1979.
Jones, Nancy Baker, and Ruthe Winegarten. *Capitol Women: Texas Female Legislators, 1923-1999*. Austin: University of Texas Press, 2000.
"Judge Hughes Declines FTC Offer." *Independent Woman*, Nov. 1950.
Kinch, Sam., Jr., and Ben Procter. *Texas under a Cloud: Story of the Texas Stock Fraud Scandal*. Austin: Jenkins Publishing, 1972.
LaForte, Robert S., and Richard Himmel. "Sarah T. Hughes, John Kennedy and the Johnson Inaugural, 1963." *East Texas Historical Journal* 27, no. 2 (1989).
Lansing, Elizabeth. "What More Do Women Want?" *Independent Woman*, Apr. 1952.
Leslie, Warren. *Dallas Public and Private: Aspects of an American City*. New York: Grossman Publishers, 1964.
Leuchtenburg, William E. *Franklin D. Roosevelt and the New Deal, 1932-1940*. New York: Harper & Row, 1963.
McCullough, David. *Truman*. New York: Simon & Schuster, 1992.
McKay, Seth S., and Odie B. Faulk. *Texas after Spindletop*. Austin: Steck-Vaughn Co., 1965.
Manchester, William. *The Death of a President, November 20-25, 1963*. New York: Harper & Row, 1967.
Marcus, Stanley. *Minding the Store: A Memoir*. Boston: Little, Brown, 1974.
Maule, Frances. "Hightide." *Independent Woman* Sept. 1950.
Mayo, John B., Jr. *Bulletin from Dallas: The President Is Dead*. New York: Exposition Press, 1967.
Montoya, Regina. "Judge Sarah Hughes: A Retrospective." *Goucher Quarterly*, summer 1987.
Moses, Carolyn Holmes. "Miss Sally, Texas' District Judge." *Independent Woman*, Apr. 1938.
Nalle, Ouida Ferguson. *The Fergusons of Texas or "Two Governors for the Price of One."* San Antonio: Naylor Co., 1946.
Navasky, Victor S. *Kennedy Justice*. New York: Atheneum, 1971.
Payne, Darwin. *As Old as Dallas Itself: A History of the Lawyers of Dallas, the Dallas Bar Associations, and the City They Helped Build*. Dallas: Three Forks Press, 1999.
æææ. *Big D: Triumphs and Troubles of an American Supercity in the 20th Century*. Rev. ed. Dallas: Three Forks Publishing Co., 2000.
Preston, Dickson J. *Talbot County: A History*. Centreville, Md.: Tidewater Publisher, 1983.
Raggio, Louise Ballerstedt, with Vivian Anderson Castleberry. *Texas Tornado: The Autobiography of a Crusader for Women's Rights and Family Justice*. Dallas: Citadel Press, 2003.
Ragsdale, Kenneth B. *The Year America Discovered Texas: Centennial '36*. College Station: Texas A&M University Press, 1987.

Richards, David. *Once upon a Time in Texas: A Liberal in the Lone Star State.* Austin: University of Texas Press, 2002.

Richardson, Rupert N., et al. *Texas: The Lone Star State.* 5th ed. Englewood Cliffs, N.J.: Prentice Hall, 1988.

Schlesinger, Arthur M., Jr. *Robert Kennedy and His Times,* vol. 1. Boston: Houghton Mifflin, 1978.

xxx. *A Thousand Days: John F. Kennedy in the White House.* Boston: Houghton Mifflin, 1965.

Seal, Mark. "Judge Sarah T. Hughes on Crime and Justice: A Supercity under Siege." *Scene,* magazine supplement to the *Dallas Morning News,* Dec. 30, 1979.

Shackleton, Robert. *The Book of Washington.* Philadelphia: Penn Publishing, 1922.

Sorensen, Theodore C. *Kennedy.* New York: Harper & Row, 1965.

Steinberg, Alfred. *Sam Rayburn: A Biography.* New York: Hawthorn Books, 1975.

Truman, Harry S. *Year of Decisions.* Garden City: Doubleday, 1955.

Vilardo, Lawrence J., and Howard W. Gutman. "The Honorable Irving L. Goldberg: A Place in History." *SMU Law Review* (Sept.-Oct. 1995).

Vrato, Elizabeth. *The Counselors: Conversations with 18 Courageous Women Who Have Changed the World.* Philadelphia: Running Press, 2002.

Weddington, Sarah. *A Question of Choice.* New York: G. P. Putnam's Sons, 1992.

"Women Have Their Day in Courtæas Lawyers." *U.S. News & World Report,* Nov. 17, 1980.

Selected Articles by Sarah T. Hughes

"Against Resolution Opposing Disarmament" (coauthored with John N. Jackson). *Texas Bar Journal* (Sept. 22, 1962).

"Buenos Aires Meeting on Status of Women." *National Business Woman* (June 1960).

"Business and Professional Women Seek to Better Their Status," *Delta Kappa Gamma Bulletin,* spring 1952.

"Character Education versus Juvenile Delinquency. *Texas Parent-Teacher,* undated.

"Crime and School Dropouts." *Texas Observer,* Dec. 27, 1963.

"For Refugee Girls: New Opportunity." *National Business Woman* (Sept. 1962).

"Ginners and Civilian Defense." *Cotton Ginners Journal* (May 1942).

"The Half-Citizen." *Kappa Beta Pi Quarterly,* Oct. 1943.

"The Half-Citizen." *Legal Chatter: A Monthly Legal Magazine,* May 1939.

"The Half-Citizen in This Democracy." *Texas Parent-Teacher,* Jan. 1941.

"How Does Your Representative Stand on Jury Service." *Texas Business and Professional Woman* (June-July 1940).

"If Democracy Survives." *Today and Tomorrow,* Mar. 1941.

"Is the Game Worth the Candle?" *Zontian,* fall 1966.

"Joint Income Proposal Is Unwise and Un-American." *Southwestern Banking and Industry* (Apr. 1942).

"The Jurist Looks at the Teacher." *Delta Kappa Gamma Bulletin,* winter 1947.

"Jury Service for Women." *Emancipator: An Independent Forward-looking Monthly,* Jan. 1943.

"Legal Aspects of Corporal Punishment in the Schools." *Delta Kappa Gamma Bulletin,* spring 1962.

"No True Juvenile Court Found in Texas." *Texas Parent-Teacher,* May 1948.

"Pre-Trial Progress in Texas: There Is Little Doubt That It Will Increase" *Texas Bar Journal* (Mar. 22, 1953).

"Problems Concerning Children Arising from Conflict in Marriage" (coauthored with John N. Jackson). *Texas Bar Journal* (Oct. 22, 1961).

"Should Women Be Left Behind?" *National Business Woman* (Oct. 1969).

"The Texas Federation Becomes of Age." *Texas Business and Professional Woman* (May 1940).

"The Unfortunate One Per Cent: Our Responsibility." Research Study Number 27, Seventeenth Annual Spring Conference of the Texas Study of Secondary Education, Jan. 1959.

"The Waiting People." *National Business Woman* (Jan. 1960).

"World Peace through World Law." *National Business Woman* (Nov. 1965).

"World Peace through World Law." *Texas Observer,* Oct. 15, 1965

Newspapers

Austin American
Austin American-Statesman

Baltimore Evening Sun
Boston Sunday Globe
Brownwood Bulletin
Bryan Eagle
Carrollton Chronicle
Chicago Tribune
Chicago Daily News
Christian Science Monitor
Dallas Dispatch
Dallas Morning News
Dallas Times Herald (originally *Daily Times Herald*)
Oak Cliff Tribune
Dallas Journal
Ferguson Forum
Fort Worth Press
Fort Worth Star-Telegram
Greenville Herald Banner
Houston Chronicle
Houston Post
Irving News
New York Times
Paris (Texas) *News*
Shreveport Times
San Angelo Times
Washington Herald
Washington Post
White Rocker

Miscellaneous

Vivian Castleberry Papers. Dallas, Texas.
Gwen Graul Papers. Dallas, Texas.
Minutes, Dallas Bar Association. Dallas, Texas.

College Yearbooks, College Publications

Donnybrook Fair. Goucher College yearbook.
The Cherry Tree. 1920. Yearbook for the George Washington University.
GWU Bulletin.
Goucher College Weekly.

Legal Citations

Bowers v. Hardwick, 478 U.S. 186 (1986).
Bradwell v. the State, 83 U.S. 130 (1872).
Buchanan v. Batchelor, 308 F. Supp. 729 (1970).
Bush v. McCollum, 231 F. Supp. 560 (1964).
Dallas v. American National Bank, N. CA3-4312B (N.D. Tex. 1971).
Dombrowski v. Pfister, 380 U.S. 479 (1965).
Dyson v. Stein, 401 U.S. 200 (1971).
Gilmore v. James, 274 F. Supp. 75 (1967).
Glover v. Cobb et al., 123 S.W. 2d, 794 (1938).
Green v. Robison, 8 S.W. 2d, 655 (1928).
Holt v. Sarver, 309 F. Supp. 302 (E.D. Ark. 1970), aff'd. 442 F. 2d 304 (8th Cir. 1971).
Interstate Circuit, Inc., et al., v. City of Dallas, 247 F. Supp. 906 (1965).
Interstate Circuit, Inc., v. City of Dallas, 390 U.S. 676 (1967).
Jefferson v. Hackney, 304 F. Supp. 1332 (1969); 406 U.S. 535 (1972).
Levy v. Louisiana, 391 U.S. 68 (1968).

Linda R. S. v. Richard D. and the State of Texas, 335 F. Supp. 804 (1971).
Memoirs of a Woman of Pleasure v. Massachusetts, 383 U.S. 413 (1975).
Miles Edward Haynes v. United States, 88 S.Ct. 722 (1968).
Price v. Johnson, 354 U.S. 266, 285 (1948).
Roe v. Wade, 314 F. Supp. 1217 (1970); 410 U.S. 959 (1973).
Roth v. United States, 354 U.S. 476 (1957).
Ruffin v. Commonwealth, 62 Va. (61 Gratt) 790, 796 (1871).
Securities and Exch. Com'n. v. National Bankers Life Co., 324 F. Supp. 189 (1971), 448 F. 2d 652 (1971), and 334 F. Supp. 444 (1971).
Shultz v. Brookhaven General Hospital, 305 F. Supp. 424 (1969).
Smith v. Allwright 321 U.S. 649 (1944).
Stein v. Batchelor, 300 F. Supp. 602 (1969).
Suggs v. Parkland, No. CA3-2486 (N.D. Tex. 1969).
Taylor v. Sterrett, 344 F. Supp. 411 (1972), 499 F. 2d 367 (1974), 532 F. 2d 462 (5th Cir. 1976), and 600 F. 2d 1135 (5th Cir. 1979).
United States v. Stone, 232 F. Supp. 396 (1964).
United States v. Wichita Falls, No. CA7-571 (N.D. Tex. 1970).
Walker v. Pointer, 394 F. Supp. 56 (1969).

Interviews by Author

Black, Carl, Sr. Jan. 2, 2003.
Castleberry, Vivian. Mar. 3, 2003.
Collins, Michael. Mar. 27, 2003.
Davis, Clarice. Sept. 19, 2002.
Figari, Ernest E., Jr. July 25, 2002.
Flowers, Terry. Mar. 7, 2003.
Frost, Hon. Martin. Aug. 22, 2002.
Graul, Dolores.
Havenstrite, Al. July 21, 1975.
Hurtekant, Joanne. Jan. 17, 2003.
James Jennings. Mar. 15, 2002.
Jones, Lois Swann. June 8, 2002.
Kuntz, Nick. Mar. 3, 2001.
Lehrer, Jim. Apr. 20, 2002.
McKool, Betty. Jan. 28, 2002.
Macon, Phyllis. July 31 and Aug. 2, 2002.
Marcus, Stanley. Sept. 26, 2001.
Mashek, John. Telephone interview, Feb. 14, 2002.
Mauzy, Oscar. June 15, 2000.
Montoya, Regina. Nov. 2, 2003.
Pederson, Rena. June 12, 2001.
Raggio, Louise. Aug. 25, 2000, Mar. 3, Apr. 24, Aug. 30, and Dec. 11, 2001.
Reyna, Ed. Mar. 4, 2002.
Sanders, Hon. Barefoot. Jan. 23, Feb. 24, and May 24, 2002.
Sanders, Jan. Apr. 26, 2002.
Shaw, Dennis. Mar. 4, 2002.
Spinuzzi, John. Apr. 16 and July 18, 2002.
Wiles, Rev. C. Preston. Nov. 18, 2002.
Wright, Rayburn. June 20, 2001.

Reference Works

The New Handbook of Texas, vols. 5 and 6, Ron Tyler, editor-in-chief. Austin: Texas State Historical Association, 1996.
R. L. Polk & Company's Baltimore City Directory, 1902-1920.
Texas Almanac and State Industrial Guide, 1952-53.
Worley's Dallas City Directory. 1920s.

Index

206–7; as B&PW international vice-president, 184; as B&PW national president, 153–56, 158–60, *333*, 401; as B&PW national vice-president, 147–49; encourages women attorneys, 179–80; favors military draft for women, 107, 158–60, 285; at Governor's Conference on the Status of Women, 315–16; on new women's movement, 302; pressures Republic Bank to appoint women, 306; promotes expanded roles for women, 101, 126–28, 283, 300–6, 316, *337–38*, 356, 366, 393, 397; promotes legislative commission on status of women, 316–17; on sex discrimination & stereotyping, 303–4; supports equality for women, 159–61, 168, 180, 234; supports women on juries, 2, 21, 64, 97–101, 127, 139–40, 147–50, 163–64, 177–79, 182, 376, 401; in Zonta Club, 29–30, 38, 45, 53, 87, 95, 97, 132, 184

World War II activities, 107–8, 114

writes articles for *Texas Observer,* 284

writes on social & legal issues, 187, 232

on youth activism (1960s), 285–86

Hughes Plan: for reform of juvenile offender programs, 114–17

Hunt, H. L.: right-wing politics of, 172, 174–75, 243–44

Hunt, Henry T.: and Colorado River hydroelectric project, 67–68, 70

Hunt, Nelson Bunker, 244

Hurtekant, Joanne: clerks for STH, 342, 375, 389–90, 392–93

Hurtekant, Kate, *342*, 393

Hutchison, Kay Bailey *(U.S. senator)*, 322, 401

Hutton, Mary Christine: on prisoners' rights, 348

hydroelectric projects: in Texas, 66–67

Ickes, Harold: and Colorado River hydroelectric project, 66–67, 69–70

illegitimate children: excluded from welfare support, 298

income tax: STH favors, 59–60

Independent Woman: on women in the draft, 159–60; on women on juries, 179

Innerarity, Dorothy, 403

Insull, Samuel, 66

Interstate Circuit, Inc. v. City of Dallas (1965), 292

Iowa Wesleyan College: presents honorary doctorate to STH, 300–1

Irons, M. R., 80

Isaacks, Maude: in Texas House of Representatives, 400

Ivins, Molly, 322

Jackson, Jim: and jail bond program, 367–68; and STH's orders, 363

Jackson, John N., 289

jails: inadequate facilities in Texas, 344–45; judiciary's hands-off attitude toward, 345, 349, 356

Jasper, John E. V.: supports STH for federal bench, 215–16

Jaworski, Leon: supports STH for federal bench, 230

Jefferson School of Law (Dallas), 85; STH teaches at, 30

Jefferson v. Hackney (1972), 297–98

Jenkins, Walter, 228, 273; and LBJ's swearing-in, 248; and nomination of STH to federal bench, 205, 209–11

Jennings, James, 251

Jester, Beauford H. *(governor)*, 139; campaigns for Truman (1948), 145; supports women on juries, 148

John Birch Society, 239, 244

Johns, Lem: and LBJ's swearing-in, 253, 255

Johns Hopkins University, 18

Johnson, Lady Bird, 228, 231; on first meeting STH, 63–64, 144, 395; and Governor's Conference on the Status of Women, 314; and Kennedy assassination, 1, 248; and LBJ's swearing-in, 253–54, 258, *336*; in presidential campaign (1960), 198, 200–1

Johnson, Lyndon B., 63, 228, 231, *335*; appoints women to federal posts, 261; attends STH's swearing-in as federal judge, 226–27; campaigns in Dallas (1960), 198–202, 219; and Dallas Republican mob, 200–2, 274–76; elected in 1964, 271–72; heart attack, 182; and Kennedy's Dallas visit, 242, 244; and loss of political power, 218; and Lower Colorado River Authority, 70–71; nominated for vice president (1960), 196; and proposed ERA, 149–50, 180–81; Sanders as legislative counsel to, 381–82; on STH's nomination to federal bench, 203–4, 206, 208, 210–15, 217–19, 223, 230; STH's relationship with, 149–50, 181–82, 199, 257–61, *336*; STH swears in as president, 1, 248–56, 259–60, *336*, 396, 398–99; STH visits at White House, 260–61, 271, 282–83; supports civil rights legislation, 271; U.S. Senate campaign (1948), 144–46, 199; as U.S. Senate majority leader, 181–82; as U.S. senator, 149–50, 157; and Vietnam conflict, 271, 283, 285; War on Poverty programs, 288, 297

Johnson, Philip C.: designs Kennedy Memorial, 279–80

Johnson, Samuel: on women, 302

Joiner, C. M. ("Dad"), 47

Jones, Clarence *(Dallas County sheriff):* breach with county commissioners, 359; as defendant in *Taylor v. Sterrett,* 346, 355–57, 360; promotes regional jail, 358–59

Jones, Lois Swan, 386–87; as STH's executor, 391–94

Jonsson, J. Erik *(Dallas mayor),* 278; Goals for

DARWIN PAYNE, professor emeritus of communications at Southern Methodist University, has published biographies of Frederick Lewis Allen and Owen Wister as well as many other books. He holds a Ph.D. in American Civilization from the University of Texas at Austin. He is currently working on a biography of Erik Jonsson, a founder of Texas Instruments and former mayor of Dallas.

Photo by Mark Payne